The Journey of a People

The Era of Restoration, 1820 to 1844

The
JOURNEY
of a
PEOPLE

☙

The ERA *of* RESTORATION, 1820 to 1844

By Mark A. Scherer

To Mary and Don Mitchell
Thanks for your serious study.
A pleasure to be in your association
Best wishes,

Mark A Scherer
22 April 2016
Kitchener

Community of Christ
SEMINARY PRESS
Independence, Missouri, USA
2013

Community of Christ
SEMINARY PRESS
Scholarly Exploration Informing Mission

Community of Christ Seminary Press publishes scholarly works of particular interest to the serious student. Always in support of the church's mission and the pursuit of truth, authors explore a wide range of issues. Their writings evidence and encourage creative thinking and inquiry in the tradition of academic freedom, which welcomes public scrutiny. Authors' methods and conclusions do not necessarily reflect official positions held by the church, the seminary, or any other church-related institution.

COPYRIGHT © 2013 COMMUNITY OF CHRIST SEMINARY PRESS
All Rights Reserved
Reproduction prohibited without written permission.

Published by Community of Christ Seminary Press,
1001 W. Walnut, Independence, Missouri, 64050, USA.

All visual images contained in this book are protected by copyright. Display or reproduction in any form is prohibited without written permission of the publisher.

Layout, maps, and design by John Hamer.

Printed in the United States of America.

Library of Congress Cataloging-in-Publication Data

Scherer, Mark Albert, 1950-
The journey of a people : the era of restoration, 1820 to 1844 / by Mark A. Scherer.
p. cm.
Includes bibliographical references (p. 499) and index.
ISBN 978-0-8309-1381-7
1. Church of Jesus Christ of Latter-Day Saints—History—19th century.
2. Mormon Church—History—19th century.   I. Title.
BX8611.S26 2008
289.309'034–dc22
2008022639

For my wife,
RITA HAWLEY SCHERER
always my Emma Hale Smith, holding me true to my obligations as professional historian and Christian believer in the essential goodness of people across space and time.

CONTENTS

List of Illustrations — ix
Preface — xiv
Acknowledgments — xv
Introduction — xix
Chapter One: The Curious Relationship between History and Faith — 1

THE EARLY PERIOD OF THE RESTORATION, 1820 to 1830

Chapter Two: The Early Nineteenth-Century Social Context — 13
Chapter Three: Early Smith Family History — 28
Chapter Four: The First Vision and Its Impact — 51
Chapter Five: Enchantment Influences in Joseph Smith's America — 68
Chapter Six: The Book of Mormon Story — 75
Chapter Seven: Organizing the Church — 121

THE MIDDLE PERIOD OF THE RESTORATION, 1830 to 1839

Chapter Eight: The Church in Kirtland, Ohio: Early Stronghold of Latter Day Saintism — 141
Chapter Nine: Establishing the Church in Zion, 1831–1833 — 165
Chapter Ten: Redeeming Zion — 208
Chapter Eleven: House of the Lord and the Latter Day Saint Pentecost — 234
Chapter Twelve: Problems in Kirtland — 256

Chapter Thirteen: Finding Sanctuary and Forging Unity at　　279
　　Far West

Chapter Fourteen: Fortress Mentality, Violence, and Expulsion　310
　　from Missouri

THE LATE PERIOD OF THE RESTORATION, *1839 to 1844*

Chapter Fifteen: Nauvoo, Illinois: Creating a New Community　345
　　on the Mississippi

Chapter Sixteen: The Evolution of Joseph Smith's Theology　　382

Chapter Seventeen: Secrecy as a Condition for Church Survival　417

Chapter Eighteen: Joseph Smith Jr., Presidential Candidate in　426
　　the Election of 1844

Chapter Nineteen: Escape, Apprehension, and Assassination　　440

Epilogue: Legacy of the Restoration Era as Foundation for the　462
　　Continuing Journey

RESOURCES

Bibliographic Essay　471
Selected Bibliography　499
Index　515
About the Author　535

LIST OF ILLUSTRATIONS

Cradles of the Restoration, 1805–1844. Map by John Hamer.	xxiii
Hill Cumorah. From John Barber and Henry Howe, Historical Collections of the State of New York, *1841. Courtesy Community of Christ Library-Archives.*	11
The United States of America in 1805. Map by John Hamer.	21
Ancestors and the immediate family of Joseph Smith Jr. Chart by John Hamer.	32
New England (county boundaries as of 1816). Map by John Hamer.	35
Lucy Mack Smith. Engraving by Frederick Piercy, Nauvoo, Illinois, in James Lindforth, ed., Route from Liverpool to Great Salt Lake Valley *(Liverpool, England: Franklin D. Richards, 1855). Courtesy Community of Christ Library-Archives.*	37
Palmyra, New York, in relation to the Erie Canal (boundaries as of 1816). Map by John Hamer.	43
Locations of Smith family homes near Palmyra, New York (boundaries as of 1829). Map by John Hamer.	47
Smith family frame home near Palmyra, New York. Courtesy John Hamer.	49
David Brainerd, missionary to Native Americans. www.wholesomewords. org/missions/biobrain.html. Courtesy Stephen Ross.	56
Elias Smith, Baptist cleric. www.mun.ca/rels/restmov/texts/esmith/es1.html. Courtesy Hans Rollman.	58
Chart illustrating details from six early accounts of the First Vision. Based on Richard P. Howard, Restoration Studies I, *"An Analysis of Six Contemporary Accounts Touching Joseph Smith's First Vision," 95-117.*	62-63
Divining rods used in seventeenth-century Europe. From Pierre LeLorrain Vallemont, La Physique Occult, *1693. Courtesy of Houghton Library, Harvard College Library. *FC6.V2427.693r.*	69
Abracadabra diagram used by Lucy Mack Smith.	70

Seer stones. The symmetrical stone was in possession of David Whitmer and subsequently his grandson George Schweich. Community of Christ ownership of these artifacts may be documented to the 1950s.   71

Joseph Smith's diggings near Jacob I. Skinner's farm in Susquehanna County, Pennsylvania. Based on an image found in Emily Blackman, History of Susquehanna County, Pennsylvania *(1873). Redrawn by John Hamer.*   73

Portraits of Emma Hale Smith and Joseph Smith Jr. Painted by David Rogers, Nauvoo, Illinois, September 1842. Originals housed at Community of Christ headquarters museum, Independence, Missouri. Courtesy Community of Christ Library-Archives.   79

The region between Palmyra, New York, and Harmony, Pennsylvania, was the cradle of the Restoration (boundaries as of 1830). Map by John Hamer.   82

Joseph Smith Jr.'s Reformed Egyptian "Caractors." Obtained by the RLDS Church in 1903 with the purchase of the Book of Mormon Printer's Manuscript from David Whitmer's heirs. Courtesy Community of Christ Library-Archives.   85

Martin Harris. Courtesy Community of Christ Library-Archives.   86

Elias Boudinot. http://en.wikipedia.org/wiki/Elias_Boudinot.   97

Title page of Ethan Smith's View of the Hebrews *(1825 edition). Courtesy Community of Christ Library-Archives.*   98

Oliver Cowdery. Courtesy Community of Christ Library-Archives.   100

Page from the original printer's manuscript of the Book of Mormon. Courtesy Community of Christ Library-Archives.   107

The "golden" plates and the densities of metals. Research by Jerry W. Nieft. Diagram by John Hamer.   112

Egbert B. Grandin print shop, Palmyra, New York. Courtesy of Church Archives, The Church of Jesus Christ of Latter-day Saints.   118

Title page of the first edition of the Book of Mormon. Courtesy Community of Christ Library-Archives.   119

Fayette, Seneca County, New York. Map by John Hamer.   125

The area around Palmyra, Manchester, and Fayette, New York. Map by John Hamer.   129

List of Illustrations   xi

The organization of the church as it has been traditionally illustrated. From T.   130
B. H. Stenhouse, The Rocky Mountain Saints *(New York: D. Appleton
and Co., 1873). Courtesy Community of Christ Library-Archives.*

Kirtland. Courtesy Community of Christ Library-Archives.   139

The vicinity of Kirtland, Ohio (boundaries as of 1831). Map by John Hamer.   142

Sidney Rigdon. Portrait from the 1870s. Courtesy Community of Christ   144
Library-Archives.

Parley P. Pratt. Courtesy Community of Christ Library-Archives.   146

The town of Kirtland, Ohio, in the 1830s. Map by John Hamer.   149

The family of Joseph and Emma Smith. Chart by John Hamer.   153

The Hiram, Ohio, mob tarring and feathering Joseph Smith Jr. From an   159
*engraving in J. H. Beadle (1882). Courtesy Community of Christ
Library-Archives.*

Title page of Book of Commandments *(1833) and* Doctrine and Covenants   164
(1835). Courtesy Community of Christ Library-Archives

Route of the missionaries to the Lamanites (boundaries as of 1830). Map by   173
John Hamer.

Missionary activities in the unorganized territory west of Jackson County,   175
Missouri (boundaries as of 1830). Map by John Hamer.

The frontier community of Independence, Missouri. Hermann J. Meyer   180
engraving, 1840s. Courtesy Community of Christ Library-Archives.

The original plat of Zion and the larger, revised plat. Maps by John Hamer.   192

The Saints were expelled from Jackson County and took refuge in neighboring   202
counties. Map by John Hamer.

Route of the "Army of Israel." Map by John Hamer.   223

Kirtland Temple. Courtesy Community of Christ Library-Archives.   240

Diagram illustrating the initials on the pulpits in Kirtland Temple. Courtesy   248
John Hamer.

Longitudinal section, Kirtland Temple, drawn March 1934 by Verdon W.   249
Upham. Courtesy Library of Congress.

Kirtland Temple Lower Court with veils suspended from ceiling, ca. 1920.   252
Courtesy Community of Christ Library-Archives.

xii THE JOURNEY OF A PEOPLE

"Facsimile no. 1" from the Book of Abraham. Times and Seasons *III, no. 9 (1 March 1842): 703.*   260

Joseph Smith's 1833 Kirtland Plat superimposed on the surrounding terrain. Map by John Hamer.   265

Kirland Safety Society notes. Courtesy Community of Christ Library-Archives.   271

Northwestern Missouri in 1835, highlighting the proposed Mormon county area. Map by John Hamer.   282

Northwestern Missouri, 1836–38. Map by John Hamer.   284

Alexander William Doniphan. Engraving by Charles B. Hall, New York City, ca. 1860. Courtesy Community of Christ Library-Archives.   285

"Sheepskin Plat" of the City of Far West, Caldwell County, Missouri, 1837. Courtesy Community of Christ Library-Archives.   291

David and John Whitmer, leaders of the church in Missouri. Courtesy Community of Christ Library-Archives.   296

The Gallatin election-day brawl in August 1838. From T. B. H. Stenhouse, The Rocky Mountain Saints, *81. Courtesy Community of Christ Library-Archives.*   306

Places of conflict in the 1838 Mormon Missouri war. Map by John Hamer.   315

Governor Lilburn Boggs of Missouri. Courtesy Community of Christ Library-Archives.   319

The massacre at Haun's Mill. From T. B. H. Stenhouse, The Rocky Mountain Saints, *97. Courtesy Community of Christ Library-Archives.*   324

The Mormon surrender at Far West. Produced ca. 1845 by Sam Brannan, proprietor of The Prophet, *a church periodical, New York City. Courtesy Community of Christ Library-Archives.*   327

The Mormon exodus from Missouri, 1838–39. Map by John Hamer.   335

Brigham Young in his late forties. Courtesy Community of Christ Library-Archives.   339

Nauvoo. From J. W. Gunnison, The Mormons, or Latter Day Saints, *ca. 1846. Courtesy Community of Christ Library-Archives.*   343

The vicinity of Nauvoo, Illinois. Map by John Hamer.   347

Nauvoo at its greatest extent, 1846. Map by John Hamer.   355

List of Illustrations

John Cook Bennett dressed as major general of the Nauvoo Legion. Courtesy Community of Christ Library-Archives.	359
Lieutenant General Joseph Smith Jr. reviewing Nauvoo Legion troops, 1844. J. H. Beadle (1882). Courtesy Community of Christ Library-Archives.	368
Mansion House in Nauvoo with the hotel wing attached at right. Courtesy Community of Christ Library-Archives.	379
Nauvoo Temple, ca. 1846. Lithograph by W. Murphy, ca. 1900. Courtesy Community of Christ Library-Archives.	393
William Marks. Courtesy Community of Christ Library-Archives.	408
Facsimile of the Kinderhook Plates. From an 1843 broadside printed in Nauvoo by Taylor and Woodruff. Courtesy Community of Christ Library-Archives.	414
Sunstone from the Nauvoo Temple. Courtesy Community of Christ Library-Archives.	419
Moonstone from the Nauvoo Temple. Courtesy Community of Christ Library-Archives.	420
Masonic apron owned by Joseph Smith Jr. Courtesy Community of Christ Library-Archives.	421
Joseph Smith's Red Brick Store in Nauvoo. Courtesy Community of Christ Library-Archives.	422
Title illustration from Joseph Smith's 1844 presidential platform. Courtesy Community of Christ Library-Archives.	432
Prospectus of the Nauvoo Expositor. Courtesy Community of Christ Library-Archives.	438
Lieutenant General Joseph Smith Jr. speaking to the Nauvoo Legion and citizens. Painted in the 1880s by John C. Hafen. Courtesy Community of Christ Library-Archives.	442
Joseph Smith III. Sketch by Sutcliffe Maudsley, ca. 1842. Courtesy Community of Christ Library-Archives.	444
Hancock County, Illinois, in 1844. Map by John Hamer.	446
The assassination of Joseph Smith. From J. H. Beadle (1882). Courtesy Community of Christ Library-Archives.	451
Presidents of the church. Chart by John Hamer.	465

PREFACE

For the past two decades many have looked to the historical writings of Richard P. Howard in his two-volume history titled *The Church Through the Years* and of Paul M. Edwards in *Our Legacy of Faith* for surveys of the church story. Researched and written in the late 1980s and early 1990s, these fine works have been very informative. Since their appearance, however, new developments have enriched the church story: institutional identity change, women ministering in the highest quorums of the church, two new church presidents, advancements in the transition from being "church as remnant" to "church in mission," a new tithing philosophy, theologian in residence, denominational seminary, field jurisdiction reorganization, the indigenous representation of the continent of Africa and of Latin America in the Quorum of Twelve Apostles, peace and justice ministries, and the "globalization of the church" as reflected by the fact that today more people—both members and friends of the church—worship in Community of Christ gatherings in languages other than English, just to mention a few.

Most of these developments are current events in the life of today's church. Other issues, such as the importance of education in the church, approaches toward people of color, and significant, new understandings of enchantment influences in the early church, celestial marriage, and polygamy are farther into the distant past. These require new interpretation based on source materials that have come to light in recent years.

Although presented in a general chronological format, many important topics in this three-volume survey receive a more focused treatment. My intent has been to produce a synthesis using as many of the best scholarly sources as possible.

ACKNOWLEDGMENTS

IN MY PERSONAL journey around the church I have observed a significant gap between the current, and ever growing, corpus of historical scholarship and the general historical knowledge of church members. The purpose of this book is to help bridge that gap. The most important contribution of this book may be to provide a synthesis of key issues from each period using the best available writings on, and provocative approaches to, the various topics, rather than blazing new interpretive trails at each historical crossroad. Of course, my own interpretation will emerge from these writings. In the final analysis, readers must weigh these interpretations and draw their own conclusions.

I want to express my indebtedness to my colleagues in the church history community who have spent years mining archives near and far for factual gems that fill to overflowing the treasure chest of historical knowledge about our religious movement. For now, let me express my appreciation to several sojourners without whom this study would have been impossible.

This study grew from the realization that the pace of significant events in our church story had increased dramatically since I became church historian. I was reminded of the need for our church history to reflect these ongoing changes and to learn from them. I followed up by approaching then-President Grant McMurray, a seasoned historian in his own right, who agreed on the need for an update. He set in motion this writing assignment and encouraged me to "think outside the box." On numerous occasions I conferred with Historian Emeritus Richard Howard and his wife, Barbara, on what direction to take this project. At various points we discussed at length interpretative approaches to critical issues. I am very grateful for their insights.

As I threw myself into this manuscript it became clear that I had to set aside other responsibilities associated with the office of church historian. This is where my friends and colleagues on the Church Heritage

Team carried much of my load. World Church archivist Ronald Romig offered valuable interpretative advice and greatly strengthened the scholarly qualities of this book with his knowledge of the church story. Assistant archivist Barbara Bernauer superbly aided my navigation of the church archives, which provided the documentary grist for each chapter. Without her professionalism, this work could not make its contribution. Artifacts manager and museum curator Joy Goodwin offered creative ideas on the use of the church's artifacts to express themes in the church story. The Church Heritage Team administrative assistant during my research, Lori McCrosson, kept everyone focused and me on task. I am truly grateful for these colleagues and their personal commitment to a far greater cause.

As a counselor in the First Presidency, Peter Judd supported this project from its inception. After his retirement from World Church employment, he voluntarily accepted the responsibility of editor and project manager. His vigilant eye for detail in my presentation of facts and his demand for accuracy and completeness in the attribution elevated this book far beyond its original presentation. Words count! And Peter constantly reminded me of my reading audience and recommended language that would better communicate the story.

I went to several trusted friends with interpretive ideas, requesting their thoughts. These included Susan Skoor, Dan Vogel, Joyce and Tim Inman, Lachlan Mackay, and Barbara Walden. They provided a valuable sounding board. I appreciate their constructive criticism. Also, I greatly needed the international perspectives of Steven Shields and Arthur Smith, who reminded me that the Community of Christ today is an international church and of my obligations as World Church historian and author to be sensitive to the needs of people who are not rooted in a truly American story.

Early in my academic career, Professor Richard McKinzie of the University of Missouri–Kansas City history department, now deceased, was a mentor for me at a pivotal time in my own journey. His encouragement gave me the confidence I needed to continue my pursuit of educational competence. Community of Christ Seminary dean Don Compier and Graceland University professor emeritus William Russell modeled the challenge of an academic to go beyond generating scholarly journal articles to publishing book-length treatments. All three men inspired me to pursue excellence. Only time will tell if I have met their high standards.

I profess to be a historian and not a theologian. Here is where I depended on my colleagues Anthony and Charmaine Chvala-Smith. They reminded me of the limitations of the historian and the liberties of the theologian in matters of faith. We had many discussions about scriptural understandings and theological beliefs in early nineteenth-century America. I especially appreciate their insightful thoughts as I assessed where early Latter Day Saintism belonged in the American tributary of the Christian mainstream.

I must offer my thanks to John Hamer and Michael Karpowicz for their creative expertise in making this book presentable to the reading public. Both are superb historians. John's years of publishing experience and Mike's computer skills were greatly tested in this project. *The Journey of a People* cover design is testament to John's detailed knowledge of church history and of my love for historic buildings. Also, the copy editing skills of Cheryll Peterman have greatly benefited this study. The depth and breadth of her editorial expertise, acquired from years of service at Herald Publishing House in Independence, Missouri, has made this a clearer presentation of the church story.

I am also indebted to the many hundreds of church-history seminar participants in various nations, who for the last several years allowed me to field test some of my ideas in their class settings. These good folks know who they are. Many students, especially those long-standing members of the Reorganized Church–Community of Christ tradition, heard some of these ideas for the first time. They frequently wondered why they had not heard them before, even though much that I presented was decades old in more-scholarly circles. I am especially appreciative of those who went through the learning progression of hearing, processing, and evaluating new understandings of the church story, even if at times it was a struggle. When asked about what makes for proper American citizenship, Thomas Jefferson said that a citizen of the new nation could not be both ignorant and free. In my opinion, this is also true of members in the Community of Christ. I believe these students similarly have been freed. I pay them tribute.

Finally, I would like to thank my family for their patience as I labored through this writing. At some of our gathering times, for example, when I was absent either physically or mentally, they understood and endured.

Not all who have assisted me in this synthesis have agreed totally with my interpretation of the church story. I graciously acknowledge that their views in some cases are quite different from my own. Any errors of fact or interpretation, and no doubt there will be some, are solely my responsibility.

Mark A. Scherer, Ph.D.
Independence, Missouri
July 2012

INTRODUCTION

IN MY STUDIES of the church story I find three significant eras in the Community of Christ journey: the Era of Restoration, the Era of Reorganization, and the Era of Worldwide Community. This volume, *The Era of Restoration*, focuses on the first period and charts the historic odyssey of a faith community beginning with its early-nineteenth-century cultural context to the assassination of its founding prophet in June 1844. This approach does not afford the reader nice, neat years of demarcation. Rather there is a transitional ebb and flow between the eras that lasts as long as a decade.

The Era of Restoration: 1820 to 1844

CENTRAL TO THE establishment of Latter Day Saintism was the aspiration to restore the primitive Christian church. Joseph Smith Jr. joined other American clerics[1] in the belief that, from the first century to the present, a great falling away brought on by human influence resulted in the dilution of the original, true gospel of Christ. The so-called Dark Ages that followed were the just reward for egregious spiritual dilutions committed by earlier generations. These clerics judged the Protestant Reformation as a meager attempt that fell far short of revealing authentic Christianity. Moving into Joseph Smith's day, the relationship between God and humans was severed and needed worthy seekers to heal the spiritual wounds with the pure and pristine gospel message.

---

1. For an excellent explanation of the various attempts by such American clerics as Elias Smith (no relation to Joseph), Lorenzo Dow, Alexander Campbell, Francis Asbury, Barton Stone, and William Miller, see Nathan O. Hatch, *The Democratization of American Christianity* (New Haven: Yale University Press, 1989), 167–70.

But the term "Restoration" meant different things to different faith groups. At times Restorationists made common claims,[2] but because their understandings were so different they tended to talk past each other. This created heated debates, intense competition for souls, and considerable tension. American Methodism under Francis Asbury (1745–1816) called for a restoration of "the original apostolic order of things." The Methodist leader firmly believed he had restored the "primitive order" of the New Testament: "the same doctrine, the same spirituality, the same power in ordinances, in ordination, and in spirit."[3]

Restorationist cleric Alexander Campbell (1788–1866), whose religious movement eventually became known as the Disciples of Christ, held a different view. Campbell argued that the only way to restore primitive Christianity was to cast off creeds, confessions of faith, and human-instituted church government as barriers that oppressed the soul. His disciples pledged their faith allegiance only to New Testament–based "Biblical government." All uses of Old Testament language were carefully expunged from writings, sermons, and church services. Campbell made a very clear distinction between Mosaic and Christian dispensations.

Different still from his contemporary Restorationists, Joseph Smith Jr. took on the challenge of "restoring the ancient order of things" by bridging both the Old and New Testament dispensations. Smith viewed other Restoration theologies as mere emulations but not the actual, true gospel. The Mormon[4] prophet could not be satisfied with anything less than the restoration of *all* things. Not like the Disciples, who saw the New

---

2. For example, all Restorationists looked with hostility toward the passive Calvinist religious experience and viewed salvation as imminently accessible and immediately available. They saw personal conversion in terms of spiritual liberation. See Hatch, *Democratization of American Christianity*, 172.

3. Francis Asbury, *The Journal and Letters of Francis Asbury*, ed. Elmer T. Clark, J. Manning Potts, and Jacob S. Payton, 3 vols. (London: Epworth Press; Nashville: Abingdon Press, 1958), 3: 492, 475–78, as found in Hatch, *Democratization of American Christianity*, 82–83.

4. In the early years of the Latter Day Saint movement detractors referred to the members as Mormons, meaning those who believed in the Book of Mormon. However, the believers also applied this name to themselves. It is used throughout this book to refer to the members of the faith movement led by Joseph Smith Jr. without any judgment or reference to the divisions that occurred following the prophet's death.

Testament church as only a model, the Latter Day Saints believed they actually were members of the original tribes of Israel.[5] In sacramental blessings a church patriarch would even identify from what Hebrew tribe each member hailed.

But Joseph Smith Jr.'s mission was also New Testament driven. In a July 1838 issue of the church's official newspaper, the *Elders' Journal*, published at Far West, Missouri, the prophet responded to twenty questions concerning his faith group's beliefs. The last question, and certainly the most important, was: "What are the fundamental principles of your religion?" Smith's answer was his most profound statement of identity of the entire Restoration Era:

> The fundamental principles of our religion is the testimony of the apostles and prophets concerning Jesus Christ, "that he died, was buried, and rose again the third day, and ascended up into heaven;" and all other things are only appendages to these, which pertain to our religion. But in connection with these, we believe in the gift of the Holy Ghost, the power of faith, the enjoyment of the spiritual gifts according to the will of God, the restoration of the House of Israel, and the final triumph of truth.[6]

Smith's response demonstrated his bridge of both the Old and New Testament dispensations.

I divide the Era of Restoration into early, middle, and late periods. The early period—from the time of the founder's early religious experiences to church organization in 1830—can only be understood in the context of the early nineteenth-century cultural milieu and its emotional-rational-emotional religious cyclical swing. During this time, social reform movements set the stage for dramatic change, especially with the opening of the American frontier.

Four interrelated issues dominate the opening period of the church story: the early family background of Joseph Smith Jr., the experience of the First Vision, the emergence of the Book of Mormon, and formal organization of the church. A close look at the historical record reveals new

---

5. Jan Shipps, *Mormonism: The Story of a New Religious Tradition* (Urbana: University of Illinois Press, 1985), 82–83.
6. *Elders' Journal* 1, no. 3 (July 1838): 44.

insights related to differing accounts of the First Vision, the existence of contemporary writings similar to the Book of Mormon, and confusion over the timing and location of events at church organization.

The middle period—from around late 1830 to 1839—was a time of triumph and tragedy, a time of both accomplished and failed expectations. During most of these years, nine hundred miles geographically separated the Kirtland, Ohio, Saints[7] from the Independence, Missouri, Saints. For nearly a decade there were two churches with one prophet, Joseph Smith Jr. Maintaining internal cohesion was a daunting challenge. At Far West, Missouri, the Saints encountered for a second time in their short history the trials of frontier American violence and state-sponsored persecution. Amid this life-threatening milieu, Joseph Smith Jr. forged a divided church into one, with one name and one administrative structure.

Church members paid a high price in lives and property in their confrontation with secular society. The theme of persecution colored their worldview as they headed east out of Far West for sanctuary across the Mississippi River. The late period of the Era of Restoration began in 1839 at Nauvoo, Illinois. Here the Latter Day Saints reached their pinnacle of achievement as a movement as they created a community mostly insulated from outside influence. In this western Illinois "river town" setting, Latter Day Saint theological speculations associated with their sacred temple quickly forced the movement to the shorelines and tributaries of the Christian mainstream. Events in this final period revealed the prophet's great vision but also exposed the limits of his influence and authority.

Before beginning the journey, however, the reader should become informed about the role of the religious historian in providing a written account such as this. Knowing the historian's liberties and limitations will make for a better understanding of the interpretive approach I take and *The Journey of a People*'s fascinating intersection of faith and history.

---

7. Although the term "Saints" might properly be used only after the church name was changed from "Church of Christ" to "Church of the Latter Day Saints" in 1834, it is used throughout this book to refer to those who followed Joseph Smith and joined the church that he founded, from its beginning in 1830. The same is true of the expression "Latter Day Saints."

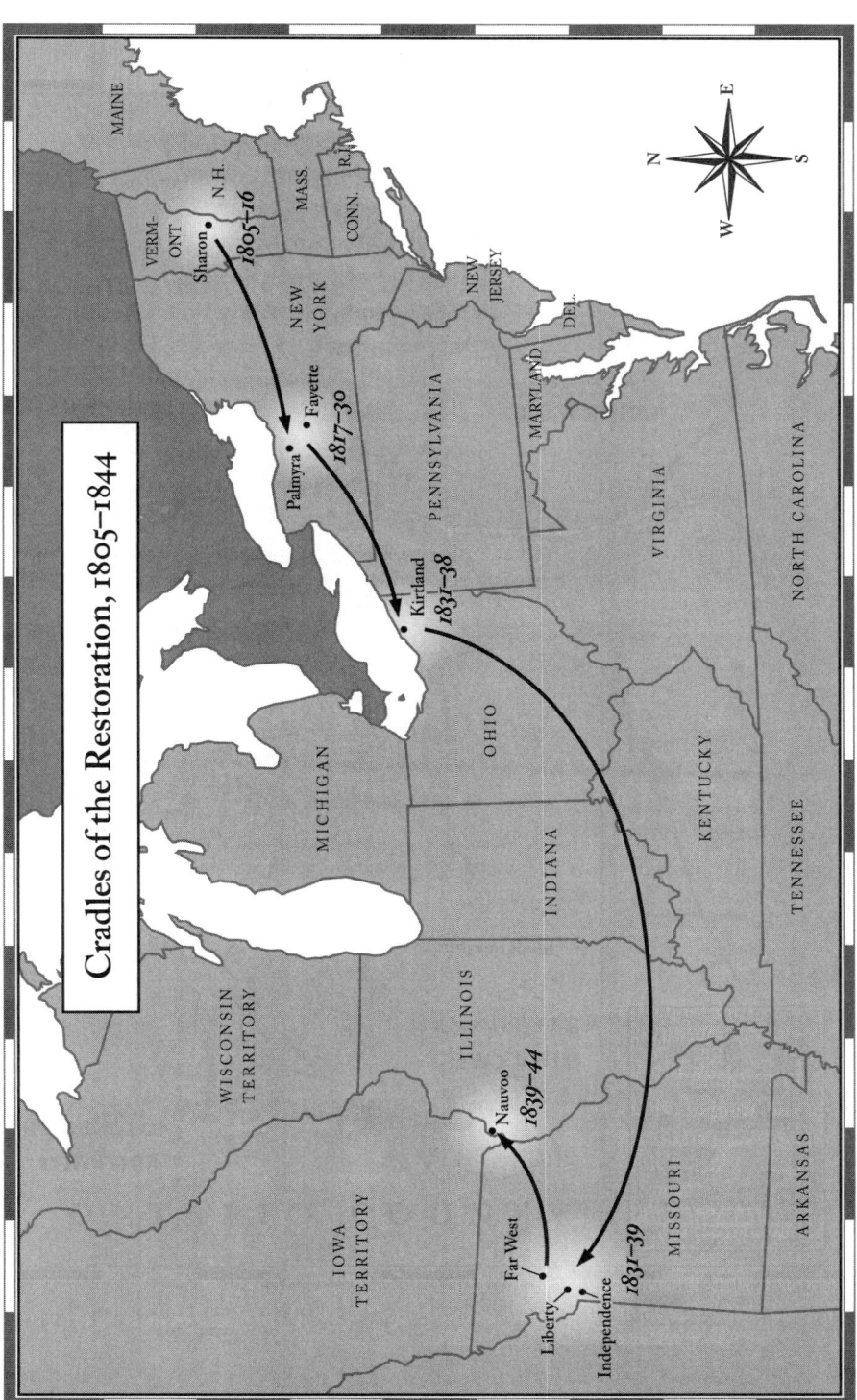

CHAPTER ONE

The Curious Relationship between History and Faith

THE JOURNEY OF A PEOPLE: *The Era of Restoration, 1820 to 1844* presents a survey of the early period of Latter Day Saint history. But readers will immediately discover that this work impacts more than their understanding of history. It prompts serious reflection on the curious relationship between history and faith. No doubt, readers will be bolstered when their faith is confirmed by historical truth. But what happens when "faithful" differs from "truthful"? What should be the proper response when sound historical inquiry causes the reader to venture onto uncharted pathways in their faith journey? The historical process can help that venture become an exciting exploration in faith as well as knowledge and understanding. This chapter offers readers some important tools for the journey.

A mature twenty-first century denominational identity is built on a healthy "historical consciousness." Without such a consciousness church members fall prey to anyone willing to tell a good story to accomplish their own personal agenda. Fiction replaces fact. For example, it is recorded that in 1834, Joseph Smith Jr.'s personal army of two hundred men, women, and children, armed to the hilt with all manner of weaponry, marched some eight hundred miles from northern Ohio to western Missouri, to forcibly liberate Zion. Later, this is described as the Latter Day Saints' blessed Army of the Lord. Then at Far West, Missouri, between 1837 and 1838, Smith's Danite henchmen are created to enforce, by violence if necessary, the "right thinking" of the membership. Yet suddenly they are referred to as a Far West Latter Day Saint community service organization. Both of these are examples of sanitization of the facts for the purpose of making a bad thing look good.

When we study our history we study ourselves. Without a mature historical consciousness, the coexistence of conflicting narratives causes a believer's sense of self to become confused.[1] Then, when the truth emerges, as it always does, innocent and unknowing members become the victims of the abuse, and set themselves up for an identity crisis that is sure to follow. Ultimately, believers wonder how this identity conflict was allowed to happen, and they become disillusioned.

The Journey of a People is a work of religious history written by a historian of religion and not a theologian. Appearances can be deceiving. A whale is not a fish even though it looks like a fish and swims under water, and a historian of religion is not a theologian, even though he or she may appear to be. Religious history is a discipline that studies the beliefs, words, and deeds of those within a faith group across space and time. It is a study that explains the blessings received, the pains and frustrations experienced, and the challenges addressed by each generation of a sect or denomination's believers.

But the study of religious history does not stand alone from the study of theology and scripture. Rather the fields of historical, scriptural, and theological inquiry complement each other. For example, it is impossible to understand the holy text without first understanding the historical context, and it is impossible to understand the holy thought without first understanding the historical thinker.

Sound religious history is not and cannot become a mere tool of parochial denominational promotion. When the expectation for the religious historian is reduced to "apologetic faith promoter," then this person is relegated to a "denominational spin meister." This, of course, is not suggesting that the historian cannot receive and should not share their personal testimony of the presence and guidance of Jesus Christ in their life. Rather it means that there must be developed an intellectual and spiritual maturity that allows for the inexorable distinction between conclusions that arise from historical inquiry and those that come from faith.

---

1. I would like to thank Matthew Naylor for his assistance with this phraseology.

So much of this church story as understood by members today is personal testimony, and ranges far beyond the historian's task to explain. Yet it is to this reality that *The Journey of a People* is written. For example, it is impossible to say for sure that on Sunday 3 April 1836, after the Kirtland House of the Lord pulpit veils were lowered, Jesus Christ, himself, appeared to Joseph Smith Jr. and Oliver Cowdery. Or whether Moses actually appeared and conferred on the two men the keys of the gathering of Israel and the leading of the ten tribes from the land of the north, only to be followed by Elias, who conferred on the two church leaders the gospel of Abraham, and then finally, Elijah who gave them the keys to priesthood authority and the charge to prepare for the Second Coming. It is impossible to say for sure what happened in the Sacred Grove in Palmyra, New York, when the young Smith put his knee to the ground and poured out his heart's desires. And it is not possible to fully verify that there were actual metallic plates so important to the Book of Mormon story. The historian can only state that all of this is to what Smith testified.

In none of these key events in the church story does the religious historian's hesitance suggest doubt that the events actually happened, but the historian is only equipped to say that records exist that testify to these events. Yet for some readers, sound historical inquiry will appear to be faith destroying. Indeed, even analyzing the Kirtland Temple epiphanies, the experience of the First Vision, or the Book of Mormon plates will be considered heresy, since for many readers specific accounts of these things are part of their personal testimony. But "asking questions" is by definition the historian's profession.[2] And providing direct answers will not be heresy unless readers have canonized their personal understanding of the church story.

Methodology

THE DISCIPLINE OF history is not a science, but an art. Historians create a design of their work through scholarly research and then draw, through the use of narrative, a picture of events as they understand them. This task would be much easier if the historian could experience all events as they actually happened, which, of course, is impossible. To address

---

2. The original Greek understanding of the term "history" means "to inquire."

this dilemma, the English historian and philosopher R.G. Collingwood (1889–1943) suggested the application of "historical imagination."[3]

Writing a history of the Community of Christ requires imagination. So let us take Collingwood's suggestion. Imagine a ten-thousand-piece puzzle on a large table. When assembled, the puzzle presents a picture that we will call "the church story." Although most pieces fit neatly together, there are some that do not. To remedy the incongruities, historians of earlier generations did their best to force the pieces into position even though clearly they would not fit. Through sound historical methodology, today's professional historians study carefully why the pieces do not fit. When they arrive at an answer, they fashion a new puzzle of the same church story. This is called historical revision or reinterpretation.

To extend this metaphor, the pieces of the puzzle are facts—both old and new. When old facts do not fit, it is because either they are misunderstood or they are not facts at all. Under no circumstances should these old pieces be discarded; instead they should be retained for future consideration and possible use as new insights emerge. These pieces are not some eccentric historian's flotsam to be cast adrift in the stream of time as extraneous but instead are extremely important; they offer clues to better understandings of the historical picture.

Sometimes historians unearth new facts that must find a place in the puzzle. At first, these new facts may appear insignificant when weighed against what is already known, but they have the potential to change the entire picture. How they tell their story is also important. This study provides a new puzzle design of a people on a journey from the past to the present.

---

3. For an excellent discussion of the philosophy of history and the historian's task, see Hans Meyerhoff, ed., *The Philosophy of History in Our Time* (Garden City, N.Y.: Doubleday Anchor Books, 1959). Meyerhoff selected writings of twenty-two leading historians of the twentieth century. Included in this anthology is Collingwood's foundational essay titled "The Historical Imagination," 66–84. Another excellent explanation of the value of "historical imagination" can be found in Van A. Harvey, *The Historian and the Believer: The Morality of Historical Knowledge and Christian Belief* (Urbana: University of Illinois Press, 1996), 115.

Faith Promotion and the Elusive Search for Truth

FINALLY, SOME EXPLANATIONS in *The Journey of a People* may be unsettling when compared with the historical perspective that nurtured so many through the generations. But *The Journey of a People* is not a cynical exposé that attempts to destroy the faith of those for whom the "old, old story" has been a firm foundation. Rather, this telling is based on what current scholarship provides, and the honesty here will hopefully exemplify the never-ending search for that elusive truth. The power of truth resides in its capacity to liberate, as is affirmed by the author of John 8:32 who wrote that "the truth shall make you free."

Due to the tentative nature of the historical enterprise, *The Journey of a People*, like almost all other histories, has a shelf life. New documentary discoveries in the months and years to come will call for yet another rewriting of the church story. Perhaps the experience of a recent eminent historian who spent years of research and writing to produce his National Book Award–winning biography of Thomas Jefferson is relevant here. In his scholarly work the author addressed the issue of "The Virginian's" alleged love affair with his slave Sally Hemings. After surveying vigilantly the historical origins of the allegation, all the known evidence, and the studies of his colleagues, he concluded that "there seems to be a clear consensus that the story is almost certainly not true.... [Jefferson's] most sensual statements were aimed at beautiful buildings rather than beautiful women." But the author kept open the possibility by stating: "In sum, the alleged relationship with Sally Hemings, if it did exist, defied the dominant patterns of his personality."[4] Shortly after his authoritative biography hit bookstore shelves, DNA testing concluded decisively that Jefferson did in fact father a child with Hemings. Serious readers still recognize this biography as meritorious even though some of the understandings have changed.

The Journey of a People reflects the interpretations from the best scholarly minds in the church history community. When quoting from

4. Joseph J. Ellis, *American Sphinx: The Character of Thomas Jefferson* (New York: Vintage Books, 1998), 365–67. For further investigation see the eleven fine essays exploring the different aspects of this issue in Jan Ellen Lewis and Peter S. Onuf, eds., *Sally Hemings & Thomas Jefferson: History, Memory, and Civic Culture* (Charlottesville: University Press of Virginia, 1999).

their sources I have endeavored to be faithful to their original spelling, punctuation, and grammar.⁵ Knowing that the advancement of historical discovery of our church story is always ongoing, at most I give this writing a "ninety-day warranty." But my hopes are that this historical interpretation will serve its readers for much longer.

Thematic History and Deconstruction

READERS MAY DISCOVER general themes emerging from the various eras of the church story. For example, it is possible to categorize the different eras of presidential leadership into periods of active reform and periods of pastoral consolidation. During periods of active reform, there is dramatic institutional change prompted either by the church leadership in "top down" decision making or from the demands of the "grassroots" membership. The change brought by these initiatives impacts institutional beliefs and even the church's identity. The change is long lasting and usually results in increased church membership. Such a period of active reform might include Joseph Smith Jr.'s years (1830–1844).⁶

Eras of pastoral consolidation place primary emphasis on strengthening the membership. Institutional decision making is directed toward preserving or clarifying beliefs as well as steadying the overall forward direction of the church. Baptismal increases result from the nurture and assurance that emanates from sensitive, pastoral leadership.⁷

Of course, characteristics of both reform and consolidation can be found in all generations of the church. The reader should be cautioned about viewing the different cycles of history in terms of being "good

---

5. Therefore I will not use [sic] to designate grammatical expressions and spellings commonly used during these earlier times but that differ from today's usage.
6. Later periods of active reform in the church story might include those of Frederick Madison Smith (1915–1946), and the years from William Wallace Smith through W. Grant McMurray (1958–2004).
7. These eras might include the years of Joseph Smith III (1860–1914) and his son Israel A. Smith (1946–1958). It is far too early to speculate on how the administration of current president Stephen M. Veazey will be categorized. Future generations will determine with greater accuracy the leadership approach that President Veazey provides the church. Obviously, they will have the benefit of time, a luxury not available for contemporary observers, to clarify their understandings and draw sound conclusions.

versus bad." Any institution, religious or otherwise, exhibits—even requires—periods of both reform and consolidation to ensure its health and prosperity. An institution that constantly demands change experiences burnout. Conversely, an institution that only consolidates and preserves dwindles from stagnancy.

Other readers may seriously question the simplicity of this cyclical interpretation, regarding it as a master narrative that commits violence to those within the church story who are victimized by such an interpretation. Possible victims might include women and people of color (who until quite recently were absent from the institutional decision-making process). The complexity of human experience defies simple explanation, and certainly the journey of this movement is very complex. This church history will provide a suitable environment to deconstruct those master themes, but hopefully it will also provide a reconstruction that signals hope for the realization of the church's best ideals.

Six Key Realities in Understanding the Historical Process

THE INFORMATION IN *The Journey of a People* is presented in as truthful a manner as possible. In researching for this project, at least six realities have become apparent. First, we can never know exactly what happened to specific people in our past. All we have are the records of those who were involved in the events as well as the accounts of those who heard about them and wrote their own versions. Even eyewitnesses differ in what they tell about a specific event. And an individual's written interpretation of events tells as much about the author as it does their subject. Furthermore, an individual may tell of an experience they had in different ways at different times and to different audiences. This behooves the historian to tell what happened based on available accounts and then to draw their own conclusions. Accounts that tell of words spoken by other people can only claim to present an approximation of what was said. In earlier years, such as those covered by this volume, methods for accurately transcribing the speeches of others were simply not available.

Second, when writing the history of a faith community, such as the Latter Day Saints, the historian can describe and assess with reasonable certainty information that is verifiable. Religious and spiritual experiences, however, as important as they are to the religious movement, remain essentially beyond the realm of historical inquiry. This means that the historian can only verify what an individual said happened to them and not what in fact happened. For example, in speaking of the prophet's messages to his followers, it is proper to say "Joseph Smith said…" because the historical record indicates that such messages were in fact dictated or written by Joseph. It is impossible for anyone, even the prophet, to tell precisely what influenced them as they wrote or spoke. Certainly the claim to divine inspiration is an important element, but it is not the only one. Saying that revelatory insight, divine counsel, and words of admonition are either "of God" or "of man," grossly oversimplifies and distorts a very complex interaction between the human and the Divine.

Third, historians seek to tell as complete a picture of events as possible. They address issues concerning how, who, when, and where events occurred and the societal and cultural influences of the times. But the most difficult question is "why." This most speculative question causes the historian to try to enter the mind of event makers, which is obviously impossible. But it is at least necessary to try in order to fully understand the subject of the study. Likewise, the process of assessing how outside factors influenced decision makers is speculative at best; but again, it is still necessary to understand and appreciate the context and outcomes of their decision making.

This is particularly important to understand in the telling of the story of a faith movement. Traditionally, Latter Day Saint history has been told from the vantage point of unwavering belief that this movement and its leaders were divinely inspired in what they said and did. This faith stance is certainly understandable, but it needs to be recognized, because it becomes a problem in the historical quest when other factors are either ignored or downplayed. This volume is written with the firm belief that all factors that could have influenced events and people should be considered, resulting in a more truthful account.

Fourth, in the Latter Day Saint movement as well as in other faith traditions, belief and theology have too often been based on specific versions of their history. Some have made specific understandings of what happened or did not happen in early years part of the foundation of their faith. This historical hazard can result in faith-shattering experiences when new facts come to light. For example, researchers have found that Joseph Smith told of his vision in the grove on more than six different occasions, with significant variations between the accounts. Also, accounts of this experience seem not to have played a significant role in the early years of the church. For some people, this information could be jarring and unsettling because they had become firmly committed to a singular understanding of this event and that it was foundational to the faith of all, including the earliest Saints.

Historical research has shown that some parts of the church story thought to be unique may not be that distinctive after all. This can also be troubling to some who see our movement's differences from others to be foundational. For example, to discover that other religious leaders had visions that resembled in some ways Joseph Smith's Sacred Grove experience in Palmyra, New York, unnerves some people, as does the knowledge that other leaders in his time also felt inspired by God to restore the primitive Christian church. Yet recognizing the separate though related roles of history and theology can prevent such things from shaking one's faith. Rather, a broader understanding for Christians may be that their faith should always be centered in Jesus Christ and that God works with people in all faith movements. Thus the reader need not be threatened or their personal testimony diminished.

Fifth, it is appropriate to comment on Joseph Smith Jr. himself and the role he played in the formative years of Latter Day Saintism. By all reports he was a strong and charismatic leader. It is obvious that he saw himself and his followers saw him as God's mouthpiece and agent in the task of restoring the truly authoritative early Christian church. They also found in him the only way to establish the kingdom of God on earth and to prepare the way for the Second Coming of Christ. Although it is not the intent of this book to be a biography of the movement's founder, it is impossible to tell the first fourteen years of the church's story without prominently featuring the movement's leader, Joseph Smith Jr.

In acknowledging Smith as prophet and seer, early Latter Day Saints, with few exceptions, saw his every word as expressing the will of God. Care is taken throughout this work to recognize that Joseph was acting under what he considered to be divine inspiration. Yet Joseph is characterized as a strong leader and one who took numerous initiatives to achieve what he saw as God's will. He was a man of uncommon spirituality, but at the same time one of common humanity.

Because of their devotion to him and the cause they saw as divinely directed, the early Saints for the most part did not distinguish between when Joseph was presuming to speak for God and when he was offering a personal opinion. This is understandable in the context of the day and also because Joseph himself did not make such distinctions—and was probably even unaware of them most of the time. His followers usually overlooked his weaknesses and, it may be said, too naively went where he directed—often taking what today we would consider as irresponsible risks for the sake of the cause. Although many have concluded that the prophet strayed from the divine will at times, the religious historian is not equipped to tell if and when this happened. Rather those value judgments should be left to individual readers (and theologians).

Finally, the worldview that prevailed on the American frontier during the early decades of the 1800s is different in many respects from that which dominates the twenty-first century. So it is important for students of history to become aware of the major differences and, as much as possible, try to see events and people through the lens of their own times. To do so in any complete sense is, of course, impossible, but the reader must try. For example, in times when enchantment and magic were commonplace, it should be no surprise to know that these factors significantly influenced Joseph Smith and members of his family. And what seems foolish and superstitious today was not a substitute for faith in those times; rather, it complemented faith. The reader must be careful not to judge people of almost two hundred years ago by today's standards.

With these understandings of the historical process, the reader is hopefully better equipped to understand the dynamics that sustained the Latter Day Saint religious tradition through to today. Therefore let the journey begin.

The Early Period of the Restoration

1820 to 1830

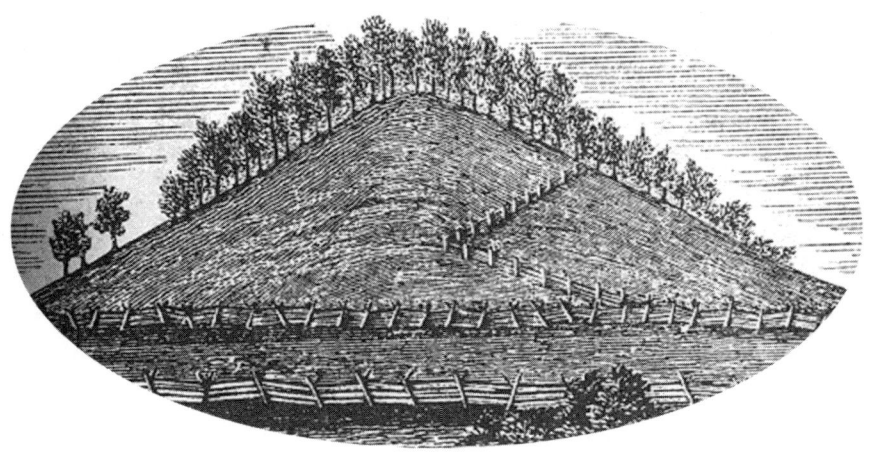

HILL CUMORAH

CHAPTER TWO

The Early Nineteenth-Century Social Context

Formative Cultural Influences

THE AMERICAN CULTURAL influences that shaped Latter Day Saint leaders and their decisions cannot be overemphasized. Nineteenth-century Americans had specific expectations in their faith journey, and the charismatic individual who could meet those expectations became a competitor amid the flourishing denominational atmosphere in their society. Each pivotal event in America's religious history was in response to contemporary influences. Joseph Smith Jr.'s great success is attributable to his ability to provide creative responses to the key religious issues that perplexed people on the American frontier. Moreover, Smith couched his responses in familiar terms; indeed, the Mormon prophet Americanized Christianity in his theology and scripture.

A crucial question is: Why did Latter Day Saintism become the quintessential American religion rather than a "footnote religion" in American social history? By comparing Joseph Smith's religion with Shadrach Ireland's (c.1717–1778) an answer begins to emerge explaining why one receives book-length treatments while the other is relegated to footnote status in the back pages of America's religious history. Although Shadrach Ireland's religious movement existed from 1753 to 1781, well more than a generation before Smith's, the events that shaped both men's stories have interesting similarities. Both were prophets with New England origins and guided their followers with their perceptions of divine revelation. Their separate theologies included "spiritual wifery," contained apocalyptic messages, and anticipated the imminent Second Coming of Jesus Christ. Prior to their deaths, both leaders predicted to their followers that their time was short. Both faith communities survived the death of their spiritual leader and then fractured amid the religious pluralism of their times.[1]

Both religions challenged the prevailing religious mood of America with unique responses to perplexing theological issues. For example, both provided communitarian solutions to the lifestyle difficulties of their separate eras. Their followers implemented their revelatory directives but with mixed results. Neither Smith's Law of Consecration and storehouse concepts of stewardship nor Ireland's creation of his Square House, a large block dwelling built by his followers as a physical focal point for their religion, could stem the secular tide of private ownership of property.

At the end of their short prophetic careers, both men made astounding theological claims. In 1844, Smith claimed the ability to remove the veil of humanity and share with his followers the true nature of God.[2] Around 1775 Ireland proclaimed that he was immortal and urged his followers to achieve physical and spiritual perfection as well. When Shadrach Ireland's health failed in early 1778, followers began to doubt his claim of immortality. Ireland's death in September disproved his claim and his movement crumbled until it was eventually absorbed into the Shaker, Baptist, and Quaker movements by 1781. Some followers of the Mormon prophet doubted his claims at the time of his incarceration at Carthage, Illinois, in 1844.

After Smith's death, his movement fractured also, but not to the point of disappearance like Ireland's. Quite the contrary, Mormon splinter groups developed, some enduring to today, while others lasted barely a generation. With all the similarities, why the difference in legacies? Certainly the answer to this question is complex, but ultimately Joseph Smith's ability to deal effectively with the perplexities of his faith and the limits of his own prophetic leadership, while lifting up his successes, sustained his

1. A very brief but informative discussion of Shadrach Ireland can be found in Stephen A. Marini, *Radical Sects of Revolutionary New England* (Cambridge, Mass.: Harvard University Press, 1982), 50–51.
2. "Conference Minutes," *Times and Seasons* 5, no. 15 (15 August 1844): 612–17, known as Joseph Smith's 7 April 1844 "King Follett Discourse."

movement after his death. That Shadrach Ireland could not do the same explained at least in part the difference in their movements' fates. Thus this study is about Joseph Smith Jr.'s religious movement and not Shadrach Ireland's.

An Age of Paradox

THE GENERATIONS OF Americans leading up to and including Joseph Smith's lived in an age of paradox. Strict Puritan fundamentalism, exposed by the extremism of the Salem Witch Trials, and the First Great Awakening, followed by the rise of rationalist deism and the strong influences and scientific ideas of Isaac Newton, eventually gave way to the intense, revivalist emotionalism of the Second Great Awakening. Formal seminaries in Andover, Massachusetts, and Princeton, New Jersey, competed with the informal "schools of the prophets"[3] that dotted the eastern seaboard. The failed control of American society by repressive English rule yielded two key documents in self-government: the Articles of Confederation, which called for strong state governments and a weaker central government, followed by the Constitution of 1789, which created weaker state governments and a strong central government.[4]

Understandably the newly emerging American society in the nineteenth century was in a state of flux. The English colonies successfully fought a war for liberation to attain life, liberty, and the pursuit of happiness, yet the new American freedoms included chattel slavery, predominantly in the South. After the 1776 revolution against Great Britain, Americans tied their financial independence to British trade. Yet in 1812, when the two nations fought again, in what some historians referred to as

3. This term did not originate with Joseph Smith Jr. Between 1750 and 1825 over five hundred clerical aspirants trained and prepared for the ministry in Protestant "schools of the prophets." This corps of ministers fostered the Second Great Awakening. See David W. Kling, "New Divinity Schools of the Prophets, 1750–1825: A Case Study in Ministerial Education," *History of Education Quarterly* 37, no. 2 (Summer 1997): 187. Smith's use of the term is an excellent example of his borrowing of commonly held secular practices for his own purposes.

4. This is a variation on a theme that the Great Awakening was America's first identity argued by William G. McLoughlin in *New England Dissent, 1630–1833: The Baptists and the Separation of Church and State*, 2 vols. (Cambridge, Mass.: Harvard University Press, 1971), 1: 329–39.

the Second American Revolution, the result was devastation of the financial security of predominantly the North. This financial disaster strongly impacted the Smith family.

In 1805, the year of Joseph Smith Jr.'s birth, Thomas Jefferson launched his second presidential administration.[5] On 23 November of that year, the Corps of Discovery, led by Meriwether Lewis and William Clark, made the fateful decision to winter in Oregon rather than begin their return trip in a vote that included participation by Clark's slave, York, and Sacagawea, the Corps' female guide.[6] In the larger American society, African Americans had to wait until 1870 to get the right to vote, through the Fifteenth Amendment, and women had to wait until the national election of 1920 for the same opportunity. On Joseph Smith Jr.'s birthday, 23 December 1805, William Clark, co-leader of Jefferson's Corps of Discovery, purchased from Clatsop tribesmen in Oregon Territory a panther skin nearly eight feet long for six small fishhooks, a worn-out file, and some spoiled fish. That Clark, Meriwether Lewis, and the other members of the Corps even took the epic journey of exploration is quite ironic. Jefferson, who commissioned the Corps, stood for a federal government limited by laws specifically defined by the Constitution. Yet he ranged far beyond those expressed powers to purchase the Louisiana Territory from Napoleon's France, thus violating his own principles of presidential authority.

Further into the political arena the state of flux continued. The presidency of James Madison, which was marred by war with Great Britain and rancorous political division, was followed by an Era of Good Feeling with his successor, another Virginian, James Monroe. In 1824, the Electoral College chose John Quincy Adams as president of the United States even though more Americans voted for his main rival, Andrew Jackson. When Jackson became president four years later, "The Tennessean" reversed government priorities by emphasizing the role of ordinary citizens over people of privilege, wealth, and class. In so doing Jackson contributed to a social environment that empowered rather than restricted religious innovation.

5. Robert V. Remini found the same relevance in associating the events of the epic journey of Lewis and Clark with the birth of Joseph Smith Jr. See Remini, *Joseph Smith* (New York: Robert V. Remini, 2002), 18.

6. Stephen E. Ambrose, *Undaunted Courage: Meriwether Lewis, Thomas Jefferson, and the Opening of the American West* (New York: Ambrose-Tubbs, 1996), 318–19.

A Divided American Intellect

IN AMERICAN LITERATURE, essayists Ralph Waldo Emerson (1803–1882) and Henry David Thoreau (1817–1862) presented with profound optimism a view of the limitless possibilities of the human spirit, the divinity of nature, and the ability of humans to discover truth. Their emphasis on transcendental thought was intended to liberate their readers spiritually, lift up the value of their heritage, and encourage an exploration of the meaning and purpose of society. Founded in New England Puritanism and modified by the spread of Unitarianism, transcendentalism acknowledged the mystical dimensions of life and promoted communal cooperatives expressed in utopian ideals. Thoreau, a master of prose, focused on moral values in his writings and encouraged his readers to live close to nature. He also promoted civil disobedience when those values were violated.

Transcendentalist Sarah Margaret Fuller (1810–1850) introduced a feminist dimension to transcendental thought by adding her "feminist principle" to utopian discussions. Fuller balanced opposites in every living being, including male and female:

> It is no more the order of nature that I should be incarnated pure in any form, than that the masculine energy should exist unmingled with it in any form. Male and female represent the two sides of the great radical dualism. But, in fact, they are perpetually passing into one another. Fluid hardens to solid, solid rushes to fluid....There is no wholly masculine man, no purely feminine woman.

Fuller also called for movement away from traditional male and female vocations in the workplace.[7]

The transcendentalists were offset, however, by stories of pessimism and doom in the writings of Edgar Allen Poe (1809–1849), Nathaniel Hawthorne (1804–1864), and Herman Melville (1819–1891). These authors were moralists also but viewed society through the lens of harsh, bleak realism. Their stories told of darkness, morbidity, and death, with sinfulness framed within the Puritan tradition. Perhaps the most pessimistic was Melville who saw evil as the great reality of his times. He strongly questioned one's ability to discern truth or to know God. Melville characterized human

---

7. Paula Blanchard, *Margaret Fuller: From Transcendentalism to Revolution* (New York: Delacorte Press/Seymour Lawrence, 1978), 222–23.

destiny as tragic and mocked the transcendentalist view of progress. For these authors, nature harbored the hazards of life and provided the arena where human weakness would bring their fall.

This era of American history offers numerous political, economic, and social confrontations pitting North versus South and East versus West. Smith's generation could not decide the proper role of the black man in their society. Some demanded immediate emancipation; some ignored the problem in hopes it would go away. Others advocated gradual emancipation, while still others, mostly in the South, referred to the "peculiar institution" as foundational to their sacred way of life. On this issue the nation was mostly divided between the North and South. Many northerners lashed out against slavery while southerners rejected their arguments by claiming that northern industrial workers lived in conditions not far removed from those of their slaves.

American society evidenced a schism between the East and West as well. Eastern coastal cities and the people of the upland and western frontier held divergent views on social priorities. In 1786, farmers of western Massachusetts, led by Daniel Shays, rebelled against eastern bankers in Boston who foreclosed on their debts. Eight years later farmers in western Pennsylvania rebelled against the imposition of an excise tax on distilleries. In western frontier regions, kegs of whiskey replaced scarce currency. Frontier settlers responded by accosting federal marshals as rumors of secession spread across the Appalachian Mountains. From the east, President George Washington led fifteen thousand troops to enforce the law and to suppress the western revolt called the Whiskey Rebellion. The relatively peaceful resolution of these conflicts helped to form the national identity.

Thus, the motto *E Pluribus Unum*—"Out of Many, One"—accurately reflected the complexity of American society, but it was more a national aspiration for the future than a catchphrase stating the reality of an American society that was far more divided than united.

The Democracy of Thomas Jefferson and Andrew Jackson

THE LIBERATING INFLUENCES of the American Revolution ranged far beyond political independence. For many, the colonial success against the most powerful nation on earth released a fierce, pent-up yearning for freedom of thought. The most important thinker of this era was Thomas Jefferson. "The Virginian's" vision for a new nation, his philosophy of governance, and his demand for the separation of church and state had a lasting impact on the first generation of Mormons. For Jefferson, the function of the state was to empower people to pursue independent thinking by limiting the restrictions on any institutions wanting to lift up democratic freedoms. This especially held true on matters of faith. Indeed, Jefferson considered his efforts toward religious freedom to be one of his greatest contributions, second only to his authorship of the Declaration of Independence.[8]

Joseph Smith's formal organization of the Church of Christ in upstate New York in April 1830 occurred early in the first presidential administration of Andrew Jackson. "The Tennessean's" grassroots political movement strongly influenced the formation of Latter Day Saintism. Central to Jacksonian democracy was the rise of the commoner and the importance of self-reliance. With the elevation of the individual also came the responsibility to perfect social institutions—an effort that could be achieved without formalized training and academic preparation. Almost nowhere could Jackson's influence be seen better than in the context of America's flourishing religious denominationalism. In the minds of many, seminary training was no longer a prerequisite for preaching the gospel. To be successful all one needed was familiarity with the Bible, a knack for public speaking, and usually a spiritual experience that empowered the

---

8. Thomas Jefferson designed his own grave marker. His obelisk at Monticello, Virginia, reads:

> HERE WAS BURIED
> THOMAS JEFFERSON
> AUTHOR OF THE
> DECLARATION
> OF AMERICAN INDEPENDENCE
> OF THE
> STATUTE OF VIRGINIA
> FOR
> RELIGIOUS FREEDOM
> AND FATHER OF THE
> UNIVERSITY OF VIRGINIA
> BORN APRIL 2. 1743
> DIED JULY 4. 1826

individual (male or female) to share the gospel. One Yale seminarian expressed horror when he heard one "gifted poundtext," who had invaded his parish, preach with great emotion:

> What I insist, upon my brethren and sisters, is this: larnin isn't religion, and eddication don't give a man the power of the Spirit. It is grace and gifts that furnish the real live coals from off the altar. St. Peter was a fisherman—do you think he ever went to Yale College? No, no, beloved brethren and sisters. When the Lord wanted to blow down the walls of Jericho, he didn't take a brass trumpet, or a polished French horn: no such thing; he took a ram's horn—a plain, natural ram's horn—just as it grew. And so, when he wants to blow down the walls of spiritual Jericho, my beloved brethren and sisters, he don't take one of your smooth, polite, college larnt gentlemen, but a plain, natural ram's-horn sort of man like me.[9]

The absence of sophisticated training in scripture and theological study prevented few ministers from taking their religion, couched in powerful sermons, on the popular circuits.

Mormon priesthood calls flourished in this empowering environment since these calls were based on potential for service and were conveyed through divine inspiration to church leaders, and not because the candidate attended a formal seminary. Only rarely were academic scholars hired to train Mormon clergy. This is not to suggest that formal education played no role in the formative years of Latter Day Saintism. In fact, church leaders established numerous educational opportunities for members and expected their participation. These opportunities were not associated, however, with local or regional academic institutions. Only in the last few years of the Era of Restoration, with the University of the City of Nauvoo, did Mormon leaders attempt to provide accredited, formal education. But even this effort was short lived as the university became one of

9. Samuel Goodrich, *Reflections of a Lifetime*, 2 vols. (New York, 1856), 1: 196–97, in Hatch, *Democratization of American Christianity*, 20. Samuel Goodrich (1793–1860) was an important newspaper publisher in Boston. His father, a Yale man, was bewildered that common people could be so arrogant as to preach in God's name. He clearly interpreted such activity as an assault on the upper segments of society. Although the actual speaker is not specifically identified in this quote, Goodrich's father made earlier references to Methodist itinerant preacher Lorenzo Dow (1777–1834), who had recently "invaded" the Goodrich family parish in Ridgefield, Connecticut.

The Early Nineteenth-Century Social Context 21

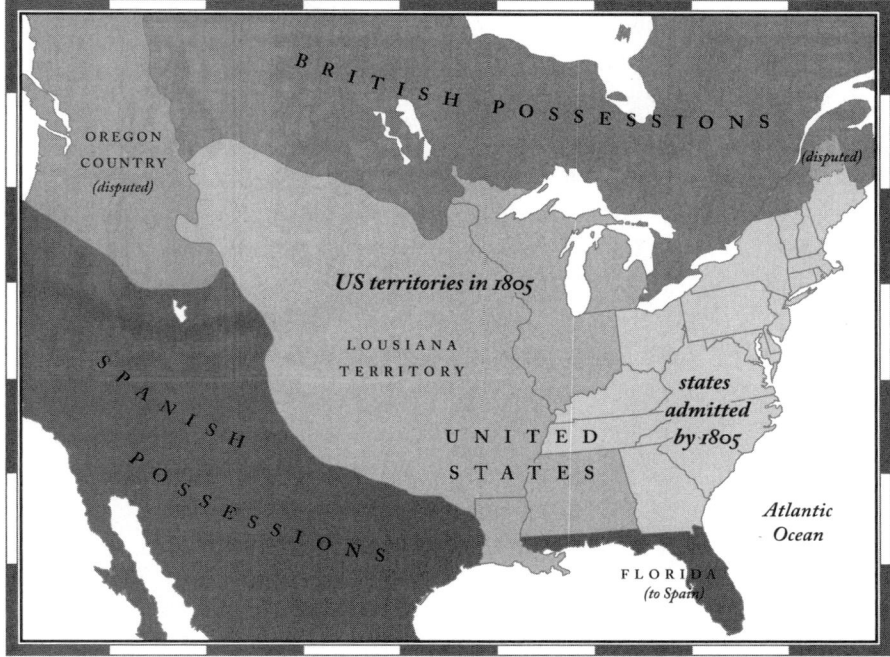

MAP BY JOHN HAMER

The United States of America in 1805

numerous "ghost colleges" that littered the American West when prosperous times expired.[10]

Andrew Jackson's political movement gained its strength from the talents and potential in people of the middling and lower classes. It is no coincidence that Mormonism was so attractive to this same segment of the American population. But one must be careful not to associate Joseph Smith too closely with all of the Jacksonian positions on popular

---

10. During this era of American history responsibility for higher education lay primarily in private hands. Community leaders saw institutions of higher education as outward signs of future prosperity and city status. To be sure, a university was a prized possession of governmental jurisdictions. A large number of new colleges were planted on the western outposts of the American frontier as a booster attraction for settlement. Although Nauvoo had denominational attractions for settlement, the fate of the University of the City of Nauvoo was essentially the same. For more on "ghost colleges" see D. W. Meinig, *The Shaping of America: A Geographical Perspective on 500 Years of History*, 3 vols. (New Haven: Yale University Press, 1993), 2: 253.

social issues of the day. The seventh president of the United States held a racial hatred for the Native American and strongly embraced Jefferson's impregnable wall of separation between church and state. It will be shown that both positions were inimical to Smith's views. For example, the Book of Mormon offered special privileges for the Native American to reclaim their American lands should the Gentile whites not repent of their sins.[11] This statement emerged about the same time as, under Jackson's executive order, Native Americans were being forcibly removed to west of the Mississippi River. Also, as Joseph Smith later campaigned for the presidency of the United States, he advocated establishment of the "dominion of the Kingdom" that would cover the entire nation.[12] Smith's intention to combine the functions of church and state under his divinely directed

---

11. Dan Vogel, in *Joseph Smith: The Making of a Prophet* (Salt Lake City: Signature Books, 2004), 356, made this observation by referring to Ether 13 (LDS edition), which is Ether 7 in the Community of Christ edition. Throughout this book, references from the Book of Mormon and Doctrine and Covenants are from the Community of Christ editions, with the LDS references added in parentheses.

12. In a General Conference on 8 April 1844, Smith declared: "*The whole of America is Zion itself from north to south, and is described by the Prophets, who declare that it is the Zion where the mountain of the Lord should be, and that it should be in the center of the land.*" *History of the Church of Jesus Christ of Latter-day Saints. Period I. History of Joseph Smith, the Prophet, by Himself*, 6 Vols. (Salt Lake City: Deseret Book Co., 1902–1932), 6: 318–19. This work is widely known in the church history community as the Documentary History of the Church. For this reason it is hereafter referred to by this title, abbreviated as DHC. Because this source will be used frequently throughout this work, an explanation of its composition is necessary. This collection is frequently cited by members of the church history community as an authoritative account of the church story during the early years. Two circumstances give the perception that the material is authored by Joseph Smith Jr. The title page states as much and the language is written in his first person voice. Thus, the impression is that the words presented are those of the prophet. Careful reading, however, reveals this collection to be a composite of the thoughts and reflections of multiple authors who either experienced the events described or had discussions with those who did. Only in the explanations of events leading up to 4 December 1831 did Joseph Smith Jr. have direct input. Of the more than 3,500 pages in the collection of volumes, this includes only 241 pages of copy amounting to less than 7 percent of the total collection. The remaining copy is the product of the sifting editorial process through the generations while still retaining the first person voice. For further explanation of this issue, see Richard P. Howard, "The 'History of Joseph Smith' in Its Historical Setting," serially presented in the *Saints' Herald* 119, nos. 7–10 (July–October 1972).

leadership ran counter to both Jackson's defense of the Union and Thomas Jefferson's separation of church and state.

Magnetism of the American Frontier

THE AMERICAN FRONTIER provided the geographic space for the development of an "American religion." The lure of the American frontier was a powerful influence since it offered opportunity to practice the gospel as the Saints understood it. Nowhere in the world was so much settlement land made so available to so many people with so few restrictions.[13] The Federal Land Act of 1820 reduced the minimum cash price to $1.25 per acre, consistent with the trend to make land acquisition more affordable.[14] High expectations for success acted as a magnet, as adventurers quickly westered to their "land of opportunity." Creating an ethos of boosterism by land companies was hardly necessary.[15] Historian Alice Felt Tyler concluded that "the frontier offered land, livelihood, and solitude to both European and American religious experiments."[16]

Social Issues in a Milieu of Change

EARLY-NINETEENTH-CENTURY Americans had a strong faith in their ability to perfect their social institutions. Advancements could be seen in transportation, agriculture, and mass production. Considerable efforts in such areas as education reform, penal reform, women's rights, and improved treatment for the mentally impaired resulted in incremental steps forward for American society in its adolescence.

Not all segments of American society benefited from these improvements. The year of church organization, 1830, was also a watershed year for voluntary immigration into America. Before this time, new arrivals were usually Protestant artisans and well-to-do farmers, generally from northern Europe and specifically from England. After 1830 Catholic peasant

13. This observation is made by many geographic historians. For example, see Meinig, *The Shaping of America*, 2: 255–56.

14. Meinig, *The Shaping of America*, 2: 243.

15. Meinig, *The Shaping of America*, 2: 255–56.

16. Alice Felt Tyler, *Freedom's Ferment: Phases of American Social History from the Colonial Period to the Outbreak of the Civil War* (New York: Harper & Row, 1962), 108.

immigrants from southern Ireland and smaller groups from Scandinavia, France, England, Poland, Italy, and Hungary arrived at American shores. These unskilled workers entered American cities and were unable to enjoy social advances. Indeed, as Joseph Smith developed his communities in Kirtland, Ohio; Independence, Missouri; and then in Nauvoo, Illinois, riots between Catholics and Protestants broke out in Philadelphia and New York. Free black immigrants also suffered from blatant discrimination.

As involuntary immigrants, black slaves suffered horrible deprivation, as has been well documented through the generations.[17] But Native Americans experienced even worse living conditions during the opening decades of the nineteenth century. Because slaves, sold on the block in the major cities, were monetary investments to their owners, they tended to receive adequate food, clothing, and shelter to ensure their survival. The removal policy of Andrew Jackson denied Native Americans even the most basic necessities for their survival. Eventually some 46,000 Native Americans were forced from their tribal lands in the South and Old Northwest by 1837, making available about 100 million acres of land east of the Mississippi for white settlement. The cost of removal in lives lost is impossible to determine. But, without a doubt, the "Trail of Tears" was the single greatest moral tragedy of Joseph Smith's generation.[18]

17. The definitive work on this topic is John Hope Franklin, *From Slavery to Freedom: A History of African Americans*, 8th ed. (New York: Alfred A. Knopf, 2000).

18. See Patricia Nelson Limerick, *The Legacy of Conquest: The Unbroken Past of the American West* (New York: W. W. Norton & Company, 1988), for an outstanding discussion of Jackson's Indian Removal program, 190–95. Initially, the death toll estimates of those Native Americans, mostly from the Five Civilized Nations (Cherokee, Creek, Seminole, Choctaw, and Chickasaw), were estimated at approximately four thousand. However, a demographic study in 1984 challenged that number as vastly underestimated. Russell Thorton, in "Cherokee Population Losses during the Trail of Tears: A New Perspective and a New Estimate," *Ethnohistory* 31, no. 4 (1985): 289–300, recalculates early demographic studies to factor in decline of birth rates and lost emigrants, or "deserters," to overall losses. Using logarithmic curves, Thorton showed losses more than twice earlier estimates, arriving at 10,138 citizens of the Cherokee nation lost during the five-year period of removal from 1835 to 1840.

Humanitarian and Social Reform Movements

THE GREAT EVILS resident in American society prompted some to establish humanitarian and utopian societies as a form of social control. Perhaps the most energetic during this era was the temperance movement. With almost religious fervor, advocates called for the elimination of alcohol because it contributed to poverty and violence. Indeed, by 1835 some three thousand ministers throughout the nation signed pledges calling for complete abstinence from hard liquor or "ardent spirits." A year later the first national convention of the American temperance movement met to rally against "demon rum." Neal Dow (1804–1897) labored long in Maine to pass the first anti-liquor law in the nation. Similar efforts on different issues by Dorothea Dix (1802–1887), advocating for specialized treatment for the insane; Horace Mann (1796–1859), winning support for educational reform; and Lemuel Shattuck (1793–1859), laying the foundation for modern public health, represent the widespread efforts to address the nation's social ills.

These issues reflect individual initiatives to improve American society. Others chose communal means to achieve those ends. John Humphrey Noyes (1811–1886) established the Perfectionists in Putney, Vermont, in 1836, then moved to Oneida, New York, where he founded his commune. Noyes believed true Christians could live without sin while maintaining high millennialist aspirations. Robert Owen (1771–1858) condemned private property and organized religion as destructive to social prosperity. Emigrating from Scotland, Owen put his ideas calling for complete communism into practice at New Harmony, Indiana, in 1825. Charles Fourier (1772–1837) argued that society's redemption lay in rejection of machinery and in closeness to nature. He established nearly fifty social groupings, called phalanxes, in New York, New Jersey, Massachusetts, Pennsylvania, and Ohio.[19]

---

19. Lawrence Foster, in *Religion and Sexuality: Three American Communal Experiments of the Nineteenth Century* (New York: Oxford University Press, 1981), focused on the different aspects of communal living within the Shaker, Oneida, and Mormon communities. Foster's significant contribution to understanding this social condition in America highlighted the uniqueness and commonalities of these movements. For further information on Robert Owen, see Arthur Bestor Jr., *Backwoods Utopias: The Sectarian and Owenite Phases of Communitarian Socialism in America: 1663–1829* (Philadelphia:

The most famous utopian experiment contemporary to the Restoration Era of Latter Day Saintism was Brook Farm in West Roxbury, Massachusetts. Transcendentalist George Ripley (1802–1880), a Unitarian minister, challenged his followers to find a more natural union between intellectual and manual labor. Followers moved to Brook Farm in search of a utopian alternative where the mind, body, and spirit were fused in a lifestyle of peaceful coexistence. Ultimately the purpose of Brook Farm was to provide a venue where people could live life to its fullest through cooperation, study, and hard work.[20] Although many of these communitarian experiments developed in the 1840s and later, their confidence in communalism reflected the mood of the nation to address social needs using a diversity of lifestyles.

The Conflicted Search for Latter Day Saint Identity

JUST AS THE nation "searched for itself" amid the conflict of values and social division, so it was also with the Latter Day Saint movement. During the Era of Restoration, as will be shown throughout this volume, Joseph Smith Jr. and the church he founded engaged the society and culture of the times and places through which they journeyed. They embraced pacifist leanings and lived within the law when to do so furthered their cause—one they saw as God's cause. Yet they took up arms and violated laws when they felt their rights were being denied. Joseph and his people became involved in local, national, and even international politics, ventured into banking and commerce, and became involved in the debate over the use or nonuse of alcoholic beverages.

The conflicted search for Latter Day Saint identity was representative of the larger society during the early nineteenth century. Latter Day Saintism, the quintessential American religion, exhibited characteristics of society's complexity. The faith movement begun by Joseph Smith Jr. reflected social themes and addressed individual concerns of certain segments of the American population. Understanding the development of

---

University of Pennsylvania Press, 1967). A useful discussion of Charles Fourier's ideas can be found in Parke Godwin, *A Popular View of the Doctrine of Charles Fourier* (Philadelphia: University of Pennsylvania Press, 1972).

20. Henry L. Golemba, *George Ripley* (Boston: G. K. Hall & Co., 1977), 91.

Latter Day Saintism is possible only if placed in the historical context of the new American republic engaged in its own search for identity as it evolved from a loose collection of British colonies in the New World to nationhood.

Joseph Smith Jr.'s family heritage demonstrates the difficulty of living during these conflicted times. Like their New England contemporaries, the Smiths had to cope with the stresses of uncertainty brought by competing national, regional, and even local priorities, a tenuous economy, and unpredictable environmental conditions. These difficult circumstances framed family decision making and shaped the Mormon prophet's upbringing.

CHAPTER THREE

Early Smith Family History

As INDICATED IN this book's Introduction, four powerful influences and events of the Restoration Era launched Latter Day Saintism as the quintessential American religious movement. These were: the early history of Joseph Smith Jr.'s family, the youth's divine encounter in a Palmyra grove, the publication of the Book of Mormon, and finally the formal organization of the church. Because these events shaped the early church story, a careful exploration of each is necessary. Much of the current, popular understanding of these times is based on faithful tradition and folklore rather than sound historical methodology.

Ancestry of Joseph Smith Jr.

Born on 23 December 1805, in Sharon, Vermont, Joseph Smith Jr. was the fourth of eight surviving children of Joseph Sr. and Lucy Mack Smith. On both sides of the family, Joseph Smith's New England heritage reflected the times. His ancestors adhered to an ethic of hard work, self-reliance, a pride of accomplishment, and a belief that perseverance would ensure their success. This "Puritan ethic" guided the family through the good times and bad.

The Mormon prophet's ancestors participated in important events in American history. On the paternal side, Robert Smith (c.1623–1693), the earliest family member to live in the New World, moved as a teenager from Toppesfield, Essex, England, to Massachusetts Bay Colony in 1638. Smith joined some fourteen thousand English immigrants between 1629 and 1642 who found in New England a haven from economic depression, poverty, and cruel religious oppression at the hands of King Charles I. Settling in this part of New England placed the Smith family in the heart of American Puritanism. Becoming prosperous, Robert moved to Boston where it is said that he built the third house there to have a cellar.[1]

In the years leading up to the 1690s, the Puritan Church in New England encountered challenges stemming from waning piety due to a decline in conversion experiences and baptismal rates. Some saw this development as the work of Satan and reacted with suspicion, paranoia, and hysteria. In 1692, a total of nineteen women were hanged and one woman was pressed to death as a result of charges brought against them alleging their practice of witchcraft. The accusers of two of the nineteen were members, at least indirectly, of Joseph Smith Jr.'s lineage. In 1691, Joseph Jr.'s great-great-grandfather Samuell Smith (1666–1748), of Boxford, Massachusetts, charged Mary Easty with performing acts of witchcraft in Topsfield, Massachusetts, five years earlier. John Gould, a Smith family in-law, accused Sarah Wilds of having committed witchcraft some fifteen years earlier. Both women were found guilty and hanged based on the charges brought by their accusers.[2] In 1773, Robert Smith's grandson, and the young prophet's great-grandfather, Samuel Smith (1714–1785), chaired a Tea Committee at Topsfield, twenty miles north of Boston, and participated in the actual Boston Tea Party.[3] Also, Samuel Smith had raised Asael (1744–1830), who was Joseph Jr.'s grandfather.

In 1767, Asael Smith married Mary Duty (1743–1836), of Windham, New Hampshire. They lived in Asael's father's house in Topsfield for their first five years together. Here Mary gave birth to their third child, Joseph, on 12 July 1771. With Joseph less than a year old, the family moved to Windham and two years later to Dumbarton, where Asael joined the revolutionary cause in July 1776. In late 1785, Asael inherited his father's farm

---

1. Donna Hill, *Joseph Smith: The First Mormon* (Garden City, N.Y.: Doubleday & Company, 1977), 16.
2. D. Michael Quinn, *Early Mormonism and the Magic World View*, rev. ed. (Salt Lake City: Signature Books, 1998), 31.
3. Mary Audentia Smith Anderson, *Ancestry and Posterity of Joseph Smith and Emma Hale, With Little Sketches of Their Immigrant Ancestors All of Whom Came to America between the Years 1620 and 1685, and Settled in the States of Massachusetts and Connecticut* (Independence, Mo.: Herald House, 1929), 51–58; Hill, *Joseph Smith*, 16.

in Topsfield and moved there. Then, in the spring of 1791, the family took the opportunity to develop a dairy farm in nearby Ipswich, a project that lasted only briefly. From Massachusetts, the close-knit Smith family made their way to Vermont, less than a year after it achieved statehood in 1791, eventually settling in the Orange County village of Tunbridge.[4] Here Joseph met his future wife, Lucy Mack (1775–1856), and they married on 24 January 1796.

The maternal side of the prophet's family also has fascinating connections to key events in early American history. Joseph Jr.'s maternal grandfather, Solomon Mack (1732–1820), played a prominent role in his upbringing and theological development. Solomon's Scottish grandfather (the prophet's great-great-grandfather), John Mack (1653–1721), immigrated to Salisbury, Massachusetts, in 1669 and eventually settled in Lyme, Connecticut. John bequeathed a large estate to his son, Ebenezer (1697–1777), but with that came the responsibility of caring for his mother, Sarah Bagley Mack (1663–unknown). These were prosperous times for Ebenezer as he married Hannah Huntley (1708–1796) and invested his inheritance wisely, at least early on. However, Ebenezer's misplaced trust with friends in a business transaction resulted in financial disaster. As soon as possible, Ebenezer indentured his four-year-old son, Solomon, to a neighbor, an arrangement that lasted almost twenty years. In his life's history, Solomon Mack described a very difficult early life:

> I lived with this man (whose name, for many reasons, I did not think proper to mention) until I was 21 years of age lacking 2 months,[5] when a difficulty took place between me and my master, which terminated in our separation.... I, however, at his request returned and fulfilled the indenture; which in consequence of being frequently abused, I had

4. On 4 March 1791, Vermont achieved statehood and became the first state not included in the original thirteen states. The Smiths moved into the nation's newest state in October of that year.

5. There is evidence that Solomon Mack was actually three years older than he thought. Lucy Mack Smith repeated her father's statement that his date of birth was 26 September 1735, but the Lyme, Connecticut, vital records date his birth to 15 September 1732. One explanation for the disparity is that by prolonging Mack's age, the owner of the indenture could extend his servant's obligation. For further explanation see Richard Lloyd Anderson, *Joseph Smith's New England Heritage: Influences of Grandfathers Solomon Mack and Asael Smith* (Salt Lake City: Deseret Book Company, 1971), 162fn10.

found my indentures in my master's custody, and I burnt them. My mistress was afraid of my commencing a suit against them, she took me aside and told me I was such a fool we could not learn you. I was totally ignorant of divine revelation or anything appertaining to the Christian religion. I was never taught even the principles of common morality and felt no obligation with regard to society and was born as others, like the wild ass's colt. I met with many sore accidents during the years of my minority.

To end his abusive indenture, Solomon secretly acquired the papers that held him in servitude. He then joined the army to fight in the French and Indian War.[6]

During this war, Solomon Mack served three tours of duty. In 1755, not yet twenty-three years old, Mack enlisted for a two-and-a-half month first tour at Fort Edward on the upper Hudson River, just south of Lake George. He served a second tour for six months under Israel Putnam and then, in 1758, a third tour at Crown Point on Lake Ticonderoga as a teamster carting military supplies.

Solomon Mack became a war profiteer during the American Revolution when he discovered that General George Washington desperately needed gunpowder to support his armies. Quickly Mack learned how to make saltpeter, a key ingredient for gunpowder, and traveled across New England earning a dollar per day teaching others his skills. But the family needed more income to survive the difficult years of the war, so during the spring of 1779, Solomon and his two sons, thirteen-year-old Jason and nineteen-year-old Stephen, joined the eighty-person crew of the privateer *Beaver*, which raided British shipping in Long Island Sound. After each victory, the common practice was to divide the booty into equal shares. This gave the Mack family three shares and the revenues necessary, with proper stewardship, to finance their future life.

In early 1759, Solomon married Lydia Gates (1732–ca. 1818), of East Hadam, Connecticut. From his difficult years soldiering and his enterprising ventures as a teamster he saved enough money to purchase sixteen hundred acres in primitive northern New York. But like his father, Solomon's naïve trust resulted in the loss of his land, and hard times set in.

6. Solomon Mack, *A Narraitve of the Life of Solomon Mack*.... (Windsor, [VT]: By the author, [1811]), 4–5.

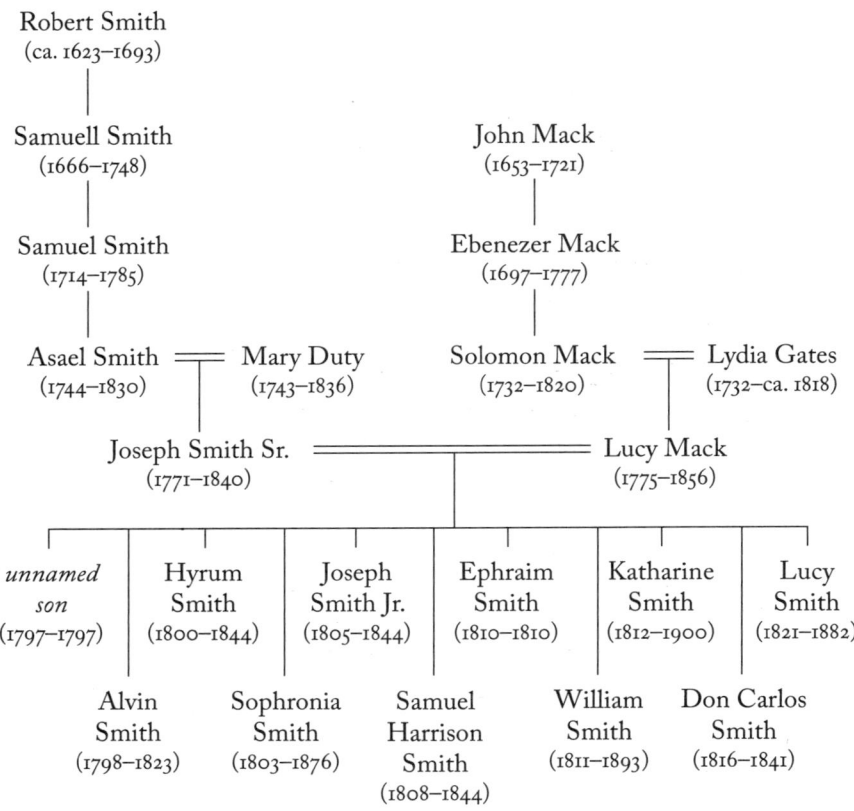

Selected ancestors and the immediate family of Joseph Smith Jr.

By now Solomon and Lydia had three children: Jason, Stephen, and Lucy. Financial difficulties haunted the family with each attempt to find relief. By 1799, Stephen Mack, a successful businessman, and Lucy, who had married Joseph Smith in January 1796, both lived near Tunbridge, Vermont. Father Solomon scraped up enough money to purchase some land so he and Lydia could be near at least two of their children.

Parentage and Difficult Times

AFTER APPROXIMATELY FIVE years, in 1804, Solomon Mack purchased a farm in Sharon, Vermont, and then rented it to his daughter, Lucy, and her husband, Joseph Smith. A year later, Lucy gave birth to their third surviving son and fourth child, named after his father, Joseph. By the time Lucy emerged from her childbearing years, she would have eight sons (an unnamed male child who died shortly after birth about 1797; Alvin; Hyrum; Joseph; Samuel Harrison; Ephraim, who lived only eleven days; William; and Don Carlos) and three daughters (Sophronia, Katharine, and Lucy).

Although finding soil suitable for farming in New England was a challenge, the young couple's future had an optimistic beginning. Joseph took part ownership of a "handsome farm" in Tunbridge, Vermont, where they lived for six years, and Lucy received a thousand-dollar dowry from her side of the family. Anticipating a prosperous life together, the enterprising couple rented out their Tunbridge farm in 1802 and moved a short distance northwest to Randolph, the commercial hub for Orange County, Vermont. There they opened a "mercantile establishment" with supplies received from Boston creditors.[7]

Times then turned on the young couple. During their first six months in Randolph, Lucy's health failed. Physicians, and even her husband, pronounced her pending death. But then, according to her memoir, Lucy prayed a mighty prayer and received a miraculous healing.[8] With Lucy's improving health, Joseph returned to his business pursuits. He learned that ginseng root was a popular aphrodisiac and treatment for the plague

---

7. In a letter to her son William, dated January 1845, Lucy recorded that she had "undertaken a history of the Family." Historian Dan Vogel speculated that Lucy must have begun her history either in late 1844 or early 1845. A version of this preliminary draft was eventually published by Orson Pratt in 1853. Thus two versions of the Smith family history are extant, namely the 1845 manuscript and the 1853 edited version. Two important contemporary studies offer valuable insights into Lucy's history. See Dan Vogel, comp. and ed., *Early Mormon Documents*, 5 vols. (Salt Lake City: Signature Books, 1996), 1: 227–450. Vogel's five-volume documentary history is a very useful collection of primary sources on which the early church story is founded. The most comprehensive study of Lucy Mack Smith is in Lavina Fielding Anderson, ed., *Lucy's Book: A Critical Edition of Lucy Mack Smith's Family Memoir* (Salt Lake City: Signature Books, 2001). Pratt's version is more readable, so all references in this study will be taken from the 1853 edited account. Because Pratt's work is popular with members of the Community of Christ, all references will be taken from the 1969 Herald House reprint of Pratt's work. See Lucy Smith, *Biographical Sketches of Joseph Smith the Prophet and His Progenitors for Many Generations* (Liverpool, England: Published for Orson Pratt by S. W. Richards, 1853; reprinted, Independence, Mo.: Herald House, 1969), 39.

8. Lucy Smith, *Biographical Sketches*, 40–41.

raging in China. The plant grew wild throughout the Green Mountains of Vermont. Because the root brought high profits to suppliers in the Asia markets, Smith saw a get-rich-quick opportunity and invested the family fortune in crystallizing and exporting it.[9] His common practice was to exchange his general merchandise with local farmers for their ginseng. Payment to Smith's suppliers for the unsold bartered goods would come with the sale of the ginseng on the China market. The plan had enough prospects for success for Smith to receive an offer of three thousand dollars from a Mr. Stevens, one of Smith's competitors. But Smith decided to ship his product to China himself—a fateful decision because, although he would receive all the profits, it meant that he also accepted all the risk.

Joseph hurried to New York City to make shipping arrangements. He went to the harbor and negotiated with a ship's captain to make the sale. Stevens soon learned of these negotiations, decided to send a shipment as well, and sent his son (whose name was not mentioned) to watch over his and Smith's cargo and to make the transaction when the ship harbored in China. On return of the ship back to New York, Joseph asked the young Stevens about the sale of his (Smith's) cargo and learned that "the sale had been a perfect failure." Lucy recorded in her family history that she could not remember the details of Stevens's excuse except to say that at the time the story was "quite a plausible tale."[10] The Smith family was devastated by the turn of events.

Not long afterward, the young Stevens hired several members of the Mack family to help with his family's ginseng business. One day, Lucy's brother Stephen[11] found his employer in a drunken stupor and asked about Smith's ginseng transaction. Caught off guard, Stevens showed Mack a trunk "exhibiting a large amount of silver and gold." Stevens said: "There, sir, are the proceeds of Mr. Smith's ginseng!" Realizing later what he had revealed, Stevens took the chest of money and fled to Canada. According

---

9. In Chinese culture, ginseng was also "considered a remedy for everything from dizziness to pleurisy." See Fawn M. Brodie, *No Man Knows My History: The Life of Joseph Smith*, 2nd ed. rev. (New York: Vintage Books, 1995), 6.
10. Lucy Smith, *Biographical Sketches*, 43–45.
11. In this episode Lucy did not identify which of her brothers, Jason or Stephen, made the discovery. However, she used Stephen's nickname, Major, as the brother who tricked the young Stevens into divulging the information.

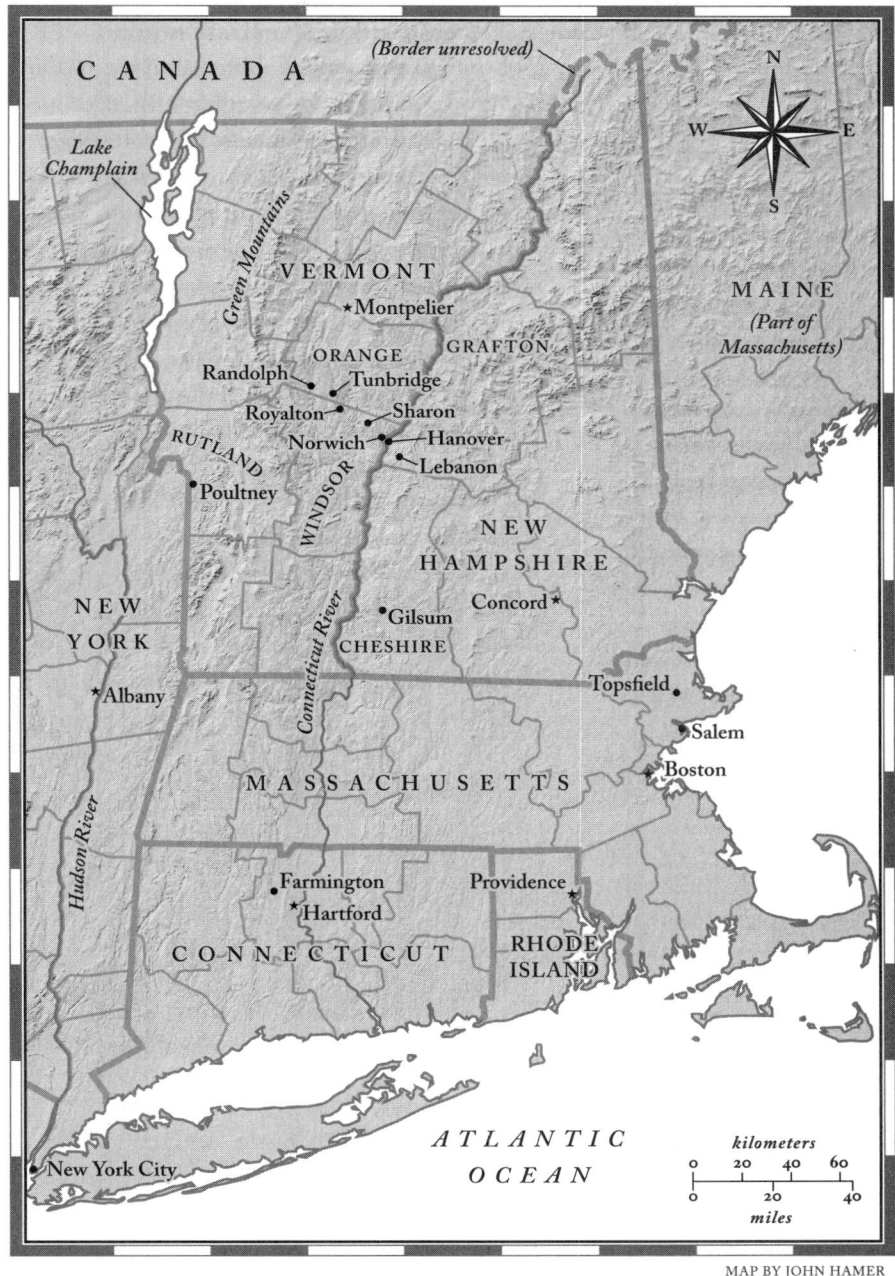

New England (county boundaries as of 1816)

to Lucy's history, her husband pursued Stevens briefly but to no avail.[12] His investment was lost, with no hope of recovery.

On his return to Randolph, Joseph and Lucy calculated their family debt at eighteen hundred dollars, including the value of their mercantile store goods purchased on credit from Boston. They had no choice but to sell their Tunbridge farm at a considerable loss (for eight hundred dollars) and to add Lucy's dowry of a thousand dollars to meet their obligations. The entire fortune was lost and their social status drastically reduced. Impoverished living conditions set in quickly—a lifestyle from which they would never fully recover.

Joseph Smith Jr.'s Early Childhood

RELATIVELY LITTLE IS known about Joseph Smith Jr.'s earliest years. By the time he was born on 23 December 1805, the family debt crisis had forced them into a tenant-farming cycle of moving from one nearby farm to the next, staying in one location no more than a two-year period. One historian described the migratory route between 1803 and 1811 as "a tiny circle around Tunbridge, Royalton, and Sharon, [Vermont]...and probably never involved a distance of more than five or six miles."[13] Then, in mid-1812, the family moved their belongings across the Connecticut River to Lebanon, New Hampshire, a distance of some twenty miles, to start yet another new life.

The farm in Lebanon became the venue for a life-shaping event for young Joseph Smith. In 1812 to 1813 a typhus epidemic spread throughout the upper Connecticut River Valley. One by one the Smith children fell victim, with Joseph's older sister, Sophronia, the first to be afflicted. Each child suffered through the illness lasting on average two weeks; but with seven-year-old Joseph the illness lingered, leaving severe complications. In her history Lucy tells that the fever symptoms abated, but in a short time the young boy complained about a sore under his left armpit. A local country doctor misdiagnosed it as a muscle sprain and applied liniment and a "hot shovel" compress as a treatment. The pain steadily increased

---

12. Lucy Smith, *Biographical Sketches*, 45–46.
13. Richard L. Bushman, *Joseph Smith and the Beginnings of Mormonism* (Urbana: University of Illinois Press, 1984), 30–31.

and swelling became noticeable. On a second visit the doctor lanced the abscess to drain the infection, which produced "fully a quart" of pus. This brought immediate relief and gave the impression that Joseph was well on the road to recovery.

However, the typhus bacteria characteristically entered Joseph's bloodstream and lodged in the upper portion of his left shinbone. This condition, called osteomyelitis, quickly developed another abscess, creating even more severe pain. This condition lasted for some three weeks when, finally, the parents called for a surgeon.

The decision for surgery was quickly made and Lucy described the procedure as follows: "The surgeon made an incision of eight inches, on the front side of the leg, between the knee and ankle. This relieved the pain in a great measure, and the patient was quite comfortable until the wound began to heal, when the pain became as violent as ever." Performing the accepted medical procedure was ineffective based on today's medical knowledge. The typhus infection was not in the soft tissues but within the tibia bone. Joseph's physical condition required a more radical solution. In this case the standard medical procedure called for amputation, a remedy commonly practiced until 1874.[14]

COMMUNITY OF CHRIST LIBRARY-ARCHIVES

Lucy Mack Smith

Fortunately for the Smith family, Dartmouth Medical College was located in Hanover, just five miles from Lebanon and the Smith family farm. The founder of this college was noted physician Nathan Smith

---

14. Abraham O. Wilensky, *Osteomyelitis: Its Pathogenesis, Symptomatology, and Treatment* (New York: Macmillan, 1934), 189, in LeRoy S. Wirthlin, "Nathan Smith (1762–1828) Surgical Consultant to Joseph Smith," *Brigham Young University Studies* 17, no. 3 (Spring 1977): 330.

(no relation), the only surgeon in the United States with the knowledge of an alternative medical procedure that involved surgical removal of the infected bone rather than complete removal of the leg. It is not known who actually contacted Nathan Smith about Joseph's medical condition, although it is entirely possible that the family's principal surgeon, a Dr. Stone, may have done so.[15]

Nathan Smith, accompanied by his partner, Cyrus Perkins, and several of his students, arrived at the Smith farm and consulted with Joseph's parents.[16] Lucy and the patient insisted that amputation was not an option. No doubt Nathan Smith told Lucy of his experimental technique and received her consent to proceed with it. Preparations were made and the seven-year-old was offered an anesthetic wine or brandy, but the patient refused. Courageously, the young boy would endure this trauma without cord restraints and in his father's arms.

Lucy described in detail the surgical procedure although she was not allowed to remain in the makeshift operating room. Instead family members sent her away into a nearby pasture. The operation began with the surgeons boring a hole with a trephine on each side of the infected area of the patient's left tibia.[17] Then the surgeons chipped out three large pieces of diseased bone. When her son screamed in pain, Lucy rushed back to the cabin and burst into the room to find the bed drenched in blood

---

15. There is no record of a "Dr. Stone" practicing medicine in New England even though both Joseph, in his 1838–1839 "Manuscript History," and his mother, Lucy, in her *Biographical Sketches*, 63, specifically identify his name. For Joseph's reference see his "Manuscript History," Book A-1, Joseph Smith Papers, LDS Church Archives, Salt Lake City, Utah, 131, in Vogel, *Early Mormon Documents*, 1: 141. William D. Morain, in *The Sword of Laban: Joseph Smith Jr. and the Dissociated Mind* (Washington, D. C.: American Psychiatric Press, Inc., 1998), 21fn5, suggested that the reference to a Mr. Stone is a "Freudian slip" due to the strong influence of seer stones in the Smith family. Morain, a Harvard trained surgeon and author of more than one hundred scientific and literary publications, analyzed the psychological impact of such a trauma on a child.

16. That students would accompany surgeons, especially as renowned as Nathan Smith, was not surprising. Amputations during this era were rather rare, as were opportunities for Nathan Smith to demonstrate his experimental technique.

17. It is probable that Lucy received firsthand explanations from her husband as her source of information. A trephine is a small cylindrical saw normally used to remove bone from the skull. See Wirthlin, "Nathan Smith," 330fn39.

from the open wound and her son "pale as a corpse, and large drops of sweat...rolling down his face, whilst upon every creature was depicted the utmost agony!"[18]

After the surgeons finished, the natural healing process would determine whether the operation was successful. Over the next three months the constant pain subsided, but additional bone fragments appeared just below the skin that required further surgery to remove. By now the affliction had taken its toll on the young boy's body, and he was so weak that he had to be carried around the farmhouse. To accelerate the long recovery, Joseph Sr. took his son to Salem, Massachusetts, to live with his brother, Jesse. Many believed that sea breezes had medicinal value. The length of the Salem convalescence is not recorded, but Joseph Jr. hobbled on crutches for three years after the surgery and limped noticeably for the remainder of his life.[19]

"The Year without a Summer"

THE SMITH FAMILY suffered mightily through the typhus epidemic of 1812–1813. But nature's wrath was not yet finished, as New Englanders soon experienced three successive crop failures. Probably

---

18. Lucy Smith, *Biographical Sketches*, 65.

19. Certainly there were unavoidable emotional scars from this dramatic event. These could well have had long-term effects on Joseph Jr. that may well have affected him throughout his life. In *The Sword of Laban*, Morain suggested this recurrence of the surgery's impact can be seen in the language of the prophet's delivery of an 1830 Fayette revelation: "Open ye your ears and hearken to the voice of the Lord your God, whose word is quick and powerful, sharper than a two-edged sword, to the dividing asunder of the joints and marrow, soul and spirit; and is a discerner of the thoughts and intents of the heart (106)." This statement was eventually printed as Section 32:1b (LDS 33:1) of the Doctrine and Covenants. See also 6:1b, 10:1b, 11:1b, and 12:1b (LDS 6:2, 11:2, 12:2, and 14:2).

In an equally provocative psychobiographical study, Robert D. Anderson, a trained psychiatrist whose interest is in applied psychoanalysis, associated Joseph Smith Jr.'s explanation of the cataclysm of the resurrection of Jesus Christ with his "barely-averted amputation of his leg and ensuing bloody operation." Anderson found this experience replayed obsessively within the Book of Mormon. He suggested the beheadings at the beginning (Laban) and ending (Shiz) and violence throughout the Book of Mormon story as psychological reflections of Smith's open surgery. See Robert D. Anderson, *Inside the Mind of Joseph Smith: Psychobiography and the Book of Mormon* (Salt Lake City: Signature Books, 1999), 25.

in May or June of 1814 the Smiths moved to Norwich, Vermont, and, according to Lucy, rented a farm from an "Esquire Moredock."[20] During this first summer, cold snaps destroyed grain crops, which were the most important source of sustenance and income. The sale of fruit from the Smiths' orchard that survived the cold weather allowed the family to eke out their bare necessities, with hopes for a better growing season the next summer. Those hopes were dashed when the climatic conditions during the summer of 1815 were no better. Of this misfortune Lucy wrote: "Mr. Smith now determined to plant once more, and if he should meet with no better success than he had the two preceding years, he would then go to the state of New York, where wheat was raised in abundance."[21]

New Englanders, who endured the following summer, referred to 1816 with disdain as "the year without a summer," the "Poverty Year," and "Eighteen Hundred and Froze to Death." Understandings of meteorology and the fragile relationship between geological events and atmospheric conditions were too primitive at that time to know that the volcanic eruption of Tambora on the Indonesian island of Sumbawa in 1815 decreased temperatures worldwide by reflection of solar radiation. This spectacular eruption jettisoned 150–180 cubic kilometers of the earth's surface into the atmosphere, making it the single greatest volcanic eruption in recorded history. It is estimated that some 92,000 lives, worldwide, were lost due to starvation caused by the 1815 Tambora eruption.[22]

20. Historian Dan Vogel speculates that the Smiths' landlord was probably Constant Murdock, one of Norwich's leading citizens. See his *Making of a Prophet*, 19.
21. Lucy Smith, *Biographical Sketches*, 67.
22. This death toll was more than twice that caused by the Krakatoa tsunami eruption of 1883 that sent only twenty cubic kilometers into the atmosphere, impacting sunsets around the world for years afterward. Scientific measurements to assess accurately the Tambora explosion were unavailable in 1815. However, today the United States Geological Survey estimates that Tambora's volcanic cloud lowered global temperatures as much as 3°C. For more information on the Tambora volcano, see W. Jacquelyne Kious and Robert I. Tilling, *This Dynamic Earth: The Story of Plate Tectonics* (Washington, D.C.: U.S. Geological Survey, 2003). A comparison of Tambora with the destruction of other cataclysmic eruptions can be found in Simon Winchester, *Krakatoa: The Day the World Exploded, August 27, 1883* (New York: HarperCollins Publishers, 2003), 4–5, and in R. J. Blong, *Volcanic Hazards: A Sourcebook on the Effects of Eruptions* (Orlando: Academic Press, 1994). Also see Klaus J. Hansen, *Mormonism and the American Experience* (Chicago: University of Chicago Press, 1981), 1–2.

Frosts, near-freezing temperatures, and foot-deep June snowstorms in the Vermont highlands to flurries as far south as Salem, Massachusetts, devastated fragile crops. Temperatures plummeted in August to nearly 30 degrees in the low-lying areas between Albany, New York, and Boston, Massachusetts, destroying corn already suffering from drought conditions. As winter approached, product scarcity forced up crop prices beyond the reach of the family's income. By fall Joseph Sr. knew the next family move would have to be out of New England.

Warning Out!

FROM 1779 TO 1817, Vermont communities were legally required to create a social safety net for the poor and indigent who settled within the village boundaries. If a family lived within the confines of the village for more than a year, they could receive at least the bare necessities for their survival. During prosperous times this obligation was borne easily; however, during difficult times, like from 1812 to 1817, the burden was a heavy one. Certainly there was a temptation to abuse this system, as poor migrants could move to wealthier areas of the state just to receive assistance from others. To counter this temptation, the state legislature provided a legal notice, called a "warning out," freeing the community from their obligation if the transient was served the notice within one year. This shifted the burden of responsibility of care for the indigent to their previous legal residence.

The warning-out procedure was directed specifically at transient families, like the Smiths, who moved frequently. Because the strict requirements of the law forced officials to initiate the warning out within one year of arrival, it behooved officials to serve transients as soon as they arrived. An extant warning-out document dates Constable John Brown serving the Smiths on 15 March 1816.[23] Thus, legal process removed any incentive for the Smiths to stay in New England if their motive was to receive public assistance in their time of extreme need. Considering their financial misfortunes, health problems, nature's wrath, and legal restrictions, the Smith family of Vermont had little to gain by staying in New England.

---

23. "A Record of Strangers Who are Warned Out of Town, 1813–1818," 53, Norwich Town Clerk's Office, Norwich, Vermont, in Vogel, *Early Mormon Documents*, 1: 666–68.

On to Palmyra, New York

THE SMITH FAMILY followed the westering migratory pattern of thousands of New Englanders during this period of American history.[24] Like so many other heads of households, Joseph had to find a climate less susceptible to the frigid New England weather, more suitable land to work, and convenient transportation for his crops. Palmyra, Ontario County, New York, seemed suitable. Lying southwest, in a warmer climate (perhaps more by perception than reality), the land had a reputation for high productivity, and the fast-growing village was a transportation hub for the newly opened Erie Canal.

In her family history, Lucy did not give the details of how she and her husband finally arrived at the decision to leave New England except to say that Joseph Sr. had learned about Palmyra from a Mr. Howard, who offered to be his traveling partner for the journey. After settling their debts, in the fall of 1816 Joseph Sr. headed for the canal town in western New York in search of prosperity for his family, and Lucy followed with the family early the next year—probably in January.

Lucy's three-hundred-mile journey in the dead of winter with her eight children—including her oldest, Alvin, at nineteen years; her youngest, Don Carlos, at ten months; and Joseph Jr. on crutches—was an insurmountable challenge to take on by herself. Nor could she leave behind her mother, Lydia Mack, who was staying with the family in Norwich. The travel route would have to include returning her mother to the Mack home in Royalton, Vermont. Knowing his wife needed help, Joseph made arrangements with his travel partner to have his cousin Luther Howard travel with Lucy and the children as teamster and guide. Along the trail she met a family named Gates, so they decided to make the journey together. Not long into the trip Lucy found Luther Howard consorting with the Gates's two daughters, drinking heavily, and abusing her children. Howard forced Joseph Jr., who could only recently walk without his crutches, out of

---

24. The best discussion of these patterns is found in Whitney R. Cross, *The Burned-over District: The Social and Intellectual History of Enthusiastic Religion in Western New York, 1800–1850* (Ithaca, N.Y.: Cornell University Press, 1982), 78–109. Cross demonstrated clearly that this migration differed from other contemporary western migrations due to the absence of vast virgin frontier tracts of land in western New York. Rather, villages like Palmyra, New York, experienced rapid growth due to the Erie Canal (79).

MAP BY JOHN HAMER

Palmyra, New York, in relation to the Erie Canal (boundaries as of 1816)

the wagon. In his 1838–1839 "Manuscript History," Joseph Jr. wrote that he "suffered the most excruciating weariness & pain." When his older brothers went to Joseph's defense, Howard beat them with his whip handle.[25]

At a small town twenty miles west of Utica, New York, with two-thirds of the difficult trip behind them, Howard attempted to commandeer the Smith wagon and team. Lucy had had enough. She found Howard in a bar room, turned to the patrons, and in a loud voice exposed his plot to leave her and her eight children without means of continuing on. In front of her audience, she turned to Howard and angrily declared, "Sir, I now forbid you touching the team, or driving it one step further. You can go about your own business; I have no use for you. I shall take charge of the team myself, and hereafter attend to my own affairs."[26] Evidently her

25. Joseph Smith, "Manuscript History," in Vogel, *Early Mormon Documents*, 1: 142.
26. Lucy Smith, *Biographical Sketches*, 70–71.

confrontation with Howard in front of an audience proved successful, since in a short time she made it to Palmyra with her children and the family possessions, but near penniless. After a nearly intolerable two-week winter expedition, averaging twenty-two miles per day, the Smith family finally reunited.

Life in Palmyra

ALTHOUGH THE GEOGRAPHY had changed, their destitute conditions remained the same. Joseph Sr. rented a small house on the west end of Palmyra Village, a canal town on the cusp of dramatic growth. To prosper, they needed a plan. Lucy wrote, "We all now sat down, and counseled together relative to the course which was best for us to adopt in our destitute circumstances."[27] Their plan was to purchase land and establish a farm in the area.

Joseph and Lucy's best times financially were 1802, in Randolph, Vermont, where they established a general store, so it should not be surprising that again they would hang a shingle in Palmyra. With an entrepreneurial spirit, and taking advantage of the canal boom and village growth trends, the Smiths set up a "cake and beer shop." Here patrons could find an assortment of gingerbread, pies, boiled eggs, root-beer, and similar items. Village resident Pomeroy Tucker told of the store's success, as the business "soon became popular with the juvenile people of the town and country, commanding brisk sales."[28] During times of community celebrations and festivals the family peddled their products through the crowds by pushcart. As an added source of income, Lucy figured that she could pay the bills by selling her hand-painted tablecloths while Joseph Sr., Alvin, Hyrum, and Joseph Jr. hired themselves out as day laborers, gardening, harvesting, clearing land, and digging wells.

---

27. Lucy Smith, *Biographical Sketches*, 71. Using census statistics and contemporary newspaper reports, historian Richard Bushman assessed the Palmyra Village population at 2,614 residents in 1810. In 1823, Palmyra divided its land and population with Macedon, New York, but the total population of the two jumped to 5,416 by 1830. See Bushman's demographic analysis in *Joseph Smith and the Beginnings of Mormonism*, 43–47.

28. Pomeroy Tucker, *Origin, Rise, and Progress of Mormonism* (New York: D. Appleton and Co., 1867), in Vogel, *Early Mormon Documents*, 3: 89.

By 1818, the family finally accumulated enough money to purchase their tract of land. Less than two miles south of town was a 3,000-acre tract parceled out in farm-size acreages. Eventually Joseph and Lucy contracted with a land agent to purchase a one-hundred-acre tract. With hard work and determination to free themselves from their poverty-stricken lifestyle, the family accomplished much by the end of their first year: they made nearly all their first annual payment, built a log house on their property, and cleared thirty acres in preparation for cultivation.[29] William recalled that, at the end of 1820, they had a sizeable acreage in production as well as an orchard planted. Now in his mid-teen years, Joseph Jr. was physically able to hire out to local farmers, thus adding to the family income. With each passing month on the farm, prosperity edged closer, yet the memory of fifteen years of abject poverty always lingered. There was still never enough for the Smiths to feel comfortable, and family members constantly searched for more money.

Leaving Alvin in Palmyra to run the cake and beer shop, in 1819 the family moved south to live in a rented "rude log house" owned by Samuel Jennings. Here they lived for more than two years. During the summer of 1820, Joseph Sr. and Alvin signed an "Article of Agreement" on one hundred acres. This practice, called "articling," allowed hardworking, productive, but cash-poor people to sign an agreement that allowed them to possess land by paying installments over a period of years. The buyer agreed to make improvements while making payments. The seller's investment was protected by contractual stipulations that allowed him to receive back the property with the improvements should the buyer default.[30]

The Smiths did not move onto their new land until they had completed construction of their own cabin, sometime between 1822 and 1823.

---

29. Lucy Smith, *Biographical Sketches*, 72.
30. For a more complete explanation of articling in its historical context, see H. Michael Marquardt and Wesley P. Walters, *Inventing Mormonism: Tradition and the Historical Record* (Salt Lake City: Smith Research Associates, 1994), 5–6. A more modern equivalent of articling is the practice of "contract for deed." This legally binding arrangement strongly favors the seller, since this person can add mandatory conditions that include scheduled improvements that would increase the property value and extend the final cost beyond a well-meaning purchaser's ability to pay. Default became a tactic to re-acquire property. This obviously benefited the seller, who retained the mandated improvements, as well as the increased equity over the length of the contract.

Certainly the timber from the thickly wooded acreage provided excellent building material. Whether they were victimized by poor economic conditions in upstate New York or by their ever-expanding family,[31] even with their best attempts to make ends meet the family became overextended. In December 1825, the Smiths defaulted on their articled property and a prosperous Quaker, Lemuel Durfee, purchased the farm. Although Durfee allowed the Smiths to stay on the farm and pay rent, once again the family faced an uncertain future.[32]

Coping with More Economic Uncertainties

For the eight years between 1817 and 1825, the Smith family lived in Palmyra but had little to show for it. The two most prominent uncertainties confronting them were familiar ones—financial and religious. In general, the Smiths had few marketable skills that would lift them out of their poverty other than their strong backs and a willingness to work. These fine qualities set them in good stead, but unfortunately their common labors commanded low wages. Joseph Sr., with some blacksmith skills, had learned coopering from his father, Asael, and taught Hyrum what he had learned. But Benjamin Saunders, a Palmyra neighbor, recalled that the Smiths "did not like to make a steady busines of it."[33] Joseph Sr. also taught school in Sharon, Vermont, but mostly relied on his knowledge of farming to earn a living.

During most of her childbearing years, Lucy Mack Smith was expecting, delivering, or nursing a baby. Not long after her marriage to Joseph in January 1796, she became pregnant and birthed her first child in 1797. The unnamed male child did not survive, but she became pregnant again, establishing a pattern that would bear eleven children in twenty-four years. Constantly on the move, creating a home, caring for her husband, and raising nine children to adulthood consumed this remarkable woman's daily

---

31. Yet another daughter, Lucy, was born in Palmyra on 18 July 1821.
32. That Durfee allowed the Smith family to stay on the property as renters suggested either his honorable intention or that nothing would be gained by taking immediate possession of the property. Rent payments continued his revenue flow.
33. Benjamin Saunders, interviewed by William H. Kelley, circa September 1884, 20, "Miscellany," Community of Christ Library-Archives, Independence, Missouri.

Early Smith Family History 47

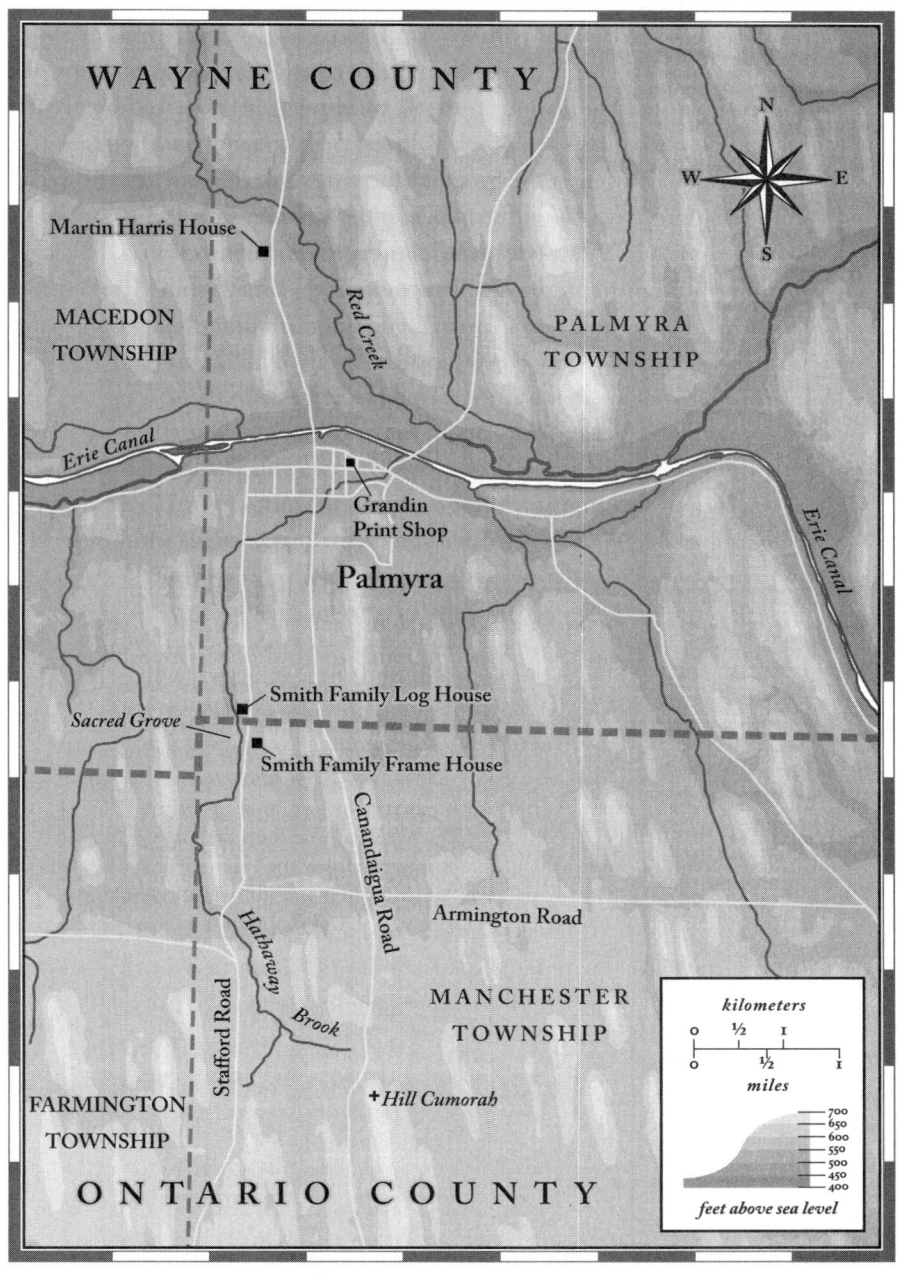

MAP BY JOHN HAMER

Locations of Smith family homes near Palmyra, New York (boundaries as of 1829)

life. No doubt she had some artistic skill, but this minimal income potential weighed against the overwhelming domestic duties that pressed heavily upon her; Lucy would have to depend on other family members as the primary wage earners.[34]

The oldest surviving Smith child, Alvin, contributed significantly to the family income. In August 1821, he almost single-handedly raised enough money to make the second property payment and pay the debt remaining from the first. Alvin accepted the task of building the frame house on their Manchester property, but his sudden death in November 1823 devastated the family, delaying completion of the house and placing an even greater burden on the other family members to make up for his lost earning power.[35] Perhaps feeling sorry for the loss of Alvin, friends and neighbors worked with the family to complete the frame house by the fall of 1825, approximately one month before they defaulted.

Hyrum, perhaps the most educated member of the Smith family, attended Moor's Charity School, an institution associated with Dartmouth College, in Hanover, New Hampshire, until the typhus epidemic. Being personal caregiver for his younger brother Joseph Jr. interrupted his attendance. While in Palmyra, Hyrum taught school, served as a trustee of the local school district, and took on the responsibility of hiring teachers.[36] He also taught in the neighboring Stafford school district. Many decades later,

34. Historian Lavina Fielding Anderson viewed Mother Smith as "a model of the early nineteenth-century republican mother, a 'moral mother' who displayed piety, dispensed values, shaped character at the domestic hearth, and brought up her [children] in the paths of civic virtue." See Lavina Anderson, *Lucy's Book*, 10.

35. Alvin contracted bilious colic and doctors administered a large dose of calomel. This common prescription was a compound of mercury and chlorine, thought to be a purgative of the supposed infected bile. Unfortunately the dose lodged in the patient's stomach. When five physicians failed to dislodge the medicine, Alvin's fate was sealed. He died on 19 November 1823. For further explanation, see Bushman, *Joseph Smith and the Beginnings of Mormonism*, 64–65.

36. In fact, Hyrum tried to hire a schoolteacher from Poultney, Vermont, named Lyman Cowdery, but because of a schedule conflict, Lyman recommended, and Hyrum hired, his brother Oliver. During the school year, Oliver lived with the Smiths. At this time Joseph and his wife, Emma, were living in Harmony, Pennsylvania. When Oliver finished his teaching obligation in Palmyra, Samuel Harrison Smith took Cowdery to Harmony and introduced him to his older brother Joseph. This launched a close relationship that lasted a decade.

S. F. Anderick, a female childhood friend and neighbor, remembered that Hyrum was "the only son sufficiently educated to teach school" and that he and Sophronia "were the most respected of the family."[37]

Until they came of age, young Joseph and his younger siblings contributed to the overall family income but in smaller amounts.[38] For example, in April 1827, Samuel Harrison worked for Lemuel Durfee to offset some of the rent the family was paying on the farm. In August of that year Joseph Jr. took his turn. In her interview Anderick recalled that people who knew the Smiths as she did wondered how such a large family could get by on so little.

For people then, as well as now, times of uncertainty prompted much theological reflection. Religion would have frequently featured in Smith family discussions, but during these times, probably more so and in very special ways. Theological issues of the day no doubt dominated evening conversations as family gathered at the hearth after a hard day's work. Heated disputes on issues relating to

COURTESY JOHN HAMER
The Smith family frame home near Palmyra

---

37. Anderick's first name is not a matter of record, but she moved to Palmyra about 1812. After the death of her mother, and her father's departure from Palmyra, Anderick remained with her uncle, Earl Wilcox, until 1828. See Arthur B. Deming Collection, *Naked Truths About Mormonism* (January 1888): 2, in Vogel, *Early Mormon Documents*, 2: 207–11.

38. Christopher M. Stafford remembered, "Old Jo claimed to be a Cooper but worked very little at anything. He was intemperate. Hyrum worked at cooperage. . . . I exchanged work with Jo [Jr.] but more with his brother [Samuel] Harrison, who was a good, industrious boy." See C. M. Stafford, *Naked Truths About Mormonism* (April 1888): 1, in Vogel, *Early Mormon Documents*, 2: 193–95. Other neighbors agreed that Samuel Harrison was an asset to the family. Hiram Jackway, who lived on Stafford Road on the southern outskirts of Palmyra Village and not far from the Smiths, stated, "Harrison was a good worker for one day or a month." See William H. Kelley Notebook, March 1881, 12, Community of Christ Library-Archives.

scriptural interpretation, preachers' sermon statements, baptism, and salvation likely sparked disagreement among family members. Finding consensus on these topics would prove difficult considering Lucy's Calvinist background and Joseph Sr.'s Universalism. In this environment, Joseph Jr. took in arguments from both sides, heard competing theologies from revivalist preachers, grew bewildered, and then sought his own answers in a nearby grove of trees.

CHAPTER FOUR

The First Vision and Its Impact

FOR MANY IN the Latter Day Saint movement today, Joseph Smith Jr.'s youthful visionary encounter at his farm near Manchester, New York, stands as the "charter event of the Restoration." Traditionally, this epiphany has been called the First Vision or the Sacred Grove Experience. A close look at the experience reveals new insights about this very special and sacred encounter. Why did the prophet take so long to record his First Vision story? How unique was having such an epiphany? How important was the spiritual experience to the first generation members of the movement? Were the vast majority of early Saints even aware of the First Vision in the opening years? What environmental circumstances influenced Joseph's portrayal of the event? When given the opportunity did Joseph tell the story consistently, and if not, then why not? And, most importantly, what place did this encounter have in the development of the religious movement founded by Joseph Smith Jr.?[1]

The Process of Joseph Smith Jr.'s Conversion

IN HIS YOUTH, Joseph Smith Jr. seemed to follow a rather predictable pattern of religious conversion in the years leading up to his First

---

1. In writing this chapter I am especially grateful for the groundbreaking research and writings of Michael Marquardt and Wesley Walters on this crucial topic. Their *Inventing Mormonism* makes a significant contribution to understanding this episode in the church story. I also acknowledge the fine research of Michael Quinn. His conclusions conflict at various points with those of Marquardt and Walters yet contribute significantly to a clearer understanding of this important topic. To all three I owe a debt of gratitude.

Vision. Historian Dickson D. Bruce Jr. explained a rather common series of experiences that people had during this era of religious enthusiasm. He identified four stages that people progressed through to arrive at their religious conversion. The first stage, or "preconversion," grew from dissatisfaction with the person's lifestyle that involved sinfulness and neglectful spirituality. When this condition could no longer be borne, the individual acknowledged the error of his or her ways and entered the second stage—"conviction." Here the person rejected sinful friends, bad habits, and worldly appetites. In the third stage, as their soul was in anguish amid their contrition and repentance, "conversion" would come through divine interdiction, usually with an epiphany or a spiritual encounter. Sometimes this experience was a vision involving heavenly personages, a heavenly whisper, or some encounter of the Spirit that led to an enlightened mind or spiritual awareness. This initiated the actual conversion, but there was more. The fourth stage would be ongoing events that provided "assurance" that the conversion experience was actually divine.[2] Although Bruce's study focused primarily on the experiences of those in the southern United States, his observations are certainly applicable to Joseph Smith's circumstances in upstate New York.

Reviewing the "Traditional Account"[3]

THE FIRST OPPORTUNITY that Joseph Smith used to record his divine encounter occurred approximately twelve years after the event. At least two reasons explain this lapse of time. First was the story's poor initial public reception in Palmyra and the surrounding upstate New York

---

2. Dickson D. Bruce Jr., *And They All Sang Hallelujah: Plain-Folk Camp-Meeting Religion, 1800–1845* (Knoxville: University of Tennessee Press, 1974), 61–69.

3. Through the years the 1842 version has been widely used throughout the Latter Day Saint movement. Yet I hesitate to call this the "official account" for two reasons. First, the Community of Christ does not take "official positions" in matters of church history; thus, to deem this account "official" is to reverse that important policy. Second, although more detail is added here, the lack of consistency with other versions calls into question the historical veracity of the specific details. However, that the details vary from account to account suggests that a spiritual encounter in fact did happen. The variations evidence legitimacy since so much is lost when the Divine Mind encounters the human mind. Confusion on details would naturally result.

countryside.[4] This lack of acceptance weighed heavily on the young man. Second, with the passage of time, other significant events in his life dwarfed the First Vision's importance. Aggressively pursuing his glass-looking and treasure seeking, angelic visitations associated with the Book of Mormon, his marriage to Emma Hale of Harmony, Pennsylvania, the translation process of the metallic plates, church and priesthood organization, church conferences, and the move to Kirtland, Ohio, all pre-empted the First Vision story. Thus, his Palmyra epiphany played a less significant role in the foundation of the church. That the prophet would take twelve years before he recorded the account becomes more understandable.

Through the generations most Latter Day Saint believers have embraced Joseph Smith Jr.'s 1842 account of the First Vision as the standard explanation for this very special event in the teenager's life. This "traditional version" appears serially in the spring 1842 issues of the Nauvoo, Illinois, church newspaper, the *Times and Seasons*. Over time, much folklore has arisen about events in upstate New York that caused the young boy to enter a wooded glen near his Manchester home in search of an answer to his question about what church to join. For some today the Grove Experience story approaches canonized status; others doubt it happened as explained in the *Times and Seasons*, and still others doubt it even happened at all. Yet it is the unquestionable long-term impact of the story that has significantly sustained the Latter Day Saint religious movement that now has spread literally around the world.

Briefly stated, during his fifteenth year Joseph was greatly excited about the religious revivals occurring near his Manchester, New York, home. As he listened to the various preachers claim to represent the "true church," he became confused as to which church to join. But in his

---

4. "History of Joseph Smith," *Times and Seasons* 3, no. 11 (1 April 1842): 748. In early versions of Smith's story, persecution was not mentioned. However, in later iterations the persecution theme became an important component of the story. Also see Lucy Mack Smith's explanation of how her young son was reviled for telling his encounter in public, in *Biographical Sketches*, 83. Mother Smith may have referred to her son's 1838–1839 "Manuscript History," where the prophet remembered being in the company of a Methodist minister who condemned the young boy "saying it was all of the Devil, that there was no such thing as visions or revelations in these days, that all such things had ceased with the apostles and that there never would be any more of them." See Joseph Smith, "Manuscript History," in Vogel, *Early Mormon Documents*, 1: 61–62.

decision to remain aloof from all the competing religions, he became restless. Then he heard the challenge of a Methodist revival preacher, identified as George Lane, to read James 1:5: "If any of you lack wisdom, let him ask of God, that giveth unto all men liberally and upbraideth not; and it shall be given him." So Joseph decided to ask for guidance in prayer.

In the 1842 account, the prophet identified only in general terms a "beautiful clear day, early in the spring of eighteen hundred and twenty" as the date when he "retired to the woods" to pray. Ensuring that he was truly alone, Joseph knelt and poured out "the desires of his heart" when suddenly he was overcome by "an astounding influence" that bound his tongue. He struggled to escape it but could not. While feeling he was doomed to destruction, a pillar of light with "the brightness of the noon day sun" appeared over his head, freeing him from his destruction.

Two personages appeared in the light and stood above him. One pointed to the other and said, "This is my beloved Son, hear him." Then, Joseph and the personage engaged in a conversation that answered his question about which church to join. The boy was told to join none of the churches, "that all creeds were an abomination in his sight; that those professors were corrupt, 'they draw near to me with their lips, but their hearts are far from me; they teach for doctrine the commandments of men, have a form of godliness, but they deny the power thereof.'" From the personage, Joseph learned many other things that he said he could not "write at this time." At that point the epiphany ended and Joseph came to his senses, finding himself lying on his back "looking up into heaven." As the boy left the grove, he knew that he had experienced a divine encounter and later wrote that he knew also that God knew it.[5]

---

5. For this description I have used the popular writing widely distributed to the church throughout the second half of the twentieth century titled *Joseph Smith Tells His Own Story*. This 32-page tract best presents what would be deemed the "traditional account" of the First Vision, the Book of Mormon story, and of church organization. Herald House, of Independence, Missouri, printed this tract until 2004. This version of the First Vision story is based, generally, on "History of Joseph Smith," *Times and Seasons* 3, no.10 (15 March 1842): 726–28, and 3, no. 11 (1 April 1842): 748–49.

The "First Vision" Experiences of Other Religious Leaders in Early American History

IN THE DAYS that followed, Joseph shared his testimony with family members and people in the surrounding community. Many years later, he claimed that his story "excited a great deal of prejudice" and that great persecution resulted from the belief that "an obscure boy only between fourteen and fifteen years of age" could not have such an experience. Joseph expressed some bewilderment about why persecution would follow his testimony when he knew in his heart it was true: "Why persecute [me] for telling the truth? I have actually seen a vision, 'and who am I that I can withstand God.'"[6] His question was a good one.

During this era of American history, claims of divine encounters were frequently recorded. On the American continent, people were having life-changing epiphanies as early as the 1700s. Connecticut-born cleric David Brainerd (1718–1747) had an encounter that paralleled Joseph Smith's in many aspects. He dated his divine experience to the early morning of 12 July 1732:

> The sun was scarce half an hour high...as I was walking in a dark thick grove, "unspeakable glory" seemed to open to the view and apprehension of my soul: I don't mean any external brightness, for I saw no such thing, nor do I intend any imagination of a body of light, somewhere away in the third heavens, or anything of that nature; but it was a new inward apprehension or view that I had of God; such as I never had before, nor anything which had the least remembrance of it. I stood still and wondered and admired!
>
> I knew that I had never seen before anything comparable to it for excellency and beauty: It was widely different from all the conceptions that ever I had had of God, or things divine. I had no particular apprehension of any one person of the Trinity, either the Father, Son, or Holy Ghost, but it appeared to be divine glory that I then beheld. And my soul "rejoiced with joy unspeakable" to see such a God, such a glorious divine being; and I was inwardly pleased and satisfied that he should be God over all forever and ever. My soul was so captivated

6. "Joseph Smith, "Manuscript History," in Vogel, *Early Mormon Documents*, 1: 62 (brackets added by Vogel).

and delighted with the excellency, loveliness, greatness, and other perfections of God, that I was even swallowed up in him, at least to that degree that I had no thought (as I remember) at first, about my own salvation, or scarce reflected there was such a creature as myself.[7]

Brainerd's spiritual experience continued into the darkness of evening before it ended. Some differences with Joseph Smith's experience are noticeable in Brainerd's explanation of his Grove Experience; nevertheless, it was just as powerful to him. Brainerd was among the most successful Congregationalist missionaries to the Native Americans of his era.[8]

Caleb Rich (1750–1821), the most important native New England Universalist preacher of his time, was born in Sutton, Massachusetts, and raised in a separatist Baptist tradition. He was one of many to be confused by competing denominational claims. With the passing of time, he contemplated his spiritual condition: "My situation appeared more precarious than a ticket in a lottery, where there was a hundred blanks to one prize." Rich could not understand why God would "for ever [suffer] the world to be thus enveloped in such a dilemma, and overwhelmed in such impenetrable darkness." After his family move in 1771 northward across Massachusetts

COURTESY STEPHEN ROSS

David Brainerd, missionary to Native Americans. Members of the Delaware tribe referred to Brainerd as a "prophet of God."

---

7. Jonathan Edwards, *An Account of the Life of the Reverend Mr. David Brainerd...*, ed. Norman Pettit (New Haven: Yale University Press, 1985), 137–39. Pettit compared the Brainerd manuscript with the 1749 edition published by Jonathan Edwards.

8. David Brainerd had a strong impact on Jonathan Edwards, one of the founders of the Great Awakening: "Only in the subsequent years when [Edwards] came to know the dying David Brainerd did he find a male model of the submissive piety he so loved." See George M. Marsden, *Jonathan Edwards: A Life* (New Haven: Yale University Press, 2003), 249.

to Warwick, along the New Hampshire border, Rich had a series of visions, causing him to pursue the ministry.

Starting with an angelic "still small voice" and then progressing to an actual conversation with Jesus Christ, Rich was told to avoid all other denominations. An angel assured him through his studies of the Bible and with heavenly advice that salvation would be his. Two years later, after his excommunication from the Baptist Church, Rich became convinced that no existing church "stood in the Apostolic rectitude or...contended for the faith once delivered to the saints" and launched his famed ministerial career preaching the Universalist doctrine of salvation for all.[9] Writing in his journal, Rich testified to the authenticity of his visionary encounter: "I could say in truth that the gospel that was preached by me, was not after man; for I neither received it of man, neither was I taught it by man, but by the revelation of Jesus Christ, through the medium of the Holy Spirit in opening my understanding to understand the scriptures."[10]

Many other religious leaders claimed similar epiphanies at the root of their ministerial careers. Historian Grant H. Palmer, in studying the original writings of eight other important clerics of this era, found that a common denominator was to have a vision during their youth that called them to the ministry.[11] For example, Eleazer Sherman, a contemporary of Joseph Smith Jr., had a vision on 10 January 1815 in which he received deliverance from his sins. The bright light signifying the presence of God and forgiveness were key themes in Joseph's First Vision explanation. This was a well-known story and was probably known to the young Smith.

Joseph most likely recalled the well-known vision of Elias Smith (no relation), the dynamic Baptist pastor in Woburn, Massachusetts, who had a dream during a logging accident in 1816. Also, in 1825, Billy Hibbard, a Methodist fire-brand preacher on the huge Litchfield, Connecticut, circuit, published his 1782 vision, received when he was twelve years old. Young Hibbard, son of a cobbler who participated in Shays's

---

9. Marini, *Radical Sects*, 71–74.
10. Caleb Rich, "A Narrative of Elder Caleb Rich," *Candid Examiner* 2, 30 April–18 June 1827, 179, in Marini, *Radical Sects*, 75.
11. Palmer studied Billy Hibbard, Abel Thornton, Jesse Lee, Lorenzo Dow, Alfred Bennett, Ray Potter, Eleazer Sherman, and Benjamin Putnam. See Grant H. Palmer, *An Insider's View of Mormon Origins* (Salt Lake City: Signature Books, 2002), 239.

Rebellion,[12] went to a "secret place to pray" and had a "grove experience" of his own. This, too, was a well-known story.

Unlike with other clerics, Joseph Smith Jr.'s First Vision did not launch his ministerial career. As will be shown, in the years immediately following his Grove Experience, the boy admitted to his frailties: "I was left to all kinds of temptations, and mingling with all kinds of society, I frequently fell into many foolish errors and displayed the weakness of youth and the corruption of human nature, which I am sorry to say led me into divers temptations, to the gratification of many appetites offensive in the sight of God."[13] It took a series of angelic epiphanies in 1823 for him to realize that his life's calling was to become a prophet of God.

COURTESY HANS ROLLMAN

Elias Smith, Baptist cleric, testified of his 1816 vision.

Assessing the Traditional Account

FROM A HISTORICAL perspective, many issues have been raised concerning the 1842 "traditional" account. These questions focus on the actual timing of the event, and especially the changes in the many different renditions over a ten-year period, from the first time Joseph recorded the event between 1831 and 1832, to the last time, in the *Times and Seasons* in the spring of 1842. A careful study by historian Richard Howard in 1980 demonstrated the different aspects of the First Vision recorded in the six major explanations (see chart on pages 62 and 63).[14] Most noteworthy was

12. Hatch, *Democratization of American Christianity*, 19–20.
13. "History of Joseph Smith," *Times and Seasons* 3, no. 11 (1 April 1842): 749.
14. Richard P. Howard, "An Analysis of Six Contemporary Accounts Touching Joseph Smith's First Vision," *Restoration Studies I: A Collection of Essays About the History, Beliefs, and Practices of the Reorganized Church of Jesus Christ of Latter Day Saints*, ed.

the central episode in the epiphany—the young boy's conversation with the personage. As Howard has observed, in the first and third of the early accounts, prior to 1840, Joseph saw only one heavenly being, and in the second, identification to whom the boy was speaking was not important enough to even mention. Only starting with the 1840 Orson Pratt account did Joseph change the story to include two separate personages, and then stayed with that number through 1842.

Chronological issues of the First Vision also have been of interest. In the different accounts, Joseph's age at the time of the encounter ranged from "about fourteen" to "sixteenth year." Michael Marquardt and Wesley Walters, after researching newspaper accounts and church records, have questioned whether a great religious revival occurred in Joseph Smith's upstate New York in the early spring of 1820, when he would have been fourteen years and three to five months old. Newspaper coverage about revivalism in western New York in 1820 was all but silent. Baptismal rates in area churches in 1820 were either flat or in decline. These two historians' studies of church records actually showed decreases in early 1820. For example, the First Baptist Church in Palmyra recorded only eight baptisms for the entire year of 1820, and only fourteen were recorded for the Presbyterians of Palmyra between February 1820 and March 1821 (including four from the Smith family).[15]

Reinterpreting the same information, historian Michael Quinn disagreed with Marquardt and Walters. Quinn suggested that if Smith's dating of the First Vision encounter were changed to the very late spring of 1820, then a chronology of events could be constructed to sustain Smith's original story. Also Quinn observed a "presentist bias" among critics of the traditional account as they superimposed modern understanding of linguistic expressions on Joseph Smith Jr.'s early-nineteenth-century generation. For example, Quinn argued that it was possible to conclude from Smith's language his reference to multiple revivals over a period of two years. This would validate Smith's chronology since revivals did happen in 1818 and 1819. Countering the observance of declining baptismal rates

---

Maurice L. Draper and Clare D. Vlahos (Independence, Mo.: Herald House, 1980), 95–117; this article includes "An Examination of Fourteen Aspects of the First Vision as Variously Treated in Six Contemporary Accounts."

15. Marquardt and Walters, *Inventing Mormonism*, 17–18.

in Palmyra churches, Quinn argued that because Palmyra's decline was minimal when compared to other districts, the Methodist revival to which Smith referred did result in some baptisms during the months surrounding the spring of 1820. Thus, having an increase in baptisms at a time of considerable decline merits the description Smith gave the period.[16]

In Oliver Cowdery's brief reference to the First Vision, in 1834, using language no doubt approved by Joseph Smith, he mentioned the importance for Smith's conversion of Methodist preacher George Lane's challenge to "ask of God." Historical documents verify that Reverend Lane did in fact lead a revival in Palmyra, but Lane's own records, as well as the records of his sponsoring Methodist Church, clearly show that Lane was appointed to the Ontario District (which included Palmyra) in July 1824. According to these same records, Lane left the area and the ministry, at least temporarily, in January 1825, due to an illness that befell his family.[17] Historians generally agree to the inaccuracy of Cowdery's 1834 reference.

Then what prompted Joseph Smith Jr. to go to James 1:5, if not George Lane's revival sermon? Quinn's studies of hymnody of the time revealed popular lyrics that could have easily prompted the young boy to search the Epistle of James. An 1811 Poughkeepsie, New York, collection titled *Usually Sung at Camp Meetings* includes the hymn with the first line "O When shall I see Jesus." Later in the hymn is a restatement of the James 1:5 scripture:

> O do not be discourag'd
>   For Jesus is your friend,
> And if you lack for knowledge,
>   He'll not refuse to lend;
> Neither will he upbraid you,
>   Though often you request.

The words of another popular hymn expressed a second aspect of the First Vision encounter:

> As at the time of noon,

---

16. D. Michael Quinn, "Joseph Smith's Experience of a Methodist 'Camp Meeting' in 1820," *Dialogue: A Journal of Mormon Thought*, paperless: E-Paper #3, expanded version. www.dialoguejournal.com/excerpts/e3.pdf

17. Marquardt and Walters, *Inventing Mormonism*, 20–21.

>   My quadrant FAITH, I take,
>   To view my CHRIST, my sun,
>   If he the clouds should break:
>   I'm happy when his face I see,
>   I know then whereabouts I be.

An additional widely distributed camp meeting hymnal included lyrics portraying yet another aspect of the First Vision:

>   ONE ev'ning, pensive as I lay,
>   Alone upon the ground,
>   As I to God began to pray,
>   A light shone all around.
>   These words with power went through my heart
>   I've come to set you free;
>   Death[,] hell[,] nor grave shall never part,
>   My love (my son) from thee.

Quinn argued that it is very likely that "Joseph sang this hymn at Palmyra's Methodist revival" and explains why the young teenager thought it appropriate to seek out God alone. That God should appear in a "pillar of light" and for Joseph to find himself "lying on [his] back, looking up into the heaven" thus came as no surprise. The boy took the words of the hymns and scripture literally. This was the expectation.[18]

Varying Accounts of the First Vision and Environmental Influences[19]

DEFENDERS OF THE traditional 1842 account rationalize the varying details of the First Vision by citing the importance of telling the story to different audiences and settings, and the passage of time. But it is also probable that in his difficult search for words to describe his experience, Joseph used his life's experiences, as anyone would, as a reservoir of details, as well as his vivid imagination, to create a story that could relate his encounter. The persuasive influence of people and the

---

18. Quinn, "Joseph Smith's Experience of a Methodist 'Camp Meeting' in 1820," 48–50.
19. See the varying accounts of the Sacred Grove Experience by Richard Howard in *Restoration Studies I*, 107–17.

	JSJ's Age	JSJ's Motivation	Location	Spiritual Captivity	Struggle with Powers	Mind Taken Away	Pillar of Light
Nov. 1832 Kirtland Letter Book by JSJ	16th year	Welfare of soul; mind distressed, mourn for sins, cry for mercy, existing denominations fell short	In the wilderness	—	—	—	Pillar of light above the brightness of the sun rested upon me and I was filled with the Spirit.
1834-35 OC/JSJ Letter to WW Phelps*	15th year	Had been aroused by Rev. Lane; perplexed over which to join	—	—	—	—	—
9 Nov. 1835 JSJ Private Journal	about 14	Did not know who was right, considered of 1st importance to be right	Silent grove	—	Knelt 3rd time; mouth opened, tongue loosed in mighty prayer	—	Pillar of fire appeared above my head, filled with unspeakable joy
1840 Orson Pratt "An Interesting Account"†	about 14 or 15	For his soul's salvation; to prepare for a future state of existence	Secret place in a grove a short distance from house	Severely tempted by the power of darkness	Sought deliverance until darkness gave way, enabled to pray in spirit	Mind caught away from the natural objects surrounding him	A bright and glorious light in the heavens above, rested upon the earth
1842 Wentworth Letter by JSJ‡	about 14	Prepare for the future; God could not be the author of confusion	Secret place in a grove	—	—	Mind taken away from the objects with which he was surrounded	A brilliant light which eclipsed the sun at noon day
1842 JSJ's "History" in the Times & Seasons**	15th year; early spring 1820	Mind greatly excited; power of the scripture	Retired to the woods	Power bound tongue; doomed to destruction; never felt before	Exerting all my powers to deliver out of the power which seized me	—	A pillar of light above the brightness of the sun which descended upon me.

This chart illustrates details from six early accounts of the First Vision. Based on Richard P. Howard, *Restoration Studies I*, "An Analysis of Six Contemporary Accounts Touching Joseph Smith's First Vision," 95-117. *Messenger and Advocate* 1, no. 3 (December 1834): 42-43;

Personages	Sins Forgiven	Denominations	Gospel Fulness	Other Instructions	JSJ's Feelings	Persecution
Saw the Lord and he spake unto me (1 personage)	Thy sins forgiven thee	None doeth good, no not one (applies to all people)	—	Go thy way; walk in my commandments; mine anger is kindling	My soul filled with love and for many days I could rejoice with great joy	I could find none who would believe the heavenly vision; family have suffered many persecutions
—	—	—	—	—	—	—
A personage appeared (1 personage)	Thy sins forgiven thee	—	—	He testified that Jesus Christ is the Son of God	—	—
2 "glorious" personages	He was informed that his sins were forgiven	All religious denominations were believing in incorrect doctrines	Promised that the fulness of the Gospel at some future time be made known	—	Leaving his mind in a state of calmness and peace indescribable	—
2 "glorious" personages	—	All religious denominations were believing in incorrect doctrines	Promised that the fulness of the Gospel at some future time be made known	—	—	—
2 personages	—	All creeds were an abomination in his sight; join none of them	—	And many other things that I cannot write at this time	When I came to myself again I found myself lying on my back, looking up into the heavens	Persecuting me, reviling me and speaking all manner of evil against me

†Orson Pratt, *An Interesting Account...*(Edinburg, Scotland); ‡*Times and Seasons* 3, no. 9 (1 March 1842): 706–707; *"History of Joseph Smith," *Times and Seasons* 3, no. 10 (15 March 1842): 726–28; 3, no. 11 (1 April 1842): 748–49.

pressures surrounding the prophet can be noted in the varying accounts of his Grove Experience. In his early accounts, for example, the story is shaped at least in part by those around him, particularly his family members. Then, as the story evolved with each retelling, institutional pressures surfaced. Two examples are particularly evident—his family and his feelings of persecution.[20]

Throughout his entire life, Joseph's family strongly influenced his decision making. This influence surfaced in his telling of his epiphany. As a young boy, no doubt Smith remembered his maternal grandfather Solomon Mack's dream where he saw a bright light and felt his soul was in peril as he pleaded for deliverance. Then Mack heard a voice call him by name during another dream some nights later when he was freed from his pain of sin. Also, both of Joseph's parents had visionary dreams. Lucy Mack Smith had a near-death dream where she saw Jesus Christ, with whom she made a pact that if she could live she would bring up her children and be a comfort to her husband.[21] Joseph Smith Sr.'s seventh and last vision, in 1819 or 1820, while living in Palmyra, was close to the time that Joseph Jr. claimed (in 1842) to have gone into the Palmyra Grove to pray. Probably Joseph Jr. and all his brothers and sisters knew each of their father's seven visions by heart.

Added to the influences of his family were the strong pressures he felt as church leader. Many years later, as Smith prepared his 1839 church history, the persecution theme pervaded the church experience. By this time, Joseph and others had endured more than a dozen "vexatious lawsuits," had fled several counties in Ohio and Missouri, and had felt the sting of property and financial loss. Thus, it is not surprising that the prophet would add his feelings of remorse and persecution into the story in later accounts:

> And though I was hated and persecuted for saying that I had seen a vision, yet it was true and while they were persecuting me reviling me and speaking all manner of evil against me falsely for so saying, I was led to say in my heart, why persecute [me] for telling the truth? I have

20. For a similar argument, see Vogel, *Making of a Prophet*, 29–31. Also see Mark D. Thomas, *Digging in Cumorah: Reclaiming Book of Mormon Narratives* (Salt Lake City: Signature Books, 2000), 48–62.

21. Lucy Smith, *Biographical Sketches*, 40–41.

actually seen a vision, "and who am I that I can withstand God" or why does the world think to make me deny what I have actually seen?[22]

This persecution theme was not mentioned in his original account of the vision in 1831–1832 probably because its powerful influence was yet to be felt. Historian Dan Vogel argued that Smith was influenced by the oppressive environment that existed as the prophet wrote at Far West, Caldwell County, Missouri, between 1838 and 1839.[23]

Reconstructing the First Vision Story

THE QUESTION THEN remains: What really happened to Joseph in the grove? It is entirely believable that he was confused about the issue of baptism, that he went into the woods to pray, and that he had an encounter with God. But it is not believable that when he came out of the woods the boy knew the exact words to describe his encounter. So much is lost when humanity is required to explain divinity.

The purpose of discussing the variations in the accounts and the probability of the First Vision being a composite explanation of Joseph's life experiences is not to call into question the legitimacy of the experience. The problem is not with the prophet but the historian. This discussion of the inconsistencies in the different explanations of the First Vision demonstrates the difficulties historians have in their ongoing and elusive search for truth. The Grove Experience is an important devotional account in the church chronicle. In matters of such faith stories, historians are limited in their observations and must defer to theologians for explanations that may be more faith-oriented than fact-oriented.

That Joseph had such an experience is easy to accept, but that it happened exactly the way he said it happened (in any of his various accounts) should be the subject of introspection. Rather it is far more

22. "Joseph Smith, "Manuscript History," in Vogel, *Early Mormon Documents*, 1: 62 (brackets added by Vogel).

23. Indeed, Vogel found it quite unusual for a young boy to experience persecution about claiming a vision at a time when so many others made the same claim. Most revivalist preachers exhorted that Jesus forgave sins, thus their wrath would have been directed at Smith due to his claims as seer, and especially for producing a scripture that was seen as competing with the Bible. Vogel suggests that Smith may have remembered this post-1827 persecution when he wrote his 1838–1839 history. See *Making of a Prophet*, 64–65.

important to find in the First Vision the key elements of Restoration heritage that are useful today. The First Vision story highlights very well the concept of prophetic revelation, God's love for all people, rejection of faith-confining creeds, the hope of forgiveness, salvation, and the search for the divine in all things. Herein lies the historical and spiritual significance of the First Vision.

It is crucial to embrace an "evolutionary development approach" to the First Vision. Of course it is important to recognize the different audiences and purposes for each explanation as justification for inconsistencies. But this was a spiritual encounter, and though one may wish for internal and external consistency in its various accounts, such requirements range beyond any human understanding to produce. Suffice it to say that as a young man Joseph Smith Jr. had a spiritual encounter that he did not fully understand. That he could not put it into words is reasonable and that he placed the event inaccurately in a distant chronology is more an indictment on his skills as historian than his skills as prophet. This may explain the dramatic variations in the different accounts when he attempted to find the right words to define such an experience, but it does not excuse the mistakes in the chronology of events. A clearer memory would have served the prophet and the movement much better.

Finally, we have seen that the First Vision's impact on the opening years of the Restoration did not have the great significance that it has had in later years. Rather, Joseph Jr. lapsed into laziness and irresponsibility in the years that followed his theophany. In a letter to Oliver Cowdery published in December 1834 in the Kirtland, Ohio, *Latter Day Saints' Messenger and Advocate*, Smith confessed:

> During this time, as is common to most, or all youths, I fell into many vices and follies; but as my accusers are, and have been forward to accuse me of being guilty of gross and outrageous violations of the peace and good order of the community, I take the occasion to remark, that, though, as I have said above, "as is common to most, or all youths, I fell into many vices and follies," I have not, neither can it be sustained, in truth, been guilty of wronging or injuring any man or society of men; and those imperfections to which I alude, and for which I have often had occasion to lament, were a light, and too often, vain mind, exhibiting a foolish and trifling conversation.

This being all, and the worst, that my accusers can substantiate against my moral character, I wish to add, that it is not without a deep feeling of regret that I am thus called upon in answer to my own conscience, to fulfill a duty I owe to myself, as well as to the cause of truth, in making this public confession of my former uncircumspect walk, and unchaste conversation: and more particularly, as I often acted in violation of those holy precepts which I knew came from God.[24]

With the great advantage of historical perspective, we today may be able to see the importance of the First Vision more clearly than did Joseph Jr. at the time it happened. Only with the passing of more than a decade, and when the circumstances presented themselves, did Joseph discover in the Sacred Grove Experience a useful testimony. Thus, perhaps we have misunderstood the Sacred Grove Experience as the primary motivation that propelled the first-generation Latter Day Saints to move forward. If not the First Vision, then what did cause these believers to uproot from their homes and take a journey of faith with the prophet?

---

24. *Latter Day Saints' Messenger and Advocate* 1, no. 3 (December 1834): 40.

CHAPTER FIVE

Enchantment Influences in Joseph Smith's America

FROM THE BEGINNINGS of the church to the present, cultural influences, both national and international, have strongly influenced its nature. The first generation of Latter Day Saints lived in a culture that included "a magical world view." There is no way to understand the advent of Latter Day Saintism without exploring the issues of enchantment that framed its beliefs. It is tempting to become judgmental and impose our twenty-first-century values on this early-nineteenth-century people. We must acknowledge, however, that these people lived in a prescientific age that did not provide clear answers to many of life's perplexing issues about which much more information exists today. When their limited scientific knowledge could not provide solutions to life's problems, they frequently resorted to parascientific solutions, which included such things as seer stones, magic chants, sacred drawings, divining rods, and talismans.

As a preface for this discussion, let us make several important observations. In Joseph Smith Jr.'s America, practicing magic rituals was not necessarily irrational or irreligious. Just as important was their belief that practicing magic rituals was not a substitute for practicing their religion. In our postmodern day, many may find these crucial distinctions difficult to make, but not so for the people of the early nineteenth century. Without this discussion, terms such as "Urim and Thummim" and "prophet, seer, and revelator," which are still used today, can be too easily misunderstood. Also without this discussion, the evolution from a theology of grace to a theology of works becomes impossible to understand completely. Indeed, the

HOUGHTON LIBRARY

Divining rods used in seventeenth-century Europe

success of Latter Day Saintism is at least in part based on Joseph Smith's amazing ability to find theological relevance in folk beliefs. This important folk-culture connecting point attracted many people to the faith.

Mystical Activities in Early Smith Family Life

LIKE SO MANY others living in these times, Joseph Smith Jr.'s family engaged in mystical dimensions of the early nineteenth century. After the Smith family lived in the Palmyra-Manchester area, neighbors accused them of neglecting their farm in favor of pursuing ritual activities. In 1845, Lucy Mack Smith responded to the charges in her biographical history of her family with a comment that acknowledged performing some magic rituals. Lucy stated:

> Let not my reader suppose that…we stopt our labor and went at trying to win the faculty of Abrac drawing Magic circles or sooth saying to the neglect of all kinds of business[.] we never during our lives suffered one important interest to swallow up every other obligation but whilst we worked with our hands we endeavored to remember the service of & the welfare of our souls.[1]

1. Lucy Smith, *Biographical Sketches*, 39. Historian D. Michael Quinn observed that the popular phrase "faculty of Abrac" linked mysticism with religion. The word "Abrac" is the first five letters of Abracadabra, a word taken from Abraxas, the Gnostic name for God. Lucy recorded this statement in her original 1845 history of Joseph Smith Jr. but it was edited out of the 1853 version. Such reference to the Smith family participa-

Lucy's denial affirmed her participation in mystical practices but not at the sacrifice of other important duties on the family farm.

Treasure Seeking to Cope with Financial and Religious Uncertainties

CONSIDERING THE DIFFICULTIES that the Smith family faced during their Palmyra years, it is not surprising that they would explore creative ways to find release from their financial woes. For those who failed to make it in the natural economy, a more suitable alternative was to pursue riches in the supernatural economy. Finding buried treasures held great attraction as people yearned for that one successful find that would bring them release from burdensome debt. For treasure seekers, financial security was just one shovelful away. Historian Klaus Hansen identified the context for the proliferation of treasure seeking in Joseph Smith's America:

```
A  b  r  a  c  a  d  a  b  r  a
A  b  r  a  c  a  d  a  b  r
A  b  r  a  c  a  d  a  b
A  b  r  a  c  a  d  a
A  b  r  a  c  a  d
A  b  r  a  c  a
A  b  r  a  c
A  b  r  a
A  b  r
A  b
A
```
Abracadabra diagram used by Lucy Mack Smith

> Treasure seeking lay at the murky intersection of material aspiration and religious desire; it possessed a dual nature: functioning at once as a supernatural economy (an alternative to a disappointing natural economy) and as a materialistic faith (an alternative to unsatisfactory abstract religion). Treasure seeking met the needs of some people who felt troubled by their culture's increasing premium on possessive

---

tion in folk enchantment that was so prevalent in her times is problematic in today's sophisticated, scientific culture. Obviously this could not have been the reason for its removal in 1853. According to Michael Quinn, the statement's deletion was possibly to avoid lending credibility to the criticisms levied against the Smith family by Philastus Hurlbut in 1833. For a further explanation of this reference see Quinn, *Early Mormonism and the Magic World View*, 68–70. Also see Lavina Anderson, *Lucy's Book*, 323, John L. Brooke, *The Refiner's Fire: The Making of Mormon Cosmology, 1644–1844* (Cambridge: Cambridge University Press, 1994), and Vogel, *Early Mormon Documents*, 1: 285.

individualism and religious voluntarism, by promising both quick wealth and a sense of power over the supernatural world.[2]

Young Joseph inherited an interest in treasure seeking from his father, who engaged in such activities in his New England days. As early as 1805, Joseph Sr. heard rumors of English pirate Captain Kidd's late-seventeenth-century excursion through the White River Valley of Vermont. This fueled speculation that the brigand secretly hid treasures in the area and launched treasure-seeking parties to pothole the banks of the White River near the Smiths' Sharon, Vermont, home. Although relatively little is known about their Vermont treasure-seeking activities, a colleague in Kirtland, Ohio, in 1837, heard the senior Smith brag: "I know more about money digging, than any man in this generation, for I have been in the business more than thirty years."[3]

COMMUNITY OF CHRIST LIBRARY-ARCHIVES
Seer stones

In 1843, Joseph Jr. petitioned in a pamphlet for the assistance of his fellow Vermonters for redress of grievances committed against his people. In a response back to Smith, one Strafford, Orange County, Vermont, resident scoffed: "You was old enough when you left here to remember a great many things about [your father] and how he used to tel[l] about your being born with a veil over your face and that he intended to procure a stone for you to see all over the world with."[4] Smith's

2. Hansen, *Mormonism and the American Experience*, 90–91.
3. James Colin Brewster, *Very Important! To the Mormon Money Diggers. Why do the Mormons rage and the People imagine a vain thing?* ([Springfield, Ill.]: n.p., [20 March 1843]), 5, in Vogel, *Early Mormon Documents*, 3: 317.
4. Green Mountain Boys to Thomas C. Sharp, 15 February 1844, 3, Thomas C. Sharp and Allied Anti-Mormon Papers, Beinecke Rare Book and Manuscript Library, Yale University, New Haven, Connecticut, in Vogel, *Early Mormon Documents*, 1: 597. New

recruitment petition was received with scorn and the Mormon prophet found no support in his home state.

Joseph directed a treasure-digging team near Harmony, Pennsylvania, in the 1820s. Rumors spread across the countryside about his successful use of his special gift to find objects that had been lost. An excellent example of Joseph's seeing abilities is Martin Harris's testimony while visiting the Smith farm in Manchester, New York, published in 1859:

> I was at the house of [Joseph Smith Jr.'s] father in Manchester, two miles south of Palmyra village, and was picking my teeth with a pin while sitting on the bars. The pin caught in my teeth, and dropped from my fingers into shavings and straw. I jumped from the bars and looked for it. Joseph and Northrup Sweet also did the same. We could not find it. I then took Joseph [Smith Jr.] on surprise, and said to him—I said, "Take your stone." I had never seen it, and did not know that he had it with him. He had it in his pocket. He took it and placed it in his hat—the old white hat—and placed his face in his hat. I watched him closely to see that he did not look one side; he reached out his hand beyond me on the right, and moved a little stick, and there I saw the pin, which he picked up and gave to me. I know he did not look out of the hat until after he had picked up the pin.[5]

But recognition of Joseph's "seeing abilities" took its toll on both his public reputation and his private life.[6] In March 1826, the young Smith was bound over in a South Bainbridge, Chenango County, New York, jail for a hearing on his alleged skills in "glass looking." The misdemeanor charge stemmed from Smith receiving money from Josiah Stowell in exchange for information on "where a band of robbers had buried on his flat a box

---

England folklore held that an infant born with a veil or caul over its head was lucky. This garment of the amniotic membrane was not only a good omen for the newly born but also for anyone who possessed one; hence, cauls were preserved and sold as good luck charms. This explanation is found in Vogel, *Making of a Prophet*, 12–13, 575fn59.

5. "Mormonism—No. II," *Tiffany's Monthly. Devoted to the Investigation of the Science of Mind, in the Physical, Intellectual, Moral and Religious Planes Thereof* 5 (August 1859): 163–70, in Vogel, *Early Mormon Documents*, 2: 303.

6. Historian Dan Vogel has identified eighteen locations across New York and Pennsylvania between 1822 and 1827 where Joseph Smith Jr. plied his trade as a treasure seeker. See Vogel's "The Locations of Joseph Smith's Early Treasure Quests," *Dialogue: A Journal of Mormon Thought* 27, no. 3 (Fall 1994): 197–231.

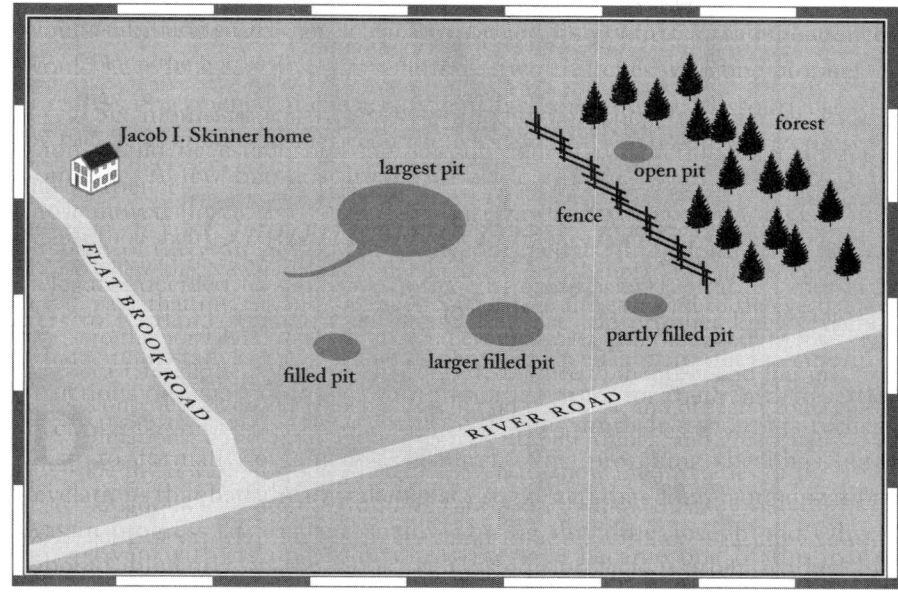

MAP BY JOHN HAMER

Joseph Smith's diggings near Jacob I. Skinner's farm in Susquehanna County, Pennsylvania

of treasure, and as it was very valuable, they [the robbers] had, by sacrifice, placed a charm over it to protect it, so it could not be obtained except by faith, accompanied by certain talismanic influences."[7] Justice Albert Neely indicted Smith with a charge of being a "disorderly person and imposter," based on a New York law that criminalized "all jugglers, and all persons pretending to have skill in physiognomy, palmistry, or like crafty science, or pretending to tell fortunes, or to discover where lost goods may be found."[8]

7. W[illiam] D. Purple, "Joseph Smith, the Originator of Mormonism. Historical Reminiscences of the Town of Afton," *Chenango Union* (Norwich, N.Y.) 30 (3 May 1877): 3, in Vogel, *Early Mormon Documents*, 4: 127–37. Justice Neely asked Purple, a physician living in South Bainbridge, New York, to take notes on the trial proceedings.

8. *Laws of the State of New York, Revised and Passed at Thirty-Sixth Session of the Legislature*, 2 vols. (Albany, N.Y.: H. C. Southwick and Co., 1813), 1: 114, in Vogel, *Making of a Prophet*, 37–38, 583fn16. This law was not enforced consistently throughout the state. Palmyra justice of the peace Abner Cole permitted Willard Chase and Joseph's brother Alvin to dig on his property. Led by Luman Walters, an itinerant necromancer, the men dug a large hole but found nothing. Cole recorded that Walters charged the two men three dollars per day for his seeing services.

Judge Neely then released his prisoner, Joseph Smith Jr., on his own recognizance and ordered him to appear before a Court of Special Sessions.

This trial never happened, however. Historian Dan Vogel speculated that because Joseph Jr. was still a minor, expressed some contrition during the initial hearing, and seemed willing to stop his scrying[9] and to leave the area, Neely may have chosen to not pursue the matter further.[10] It is possible that Judge Neely and the Smiths arranged an out-of-court settlement, enabling the young man to take "leg bail." That Smith returned to Bainbridge on numerous occasions, including for his marriage to Emma Hale just months after the trial, suggested that the young man felt he had paid his debt to society.

Peter G. Bridgman, Stowell's nephew and Joseph's chief accuser, saw his uncle's family resources being squandered, so he brought the charges. Bridgman could take some satisfaction in that the impact of the hearing was enough to destroy Smith's reputation. This "labeling" strategy, a legal tactic dating back to the early 1700s in New England, worked successfully, as Smith's future in-laws rejected his claims to be a seer. This brush with the law drove a lasting wedge in their relationship.[11] Joseph Smith Jr.'s active seven-year career of treasure seeking built his reputation as one among many upstate New York scryers to be known for his skilled use of a seer stone. Understanding Smith's treasure-seeking activities is an important key to understanding the discovery, recovery, and translation process of the metallic plates of the Book of Mormon.

---

9. Scrying is seeing or predicting the future through use of a physical object.
10. Vogel, *Making of a Prophet*, 85.
11. This practice of using charges to smear a person's reputation dates back to the pre-Revolution days. An effective way of repressing occult believers was to levy charges, bring the accused to trial, find them innocent, and then release them. Indictments and trials branded accused witches for their entire lives. The trial sent signals to anyone who would dare be associated with these people as well. For more on this "labeling" practice, see Jon Butler, "Magic, Astrology, and the Early American Religious Heritage, 1600–1760," *American Historical Review* 84, no. 2 (April 1979): 344–45.

CHAPTER SIX

The Book of Mormon Story

Discovery of Ancient Plates[1]

FOR GENERATIONS OF people around the world the Book of Mormon has been the foundation of their faith. They find this unique scripture's legitimacy in its miraculous discovery and divine translation, the testimonies of those who witnessed the plates, and the scripture's message that Jesus is the Christ.

According to Joseph Smith Jr., on the night of 21 September 1823, as he prayed for forgiveness, his bedroom filled with light. The angel Moroni,[2] in a brilliant white robe, appeared to Joseph, standing at his bedside. Moroni called Joseph by name and announced that he was a messenger from God and that there was a work for the youth to do. The angel described an ancient record written on golden plates buried in a nearby hill, and that it contained the record of the fullness of the gospel as it had been delivered to an ancient people. Through the night, the young boy experienced three visitations that were essentially the same. On the last visitation the angel warned him that Satan would tempt him "to get the plates for the purpose

---

1. This traditional account is based on Joseph Smith Jr.'s first record of these events written in 1832. It has fewer details than later accounts, but I believe it is more accurate. Joseph Smith's 1832 "History of Book of Mormon Origins" is found in his *Letterbook*, 1: 1–6, Joseph Smith Papers, located in the LDS Church Archives, in Vogel, *Early Mormon Documents*, 1: 29–30. This account is also consistent with the popular pamphlet, *Joseph Smith Tells His Own Story*, 11–13.

2. Accounts vary as to the name of the angel that appeared at Joseph's bedside. Although the traditional account identifies the angel as Moroni, at least two other accounts use the name Nephi. For the Nephi account see "History of Joseph Smith," *Times and Seasons* 3, no. 12 (15 April 1842): 753. Also see Lucy Smith, *Biographical Sketches*, 84.

of getting rich." Moroni cautioned that Joseph's only motive to receive the plates should be "to glorify God."

Because these visitations lasted until dawn, Joseph was exhausted, but he just had to tell his father what had transpired. Later that morning Joseph's work in the field was a struggle and rather unproductive. Joseph Sr. noticed his son's difficulties and told the boy to return home to rest. During his walk back to the house Joseph collapsed from his fatigue. While he was unconscious he received yet another visitation that was essentially the same as the night before.[3] When he told his father about the epiphany, Joseph Sr. confirmed it was of God and told the boy to follow the angel's directions.

Almost immediately Joseph went to nearby Hill Cumorah and found the plates in a stone box, just as he had been shown. When he pried open the heavy lid Joseph found not only the metallic plates but also a sword and two transparent stones in silver bows fastened to a breastplate that he eventually called the "Urim and Thummim."[4] When he reached down to

---

3. In Lucy Mack Smith's account she mentioned that the angel chastised the boy for not telling his father about the epiphany from the previous night. The messenger asked young Joseph: "Why did you not tell your father that which I commanded you to tell him?" Joseph replied, "I was afraid my father would not believe me." The angel rejoined, "He will believe every word you say to him." See Lucy Smith, *Biographical Sketches*, 88–89.

4. In biblical days the Urim and Thummim was used in the process of casting lots by oracles who inquired about spiritual mysteries. Their questions had to be posed in the form of a "yes-no" question or an "either-or" response. The term "Urim and Thummim" has Old Testament roots; for example, the Urim and Thummim as the breastplate of judgment (Exodus 28:30, Leviticus 8:8); the Urim and Thummim would be with the Holy One (Deuteronomy 33:8); and the priest would have access (Ezra 2:63, Nehemiah 7:65). The Book of Mormon reference to the Urim and Thummim had a more modern use, namely "interpreters." For example, no one can look in them unless commanded. Whoever is commanded is called a seer (Mosiah 5:73–74; LDS 8:13). In the same chapter, the interpreters are prepared for the unfolding of mysteries (Mosiah 5:83; LDS 8:19). Also, interpreters are for the preservation of records to be handed down from one generation to another (Mosiah 13:2; LDS 28:20). Finally, the interpreters were to be sealed up with the record (Ether 1:99; LDS 4:5). In the Book of Alma (17:71; LDS 37:38) the term "director" refers to a ball. Joseph Smith Jr. and Lucy Mack Smith expressed their own understanding of the scriptural references in their description and explanation of the Urim and Thummim and its purpose. There are no references in the Bible to suggest that the Urim and Thummim were spectacles into which a seer peered; nor are there any references to glasses affixed to a breastplate. A lack of specificity allowed

retrieve the ancient artifacts, Moroni appeared and told him "the time for bringing them forth had not yet arrived" but to return each year until the time was right.[5]

Joseph's maturation process lasted four years; it would be that long before he would be allowed to retrieve the plates. During this time of preparation the boy experienced family deaths, financial deprivation and loss of the family residence, treasure seeking ventures, a brush with the law, more basic education, and his marriage to Emma Hale of Harmony, Pennsylvania.

Retrieving the Plates

THOSE CLOSE TO the Smiths, and even some of their detractors, knew about Joseph Jr.'s yearly visit to Hill Cumorah. In late September 1827, in Colesville, New York, a family friend, Joseph Knight, and Josiah Stowell, Joseph's former treasure seeking employer from South Bainbridge, New York, arrived at the Smiths' Manchester farm to discuss the plates. At this time rumors circulated that a neighbor, and competing treasure seeker, Samuel Lawrence, intended to prevent Joseph's next visit. On 21 September Joseph Jr. asked his father to spy on the nearby Lawrence farm for any indication that there might be trouble. Joseph Sr. returned that afternoon with nothing to report.

As evening fell Joseph and his wife of less than a year, Emma Hale, prepared for the sacred Cumorah visit. Although the family had gone to bed, Lucy stayed up, and after midnight Joseph Jr. came into her room and asked for a box with a lock. Lucy could not provide it but she knew its purpose. Joseph responded, "Never mind. I can do very well for the present without it—be calm—all is right."[6] Then Emma appeared in her riding

---

the prophet the freedom to give his own interpretation to what "Urim and Thummim" actually meant. Eventually, Joseph Jr. would refer to his seer stone as the Urim and Thummim, possibly suggesting that its use was more important than a physical description of the holy artifact. An excellent discussion of the Urim and Thummim is found in Kenneth Sowers Jr., "The Mystery and History of the Urim and Thummim," *Restoration Studies II*, ed. Maurice L. Draper and A. Bruce Lindgren (Independence, Mo.: Herald House, 1983), 75–79.

5. *DHC*, 1: 11–16.
6. Lucy Smith, *Biographical Sketches*, 114

clothes and together the young couple rode into the countryside in Joseph Knight's wagon.

Joseph retrieved the plates, but he and Emma did not return to the farm until after breakfast the next morning. They came home empty-handed because, fearing that robbers lurked near the farm, Joseph had lodged the plates in a decayed birch log about three miles from home. He really needed a locked box for safe storage so he asked his mother, who then recommended a good carpenter. Unfortunately there was no money to pay for the box. While they pondered what to do, Lucy wrote in her family history that a Mr. Warner rode up to the farm reporting that the widow Wells, living in nearby Macedon, needed a well dug and requested that young Joseph provide the labor. Her willingness to pay good money prompted Joseph to leave immediately. Although money would hopefully become available to purchase the storage box, Lucy wrote that eventually Hyrum emptied a box with lock and key for Joseph's use.[7]

While Joseph dug the well in Macedon, his father learned of a plot to steal the plates. Emma rushed to her husband to sound the alarm and pleaded with him to return. Lucy reported that Joseph immediately peered into his Urim and Thummim and saw that the plates were still safely hidden. On his return to the family farm he reported that they were still secure. But fearing the worst, Joseph headed for Cumorah to retrieve the plates from the birch log.

Evidently, suspicious men followed him through the woods because after Joseph placed the plates in a linen cloth and walked just a short distance toward home, a man surprised Joseph with a blow to the head with his gun. Joseph responded with a blow of his own that knocked the man down, and then, with the plates under his arm, ran away as fast as he could. After about a half mile, Joseph was attacked a second time and then a third time before he arrived back at the farm. In running this gauntlet Joseph suffered only a dislocated thumb, but the plates arrived home safely, at least for a time.

After a brief rest, Joseph related his experience to his father and Joseph Knight, and to Josiah Stowell. The two visitors went after the brigands but without success, and Joseph Sr. reset his son's thumb. The family

---

7. Lucy Smith, *Biographical Sketches*, 116–20.

The Book of Mormon Story

COMMUNITY OF CHRIST LIBRARY-ARCHIVES
Portraits of Emma Hale Smith and Joseph Smith Jr.

now hoped that life on the farm could return to normal, with the plates in safekeeping. Years later, in her biographical history, Lucy stated that one afternoon, while the family was working in the field, Joseph Jr. called her from her work to view his sacred find. Lucy gave a detailed account of what she saw:

> He handed me the breastplate spoken of in his history. It was wrapped in a thin muslin handkerchief, so thin that I could see the glistening metal, and ascertain its proportions without any difficulty. It was concave on one side and convex on the other, and extended from the neck downwards as far as the center of the stomach of a man of extraordinary size. It had four straps of the same material for the purpose of fastening it to the breast, two of which ran back to go over the shoulders, and the other two were designed to fasten to the hips. They were just the width of two of my fingers, (for I measured them,) and they had holes in the end of them, to be convenient in fastening. The whole

plate was worth at least five hundred dollars. After I had examined it, Joseph placed it in the chest with the Urim and Thummim.[8]

Knowing there were jealous people still in search of the plates, the family decided to hide them in the hearth stonework of the farmhouse. In case of a burglary, surely no one would ever look there.

Not long thereafter, those inside the farmhouse heard riders in the distance approaching and anticipated their intent to steal the plates, so the family organized their defense. When the mob arrived, Joseph Jr. threw the door open and yelled a signal, giving the impression that a legion of troops was there to defend the home. At that moment all the male members of the family charged from the house. This startled the trespassers and they bolted away—the stratagem worked.

Then the family learned of plans for another robbery attempt.[9] This time there would be no defense. When the intruders rummaged around outside and in the cooper shop, they found the box and broke it open only to find it empty. To outwit the robbers Joseph Jr. had placed the box underneath floorboards of the cooper shop. But before doing so he removed the contents, wrapped them in cloths, and hid them in the flax stored in the shop. This last-minute maneuver saved the contents. Lucy speculated that Willard Chase's sister, Sally, a respected glass looker, prompted intruders to search the Smiths' cooper shop for the plates.[10] Lucy inferred that only because Joseph Jr.'s powers were greater than Sally's did the plates remain hidden.

The Chases and Smiths shared a farm property line in Manchester and lived less than a mile from each other. As time passed they dug together for buried treasures, suggesting that Chase had more confidence in Joseph's adeptness than his younger sister Sally's. In fact, his sister claimed only to find the location of treasures but admitted that her power did

---

8. Lucy Smith, *Biographical Sketches*, 124.
9. Lucy did not tell how Joseph discerned any of this information although she frequently reminded the reader that Joseph Jr. always kept his Urim and Thummim close to him.
10. Lucy Smith, *Biographical Sketches*, 125–26.

not extend to fending off the treasure's spirit guardians."[11] Joseph Jr. claimed both powers.

No doubt news of the attacks at the Smith farm reached the streets of Palmyra Village and generated considerable interest. The well-to-do Palmyra farmer Martin Harris became quite curious about young Smith's seeing abilities. Harris interpreted Smith's activities to be the work of the Lord and gave him fifty dollars in silver to cover his debts. Over time, Martin Harris would play a crucial role in financing the printing of the Book of Mormon.

First Attempts at Translation Frustrated

IN DECEMBER 1827, Joseph began translating the sacred writing. He did so with his wife, Emma, as the scribe, but the unsafe environment of the Smith family farm was not conducive for translation. Joseph and Emma needed a change of venue, so Emma sent word to her family in Harmony, Pennsylvania, where they desired to move. Emma may have been uncertain of her reception back home, since she and Joseph had eloped. Also, just a year earlier the Chenango County, New York, trial had destroyed her husband's reputation. All this created fears that the Hale family would not accept him. But they responded to Emma's peace gesture with enthusiasm.

Shortly before Harris made his donation to Joseph to cover his expenses, Emma's brother Alva Hale arrived with greetings from the Hale family and offered to assist with the move of his sister and brother-in-law. Extra care had to be taken to transport the plates, so Joseph placed them in an Ontario windowpane box and put the box in a forty-gallon cask of beans. Then the cask and the couple's other possessions were loaded onto their wagon.

The Wagon Ride to Harmony, Pennsylvania

IT TOOK FOUR days for Joseph, Emma, and her brother Alva to travel the 128 miles from Manchester, New York, to Harmony, Pennsylvania, in December 1827. The route took them through southern New York

---

11. Dan Vogel makes this observation in *Making of a Prophet*, 37.

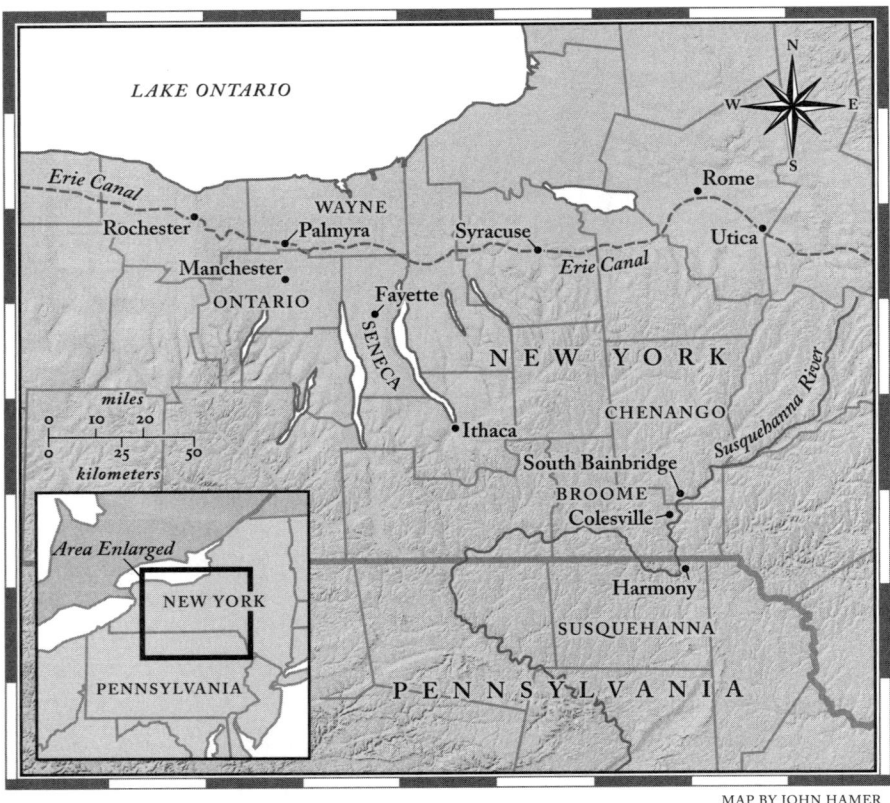

MAP BY JOHN HAMER

The region between Palmyra, New York, and Harmony, Pennsylvania, was the cradle of the Restoration (boundaries as of 1830).

countryside that constantly reminded them of the once-present pre-Columbian Americans who lived there. It is likely that Joseph passed the time in silence, vividly imagining great battles between the inhabitants who left piles of bodies buried in sacred mounds. Popular folklore recorded in local newspapers even provided the details of unfortunate mound builders "killed in battle and hastily buried."[12] Local residents believed the mound builders were a white-skinned, Christian people who were destroyed by more primitive tribes. There were eight mounds within a twelve-mile

12. *Palmyra Register*, 21 January 1818, in Dan Vogel, *Indian Origins and the Book of Mormon: Religious Solutions from Columbus to Joseph Smith* (Salt Lake City: Signature Books, 1986), 25.

radius of Smith's Manchester farm, and burial, fortification, and sacrificial mounds were sprinkled along the way to Harmony.[13]

As they approached Emma's home village, the familiar surroundings would have warmed her heart; Joseph would have been more anxious, however. After their greetings the couple moved in with Emma's parents, Isaac and Elizabeth Hale, but only temporarily. The Hales had lots of questions for the couple and for Joseph specifically. No doubt they asked about their future plans, especially since Emma was three to four months pregnant and was probably showing it.

It did not take long for Isaac to ask Joseph about his treasure seeking, since the young man's reputation was far from repaired. Isaac asked to see the plates about which he had heard so much, but Joseph responded with only the box that contained them. Father Hale described the container as a "common sized window-glass" box measuring approximately ten inches by twelve inches. Joseph allowed Isaac to heft the box but not to look inside. Joseph told his father-in-law that only a few privileged people would get to see them. Isaac wondered aloud who would be the first to see them. Joseph replied to his father-in-law, "A young child."[14] Later Joseph explained further to Joshua McKune, who had also married into the Hale family, that Smith's firstborn child would be a male and would "translate the characters, and hieroglyphics, upon the Plates into our language at the age of three years."[15] Joseph's prophecy was only partly correct. On 15 June 1828 Emma gave birth to a male child they named Alvin, but he died shortly after birth.

Over time Isaac grew perturbed by Joseph's secrecy about the contents of the box. Out of frustration he exclaimed, "If there was anything in my house of that description, which I could not be allowed to see, he must take it away; if he did not, I was determined to see it."[16] The threat reminded Joseph of the same problem in Manchester and convinced him

---

13. Brodie, *No Man Knows My History*, 19.
14. "Mormonism," *Susquehanna Register, and Northern Pennsylvanian* 9 (1 May 1834): 1, in Vogel, *Early Mormon Documents*, 4: 286.
15. "Mormonism," in Vogel, *Early Mormon Documents*, 4: 326.
16. "Mormonism," in Vogel, *Early Mormon Documents*, 4: 286–87.

to hide the plates. Using the same solution as before, he hid them in a nearby stand of woods.

The deteriorating family relationship could be repaired only with the young couple's move out of the Hale house. Emma's brother Jesse had lived in a house owned by Isaac and Elizabeth located approximately 450 feet west of the Hale house, near the Susquehanna River. Before the couple arrived from Manchester, Jesse had vacated the house when he finished construction on his own. This became the couple's first home. When they were comfortably settled in, the translation process—the reason for moving to Harmony in the first place—could begin, with Emma as the first scribe.

In January 1828, the Smiths received visitors from Palmyra—Hyrum and Martin Harris. Joseph was happy to see his older brother and his financial supporter as they updated each other on their activities. In their discussions Harris shared an epiphany he had received commissioning him to seek verification of the transcribed writings by the academic community of New York. Perhaps the prosperous Palmyra farmer contemplated further investment in the translation project. Writing in his 1832 account, Joseph explained the visitation, stating that the Lord had appeared to Harris in a vision and showed him the marvelous work that Smith was about to do, and Harris immediately came to Harmony and said the Lord had shown him that he must go to New York City with some of the characters.[17] Harris left Harmony with a piece of paper measuring 3 ¼ inches long and 8 inches wide. On it Smith placed letters from the plates and labeled the top of the page "Caractors." Harris could not say whether Joseph copied from memory, from the actual plates, or from other writing, since the prophet drew a curtain in the corner of the room for secrecy.

Harris began his tour by showing the page to scholars in Utica, Albany, and eventually New York City. Field testing his writings provided Smith with a "no lose" situation. If the scholars who inspected his writing sample judged them to be authentic, it would legitimize his reputation as a prophet of God. On the other hand, if the scholars admitted they could not read the letters, then Joseph could claim to Harris and others his superior prophetic gifts over the best scholarly minds in America.

17. For the original language Smith used in his 1832 history see Dean C. Jessee, ed., *The Papers of Joseph Smith: Autobiographical and Historical Writings*, 2 vols. (Salt Lake City: Deseret Book Company, 1989), 1: 9.

The Book of Mormon Story   85

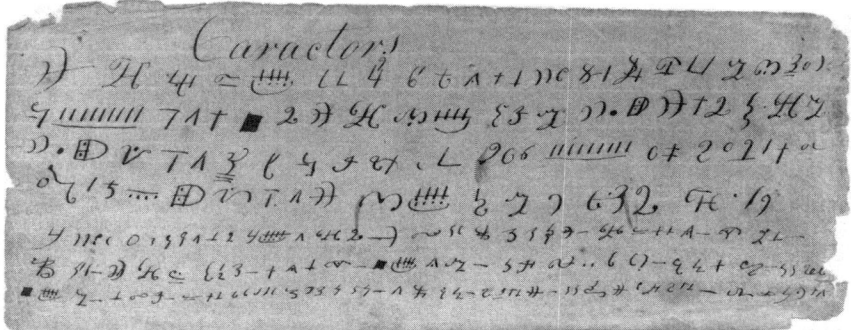

COMMUNITY OF CHRIST LIBRARY-ARCHIVES

Joseph Smith Jr.'s Reformed Egyptian "Caractors." This is believed to be the only authentic extant manuscript copy, thought by some to be in the hand of Joseph Smith Jr.

Harris's experience in New York City was the perfect test case for Smith's "reformed hieroglyphics." While in Manhattan, Harris stopped at the office of American antiquities scholar Samuel Latham Mitchell (also Mitchill; 1764–1831), who, after a short review, deferred his judgment to Professor Charles Anthon (1797–1867), classical studies scholar at Columbia University. Anthon studied the writings and quickly determined that "they contained anything but 'Egyptian Hieroglyphics.'" Instead he said the letters combined characteristics of "Egyptian, Chaldeak, Assyriac, and Arabic" while other figures were not identifiable. Amazed with this find, Anthon agreed to authenticate the writings with a signed letter, and gave it to Harris. As Harris prepared to leave, Anthon asked him about the origins of what he had just authenticated. Harris offered a brief recital of the story of the plates' discovery. According to Joseph Smith's 1839 history, Anthon destroyed the letter and scoffed "that there was no such thing now as ministering angels, and that if I would bring the plates to him, he would translate them."[18] After a few more exchanges Harris left Anthon and reported back to Smith in Harmony.

If Joseph's plan was to convince his financial benefactor of the plates' authenticity, then the plan worked. Considering his previous epiphany and now the events in Anthon's office, Harris was convinced more than ever. He even volunteered to be a scribe, which delighted Emma, who was

18. Joseph Smith Jr., "Manuscript History," in Vogel, *Early Mormon Documents*, 1: 70.

enduring the discomforts of pregnancy. Now the translation could continue in earnest.

Between 12 April and 14 June 1828, Smith and Harris worked on the first 116 manuscript pages. Since Emma's childbirth neared, it seemed a good time to take a break from the work. Being gone for such a long time from his Palmyra farm was quite a sacrifice for Martin Harris. Feeling the need to justify his efforts, he pressured the "Seer" for permission to take the manuscript back to Palmyra to show his wife and others the fruits of his labor. This way he could justify his expenditure of time. Seeking divine permission through his seer stone, Smith rejected the first two requests; however, with the third request permission came, but with conditions. The scribe could show the manuscript to only five specified family members.[19]

COMMUNITY OF CHRIST LIBRARY-ARCHIVES
Martin Harris

Harris left Harmony on 14 June, and the next day Emma had a difficult birth. The child, a boy they named Alvin after Joseph's oldest brother, survived only a few hours. Over a period of fourteen days Emma lay near death but then began her slow recovery. Harris's time away extended beyond what was expected and made Joseph very nervous. The sacred manuscript was out of his possession, and so with Emma improving, Joseph decided to go back to Manchester to see his family and check on Harris and the manuscript.

Traveling mostly by stagecoach, Smith finally arrived at his parents' home. Exhausted, he sent for Harris almost immediately; when he failed to show, Joseph suspected the worst. Harris arrived at the farmhouse at noontime with the news that he had lost the manuscript. Joseph cried out, "Oh, my God! All is lost! All is lost! What shall I do?" He wept aloud,

19. These people were his wife, Lucy; his brother, Preserved; his father, Nathan; his mother, Rhoda; and his wife's sister, Polly Harris Cobb.

pacing back and forth. Then he went to his seer stone for assistance but found none.

Now Joseph had to return to Harmony and share the bad news with Emma. He feared what the two traumas—the loss of their son and the loss of the manuscript—might do to his wife. These two losses plunged Joseph into deep despair. When he returned to Harmony he was not surprised to find that an angel had taken away the plates, spectacles, and vestment. Also gone was his gift for "seeing." No further progress could be made, and Joseph even contemplated giving up on the entire project.

These agonizing times set Joseph adrift wondering what to do next or how to regain favor with God and with his friends. His treasure seeking damaged further his personal reputation with people in New York and Pennsylvania, and the loss of the manuscript destroyed his relationship with God. The loss of his son, Alvin, was a clear sign of God's displeasure. Only the survival of his wife, Emma, offered a glimmer of hope. During these difficult times, Joseph began attending the local Methodist congregation, perhaps to gain favor with his in-laws, perhaps to please Emma, but perhaps also to find spiritual solutions to his life's crisis.[20] Unfortunately, Joseph's treasure-seeking reputation preceded him, and that he was poorly received by local Methodist ministers only encouraged him to continue seeking God's will.

By July 1828, the "little season" of rejection by the angel ended when Joseph was informed that his gift of translation "is now restored unto you again, therefore see that you are faithful and continue on unto the finishing of the remainder of the work of translation as you have begun."[21] The instruction also resolved the dilemma of what to do to recover the lost story: "Behold, I say unto you, that you shall not translate again those words which have gone forth out of your hands; for, behold, [the thieves] shall not accomplish their evil designs in lying against those words."[22]

From this experience he had learned the lessons of his disobedience, and a new confidence spurred the young man to reengage the translation process with renewed vigor. He completely immersed himself in

---

20. This is basically the observation of Dan Vogel in *Making of a Prophet*, 128.
21. Doctrine and Covenants 3:1c (LDS 10:3).
22. Doctrine and Covenants 3:6a (LDS 10:30–31).

translating what he understood as God's word into an American scripture named the Book of Mormon, after one of its major figures.

The Translation Process[23]

LITTLE IS KNOWN about the actual translation process except what can be pieced together by witnesses and personal remembrances.[24] Joseph Smith did not feel it necessary to give details about his methodology, and said as much from his earliest explanation of the process published on 25 October 1831[25] to his last known statement on the subject published five months after his death in the *Times and Seasons*.[26] However, the consistency of explanations, from both supporters and detractors, makes it possible to give an account of how the Book of Mormon came into being.

Essentially two methods emerged from these explanations: seeing through two clear stones in a silver bow and seeing through a chocolate-colored opaque stone about the size of an egg. Three accounts reference the stones in a silver bow. Oliver Cowdery and Martin Harris referred to the Urim and Thummim that Joseph "obtained with the plates," thus making

23. Translation—the turning of something spoken or written in one language into another—usually implies that the translator has command of both languages. Joseph never claimed to be able to understand the language of the writings on the plates. So translation as it is applied to Smith's production of the English text of the Book of Mormon is to be understood more as a spiritual than a linguistic process.

24. For an excellent discussion of this important topic see James E. Lancaster, "By the Gift and Power of God," *Saints' Herald* 109, no. 22 (15 November 1962): 14–18, 22, 23; published in revised form as "The Method of Translation of the Book of Mormon," *The John Whitmer Historical Association Journal* 3 (1983): 51–61; also found in *Restoration Studies III*, ed. Maurice L. Draper and Debra Combs (Independence, Mo.: Herald House, 1986), 220–31; and as "The Translation of the Book of Mormon" in *The Word of God: Essays on Mormon Scripture*, ed. Dan Vogel (Salt Lake City, Signature Books, 1990), 97–113.

25. At a church conference located just fifteen miles south of Kirtland at Orange, Cuyahoga County, Ohio, on this date, Joseph Smith Jr. met with the priesthood and congregational membership and stated: "It was not intended to tell the world all the particulars of the coming forth of the book of Mormon, & also said it was not expedient for him to relate these things." See *Far West Record*, entered under the date 25 October 1831, by Oliver Cowdery, Clerk of the Conference, as found in Donald Q. Cannon and Lyndon W. Cook, eds., *Far West Record: Minutes of The Church of Jesus Christ of Latter-day Saints, 1830–1844* (Salt Lake City: Deseret Book Company, 1983), 23.

26. "History of Joseph Smith," *Times and Seasons* 5, no. 21 (15 November 1844): 707.

a distinction between the silver-bowed stones and the egg-shaped stone. Oliver Cowdery, the principal scribe, referred twice to the translation process: "These were days never to be forgotten—to sit under the sound of a voice dictated by the *inspiration* of heaven, awakened the utmost gratitude of this bosom! Day after day I continued, uninterrupted, to write from his mouth, as he translated, with the *Urim* and *Thummim*, or, as the Nephites whould have said, 'Interpreters,' the history, or record, called 'The book of Mormon.'"[27]

Also, in her family biography, Lucy Mack Smith told the story of the Urim and Thummim's discovery and purpose. "There were two stones in silver bows, and these stones fastened to a breastplate, constituted what is called the Urim and Thummim, deposited with the plates; and the possession and use of these stones were what constituted Seers in ancient or former times; and that God had prepared them for the purpose of translating the book."[28] Even with these details more specifics are needed.

Perhaps the most complete explanation of the silver-bowed stones method came from the prophet's younger brother, William, in an 1891 interview given to J. W. Peterson and W. S. Pender of the Reorganized Church of Jesus Christ of Latter Day Saints. Some years later Peterson gave this account of William's explanation:

> The Urim and Thummim were set in a double silver bow which was twisted into the shape of the figure eight, and the two stones were placed literally between the two rims of the bow. At one end was attached a rod which was connected with the outer edge of the right shoulder of the breastplate. By pressing the head a little forward, the rod held the Urim and Thummim before the eyes much like a pair of spectacles. A pocket was prepared in the breastplate on the left side, immediately over the heart. When not in use the Urim and Thummim was placed in the pocket, the rod being of just the right length to allow it to be so deposited. This instrument could, however, be detached from the breastplate, and his brother said that Joseph often wore it detached when away from home, but always used it in connection with the breastplate when receiving official communications, and usually so

---

27. Letter from Oliver Cowdery to W. W. Phelps, 7 September 1834, *Latter Day Saints' Messenger and Advocate* 1, no. 1 (October 1834): 14.

28. Lucy Smith, *Biographical Sketches*, 84.

when translating, as it permitted him to have both hands free to hold the plates. In answer to our query, William informed us that he had, himself, by Joseph's direction, put the Urim and Thummim before his eyes, but could see nothing, as he did not have the gift of Seer. He also informed us that the instruments were too wide for his eyes, as also for Joseph's, and must have been used by much larger men. The instrument caused a strain on Joseph's eyes, and he sometimes resorted to the plan of covering his eyes with a hat to exclude the light in part.[29]

William Smith never scribed for his older brother, nor was he an eyewitness to the translation process, and no doubt his memory struggled to span the sixty years to recall such detail. Also William Smith's 1891 remembrance is inconsistent with his explanation made in 1883: "The manner in which this [the translation] was done was by looking into the Urim and Thummim, which was placed in a hat to exclude the light, (the plates lying nearby covered up), and reading off the translation, which appeared in the stone by the power of God."[30] A year later, in June 1884, William addressed the translation methodology issue again in a sermon in Deloit, Iowa. *Saints' Herald* editors felt the sermon should be published, so it appeared in the 4 October 1884 issue. William enlightened the gathered congregation by stating: "When Joseph received the plates he also received the Urim and Thummim, which he would place in a hat to exclude all light, and with the plates by his side he translated the characters, which were cut into the plates with some sharp instrument, into English. And

---

29. John W. Peterson (1865–1932) was born at Salt Lake City, Utah. He was baptized a member of the RLDS Church in 1880 at Harlan, Iowa. After holding several priesthood offices, he was ordained a seventy in 1892. He married Lillie F. Ackerly in 1894. Peterson died in Washington State in August 1932. William S. Pender (1861–1913) was born at Muscatine, Iowa. He was baptized into the RLDS Church at Columbus, Kansas, before 8 August 1886, when he was ordained an elder at the same place. In 1891 he was ordained a seventy. He died during a visit to the place of his birth and early childhood in January 1913. Peterson and Pender interviewed William Smith at his residence at Osterdock, Clayton County, Iowa, on 4 July 1890. About thirty years later (1 May 1921), Peterson gave this account of the interview. The original one-page document is typed with handwritten corrections and signature by J. W. Peterson. See "Statement of J. W. Peterson Concerning William Smith," 1 May 1921, Miscellaneous Letters and Papers, Community of Christ Library-Archives.

30. William Smith, *William Smith on Mormonism....* (Lamoni, Iowa: Herald Steam, 1883), 10–12, Vault Pamphlet Collection, Community of Christ Library-Archives.

thus, letter by letter, word by word, sentence by sentence, the whole book was translated."[31]

William Smith's 1883 and 1884 accounts, however, are consistent with those of so many others who actually witnessed the process. Emma Smith's 1879 interview with her sons Joseph III and Alexander Hale offered her explanation of how Joseph Smith translated the Book of Mormon story:

> In writing for your father I frequently wrote day after day, often sitting at the table close by him, he sitting with his face buried in his hat, with the stone in it, and dictating hour after hour with nothing between us.... He had neither manuscript nor book to read from.... If he had had anything of the kind, he could not have concealed it from me.... The plates often lay on the table without any attempt at concealment, wrapped in a small linen tablecloth, which I had given him to fold them in.... Oliver Cowdery and your father wrote in the room where I was at work.[32]

Two years later, in 1881, David Whitmer also remembered Joseph dictating the Book of Mormon with the hat and stone: "[Joseph] did not use the plates in the translation, but would hold the interpreters to his eyes and cover his face with a hat, excluding all light, and before his eyes would appear what seemed to be parchment." Since the characters written on the parchment would be the same on the plates, the Seer vocalized word for word what he saw. The scribe then recorded it. Observing the same translation process in Harmony, Joseph Knight agreed:

> Now the way he translated was he put the urim and thummim into his hat and Darkned his Eyes then he would take a sentence and it would apper in Brite Roman Letters then he would tell the writer and he would write it[.] then...the next sentance would Come and so on But if it was not Spelt rite it would not go away till it was rite[,] so we see it was marvelous[.] thus was the hol [whole] translated.[33]

---

31. "The Old Soldier's Testimony," *Saints' Herald* 31, no. 4 (4 October 1884): 644. C. E. Butterworth reported the details of the sermon to the *Herald* for publication.

32. Joseph Smith III, "Last Testimony of Sister Emma," *Saints' Herald* 26, no. 19 (1 October 1879): 289–90; also see *Saints' Advocate* 2, no. 4 (October 1879): 49–52.

33. Joseph Knight Sr., "Manuscript of the History of Joseph Smith," circa 1835–1847, LDS Church Archives, in Vogel, *Early Mormon Documents*, 4: 17–18 (brackets added by Vogel).

Whether or not the plates were physically present, the translation process of the sacred writings was just as miraculous as their discovery and recovery.[34] It is very important to note that the actual translation process ranges far beyond the scope of historical scholarship.

The Book of Mormon Story Basics

THE FIFTEEN BOOKS that compose the Book of Mormon trace the history of three ancient Jewish peoples who lived in the Holy Land and migrated by sea to a new home. The story of the Book of Mormon begins in the days leading up to the Babylonian destruction of Jerusalem and tells how God intervened to allow one special, extended family, led by their patriarch, Lehi, to escape on a faith journey that eventually took them to a distant land.

Chronologically, the first civilization was the Jaredites, who assumed the name of Jared and his sibling, known only as the Brother of Jared. The Jaredite story encompasses a time frame assumed to be from 2350 BCE to 400 BCE, and appears in the Book of Ether. The story tells how these people sailed on a faith journey from the Holy Land to a faraway land. Some believe their possible landing site was on the west coast of Mexico. Speculations suggest that the Jaredite people might have been the Olmecs or perhaps even the Mayans.

The story of the second migration of peoples, known as Nephites and Lamanites, is found throughout the Book of Mormon but mostly during the years 600 BCE to 421 CE. According to some researchers, the landing site for these peoples was along the west coast of Guatemala. The Nephites may have been the progenitors to the Toltec or Aztec civilizations, while the Lamanites became the Native Americans.

The people of the third migration had two names: Mulekites and Zarahemlites. Their story extends from 586 BCE to 421 CE. Their narrative is found in the Book of Omni. Some suggest a possible landing site for this migratory people as the southern coast of Mexico, near the state of Oaxaca.

---

34. See Lancaster, "The Method of Translation of the Book of Mormon," *John Whitmer Historical Association Journal* 3 (1983): 51–61; also found in *Restoration Studies III*, 220–31, and in Vogel, *Word of God*, 97–113.

The Book of Mormon provides less information about this people, and no speculations exist about the successor civilization to the Mulekites.[35]

Book of Mormon language uses many biblical expressions and texts borrowing extensively, for example, from Isaiah.[36] Conflicts, warring tribes, and periods of peace dominate the storyline. There are great clashes between forces for good and evil, familial devotion, and sibling rivalry. Heroic figures like Nephi, Abinadi, and Moroni prevail over villains like Laman, Korihor, and Gadianton. Prophecies are fulfilled, loyalty and honor are rewarded, and deception and betrayal are punished. The narrative provides faith stories, morality plays, and sermons. But the most significant Book of Mormon story is an account of the resurrected Christ's visit among these New World peoples shortly after the Crucifixion. The Book of Mormon lifts up strict pacifism as expressed in the lifestyle of a small group of people called the Anti-Nephi-Lehies[37] yet tells of great violence—the book begins with the beheading of Laban[38] and ends with the beheading of Shiz.[39]

The Book of Mormon connected well with early nineteenth-century American values. Reading the Third Book of Nephi, for example, one could

---

35. I would like to thank Harry M. Steede of Independence, Missouri, for his insights on Book of Mormon geography, especially relating to the possible landing sites of the three migrations. Other Book of Mormon devotees have claimed a westward rather than eastward migration, identifying settlement sites on the east rather than west coast of the Americas. Despite extensive efforts to prove that early inhabitants of the Americas were those described in the Book of Mormon who came from the Holy Land, there is no support for these theories among today's archaeologists and anthropologists, who have the greatest respect among their scholarly colleagues.

36. Twenty-one complete chapters of Isaiah and segments of many other chapters are recorded in the Book of Mormon. Some of these passages are from what modern scholars refer to as "Second Isaiah," thought not to have been written until several decades after the departure of Lehi and his family from Jerusalem. See, for example, parts of Isaiah 52 to 54 found in Mosiah 7:77–80 (LDS 12:21–24) and 8:67–69 (LDS 15:29–31) and in III Nephi 7:43–45 (LDS 16:18–20), 9:70–83 (LDS 20:32–45), and 10: 9–25 (LDS 22:1–17). Book of Mormon passages from Isaiah are taken from the King James translation of the Bible. For a discussion of Isaiah passages in the Book of Mormon, see David P. Wright, "Isaiah in the Book of Mormon: Or Joseph Smith in Isaiah," in *American Apocrypha: Essays on the Book of Mormon*, ed. Dan Vogel and Brent Lee Metcalfe (Salt Lake City: Signature Books, 2002), 157–234.

37. Alma 14:26–28 (LDS 24:5–6).

38. I Nephi 1:120 (LDS 4:18).

39. Ether 6:104 (LDS 15:30).

conclude that America is the New Jerusalem, thus confirming a long-held Puritan belief in the mission and future of the nation.[40] Commentaries on contemporary issues of American governance are revealed in a discussion about the need to appoint honest judges during the reign of Mosiah:

> Let us appoint judges, to judge this people according to our law, and we will newly arrange the affairs of this people, for we will appoint wise men to be judges, that will judge this people according to the commandments of God.
>
> Now it is better that a man should be judged of God than of man, for the judgments of God are always just, but the judgments of man are not always just;
>
> Therefore, if it were possible that ye could have just men to be your kings, who would establish the laws of God, and judge this people according to his commandments; yea, if ye could have men for your kings, who would do even as my father Benjamin did for this people, I say unto you, If this could always be the case, then it would be expedient that ye should always have kings to rule over you.[41]

This discussion is reminiscent of James Madison's observation in the Federalist Papers presented in October 1787. In Federalist #51, writing also to the people of New York, under the pseudonym "Publius," Madison addressed the same need for honesty and integrity in government:

> Ambition must be made to counteract ambition. The interests of the man must be connected with the constitutional rights of the place. It may be a reflection on human nature, that such devices should be necessary to control the abuses of government. But what is government itself, but the greatest of all reflections on human nature? If men were angels, no government would be necessary. If angels were to govern men, neither external nor internal controls on government would be necessary.[42]

Joseph Smith Jr.'s generation read that at various points in this ancient history these Hebrew tribes placed great confidence in democracy

---

40. III Nephi 10:1–3 (LDS 21:22–24).
41. Mosiah 13:14–17 (LDS 29:11-13).
42. Roy P. Fairfield, ed., *The Federalist Papers: A Collection of Essays Written in Support of the Constitution of the United States*, 2nd ed. (Baltimore: Johns Hopkins University Press, 1986), 160.

and majority rule: "Now it is not common that the voice of the people desireth anything contrary to that which is right; but it is common for the lesser part of the people to desire that which is not right."[43] Indeed, the expression "voice of the people" frequents the pages of the American scripture.[44] Through the voice of the people during times of prosperity, laws were passed,[45] government was held in check,[46] citizens petitioned their government and held referendums,[47] disputes were settled,[48] liberties were protected,[49] judges and governors were chosen,[50] eminent domain was determined,[51] and civilians controlled the military.[52]

The Book of Mormon admonished the people to use their voice wisely because they would be held accountable in their decision making. Of course, this was an important issue during the contentious political debates of the early nineteenth century. If the people, through the use of their "voice" in government, chose wrongly, then God's wrath would visit them to hold them accountable:

> Therefore this shall ye observe, and make it your law to do your business by the voice of the people. And if the time comes that the voice of the people doth choose iniquity, then is the time that the judgments

43. Mosiah 13:35 (LDS 29:26).
44. The expression "voice of the people" was in popular use during Smith's generation. The concept of democracy was known in the Greek city-states. The term "democracy" has Greek derivation, from *demos* referring to "people" and *kratis* referring to "vote." Thus, literally, democracy means "people vote." Put together, *demos* and *kratis* form the Anglicized term. There is little evidence that the different cultures of the Book of Mormon would have known the Hellenistic world and democracy. The expression "voice of the people" can be found in Mosiah 5:12, 10:2, 13:4, 13:34, 13:35, 13:36, 13:37, 13:40; Alma 1:56, 1:57, 1:60, 2:23, 8:28, 15:22, 15:23, 23:7, 23:8, 23:18, 23:20; Helaman 1:5, 1:6, 1:38 (LDS Mosiah 7:9, 22:1, 29:2, 29:25, 29:26, 29:26, 29:27; 29:29; Alma 2:3, 2:4, 2:7, 4:16, 10:19, 27:21, 27:22, 51:7, 51:7, 51:15, 51:16; Helaman 1:5, 1:6, 2:2).
45. Alma 1:56 (LDS 2:3).
46. Mosiah 13:40 (LDS 29:29) and Alma 1:60 (LDS 2:7).
47. Alma 15:22 (LDS 27:21).
48. Alma 23:7 (LDS (51:7).
49. Helaman 1:8 (LDS 1:8).
50. Helaman 1:5, 38 (LDS 1:5, 2:2).
51. Alma 15:23 (LDS 27:22).
52. Alma 21:69 (LDS 64:34).

of God will come upon you; Yea, then is the time he will visit you with great destruction, even as he has hitherto visited this land.[53]

The Book of Mormon addressed other important political issues of the times such as Jacksonianism and anti-monarchicalism; social issues including racism and care for the poor and indigent; and the theological issues of Calvinism, atonement, the Resurrection, Christian primitivism, and trinitarianism.

The Book of Mormon represented an Americanization of the Judeo-Christian tradition. No longer did the American citizenry have to look half a world away to the Holy Land for the lessons of the Bible; now those lessons could be found in their own lands. The ability to relate the Mormon scripture to the everyday lives of the reader, especially in the context of popular belief, reflects a key characteristic of Joseph Smith Jr's religious genius—that is, his ability to apply his sense of the divine will to the needs of the times.[54]

Nineteenth-Century Cultural Influences, Genre Books on Native American Origins, and Book of Mormon Authorship

AT THE END of the nineteenth century, some inquirers began to look closely at the traditional understanding of the Book of Mormon's origins for evidences of human authorship.[55] Today, scholars note the

---

53. Mosiah 13:36–38 (LDS 29:26–27).

54. There is certainly nothing new in this conclusion. American social historian Harold Bloom made this same observation in his insightful analysis of religion fifteen years ago in *The American Religion: The Emergence of the Post-Christian Nation* (New York: Simon & Schuster, 1992), 84, 101, 113, 126. Bloom seemed influenced in his conclusion by Fawn Brodie, who observed the same more than forty-five years earlier in her classic biography *No Man Knows My History*, 403.

55. Perhaps the most well-known inquiry was that of Brigham H. Roberts whose three scholarly essays, "Book of Mormon Difficulties," "A Book of Mormon Study," and "A Parallel" resulted in the landmark *Studies of the Book of Mormon*, published posthumously in the 1920s. Roberts posed, and then addressed, questions about the Book of Mormon origins and authorship that are still relevant today. See B. H. Roberts, *Studies of the Book of Mormon*, ed. Brigham D. Madsen, 2nd ed. (Salt Lake City: Signature Books, 1992).

strong cultural influences from Joseph Smith's America on the Book of Mormon storyline.

Claiming that the Native American had Hebrew ancestry was nothing new in the early nineteenth century. Such speculations preceded the Book of Mormon by several generations. Five popular and important works laid the foundation for Joseph Smith Jr.'s assertions. In 1768 James Adair (c.1709–c.1783) finished his *History of the American Indian.* Published in 1775, this popular study provided firsthand experiences with southern tribes of North America. Adair concluded his analysis of their customs, languages, and history by speculating that the original inhabitants could trace their ancestry to ancient Jews. A similar study published in Philadelphia, Pennsylvania, in 1799 by Charles Crawford, titled *Essay upon the Propagation of the Gospel, in which there are facts to prove that many of the Indians in America are descended from the Ten Tribes,* added to the collection of works connecting America's original inhabitants to the Middle Eastern Holy Land.

Elias Boudinot (1740–1821) promoted the Native American–Hebrew relationship in *A Star in the West; or a Humble Attempt to Discover the Long Lost Tribes of Israel in Preparatory to the Return to Their Beloved Jerusalem* and published his work in 1816. Later Boudinot, a former member of the Second Continental Congress, was elected first president of the American Bible Society. Another work with widespread popularity was by Josiah Priest (1788–1851) titled *The Wonders of Nature and Providence Displayed Compiled from Authentic Sources, Both Ancient and Modern, Giving an Account of Various and Strange Phenomena Existing in Nature,* published in Albany, New York, in 1826. Priest summarized the writings of Adair and Boudinot, and then generally agreed with them, declaring his own observations in a list of twelve specific claims about the Hebrew origins of the Native American.[56]

Elias Boudinot

---

56. Josiah Priest, *The Wonders of Nature and Providence Displayed....* (Albany, N.Y.: By the Author, 1826), 377–407.

Congregationalist pastor Ethan Smith (1762–1849) provided the most impressive early nineteenth-century argument for the Native American–Hebrew connection in his *View of the Hebrews; or the Tribes of Israel in America*. First published in Poultney, Vermont, in 1823, Ethan Smith's treatise had such widespread popularity that he reprinted it in 1825. *View of the Hebrews* has a remarkable similarity to the Book of Mormon. Both books advocate the Native American–Hebrew connection, and both begin with events surrounding the destruction of Jerusalem. Ancient writings, for Ethan on "parchment" and Joseph on "golden plates," were buried and then discovered and provide the original source for both stories. Several years before the Book of Mormon was published, Ethan Smith wrote: "In resemblance of the Urim and Thummim, the American Archimagus wears a breast plate made of a white conch-shell with two holes bored in the middle of it, through which he puts the ends of an otter skin strap, and fastens a buck horn white button to the outside of each, as if in imitation of the precious stones of the Urim."[57] Joseph Smith Jr. told of transparent stones in a silver bow fastened to a breastplate. Ethan Smith said his ancient writings were "hieroglyphical paintings"[58] while Joseph Smith described his ancient

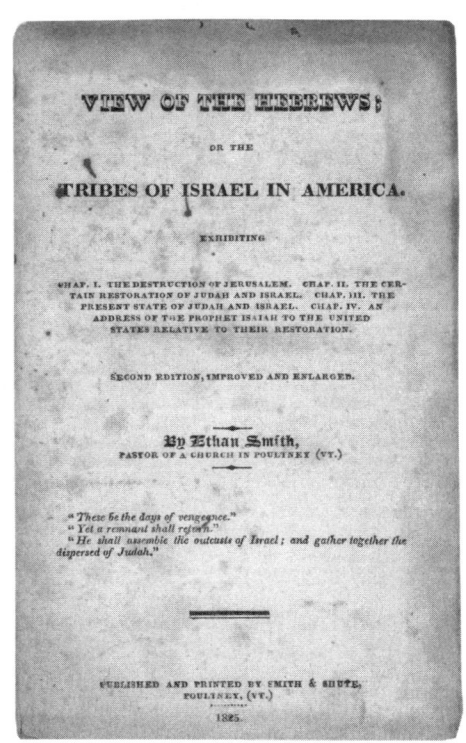

COMMUNITY OF CHRIST LIBRARY-ARCHIVES

Title page of Ethan Smith's View of the Hebrews

---

57. Ethan Smith, *View of the Hebrews* (Poultney, Vt.: Smith and Shute, 1825), 150.

58. Ethan Smith, *View of the Hebrews*, 182.

writings as "reformed hieroglyphics." Lifting up the importance of gentile Americans in teaching Native Americans the gospel, Ethan Smith wrote that the "white men would naturally teach them (if they taught any thing,) that Jesus Christ the Son of God is the Saviour of the world" and should prepare to lead others in the last days.[59] Similarly, Joseph Smith claimed that America was the Promised Land and the purpose of the Book of Mormon was to teach the gospel in the last days to the Lamanites.

Both *View of the Hebrews* and the Book of Mormon addressed the issue of polygamy. Ethan Smith wrote that the Delaware Indians "had become so foolish, and so wicked, that they would take a number of wives at a time; and turn them away at pleasure!"[60] While in the Book of Mormon, the Nephite people

> begin to wax in iniquity; they understand not the scriptures: for they seek to excuse themselves in committing whoredoms, because of the things which were written concerning David, and Solomon his son. Behold, David and Solomon truly had many wives, and concubines, which thing was abominable before me.[61]

Whether or not Joseph Smith Jr. actually read any of the five popular writings mentioned is impossible to determine. However, the notion that the Native American could trace his roots to the Holy Land pervaded the Seer's popular culture.

The Pivotal Role of Oliver Cowdery

OLIVER COWDERY'S IMPORTANT role in the production of the Book of Mormon cannot be overstated. Joseph Smith Jr. had at least three years to contemplate what the book might contain before his first attempt to translate. But one huge problem was finding suitable scribes. Translation was slow and laborious when Emma and Martin Harris assisted. Between 12 April and 14 June 1828, the initial 116 pages progressed at an average of about two pages per day. This pace continued after the process resumed in the fall of 1828 with Emma, her brother Reuben, and

---

59. Ethan Smith, *View of the Hebrews*, 104–5, 228.
60. Ethan Smith, *View of the Hebrews*, 104–5.
61. Jacob 2:32–33 (LDS 2:23–24).

Joseph's younger brother Samuel Harrison as scribes. But when Oliver Cowdery arrived at the Smith home in Harmony, Pennsylvania, the process of translation accelerated dramatically. With Cowdery's assistance in the spring of 1829, the pace increased to approximately six to eight pages per day.

One must ask why the translation pace nearly quadrupled. Oliver Cowdery's family background may provide valuable clues. The Cowdery family roots were in Poultney, Rutland County, Vermont, where Oliver lived for twenty-two years, until 1825. Church records show that Keziah, Oliver's stepmother, was a member of the Poultney Congregational Church, along with Oliver's three sisters, when Ethan Smith was pastor. During Ethan Smith's five-year tenure as pastor in the Poultney congregation (November 1821 to December 1826) he wrote and published twice his *View of the Hebrews*. In early 1827 Ethan Smith visited Palmyra about the same time Joseph Smith married Emma Hale in South Bainbridge, New York.[62] Following the wedding, the young couple returned to upstate New York and could have been in Palmyra during Ethan Smith's visit.

COMMUNITY OF CHRIST LIBRARY-ARCHIVES
Oliver Cowdery

After the Smith family lived in the Palmyra area, community leaders noted the academic training of Hyrum Smith and selected him as trustee

---

62. The *Wayne Sentinel*, a local newspaper, showed Ethan Smith identified as having letters posted to him in the Palmyra Post Office. This list is dated 5 January 1827. For a more in-depth explanation of this possibility, see Brigham D. Madsen's "Introduction" to B. H. Roberts, *Studies of the Book of Mormon*, 27.

for the local school.⁶³ One of his assigned duties was to hire teachers. Lyman Cowdery, Oliver's older brother, learned about the need for a school instructor in Manchester and contacted Hyrum for an interview. When Lyman, who was practicing law in nearby Wayne County, realized he had a schedule conflict, he recommended his younger brother, Oliver, for the position. Hyrum hired Oliver and offered to board him at the Smith farm. While living with the Smiths, Oliver heard the fascinating stories of angel visitations and the discovery of the golden plates. He asked for "the privilege of writing for Joseph."⁶⁴ At the conclusion of the school term, in early April 1829, Samuel H. Smith and Cowdery went to Harmony, where Samuel introduced the two men. There seemed to be an immediate bonding of trust between the two. Together Joseph and Oliver completed the entire Book of Mormon transcript in just ninety days.

Although Joseph Smith Jr.'s knowledge of *View of the Hebrews* remains a question, Oliver Cowdery's familiarity with Ethan Smith's novel seems beyond question. One can anticipate Cowdery's assistance at various opportunities during the time the two men worked on the manuscript. Indeed, Joseph prophesied of Cowdery's gift to translate:

> And, therefore, whatsoever you shall ask me to tell you by that means, that will I grant unto you, and you shall have knowledge concerning it; remember, that without faith you can do nothing. Therefore, ask in faith. Trifle not with these things; do not ask for that which you ought not; ask that you may know the mysteries of God, and that you may translate and receive knowledge from all those ancient records which have been hid up, that are sacred, and according to your faith shall it be done unto you.⁶⁵

At one point, as Cowdery yearned to actually translate, Smith hesitantly consented but refused Cowdery the use of his seer stone. Instead Cowdery

---

63. In summer and fall of 1812 Hyrum, age eleven, attended Moor's Charity Academy in Hanover, New Hampshire. This academy, although established for those who could not afford higher education, was associated with the prestigious Dartmouth College. By 1828 Hyrum was teaching school in Manchester Township. See Bushman, *Joseph Smith and the Beginnings of Mormonism*, 32.
64. Lucy Smith, *Biographical Sketches*, 151–52.
65. Doctrine and Covenants 8:3d–f (LDS 8:9–11).

was to use faithfully the "gift of Aaron"[66] given him by God to translate. Unfortunately for Oliver his efforts failed. Joseph responded with words of patience and encouragement, explaining to Oliver that in the future "you must study it out in your mind." Joseph explained further that Oliver would know if his interpretation was right because his bosom would burn if it were so, and if it were wrong, then he would have no such feeling.[67]

Currently there is no convincing evidence that proves Cowdery actually wrote segments of the Book of Mormon story. However, it is entirely possible and certainly reasonable to conclude that when Joseph struggled with interpretive language, Oliver, whose educational background far exceeded the prophet's, could have used his extensive gifts and personal background experience to contribute significantly to the story construction.[68]

DNA Studies and the Book of Mormon

MORE RECENTLY THE scientific community has addressed the possibility of pre-Columbian Jewish migrations to the American continent and Pacific islands. The early hope of some was that DNA studies would identify an undeniable genetic link between ancient Jewish populations and the Amerindian and native Pacific island populations. Such a connection could finally establish the Book of Mormon as a possible historical record of these people. When the results of these studies rejected Book of Mormon claims, a debate emerged over the DNA analysis conclusions.[69]

66. Doctrine and Covenants 8:3b (LDS 8:6–7).

67. Doctrine and Covenants 9:3a–d (LDS 9:7–9).

68. Suggesting Cowdery's involvement is not new. In an 1897 letter to Dietrich Willers Jr., a historian preparing his *Centennial Historical Sketch of the Town of Fayette*, Lee Yost, a Michigan merchant and former resident of Fayette, New York, promoted the Cowdery thesis. Having familiarity with the translation process and Cowdery's involvement, Yost wrote: "Now my idea of this is that in the First Cowdery had a goo[d] deal to [do] with the writing of the Mormon Bible." See Lee Yost to Dietrich Willers Jr., 18 May 1897, Willers Papers, Seneca Falls Historical Society, Seneca Falls, New York, in Vogel, *Early Mormon Documents,* 5: 290 (brackets added by Vogel).

69. Discounting such scientific theorization, see Hugh Nibley, *Lehi in the Desert: The World of the Jaredites; There Were Jaredites,* ed. John W. Welch, Darrel L. Matthews, and Stephen R. Callister (Salt Lake City: Deseret Book Company and the Foundation for Ancient Research and Mormon Studies, 1988), and Ted E. Brewerton, "The Book of

In an extensive study, Simon G. Southerton[70] profiled more than seven thousand people throughout the Americas and the Polynesian islands. His methodology focused on the genetic markers of both paternal and maternal lineages. Southerton knew that "if Israelites found their way to America and Polynesia before Columbus, the genetic signs of their presence would have been carried among their living descendants."[71] Southerton could find no genetic connection. Instead he confirmed anthropological and archaeological research that the molecular pedigrees of Native Americans cluster on the Asian branch of the human family tree.[72]

With emphatic disagreement apologists have argued that genetic scientists have neglected scriptural and historical evidence that would challenge their scientific conclusions. For example, one Web-based author criticized:

> The Lord explicitly forbade intermarriage between Israelites and the inhabitants of Palestine, commanding: "Neither shalt thou make marriages with them; thy daughter thou shalt not give unto his son, nor his daughter shalt thou take unto thy son" (Deuteronomy 7:3). The spiritual and social separation between Israel and the surrounding nations is a frequent scriptural theme. Limited intermixing occurred between Israel and surrounding kingdoms during the captivity in Egypt and the early period of the Kingdom of Israel, mainly consisting of the

---

Mormon: A Sacred Ancient Record," *Ensign* 25 (1995): 30–31. Emory University researcher Douglas Wallace was among the first to explore Native American origins by focusing on their mitochondrial (maternal) DNA. But the breakthrough for understanding this issue occurred in 1990. See Theodore G. Shurr, Scott W. Ballinger, Yik Y. Gan, et. al., "Amerindian Mitochondrial DNAs Have Rare Asian Mutations at High Frequencies Suggesting They Derived from Four Primary Maternal Lineages," *American Journal of Human Genetics* 46 (1990): 613–23. A decade later Shurr followed with "Mitochondrial DNA and the Peopling of the New World," *American Scientist* 46 (2000): 246–53.

70. In Southerton's authoritative *Losing a Lost Tribe: Native Americans, DNA, and the Mormon Church* (Salt Lake City: Signature Books, 2004), he observed: "Many people do not appreciate how closely related the plant and animal kingdoms are on a molecular level, but the structure and language of DNA is remarkably conserved in both plants and animals" (viii). DNA is an abbreviation of deoxyribonucleic acid, one of the most basic building blocks of the human genome.

71. Southerton, *Losing a Lost Tribe*, 129.

72. Southerton, *Losing a Lost Tribe*, 88.

assimilation of foreign wives. Nonetheless, the continued emphasis on separation between Israel and its neighbors would make it foolish to expect genetic "regional affiliation" markers gathered from a composite of Canaanites, Egyptians, Phoenicians, Philistines, and other groups then inhabiting the ancient Near East, to represent a definitive test of early Israelite ancestry.[73]

An alternative view of the Book of Mormon story saw the ancient Lamanites located in a limited geographic region around the Isthmus of Tehuantepec in Central America. This argument narrowed the Book of Mormon story to a lineage history of the Maya rather than it being a hemispheric history.[74]

But because of the scientific advances in genetic research, Southerton observed that even "a miniscule Lehite colony" amid a multicontinental population could be detected. However, to date neither he nor any other professionally trained scientist has discovered sustained genetic evidence linking the Amerindian to ancient Middle Eastern peoples.[75]

The Witnesses of the Book of Mormon Plates: "Seeing is believing, but feeling is truth"

THE NEXT BOOK OF MORMON issue to be addressed relates to those who witnessed the plates. Joseph felt the need for others to see the plates so he would have added support against the anticipated flood of criticism when the book came off the press in March 1830. The Seer thus prepared eleven men for a visionary encounter. The first three witnesses were Oliver Cowdery, David Whitmer, and Martin Harris. Then came the

---

73. *http://www.fairlds.org*. This Web site is sponsored by the Foundation for Apologetic Information and Research (FAIR). FAIR is staffed completely by students of the scriptures, ancient languages, early Christian history, early LDS history, and LDS doctrine and apologetics.

74. See John L. Sorenson, *An Ancient American Setting for the Book of Mormon* (Salt Lake City: Deseret Book Company, 1985).

75. The best summary of genetic studies of the Book of Mormon is Thomas W. Murphy, "Lamanite Genesis, Genealogy, and Genetics," in Vogel and Metcalfe, *American Apocrypha*, 47–77. Murphy agreed with Southerton's conclusion and added: "The term Lamanite is a modern social and political designation that lacks a verifiable biological or historical underpinning linking it to ancient American Indians," 68.

experiences of eight other witnesses: Christian Whitmer, Jacob Whitmer, Peter Whitmer Jr., John Whitmer, Hiram Page, Joseph Smith Sr., Hyrum Smith, and Samuel Harrison Smith. When publishing the work in 1830, the Seer placed their attested testimonies in the back of the book for all to read.[76] Weighing our traditional understanding as expressed in their recorded testimony with how these men explained their experience is a fascinating study.

To historically appreciate the testimonies of the three and the eight witnesses, one must understand the context and cultural influences on them. Today, those who interpret the Book of Mormon as literal history are bolstered by the testimony of two sets of witnesses. Smith's rationale for selecting each of the witnesses is subject to considerable speculation. Family relations must have been a consideration since almost all were either Smiths or Whitmers or related by marriage.[77] Only Martin Harris stood outside the two extended families, but as soon-to-become primary financier, his involvement was crucial to the success of the Book of Mormon project.

The three witnesses—Oliver Cowdery, David Whitmer, and Martin Harris—were very close to the Seer and at least two were experienced visionaries. Both Cowdery and Harris claimed to see the plates in their own visions prior to meeting with Smith for that purpose.[78] By late June

---

76. More recent editions of the Book of Mormon place these testimonies at the front.

77. Hiram Page married Catherine Whitmer, sister to the Whitmer witnesses, on 10 November 1825. Cowdery married Elizabeth Ann Whitmer, sister to the Whitmer witnesses, on 18 December 1832.

78. Mary Musselman Whitmer (1776–1856), mother of the Whitmer witnesses, also claimed to see the plates in a vision in early June 1829 at her Fayette, New York, farm. Her grandson, John C. Whitmer, in an 1888 interview with Andrew Jenson and Edward Stevenson, remembered that his grandmother said she went into the family barn to milk her cows when a man appeared before her. According to her testimony, he took the plates from his knapsack, then turned the leaves for her inspection until she was satisfied. The personage along with the plates then disappeared. Jenson and Stevenson reported their interview in separate writings. See Andrew Jenson, "Still Another Witness," *Historical Record* 7 (October 1888): 621, in Vogel, *Early Mormon Documents*, 5: 261–62; and Edward Stevenson, Interview of David Whitmer (4) 2 January 1887, Richmond, Missouri, *The Juvenile Instructor* 24 (1 January 1889), in *David Whitmer Interviews: A Restoration Witness*, ed. Lyndon W. Cook (Orem, Utah: Grandin Book Company, 1993), 217–18.

1829, Smith approached the end of the translation process and wanted to add the witnesses' testimonies before the manuscript could be sent to the printer. At Oliver Cowdery's request David Whitmer brought Joseph and Oliver back from Harmony to the Whitmer farm in Fayette, New York. After their arrival David and Oliver pressed Joseph to view the plates. Evidently Joseph had no qualms about David and Oliver, but Lucy Mack Smith stated that Joseph first admonished Martin by stating: "Martin Harris, you have got to humble yourself before God this day, that you may obtain a forgiveness of your sins. If you do, it is the will of God that you should look upon the plates, in company with Oliver Cowdery and David Whitmer."[79]

Shortly thereafter, the four men "repaired to a grove, a short distance from the house, where they commenced calling upon the Lord, and continued in earnest supplication, until he permitted an angel to come down from his presence, and declare to them, that all which Joseph had testified of concerning the plates was true."[80] Joseph Jr. provided more detail about the experience in his 1838–1839 account of these events. He recorded that the four men on bended knee prayed for light. Nothing happened so they prayed a second time. Again, nothing happened. Then, Harris, feeling he was to blame, perhaps since only he had been admonished earlier, dismissed himself and walked a distance away from the other men. With Harris gone, the others knelt and prayed again, and then "beheld a light above us in the air of exceeding brightness, and behold an angel stood before us; in his hands he held the plates which we had been praying for…to have a view of: he turned over the leaves one by one, so that we could see them, and discern the engravings thereon distinctly."[81]

Joseph then went to Harris and together they prayed. The Seer wrote that "the same vision was opened to our view; at least it was again to me, and I once more beheld, and seen, and heard the same things; whilst at the

---

79. Lucy Smith, *Biographical Sketches*, 164. It is interesting that Joseph Smith would set conditions for Harris and not the other two men. By doing this the Seer made Harris responsible for his own vision, thus relieving himself of any responsibility should Harris have an unsuccessful experience.

80. Lucy Smith, *Biographical Sketches*, 164.

81. Joseph Smith, "Manuscript History," in Vogel, *Early Mormon Documents*, 1: 84–85.

COMMUNITY OF CHRIST LIBRARY-ARCHIVES

Page from the original printer's manuscript of the Book of Mormon (manuscript page 399; III Nephi 9:89–103 [21:4–17 LDS])

same moment, Martin Harris cried out... "'Tis enough, 'tis enough; mine eyes have beheld, mine eyes have beheld.' And jumping up he shouted, Hosanna, blessing God; and—otherwise rejoiced exceedingly."[82]

Tradition suggests that all three witnesses plus Joseph Smith Jr. had the same vision. However, from their separate explanations it is clear that this was not the case. For example, years later in 1877, David Whitmer said that the angel laid the plates on a table along with the Urim and Thummim, ball or director, and the sword of Laban.[83] Also Whitmer explained that the epiphany occurred as the men were "sitting upon a log...talking"[84] rather than praying as Joseph wrote.

The encounter of the eight witnesses was considerably different from that of the three. The three witnesses had their viewing near the Whitmer farm in Fayette and the eight had theirs near the Smith farm in Manchester. The three witnesses received revelatory sanction for their viewing[85] while the eight witnesses were not commissioned by revelation to view the plates. No angelic visitation accompanied the viewing by the eight; instead Joseph revealed the plates to them. The three did not claim to handle the plates during their vision, while the eight did. However, from the later writings of the eight, only three claimed to actually handle the plates. It is possible that Joseph felt an increased number of witnesses added credibility to his claims and could spread responsibility for deflecting criticism that was sure to come. Claiming to feel the plates added more credibility to their witness.

82. Joseph Smith, "Manuscript History," in Vogel, *Early Mormon Documents*, 1: 85.

83. This account is repeated by E. C. Briggs in his 4 June 1884 letter to Joseph Smith III. See *Saints' Herald* 31, no. 25 (21 June 1884): 396.

84. Edward Stevenson, Journal, 24: 30–37, entry of 9 February 1886, LDS Church Archives, in Vogel, *Early Mormon Documents*, 5: 160. Writing from Palmyra on 29 November 1829, Oliver Cowdery described the physical setting of the Three Witnesses epiphany, stating: "It was a clear, open beautiful day, far from any inhabitants, in a remote field, at the time we saw the record...." Different from the traditional explanation, Cowdery did not mention that Harris had separated from the others at the time of the viewing. Cowdery's remembrance was just five months after the June epiphany. *Gospel Luminary* 2, no. 49 (10 December 1829): 194. I thank historian Erin Jennings for bringing this newly discovered source to my attention.

85. Doctrine and Covenants 5:1a (LDS 5:1). Here Martin Harris is identified as a witness to view the plates. Section 5:3b–e (LDS 5:11–16) indicates that three will be allowed to be witnesses. Dan Vogel argues this point in *Making of a Prophet*, 469.

Plain Sight and Second Sight[86]

CAREFUL ANALYSIS OF the testimonies of the three and the eight witnesses, as well as their separate statements in the years that followed, strongly suggests the visionary nature of their experiences. All eleven witnesses plus Joseph Smith shared a worldview that included guardian spirits protecting slippery treasures that moved through the earth just beyond the reach of diggers. Although none denied their visions of the plates, several admitted that the experience was seen with visionary eyes and not natural eyes. This phenomenon is known as "second sight." It is the sight afforded, for example, Martin Harris, who likened his vision of the plates to seeing a city through a mountain.[87] Contemporary expressions used by the witnesses such as "seeing with spiritual eyes" or "seeing with the eyes of understanding" make the distinction between plain or natural sight and second sight.

Shortly before the Book of Mormon came off the press, the chief typesetter, John H. Gilbert, remembered a visit by Martin Harris at the Grandin print shop, where Gilbert worked. Having set the type, Gilbert knew the Book of Mormon story well. As Gilbert recalled: "Martin was in the office when I finished setting up the testimony of the three witnesses. I said to him,–'Martin, did you see those plates with your naked eyes?' Martin looked down...for an instant, raised his eyes up, and said, 'No, I saw them with a spir[i]tual eye.'"[88] Approximately a year later, in March 1831, Harris addressed a meeting in Painesville, Ohio, where he claimed to know "all about the gold plates, Angels, Spirits, and Jo Smith—he had seen and handled them all, *by the power of God!*"[89] Even the three witnesses of the eight who later actually claimed the privilege of handling the plates

---

86. A more complete explanation of this interesting phenomenon can be found in Palmer, *An Insider's View*. Palmer's sixth chapter titled "Witnesses to the Golden Plates" analyzes in detail the differences between "seeing with the natural eye" and "seeing with spiritual eyes," 175–213.

87. Stephen Burnett to Lyman E. Johnson, 15 April 1838, in Vogel, *Early Mormon Documents*, 2: 292.

88. John H. Gilbert, "Memorandum, made by John H. Gilbert Esq, Sept. 8th, 1892 Palmyra, N.Y.," 5, Palmyra King's Daughters Free Library, Palmyra, New York, in Vogel, *Early Mormon Documents*, 2: 548 (brackets added by Vogel).

89. *Painesville Telegraph*, 15 March 1831, [3], in Palmer, *An Insider's View*, 199.

admitted that an angel facilitated the event. John Whitmer's account is representative. In 1839, he told church member Theodore Turley: "I handled those plates; there were fine gravings on both sides...they were shown to me by a supernatural power."[90]

Disagreements on when, where, and how their visions happened require close inspection. After the three viewed the plates near the Whitmer farm in Fayette, the eight witnesses met with Joseph at the Smith farm in Manchester to view the plates. John Whitmer testified that the eight witnesses were divided into two groups of four before viewing the plates. Lucy Mack Smith said the eight saw the plates together as they "repaired to a little grove...as Joseph had been instructed that the plates would be carried there by one of the ancient Nephites. Here it was that those eight witnesses...looked upon and handled them."[91] Whitmer's claim that the two groups of four viewed the plates inside the Smith home contradicts other sources, however.[92]

Assessing the Composition and Dimensions of the Nephite Plates

WHAT DID THE three and eight witnesses actually see when they were shown the Book of Mormon plates? Weighing the traditional account with modern scientific knowledge adds further insight into the

90. *DHC*, 3: 307.

91. Lavina Anderson, *Lucy's Book*, 455–56, Vogel, *Early Mormon Documents*, 1: 395–96, 248. In a less-than-objective yet interesting account, Illinois governor Thomas Ford wrote in his 1854 state history his understanding of the testimony of the eight witnesses that Joseph Smith Jr. set an empty box in front of the men and told them that it contained the sacred plates. One by one the men peered into the box, finding it empty. When the men admitted not seeing anything, Smith scolded them stating: "O ye of little faith! How long will God bear with this wicked and perverse generation? Down on your knees, brethren, every one of you, and pray God for the forgiveness of your sins, and for a holy and living faith which cometh down from heaven." The men quickly launched into a period of meditation praying "two hours with fanatical earnestness." After their time of supplication, Smith told them to look again. They did so and this time everyone saw the plates. See Thomas Ford, *History of the State of Illinois, from Its Commencement as a State in 1818 to 1847* (Chicago: S. C. Griggs and Co., 1854), 258.

92. See Dan Vogel's observations of John Whitmer's April 1878 interview with P. Wilhelm Poulson in *Early Mormon Documents* 5: 247–49.

story. On several occasions Joseph Smith gave the dimensions of the plates as six inches in width, eight inches in length, and six inches thick. Those who viewed the plates claimed that they had the "appearance of gold."[93] In his letter to John Wentworth, editor of the *Chicago Democrat*, published in the Nauvoo *Times and Seasons* in March 1842, Smith wrote:

> These records were engraven on plates which had the appearance of gold, each plate was six inches wide and eight inches long and not quite so thick as common tin. They were filled with engravings, in Egyptian characters and bound together in a volume, as the leaves of a book with three rings running through the whole. The volume was something near six inches in thickness, a part of which was sealed. The characters on the unsealed part were small, and beautifully engraved. The whole book exhibited many marks of antiquity in its construction and much skill in the art of engraving.[94]

Joseph told that, when he retrieved the plates in late September 1827, three lurking men accosted him on the way back to Emma and the wagon. For quite a distance with the plates in tow, and after each separate scuffle along the way, he outran these men; then for safekeeping he lifted them into a hollow tree top.[95] Next, to transport the plates to Harmony, Pennsylvania, Joseph placed them in a barrel of beans.[96] Finally, one day while translating in Harmony, Oliver and Joseph took a break and decided to go for a walk. The men left the plates on a table, covered in cloth. In their absence Emma said that she moved them so she could clean the table.[97]

---

93. For example the eight Book of Mormon witnesses testified that the plates had the appearance of gold. Joseph used this expression in "Church History," *Times and Seasons* 3, no. 9 (1 March 1842): 707. Also see Joseph Knight Sr., "Manuscript of the History of Joseph Smith," in Vogel, *Early Mormon Documents*, 4: 15.

94. "Church History," *Times and Seasons* 3, no. 9 (1 March 1842): 707.

95. Martin Harris interview with Joel Tiffany, 1859, in Vogel, *Early Mormon Documents*, 2: 306.

96. In neither of these stories did Joseph did tell what happened to the breastplate, Urim and Thummim, and sword of Laban, also found in the stone box in Hill Cumorah.

97. This is a reconstruction of the explanation that Emma Hale Smith Bidamon gave to her son Joseph Smith III, in February 1879. See Joseph Smith III, "Last Testimony of Sister Emma," 290.

THE "GOLDEN" PLATES AND THE DENSITIES OF METALS

Dimensions of the metallic plates:

6 × 8 × 6 inches

15.24 × 20.32 × 15.24 centimeters

Approximate volume of the plates:

4,700 cm³

Density of minerals and alloys:

Gold (Au): 19.32 g/cm³
Lead (Pb): 11.3 g/cm³
Tin (Sn): 6.55 g/cm³
Yellow Brass (65% Cu, 35% Zn): 8.47 g/cm³

Mass of the plates
  assuming a solid block:
    Gold: 200 lbs.
    Lead: 117 lbs.
    Tin: 68 lbs.
    Yellow Brass: 88 lbs.

  assuming plates have 15% less mass than a solid block:
    Gold: 170 lbs.
    Lead: 100 lbs.
    Tin: 58 lbs.
    Yellow Brass: 75 lbs.

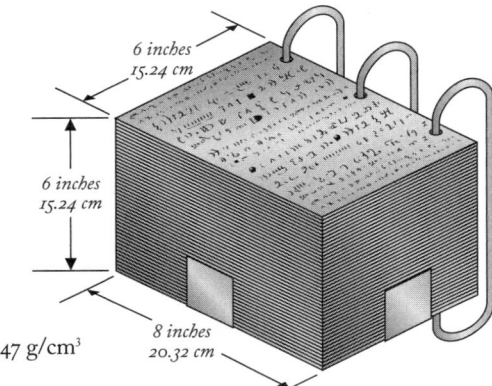

While being described as having "the appearance of gold," one must ask if it is possible that the plates were actually gold. A solid block of gold based on the dimensions that Joseph provided would weigh approximately 200 pounds. But since the plates were not in a solid block but leafed, were etched, and had three holes with rings, it is necessary to recalculate the actual weight. Subtracting ten to fifteen percent, a reasonable estimate for these conditions, plates of gold would weigh between 170 and 180 pounds.[98] That Joseph and Emma could have handled the plates so manageably on each occasion, though weighing at least 170 pounds, and that it was not an issue or even mentioned, seems to defy physical science.

These calculations should not question the existence of the plates, however. On too many occasions the scribes remembered the plates being

---

98. Of course these figures are very speculative. These statistical measurements were calculated with the assistance of Jerry W. Nieft, Ph.D., in March 2001. Metallic densities were taken from periodic tables in *Handbook of Chemistry and Physics* (Cleveland, Ohio: The Chemical Rubber Publishing Company, 1962).

present during their translation sessions. Of course, the plates were either shrouded in cloth or placed inside a box. Some of Smith's contemporaries, for example, his father-in-law, Isaac Hale, hefted the box after being told the plates were inside. Others thumbed the metallic pages while covered in cloth. Emma Smith claimed she saw the plates wrapped in a small linen tablecloth and even moved them across a table.[99] These circumstances clearly were not "second sight" experiences.

From such firsthand accounts it is reasonable to conclude that the plates did exist, but were probably not made of gold. Lead sheets at the stated dimensions would weigh 100 pounds, brass sheets would weigh 75 pounds, and tin sheets would weigh 58 pounds. Martin Harris, interviewing with New York City editor Joel Tiffany in 1859, gave a very detailed description of the plates. Harris claimed: "I hefted the plates many times, and should think they weighed forty or fifty pounds."[100] Finally, when asked in 1884, in a public setting to estimate the weight of the plates, William Smith responded: "As near as I could tell, about sixty pounds."[101]

A Spectrum of Opinion on the Book of Mormon

EXPLORATIONS INTO THE Book of Mormon story have only grown through the years. Consensus has not developed on whether or not the Book of Mormon is an authentic history of pre-Columbian peoples in the New World. Today we can summarize three general positions about the scripture's origins and authorship. The first is that the Book of Mormon is the literal history of ancient America written by prophets of God as they were inspired to do so and handed down from one generation to the next until they were buried at Hill Cumorah. Through divine intervention the plates were given to Joseph Smith Jr. whose inerrant translation became the exact Word of God and another scriptural testament to the divinity of Jesus Christ.

---

99. "Statement of J. W. Peterson Concerning William Smith," 1 May 1921, 1, Miscellaneous Letters and Papers, Community of Christ Library-Archives; Also found in William Smith, "The Old Soldier's Testimony," 644. Emma Hale Smith Bidamon also thumbed the pages as indicated in Joseph Smith III, "Last Testimony of Sister Emma," 290.
100. Harris interview with Joel Tiffany, 1859, in Vogel, *Early Mormon Documents*, 2: 306.
101. William Smith, "The Old Soldier's Testimony," 644.

The far opposite position completely rejects any possible divine origin in the writings. Instead, this approach discards the Book of Mormon's scriptural legitimacy and sees the writings as a charade with Joseph Smith Jr. as an imposter. Proponents of this view read the Book of Mormon as a mere genre novel, just one of many contemporary writings of Smith's generation that focus on the origins of the American Indian.

Between these two extremes are conclusions that emphasize to varying degrees the role of Joseph Smith in the book's writing while not necessarily ruling out divine inspiration. Among these approaches, five strong influences on Joseph Smith Jr. are important. The first focuses on the powerful presence of the Bible that permeated the Smith family worldview. Interpretation of various scriptures undoubtedly frequented family discussions throughout young Joseph's life. Like their neighbors, Joseph Sr. and Lucy Mack Smith would use the Bible as the key instructional tool in teaching their children to read and write. Thus it is not surprising that biblical (and even apocryphal) stories, linguistic expressions, and moralistic themes were so noticeable in the Book of Mormon text.[102]

The second influence emanates from the early nineteenth-century cultural environment. American myths and antiquities, so pervasive in New York and Pennsylvania, shaped Joseph Smith Jr.'s generation. The influence of treasure seeking, money digging, and mystical influences impacted everyone to some degree. Folklore writings of the times, whether found in private collections, local newspapers,[103] or in nearby libraries, had a powerful influence on the young man. Often those cultural influences found expression in the Book of Mormon origins and story.

The third influence is Joseph Smith Jr.'s strong family ties, which shaped his character and thus the Book of Mormon story. As the middle child in a tension-filled family, Joseph felt a strong obligation to resolve bitter theological and scriptural arguments between family members and used the Book of Mormon as a tool to do just that. Some scholars suggest

---

102. An excellent essay on the recurrence of biblical expression within the Book of Mormon is David P. Wright, "Isaiah in the Book of Mormon," in Vogel and Metcalfe, *American Apocrypha*, 157–234.

103. For example, two newspapers in Palmyra posted frequent articles on Native American folklore. See the *Palmyra Register*, January 1818, and the *Palmyra Herald*, February 1823, for such articles.

that Book of Mormon characters, and even name selections, were subconscious reflections of Smith family members and those around him.[104] This American scripture launched a new religious alternative for his family. Claiming prophetic authority, Joseph achieved family harmony by baptizing and eventually assigning family members to key responsibilities within the new church.

Joseph Smith Jr. drew a fourth powerful influence from his believers—those who embraced Book of Mormon teachings and found spiritual sustenance in its verses. For these people, an undeniable and powerful spirit pervaded its pages to assure them the writings were true. Moralistic stories modeled in the lives of the book's main characters addressed key theological and social issues of the day.

But proclaiming a second scripture was quite offensive to defenders of the Bible as the sole scripture within the Judeo-Christian tradition. One noted contemporary cleric, Alexander Campbell (1788–1866), whose reform efforts led to the emergence of the Disciples of Christ, used his church newspaper, the *Millennial Harbinger*, to launch a stinging critique arguing that Joseph Smith,

> through his stone spectacles, wrote on the plates of Nephi, in his book of Mormon, every error and almost every truth discussed in New York for the last ten years. He decides all the great controversies—infant baptism, ordination, the trinity, regeneration, repentance, justification, the fall of man, the atonement, transubstantiation, fasting, pennance, church government, religious experience, the call to the ministry, the

---

104. Lemuel, Nephi's older brother, is a biblical name but also happens to be the name of Joseph Jr.'s neighbor, Lemuel Durfee, who testified to Philastus Hurlbut that Joseph Jr. possessed an immoral character. Durfee was one of Smith's strongest Palmyra critics. Fawn Brodie makes this observation in *No Man Knows My History*, 43fn.

Robert D. Anderson suggests that Smith "stacked" the story of the conversion of the four sons of Mosiah with the conversion of the four Smith family members to Presbyterianism during the revival period in Palmyra. See Anderson's *Inside the Mind of Joseph Smith*, 144. William D. Morain notes the similarity between the death from natural causes of Nephi's father-in-law, Ishmael, and his real life father-in-law, Isaac Hale. Then Morain raises the possibility that as Ishmael was the first person to die among the righteous family members leaving Jerusalem, this was Smith's subliminal fantasy wish-fulfillment to eliminate Isaac at the first convenient juncture in the storyline, especially considering their rocky relationship shortly after he and Emma eloped. See *The Sword of Laban*, 102.

general resurrection, eternal punishment, who may baptize, and even the question of free masonry, republican government, and the rights of man.[105]

Ironically, Campbell listed the exact attributes that popularized and sustained Smith's religious movement. The inspiration of which Campbell was so critical actually reflected Smith's genius as a religious leader as he sought God's will in providing answers to people's daily struggles and meeting their spiritual needs. The prophet and his people drew strength from each other to accomplish their purposes in their perceived divine plan.

The last influence of this middle-ground view between those who view the Book of Mormon as the literal inerrant Word of God and those who render the work a fraud was Joseph's use of his vivid imagination to carry him through both good times and bad. The young man was the most gifted storyteller in a family of gifted storytellers. His resourcefulness was a substitute for his lack of formal education, but it also empowered him to identify with those just like him on the American frontier. As Smith used his abilities, along with his experience of divine inspiration, to resolve, through the Book of Mormon storyline, perplexing issues in his own mind, he also resolved them for thousands of Book of Mormon believers.

Considering carefully the impact of these five powerful influences, according to this view the Book of Mormon was a direct reflection of the mind and spiritual giftedness of Joseph Smith Jr., its author, the role he claimed on the title page (see image on page 119). The American scripture was a product of the unexplainable interplay of the divine and the human. In no way does this middle-ground explanation denigrate the significant role of the Book of Mormon on the progress of Smith's followers then or in the lives of believers still today. Rather, that the Book of Mormon speaks so powerfully as scripture to millions of people around the world shows the writing's strong spiritual quality.

Today the time-worn division between Book of Mormon "believers" and "non-believers" is, to many people, less and less relevant. Whether or

---

105. Alexander Campbell, *Millennial Harbinger*, 10 February 1831, 93, in Richard S. Van Wagoner, *Sidney Rigdon: A Portrait of Religious Excess* (Salt Lake City: Signature Books, 1994), 137.

not one is caught up in this dichotomy, the Book of Mormon is a fact of American religious history. For converts in the nineteenth and many in the twentieth and twenty-first centuries, the Book of Mormon redirected people's lives as it Americanized the Judeo-Christian gospel. No longer were believers geographically separated from biblical events that happened in a distant Holy Land in the Middle East. With the Book of Mormon, those same sacred events could be found in the pre-Columbian historical roots right where they resided. With the Book of Mormon, America became a second Holy Land.[106]

Disposition of the Plates and Publication of the Book of Mormon

TRADITION HAS IT that the plates disappeared as miraculously as they were discovered. On 2 May 1838, Joseph Jr. stated that the plates remained safely in his possession while he completed the manuscript. Then he returned them to an angel according to previously determined arrangements.[107] The actual date for this event has not been documented. Likewise, the actual date the translation process concluded is also in

---

106. A current focus of Book of Mormon study in Community of Christ is on exploring how the text informs identity and mission today. This emphasis is not so much on the origins of the book as on rediscovering its vital message to contemporary readers in addition to its nineteenth-century relevance. When approached from this perspective, the Book of Mormon can be viewed as a powerful prophetic text that, in addition to its witness of Jesus Christ, warns against aspects of human societies that continue to result in economic injustice, skepticism, violence, and war.

107. "History of Joseph Smith," *Times and Seasons* 3, no. 13 (2 May 1842): 772. Another account of the disposition of the plates passed through the generations. This stated: "When Joseph got the plates, the angel instructed him to carry them back to the Hill Cumorah, which he did. Oliver says that when Joseph and Oliver went there the hill opened and they walked into a cave, in which there was a large and spacious room. He says he did not think at the time whether they had the light of the sun or artificial light, but that it was just as light as day. They laid the plates on a table; it was a large table that stood in the room. Under this table was a pile of plates as much as two feet high; and there were altogether in this room more plates than probably many wagon loads; they were piled up in the corners and along the walls." *Juvenile Instructor* (September 1922): 488–89. This account appears as part of an editorial by George Q. Cannon titled, "The Sword of Laban." He attributed it to Brigham Young.

Egbert B. Grandin's print shop (located on upper floor to the left)

doubt.[108] A reasonable estimate is sometime in the last two weeks of June 1829.

Before the translation was complete Joseph addressed the looming problem of publishing the Book of Mormon. The first step was to acquire a legal copyright. On 11 June 1829 he registered the book with R. R. Lansing, clerk of the Northern District of New York, and obtained the ownership writ. Then Smith, along with Martin Harris, opened negotiations with various upstate New York publishers to begin actual printing. First, he approached Egbert B. Grandin, a local printer in Palmyra, but without success. Grandin anticipated how poorly received the Book of Mormon would be in the Palmyra/Manchester area and considered the risk of payment default too great. This forced Joseph and Martin to travel twenty-five miles northwest to Rochester to negotiate with Thurlow Weed, publisher of the *Rochester Telegraph*. But Smith's reputation preceded his arrival and Weed flatly rejected the project. Last, Smith and Harris approached Elihu Marshall, also a Rochester publisher, who agreed to print the book. Evidently Smith and Harris grew leery of traveling and feared the distance

108. Lucy Mack Smith identified the completion date prior to the vision of the three witnesses; see *Biographical Sketches*, 163; David Whitmer gave the date of 1 July 1829. Whitmer's determination is given in his *An Address to All Believers in Christ By A Witness to the Divine Authenticity of the Book of Mormon* (Richmond, Mo.: David Whitmer, 1887), 33, and in his interview in the *Kansas City Journal*, 5 June 1881.

could jeopardize their ability to protect the manuscript. So they returned to Palmyra and bargained again with Grandin. This time they struck a deal. Harris would put up his farm to secure the $3,000 cost of printing 5,000 books.[109]

Evidently, Joseph and Oliver reviewed the finished original manuscript and determined how difficult it would be for typesetter John H. Gilbert to decipher the writings. A readable manuscript was needed, so Cowdery set to the task of making another copy, referred to today as the Printer's Manuscript.[110] Of course security was also an important issue. Joseph had been victimized once already and lived in sus-

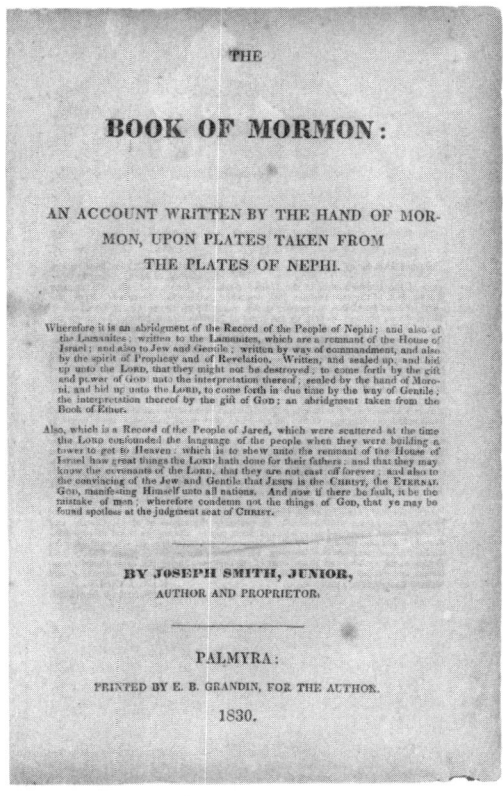

COMMUNITY OF CHRIST LIBRARY-ARCHIVES

Title page of the first edition of the Book of Mormon

---

109. This action by Harris eventually cost him his marriage. With a marriage already failing, Lucy Harris accused her husband of being duped by Joseph Smith, declared the Seer as a "grand impostor," and claimed the farm collateral was a scheme "to induce Mr. Harris to give his property into Joseph's hands that he might by robbing her husband make himself rich." See Lucy Mack Smith, Preliminary Manuscript, as found in Vogel, *Early Mormon Documents*, 1: 354–55.

110. Today, the Printer's Manuscript of the Book of Mormon is located in the archives of the Community of Christ in Independence, Missouri. The Original Manuscript was placed in the cornerstone of the Nauvoo House. However, it was found to be almost completely destroyed by the elements when recovered later. Fragments of the Original Manuscript are currently housed in the First Presidency's vault of the Church of Jesus Christ of Latter-day Saints in Salt Lake City, Utah.

picion that thieves always lurked nearby with the intent of stealing his writings. A second copy would ease his mind. Not surprisingly, he allowed only a few sheets of the printer's manuscript to be provided for publishing purposes. Only when he felt absolutely confident did the Seer allow Gilbert to take home the entire manuscript, where he added capitalization and punctuation. All told the printing process ran from August 1829 to March 1830, with the entire first issue completed by summer.[111]

The first copies of the Book of Mormon hit the dusty streets of Palmyra in the spring of 1830. The poor reception and slow sales were problematic, especially for Martin Harris, who stood to lose his Palmyra farm. The price per book was set too high for the low demand. But how does one set an appropriate price on sacred writings? Here again Joseph depended on divine direction. He was told to set the price initially at $1.50 per book; but with sagging sales among skeptical Palmyrans, Joseph was then inspired eventually to drop the price to one dollar per book.[112]

When word of the price being set by revelation leaked to the public, it only added to the skepticism. But with the Book of Mormon completed and published, the Seer turned his attention to other matters, including establishing a church.

111. In addition to the 5,000 copies in this first printing, later editions of the Book of Mormon were published in Kirtland (1837) and Nauvoo (1840).

112. John A. Clark to Dear Brethren, dated 31 August 1840, *The Episcopal Recorder* (Philadelphia) 18 (12 September 1840): 98–99, as found in Vogel, *Early Mormon Documents*, 2: 269–71. John A. Clark was pastor of Palmyra's Zion's Episcopal Church in 1824, and eventually moved to Philadelphia. After a visit in Palmyra in August 1840, he wrote several letters to *The Episcopal Recorder* "detailing some facts connected with the rise and origin of Mormonism." Two letters of the ten he wrote included information he received from interviews with Martin Harris, including these price quotes.

CHAPTER SEVEN

Organizing the Church

During the spring of 1829, Joseph Smith Jr.'s thoughts turned to formally organizing a church. The preaching, healings, and revelations that had already taken place suggested that church organization was in progress, at least informally. During this time, Joseph and Oliver labored diligently on the Book of Mormon project. As they worked on the account of Jesus' ministry in the Third Book of Nephi, perhaps they pondered the need for a restoration of the church in the modern day. But the lack of priesthood authority to take this action weighed heavily upon them, so they prayed for divine direction. Eventually, both men offered their explanations of their divine encounter, with Cowdery writing first. In a letter to William W. Phelps dated 7 September 1834, he stated:

> The Lord, who is rich in mercy, and ever willing to answer the consistent prayer of the humble, after we had called upon him in a fervent manner, aside from the abodes of men, condescended to manifest to us his will. On a sudden, as from the midst of eternity, the voice of the Redeemer spake peace to us, while the vail was parted and the angel of God came down clothed with glory, and delivered the anxiously looked for message, and the keys of the gospel of repentance!—What joy! what wonder! what amazement! While the world were racked and distracted—while millions were grouping as the blind for the wall, and while all men were resting upon uncertainty, as a general mass, our eyes beheld—our ears heard. As in the "blaze of day;" yes, more—above the glitter of the May Sun beam, which then shed its brilliancy over the face of nature! Then his voice, though mild, pierced to the center, and his words, "I am thy fellow servant," dispelled every fear. We listened—we gazed—we admired! 'Twas the voice of the angel

from glory—'twas a message from the Most High! and as we heard we rejoiced, while his love enkindled upon our souls, and we were rapt in the vision of the Almighty! Where was room for doubt? No where: uncertainty had fled, doubt had sunk, no more to rise, while fiction and deception had fled forever!

But, dear brother think, further think for a moment, what joy filled our hearts and with what surprise we must have bowed, (for who would not have bowed the knee for such a blessing?) when we received under his hand the holy priesthood, as he said, "upon you my fellow servants, in the name of Messiah I confer this priesthood and this authority, which shall remain upon earth, that the sons of Levi may yet offer an offering unto the Lord in righteousness!"

I shall not attempt to paint to you the feelings of this heart, nor the majestic beauty and glory which surrounded us on this occasion; but you will believe me when I say, that earth, nor men, with the eloquence of time, cannot begin to clothe language in as interesting and sublime a manner as this holy personage. No; nor has this earth power to give the joy, to bestow the peace, or comprehend the wisdom which was contained in each sentence as they were delivered by the power of the Holy Spirit! Man may deceive his fellow man; deception may follow deception, and the children of the wicked one may have power to seduce the foolish and untaught, till nought but fiction feeds the many, and the fruit of falsehood carries in its current the giddy to the grave; but one touch with the finger of his love, yes, one ray of glory from the upper world, or one word from the mouth of the Savior, from the bosom of eternity, strikes it *all* into insignificance, and blots it forever from the mind! The assurance that we were in the presence of an angel; the certainty that we heard the voice of Jesus, and the truth unsullied as it flowed from a pure personage, dictated by the will of God, is to me, past description, and I shall ever look upon this expression of the Savior's goodness with wonder and thanksgiving while I am permitted to tarry, and in those mansions where perfection dwells and sin never comes, I hope to adore in that DAY which shall never cease![1]

Looking closely at Cowdery's explanation reveals the feelings of peace during the epiphany, being in the presence of an angel, hearing the voice of Jesus, and the delivery of the priesthood of the sons of Levi to the two

---

1. Oliver Cowdery to William W. Phelps, 7 September 1834, *Latter Day Saints' Messenger and Advocate* 1, no. 1 (October 1834): 15–16.

men in the name of the Messiah. It also reveals the problems of lack of complete understanding due to the human condition.

Eight years later, Joseph Smith Jr., writing in his history, offered a similar version but added more. For example, Joseph specifically dated the epiphany as happening on 15 May 1829. He told of a heavenly messenger instructing him and Oliver to first baptize, then ordain, each other to the priesthood, after the order of Aaron. Joseph's account also indicated that both received the gift of prophecy following their baptisms and ordinations and that, at some future time, the Melchisedec priesthood would be conferred. Smith placed his explanation in the church newspaper, *Times and Seasons*, in 1842, adding to the story what served the needs of the church at that time in Nauvoo, Illinois.[2]

Joseph and Oliver now felt their most important concern was the need for permission to establish a church, and that could come only from God. Instruction came in the months leading up to church organization. Joseph explained, stating:

> In this manner did the Lord continue to give us instructions from time to time, concerning the duties which now devolved upon us, and among many other things of the kind, we obtained of him the following, by the spirit of prophecy and revelation; which not only gave us much information, but also pointed out to us the precise day upon which, according to his will and commandment, we should proceed to organize his church once again, here upon the earth.[3]

This gave impetus to a religious movement that within five generations would span the globe and shape the faith journey of millions of people.

---

2. "History of Joseph Smith," *Times and Seasons* 3, no. 19 (1 August 1842): 865–66.
3. *Times and Seasons* 3, no. 23 (1 October 1842): 928–29. This was titled "Articles and Covenants of the Church given in Fayette, New York," and was entered in the Doctrine and Covenants as Section 17 (LDS 20). This section is a compilation of numerous statements of instruction concerning the organization of the church before and after formal organization on 6 April 1830. Clearly, church organization evolved over a period of years. Events of early April 1830 only began that process.

Fayette or Manchester?

THE TRADITIONAL STORY of church organization has it that on 6 April 1830 the church was formally organized at the farm of Peter Whitmer Sr. in Fayette, Seneca County, New York, located at least twenty-five miles south of the Manchester/Palmyra area. This story, so sacred to future generations, first appeared in the May 1834 edition of *The Evening and the Morning Star* in a statement communicating "Minutes of a Conference of the Elders of the church of Christ, which church was organized in the township of Fayette, Seneca county, New-York, on the 6th of April, A. D. 1830."[4] Unfortunately, no minutes of the actual organizational meeting exist that tell in detail the venue or the business church leaders transacted on that day. Only from fragments of testimonies by individuals present and what was published later about the organizational meeting can events be reconstructed with some degree of accuracy.

Published statements, historical circumstances, and personal remembrances strongly suggest that the Church of Christ was officially organized on 6 April 1830 in the Smith log cabin in Manchester Township, Ontario County, and not in Fayette, Seneca County. In July 1830, just three months after church organization, John Whitmer recorded six inspired statements that were given on organization day. In the following year, these statements were prepared for the *Book of Commandments* as chapters 17 through 22 with heading statements that specifically identified Manchester as the location where they were given. In late July 1833, the *Book of Commandments* went to press in Independence, Missouri. However a mob destroyed the church press and the book was never published.[5] Later these six statements were combined into one and placed in the first edition of the Doctrine and Covenants in 1835, and arranged as Section 21. They were directed to men who participated in the organization procedures, specifically Oliver Cowdery, Hyrum Smith, Samuel H. Smith, Joseph Smith Sr.,

---

4. "Communicated," *The Evening and the Morning Star* 2, no. 20 (May 1834): 160. This is the earliest known published statement to establish Fayette, New York, as the venue for organization.

5. Some printed pages were salvaged and bound, thus preserving an unknown number of copies of the *Book of Commandments*. This book, like its successor the Doctrine and Covenants, contained instruction and counsel to individuals and to the church, given by Joseph Smith Jr., the prophet.

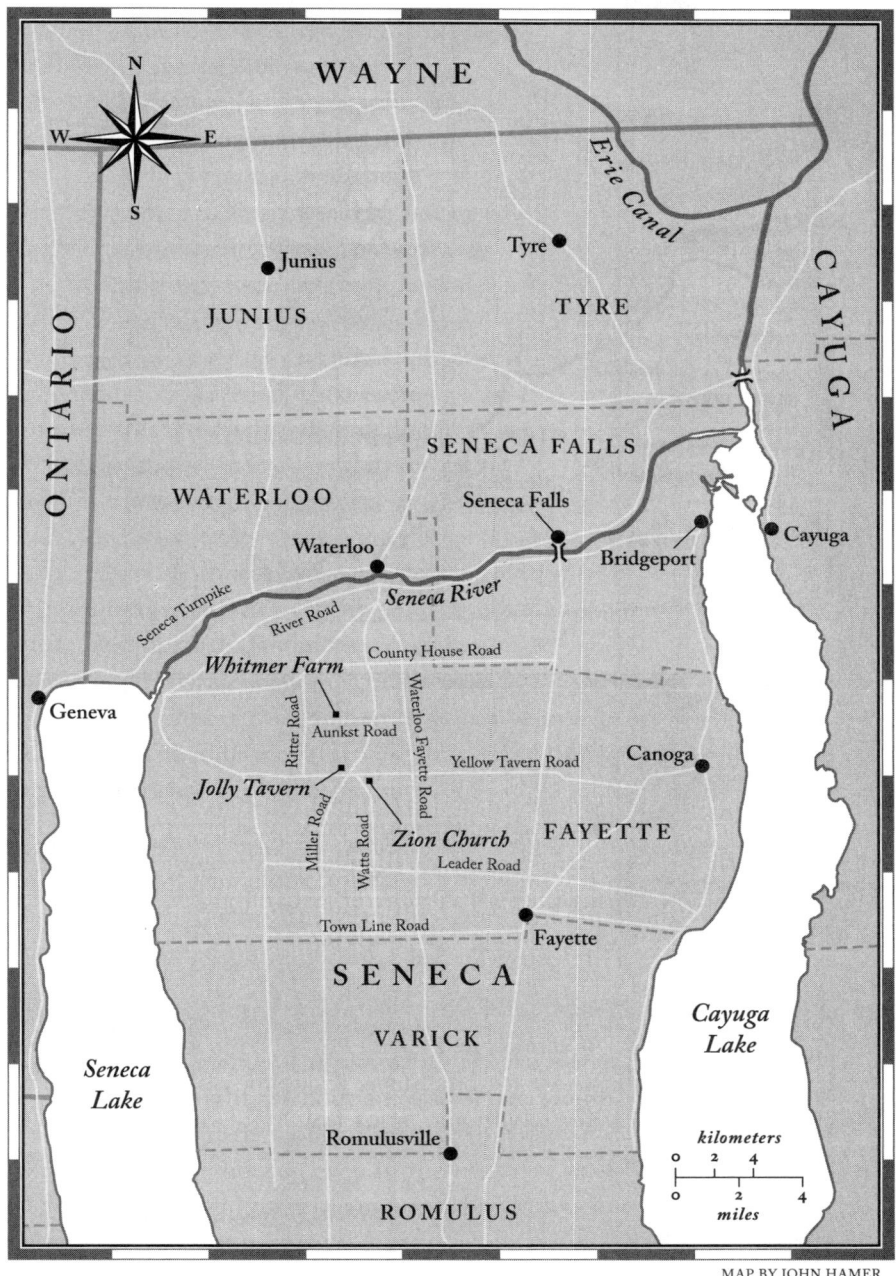

Fayette, Seneca County, New York

Joseph Knight Sr., and Joseph Smith Jr. Consistent with the six statements in the *Book of Commandments*, all references in the church's Independence, Missouri, newspaper, *The Evening and the Morning Star*, between 1832 and 1833, referred to the organizational meeting in Manchester Township in upstate New York.

Also, Orson Pratt's 1840 missionary tract titled *Interesting Account of Several Remarkable Visions...* identified Manchester as the venue for church organization,[6] as did Joseph Smith Jr.'s 1842 letter to John Wentworth, published in the Nauvoo *Times and Seasons*: "On the 6th of April, 1830, the 'Church of Jesus Christ of Latter-Day Saints,' was first organized in the town of Manchester, Ontario co., state of New York."[7] Since the church name at the founding was Church of Christ, and did not become the Church of Jesus Christ of Latter Day Saints until 1838, Smith's reference was anachronistic. Of course, it is possible that the prophet was simply referring to the existing church in his Wentworth letter. But this was not the only time he did this in his writings. Joseph Jr. wrote in his "Manuscript History," "I then laid my hands upon Oliver Cowdery and ordained him an Elder of the 'Church of Jesus Christ of Latter Day Saints.'"[8] Here he was referring to an event that occurred before 1838.

Historical circumstances placed Joseph Jr. and Hyrum Smith in Manchester in early April 1830. Joseph Knight Sr. of Colesville, New York, also a recipient of a *Book of Commandments* instruction, and close family friend, brought Joseph Jr. by wagon from Harmony, Pennsylvania, to Manchester shortly before organization day. During his time with the Seer, Knight remembered Joseph saying that "there must Be a Church Biltup

---

6. O[rson]. Pratt, *Interesting Account of Several Remarkable Visions, and of the Late Discovery of Ancient American Records* (Edinburgh, Scotland: Ballantyne and Hughes, 1840), 23–24, Vault Pamphlet Collection, Community of Christ Library-Archives. Evidently to enforce conformity, church leaders changed the location to Fayette in an 1848 reprint: "And on the sixth of April, in the year of our Lord one thousand eight hundred and thirty, the 'Church of Jesus Christ, of Latter-day Saints' was organized in the town of Fayette, Seneca County, State of New York, North America." Orson Pratt, *Remarkable Visions*, 1848, pamphlet series, no. 6 (Liverpool: R. James, 1851), 12, in Marquardt and Walters, *Inventing Mormonism*, 159–60, 169fn39.

7. "History of the Church," *Times and Seasons* 3, no. 9 (1 March 1842): 708.

8. Joseph Smith, "Manuscript History," A-1, 37, in Jessee, *Papers of Joseph Smith*, 1: 303.

[built up]."⁹ Knight did not record any details about the actual meeting but did recall the baptisms associated with the charter gathering: "I had ben there several Days. Old Mr Smith and Martin Harris Come forrod [forward] to Be Babtise[d] for the first. They found a place in a lot a small Stream ran thro and they ware Babtized in the Evening because of persecution. They went forward and was Babtized Being the first I saw Babtized in the new and everlasting Covenant."¹⁰ Knight mentioned nothing about traveling twenty-five miles south to Fayette; rather he wrote that after he acquired his allotment of "mormon Books" he returned back to his family in Colesville, New York.¹¹

Personal accounts from people who lived in the Manchester area and observed the proceedings placed organizational events there. Three examples are Cornelius R. Stafford, Benjamin Saunders, and William Smith. C. R. Stafford was born and raised in Manchester and lived near the Smith family farm. Recalling the baptismal service at the time of organization, he wrote, "I saw old Jo Smith, his wife [Lucy Smith], and Mrs. [Sarah Witt] Rockwell baptized by prophet Jo Smith."¹²

Among those gathered at the Smith log cabin for the organizational activities was Benjamin Saunders, another of Smith's neighbors. Like Stafford, Saunders remembered when the "[Smiths] held meetings at their house. I was there when they first baptized. Oliver Cowdery did the baptizing. Old brother [Joseph Smith Sr.] was baptized at that time and I think old Mrs. Rockwell."¹³ Neither Stafford nor Saunders affiliated with the church. One must wonder if non-believing neighbors would have traveled twenty-five miles each way (fifty miles total) from Manchester to

---

9. "Joseph Knight Sr., "Reminiscence," in Vogel, *Early Mormon Documents*, 4: 21 (brackets added by Vogel). Lucy Smith remembered that these baptisms occurred in the morning of organizational day; see her *Biographical Sketches*, 181. However, Joseph Smith Jr.'s 1839 "Manuscript History" agreed with the Knight account that the baptisms were in the evening.

10. Dean Jessee, "Joseph Knight Recollection of Early Mormon History," *Brigham Young University Studies* 17, no. 1 (Autumn 1976): 37 (brackets added by Jessee).

11. Vogel, *Early Mormon Documents*, 4: 22.

12. Vogel, *Early Mormon Documents*, 2: 197 (brackets added by Vogel). Stafford's son, Royal M. Stafford, attested to this statement.

13. Saunders, Interview, 1884, 26.

Fayette just to witness the baptisms of their neighbors into a religion in which they had relatively little interest. Their participation would be more understandable, however, if it required a brief wagon ride less than a mile each way.

Finally, William Smith, Joseph Jr.'s younger brother, who at the time had just had his nineteenth birthday, wrote many years later that the church was organized in Hyrum Smith's small log house in Manchester.[14] William's reference to Hyrum living in the log home is chronologically accurate since Hyrum, the oldest surviving child, moved into the old log cabin after his family moved into their frame farmhouse just several hundred yards to the south. This log cabin was a popular venue for family activities and became a refuge when the Smiths were evicted from the frame house just before church organization.

Reasons for the Confusion

CLEARLY, IDENTIFYING THE motives for people's actions in historical circumstances is perhaps the most subjective exercise in the subjective discipline of history. Understanding how and why the location of church organization became confused is speculative at best.

That such an important occasion as church organization would be confused seems improbable unless writers inadvertently blurred the formative events happening in the weeks and months that followed 6 April 1830 into a sacred, although rather historically inaccurate, storyline. The Whitmer farm in Fayette, New York, was the site of many pivotal happenings during this period. On 11 April, the Sunday that followed organization day, the first congregation—the Fayette Branch—was formally recognized, and Oliver Cowdery gave his first "public discourse."

The next church conference, held on 9 June, again met in Fayette. Here Joseph Smith Jr. read "the Articles and Covenants of the Church of Christ." Those in attendance voted unanimously to approve this statement as their confession of faith. At this June conference, delegates again accepted the leadership of Joseph and Oliver as well as the Book of Mormon as a primary scripture of the church. As on organization day, 6 April, a baptismal service was held. Yet many of those baptized at this Fayette

---

14. William Smith, *William Smith on Mormonism*, 13–15.

Organizing the Church

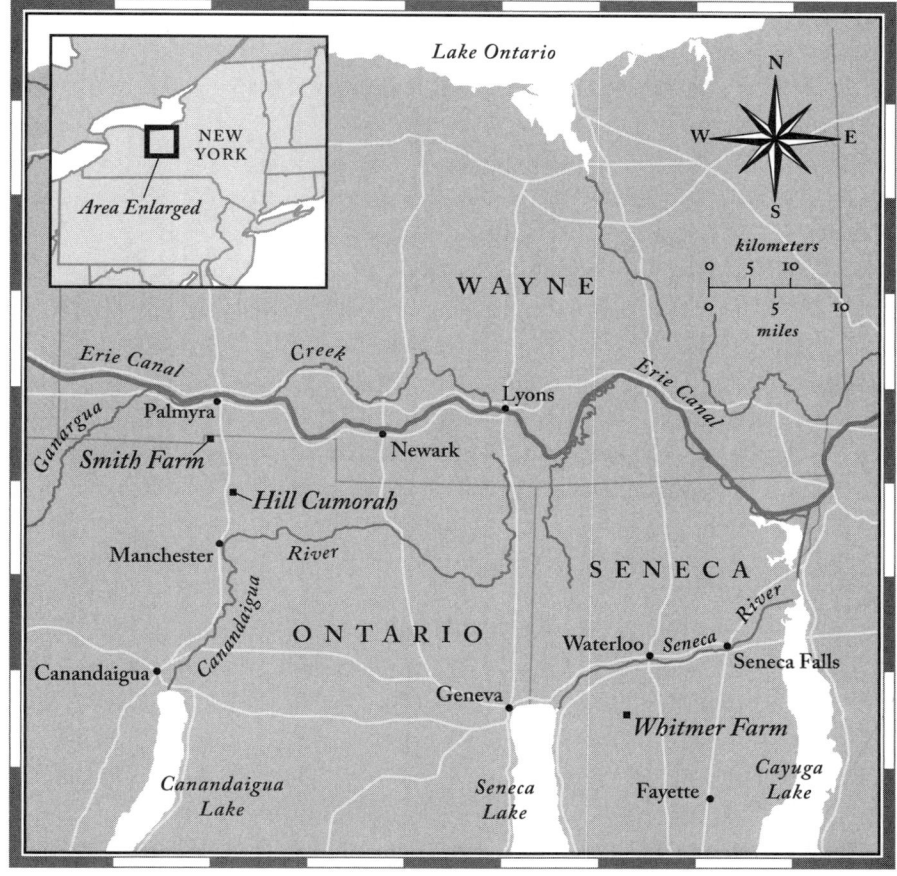

The area around Palmyra, Manchester, and Fayette, New York

conference hailed from the Manchester area, including Jerusha Barden Smith (Hyrum's wife) and William, Don Carlos, and Katharine Smith (Joseph Jr.'s brothers and sister). This baptismal service even included members of the Rockwell family, specifically Porter, Caroline, and Electa Rockwell (all children of Sarah Rockwell who was baptized on 6 April in Manchester).

The 26 September conference, also held in Fayette, included more historic decisions in the life of the church, including the commissioning of the first official missionaries to the Lamanites, as prayers were given for Oliver Cowdery and Peter Whitmer Jr. Participants in the conference

COMMUNITY OF CHRIST LIBRARY-ARCHIVES

The organization of the church as it has been traditionally illustrated

testified to the dramatic outpouring of the Holy Spirit among them. Oliver Cowdery ordained Newel Knight a priest, and those in attendance observed that the number of members had jumped from thirty-five at the June conference to sixty-two.

Sustained growth in members and the perceived powerful movement of the Holy Spirit characterized the Fayette meetings and conferences held in the spring of 1830. Such positive events occurring at or near the Whitmer farm left a lasting impression. This may partially explain why, with the passing of over fifty years, in 1887 David Whitmer associated the organization of the church with Fayette:

> Now, when April 6, 1830, had come, we had then established three branches of the "Church of Christ," in which three branches were about seventy members: One branch was at Fayette, N. Y.; one at Manchester, N. Y., and one at Colesville, Pa. It is all a mistake about the church being organized on April 6, 1830, as I will show. We were as fully organized—spiritually—before April 6th as we were on that day. The reason why we met on that day was this; the world had been telling us that we were not a regularly organized church, and we had no right to officiate in the ordinance of marriage, hold church property, etc., and that we should organize according to the laws of the

land. On this account we met at my father's house in Fayette, N. Y., on April 6, 1830, to attend to this matter of organizing according to the laws of the land; you can see this from Sec. 17 Doctrine and Covenants: the church was organized on April 6th *"agreeable to the laws of our country."*[15]

Perhaps assuming David Whitmer's statement as firsthand evidence, Inez Smith Davis continued the Fayette tradition in *The Story of the Church*, first published in 1934.[16] The Reorganized Church then sealed the tradition by including it in the 1952 edition of the Doctrine and Covenants.[17] But Whitmer's quote above raises the final issue of this analysis—legal incorporation.

The Issue of Legal Incorporation

CHURCH FOUNDERS OBSERVED an important legal practice by choosing 6 April to launch their movement. In the state of New York, the first Tuesday of April was set aside as a day to perform legal functions. The law did not limit meetings to only the first Tuesday, as "special meetings" were also convened.[18] However, regularly scheduled

---

15. David Whitmer, *An Address to All Believers*, 33. Whitmer incorrectly places Colesville in Pennsylvania; it is actually in New York.

16. Inez Smith Davis, *The Story of the Church: A History of the Church of Jesus Christ of Latter Day Saints, and of Its Legal Successor, the Reorganized Church of Jesus Christ of Latter Day Saints*, 6th ed. (Independence, Mo.: Herald House, 1959), 81–82.

17. Preface to Section 17 (LDS 20).

18. For example:

> At a special town meeting held at the Presbyterian Meeting House in the Village of Palmyra on May 4th, 1830, present: Frederick Smith, Esq., one of the Justices of the Peace for the Town of Palmyra. On motion: Voted that James White serve as clerk of said meeting.
>
> The meeting then proceeded to elected by ballot a person to fill the vacancy of one Commissioner of Highways caused by the neglect of Benjamin Cole to take the necessary oath within the time prescribed by law. Thereupon George W. Cuyler was declared to have been duly elected to fill said vacancy. On motion, the meeting then adjourned without delay.
>
> James White, Clerk and Frederick Smith
> I certify the above to be a true copy.
> M. W. Willcox, Clerk

town meetings and local elections of constables, justices of the peace, and road overseers were usually performed on or associated with this day. For example, the Town of Palmyra convened their annual town meeting at the Presbyterian meeting house at the same time Joseph Smith Jr. convened his followers in Manchester a few miles to the south.[19] Town officials for Palmyra, including a supervisor, three assessors, clerk, commissioners of highways, and even an "overseer of the poor," were elected on that day.[20]

    Joseph Willcox's mark: A round hole in the right ear. Recorded August 12th, 1830.

Minutes of this special meeting were provided by Michael Marquardt. They can be found at www.palmyrany.com/minutes/TB/1830.htm. Note the identifying mark for Joseph Willcox.

19. The Western Presbyterian Church is still located at the corner of Canandaigua Road and Main Street in Palmyra. Known locally as "church corner," this historic intersection today has four churches located there. Besides the Presbyterian Church, the First United Methodist Church, the First Baptist Church, and Zion's Episcopal Church are situated at this intersection. Today a commemorative plaque outside the church noted that on 5 April 1849, the British world leader Winston Churchill's maternal grandparents were married in the Western Presbyterian Church.

20. Although lengthy and detailed, the minutes of the 6 April 1830 Palmyra town meeting are reproduced here to give the reader an idea of what kinds of business was transacted at such meetings.

    Town of Palmyra Minutes — 1830

    At the annual town meeting of the inhabitants of the Town of Palmyra held at the Presbyterian Meeting House on Tuesday, April 6th, 1830, present: Frederick Smith, Alexander R. Tiffany, Ambrose Salisbury, and William Willcox, Esquires, Justices of the Peace of said town and Inspectors of said election.

    Voted that we choose but three assessors.
    Voted that we choose but four constables.
    Voted that we choose the Town Sealer by ballot.
    Voted that the other officers to be chosen at this meeting be chosen by ayes and noes.
    Voted that the time of holding the annual town meeting of this town be on the first Tuesday of April.

    The following persons having received the greatest number of votes are declared duly elected to the several and respective offices:

    Ambrose Salisbury — Supervisor
    Marlin W. Willcox — Town Clerk
    Lyman Reeves, William Rogers, Jr., & Wells Anderson — Assessors

Thus, it is not surprising that the church was organized on 6 April 1830, since this was the first Tuesday.

The timing of the Manchester meeting was consistent with David Whitmer's proposed rationale for organization to be in agreement with

> George Culver, Benjamin Cole, and Sidney S. Durfee — Commissioners of Highways
> Maltby Clark, James Hubbell, and Ovid Sovell — Commissioners of Common Schools
> Lewis Foster, Theron R. Strong, and Jonathan S. Eggleston — Inspectors of Common Schools
> James White — Justice of the Peace
> Caleb Beal and Eldridge Havens — Overseers of the Poor
> Truman Heminway — Collector
> Truman Heminway, Merit Sherman, Francis Bortle, & Erasmus D. Robinson — Constables
> Pomeroy Tucker — Town Sealer
>
> Voted that the following persons serve as Overseers of Highways in the several road districts for which they are severally chosen:
>
> | No. | | No. | |
> |---|---|---|---|
> | 1 | David S. Jackways | 14 | George P. Stephens |
> | 2 | Orlando Saunders | 15 | Oliver Durfee |
> | 3 | Stephen Willcox | 16 | Paul Jagger |
> | 4 | James P. Horton | 17 | Benjamin Cole |
> | 5 | William Rogers, Jr. | 18 | James R. Sandford |
> | 6 | Clark Wright | 19 | Jacob Norris |
> | 7 | Thomas Goldsmith | 20 | James Green |
> | 8 | Merit Sherman | 21 | William Durfee |
> | 9 | Luther Sandford | 22 | Walter Sherwood |
> | 10 | David P. Daggett | 23 | Thomas Eggleston |
> | 11 | Edward S. Townsend | 24 | Elery Hicks |
> | 12 | Aretus Lapham | 25 | Rufus Sweezy |
> | 13 | Abner Z. Lakey | 26 | Henry Vaughn |
>
> Voted that we choose one Pound Master.
> Voted that the vote to choose a Pound Master be reconsidered.
> Voted that the sum of $150 be raised for the support of the poor of said town.
> Voted that Fence Viewers be allowed $.75 per day for their services.
> Voted that this meeting stand adjourned until the first Tuesday of April next, then to be opened at Ambrose Salisbury's dwelling house at 10:00 a.m.
>
> Marline W. Willcox, Town Clerk
> Frederick Smith, A. R. Tiffany, and A. Salisbury
> I certify the above to be a true copy. M. W. Willcox, Town Clerk
>
> These minutes can be found at www.palmyrany.com/minutes/TB/1830.htm.

"the laws of the land." However, two other references he made were not historically accurate. First, the three branches to which he referred were established shortly after organization, and not before.[21] Second, Whitmer expressed concern about the legality of marriages performed and of property acquired by the church. This concern could only apply, however, to possible future events as there is no documentary evidence of any marriages performed or property acquired in the name of the Church of Christ before organization. These mistakes were easily made considering that his reminiscences extended over a fifty-year period.

The existing laws for the State of New York in 1830 required that in order for a church to be incorporated, the minister or leader of the group had to post public notice of the time and date for male members to meet to elect trustees. This posting had to occur at least fifteen days before the day of election, and notice was to be given at least two successive Sabbaths or days on which the church, congregation, or society should meet for public worship before the day of election.[22] This would have been impossible for Joseph Smith Jr. to accomplish since at this time he was either in Harmony, Pennsylvania, or traveling back to Manchester, New York. Although the law provided for another believer to post notice, there is no evidence that this was done.[23]

---

21. Actually, all three branches were formed after church organization. "Soon after the book of Mormon came forth, containing the fulness of the gospel of Jesus Christ, the church was organized on the sixth of April, in Manchester; soon after, a branch was established in Fayette, and the June following, another in Colesville, New York. We shall not give, at this time, the particulars attending the organization of these branches of the church.... Twenty more were added to the church in Manchester and Fayette, in the month of April; and on the 28th of June, thirteen were baptized in Colesville.... In October, (1830) the number of disciples had increased to between seventy and eighty." "Rise and Progress of the Church of Christ," *The Evening and the Morning Star* 1, no. 11 (April 1833): [167].

22. *Laws of the State of New York, Revised and Passed at the Thirty-Sixth Session of the Legislature* (Albany, N.Y.: H.C. Southwick & CO, 1813), 2: 214, in Marquardt and Walters, *Inventing Mormonism*, 162–63fn56.

23. The following is an extract from New York state law pursuant to incorporation of the Church of Christ. "An Act to provide for the Incorporation of Religious Societies," passed April 5, 1813:

...which certificate being duly acknowledged or proved by one or more of the subscribing witnesses, before the chancellor or one of the judges of the court

Investigations of county and state records show that no incorporation papers were filed on behalf of the Church of Christ. This may be

> of common pleas of the county, where such church or place of worship of such congregation shall be situated, shall be recorded by the clerk of such county in a book to be by him provided for that purpose...
> III. And be it further enacted, That it shall be lawful for the male persons of full age, belonging to any other church, congregation or religious society, now or hereafter to be established in this state, and not already incorporated, to assemble at the church meeting house, or to the place where they statedly attend for divine worship, and, by plurality of voices to elect any number of discreet persons of their church, congregation or society, not less than three, nor exceeding nine in number, as trustees, to take the charge of the estate and property belonging thereto, and to transact all affairs relative to the temporalities thereof; and that at such election, every male person of full age, who has statedly worshipped with such church, congregation or society, and has formerly been considered as belonging thereto, shall be entitled to vote, and the said election shall be conducted as follows: The minister of such church, congregation or society, or in case of his death or absence, one of the elders or deacons, church wardens or vestry men thereof, and for want of such officers, any person being a member or stated hearer in such church, congregation or society, shall publicly notify the congregation of time when, and place where the said election shall be held, at least fifteen days before the day of election; that the said notification shall be given for two successive sabbaths or days on which such church, congregation or society, shall stately meet for public worship, preceding the day of election; that on the said day of election, two of the elders or church wardens, and if there be no such officers, then two of the members of said church, congregation or society, to be nominated by a majority of the members present, shall preside at such election, receive the votes of the electors, be the judges of the qualifications of such electors, and the officers, to return the names of the persons who, by plurality of voices, shall be elected to serve as trustees for the said church, congregation or society; in which certificate the name or title by which the said trustees and their successors shall forever thereafter be called and known; shall be particularly mentioned and described; which said certificate, being proved or acknowledged as above directed, shall be recorded as aforesaid; and such trustees and their successors shall also thereupon, by virtue of this act, be a body corporate, by the name or title expressed in such certificate; and the clerk of every county for recording every certificate of incorporation by virtue of this act, shall be entitled to seventy-five cents, and no more." From *Laws of the State of New-York, Revised*, 2: 212, 214.
>
> See also *Laws of the State of New-York* (Albany: J. Buel, 1819), 34, and *Laws of the State of New-York* (Albany: E. Croswell, 1826), 34–35. Provided through electronic communication by Michael Marquardt, 14 January 2006. Also see Marquardt and Walters, *Inventing Mormonism*, 162–63fn56.

because legal requirements were not followed. Another possibility is that in the state of New York people were free to organize as a voluntary unincorporated religious society or church with no trustees.[24] No matter how well-intentioned church leaders were in wanting to meet state requirements for their legal existence, ultimately the meeting on 6 April 1830, in Manchester, Ontario County, New York, for the purposes of incorporation was more "spiritual" than legal. Perhaps the issue of church incorporation should be best understood in the context of the establishment clause in the First Amendment of the United States Constitution, guaranteeing freedom of religion.[25] In no way do these observations reduce the enormous importance of organizational events and their foundational role in the life of the early church.

Like the accounts of so many of the church's formative events, the chronological and geographical explanations of church leaders conflicted with the records they left behind. Why did these mistakes occur so frequently? Identifying what actually did happen amid conflicting information takes time, and determining the intent of individuals nearly two centuries distant is a difficult historical enterprise indeed.

At least two explanations may account for the frequent historical inaccuracies. First, these people were constantly being uprooted. Often accosted by detractors and forced out of their homes, their deep-seated emotions may have repressed some painful memories and reshaped others. Writings were lost and important details in their stories were forgotten along the difficult trails of their sacred journey. Second, decision makers and their scribes were quite willing to change their historical and scriptural records to suit their needs. Such was the case when Joseph Smith Jr. told his story of the First Vision to different audiences and at different times. Thus, as giants in the foundation of their church and as great spiritual leaders who met the needs of their followers, most recorders of the early church story were better theologians than they were historians.

Debating presumably minor details might seem inconsequential, so does it make any difference when weighed with the larger life of the church and its future mission? The answer is yes, because a church's authenticity is

---

24. Marquardt and Walters, *Inventing Mormonism*, 164.
25. Marquardt and Walters, *Inventing Mormonism*, 163.

deeply rooted in its identity and its story is a key revelation of that identity. Thus, to promote a false history is to promote a false identity, and to promote a false identity is to jeopardize authenticity.

Conclusion to the Early Period of the Restoration

FOUR KEY EVENTS shaped the early Restoration era: the family history of Joseph Smith Jr., the First Vision and its impact, the Book of Mormon, and the formal organization of the church. Many of the major themes resident in the years of the early national period of American history are expressed in the Seer's family history. The Smith family can be traced back to English immigration and colonization, New England Puritanism, the French and Indian War, and the American Revolution.

Like so many other families during those times the Smiths endured the pangs of poverty, which seemed ever present. They found themselves subject to the whims of a fragile New England economy and confronted their very survival when challenged in bad times while they prospered during the good. As tenant farmers they were particularly susceptible to their environment, but they exhibited an entrepreneurial spirit as well.

Somehow the Smiths never fully benefited from the presence of education in their family. They embraced the need for learning, as both Father and Mother Smith were educators in their early years. Hyrum, the best educated in the family, attended a charity academy affiliated with the prestigious Dartmouth College, albeit for a short time. Palmyra citizens recognized Hyrum's credentials, installed him as an education commissioner, and entrusted him with hiring their instructors—no small responsibility. Unfortunately, the family could not build on Hyrum's reputation. Too many circumstances lessened the chances for the Smiths to rise out of their impoverished status in the community.

Amid all else, the Smiths were a very religious family. They experimented in mysticism but no more or less than so many of their friends. Enchantment influences complemented their faith journey in search of the unknown. The family religious heritage was basically polarized between the Calvinist Macks and the Universalist Smiths. This conflict persisted through the years and created many tense moments. Their confrontation with abject poverty and social marginalization wherever they migrated, and their inability to find denominational consensus, significantly contributed to their family dysfunction. The religious revivals that inflamed upstate New York during these times created a fertile environment for various Smith family members to experience dreams and visions. Future generations of church believers would find great meaning in young Joseph's encounter in a grove near Palmyra.

Perhaps better than anything else in the early years of the Restoration movement, the Book of Mormon exhibited the creativity and spiritual discernment of Joseph Smith Jr. The storied themes of this book reflect the strong influences of his family and friends, his culture, and other books of the times that dealt with the origins of Native Americans. Yet more than this, the book contained a theology that embraced New Jerusalem themes of Puritanism and created an American version of the Judeo-Christian tradition.

Early in the history of the Restoration, the Book of Mormon became the single most important reason for joining the Latter Day Saint movement. But those who embraced the Book of Mormon and its theological teachings needed a community to which they could belong. Joseph Smith Jr. and his family, in response to his sense of divine inspiration, led the organization of a new church. In addition to the satisfaction of being faithful to the Spirit's guidance, as they understood it, they also received the respect for which they yearned, resolved family disputes by achieving consensus, and found an avenue for salvation of their souls.

For the generations that followed, the traditional account of how church leaders accomplished church organization has been more a matter of tradition than historical fact, and for the first generation, more a matter of spirituality than legality. The framers of church organization initially followed legal requirements but then, when the occasion seemed to require, veered away to suit their own particular needs. This established an important precedent that the prophet used as he moved his church through Ohio, Missouri, and Illinois. As with the Smith family, believers found within the church tenets and ecclesiastical structure an opportunity to attain their salvation. Baptism meant joining in a sacred journey that required believers to build communities of faith based on divine principles as interpreted to them through their prophet, seer, and revelator, Joseph Smith Jr.

The Middle Period of the Restoration

❧

1830 to 1839

KIRTLAND

CHAPTER EIGHT

The Church in Kirtland, Ohio: Early Stronghold of Latter Day Saintism

THE SEPTEMBER 1830 church conference in Fayette, New York, commissioned a special missionary team to share the Book of Mormon with the Native Americans on the borders of the nation.[1] A few weeks later, the team of Parley Pratt, Oliver Cowdery, Peter Whitmer Jr., and Richard Ziba Peterson, historically referred to as the "Lamanite Missionaries," headed westward on the rather well-worn trails out of upstate New York and into northeastern Ohio. There they found former Campbellite minister Sidney Rigdon and his followers living in a land that had a rich but contentious history. English King Charles II, who reigned from 1660 to 1685, had granted the land to his colony of Connecticut. Following the American Revolution, the American government had little money to pay the newly created states for their service to win liberation from England. Instead, the federal government awarded sizeable tracts of land from the new frontiers achieved through victory. In complicated negotiations, Connecticut gained ownership of a four-million-acre tract of land stretching westward along the southern shoreline of Lake Erie for 125 miles. Appropriately the geographic region was referred to as the Connecticut Western Reserve.[2]

---

1. Doctrine and Covenants 27:3a–d (LDS 28:8–9).
2. A brief but excellent summary of the early historical origins of the Connecticut Western Reserve, also known as New Connecticut, can be found in Van Wagoner, *Sidney Rigdon*, 16–17.

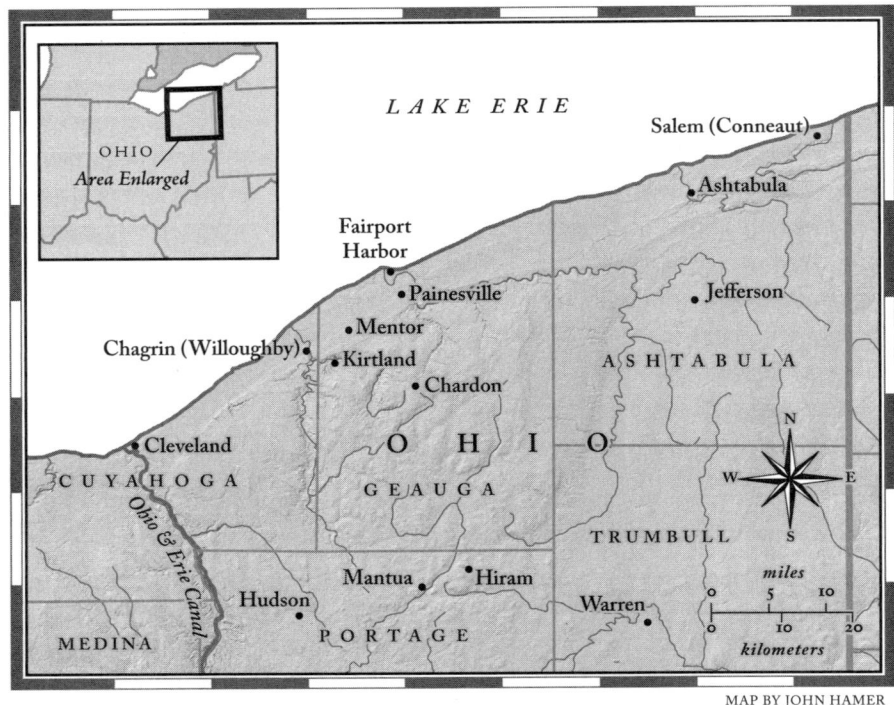

MAP BY JOHN HAMER

The vicinity of Kirtland, Ohio (boundaries as of 1831)

After the War for Independence, numerous agents from joint-stock companies quickly invaded the wilderness of the Western Reserve. They hoped to turn a handsome profit on land sales to the thousands of people from the large eastern cities and rural farmlands who were packing their wagons to find prosperity in the newly opened reaches. One company was the Connecticut Land Company, who commissioned Moses Cleaveland to survey the tract into townships. Cleaveland's colleague Turhand Kirtland established a community northeast of Cleaveland's Lake Erie settlement. Locating his small village six miles away from the lake shielded the original settlers from the harsh winter winds blowing off Lake Erie, yet positioned them close enough to benefit from the lake's lifeline of commerce. In 1811, just eight years after Ohio achieved statehood,[3] the area's first permanent white settlers raised their log cabins in Kirtland's clearing

---

3. Ohio entered the union as the seventeenth state on 1 March 1803.

along a branch of the Chagrin River. By the end of the decade, nearly five hundred claimed Kirtland as their residence; and by the time the Lamanite Missionaries arrived in the fall of 1830, the community had more than doubled, to more than a thousand. The village included grist, carding, and sawmills, a hotel, and a mercantile store. In time, settlers identified with the all-important mills and named their village Kirtland Mills.

Settlement Practices

THE ESTABLISHMENT OF Kirtland Mills followed the rural settlement patterns of hundreds of contemporary wilderness communities in America during the 1830s. Historical geographer Donald Meinig identified the combination of conditions that led to successful settlement during this era:

> 1. the huge expanse of good-quality lands made available at a very modest price;
>
> 2. the essential emptiness of the area, its familiarity in kind and ready domestication by established systems of pioneering;
>
> 3. the prevailing principle that beyond establishing the most elementary frameworks for public order, the government was not to control or manage the processes of settlement and development but leave all to private initiative; and
>
> 4. the concurrent revolution in transportation facilities that ensured ever-more efficient connections between new places in the continental interior and the great entrepôts of world commerce.[4]

Although having their own religious motivations, the Latter Day Saints in the Kirtland, Ohio, area participated in larger emigration patterns described by then-contemporary French observer Michael (also Michel) Chevalier, as two "great masses...[of] the New England and Virginia columns" emigrating westward, who "planted themselves in the wilderness, each in a manner comfortable to his nature and condition."[5] While

---

4. Meinig, *The Shaping of America*, 2: 255.
5. Michael Chevalier, *Society, Manners and Politics in the United States: Being a Series of Letters on North America* (Boston: Weeks, Jordan, 1839), 109–114, in Meinig, *The Shaping of America*, 2: 264. The French Ministry of Interior sent Chevalier on a two-year assignment to examine canals, railroads, banks, and other facilities and institutions in America.

the southern region of Ohio attracted Chevalier's "Virginia column," the northern region, or the Western Reserve, attracted New England–stock families, including the Crarys, the Morleys, and the Whitneys.

Sidney Rigdon and Early Theological Themes

WITH THE PASSING of a few years in the Western Reserve, Campbellite preacher Sidney Rigdon was the area's most important religious figure. Born on 19 February 1793 in Pennsylvania, Sidney was the youngest of four children. His love for reading the Bible, history, and studying English grammar foreshadowed his future in religious studies. By the time he reached his mid-twenties, he received his license as a Baptist preacher and became known for his spell-binding eloquence. After several discussions with Alexander Campbell, Rigdon affiliated with his movement, which eventually became the Disciples of Christ, and accepted an invitation to pastor a congregation in Mentor, Ohio. Rigdon's influence quickly spread to nearby Kirtland where, together with his members in Mentor, he created a large following.

COMMUNITY OF CHRIST LIBRARY-ARCHIVES
Sidney Rigdon

Two primary theological themes in Sidney Rigdon's faith were communalism and millennialism. Rigdon—like members of Joseph Smith's family—was convinced of the need to "restore the ancient order of things," that is, to recreate the primitive Christian church. In his view, the best way to accomplish this was by calling believers to lay their possessions "down at the Apostles' feet" and to introduce his "common stock system." The charismatic preacher called for a small communal society based on Acts 2. In February 1830, Rigdon planted communal settlements in Kirtland under the leadership of Isaac Morley; in Mayfield, Ohio, under the leadership of Lyman Wight; and in Chardon, Ohio, under the leadership of Edison Fuller.[6] Together they called their collective experiment "the Family" and covenanted "to renounce private property and share all goods."[7] This reordering of wealth would continue to echo throughout Latter Day Saintism during its infant years.

In the Western Reserve, Sidney Rigdon was one of the most vocal proponents of millennialism, a belief in the imminent Second Coming of Christ. But Rigdon's view of the societal conditions and timing of the millennial reign differed significantly from Alexander Campbell's view and put considerable theological distance between the two clerics.[8] Other points of disagreement between Campbell and Rigdon surfaced over gifts of the Holy Spirit, such as speaking in tongues (glossolalia), interpretation of tongues, visions, and healing. Campbell also rejected claims of authority to perform sacramental ordinances and the ancient miracles.[9]

Rigdon and Campbell parted ways by August 1830. Serendipitously, amid this theological searching in Rigdon's "Family," the Lamanite Missionaries arrived in the Kirtland area. Parley Pratt looked forward to introducing his old friend and mentor, Sidney Rigdon, to his colleagues, to his church, and especially to the Book of Mormon, Pratt's chief proselytizing tool. Actually, Rigdon had already heard about the "golden bible" from the numerous visitors from upstate New York. Also, several Western Reserve

6. Ronald E. Romig, "Law of Consecration: Antecedents and Practice at Kirtland, Ohio," in *Restoration Studies VI*, ed. Wayne Ham and Joni Wilson (Independence, Mo.: Herald House, 1995), 193, 195, 201fn12.

7. Van Wagoner, *Sidney Rigdon*, 50–51.

8. Both Rigdon and Campbell agreed on the millennial return of Jesus Christ, however they had a serious disagreement on the timing of the sacred event. Campbell had confidence that with the ultimate Christianization of the world and the perfection of human institutions, Christ's return would be a capstone upon the foretold thousand-year reign. His was a postmillennial view of the Second Coming. Rigdon had far less confidence in human decision making and believed that only Christ's return could initiate the thousand year reign. Thus Rigdon's view of the Second Coming was pre-millennial. For a more in-depth explanation of millenarianism, see Grant Underwood, *The Millenarian World of Early Mormonism* (Urbana: University of Illinois Press, 1993).

9. Richard Bushman has observed that "the Enlightenment drained Christianity of its belief in the miraculous, except for Bible miracles." See Bushman, *Joseph Smith and the Beginnings of Mormonism*, 7. Also see Van Wagoner, *Sidney Rigdon*, 52–53.

and New York newspapers had reported the details of the Palmyra discovery as early as 1827.[10]

Rigdon's first impression of the Book of Mormon was less than favorable, but he resolved his problems by mid-November 1830 and was baptized on his belief in the American scripture as well as the testimonies of the missionaries.[11] The impact of Rigdon's conversion in November 1830 cannot be overstated. When he shared his personal experience with his parishioners, he could hardly hold back his emotion. Soon large numbers converted on Rigdon's testimony. Still Rigdon had not actually met the prophet; so accompanied by the Painesville, Ohio, hatter Edward Partridge, they went to Fayette, New York, arriving on 10 December. There the two inquirers found the prophet and heard his testimony. The next day Smith baptized Partridge in the nearby Seneca River. Later,

COMMUNITY OF CHRIST LIBRARY-ARCHIVES
Parley P. Pratt

---

10. An excellent source for further information on this is "History of Orson Hyde," *The Latter-Day Saints' Millennial Star* 26 (19 November 1864): 744, in Microfilm Collection, Community of Christ Library-Archives. Hyde apprenticed in the Rigdon home and even accompanied Rigdon on a preaching tour through Elyria and Florence, Ohio. Hyde pastored a group of Rigdonite converts in Florence while teaching school in that Western Reserve community. Thus, Hyde was in a strong position to know Rigdon's acquaintance with the Mormon scripture. For contemporary newspaper accounts see *Rochester Advertiser and Telegraph*, 31 August 1829, the *Gem*, 5 September 1829, and the *Painesville (Ohio) Telegraph*, which cited the *Palmyra (New York) Freeman*, 22 September 1829. For further explanation see Van Wagoner, *Sidney Rigdon*, 65fn27.

11. The greatest difficulty Rigdon had was in putting away his belief in the Bible as the only word of God. He had to convince himself that the Book of Mormon could also be included as scripture, a difficult conclusion coming out of his strong Baptist background.

Smith described Partridge as "a pattern of piety, and one of the Lord's great men."[12]

These were fortuitous times for Sidney Rigdon and Joseph Smith Jr., for they fulfilled each other's needs. Rigdon, the scholar, searched for a religious vision with which he could lead his people; and Smith, the unlearned, needed credibility and a place where he could implement his vision for the future. Both were charismatics who could captivate people's imagination. Rigdon's most effective ministry came from his pulpit, while Smith's came from his handshake. Rigdon searched for a new religious framework, while Smith searched for a following. With Rigdon's conversion, more than three hundred people joined the movement within a two-month period. This almost doubled the size of the movement. Together the two men teamed up to advance the newly organized Church of Christ, an American sect that proved capable of competing with the more-established religions on the American frontier.

Building the Kirtland Community

AS THE SECOND conference of the church convened in Fayette, New York, in late September 1830, Joseph announced his decision to formally begin a "pilgrimage," or holy journey, westward. In a revelatory statement given on 2 January 1831, the prophet told his followers that they should "go to the Ohio."[3] But there were practical questions associated with this decision. For example, what would be the disposition of the disciples' property, especially the farms that could not be sold? Who would take care of the poor and needy unable to afford the move? How would the few church resources be administered? Where would the followers settle once they arrived? The prophet asked his people to have faith that God would provide. However, the realities of community building turned out to be more difficult than even the prophet expected.

12. *DHC*, 1: 128. Edward Partridge was born to William and Jemima Partridge on 27 August 1793 in Pittsfield, Berkshire County, Massachusetts. He began a four-year apprenticeship as a hatter at age sixteen. At the completion of his training, Partridge was caught up in the religious fervor of the times and heard Campbellite minister Sidney Rigdon preach. In 1828, Rigdon baptized Partridge and his wife, Lydia, and the couple joined Rigdon's following in Mentor, Ohio.

13. Doctrine and Covenants 38:7b (LDS 38:32).

Joseph Smith's arrival in Kirtland began with an answer to a prayer. Riding by sleigh with his wife, Emma, Sidney Rigdon, and Edward Partridge, the group pulled up to the hitching post of general store owner Newell K. Whitney on 1 February 1831. To the surprise of the other passengers Smith quickly jumped out and ran into the store, approached the owner, and said, "Newell K. Whitney, thou art the man. You have prayed me here; now what do you want me to do?" With astonishment Whitney responded, "You have the advantage of me; I do not know you." Joseph smilingly replied, "I am known as the Prophet Joseph Smith." At this time Whitney and his wife, Elizabeth Ann, had not been baptized, but with this encounter, they soon would be.

Over the next few months, the New York church members obeyed the commission "to go to the Ohio." This required them to leave behind their homes and farms, dispensing of them as best they could. In all, some two hundred people westered by foot, stagecoach, sleigh, or wagon. Some traveled on the canal system or even on steamboats that navigated along the shores of Lake Erie. From Fairport Harbor, the Saints disembarked with all their possessions and trundled southwest nearly twenty miles to Kirtland.

The large number of immigrants moving into the small Kirtland area was bound to raise suspicions among nonbelievers. Western Reserve newspaper editors sensationalized stories about the newly arrived Saints and their prophet in order to sell papers. The most vicious critic in the Western Reserve was Eber D. Howe, editor of the Painesville, Ohio, *Telegraph*. Howe referred to the Book of Mormon as "the gold bible" and the Smith family as "money diggers."

Because Mormon beliefs varied from the widespread Protestant beliefs throughout the Western Reserve, Howe found an opportunity to separate the Saints from others in the Kirtland community. For example, most people on the American frontier believed that the Bible was the only record of the Word of God and that manifestations of the Spirit, such as miracles and speaking in tongues, had all ended during the early apostolic era. The larger frontier Christian community also believed that local congregations granted authority to preach and to perform sacramental functions. Mormons held radically different views, asserting that the Book of Mormon, and eventually the Doctrine and Covenants, were also scripture;

The Church in Kirtland, Ohio: Early Stronghold of Latter Day Saintism   149

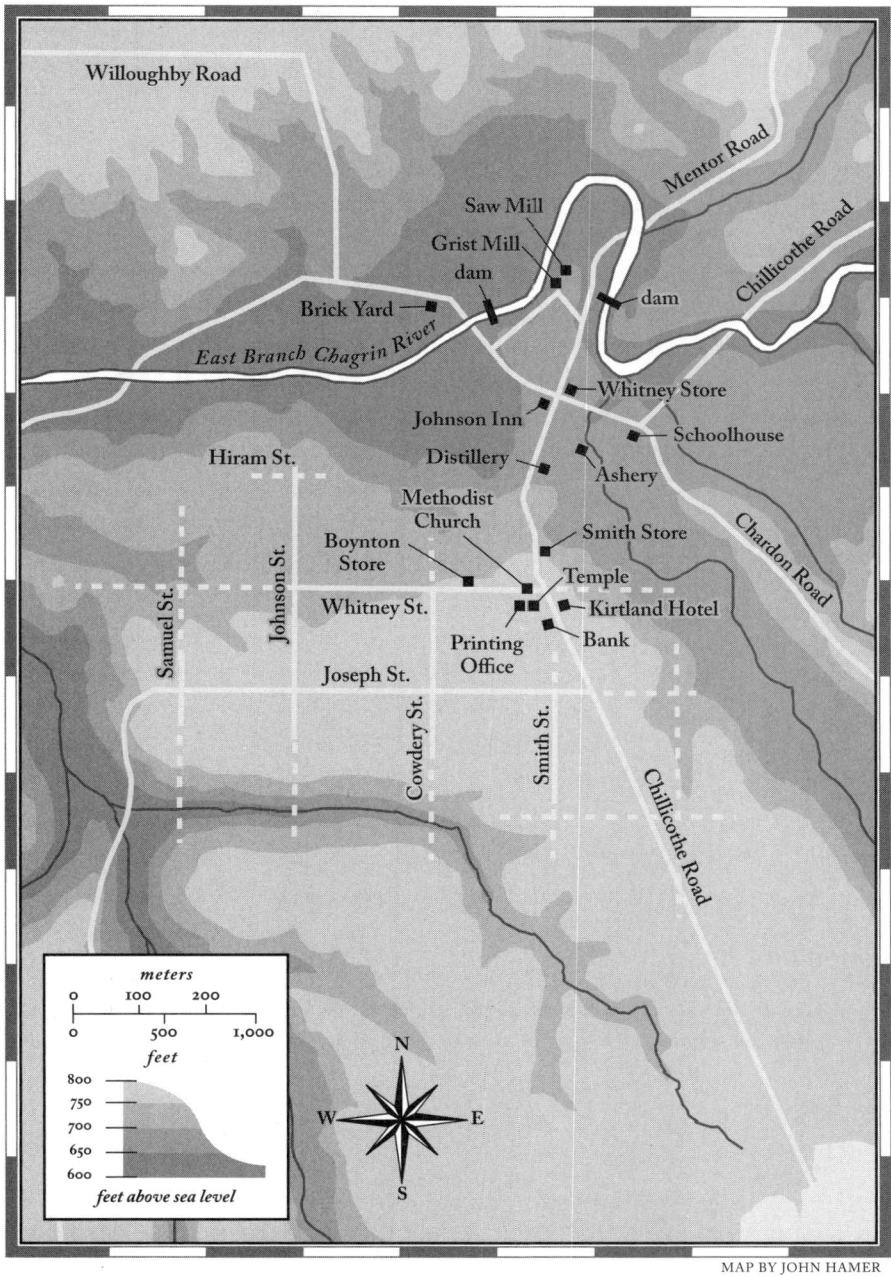

The town of Kirtland, Ohio, in the 1830s

that spiritual manifestations, including prophetic revelation, continued; and that only God, through the prophet, provided priesthood authority to perform sacramental functions. Since most found these beliefs to be quite strange, the Mormon claim to be "the only true church" was actually offensive. The history of the Saints in Kirtland can only be understood in the context of what both connected them with and separated them from their neighbors.

Law of Consecration and Stewardship

ADDED TO THEIR unusual religious beliefs was the Saints' communal lifestyle, pursued during the opening months of their settling in the Western Reserve. In February 1831, Smith provided the Law of Consecration and Stewardship, which called the members to consecrate all their possessions to the church for the purpose of eliminating poverty and relieving debt among believers. This stewardship plan required total consecration as well as a yearly donation of any surplus profits to a storehouse that would become a reservoir to assist future needs. All good church members were to make such sacrifices, and in return, families were promised an "eternal inheritance." With their obedience, the prophet assured them by proclaiming "great shall be thy reward."[14] Here the word of God delivered by the prophet was quite clear—those who abide by the law shall be saved, and those who do not must be cast out of the church.[15] Smith's hopes were to eliminate poverty, inequalities in wealth, and wasteful

---

14. Doctrine and Covenants 42:18b (LDS 42:65). The promise of an eternal inheritance, where the prophet guaranteed followers citizenship in God's eternal city at the Second Coming, proved to be a powerful motivational tool. With heavy millennialist overtones, such assurances evidenced Smith's belief in his ability to impact individuals' condition in the afterlife.

15. Doctrine and Covenants 42:11 (LDS 42:37–39):

   And it shall come to pass that he that sinneth and repenteth not, shall be cast out of the church, and shall not receive again that which he has consecrated unto the poor and the needy of my church, or, in other words, unto me; for inasmuch as ye do it unto the least of these, ye do it unto me; for it shall come to pass that which I spake by the mouths of my prophets shall be fulfilled; for I will consecrate of the riches of those who embrace my gospel, among the Gentiles, unto the poor of my people who are of the house of Israel.

consumption among the membership, as well as fund church operations and construction of church buildings.

Although the vast majority of church members were poverty stricken, a very few possessed considerable resources. Still the expectations were for them to commit their wealth for redistribution under the Law of Consecration. When that did not happen to church leaders' satisfaction, they faced judgment. Such was the case on 16 June 1836 when Preserved Harris, brother of Martin Harris, was charged, found guilty, and disfellowshipped in a church tribunal with "want of benevolence to the poor and charity to the church."[16] Leaders had to approach this problem with great care since to disfellowship a person of wealth also removed a key source of income.

With the passing years the heavy weight of the House of the Lord construction project, the publication of numerous resources, the expenses of church leaders, and the heavy demands of the needy all took their toll on church coffers. By the summer of 1834, with the failed Zion's Camp march, it was becoming clear that a new interpretation of stewardship giving would be needed.

Finally, the communal directives of the Law of Consecration butted up against the powerful forces of private ownership in the secular Jacksonian society. Under the weight of those forces, Smith's "more perfect law" faltered. The realities of a church membership living on the margins of society, with little surplus to consecrate, meant that there would be few resources to redistribute. Strong resistance from the gentile community and their competition for increasingly scarce land resources in Kirtland, and later in Independence, Missouri, hindered full achievement of the Law of Consecration's worthy goals.

Thus, what began as a divinely commissioned redistribution of wealth based on justified wants and needs, circumstances, and skills of individual members now required reinterpretation. In 1833, the prophet adjusted functional stewardship practices to conform better to the laws of the land.

16. In the same tribunal Elder Isaac McWithy faced similar charges but had the charges dropped. After hearing numerous testimonies to his guilt, McWithy then faced his accusers and declared that "he had relieved the wants of the poor, and did so many good things that he was astonished that he should hear such things as he had heard today, because he did not give all the[y] had got to one man. If he had done wrong, he asked forgiveness of God and the Church." See *Kirtland Council Minute Book*, 16 June 1836, transcript, Community of Christ Library-Archives, 212–18.

For example, deeds that could not be broken replaced leaseholds. By June 1834, Smith announced that the Law of Consecration was suspended until such a day as Zion could be redeemed.[17] Four years later, in July 1838, the prophet reinstituted a modified form of stewardship calling for members to consecrate all "surplus" property into the hands of the bishop, and to pay "one tenth of all their interest" each year as long as they should live.[18] The notable variations in the stewardship philosophies during this era reflected the ongoing search for scarce revenues to fund the church's programs.

Smith Family Issues in Kirtland

JOSEPH AND EMMA arrived in Kirtland without making arrangements for their housing. Establishing a home there for the family was a particular challenge for the prophet. The short-term solution was to accept temporary quarters until a dwelling could be built. They soon received two invitations, one from the Algernon Sidney Gilbert family and the other from the Whitneys. Since the Gilberts were already sharing their home with a family, Joseph and Emma decided to move in with the Whitneys, where they stayed for a month. During this time, Emma and Elizabeth Ann Whitney, Newell's wife, struck up a close friendship. But living with others was not satisfactory to Emma. Responding to her need, Joseph gave instruction that called for the construction of a house for the prophet and his family.[19] Workers responded, and the couple moved into a single-room dwelling in the Morley settlement in the early spring of 1831.

Emma endured the travels from New York in the dead of winter, the move into the Whitney home, and then the move into her own small cabin, all while pregnant. On the last day of April she delivered twins and named them Thaddeus and Louisa. Possibly born premature, the infants died after just three hours of life. The devastating loss of the twins, compounded by the loss of their first-born, Alvin, on 15 June 1828, under similar

---

17. Doctrine and Covenants 102:3c, f (LDS 105:9–10, 13–14).
18. Doctrine and Covenants 106:1b (LDS 119:4).
19. Doctrine and Covenants 41:3a (LDS 41:7): "And again, it is meet that my servant Joseph Smith, Jr., should have a house built, in which to live and translate."

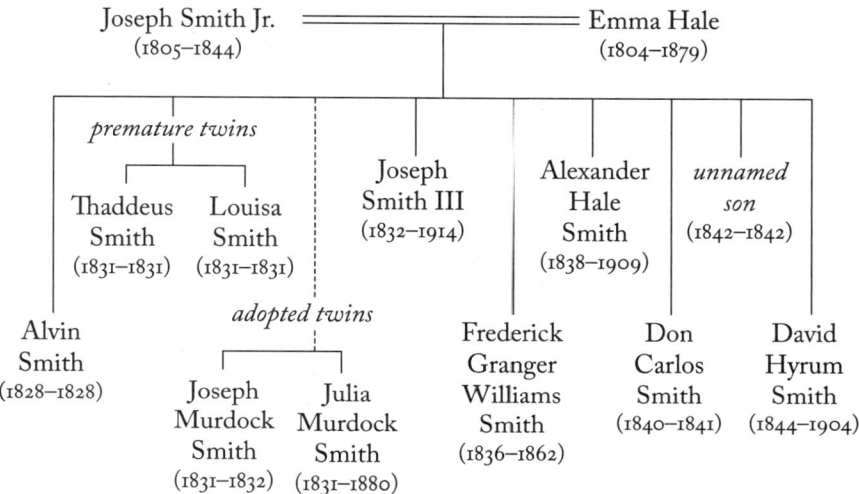

The family of Joseph and Emma Smith

circumstances, was a heavy burden for the young couple to carry.[20] However, just the day after their twins died, Julia Clapp Murdock, the wife of John Murdock, died while giving birth to twins.[21] Their names were Joseph

20. Alvin Smith, first child born to Joseph and Emma Smith, was buried in the McKune Cemetery, located today in Oakland, Susquehanna County, Pennsylvania. According to Sophia Lewis, who was present at the birth, the child was "still-born and very much deformed." See Vogel, *Early Mormon Documents*, 4: 298.

21. John and Julia Murdock settled in the Kirtland area in 1820. After several years they joined Sidney Rigdon's Campbellite fellowship. On 14 November 1830, shortly after the arrival of the Lamanite Missionaries, Parley Pratt baptized John Murdock who was ordained the same day to the priesthood office of elder. The following day Julia received baptism. Julia died on 30 April 1831. John wrote about the loss of his wife in his autobiography: "I moved my family to Brother C [Caleb] Baldwins, in Warrensville, in Dec. and my wife died 30th of Apl and left 5 living children, two of them but 6 hours old." John Murdock, *An Abridged Record Of The Life Of John Murdock, Taken From His Journal By Himself. Containing An Account Of His Genealogy And That Of His Children, As Also His Travels, Experience, Ordinations, Callings, Preaching, Blessings, Endowments And Etc.*, typescript, Community of Christ Library-Archives. The scene created an indelible memory in six-year-old son John Riggs Murdock, who recalled: "Fresh in my memory is the death of my dear mother, which occurred in Warrensville Township, which joins Orange Township. There was a dreadfully sad scene among her poor children following her death. It was simply heartrending to hear little Phoebe, only two years old, cry out for her mother as if her little heart would break. We were staying

and Julia. Because Emma could nurse them, she took them in while their natural father considered the difficulties of caring for his family of five small children. After nine days of caring for the Murdock twins, Joseph and Emma consented to adopt them permanently as their own.

Stirring Public Passion in the Western Reserve

WHEREVER THE PROPHET went he stirred the passions of both believers and nonbelievers. By fall 1831, the Smiths of Kirtland, Ohio, were the focus of social life and ecclesial interest. Joseph's reputation as a cleric spread throughout the countryside. People heard how he had miraculously cast out the devil plaguing a Colesville, New York, friend.[22]

But of greater interest to those in the Kirtland area was Joseph's healing of Elsa Johnson of Hiram, Ohio. Out of curiosity, Elsa and her husband, John, accompanied by Methodist preacher Ezra Booth, came to Kirtland to learn more of Smith's religious beliefs. According to the story, as the Johnsons, Smiths, and Booth chatted, Joseph noticed that Elsa's rheumatic arm hung uselessly to her side. Assessing the condition, Joseph walked across the room, took Elsa by the hand, and said solemnly: "Woman, in the name of the Lord Jesus Christ I command thee to be whole."

---

at a neighbors when Father came and told us the sad news. He wept most bitterly; for he realized all the sorrow of the situation." J. M. Tanner, *John Riggs Murdock* (Salt Lake City: The Deseret News, 1909), 9, in S. Reed Murdock, *John Murdock: His Life and his Legacy...* (Layton, Utah: Summerwood Publishers, 2000), 68.

22. In April 1830, Joseph Smith Jr. visited the Knight family, living in Colesville, Broome County, New York. Joseph Knight had employed the young Smith four years earlier, thus establishing a close relationship. When the prophet arrived at the Knight home, several gathered also to meet the Palmyra prophet because they knew that Joseph Knight's son, Newel (also Newell), was "suffering very much in his mind, and his body acted upon in a very strange manner; his visage and limbs distorted and twisted in every shape and appearance possible to imagine; and finally he was caught up off the floor of the apartment, and tossed about most fearfully." Joseph was shocked when he first observed the young man's condition. When Newel gathered his strength he begged the prophet to cast out the devil. Amid the onlookers, Joseph took Newel's hand and said: "If you know that I can, it shall be done." Almost immediately Newel's body relaxed as his family and friends lifted him back onto his bed. After a short convalescence, Newel traveled to Fayette and was baptized at the Whitmer farm in late May. See *DHC*, 1: 82–83. Historian Richard Bushman identified this exorcism as the first miracle performed in the church. See his *Joseph Smith and the Beginnings of Mormonism*, 154.

Then the prophet immediately left the room. Startled by the presumption of such a spiritual gift, his declaration stopped all conversation in the room, at which time Elsa raised her arm over her head for the first time in years. The next day she returned home and did her washing with little pain or difficulty.[23] The observers converted to the church upon the experience.

Each day, visitors arrived at the Smith home, costing the family their much desired privacy. Joseph had begun revising the Bible and took this task seriously. He viewed himself not only as God's mouthpiece but also God's penman, commissioned to correct a corrupted scripture. In doing so he felt inspired to recover lost parts of the text that provided support for doctrines and principles that were integral to the beliefs and practices of the restored church. The prophet received the able assistance of Oliver Cowdery and John Whitmer. But when the two church leaders accepted missionary assignments, the newly converted Sidney Rigdon made one of his most important contributions to the Restoration Era—the restoring of the biblical scripture. With his considerable knowledge of the Bible, he assisted Smith in a biblical rewrite eventually known as Joseph Smith's "New Translation" of the Bible.[24]

In early September 1831, the Smith family accepted an invitation from the Johnsons to move, at least temporarily, to their farm in Hiram, Portage County, Ohio, about thirty miles southeast of Kirtland. In the Johnson home, Joseph, Emma, and their two infant children joined with John, Elsa, and their daughter, Nancy Marinda.

Good times and bad followed the couple to Hiram, however. On the first day of November, the prophet convened a conference of the church there. During the conference, discussions focused on the issue of preserving and organizing Smith's revelations. The decision was to print the *Book of Commandments*, a compilation of the revelations up to that date. Because the church press was being set up in Independence, Missouri, Oliver Cowdery was commissioned to transport the collection to publisher

---

23. *DHC*, 1: 215–16fn.
24. This work was not distributed during Joseph's lifetime, but was published by the RLDS Church in 1867. In more recent times it has come to be referred to as the "Inspired Version." Detailed information on the textual development of Smith's version of the Bible can be found in Richard P. Howard, *Restoration Scriptures: A Study of Their Textual Development*, 2nd ed. (Independence, Mo.: Herald House, 1995).

William W. Phelps. Cowdery left on 15 November with the materials, while Joseph focused on revising the Bible with Sidney Rigdon and preaching throughout Ohio.

In late January 1832, Joseph called for another conference—this one to meet in Amherst, Ohio. Here, Smith consolidated his leadership by instituting more church organization and structure. He felt the need to be sustained by church members as president of the high priesthood. After the conference, the prophet and Rigdon returned to the Johnson farm. The order of the day was to revise the New Testament, with Sidney as scribe. As the two men labored on the text of John 5:29, they pondered the true nature of the afterlife. On 16 February, a dozen men arrived for a visit, including early convert Philo Dibble.[25] According to Dibble, as Smith spoke and Rigdon wrote, the two men received a vision of the heavens. In this vision, the men were shown not just one heaven, but three—celestial, terrestrial, and telestial. This encounter became known as the Vision of the Three Glories. Briefly summarized, the celestial, or the glory of the sun, the highest heaven, was reserved for the church of the Firstborn, or those to come forth in the first resurrection. The terrestrial glory, or the glory of the moon, was for those who died without the gospel but accepted it in the next life. The lowest glory of heaven, the telestial, or glory of the stars, was designated for those "who received not the gospel of Christ, neither the testimony of Jesus," or most of earth's inhabitants. Hell, the fourth state of existence in the afterlife, was reserved only for the "sons of perdition."

The Smith-Rigdon version closely paralleled the view of Swedish theologian Emmanuel Swedenborg (1688–1772), who argued for the same three heavenly states. In his widely distributed writings, Swedenborg used human anatomy as his model, suggesting that the highest state of heaven was the head, the middle heaven was the body, and the lowest was the feet. The Smith-Rigdon use of the firmament also closely resembled contemporary Scottish philosopher-scientist Thomas Dick (1774–1857), well-known for his views of the afterlife. Dick speculated that heavenly bodies, such as planets, could be populated and thus become possible locations for the varying degrees of a pluralist heaven.

---

25. Philo Dibble (1806–1895) was baptized on 16 October 1830.

The Church in Kirtland, Ohio: Early Stronghold of Latter Day Saintism 157

Few doubt Smith's knowledge of both Swedenborg's and Dick's theories. Articles on the plurality of worlds appeared in Palmyra-area almanacs and newspapers as early as 1823. Oliver Cowdery even quoted Thomas Dick extensively in the February and March 1837 issues of the Kirtland, Ohio, *Latter Day Saints' Messenger and Advocate*.[26] The appearance of these articles coincided with the evolutionary development of Smith's insights about the cosmos and what happens to the soul in the afterlife. Not surprisingly, historians and theologians have connected these philosophical theories and Latter Day Saint theology.[27]

During the hour-long epiphany in Johnson's Hiram, Ohio, home, the witnesses neither spoke nor moved, but simply observed the two men. Dibble wrote that "Joseph wore a black suit, but his face shone as if transparent. At intervals, Joseph described to Sidney what he saw. Sidney replied, 'I see the same.' Then Sidney described what he saw and Joseph replied, 'I see the same.'" Dibble described the demeanor of the participants by stating: "Joseph sat calmly and firmly all the time in the midst of a magnificent glory, but Sidney sat limp and pale, apparently as limber as a rag, observing which, Joseph remarked, smilingly, 'Sidney is not used to it as I am.'" Eventually this experience was entered into the Doctrine and Covenants as Section 76. If Dibble is correct, then the written language is substantially from Rigdon who "stayed up all night to record what they had seen."[28]

26. For a broadened discussion of the similarities between the Latter Day Saint concept of the three heavens and Emmanuel Swedenborg's concept, see Quinn, *Early Mormonism and the Magic World View*, 14–15, 219. On the use of Thomas Dick's writings see Oliver Cowdery, "The Philosophy of Religion," *Latter Day Saints' Messenger and Advocate* 3, no. 5 (February 1837): 461–63, and continued in the next issue, no. 6 (March 1837): 468–69.

27. Articles explaining Swedenborgian concepts of the afterlife appeared in Palmyra newspapers during the time the Smiths resided in upstate New York. See "Remarkable VISION and REVELATION; as seen and received by Asa Wild of Amsterdam (New York)," *Wayne Sentinel* (Palmyra, New York), 22 October 1823, [4]. Also see "SWEDENBORGIANS," *The Reflector* (Palmyra, New York), 16 March 1830, 87. Both newspaper sources are cited from Quinn, *Early Mormonism and the Magic World View*, 485fn363. Also see John L. Brooke's observations on the Swedenborgian influence in his *The Refiner's Fire*, 95–99.

28. Philo Dibble, *History of the Life of Philo Dibble, Sr.* (n.p., n.d.). A version of Dibble's account is found in Van Wagoner, *Sidney Rigdon*, 112. However, Van Wagoner advises

Jealousies and suspicions within the membership surfaced while Joseph and Sidney lived in Hiram, Ohio. Ezra Booth, annoyed by the prophet's ebullient personality, charged Joseph with "a want of sobriety, prudence, and stability…a spirit of lightness and levity, and temper of mind easily irritated, and an habitual proneness to jesting and joking."[29] Others suspected that the Law of Consecration was a disguised "land grab" by Joseph Smith to gain control of the countryside. Some even questioned the prophet's morality.

Anger boiled over late on Saturday evening 24 March 1832. Joseph and Emma, exhausted from caring for the twins who were deep into the throes of measles, finally fell asleep, when a dozen men sneaked into the Johnson farmhouse and dragged Joseph into a nearby field. Another contingent of attackers wrested Sidney Rigdon from his log cabin, located across the road. In the front yard, a mob numbering between fifty and sixty knocked Sidney unconscious while Joseph put up a valiant fight, kicking one attacker to the ground. Mob leaders induced a Dr. Dennison, a respected physician from the local community, to join the mob and to castrate Smith. Dennison took pity and refused, so the mob took vengeance by stripping Joseph and scratching him until he bled. Then they attempted to force him to swallow poison. The mobbers could not force open his mouth with the vial, although they did break a front tooth, leaving the prophet with a lisp for the remainder of his life. Finally, the mob poured pitch tar all over his head and body and then rolled him in a feather tick. They left him motionless on the frozen ground.

Disoriented, Joseph struggled to stand, and then stumbled back to the house. From a distance it appeared that Joseph was covered in blood. When Emma first saw her husband, she fainted at the sight. Throughout the night his friends worked diligently to remove the tar and to bandage his wounds. When the sun rose, Joseph prepared and gave his Sunday morning sermon from the front steps of the Johnson farmhouse. In the congregation that gathered, Joseph recognized some of his attackers, who

---

caution on the veracity of Dibble's claim. Also see Marquardt, *The Joseph Smith Revelations*, 191.

29. Ezra Booth to Rev. I. Eddy, 21 November 1831, in Linda King Newell and Valeen Tippets Avery, *Mormon Enigma: Emma Hale Smith* (Urbana: University of Illinois Press, 1994), 41.

The Church in Kirtland, Ohio: Early Stronghold of Latter Day Saintism

COMMUNITY OF CHRIST LIBRARY-ARCHIVES

The Hiram, Ohio, mob tarring and feathering Joseph Smith Jr.

could hardly believe Smith's courage and determination. In his address, Smith had an excellent opportunity to identify and accuse his attackers but chose otherwise.

Mobbers brutalized Sidney even more than Joseph. Rigdon received several severe blows to the head and was dragged over a wood pile and frozen plough furrows. He did not regain consciousness for several days and the effects of this beating lasted throughout Rigdon's life.[30]

30. For excellent analysis of the long-term effects of the beating on Rigdon, see Van Wagoner, *Sidney Rigdon*, 116–18. Van Wagoner mentioned an early childhood injury similar to the blows to the head Rigdon received during the attack. When he was seven years old, Rigdon fell from his horse but caught his foot in the stirrup. The horse dragged Rigdon a considerable distance before his rescue, 116–17.

But the worst victim of the attack was its most vulnerable—the feverish twin, Joseph. As the attack was happening, the cold night air only aggravated the baby's sickly condition. For the next six days, Emma did what she could to reduce the symptoms but could only watch with a mother's anguish as the infant succumbed to the fever on Friday 29 March 1832.

Neither the physical humiliation nor the loss of baby Joseph slowed down the prophet. Within three days of the child's passing, the prophet went on a mission and left Emma to move back by herself to their home in Kirtland. On Smith's arrival back to the area weeks later, Joseph, Emma, and Julia returned to the Johnson farm briefly and then moved back again to Kirtland to Newell Whitney's store.

In October 1832, with Emma more than eight months pregnant, Joseph left again for Albany, Boston, and New York City. While strolling through lower Manhattan, admiring the tall buildings and bustling city life, Joseph came upon a beautiful church whose architecture left an indelible mark on his mind. Although delighted to hear from her husband, Emma prepared for the birth of another child without his presence. On 6 November 1832 in the Whitney store in Kirtland, Ohio, she delivered again. This child would be the couple's first natural-born child to survive and to live a long and productive life. Shortly after the difficult delivery, Joseph arrived back at Kirtland to his wife, Emma; his daughter, Julia; and now his newborn son, whom they named Joseph.

The Ecclesiastical Structure of the New Church

OVER TIME, KIRTLAND, Ohio, became the seat of the church—the location where church organization would flower. Considering the small size of the church in New York, creating a church authority with Joseph Smith Jr. as first elder and Oliver Cowdery as second elder seemed to suffice. However, when the church moved to Kirtland, greater numbers meant greater needs in church governance. Smith's first action within days of his arrival in Kirtland was to define the ministerial function of bishop, ordaining Edward Partridge to the task of instituting the Law of Consecration and Stewardship.[31] Then Joseph set in order the high priesthood at the Kirtland Conference on 3 June 1831 and received high

---

31. Doctrine and Covenants 41:3c (LDS 41:9).

priesthood authority from the hands of Lyman Wight.[32] As stated earlier, at the Amherst Conference near Hiram, Ohio, on 25 January 1832, Smith was ordained president of the high priesthood, with the acknowledgment repeated in Independence, Missouri, the following April. Not until 1835 did church officers use the term "Melchizedek [also Melchisedec] priesthood" to describe the different offices of this ecclesiastical order.[33] The primary motivation for these actions, along with the opening of a School of the Prophets in late January 1833, was to prepare church ministers for mission.

On 18 March 1833, Sidney Rigdon and Frederick Granger Williams were ordained as Joseph's counselors.[34] In Kirtland, Smith prophesied: "And again, verily I say unto thy brethren Sidney Rigdon and Frederick G. Williams, their sins are forgiven them also, and they are accounted as equal with thee [the prophet] in holding the keys of this last kingdom."[35] By the end of 1833, Joseph ordained his father as patriarch of the church, a position yet to be defined by the prophet, but presumably to focus on spiritual needs of the people. During Joseph Sr.'s ordination blessing, Joseph Jr. stated:

---

32. Approximately fifty elders met in this conference and had a Pentecostal experience. Church historian John Corrill described the visionary encounter: "Some curious things took place. The same visionary and marvellous spirits, spoken of before, got hold of some of the elders; it threw one from his seat to the floor; it bound another, so that for some time he could not use his limbs nor speak; and some other curious effects were experienced, but, by a mighty exertion, in the name of the Lord, it was exposed and shown to be from an evil source." See John Corrill, *A Brief History of the Church of Christ of Latter Day Saints, (Commonly Called Mormons;) Including an Account of Their Doctrine and Discipline; with the Reasons of the Author for Leaving the Church* (St. Louis: Printed for the Author, 1839), 18.

33. Historian Gregory Prince has observed that numerous contemporary sources referenced these events as formulating "the order of Melchisedek." But specific reference to the Melchizedek Order was not made until 1835. See "A Vision," *The Evening and the Morning Star* 1, no. 2 (July 1832): [2-3]. See Gregory A. Prince, *Having Authority: The Origins and Development of Priesthood During the Ministry of Joseph Smith* (Independence, Mo.: Independence Press, 1993), 40. Anachronistic references were not uncommon during this era.

34. Originally Joseph Smith Jr. selected Jesse Gause to join with Sidney Rigdon as counselor in what later came to be called the First Presidency, but the prophet quickly replaced Gause with Frederick Granger Williams. Rigdon remained as counselor for nearly the entire Restoration Era.

35. Doctrine and Covenants 87:3a (LDS 90:6).

He [Joseph Sr.] shall be called a prince over his posterity, holding the keys of the patriarchal priesthood over the kingdom of God on earth, even the Church of the Latter Day Saints; and he shall sit in the general assembly of patriarchs, even in council with the Ancient of Days when he shall sit and all the patriarchs with him—and shall enjoy his right and authority under the direction of the Ancient of Days.[36]

To address church policy issues impossible to resolve by other administrative bodies, Smith established the Kirtland High Council on 17 February 1834. Twelve high priests and the First Presidency performed judicial functions having both original and appellate jurisdiction. This important body settled problems such as breach of contract between members, child and spouse abandonment, failing to attend church functions, violations of the Word of Wisdom and the Law of Consecration and Stewardship, and slandering of church leaders. A second high council was formed to preside over the Missouri church on 7 July 1834, appointing David Whitmer as president, and John Whitmer and William W. Phelps as counselors.

On 5 December 1834, Joseph Smith ordained Oliver Cowdery as assistant president of the high priesthood. According to Cowdery's notes, the prophet declared that, as assistant president, Cowdery was "to assist in presiding over the whole church, and to officiate in the absence of the President."[37] The position of assistant president was sustained through the years as Joseph ordained Hyrum to assume this position on 19 January 1841 in Nauvoo, Illinois.

The call to apostolic ministry dates back to 1829, a year before the church was organized, when Joseph and Oliver claimed ordination through a spiritual manifestation. With this authority, Smith commissioned the three Book of Mormon witnesses, David Whitmer, Oliver Cowdery, and Martin Harris, to select the original Quorum of Twelve Apostles. On 14 February 1835, the committee announced their selections, and over the next several days they filled the quorum. They chose Lyman E. Johnson,

36. Patriarchal Blessings Book 1, LDS Church Archives; copy in Irene Bates Collection, in Prince, *Having Authority*, 62.
37. "Manuscript History of the LDS Church," Book A-1, 5 December 1834, in Cowdery's handwriting, LDS Historical Department, Salt Lake City, Utah, in D. Michael Quinn, "Joseph Smith III's 1844 Blessing and the Mormons of Utah," *John Whitmer Historical Association Journal* 1 (1981): 13.

Brigham Young, Heber C. Kimball, Orson Hyde, David W. Patten, Luke S. Johnson, William E. McLellin, John F. Boynton, Orson Pratt, William Smith, Thomas B. Marsh, and Parley P. Pratt. Joseph took this opportunity to make the distinction between the traveling and standing ministries. The Council of Twelve Apostles received a commission to travel and to consider the world as their mission field.

Just two weeks after the organization of the apostolic quorum, the prophet directed his attention to the priesthood office of seventy. The seventies, taken from the tenth chapter of the Gospel of Luke, were called to be proselytizing witnesses and to assist the apostles. The first seventies were drawn from those men who proved their intense loyalty by enduring the frustration and hardship of the 1834 Zion's Camp march. This failed attempt to regain by force lands lost in Independence, Missouri, lasted from May through July (to be explained later).

Lack of definition in his use of the terms "high priesthood," "high priest," and the "order of Melchisedec" reflected the uncertainty of even the prophet himself. Historian Richard L. Bushman's suggestion that "experience may have outrun comprehension"[38] is a reasonable explanation of the confusion. Just as Joseph Jr.'s understanding of the Grove Experience evolved over time and produced several different explanations, creating an enduring priesthood structure that would meet the needs of a growing church also took time.

By summer 1835, the prophet concretized priesthood structure with the publication of the Doctrine and Covenants. This book of scripture evolved from the *Book of Commandments*, which was destroyed by an angry mob in Independence, Missouri, before it was even published. Because the pages of the *Book of Commandments* were strewn in the streets outside the church printing house, few church members had actually read its pages. The need for an expanded open canon of scripture became more evident with time. Thus, decision makers took various parts of the *Book of Commandments* and included them in a new compilation of inspired statements, doctrinal lectures on faith, and specific "Covenants and Commandments of the Lord" as determined by delegates to an official general assembly in

---

38. Richard Lyman Bushman, *Joseph Smith: Rough Stone Rolling, A Cultural Biography of Mormonism's Founder* (New York: Alfred A. Knopf, 2005), 159.

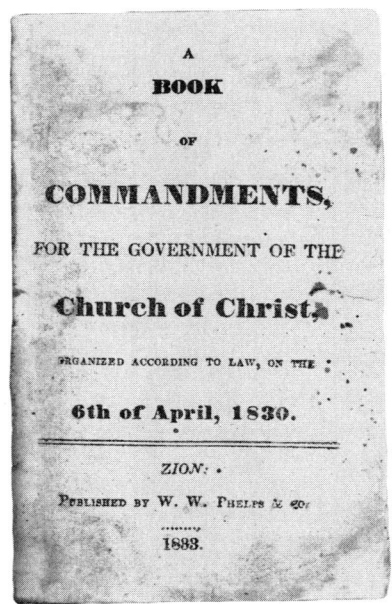 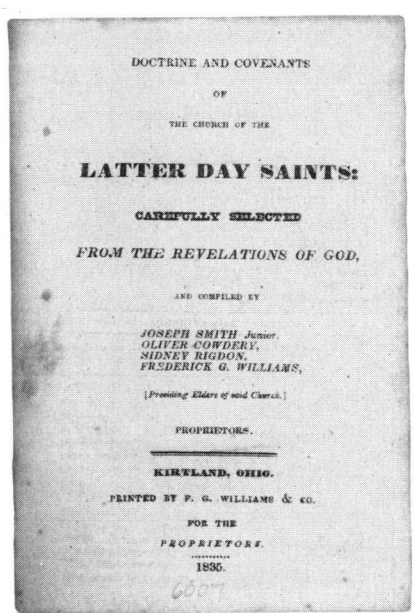

COMMUNITY OF CHRIST LIBRARY-ARCHIVES

Title page of Book of Commandments *(1833) and* Doctrine and Covenants *(1835)*

Kirtland, Ohio, on 17 August 1835.[39] These delegates adopted this collection of writings known as the Doctrine and Covenants as authentic and binding on the church as a whole, including the priesthood quorums.

---

39. A comparison of section 2 of the 1835 Doctrine and Covenants with chapter 24 of the *Book of Commandments* shows the addition of the office of high priest, bishop, and high councilor. This is an example of how Joseph Smith changed the text of his instructions based on new insights into church organization and governance. See Howard, *Restoration Scriptures*, 160.

CHAPTER NINE

Establishing the Church in Zion, 1831–1833

Creating Sacred Community

THE STORY OF the church in Independence, Jackson County, Missouri, is a story of community building. Located on the then-western border of the United States, this newly created frontier town became Mormonism's most serious attempt to create sacred community. Here the original church members encountered the enormous challenge of fulfilling their divinely commissioned mandate to move to Zion and prepare for the Second Coming of Christ.

Early on, Joseph Smith Jr. became intrigued by the scriptural admonition to usher in the millennial reign. The young prophet felt he was especially groomed to assist in that process, but how to accomplish the task remained an enigma. Leaders of other religious groups pursued their own ways to facilitate Christ's return. For example, Theophilus Ransom Gates, the impoverished Connecticut farmer turned popular, self-appointed preacher, published widely in Christian journals that the millennium would be explicitly individualist. According to Gates, the Holy Spirit would work within the individual Christian and outside all religious institutions. Particularly unnecessary were any "prophets" who allegedly spoke for God.[1]

Of course, Joseph Smith rejected Gates's view. Rather, he felt the best way to prepare for the Advent of Christ was to establish sacred

---

1. Hatch, *Democratization of American Christianity*, 176.

community. But this would be a hybrid community based on Old and New Testament beliefs couched in a contemporary American cultural setting. In no metaphysical sense, Smith named this special community the literal Center Place of Zion. That he would perceive God as choosing the new American nation as the geographic center for the redemption of the world is quite understandable. The theology of Joseph Smith's religious movement, priesthood qualification and organization, hymnody, scripture, and even many of the sacraments would be best understood in an early nineteenth-century American social context.[2] Smith drew from his seventeenth-century New England Puritan roots by attempting to make real their vision of "the city on a hill."

Church members who migrated to Independence in the early 1830s intended to replicate the same covenant made with God by the Children of Israel in their flight out of Egypt.[3] These Saints, too, would search for the Promised Land, to be found, of course, somewhere in the New World. Likewise, they held great aspirations to become God's people, but living in this New Covenant demanded adherence to the principles and practices of the "Primitive Church." Christian primitivism was the popular belief in the possibility of restoring the "ancient order" of the original first-century apostolic church. Achieving this required stripping away all doctrinal and administrative vestiges of modernity that had contaminated

---

2. The emphasis placed on Joseph Smith's Americanization of the gospel is not new. Historian Klaus Hansen made this argument as early as 1967. See his *Quest for Empire: The Political Kingdom of God and the Council of Fifty in Mormon History* (East Lansing: Michigan State University Press, 1967), 8–9.

3. Examples of this identification with the Children of Israel abound in early Latter Day Saint literature. For example, see the "The Sixth of April," *The Evening and the Morning Star* 1, no. 11 (April 1833): [5]:

> On the 6th of April, between seventy and eighty ordained members, representing more than five hundred members of the church of Christ, met for instruction, serving God, &c. in the land of Zion, and spent the day, from ten till four o'clock, very agreeably.
>
> It affords us much pleasure to record this little fact. When the foundations of this earth were laid, the morning stars sang together, and all the sons of God shouted for joy: the Passover was kept solemnly by the children of Israel, and so let the solemnities of eternity rest upon our minds, since the Lord has been so merciful as to re-establish his church for the last time, in these last days.

"the one true church." Joseph's followers knew that their day—the new dispensation—had finally arrived, and now they were to be the builders of the New Jerusalem.

As scriptural literalists, the Saints understood full well the prophecy from Isaiah that "I [the Lord] will proceed to do a marvellous work among this people, even a marvellous work and a wonder."[4] They also knew well Ezekiel's prophecy stating:

> Take thee one stick, and write upon it, For Judah, and for the children of Israel his companions: then take another stick, and write upon it, For Joseph, the stick of Ephraim, and for all the house of Israel his companions: And join them one to another into one stick; and they shall become one in thine hand. And when the children of thy people shall speak unto thee, saying, Wilt thou not shew us what thou meanest by these? Say unto them, Thus saith the Lord God; Behold, I will take the stick of Joseph, which is in the hand of Ephraim, and the tribes of Israel his fellows, and will put them with him, even with the stick of Judah, and make them one stick, and they shall be one in mine hand. And the sticks whereon thou writest shall be in thine hand before their eyes. And say unto them, Thus saith the Lord God; Behold, I will take the children of Israel from among the heathen, whither they be gone, and will gather them on every side, and bring them into their own land: And I will make them one nation in the land upon the mountains of Israel; and one king shall be king to them all: and they shall be no more two nations, neither shall they be divided into two kingdoms any more at all: Neither shall they defile themselves any more with their idols, nor with their detestable things, nor with any of their transgressions: but I will save them out of all their dwelling places, wherein they have sinned, and will cleanse them: so shall they be my people, and I will be their God.[5]

Reading from the Book of Mormon, their uniquely American scripture, only confirmed the Saints' understanding of the times in which they lived:

---

4. Isaiah 29:14 KJV.
5. Ezekiel 37:16–23 KJV. Although most of today's students of scripture reject this "stick of Joseph" interpretation, the first generation Saints embraced it fully.

> A seer will I raise up out of the fruit of thy loins; and unto him will I give power to bring forth my word unto the seed of thy loins; And not to the bringing forth my word only, saith the Lord, but to the convincing them of my word, which shall have already gone forth among them. Wherefore, the fruit of thy loins shall write; and the fruit of the loins of Judah shall write; And that which shall be written by the fruit of thy loins, and also that which shall be written by the fruit of the loins of Judah, shall grow together, Unto the confounding of false doctrines, and laying down of contentions, and establishing peace among the fruit of thy loins, And bringing them to the knowledge of their fathers in the latter days; And also to the knowledge of my covenants, saith the Lord. And out of weakness he shall be made strong, in that day when my work shall commence among all my people, unto the restoring thee, O house of Israel, saith the Lord. And thus prophesied Joseph, saying: Behold, that seer will the Lord bless; And they that seek to destroy him, shall be confounded: For this promise, of which I have obtained of the Lord, of the fruit of thy loins, shall be fulfilled. Behold, I am sure of the fulfilling of this promise. And his name shall be called after me; and it shall be after the name of his father. And he shall be like unto me; for the thing which the Lord shall bring forth by his hand, by the power of the Lord shall bring my people unto salvation; Yea, thus prophesied Joseph, I am sure of this thing, even as I am sure of the promise of Moses: for the Lord hath said unto me, I will preserve thy seed for ever. And the Lord hath said, I will raise up a Moses; and I will give power unto him in a rod; And I will give judgment unto him in writing.[6]

Added to this Book of Mormon scripture were two prophetic statements. The first, given in Fayette, New York, in September 1830, called for missionaries to

> go unto the Lamanites, and preach my gospel unto them; and inasmuch as they receive thy teachings, thou shalt cause my church to be established among them, and thou shalt have revelations, but write them not by way of commandment. And now, behold, I say unto thee, that it is not revealed, and no man knoweth where the city shall be

---

6. II Nephi 2:17–33 (LDS 3:11-17).

built, but it shall be given hereafter. Behold, I say unto thee that it shall be on the borders by the Lamanites.[7]

Six months later the Saints still did not know where the city of Zion would be established, but in subsequent instruction were told to have patience:

> Thou shalt ask, and it shall be revealed unto thee in mine own due time, where the New Jerusalem shall be built. And, behold, it shall come to pass, that my servants shall be sent forth to the east, and to the west, to the north, and to the south; and even now, let him that goeth to the east, teach them that shall be converted to flee to the west; and this in consequence of that which is coming on the earth, and of secret combinations. Behold, thou shalt observe all these things, and great shall be thy reward; for unto thee it is given to know the mysteries of the kingdom, but unto the world it is not given to know them.[8]

Even with its uncertainty this message became one of the many proselytizing tools for early church missionaries. Converts were captivated by four revelatory admonitions given between April and June 1829, all introduced by the claim that "a great and marvelous work" was about to come forth.[9]

Connecting their prophet Joseph's teachings to the Bible, the tribes of Israel, and the Book of Mormon required little imagination for these believers. But what was that great and marvelous work? How would the disciples prepare for it? And then how would they fulfill their calling to usher it in? Finding the answer became their life's purpose because the stakes were very high for believers who just knew that the Christian church was on the brink of disintegration. Even more important for them was their personal salvation. The sacred community was the physical location of the interplay between life in this world and life in the next; this was to be a sacred community, indeed. The way they lived out their millennial expectation separated the Mormons from other primitivist restoration churches.

---

7. Doctrine and Covenants 27:3a–d (LDS 28:8–9).
8. Doctrine and Covenants 42:17b–18b (LDS 42:62–65).
9. Doctrine and Covenants 6:1a; 10:1a; 11:1a; and 12:1a (LDS 6:1; 11:1; 12:1; and 14:1).

"Go unto the Lamanites"

EARLY CHURCH MEMBERS pinned their salvation on one man—Joseph Smith Jr., their modern day Moses—to lead them to that Promised Land. Through their American scripture, the Book of Mormon, they could assist the "remnant of Israel" to come to the same understandings. They claimed that this book not only identified the Native American as that remnant but also told their own history. Thus, the Book of Mormon became an important proselytizing tool, at least during the early years. The church conference held in late September 1830 in Fayette, New York, commissioned the first Latter Day Saint missionaries to take the gospel to the Native Americans. Who specifically was to go and their destination was yet to be determined, as the prophet shared only that the New Zion was located "on the borders by the Lamanites."[10] Then, Joseph filled in the details. He identified the second elder, Oliver Cowdery, as mission leader, whose purpose was to "go unto the Lamanites" and preach the gospel, and also establish a church among them.[11] Three other missionaries to join Cowdery were Parley P. Pratt, Peter Whitmer Jr., and Richard Ziba Peterson. The team embarked on their twelve-hundred-mile journey to the western border of the United States in October 1830.

By the time the team arrived in Independence, Missouri, they had experienced a roller coaster pattern of successes and failures. The team left with the divine assurance of success in the Fayette conference, followed by failure near Buffalo, New York, by tremendous success at their next stop, Kirtland, Ohio, and by failure once again in Sandusky and Cincinnati, Ohio—all before their arrival in Independence. The first opportunity to share the Book of Mormon with the Lamanites occurred near Buffalo. The Cattaraugus tribe kindly received the Mormon missionaries, who spent part of one day instructing them on the sacred history of their ancestors. In his autobiography Parley Pratt did not mention any baptisms, thus suggesting questionable success of the first encounter. Pratt wrote only that they left two copies of the Book of Mormon with the tribal members who

---

10. *Book of Commandments* 30:9.
11. *Book of Commandments* 30:7.

could read and then pressed on.[12] Because of their belief in the divine origins of the Book of Mormon and their revelatory commission, the failure to make converts in their first encounter must have been a surprise.

Contemplating the next leg of their journey, the team traveled two hundred miles farther westward to Kirtland, Ohio, to meet with Pratt's friend and former instructor Sidney Rigdon. Within just a few weeks of proselytizing, the team baptized 127 people. Among the converts would be several key leaders besides Rigdon, including Isaac Morley, John Murdock, Lyman Wight, and Edward Partridge. Also among the new converts was a future counselor to the prophet, Frederick Granger Williams, a physician whose skills could prove useful on the difficult journey; so he joined them in their trek westward.

Their next stop was fifty miles west of Kirtland, possibly Strongsville, Ohio.[13] Here they continued their proselytizing, making some friends but also some enemies. Pratt wrote of his arrest during this stop, and of his harrowing escape. He claimed the sheriff's warrant was based on "a very frivolous charge" supported by "false witnesses." The intent of his accusers was, as Pratt described, to test the "powers of [his] apostleship."[14] At the initial hearing, Pratt made no defense in the presence of his accusers and scoffed at the charges. The magistrate bound Pratt over for trial and placed him under house arrest. The trial went through the first day without decision and was adjourned until the next day. On the morning of the second day, an officer took Pratt to breakfast at a local inn where Pratt found his colleagues. He whispered to them to continue on the journey and that he would catch up with them. They left without incident.

During the breakfast, Pratt admired the officer's big bull dog. The Mormon missionary learned that the officer had trained his powerful dog to chase down escapees. As they ate breakfast, Pratt planned his escape.

---

12. Parley P. Pratt Jr., ed., *Autobiography of Parley Parker Pratt* (Salt Lake City: Deseret Book Company, 1976), 47.

13. In his autobiography, Pratt did not specify the exact location where this incident occurred. This speculation is based on the route of Pratt's return trip, which appeared to be a retracing of his outbound route.

14. Pratt did not become an apostle until 12 February 1835. It is possible that his accusers were making the statement cynically since the claim of the restoration of the twelve apostles during Pratt's generation was viewed with great skepticism by nonbelievers.

Evidently the officer had such confidence in the dog that he did not brandish a weapon. So when the two men emerged from the inn, Pratt turned to the officer, thanked him for the lodging and the breakfast, and stated: "I must now go on my journey; if you are good at a race you can accompany me." Then Pratt calmly walked away. The officer stood confounded as Pratt picked up his pace, anticipating that the officer would release the bull dog at any moment. Then Pratt went into a full sprint "like that of a deer." When the officer released his dog, the gap closed quickly as Pratt made it into the nearby woods. The officer urged on the dog by yelling, "Stu-boy, stu-boy...down with him" and clapping his hands. Pratt's quick thinking may have saved him. Just as the dog was about to pounce, the missionary stopped, turned to the approaching dog, and imitating the officer's voice, yelled, "Stu-boy, stu-boy...down with him" and pointed forward. Obediently the dog continued his sprint through the trees. By now deep into the woods, Pratt abruptly changed his direction away from both man and dog, never to see or hear from either again.[15]

Not long after his escape, Pratt met up with his fellow travelers and together they continued their trek. The next stop on their journey was Sandusky, Ohio, where the team preached to the Wyandotte Indians, a Native American tribe victimized by the Indian Removal Act passed on 28 May 1830. This act provided legal cover for those wanting desirable ancestral homelands of the original occupants.[16] The missionary team spent several days with the tribe, who prepared for their removal to the western territories. Again, the missionaries were well received but recorded no baptisms.

The missionaries continued on to Cincinnati, Ohio, where they spent several days preaching but again with little success. About 20 December, they took passage on an Ohio River steamer bound for St. Louis, Missouri. At Cairo, Illinois, located at the confluence of the Ohio and Mississippi Rivers, their boat encountered treacherous ice floes. The danger was reason enough for the captain to dock his steamer and await safer travel conditions. Because of their unscheduled delays in Kirtland and Sandusky, the missionary team set out on foot and headed north to St. Louis. Heavy rain

15. Pratt, *Autobiography*, 49–51.
16. For more on the plight of the Native American during this era of church history, see Dee Brown, *Bury My Heart at Wounded Knee: An Indian History of the American West* (New York: Harcourt/Holt, Rinehart & Winston, 2007).

Establishing the Church in Zion: 1831–1833

MAP BY JOHN HAMER

Route of the missionaries to the Lamanites (boundaries as of 1830)

and snow made travel difficult. At times they plodded through three-foot drifts but always preached along the way to anyone who would listen. The men finally arrived and recuperated briefly in St. Louis.

After the first of the year, they launched out again on foot, heading west. They passed through St. Charles, toward Independence, and covered some three hundred miles. This last leg of the trek was especially difficult since they were without trails or roads and found few homes to shelter them from the elements. Pratt wrote, "We travelled for whole days, from morning until night, without a house or fire, wading in snow to the knees at every step, and the cold so intense that the snow did not melt on the south side of the houses, even in the mid-day sun, for nearly six weeks."[17] After much difficulty, the team arrived in Independence, Jackson County, Missouri, on 15 January 1831.

17. Pratt, *Autobiography*, 52.

Early Missionary Efforts in Jackson County, Missouri

THE LAMANITE MISSION took four months of travel, mostly on foot, from western New York to the western border of the United States. In his enthusiasm, Pratt may have exaggerated that his team preached to "tens of thousands" of Gentiles and baptized and confirmed "many hundreds of people," organizing them into "churches of Latter Day Saints."[18] But they were the "Lamanite" missionaries and they had preached to two Native American nations. They also succeeded in finding in Independence a suitable location to stage an aggressive proselytizing campaign "among the Lamanites."

Not long after arriving in Independence, the missionary team divided forces. They had exhausted their resources just to get there, so Whitmer and Peterson found work as tailors while Cowdery, Pratt, and Williams, with Book of Mormon in hand, ventured out into Unorganized Territory some twenty miles west of Independence. During the first night in the western territory, the three stayed in the camp of a Shawnee tribe. The following day they crossed the Kansas River to preach and teach among the Delaware tribe. The three missionaries stayed with a Mr. Pool, retained by the federal government as a blacksmith, who eventually became their translator. For several days, as the team proselytized, more tribal members came to hear the Book of Mormon story.

Although the stories piqued their interest, the details of the Book of Mormon could not match the greater needs of this dislocated people. The Delaware were newly arrived and the snow was deep and threatened their tribal livestock. They had houses to build, fences to erect, and a council house to construct, all before they could take seriously the intricacies of the Book of Mormon. The chieftain, however, did invite Cowdery and the others to return to tell them more.[19] As with the Wyandotte, the missionaries left copies of the Book of Mormon with those among the Delaware who could read. With some enthusiasm, tribal elders even began to spread the

---

18. If Pratt meant this reference literally, his reminiscence would have been anachronistic, since the name "The Church of the Latter Day Saints" was not officially adopted until 3 May 1834. Thus one must assume that Pratt's reference here is informal.

19. Oliver Cowdery provided the text of his "Speech to the Delawares" and gave the Delaware chief's reply in *DHC*, 1: 183–85.

Establishing the Church in Zion: 1831–1833 175

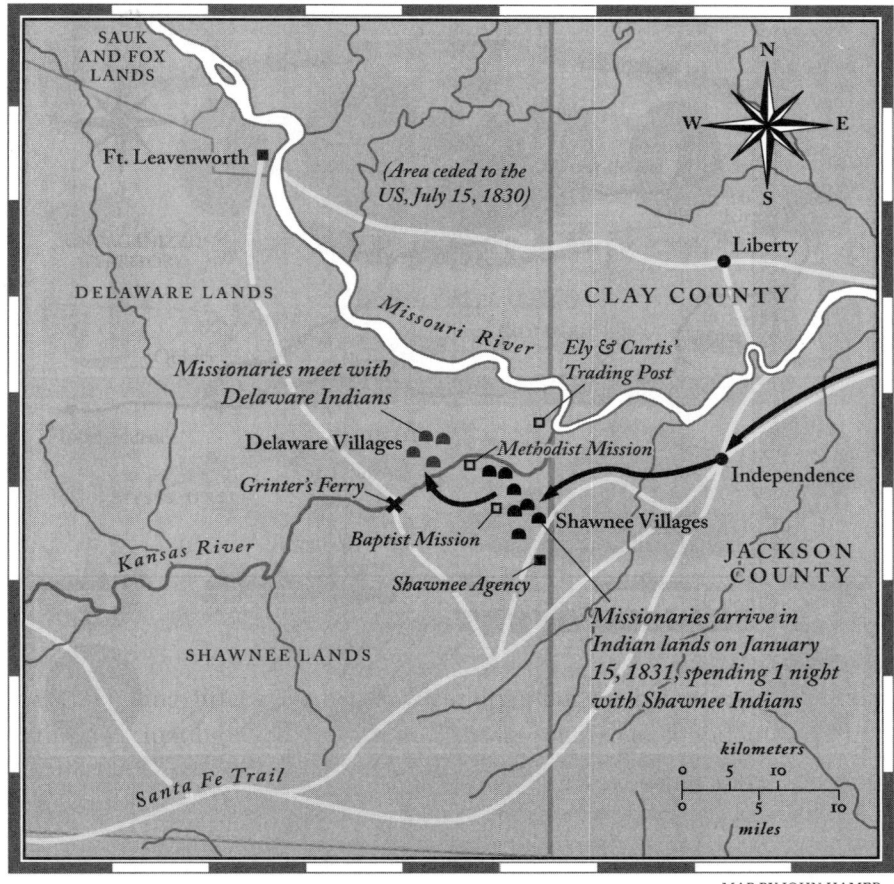

MAP BY JOHN HAMER

Missionary activities in the unorganized territory west of Jackson County, Missouri (boundaries as of 1830)

Book of Mormon story themselves. For the first time, the missionary team felt they were making substantive progress in converting the Lamanites to the gospel. Large numbers of baptisms had yet to happen, but the prospects seemed very encouraging.

The Mormon missionaries were jubilant about their inroads with the Delaware, but their enthusiasm was short lived. A federal law prohibited contact between Native Americans and whites on Indian lands without a special license from the superintendent of Indian Affairs, General William

Clark.[20] Because they had not obtained permission during their recuperation in St. Louis in early January, they did not have the required papers to allow them to circulate legally among the Native Americans.

Shawnee Indian agent Richard Cummins had enforced the restriction on other interlopers the previous fall and had little patience now with these missionaries. Cummins ordered them out of the territory on threat of imprisonment. Appeals were necessary, so independently both Cummins and Cowdery pleaded their cases through letters to Clark's office. Upholding his responsibilities, Cummins rationalized: "I have refused to let them stay or, go among the Indians unless they first obtain permission from you, or some of the officers of the Genl. Government who I am bound to obey."[21] Also writing to Superintendent Clark, Oliver Cowdery declared:

> As I have been appointed by a society of Christians in the State of New York to superintend the establishing Missions among the Indians I doubt not but I shall have the approbation of your honour and a permit for myself and all who may be recommended to me by that Society to have free intercourse with the several tribes in establishing schools for the instruction of their children and also teaching them

---

20. William Clark served two terms as superintendent of Indian Affairs headquartered in St. Louis. His first appointment began in 1808 and ended in 1813. He served as the last governor of Missouri Territory until statehood in 1821. Clark concluded his career of government service by resuming his superintendence of Indian Affairs from 1821 until his death in 1838. The Lamanite Missionaries arrived in St. Louis during Clark's second tour of duty as superintendent. Native American relations, both warlike and peaceful, were always of great interest to Clark. The Great Explorer helped suppress uprisings against the Winnebago and Black Hawks; and after the War of 1812, he negotiated a number of important peace treaties with Native American tribes. Weighing the reputations of the two explorers, most contemporaries held Clark in higher esteem because of the mysterious death of his partner, Meriwether Lewis, on 11 October 1809. Today, historians remain in doubt whether Lewis committed suicide or was murdered. In 1889–1891, historian Henry Adams, in his multivolume history of Thomas Jefferson, hardly mentioned the Lewis and Clark expedition. This may be because of the controversial circumstances of Lewis's death; but more important, Clark's service as superintendent was far more well-known to Adams's generation and received much greater appreciation. For more explanation on this observation see Ambrose, *Undaunted Courage*, 484.

21. Warren A. Jennings, "The First Mormon Mission to the Indians," *The Kansas Historical Quarterly* 37 (Autumn 1971): 298.

the Christian religion without intruding or interfering with any other Mission now established.[22]

The team held out little hope that their letter would get them their authority, so on 14 February 1831 they decided that one of them should go to St. Louis, make personal appeal, and then return with the required legal papers. Pratt got the nod and left the following day. He covered an exhausting thirty miles per day.

The record is unclear about the time Pratt actually spent in St. Louis. Presumably, he argued his case at Clark's office, but his pleadings would not have been with Clark himself since the Great Explorer left St. Louis in November 1830 and did not return until the following March. However, Pratt could have met with Clark's subagent, John Ruland, who had the authority to grant permission. That the missionaries never received the papers suggests that either Ruland supported Cummins's decision and rejected Pratt's appeal or that Ruland overturned Cummins's decision and sent the papers by courier, but that they were lost in transit. There is no evidence of a decision from Clark's office either way.

Oliver Cowdery understood that Pratt would return to Independence with the papers. Instead Pratt continued on east to share the hopeful news at church headquarters in Fayette, New York.[23] Pratt's optimism for the mission's success was based more on potential than achievement. The missionaries had exhausted their financial resources and were in short supply of their American scripture. Following the prophet's instructions, they presented the Book of Mormon story directly to the Cattaraugus, Wyandotte, and Delaware tribes resulting in few, if any, Lamanite baptisms. Finally, federal government officials forced the missionaries out of the territory.

Basically retracing his route home, Pratt took a week-long steamboat passage from St. Louis to Cincinnati then walked the 250 miles to Strongsville, Ohio.[24] Here Pratt was stricken with measles, convalesced

---

22. Jennings, "First Mormon Mission," 298.
23. Pratt could not have known that by this time Joseph Smith was moving the church headquarters to its temporary location, Kirtland, Ohio.
24. In his autobiography, Pratt probably misspelled the name of this Ohio community. Today's spelling is Strongsville. See Pratt, *Autobiography*, 58.

for several days, and then rode on horseback the remaining distance to Kirtland, arriving in mid-March 1831; here he learned that, in response to revelation,[25] church headquarters had moved there. When Pratt rode into Kirtland, a throng of hundreds gathered to hear his story. He excited his audience and encouraged the Saints to gather to Jackson County. Convinced also of the importance of the journey, the prophet prepared for his first visit to Independence.

From "Lamanite" to "Gentile" Missionaries

OLIVER COWDERY AND the other missionaries in Jackson County did not sit idly by awaiting word from either Pratt or the prophet. Two important observations should be made at this point. First, the missionaries meeting such strong resistance during their brief excursion into Unorganized Territory should have alerted them to the "clash of cultures" that would result during their sacred community building that lay just beyond the horizon. Second, the significant outcome of the legal obstacles preventing the team from preaching to the Lamanites actually changed the original purpose of the mission from taking the Book of Mormon to the Native American, to whom the book was written, to proselytizing the Gentiles in western Missouri. Undaunted by their circumstances, Joseph Smith's "Lamanite Missionaries" became the "Gentile Missionaries" and began an aggressive effort to convert white settlers in western Missouri at a pivotal time in Mormon history as well as the history of the region.

Missouri state government officials drew the original boundary lines for Jackson County on 15 December 1826. With the newly created circuit court for western Missouri, established in Independence in March 1827, plans were made and then implemented for the frontier community to be

---

25. See Doctrine and Covenants 38:7a–d (LDS 38:31–33):

> And that ye might escape the power of the enemy, and be gathered unto me a righteous people, without spot and blameless: wherefore, for this cause I gave unto you the commandment, that you should go to the Ohio; and there I will give unto you my law; and there you shall be endowed with power from on high, and from thence, whosoever I will, shall go forth among all nations, and it shall be told them what they shall do; for I have a great work laid up in store, for Israel shall be saved, and I will lead them whithersoever I will, and no power shall stay my hand.

the seat of government for the county. Three months later Independence was platted and town lots were sold as settlers took advantage of the numerous clear springs providing abundant supplies of water. Geographically, Independence was well situated, being close to Missouri River traffic and, a decade later, a jumping off point for three transcontinental routes—the Santa Fe, California, and Oregon Trails—that would shape the nation, its history, and its people.

In the months following Pratt's departure, the Independence, Missouri, economy received the boost of a lawyer, miller, and various merchants, all but guaranteeing the future of the settlement and its prominence on the western border of the United States.[26] As with original settlers in other newly opened territories in the American West, the names they chose for their jurisdictions signified the values of a proud, patriotic people and the national leaders they admired most: Independence, Liberty, Columbia, and Jefferson City, and the counties of Lafayette, Jackson, and Clay. For the original white settlers, Independence brimmed with optimism and prosperity, that is, until the Mormon migrations threatened them.

A Clash of Cultures

MEMBERS OF THE fledgling religious movement heard the call of their prophet, Joseph Smith, to establish the New World Jerusalem on the prairie of the American frontier. The Saints were attracted particularly to millenarian prophecy specifying that the Second Coming would be initiated on the American continent. Over time, adherence to that spiritual direction became a test of fellowship. When Smith prophesied the creation of Zion out West, he commissioned the members to claim their inheritance there.[27] As stated earlier, frequently church leaders placed followers in the role of the tribes of Israel.[28] Declaring an inheritance in

---

26. Sherry Lamb Schirmer and Richard D. McKinzie, *At the River's Bend: An Illustrated History of Kansas City, Independence, and Jackson County* (Woodland Hills, Calif.: Windsor Publications, Inc., 1982), 15.

27. See Doctrine and Covenants 55:2b, 63:13b, 64:6b, and 87:7b (LDS 55:5; 63:48; 64:30; and 87:30).

28. For example, see William W. Phelps, "To the Saints," *The Evening and the Morning Star* 1, no. 6 (November 1832): [6]. "Have you fulfilled the commandment, which saith: Behold I the Lord have appointed a way for the journeying of my saints, and behold

COMMUNITY OF CHRIST LIBRARY-ARCHIVES
The frontier community of Independence, Missouri (view from south)

Missouri, such as identified in Ezekiel 48:29, "This is the land which ye shall divide by lot unto the tribes of Israel for inheritance, and these are their portions, saith the Lord God," exemplified Joseph's theological and motivational genius.

The early disciples understood their inheritance in the context of removing to the sacred geography of Zion, but it was far more than that. An inheritance was also a divine promise of safety and security in both this life and the next depending on their willing response to be God's chosen people. But to receive their inheritance involved a process. On their arrival in Independence, the bishop in Zion, Edward Partridge, would locate the family on a particular tract of land where, through their hard work, the family would contribute their surplus to the church storehouse. From their designated plot of land in Zion they would live in righteousness and await Christ's coming. An inspired statement addressed to the elders who had come to Independence in July 1831 offered detailed instruction:

> Hearken, O ye elders of my church saith the Lord your God, who have assembled yourselves together, according to my commandments, in

---

this is the way: That after they leave the canal, they shall journey by land, inasmuch as they are commanded to journey and go up unto the land of Zion; and they shall do like unto the children of Israel, pitching their tents by the way?"

> this land which is the land of Missouri, which is the land which I have appointed and consecrated for the gathering of the Saints: wherefore this is the land of promise, and the place for the city of Zion. And thus saith the Lord your God, If you will receive wisdom here is wisdom. Behold, the place which is now called Independence, is the Center Place, and the spot for the temple is lying westward upon a lot which is not far from the courthouse; wherefore it is wisdom that the land should be purchased by the Saints; and also every tract lying westward, even unto the line running directly between Jew and Gentile. And also every tract bordering by the prairies, inasmuch as my disciples are enabled to buy lands. Behold, this is wisdom, that they may obtain it for an everlasting inheritance.[29]

This revelation sealed the enduring gift of inheritance in both this life and the next.

The inheritance was also tied to the Law of Consecration and Stewardship to be fulfilled in Zion; thus, the divine promise proffered economic salvation. Here the storehouse principle provided for resources to be distributed equitably between rich and poor believers. At a time in American history when destitution was just an ill-timed crop frost, hailstorm, or debilitating illness away, an inheritance held out great promise and security.

Smith bestowed God's protection on those willing to take the sacred journey to Zion. Recipients of their inheritance received the promise of physical safety amid the violence of American frontier life. This assurance removed much of the fear associated with trekking to an unknown land nearly a thousand miles away.

> Behold, I, the Lord, have made my church in these last days, like unto a judge sitting on a hill, or in a high place, to judge the nations; for it shall come to pass, that the inhabitants of Zion shall judge all things pertaining to Zion; and liars, and hypocrites shall be proved by them, and they who are not apostles and prophets shall be known. And even the bishop, who is a judge, and his counselors, if they are not faithful in their stewardships, shall be condemned, and others shall be planted in their stead; for, behold, I say unto you that Zion shall flourish, and the glory of the Lord shall be upon her, and she shall be an ensign unto the people, and there shall come unto her out of every nation under

---

29. Doctrine and Covenants 57:1a–g (LDS 57:1–5).

heaven. And the day shall come, when the nations of the earth shall tremble because of her, and shall fear because of her terrible ones. The Lord hath spoken it. Amen.[30]

Such divine assurances made the sacrifices of uprooting and moving to the remote western reaches of the United States easier to bear.

But most important, an inheritance was a millennial expression of personal salvation based on a doctrine of works. Believers who went "to build up Zion" as God's people secured their salvation at Judgment Day. Those who opposed them would suffer condemnation of their soul and pay an eternal price at the Second Coming while those with inheritances would be protected from God's wrath. Through the use of the inheritance, the prophet could discern the member's commitment by separating those loyal enough to make the difficult journey from those unwilling to make the sacrifices. The concept of inheritance, therefore, was an early expression of Smith's theology of works that would flower during the Nauvoo era a decade later.

Adherents westered to Zion mostly in wagon trains and used their common faith, and even geographic origins, to bind them together as God's chosen people. They traveled as individuals and families, but also as communities. In March 1831, it came time for the faithful to heed the call of their prophet to take the scriptures of Isaiah, Ezekiel, and II Nephi literally, and move westward to Zion. Joseph wrote his brother Hyrum at Colesville, in south-central New York, to bring the believers to Kirtland as soon as possible.

The sixty Saints, under their leader, Newel Knight, left Colesville and headed for Kirtland, Ohio. They floated the Cayuga and Seneca Canal to reach the Erie Canal and proceeded to Buffalo, where they wintered for several weeks due to harsh weather. By mid-May 1831, they reached Kirtland and were told to settle in nearby Thompson, Ohio, on the land controlled by newly converted Leman Copley. Copley followed the prophet's stewardship precepts by turning over his property to the church to be used as the leaders saw fit, but then Copley became disaffected and broke

---

30. Doctrine and Covenants 64:7c–8b (LDS 64:37–43).

the arrangement.³¹ He brought suit and won a judgment necessitating the removal of the Colesville community from his property.³² When Copley rejected his membership, Smith told the Colesville Saints to continue on west to lay the foundations for a primary gathering place in Independence, Missouri. Adhering to the command of their prophet, two dozen Colesville wagons trundled off to the Ohio River, continuing their sacred journey to secure their inheritance in Zion and to prepare for the Second Coming. The settlement left shortly after the church's fourth General Conference in early June 1831.

Also after the June 1831 conference, Joseph, Sidney Rigdon, Martin Harris, Edward Partridge, W. W. Phelps, Joseph Coe, Algernon Sidney Gilbert, and Gilbert's wife, Elizabeth, left Kirtland to visit Independence. Coincidentally the prophet's party booked passage on the same riverboat as the Colesville members, so together they traveled downriver to the Mississippi River, and then at St. Louis, on to the Missouri River. Since the Smith party traveled lighter, they decided they could make faster time on the trail. So Smith, Martin Harris, Edward Partridge, and Joseph Coe walked into Independence in late July, arriving several days ahead of those on the Colesville steamboat.

The Mormon leaders' initial reactions to Jackson County, Missouri, were quite mixed. They were overjoyed to meet with the missionaries, but were quite unimpressed with the Missouri citizens. Those who initially settled in Jackson County hailed mostly from Virginia, Kentucky, and Tennessee. Like Smith, these earlier immigrants were attracted by the "lay of the land." Strongly impacted by the western Missouri woodlands, reminiscent of their eastern homeland, Jackson County offered the lifestyle with which they were most familiar. The loose sod of cleared eastern forests broke easier than the baked-hard prairies to the west. The hardwoods had provided building supplies for their log cabins and eventually their

---

31. Actually Bishop Edward Partridge contracted for a loan to pay off Copley's debt. Copley was still in the process of purchasing the land and had not yet consummated the transaction. For more information, see Newell Knight's personal journal titled *Scraps of Biography* (Salt Lake City: Juvenile Instructor Office, 1883), 69.

32. A more complete explanation of the Law of Consecration and Stewardship, a revelatory mandate to provide property to the church for its use, will be provided later. That Copley won back his property in a lawsuit tested in Ohio courts should have signaled to church leaders the legal problems soon to come in Jackson County, Missouri.

sawmills.[33] They were "people of the forest." Also, they were hard living, rugged individualists who emulated the values of Andrew Jackson. They prided themselves with their pioneer heritage, inbred from early generations who had migrated from the populated Atlantic seaboard regions. The first white settlers of Jackson County were hardened with a restless instinct and driven to prosperity through self-advancement.[34]

Generally, Joseph Smith and his followers were "people of the village."[35] The Mormons originated from small northeastern communities, where collective values were as important as individual ones. The lifestyle, deeply rooted in the early English immigrant experience where people depended on each other for survival, was much more communal. Evidence of the cultural divide became noticeable early in the Mormon experience in Jackson County. On his arrival in late July 1831, the prophet had an unfavorable first impression of the pioneer Jackson County residents:

> Coming as we had from a highly cultivated state of society in the east, and standing now upon the confines or western limits of the United States, and looking into the vast wilderness of those that sat in darkness; how natural it was to observe the degradation, leanness of intellect, ferocity, and jealousy of a people that were nearly a century behind the times, and to feel for those who roamed about without the benefit of civilization, refinement, or religion.[36]

As the Missouri citizens had similar impressions of the newly arrived Mormons, confrontations were bound to happen.

The Importance of Sacred Geography

ANY DOUBTS, HOWEVER, about the sacredness of western Missouri geography were put to rest when Joseph received confirmation through revelation that this would be "the land appointed...and consecrated for the

33. Schirmer and McKinzie, *At the River's Bend*, 18.
34. Ray Allen Billington and Martin Ridge, *Westward Expansion: A History of the American Frontier*, 5th ed. (New York: Macmillan Publishing Co., 1982), 409–12.
35. Historian Paul M. Edwards invoked this term. See his explanation in *Our Legacy of Faith: A Brief History of the Reorganized Church of Jesus Christ of Latter Day Saints* (Independence, Mo.: Herald House, 1991), 57.
36. *DHC*, 1: 189.

gathering of the Saints."[37] Jackson County was to be the actual location of the Center Place of Zion, the New Jerusalem. Smith must have anticipated this because before he left Kirtland a month earlier he commissioned eleven teams of missionaries, traveling two by two, to Independence. They were to preach along the way, and when they arrived in Independence they, too, would receive their inheritances. When they completed their commitments, the few missionaries who remained behind provided the ecclesiastical foundation for the Missouri church to take its place in Zion and to await the arrival of the Kirtland church.[38]

On 25 July 1831, several days after Smith's party arrived in Independence, the Colesville Saints off-loaded their possessions at the Missouri River wharf, then flatboated up the Big Blue River. They planted their settlement between Independence and the western border of the United States. Young emigrant Emily Austin recalled that they resorted

> to flat boats to take us up the river to the mouth of the Big Blue, in Jackson county, and to the ferry landing, and here we disembarked and our journey was ended, except for a few miles by land into the country. And as I had been informed of the direction, I walked on in advance of the company, not intending to lose sight of those who were shortly coming. I walked on slowly, thinking how strange it was to think of this being the Hill of Zion.[39]

The mysticism of being in Zion had a powerful impact. Austin's statement revealed the wonderment that set in upon the new settlers' arrival in Independence. The struggles of the 900-mile sacred journey quickly yielded to the struggles of building sacred community.

37. Doctrine and Covenants 57:1a (LDS 57:1).
38. Eventually the separation between the two churches would become a source of conflict remedied only by prophetic direction (see Doctrine and Covenants 85 [LDS 88]) and the eventual merger at Far West, Caldwell County, Missouri, in 1837–1838.
39. Emily Austin, *Mormonism; or, Life Among the Mormons* (Madison, Wis.: Cantwell, 1882), 65.

Building the Sacred Community on Sacred Land

AFTER A FEW days of touring the area, on 2 August 1831, the prophet appointed Sidney Rigdon to dedicate the land in Kaw Township to be occupied by the Colesville Branch and to lay the first log for a common building. The very next day Sidney and Joseph dedicated a heavily wooded tract of land on a rise just west of the Independence courthouse to be the location for the temple in Zion. During the dedication service, Joseph stripped some bark from a sapling and dropped a rock next to it to mark where the temple would be built. That the church did not own the land at the time seemed of little consequence, since the Second Coming and the initiation of God's law would preempt all human designs. However, the following December, Bishop Edward Partridge purchased from Jones Hoy Flournoy a 63-plus-acre tract of land that included the spot for a temple. The actual location of where Joseph barked the tree and dropped the rock is not well documented. Determining the specific location would remain a source of controversy for generations to come. Consecrating land in Independence, Missouri, exemplifies Joseph's practice of identifying sacred geography wherever he led his people throughout the Mormon journey.

On 4 August 1831, the first General Conference of Joseph Smith Jr.'s Missouri church was held in the home of new convert Joshua Lewis in Kaw Township. Approximately thirty members and fourteen elders received the Communion, followed by the prophet's sermon calling the membership to righteous living. In the days that remained before the prophet's entourage departed for Kirtland, Joseph attended a funeral for Polly Knight[40] and gave the last of four revelatory messages[41] that he delivered during his stay in western Missouri.

---

40. Polly Knight was the wife of Joseph Knight Sr. and the mother of Newel Knight, who led the Colesville Saints to Missouri. Her health failed as the trek to Zion progressed but she would not consent to stop traveling. Her greatest desire was to set her feet upon the land of Zion. Newel Knight, fearing she should die before arriving at their destination, went on shore at one point during the trip and bought lumber to make her coffin. Joseph Knight claimed that his wife was the first church member to die. See Newell Knight, *Scraps of Biography*, 70.

41. Doctrine and Covenants Section 57 (LDS 57) dedicated the "spot for the temple"; Section 58 (LDS 58) called for the laying of the foundations for Zion; Section 59 (LDS 59) offered blessings to those whose feet stand upon the land of Zion; and Section 60

Issues in Kirtland pressed for Joseph's return so he left on 9 August 1831, but the number of pilgrims arriving in Independence increased dramatically. Actually, the Colesville church members were an advance party of much larger migrations of followers headed west. With the passing of just a year, waves of Mormons seeking their inheritances arrived in Zion. Editor William W. Phelps reported in the church newspaper, *The Evening and the Morning Star*, that by November 1832 more than eight hundred Saints had gathered in Zion to receive their inheritances.[42]

During the spring of 1832, Joseph Smith made his second trip to Independence. Newell K. Whitney, Peter Whitmer Sr., and Jesse Gause joined in the prophet's journey. On 24 April 1832, the team arrived by stage coach. Two days later Joseph convened a conference to acknowledge his presidency of the high priesthood, just as he had done in Amherst, Ohio, for the Kirtland church a few months earlier. During his brief stay in Independence, the prophet spent two days at the Colesville settlement to bolster spirits. Also, on 1 May 1832, church leaders made the important decision for Phelps to use the church press to print three thousand copies of the *Book of Commandments*, a first attempt to organize a collection of Smith's revelatory statements,[43] and to print hymns selected by the prophet's wife, Emma Hale Smith.

(LDS 60) counseled those traveling from and to Zion, and cautioned against hesitance to bear their witness.

42. "The Gathering," *The Evening and the Morning Star* 1, no. 6 (November 1832): [5].

43. Earlier, at the 1 November 1831 Hiram, Ohio, conference, delegates, listed as less than a dozen elders, "made a request desiring the mind of the Lord" and determined that ten thousand copies would be most appropriate. See *Far West Record*, 26–27. This huge number ranged far beyond what could be afforded financially by the fledgling church and established a mandate that burdened the capabilities of W. W. Phelps, church printer in Independence, Missouri.

But another practical reality factored into the reduction—a scarcity of paper. The church's Independence press was the westernmost press in the United States and experienced difficulty in meeting expectations due at least in part to limited paper supplies. To meet this need the prophet purchased a supply of paper in Wheeling, West Virginia, and brought it to Zion during his spring 1832 trip. See *DHC*, 1: 243–44. Perhaps realizing these difficulties, on 30 April 1832, the Literary Firm, a committee tasked with coordinating the publication of the church resources, eased the pressure on Phelps and his press operation by reducing the ten thousand number to three thousand. Certainly this was a far more reasonable expectation. See *Far West Record*, 46.

Much to the chagrin of the Independence disciples, Joseph left them on 6 May 1832. But the prophet's actions during his visit removed any doubts among local citizens about the permanence of the Church of Christ's presence in Jackson County. His followers were there to stay. Just a month later Editor Phelps had the church printing press running, and he published the first issue of *The Evening and the Morning Star*. The church press being less than twenty miles from the United States border, and at least a hundred miles farther west than any other press, made the *Star* the westernmost mode of printed communication in the entire nation.

The Looming Problem of Numbers

BY EARLY 1833, hundreds of Mormons had gathered to Zion. The impact of these large numbers—the result of aggressive and successful evangelization—was considerable. The economic impact could be felt by all who settled in western Missouri. In the second issue of the *Star*, Phelps's concerns surfaced about the unmanageable numbers of migrants entering Jackson County:

> It is about one year since the work of the gathering commenced, in which time between three & four hundred have arrived here and are mostly located upon their inheritances, and are generally in good health and spirits and are doing well. The expenses of journeying and settling here, together with the establishing of a printing office and store, have probably exceeded the expectations of our brethren abroad, and although Zion, according to the prophets, is to become like Eden or the garden of the Lord, yet, at present it is as it were but a wilderness and desert, and the disadvantages of settling in a new country, you know, are many and great: Therefore, prudence would dictate at present the churches abroad, come not up to Zion, until preperations can be made for them.... The prospect for crops, in this region of country, is, at present, tolerable good, but calls for provisions will undoubtedly be considerable, for besides the emigration of the whites, the government of the United States is settling the Indians, (or remnants of Joseph) immediately to the west, and they must be fed.[44]

---

44. "The Elders in the Land of Zion to the Church of Christ Scattered Abroad," *The Evening and the Morning Star* 1, no. 2 (July 1832): [5].

By this time the church owned nearly two thousand prime acres in western Missouri. Although land sales promised to line the pockets of real estate speculators, much to the Missouri citizens' great frustration the Mormon purchases took valuable land off the market and began to drive up property values. Competition for good land became a constant source of irritation.

Politically, the challenge of such a large number of emigrants was daunting for the Missourians. The possibility of a political takeover of local government had to be avoided at all costs. The Missourians knew that the time would come when the Mormons would outnumber their votes. Controlling influential local government positions would negate the sacrifices of the earliest settlers in moving from their eastern homes to the Missouri frontier.

Theologically, Mormons considered themselves a chosen people commissioned to "build up the City of God" and to usher in the Second Coming. They were not afraid to communicate to Gentiles that the specific reason for their settlement in Jackson County was to receive their spiritual inheritance of salvation. Indeed, in instruction given on 8 August 1831, the day before he left Independence, the prophet admonished them about remaining silent.[45] Years later, in 1846, Mormon apostle Orson Pratt could have been referring to the perceived theological superiority of early church members who settled in Zion as he succinctly contrasted the Mormon "Doctrine of the Saints" with the "Doctrine of Sectarians" stating:

---

45. See Doctrine and Covenants 60:3d–4d (LDS 60:12–17):

> And now I speak of the residue who are to come unto this land. Behold, they have been sent to preach my gospel among the congregations of the wicked; wherefore, I give unto them a commandment thus:
> Thou shalt not idle away thy time; neither shalt thou bury thy talent that it may not be known. And after thou hast come up unto the land of Zion, and hast proclaimed my word, thou shalt speedily return, proclaiming my word among the congregations of the wicked. Not in haste, neither in wrath nor with strife; and shake off the dust of thy feet against those who receive thee not, not in their presence, lest thou provoke them, but in secret, and wash thy feet as a testimony against them in the day of judgment. Behold, this is sufficient for you, and the will of him who hath sent you. And by the mouth of my servant Joseph Smith, Jr., it shall be made known concerning Sidney Rigdon and Oliver Cowdery, the residue hereafter. Even so. Amen.

"He that believeth and is baptized shall be saved: he that believeth not shall be damned."[46] On this there could be no compromise.

The large Mormon presence, increasing almost daily, purchasing the best lands, jeopardizing the political interests of the citizens, and asserting theological exclusiveness created a volatile atmosphere in Jackson County. Isolated incidents of violence broke out in the early spring of 1832. Mormons reported burned haystacks and broken windows, while legal authorities ignored their complaints. Over time, the resistance became better organized and more violent. On 18 April 1833, a mob attacked one Mormon family with whips.

Sacred City Planning

THE VIOLENT ATMOSPHERE did not prevent Joseph Smith from developing his plans for the world's Holy City in America. On 25 June 1833, he sent his "Plat of the City of Zion" to church leaders in Independence. Although this plan did not subsequently assume revelatory sanction, his ideas for the sacred city may have emerged from his readings of Revelation 21 or Ezekiel 48.[47] Smith's plan called for a one-square-mile city divided into ten-acre blocks. Each block would be subdivided into half-acre lots, with one house per lot arranged on alternate streets so they would not face each other. At the city center was a temple complex reserved for twenty-four temples to be placed on two of three fifteen-acre blocks. Smith intended for each temple to fill a particular spiritual function in the church. This sacred ground was to be the most holy site in the "Center Place of Zion." To accommodate the Zionic stewardship plan, there were to be storehouses placed on acreages immediately north of the complex of temples. Streets of Zion were to be 135 feet wide—as the lore of the times suggested, this was the distance necessary for a teamster to make comfortably a 180-degree turn with his wagon. All residents were to live inside the city limits. Because their barns and stables were to be located

---

46. Orson Pratt, *The Prophetic Almanac for 1846* (New York: New York Messenger, 1846), n.p. Community of Christ Library-Archives.

47. This is Richard H. Jackson's observation in his excellent analysis of Mormon community building. See his "The Mormon Village: Genesis and Antecedents of the City of Zion Plan," *Brigham Young University Studies* 17, no. 2 (Winter 1977): 224.

on the city outskirts, Joseph must have had concerns for cleanliness in the Holy City. Mormon-owned farmland surrounded the sacred community.[48]

The margin notes scribbled on Smith's Plat of Zion reveal the millennial influence of the times. Smith proposed a city population of fifteen to twenty thousand saved souls in the City of Refuge. These numbers would result in a very high population density. According to the design, in Zion there were to be forty-two blocks with each containing twenty lots. There were also four larger blocks containing thirty-two lots. With only one house allowed for each lot, this plan would calculate to sixteen people per household with a maximum population of fifteen thousand, and twenty-one people at twenty thousand.[49] The closeness of community evidently facilitated the commonness of purpose and enhanced the spiritual condition of the people.

Joseph had second thoughts about his initial plan for settling his sacred city and sent a second plan to the Saints in Independence on 6 August 1833. His new plat extended the boundaries of the New Jerusalem to accommodate an increased total number of lots. Perhaps salvation would be extended to more people. He eliminated the storehouse designation, which showed his evolved thinking about his stewardship plan. Smith also reoriented the two temple blocks and reduced their size from fifteen to ten acres each.

Joseph Smith's overall attempt to redraw the map of Independence is significant in three ways. First, his concern showed the extent to which he asserted his prophetic leadership. A prophet of God needed also to be

48. Jackson suggested that the vast majority of initial settlements in America were laid out according to a definite plan. The grid pattern prescribed by Joseph Smith for the City of Zion contained some variations but little from those used throughout trans-Appalachia. Perhaps the most unique characteristic was the uniformity of the street width. Most town planners narrowed side streets to no more than ninety-nine feet. The plan for Far West, Missouri, laid out three years later, conformed to cityscapes across the Midwest. Smith ordered four large streets measuring 132 feet wide bordering a central square. Far West side streets narrowed to eighty-two and a half feet. All Nauvoo, Illinois, streets were uniform at fifty feet in width. See Jackson, "The Mormon Village," 238–39.

49. One can assume that each dwelling would include both nuclear and extended families. The population density of the lots in Zion gave hints of the primacy of the family in Mormon culture, a legacy that continues today in the LDS Church.

192   THE JOURNEY OF A PEOPLE

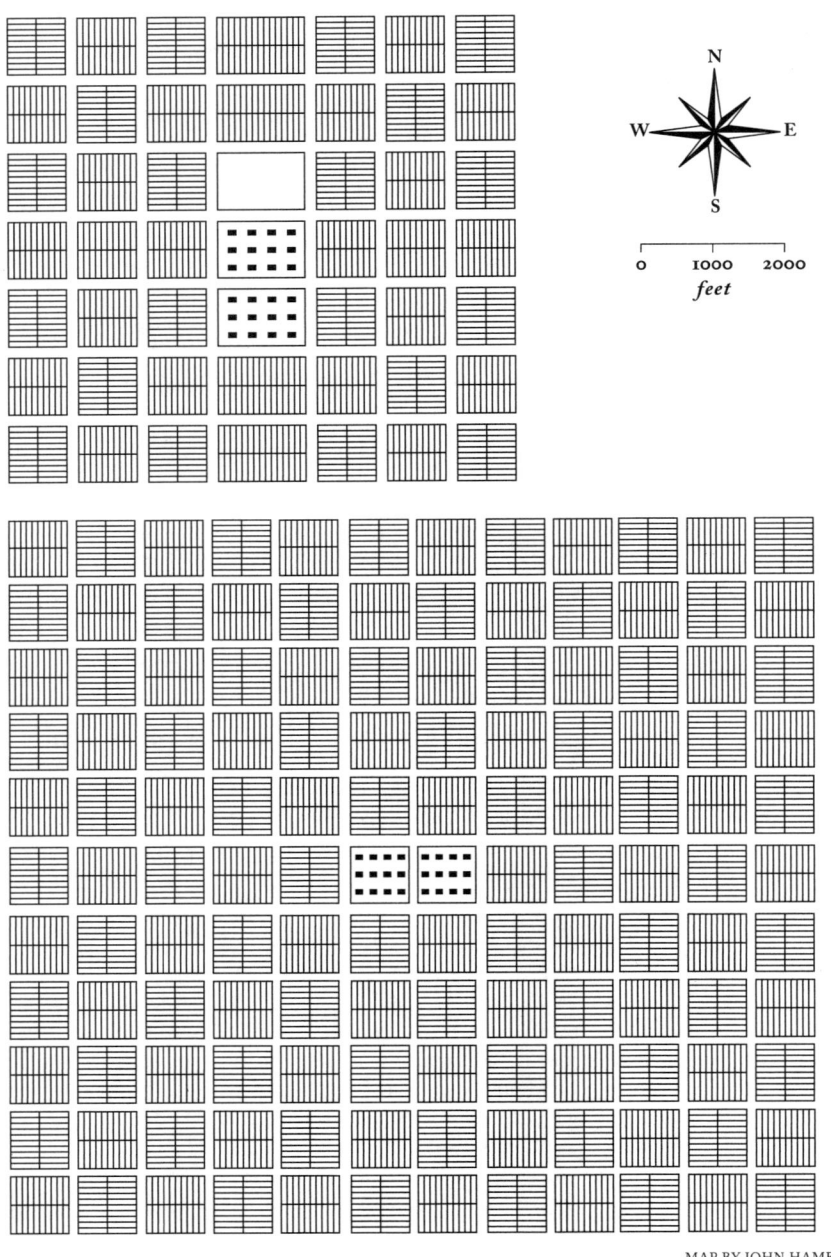

MAP BY JOHN HAMER

The original plat of Zion (top) and the larger, revised plat (bottom)

a city planner—especially for the Holy City. He later used the skills he learned in developing Zion to plan communities at Far West, Missouri, and Nauvoo, Illinois. Smith did not resort to specific details of the Plat of Zion in laying out his later cities; nevertheless, he did benefit from dealing with issues of where and how to accommodate the living needs of his people as they moved from one sacred community to the next along their journey.

Second, producing the Plat of Zion expressed Joseph Smith's penchant for connecting sacred geography to his evolving theology. He was not satisfied with theoretical religious practices; rather, his belief systems required physical appearance. Expressing Mormon theology went beyond just the planning of sacred communities; even the movement's most important buildings required architectural designs that conveyed both the values of his religious movement and the prophet's "Holiness to the Lord" tribute.[50]

Third, the Saints' privation grew severe long before Smith's second plat arrived in Independence. However, the prophet's redesign plan demonstrated his lack of understanding of the practical problems the followers had in their living circumstances in Zion between 1832 and 1833. He assumed that he could reorder the lives of Independence, Missouri, residents—both believers and nonbelievers—from Kirtland, Ohio, some nine hundred miles away. The physical separation from the Missouri church hindered him from making decisions based on updated information.[51]

Had the Missouri members attempted implementation of the 25 June plat and its revision of 6 August, they would have been compelled to buy up much more land around the central part of the town of

50. The prophet placed "Holiness to the Lord" above the entrance to the Nauvoo Temple. Members of the Reorganization continued this practice when they placed it above the Stone Church at Plano, Illinois, after the community became the location of its church headquarters in 1866.

51. There is the hazard of being overly judgmental here. Today, one must speculate about the thinking of a man living nearly 175 years earlier without the benefit of personal interview, while taking into account the dramatic cultural differences between then and now, and accepting the changed worldview of the passing generations. Still, it is possible to raise important questions: Did the prophet's anticipation of the imminent Second Coming prompt him to preempt the legal city plan, and was Smith influenced by a newly emerging transcendental intellect that acknowledged the existence of a higher power than that of organic law?

Independence. To the frustration of non-Mormon settlers, the attempt to purchase would have inflated prices. So in pushing forward on such a project the Saints would have quickly confronted the hostility of the Missouri citizens, who had already refused to sell out to the Mormon colonizers. This impasse would have incited further violence. The Missouri citizen demands for evacuation alone would have convinced Missouri Mormon leaders to place a hold on any implementation. The fact of the plats underscores the wide divide, both geographically and culturally, between church leaders in Kirtland and Independence and early settlers in Jackson County. In the explosive atmosphere during the summer of 1833, the physical expulsion of the Latter Day Saints required only a spark.

Volatility of the Printed Word

Two articles in the church's newspaper, *The Evening and the Morning Star*, turned impassioned fears into organized violence. The first article appeared on the front page of the July 1833 issue and warned believers to "Beware of False Prophets." This reference grew from several emotional exchanges between Mormons and other religious leaders in Jackson County about the rightness of church beliefs. Editor William W. Phelps must have discerned a need of his church member readership for counsel and encouragement to help them remain strong in the faith. Rhetorically, Phelps posed the questions:

> Brethren in the church of Christ, did you ever hear of a true prophet, that persecuted any one for his religion, whether pure or of man? Did you ever hear, or have you ever read of a true prophet, that spake evil of any man, or that would lie to further the cause of God, or any thing else? If you have, brethren, then has the hypocrite an excuse for leaving his own fault unexposed, and, publishing his neighbor's to the world![52]

To the predominant surrounding religious culture, Phelps's cautionary language turned inflammatory when he suggested that churchmen who criticized Mormons were "false prophets." Understandably this broadside struck sensitive nerves in the pastorates of other local churches.

---

52. "Beware of False Prophets," *The Evening and the Morning Star* 2, no. 14 (July 1833): [105].

The second article reached beyond local denominational disputes to the ubiquitous national slavery issue. As with "Beware of False Prophets," this second writing only added to the emotionally charged atmosphere. In his article Phelps quoted the laws of Missouri concerning prohibitions of free negroes and mulattoes from coming into or settling in the state under any pretext whatever without a certificate "evidencing that he is a citizen." Ironically, his opening phrase, "To prevent any misunderstanding...," had just the opposite effect. But most offensive was his poorly worded article title, "Free People of Color," that seemed to confirm gentile suspicions about Mormon views on slavery.[53]

One must wonder about the motives for choosing this article title. William W. Phelps, a veteran anti-Masonic political publisher, certainly knew better than most the power of the printed word and its impact on his readership. He was also quite aware of the hot-tempered mood of Jackson County citizens by the summer of 1833. Still, he chose the title "Free People of Color," injecting into an already unstable atmosphere clearly the most divisive issue in American society. His word choice elevated the rationale for persecution to a new level for original settlers prone to read only the headlines of a newspaper, and especially a Mormon one.

Perhaps Editor Phelps anticipated the arrival to Independence of free church members of color. Obviously this conjured up in the mind of the larger gentile population hundreds of free black Mormons moving to Jackson County. Actually, there was no evidence of such baptisms occurring or of migrations of people of color coming to Jackson County. One can only speculate that Phelps based his belief on either bold assumption about the success of proselytizing among free people of color, or on false rumor.

Indeed, in 1839, Parley P. Pratt, a member of the original Lamanite Mission to Jackson County, and by then a member of the Council of Twelve Apostles, knew the progress of the church quite authoritatively. Reflecting back on the persecution of the Church of Christ in Zion, Pratt stated emphatically: "In fact one dozen free negroes or mulattoes never have belonged to our Society in any part of the world, from its first organization to this day, 1839." Pratt continued his searing indictment of the

---

53. "Free People of Color," *The Evening and the Morning Star* 2, no. 14 (July 1833): 109.

Missouri gentile persecutors on this issue by claiming, "The statement concerning our invitation to them [free blacks and mulattoes] to become Mormons, and remove to this state, and settle among us, is a wicked fabrication."[54] Yet it was to these nonexistent church members that Phelps supposedly counseled caution.

A more likely motivation for the word choice in his article title may have been that Phelps had a concern about nonmember African Americans moving into Jackson County. In the last paragraph of "Free People of Color," Phelps summarized the chattel status of the slave in the eyes of Missouri state law: "Slaves are real estate in this and other states, and wisdom would dictate great care among the branches of the church of Christ, on this subject." The only sentence that might have defused the article was its last: "So long as we have no special rule in the church, as to people of color, let prudence guide, and while they, as well as we, are in the hands of a merciful God, we say: Shun every appearance of evil." But in irrational and emotionally charged times, even this statement could be interpreted as aiding and abetting or, worse, luring African Americans into the state.

Those wanting to expel the Mormons easily found in these articles ample reason to move against their peculiar and unwanted neighbors. Powerful community forces aligned against the Mormons. Respected local government and religious leaders were among eighty citizens who signed a "Secret Constitution" calling for a meeting on 20 July to determine their course of action. Clearly the citizen reaction caught Phelps by surprise, so to allay fears and set the record straight on his "Free People of Color" article, on 16 July he published a handbill titled "The Evening and the Morning Star Extra.----." From this handbill much can be learned about early church members' attitudes toward slavery and the possibility of free African Americans joining the church, as well as their attempts to reconcile with their gentile neighbors to save their community in Zion. The handbill text is provided here in its entirety:

> Having learned, with regret, that an article entitled FREE PEOPLE OF COLOR, in the last number of the Star, has been misunderstood, we feel in duty bound to state, in this Extra, that our intention was not only to stop free people of color from emigrating to this state, but to

---

54. Parley Parker Pratt, *History of Late Persecutions of the Church of Latter Day Saints* (1840), 28, Vault Collection, Community of Christ Library-Archives.

prevent them from being admitted as members of the church. In the first column of the 111th page of the same paper, may be found this paragraph: "Our brethren will find an extract of the law of this state, relative to free people of color, on another page of this paper. Great care should be taken on this point. The saints must shun every appearance of evil. As to slaves we have nothing to say. In connexion with the wonderful events of this age, much is doing towards abolishing slavery, and colonizing the blacks in Africa."

We often lament the situation of our sister states in the south, and we fear, lest, as has been the case, the blacks should rise and spill innocent blood: for they are ignorant, and a little may lead them to disturb the peace of society. To be short, we are opposed to have free people of color admitted into the state; and we say, that none will be admitted into the church, for we are determined to obey the laws and constitutions of our country, that we may have that protection which the sons of liberty inherit from the legacy of Washington, through the favorable auspices of a Jefferson, and Jackson.[55]

From Phelps's clarification, it is possible to conclude that it was not Mormon policy to incite rebellion between slave and master; nor did the church encourage black migration into their community or even invite African Americans to join the movement. Phelps intended for the reader to see church members as law-abiding citizens who saw peace and stability as important to their success and prosperity. Phelps and his helpers posted the "Extra" handbills around Independence, but with emotions running high, the bills were quickly torn down. Missourians had decided the time for public denials was over.

Failure of Negotiations and Frontier Vigilantism

BY SATURDAY 20 July, the Secret Constitution had circulated throughout Jackson County. To keep the peace, this document declared five conditions required of church members:

1. That no Mormon in future move and shall settle in this county.

---

55. Chad J. Flake and Larry W. Draper, eds., *A Mormon Bibliography, 1830–1930: Books, Pamphlets, Periodicals, and Broadsides Relating to the First Century of Mormonism*, 2nd ed., rev. and enl., 2 vols. (Provo, Utah: Brigham Young University Press, 2004), 1: 376.

2. That those now here, who shall give a definite pledge of their intention within a reasonable time to remove out of the county, shall be allowed to remain unmolested until they have sufficient time to sell their property and close their business without any material sacrifice.

3. That the editor of the "Star" be required forthwith to close his office, and discontinue the business of printing in this county; and as to all other stores and shops belonging to the sect, their owners must in every case strictly comply with the terms of the second article of this declaration, and upon failure, prompt and efficient measures will be taken to close the same.

4. That the Mormon leaders here, are required to use their influence in preventing any further emigration of their distant brethren to this county, and to counsel and advise their brethren here to comply with the above requisitions.

5. That those who fail to comply with these requisitions, be referred to those of their brethren who have the gifts of divination, and unknown tongues, to inform them of the lot that awaits them.[56]

Armed with this signed document, as well as weapons to enforce their demands, hundreds of angry citizens gathered in the street in front of the Mormon newspaper office, not far from the county courthouse. Representatives from both sides negotiated the future of the Church of Christ in Jackson County. Church negotiators included William W. Phelps, Edward Partridge, Sidney Gilbert, John Whitmer, Isaac Morley, and John Corrill. A committee of thirteen represented the crowd that gathered, demanding immediate sale of Mormon lands, removal from the county, and a promise to stop future migrations. The Mormon negotiators asked for three months to consider citizen demands since they would have to communicate with church leaders back in Ohio. The disgruntled local committee gave them fifteen minutes.

The Mormon representatives flatly refused these demands, igniting a swift mob response. Ruffians rushed the printing office and turned the Phelps family out into the street. Then they attacked the press office, pied the type, and scattered printed materials into the street. Last, they ripped

---

56. "Regulating the Mormonites," *Daily Missouri Republican* (St. Louis, Missouri) 12 (9 August 1833): 2–3. *www.sidneyrigdon.com/dbroadhu/MO/Misr1833.htm*. A rich resource of early Missouri documents can be found at this Web site sponsored by historian Dale Broadhurst.

off the office roof and tore down the walls. The whole ordeal lasted less than an hour.

One of the church negotiators, Sidney Gilbert, owned a general store a few doors north of the printing office. The mob turned its attention to his store and ransacked the place, destroying much of his merchandise. Eventually, they moved on to the Mormon-owned blacksmith shop of Robert and Hannah Rathbun and vented their anger there. Before the melee concluded, the mob took Bishop Edward Partridge and church member Charles Allen into the public square and tarred and feathered them, then promised more violence until every Mormon left the area.

An Uneasy Peace and the Church Response

AN UNEASY PEACE fell over Independence for the next three days. Church members gathered up unfinished copies of the *Book of Commandments* and any other papers strewn from the wreckage of the church printing office. The cessation of violence did not last long, as reprisals flared again on the following Tuesday, 23 July. Ruffians then forced an assembly of church leaders into the public square of Independence. Under duress the leaders signed an agreement committing to an evacuation procedure where one group of disciples would leave before 1 January 1834 and the remainder by April. John Corrill and Sidney Gilbert would remain behind as agents to sell all church-associated properties.

Oliver Cowdery immediately left for Kirtland to explain how the dispossessed were suffering in Zion. On Cowdery's arrival, Joseph Smith called for a church council to consider an appropriate response. Council members agreed to three important actions: First, the colonists in Zion should seek their right to redress their grievances under the law. Second, those leaders who actually signed the agreement should leave Independence immediately. Third, church members should refuse to sell their lands in Zion.

Since Missouri members signed the agreement under duress, church leaders knew its terms were not legally binding. The injured parties would stake their hopes on the Missouri state government. When the Missouri church leaders finally received the prophet's orders from Kirtland, they petitioned directly to Missouri governor Daniel Dunklin for state assistance. As a legal issue for the state, the governor sent the plea for redress of grievances to the attorney general, who referred the matter to local courts. To represent them, the church retained the Richmond, Missouri, law firm of Doniphan, Atchison, Rees, and Wood toward the end of October. Also, for their own protection, church leaders ordered each Mormon settlement to prepare for the defense of their homes and families.

Meanwhile, church representatives went south to newly created Van Buren County to explore resettlement possibilities there, and another contingent headed north to Clay County for arms and ammunition. On 20 October the Missouri church leadership decided to defend itself against attack. All Jackson County braced for violence between the two armed camps. Hostilities broke out on 31 October when Missourians raided the Whitmer settlement approximately eight miles west of Independence on the Big Blue River. The settlement defenders were overwhelmed by the forty to fifty attackers. Ten cabins were demolished and several men were scourged as the survivors fled to the safety of the nearby woods.

When the fighting subsided and families returned, they found their loved ones brutalized by the vigilantes. Church leaders recognized the attackers and brought charges to the local justice of the peace to hold them accountable.[57] The justice would not entertain the charges, signaling to all that the local courts would not offer protection. Each church settlement posted pickets for their safety. Soon after, another skirmish left a Missouri citizen wounded, leaving both sides preparing for all-out war.

Homeless church members were ordered to camp on their Temple Lot west of the public square. With each day the encampment grew larger as victimized believers gathered only with what they could carry. On 4 November, the capture of an important church-operated ferry on the Big Blue precipitated a pitched battle of nearly eighty men almost equally divided in

---

57. Finding no satisfaction in court by this late date should have been no surprise to petitioners. John Corrill described the determination of church members to adhere to the direction of Joseph Smith (and Missouri governor Daniel Dunklin) to find redress in the local courts. Their attempts not only failed but inflamed an already violent atmosphere. Corrill wrote that church members petitioned the governor for protection "but he said we must appeal to the civil law for redress. This we tried, but found it of no use for as soon as the people found out we had petitioned the Governor for protection, and that we were about to appeal to the law for redress, they became very angry, and again commenced hostilities." See Corrill, *A Brief History*, 19.

a nearby field. With the exchange of volleys the citizens broke ranks, and when the smoke cleared two Missourians were dead. One Mormon defender, Andrew Barber, died of his wounds the next day, and Philo Dibble's wounds crippled him for life. After the engagement at the Big Blue, several church leaders were imprisoned in the Independence jail.

Exodus from Zion

STATE OFFICIALS COULD not allow civil war on their western border, especially as rumors spread that the believers were seeking an alliance with Indian tribes, so Lieutenant Governor Lilburn W. Boggs, an Independence, Missouri, resident, volunteered to mediate the crisis. Abuses continued, however. With their hopes for building up the City of God dashed, church members evacuated Jackson County. Some Saints went to counties south and east of Independence, but most headed north to Wayne's Landing and other portages and crossed the Missouri River into Clay County. Jailers released the church leaders and allowed them to join in the exile.

By mid-November 1833, what began as a great experiment to build up the kingdom of God ended in failure. While the exiles camped along the bank of the Missouri River in Clay County, an early morning meteor shower filled the sky. The church members took the telestial event as a favorable sign from heaven. They vowed to return to Zion to regain their inheritances. But for now they would find refuge across the river. Standing on the north bank they could easily see their sacred homeland. They were so close to their Zion, yet so far.

Lessons from the Mormon Failure in Zion

WHAT WENT WRONG? The Missouri Saints responded faithfully to their prophet's call to gather to Zion, to build up the sacred community, to receive their inheritance, and to prepare for the Second Coming. As best they could they consecrated what little property that remained from their journey from the east. Within their fellowship they were basically of one heart and one mind about their purposes. The necessary institutional requirement to create the Missouri church, with its elaborate administrative and priesthood structure, was in place.

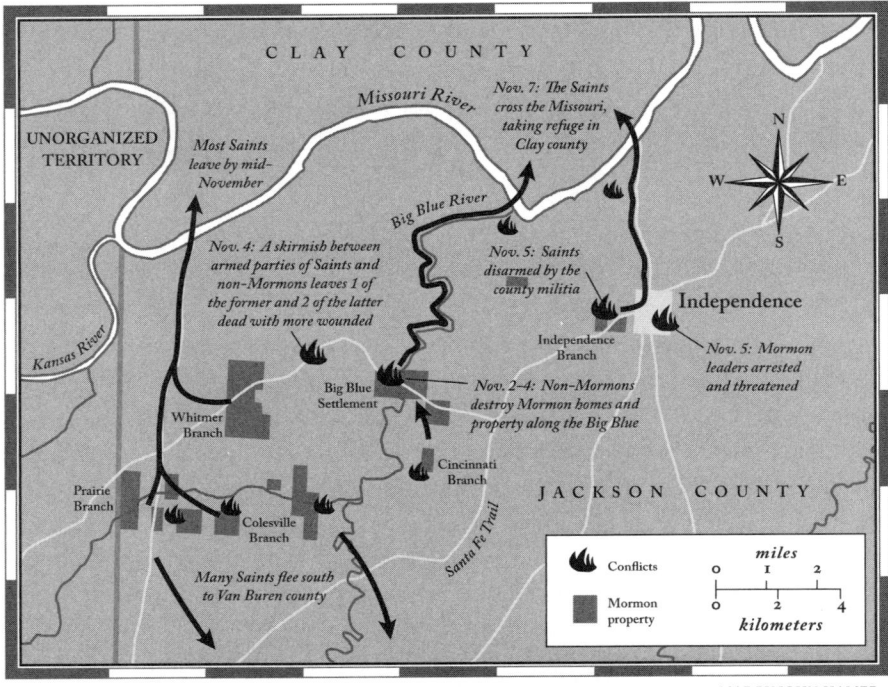

MAP BY JOHN HAMER

The Saints were expelled from Jackson County and took refuge in neighboring counties.

Perhaps the answer was all around the Mormons. Their theology of exclusion was founded on their belief of being the "only true primitive Christian church" centered in what they perceived as a corrupt American society. They viewed mainstream churches, defiled by modern innovations, as part of the problem rather than the solution. Where other Americans saw their God as a source of spiritual redemption, disciples of the Church of Christ felt God's wrath would be visited on the unbeliever. To protect themselves from the evils of society and to maintain their spiritual purity, Mormons closed ranks within their community. Eventually, those moving to the farthest western reaches of the United States, whether consciously or unconsciously, facilitated their isolation.

The Mormon community aspired to be one of civility, symbolically planted amid the wilds of the American frontier and among those they perceived as uncouth and unrefined. Prophetic revelation from the one "mighty and strong"[58] was supposed to provide stability, direction for living, and a constant reminder that they were God's chosen people. The ecclesiastical structure of the church leadership in Missouri took responsibility for the stewardship administration of their community. The bishop, a member of the higher order of the Mormon bicameral priesthood, held the consecrated reigns of fiscal management and economic development of the community as well as responsibility for the welfare of its church member citizens.

Mormon communitarianism took its inspiration from scripture, and Joseph Smith looked with interest on Sidney Rigdon's social experiment in Kirtland, Ohio, based on Acts 2:

> All that believed were together, and had all things common; And sold their possessions and goods, and parted them to all men, as every man had need. And they, continuing daily with one accord in the temple, and breaking bread from house to house, did eat their meat with gladness and singleness of heart, Praising God, and having favour with all the people. And the Lord added to the church daily such as should be saved.[59]

But the prophet would put a different stamp on such stewardship concepts as he initiated a total consecration of church members' possessions:

> The priests and teachers shall have their stewardships, even as the members; and the elders, or high priests who are appointed to assist the bishop as counselors, in all things are to have their families supported out of the property which is consecrated to the bishop, for the good of the poor, and for other purposes, as before mentioned, or they are to receive a just remuneration for all their services; either a stewardship, or otherwise, as may be thought best, or decided by the counselors and bishop. And the bishop also shall receive his support, or a just remuneration for all his services, in the church.[60]

---

58. Isaiah 28:2.

59. Act 2:44–47 KJV.

60. Doctrine and Covenants 42:19a–c (LDS 42:70–73).

Clearly the strongest scriptural source of support for the design of the Mormon community could be found in their American scripture, the Book of Mormon:

> And it came to pass in the thirty and sixth year, the people were all converted unto the Lord, upon all the face of the land, both Nephites and Lamanites, and there were no contentions and disputations among them, and every man did deal justly one with another; And they had all things common among them, therefore they were not rich and poor, bond and free, but they were all made free, and partakers of the heavenly gift.[61]

This book of scripture, permeated with communitarian principles, provided the initial motivation for church colonization on the American frontier.[62]

For all the differences in their worldviews, church members and the Missouri citizens were more alike than each perceived. Both the Mormons and the Missourians confronted a hostile wilderness environment when they arrived in newly created Jackson County. Both had exhausted their personal resources in a total commitment to survive their journey and competed for those same limited resources. Both heralded their Revolutionary War heritage as empowering their differing lifestyles. Both appealed to republican virtues to support their separate worldviews. Neither recognized the worth of black people in American society but saw them as either having the "curse of Cain" or as having potential for human servitude. Finally, fundamentalist religious values were important to both populations. For all these commonly held experiences, better communications on both sides would have created at least the potential for accommodation of each other's needs. Because neither side was willing to engage in the other's concerns, there was a sense of inevitability in the outcome.

61. IV Nephi 1:3–4 (LDS 1:2–3).
62. Kenneth H. Winn, *Exiles in a Land of Liberty: Mormons in America, 1830–1846* (Chapel Hill: The University of North Carolina Press, 1989), 57. Winn explained that communal Mormonism took on a popular republican quality rather being countercultural. Winn's classical republican views of Mormon communitarianism add significantly to this discussion, especially when both Mormons and Missourians saw each other as threats to the same classical republican virtues of libertarianism, religious pluralism, and market capitalism so important to their day. For specific explanations of republican ideology in the context of Jacksonian America, see Winn's third chapter titled "Social Disorder and the Resurrection of Communal Republicanism among the Mormons," 40–62.

Perceptions thus became reality and the Saints would lose out in a recurring clash of cultures.

Independence, Missouri, as the Garden of Eden

THERE IS NO better example of Smith's Americanizing the Judeo-Christian tradition than his identification of Independence, Missouri, as the location of the original Garden of Eden. On his arrival in Jackson County in late July 1831, Joseph was greatly impressed by his surroundings. This newly settled region of the country was situated at the edge of large stands of hardwood, deciduous forests. To the west of Independence lay hundreds of miles of treeless prairie deemed uninhabitable by the popular contemporary myth of the "Great American Desert."[63] Considering that Independence was strategically located near the Missouri River's bend, that the State of Missouri had recently platted the community and declared it to be the government seat for Jackson County, and that its location placed its residents in close proximity to recently removed Native Americans to whom the Book of Mormon was written, it is not surprising that Smith factored geography into his theology just as he would do at every stop along the journey. Only months before his trip to Independence, the prophet foretold of the Holy City of Zion's location somewhere in the western United States:

> Wherefore, I the Lord have said, Gather ye out from the eastern lands, assemble ye yourselves together ye elders of my church; go ye forth unto the western countries, call upon the inhabitants to repent, and inasmuch as they do repent, build up churches unto me; and with one heart and with one mind, gather up your riches that ye may purchase an inheritance which shall hereafter be appointed unto you, and it shall be called the New Jerusalem, a land of peace, a city of refuge, a place of safety for the saints of the most high God; and the glory of the Lord shall be there, and the terror of the Lord also shall be

---

63. During the 1820 Yellowstone Expedition of this vast geographic region, Major Stephen Long (1784–1864) inscribed on his map the words "Great Desert." This followed Zebulon Pike's (1779–1813) prediction that "these vast plains of the western hemisphere, may become in time equally celebrated as the sandy deserts of Africa." See Meinig, *The Shaping of America*, 2: 76.

there, insomuch that the wicked will not come unto it; and it shall be called Zion.[64]

With great anticipation his followers awaited the prophet's specific designation of this sacred city, since within its gates could be found their inheritance in the kingdom of God.

As Joseph Smith and his missionary team approached Independence from the east, certainly the designation of Zion was on the prophet's mind. That his first impressions of the area were less than favorable was not surprising. Independence was located on the remote western border of the United States. The first white gentile inhabitants of the region were rough pioneers. As mentioned earlier, Smith described these gentile settlers as having a "leanness of intellect, ferocity, and jealousy of a people that were nearly a century behind the times... [and] without the benefit of civilization, refinement, or religion."[65]

Of the land, his description was much more favorable, observing the beauty of flowers and rolling hills, the "luxuriant forests" with rich, fertile soil, and an abundance of wild game.[66] After receiving this revelatory insight Smith identified Independence as the "Center Place" and even plotted where the temple in Zion should be constructed: on land "lying westward, upon a lot which is not far from the courthouse."[67] But the prophet did not stop here. The combination of such beautiful land and his propensity to link geography with his religion was too much to resist; thus, some have claimed that Smith later concluded that this land was also the location of the actual Garden of Eden and more.[68]

64. Doctrine and Covenants 45:12a–d (LDS 45:64–67).

65. *DHC*, 1: 189.

66. *DHC*, 1: 197.

67. Doctrine and Covenants 57:1a–d (LDS 57:1–3).

68. Brodie, *No Man Knows My History*, 211. Other church leaders recalled many decades later Smith's declaration of Jackson County to be also the launching point for Noah's Ark. However, such remembrances must be understood as circumstantial and strongly tainted by the tellers' own theological speculations. Responsible historians struggle to determine what the Seer actually taught and what later church leaders promoted using their alleged private conversations with the prophet as the only source of their teachings. For an example of this speculation, see Heber C. Kimball, "Advancement of the Saints...." *Journal of Discourses* 10 (1865): 235. Kimball gave this discourse to a congregation of believers in Provo City, Utah, on 27 June 1863, the nineteenth anniversary

The lure of such a theology in convincing families to uproot their lives and to embrace Mormonism promoted the faith in unique ways and created crucial separation from competing churches. The designation of Independence, Jackson County, Missouri, as the actual site of the Holy City of Zion and the Garden of Eden seemed consistent with Smith's other conclusions, especially considering his felt need to find answers to difficult scriptural questions, his impressions about the sacredness of western Missouri, and his practice of closely linking land and theology—all vital distinctives of his Americanized Judeo-Christian gospel.

---

of the death of Joseph Smith Jr. Acknowledging that people in the audience knew the prophet, Kimball reminded them about the Seer's teaching: "And I will say more, the spot chosen for the garden of Eden was Jackson County, in the State of Missouri, where Independence now stands; it was occupied in the morn of creation by Adam and his associates who came with him for the express purpose of peopling this earth." Believer Charles Walker claimed Joseph Smith told "Dimic B Huntington while his boots were being mended, that Noah built the Ark in the Land where South Carolina is now." See A. Karl Larson and Katherine Miles Larson, eds., *Diary of Charles Lowell Walker*, 2 vols. (Logan: Utah State University Press, 1980), 2: 730.

CHAPTER TEN

Redeeming Zion

Tensions from Without and Within

THE ARRIVAL OF the Saints and their prophet at the American frontier fueled the volatile atmosphere. Joseph Smith inflamed the passions. It seemed that people either revered Joseph Smith Jr. as a prophet of God or despised him as a religious charlatan. With his move away from New York, Smith hoped to put behind him a checkered past that included brushes with the law and charges of indolence and vagrancy. Unfortunately for the young visionary, the move to Kirtland could not completely extinguish his past, as problems arose from outside and within the movement.

The tar and feathering incident in Hiram, Ohio, in March 1832 is just one example in a lengthy history of persecution that Joseph Smith endured during his lifetime. Perhaps the most notable critic of the Mormon prophet during the early Kirtland period was Alexander Campbell, founder of the movement eventually called the Disciples of Christ. Campbell's attack was not surprising. Both spiritual leaders headed up frontier American religions, and Smith's great success lured away members as well as potential converts to Campbell's movement. And of course Sidney Rigdon, a prominent Disciple, was now a popular leader within Joseph Smith's movement.

During the early 1830s, Mormon missionaries successfully proselytized in northern New York. On 13 March 1833, Methodist preacher

Doctor Philastus Hurlbut[1] met Joseph Smith Jr. and, having read the Book of Mormon, was baptized. Five days later, Sidney Rigdon ordained Hurlbut an elder and sent him into the Pennsylvania mission field. Church leaders abruptly recalled Hurlbut on charges that he talked obscenely to a woman. Less than a month after his ordination, on 2 June 1833, he was excommunicated. Shortly thereafter, Hurlbut moved back to Pennsylvania and launched a vicious attack on Mormonism.

Hurlbut's primary purpose was to prove the Book of Mormon was false. Soon after his arrival back in Pennsylvania, he learned about a romance novel that contained a similar storyline to that of the Book of Mormon. Its author, Solomon Spaulding (1761–1816), hailed from Ashford, Connecticut, but had moved to Amity, Washington County, Pennsylvania.[2] Spaulding's novel, titled *Manuscript Found*, is a fictitious story about a shipload of Roman soldiers who set sail for Britain during the days of Constantine. They were blown off course and ended up on the east coast of North America. The narration is provided by a Roman soldier named Fabius who writes his story as a historical account. Through the generations, historians have noted the many parallels between *Manuscript Found* and the Book of Mormon. For example, both introductions include discoveries of secretly buried, ancient writings in stone boxes. Also, both writings were purportedly translated from histories written by authors while they lived in America before the Christian era.[3]

In an attempt to discredit Joseph Smith Jr., Hurlbut accused Sidney Rigdon of stealing the unpublished manuscript and giving it to Smith sometime before 1829. Hurlbut then claimed that Smith used this manuscript as the primary source for the Book of Mormon. Then, in an inflammatory public exchange, Hurlbut threatened the life of the Mormon prophet. In January 1834, Smith moved against Hurlbut in a court of law and won a judgment that included a $200 fine and for Hurlbut to observe a "cooling off period" that required him to keep the peace for six months. Hurlbut responded by turning his materials over to Eber D. Howe,

1. Hurlbut (also Hurlburt) was not a medical doctor as his name might suggest; rather, "Doctor" was his first name, given him by his parents.
2. Spaulding's name has been spelled in numerous sources as Spalding.
3. See David Persuitte, *Joseph Smith and the Origins of the Book of Mormon* (Jefferson, N.C.: McFarland & Company, 1985), 247–55, and Van Wagoner, *Sidney Rigdon*, 140fn22.

editor of the Painesville, Ohio, *Telegraph*, who published the Hurlbut claims in *Mormonism Unvailed* later that year. Combining his own arguments with Hurlbut's, the *Telegraph* editor hounded the Mormon prophet incessantly.[4]

As if countering attacks from outside the movement was not enough to create concerns, Joseph Smith Jr. also had to deal with problems from within. Early in 1831, he was forced to confront a challenge to his prophetic leadership when Laura Hubble circulated revelations she had received through the use of her seer stone. Hubble's challenge was reminiscent of similar circumstances the previous September when Hiram Page also claimed to have revelations through a stone.[5] Through a revelation of his own, Smith declared that only the prophet could speak for God.[6]

In August 1831, shortly after the death of Polly Knight, wife of Joseph Knight, possibly the first deceased church member, Ezra Booth, the Methodist minister who witnessed the miracle healing of Elsa Johnson, defected from the church, accusing Smith of being a false prophet. This required Joseph, Sidney, and others to journey to northeastern Ohio to defend against Booth's allegations.

Not long after Joseph and Sidney experienced the Vision of the Three Glories in February 1832, the Mormon prophet realized that the composition of the presidency of the high priesthood should include two counselors. Now he could formally appoint assistants to help him carry

---

4. Eber D. Howe, *Mormonism Unvailed* (Painesville, Ohio: E. D. Howe, 1834). The Spaulding-Rigdon theory has been roundly disproved today. Even the most skeptical scholars of the historical origins of the Book of Mormon have discredited the theory. See Brodie, *No Man Knows My History*, 444–56; Richard P. Howard, "Beating Solomon Spaulding's Poor, Dead Horse One More Time," *Saints Herald* 124, no. 9 (September 1977): 549; and Dan Vogel, *Indian Origins and the Book of Mormon: Religious Solutions from Columbus to Joseph Smith* (Salt Lake City: Signature Books, 1986), 4. More recently, historian Richard K. Behrens has observed that the close connection of Book of Mormon narrative to the Spaulding manuscript may have been made through Hyrum Smith. Both Spaulding and Hyrum attended lectures at Dartmouth College in Hanover, New Hampshire, when professors broached this topic. See his "Dartmouth Arminianism and Its Impact on Hyrum Smith," *John Whitmer Historical Association Journal* 26 (2006): 174–75, 179.
5. Doctrine and Covenants 27 (LDS 28).
6. Doctrine and Covenants 43 (LDS 43).

the heavy burden of presidential leadership. During these formative years of church organization, what Joseph Smith Jr. needed most was stability among those closest to him—people whom he could rely on for sound advice. Sidney Rigdon and Jesse Gause, his presidential counselors, fell short of his expectations at this crucial time.

Sidney Rigdon's Emotional Outburst and Smith's Repudiation

ALTHOUGH SIDNEY RIGDON'S loyalty during these early years was unquestioned, he was susceptible to violent mood swings. Since his move from Mentor to Kirtland, he had neglected to arrange for a permanent dwelling for his large family. Instead, he relied on the Saints to temporarily house his family, causing them to be bounced from one household to the next. In the early summer of 1832, Rigdon had just returned from a lengthy journey to Independence, Missouri. When he arrived at the Reynolds Cahoon residence, where his family was staying, he discovered a disconsolate wife and, with his daughter, Nancy, quite ill, a suffering family. Physically exhausted and under enormous stress, Rigdon accepted the invitation to speak at a prayer service in Joseph's barn on 5 July. Rigdon arrived late to the meeting and burst in quite agitated. Lucy Mack Smith described the scene:

> At last [Rigdon] came in, seemingly much agitated. He did not go to the stand, but began to pace back and forth through the house. My husband said, "Brother Sidney, we would like to hear a discourse from you to-day." Brother Rigdon replied, in a tone of excitement, "The keys of the kingdom are rent from the church, and there shall not be a prayer put up in this house this day." "Oh! no," said Mr. Smith, "I hope not." "I tell you they are," rejoined Elder Rigdon, "and no man or woman shall put up a prayer in this place to-day."
>
> This greatly disturbed the minds of many sisters, and some brethren. The brethren stared and turned pale, and the sisters cried, Sister Howe, in particular, was very much terrified: "Oh, dear me!" said she, "what shall we do? what shall we do? The keys of the kingdom are taken from us, and what shall we do?" "I tell you again," said Sidney,

with much feeling, "the keys of the kingdom are taken from you, and you never will have them again until you *build me a new house.*"⁷

Charles C. Rich, who also witnessed Rigdon's emotional outburst, added that the distraught preacher declared that God had rejected the movement and for everyone to go home.

To address this embarrassing eruption, Hyrum borrowed Rich's horse, immediately rode to Hiram, Ohio, and informed Joseph. Quickly the two returned to Kirtland. The prophet told members to attend his sermon on the following Sunday when he would respond to Rigdon's claim. In this heavily attended church service, the prophet allayed everyone's fears by "denouncing the doctrine of Rigdon's as being false, took [Rigdon's] license from him and said, 'The Devil would handle him as one man handles another—the less authority [Rigdon] had the better.'"⁸ Rigdon, one of Joseph's two counselors, lost his priesthood over the incident; Joseph later restored it and his position as counselor but only after Rigdon repented in public for his unacceptable performance.

The Defection of Jesse Gause

THAT JOSEPH JR. would choose Sidney Rigdon as one of his counselors is of no surprise, even with his emotional problems. Next to the prophet, Rigdon was the most powerful religious leader in Kirtland. But Smith's selection of Jesse Gause (also Gauze) would be an unsolved mystery. The exact date of Gause's conversion is unknown, but his credentials made his choice as counselor understandable.⁹ With a strong background

---

7. Lucy Smith, *Biographical Sketches*, 238. Rigdon may have been repeating the revelatory counsel used by the prophet to build his home. That certainly worked for the prophet, and Rigdon's family needs were just as desperate. No doubt Rigdon's wife, Phebe, pressured Sidney with complaints about his inadequate provision for his family. Finally, Rigdon may have suffered from a bipolar psychological flare-up prompted by the enormous pressures that weighed so heavily on him.

8. Charles Coulson Rich, "History [of] Charles Coulson Rich," MS, 3–4, Charles Coulson Rich Papers, LDS Church Archives, in Leonard J. Arrington, *Charles C[.] Rich: Mormon General and Western Frontiersman* (Provo, Utah: Brigham Young University Press, 1974), 21.

9. Jesse Gause was born in 1784 and joined the Quaker movement in 1806. In approximately 1829 he moved to a Shaker village in Massachusetts, and from that village to North Union village, just sixteen miles southwest of Kirtland. It is possible that Gause

as a Quaker, and even some leadership experience among the Shakers, at a time when the prophet was launching his Law of Consecration, Gause's knowledge and skills appeared desirable. The historical record provides no direct information as to why Gause apostatized, but his defection added to the instability within the highest leadership level of the fledgling church.[10] The brevity of Gause's tenure as counselor and the selection of the highly qualified Frederick Granger Williams as his replacement repaired any damage caused by Gause's excommunication on 3 December. Rather, Smith looked to friendships and extended family as crucial allies to forge an alternative religious and civic society that would be founded on his newly emerging church.[11]

Much was accomplished in 1832, including acknowledgment of Joseph as president of the high priesthood in both the Ohio and Missouri churches and the survival of his namesake child. However, for Joseph Smith Jr., the year was his most difficult thus far as church leader. It began with brutal tar and feathering and the loss of his adopted son and ended with the excommunication of one of his closest advisers. His problems within the church continued into the new year.

Persisting Tensions between the Ohio and Missouri Churches

AMONG THE MEMBERSHIP, it became quite clear that the relationship between Sidney Rigdon and Edward Partridge had grown contentious. Although specific details were never exposed, it is possible that Rigdon was critical of Partridge consecrating only a portion

---

learned of Joseph Smith's religion during the prophet's proselytizing trip to North Union in March 1831. For more on Gause see D. Michael Quinn, "Jesse Gause: Joseph Smith's Little-Known Counselor," *Brigham Young University Studies* 23, no. 4 (Fall 1983): 487–93.

10. Michael Quinn speculates that the circulating rumors about polygamy and the prophet's possible involvement may have discouraged Gause. See Quinn, "Jesse Gause," 492.

11. Historian Steven Epperson observed that "Smith plumbed the depths of his needs and those of his contemporaries, and then proclaimed his friendship the grand fundamental principle of Mormonism." See his "The Grand Fundamental Principle: Joseph Smith and the Virtue of Friendship," *Journal of Mormon History* 23, no. 2 (Fall 1997): 104–105.

of his family business possessions in the Kirtland area. Also, Rigdon may have held Partridge accountable for mismanaging church finances in Missouri. For example, Partridge declined to advance funds for Smith and Rigdon's 1831 trip to Independence. Finally, Rigdon may have become frustrated with Partridge's inability to resolve legal lease issues with church members arriving in Zion.[12]

All these contentions should be understood in the context of the jurisdictional conflict between the church in Kirtland and the church in Missouri. It took the personal involvement of the prophet to mediate the conflict between the three church leaders. In a public display in a late April 1832 conference in Independence, Partridge and Smith reconciled their differences. Smith wrote optimistically: "The right hand of fellowship was given to me by the Bishop, Edward Partridge, in behalf of the Church. The scene was solemn, impressive and delightful. During the intermission, a difficulty or hardness which had existed between Bishop Partridge and Elder Rigdon, was amicably settled, and when we came together in the afternoon, all hearts seemed to rejoice."[13] Actually, eruptions between Rigdon and Partridge continued.

As Joseph and the church entered into 1833, tensions from within persisted. The great expectations of establishing the church in Zion went unfulfilled. Joseph sensed the need to send assurances to the Saints in Zion. His statement through revelation extended an "olive leaf" to William W. Phelps.[14] Although this had a positive effect in addressing difficult Law of Consecration issues, time would show that the prophetic counsel would not remedy all the problems that existed between Independence and Kirtland.

---

12. On one occasion, Partridge lost track of sixty dollars of church funds. An excellent discussion of these issues is found in D. Brent Collette, "In Search of Zion: A Description of Early Mormon Millennial Utopianism as Revealed through the Life of Edward Partridge" (master's thesis, Brigham Young University, 1977), 49–53.

13. *DHC*, 1: 267.

14. Doctrine and Covenants 85 (LDS 88). This admonition covered a wide range of topics for the members of both the Independence and Kirtland churches to ponder. In essence, Smith encouraged both memberships to keep in perspective key issues that pertained to their mission and to the afterlife. Thus the counsel redirected the members from their disagreements related to their varying circumstances toward a common goal.

These were difficult times throughout the church, but especially in Independence. Baptisms among the Native Americans were near nonexistent, and tensions generated by an exclusivist theology tended to offend rather than to attract potential converts. The poor reception of the Book of Mormon among Jackson County citizens reflected less the zeal of those who testified to it as the "fullness of the gospel" and more to primacy of the Bible as the sole source of the Word of God. Moreover, the citizens were put off by the Book of Mormon's acknowledgment that Native Americans were a people of worth and purpose. The application of the Law of Consecration and Stewardship met resistance and faltered, especially over the disposition of property rights of those who withdrew from the covenant. More members migrated to Zion than could be accommodated by the storehouse principle, a vital component of the Law of Consecration. Most elders sent to assist in the work in Independence returned to Kirtland rather than settling permanently. Not recognizing the nearly impossible circumstances of living encountered by the western church leadership, Joseph tended to micromanage details from Kirtland while holding its leaders in Independence, like Edward Partridge, accountable. The prophet had already chastised Partridge as early as September 1831 during the preparations for his move to Independence.[15]

The tensions between Kirtland and Independence boiled over and an exchange of letters between the two church leaderships revealed a significant rift. In a letter dated 11 January 1833, the prophet scolded William W. Phelps and others with warnings of calamities that would befall them unless they changed their behavior:

> For if Zion will not purify herself, so as to be approved of in all things, in His sight, He will seek another people; for His work will go on until Israel is gathered, and they who will not hear His voice, must expect to feel his wrath.... Our hearts are greatly grieved at the spirit which is breathed both in your letter and that of Brother Gilbert's, the very spirit which is wasting the strength of Zion like a pestilence; and if it is not detected and driven from you, it will ripen Zion for the threatened judgments of God.[16]

---

15. Doctrine and Covenants 64:3d (LDS 64:17). The historical record is unclear on what sins Partridge committed to merit inclusion in the Doctrine and Covenants.

16. *DHC*, 1: 316–17.

Missouri leaders Sidney Gilbert, John Corrill, and William W. Phelps sent numerous letters expressing their frustration with the constraints placed on their decision making. This stinging criticism from Independence prompted Kirtland leaders to call a special conference of high priests to address the issues. Their decision was to appoint Orson Hyde and Hyrum Smith to draft a response calling for Bishop Partridge to rebuke those causing the difficulties. This letter revealed the lack of sympathy among the Kirtland high priests:

> Brother Phelps requested in his last letter that Brother Joseph should come to Zion; but we say that Brother Joseph will not settle in Zion until she repent, and purify herself, and abide by the new covenant [Law of Consecration], and remember the commandments that have been given her, to do them as well as say them....
> Let the Bishop read this to the Elders, that they may warn the members of the scourge that is coming, except they repent.... Tell them that they have not come up to Zion to sit down in idleness, neglecting the things of God, but they are to be diligent and faithful in obeying the new covenant.[17]

This response from the high priests affirmed Joseph's desire for administrative control. Ironically, Independence leaders were more than happy for Joseph to exert his prerogative if he would just move to Zion as he intimated earlier. Unfortunately for them that would never happen.

By summer 1833, although the Saints knew they were not welcome in Jackson County, still they came, and in large numbers. By fall, twelve hundred Saints had followed the prophet's admonition to gather to Zion. Missouri, not Ohio, had the largest concentration of Mormons. Expectations of the Missouri Saints were that their prophet and his family would join them in Zion. Instead he made only periodic visits and suggested it might be at least five years before the move to Zion would be complete.[18] The Orson Hyde–Hyrum Smith letter set the conditions on which the prophet

---

17. *DHC*, 1: 319–20.
18. In a revelatory statement the prophet told Frederick Granger Williams not to sell his farm in Kirtland. "I do not will that my servant Frederick G. Williams should sell his farm, for I, the Lord will to retain a strong hold in the land of Kirtland, for the space of five years, in the which I will not overthrow the wicked, that thereby I may save some" (Doctrine and Covenants 64:4c [LDS 64:21]).

would eventually move to Zion. Until then, the Saints in Independence would have to accept Joseph's solution—two churches with one prophet.

As 1834 opened, the evacuation of Jackson County, Missouri, caused by the clash of cultures between the Mormons and Missouri citizens, was complete. A few Saints scattered into the counties south of Zion[19] but most moved north across the Missouri River into Clay County. On the first day of the year, Bishop Partridge convened a church conference where delegates decided to send Lyman Wight and Parley P. Pratt as messengers to Kirtland. Their mission was to ensure the prophet knew exactly what circumstances the Missouri members faced and to get specific instructions on what to do next. Smith's orders were for the Saints to settle as close to Zion as possible, and under no circumstances were they to sell their property.

Wight and Pratt also intended to rally support for the redemption of Zion. But on their arrival in Kirtland in late February 1834, they found conditions for the church there in disarray as well. To physically intimidate the Saints, a Kirtland mob had gathered northwest of the community and fired a dozen rounds of cannon shells that burst within view for all to see. Mormons braced for an attack that did not come.

Making matters worse, the high cost of living saddled the Saints with heavy debt. The Kirtland members were already more impoverished than their neighbors, since their gathering had exhausted most of their personal resources. Inflationary conditions made it more difficult to acquire land and caused a jump in food prices. Also, the costs of constructing the House of the Lord, establishing a church press, and the later purchase of several Egyptian artifacts imposed great hardship on believers throughout their stay in Kirtland.

Gentile businessmen compounded the Saints' woes by refusing to hire them as day laborers, nor would they mill their grain. Then several businessmen bought up all the grain on hand and refused to sell any to the Saints in hopes of driving them away. Only the availability of food resources in nearby Portage County forestalled starvation.

---

19. These included Cass, Bates, and Vernon Counties.

The Army of Israel and the Redemption of Zion

IN A CHURCH service on 23 February, Wight and Pratt testified to the trials and tribulations of the Missouri Saints. Their presentation stirred the Kirtland Saints to action and forced the hand of the prophet, who was in an untenable situation. More encouragement to stand true to their beliefs would not bolster the spirits of the Saints in Zion. Not even sending more money, even had it been available, would return them to the sacred homeland.[20] It was time for action. Joseph Smith Jr. responded to the difficult circumstances in Independence and in Kirtland with a call to liberate Zion.

The burden of church leadership pressed down on Joseph Smith. Throughout his fourteen-year tenure as prophet-president he always sought guidance from God during difficult times. This time would be no different. Proceeding under God's protection and command, church member obedience was expected. The enabling instruction for the liberation of Zion came on 24 February 1834, just two days after Wight and Pratt's arrival. The inspired message designated leaders, identified a recruitment plan, and even established the size of the army necessary to be successful.[21] It seemed that church members had met Smith's understanding of the requirement for "turning the cheek" three times.[22]

---

20. Smith had sent a fifty-dollar United States note to the Missouri Saints earlier. See "History of Joseph Smith," *Times and Seasons* 6, no. 14 (1 August 1845): 976.

21. Doctrine and Covenants 100 (LDS 103).

22. "And if any nation, tongue, or people should proclaim war against them, they should first lift a standard of peace unto that people, nation, or tongue, and if that people did not accept the offering of peace, neither the second nor the third time, they should bring these testimonies before the Lord; then, I, the Lord, would give unto them a commandment, and justify them in going out to battle against that nation, tongue, or people, and I, the Lord, would fight their battles, and their children's battles and their children's children until they had avenged themselves on all their enemies, to the third and fourth generation; behold, this is an ensample unto all people, saith the Lord, your God, for justification before me" (Doctrine and Covenants 95:6c–f [LDS 98:34–38]). For an explanation of early militant attitudes of the prophet, see Graham St. John Stott, "Just War, Holy War, and Joseph Smith Jr.," *Restoration Studies IV*, ed. Marjorie B. Troeh and Eileen M. Terril (Independence, Mo.: Herald House, 1988), 134–41.

Legality may not have been a concern to those who were "going to fight the battle of the Lord and redeem Zion,"[23] but perhaps it was for the prophet. From earlier communications, church leaders found a shred of hope that legal action could be taken.[24] Missouri governor Daniel Dunklin (1790–1844) seemed to raise hope for the Saints' protection in their return to their lands under his responsibility to maintain law and order. However, Dunklin felt that he did not have the authority to place a "standing army" in Jackson County. Dunklin's language provided only a thin veil of legitimacy in raising the army and marching to Zion.[25] The Army of Israel, as the marchers would be known, could be gathered legally (only in Missouri) to assist the Missouri governor in the fulfillment of his duties "to maintain law and order."

Assured that they were in the service of God, called to liberate Zion, early volunteers joined with zeal as Joseph announced a 1 May departure date for the first companies. In his diary Reuben McBride recorded a song composed for the march:

> Hark and listen to the trumpiters,
> they sound for volunteers
> on Zions bright and flowery mound
> behold their officers
> their garment white their armars bright
> with courage bold they Stand
> inlisting Soldiers for their king
> to march to Zion's land
> It sets my hart all on a flame
> a soldier to be

---

23. The Chagrin, Ohio, postmaster, J. M. Henderson, overheard this reference to the Zion's Camp marchers and mailed it in a warning to the postmaster in Independence, Missouri. Eventually, this statement was published in the influential Columbia, Missouri, newspaper, the *Missouri Intelligencer and Boone's Lick Advertiser*, on 7 June 1834; see Roger D. Launius, *Zion's Camp: Expedition to Missouri, 1834* (Independence, Mo.: Herald House, 1984), 51.

24. Church leaders received this intelligence from a "Brother Elliott, of Chagrin" in "History of Joseph Smith," *Times and Seasons* 6, no. 14 (1 August 1845): 976.

25. From the "City of Jefferson" (Jefferson City, the Missouri capital) Governor Daniel Dunklin responded to church leaders' petition for redress on 4 February 1834. "History of Joseph Smith," *Times and Seasons* 6, no. 14 (1 August 1845): 977.

> I will inlist gird up my arms
> and fight for liberty
> we want no cowards in our band
> who will their Colours fly
> we call for valient harted men
> who are not afraid to die.[26]

But the enthusiasm for armed intervention reached only so far into the church community. Smith's 24 February instruction called for as many as five hundred to effect liberation, but at the outset only 150 arrived in Kirtland for enlistment.

So Joseph sent his brother Hyrum on a recruitment tour into Michigan. Accompanied by Lyman Wight, the two church leaders spoke in congregations and to church families, soliciting their support. Their experience was similar to the Kirtland flank. The timing of the recruitment conflicted with spring planting and the need to feed families in the coming year. This, along with the prospects of a difficult nine-hundred-mile journey and the real possibility of falling in battle, meant that only the strongest supporters heeded the call to battle for the Lord.

Besides the timing issue and low recruitment, another significant problem was financial. The money needed to supply the Army of Israel did not flow into Kirtland any more than did the recruits. Smith sent out emissaries to find resources. Orson Hyde's experience in upstate New York revealed the problems among the membership in financially supporting the prophet's fiery admonition and the march. In late March 1834, Hyde wrote the prophet about the Saints' hesitance to donate some $2,000 to the cause. Feeling the frustration as the 1 May departure fast approached, Joseph and his counselors warned the New York Saints that God would "take away their talent,...and shall prevent them from ever obtaining a place of refuge, or an inheritance upon the land of Zion." They concluded this message stating: "We therefore adjure you to beseech them, in the name of the Lord, by the Son of God, to lend us a helping hand; and if all this will not soften their hearts to administer to our necessity for Zion's sake, turn your back upon them, and return speedily to Kirtland; and the blood of

---

26. Launius, *Zion's Camp*, 52–53; also see Leonard J. Arrington, *Brigham Young: American Moses* (New York: Alfred A. Knopf, 1985), 40–41.

Zion be upon their heads, even as upon the heads of her enemies."[27] By the departure date, Joseph had received just $160 of the $2,000 expected, and eventually left Kirtland with $190 to finance the march to Zion, although more funds eventually trickled in.

As volunteers arrived, Joseph assigned them to their companies. On the departure date they would be staggered so as not to startle people along the trail. Companies ranged in number from just a few to well more than a hundred, with an advance group leaving on 1 May. At New Portage, Ohio, about fifty miles southwest of Kirtland, the advance party established a staging camp and then received each company bound for Missouri. Participants contributed all their money to a common treasury, and Frederick Granger Williams administered the funds to finance the journey. The main complement of the Army of Israel that followed numbered about 125 men and three women. Now Joseph was ready for the long, difficult march to liberate Zion.

The main body of troops, led by Joseph Smith, traveled some six hundred miles in just thirty days. The torrid pace took its toll on life and limb. The normal difficulties of spring travel included fording swollen creeks and muddy trails and, combined with the bad food and tainted water, led to bickering. On numerous occasions, the prophet chastised those who grumbled and even threatened others. More seriously, cholera, a waterborne disease, spread throughout the ranks and took a heavy toll on morale, causing marchers to wonder why they had been commissioned of the Lord to liberate Zion only to die from the dreaded disease.

At various points in the journey, the difficulties of travel were interrupted with amazing occurrences. Two occasions demonstrate how leaders reminded the volunteers they were on a divine mission. On Tuesday 27 May, Brigham Young came across a rattlesnake and prepared to kill it when he was inspired to order a soldier to "take this snake and carry it off and tell it not to come back again; and say to its neighbors do not come into our camp to-night, lest some one might kill you!" The soldier did as he was ordered.[28]

---

27. *DHC*, 2: 48–49.
28. M. R. Werner, *Brigham Young* (New York: Harcourt, Brace and Company, 1925), 98–99.

The marchers passed numerous Indian mounds and burial sites along the journey. On 3 June near Naples, Illinois, Joseph and his army reached the Illinois River. While encamped on its banks, the prophet and several of his lieutenants scurried up one rather steep mound to survey the countryside. When they reached the peak, they discovered what appeared to be three stone altars. With their curiosity aflame, they dug next to the piling, and twelve inches down they unearthed a human skeleton with an arrow through its ribs. Immediately, Joseph divined that the arrow was "Lamanitish" and the man was

> a white Lamanite, a large thick set man, and a man of God. He was a warrior and chieftain under the great prophet Omandagus, who was known from the hill Cumorah, or Eastern sea, to the Rocky Mountains. His name was Zelph. The curse was taken from him, or at least, in part; one of his thigh bones was broken, by a stone flung from a sling, while in battle years before his death. He was killed in battle, by the arrow found among his ribs, during the last great struggle of the Lamanites and Nephites.[29]

The next day, the marchers reached the Mississippi, taking almost two full days to ferry across the mile-and-a-half-wide river. With fewer than 125 people in his troop when the prophet left Kirtland, overall troop numbers increased by fifty due to productive recruitment efforts en route.

Before he left Kirtland, Joseph commissioned his brother Hyrum and Lyman Wight to recruit among the Saints in Michigan and northern Illinois. They planned to rendezvous at the Salt River near Louisiana, Missouri. On Saturday 7 June 1834, the main body arrived at the designated site, known as the Allred settlement. Clearly, morale among Joseph's ranks sagged, and even for their leader, although he tried not to show it. The prophet recognized that the small numbers confronted a huge task—the redemption of Zion. However, he hoped that Hyrum and Lyman would swell the ranks. Even with the uncertainties of frontier travel, surprisingly, Joseph had only to wait a day for the arrival of the Smith-Wight column. The embrace of the two brothers lifted each other's spirits as well as those of the united army. The total number of Zion's Camp marchers reached

---

29. "History of Joseph Smith," *Times and Seasons* 6, no. 20 (1 January 1846): 1076.

Redeeming Zion 223

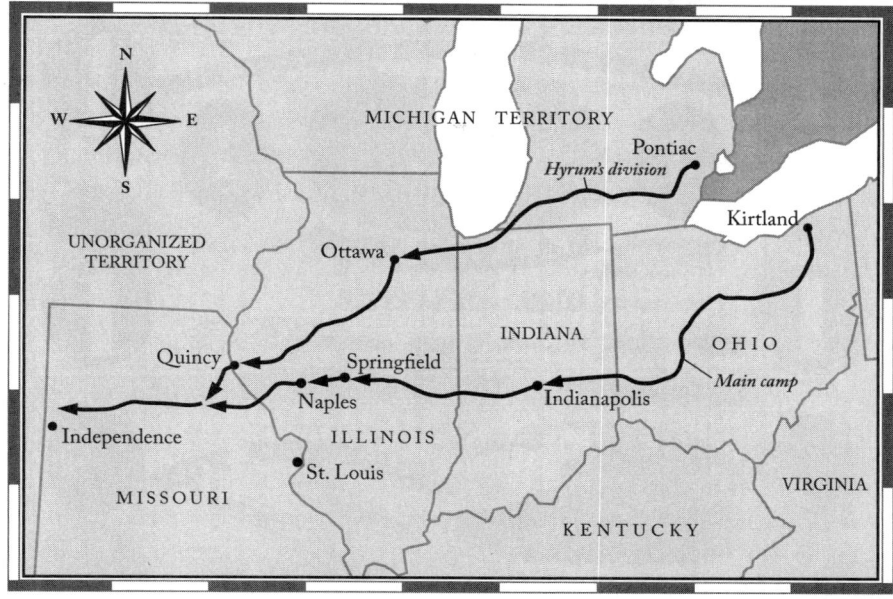

MAP BY JOHN HAMER

Route of the "Army of Israel"

223, including fifteen women and children, but far below expectations.[30] Still, anticipating God's assistance, the prophet felt confident that the small numbers and their sacrifices would bring success.

Joseph took the next five days to rest his troops and reorganize the expedition to increase efficiency and prepare for the crucial days that lay just ahead. Marcher Levi Hancock fashioned a flag out of white cloth tipped in red, emblazoned an eagle, printed PEACE in big letters on it, and then hoisted it onto a flagstaff. Quite impressed, Joseph ordered it carried before the troops as they ventured into Missouri. While it was on the eastern side of the state, the expedition was more of a curiosity than a threat, especially with the message sent with the unfurled flag.[31]

---

30. The contribution of the women and children to the Zion's Camp march should not be underestimated. For more information, see Andrea G. Radke, "We Also Marched: The Women and Children of Zion's Camp, 1834," *Brigham Young University Studies* 39, no. 1 (2000): 147–65.
31. Levi Hancock, "Autobiography of Levi Ward Hancock, 1803–1836," 55. See *New Mormon Studies CD-Rom: A Comprehensive Resource Library*.

A Sense of Betrayal and a Fateful Decision

WHAT APPEARED TO some as an invading army traversing the state caused considerable unease in Jefferson City as it moved westward. Governor Daniel Dunklin could only wait so long before responding. On 12 June, as the camp prepared for the trek across Missouri, Joseph sent Orson Hyde and Parley Pratt to remind the governor of his assumed offer of assistance to execute the laws to maintain law and order. Historian Roger Launius noted the strategic selection of Hyde and Pratt. The two eloquent men were fierce debaters—the coarse, frontiersman Orson Hyde complemented by the neatly dressed, elegant Parley Pratt.[32]

When Hyde and Pratt arrived at the governor's mansion, they found a hesitant politician rather than a forceful chief executive. Again, Dunklin affirmed that the local courts had the jurisdiction to handle the matter, knowing full well that the Jackson County officers of the court had participated in the mob action that initiated the grievances. Dunklin suggested that the Mormons sell their property and move elsewhere. The two Mormon ambassadors expressed outrage. As he was leaving, Pratt turned to the governor and vented his frustration:

> We would hold no terms with land pirates and murderers. If we could not be permitted to live on the lands which we had purchased of the United States, and be protected in our persons and rights, our lands would, at least, make a good burying ground, on which to lay our bones; and like Abraham's possession in Canaan, we should hold on to our possessions in the county of Jackson, for this purpose at least.[33]

Pratt's threat did not go unnoticed. Although Dunklin wanted to maintain the peace, the Missouri lieutenant-governor was a rabid Mormon-hater and was fully aware of the stakes should Zion's Camp reach Jackson County unopposed. Dunklin's lieutenant-governor was Jackson Countian Lilburn W. Boggs.

Orson Hyde and Parley Pratt arrived back at the main encampment during the morning of 14 June and delivered the bad news to Joseph Smith about Dunklin's lack of support. Now Smith and the Zion's Camp lead-

---

32. Launius, *Zion's Camp*, 113.
33. Pratt, *Autobiography*, 115.

ership faced a crisis decision, not only about the future of the march but also the fate of Zion itself. Should the march continue illegally or should they return to Kirtland? Three factors weighed heavily in the two-hour-long council. First was Joseph's revelatory command that had prompted the mission to liberate Zion. Even with the loss of state support, church leaders knew their mission was ordained of God; therefore, their success would be jeopardized only by their lack of perseverance and faithfulness. Second, the huge personal sacrifices of those who heard the prophet's call and responded would be in vain with the decision to retreat without battle. A third factor was the status of the Saints' inheritances should Zion not be freed—would they be lost or retained? Perhaps because the prophet had not received specific light to answer this question, and considering the other circumstances, Joseph Smith determined that the march should continue anyway. From that moment forward, Zion's Camp was an invading army and "little better than the Jackson Countians who acted so harshly the previous October."[34]

The Drums of War

AN ATTEMPT ON 16 June 1834 to find a peaceful compromise between the marchers and the Missourians failed and assured confrontation.[35] To keep secret Smith's two-hundred-soldier invasion force was impossible. Rumors of war spread quickly to Jackson County citizens, who appealed for troops from neighboring counties and geared for all-out war.

On 19 June, the Army of Israel marched through Richmond, Ray County, Missouri, and continued to just ten miles northeast of Liberty, in Clay County. Smith chose a field near the floodplain between the Little and Big Branches of the Fishing River. The gentle stream was but a few feet deep as marchers pitched their tents and built their fires. Throughout the camp, the close proximity to Zion raised spirits, but as the sun began to set, the marchers were startled when five angry Missouri citizens rode into

---

34. Launius, *Zion's Camp*, 115.
35. Scott H. Partridge, "The Life of Edward Partridge," unpublished biography, 173, Community of Christ Library-Archives; *DHC*, 2: 96–97; Roger D. Launius, *Alexander William Doniphan: Portrait of a Missouri Moderate* (Columbia: University of Missouri Press, 1997), 21–22.

camp with a warning that a powerful citizen army had gathered across the river and was prepared to repel the Mormon invaders.

Joseph learned that the opposing army was composed of fresh volunteers from Jackson, Ray, and Clay Counties and outnumbered his troops by nearly two to one.[36] It was now dusk. As the intruders left the camp as abruptly as they came, Heber C. Kimball noted an ominous, dark cloud appear on the western horizon. Just twenty minutes later, the heavens opened with a torrential hailstorm. Hail pelted both camps but mostly that of the Missourians. Huge pieces of ice even broke off gunstocks, and powerful winds pulled up tent stakes and drove off horses. Dangerous lightning streaked overhead. Tree branches fell all around, causing some of the Mormons to scurry for shelter in a nearby Baptist church.

The storm's fury lasted through the night. At daybreak on 20 June, Smith surveyed the damage and quickly noted the swollen river. What originally was a shallow, placid stream not much more than ankle deep was now between thirty and forty feet deep. With the swift current, there no was way to safely cross the river, so both armies withdrew to fight another day. The prophet interpreted events as God's intervention: "The earth trembled and quaked; the rain fell in torrents, and, united, it seemed as if the mandate of vengeance had gone forth from the God of battles to protect his servants from the destruction of his enemies, for the hail fell on them, and not on us, and we suffered no harm except the blowing down of some of our tents and getting some wet."[37] Once again the prophet spoke in Old Testament terms and compared his army to the House of Israel escaping from Pharaoh's armies through divine intervention.

Reconciliation Efforts[38]

DURING THE DAYS before the Saints approached the Fishing River, peacemakers from both sides sought compromise by exchanging proposals to reconcile differences and avoid war. At the direction of

---

36. The army of Missouri citizens included two hundred from Jackson County, sixty from Ray County, and seventy from Clay County. "Extracts from H. C. Kimball's Journal," *Times and Seasons* 6, no. 2 (1 February 1845): 790.
37. "History of Joseph Smith," *Times and Seasons* 6, no. 21 (15 January 1846): 1091.
38. An excellent account of these negotiations is found in Launius, *Zion's Camp*, 127–33.

Governor Dunklin, Fifth Circuit Court judge John F. Ryland, of Lexington, Missouri, hosted the negotiations at the Liberty, Missouri, Courthouse, and Clay County judge Joel Turnham presided. A thousand citizens gathered to witness the deliberations. The first proposal came from the Jackson Countians in an offer to "buy all the land in the county of Jackson, and also all the improvements which the said Mormons had on any public lands in said county of Jackson, as they existed before the first disturbances between the people of Jackson and the Mormons, and for such as they made since." To facilitate this offer, a committee of "three disinterested arbitrators," to be chosen by both sides, would survey the church holdings and establish fair market values. On the committee's absolute decision, Jackson Countians would then pay double the value within thirty days. With payment completed, the Saints were to promise to never return to the county. As an addendum to the offer, the Jackson County negotiators proposed that any further lands sold to Mormons would require the purchaser to pay the double valuation also.[39]

The prospect of the Mormons returning to Jackson County through further land purchases, even with the proposal of a double valuation, was simply too difficult to fathom. When the reconciliation proposals were read, the crowd of a thousand exploded in an uproar. Amid the chaos, W. W. Phelps, William McLellin, and several other Mormon representatives huddled to consider their response to the offer. After order was restored, they announced that they were not in a position to accept or reject the offers but would discuss the details with church leaders and provide Judge Turnham a quick response. The Mormon negotiators also promised that the Mormon army desired no hostilities and would not enter Jackson County before the announcement of their decision.

But neither side was in the mood for compromise because everyone knew Jackson County's religious significance, and they knew that the Mormons would never sell their properties. Also, the enormous cost of buying the property of Jackson County citizens was far beyond the resources of

---

39. The actual language of this proposition stated that Missouri citizen lands could be sold to Mormons. Although that option was expressed, removal of Mormons was the whole purpose of the negotiations and the citizens could simply refuse to sell to them, which would accomplish their purpose. See "Propositions of the People of Jackson to the 'Mormons,'" *The Evening and the Morning Star* 2, no. 22 (July 1834): 175.

the impoverished religious sect, nor could church leaders have the resources available within thirty days. The same confrontation with reality existed for Jackson County citizens. Negotiators were quite presumptuous that residents would sell their properties to the Mormons, even at inflated prices, let alone the assumption that citizen resources were available to purchase Mormon lands that, for many, were already in their possession. Thus, the Jackson County proposals seemed to be more form than substance.

When the Mormon negotiators shared the details with church leaders, surprisingly Joseph considered the propositions fair but felt the committee inaccurately identified, and thus shorted, Mormon properties. But the prophet never seriously considered the proposals; instead he construed the propositions as an attempt to cover up unlawful conduct by the Jackson County mobbers. Rejection of the offers came in a note signed by Phelps, McLellin, and the others, but kept open the possibility for reconciliation, declaring that the Zion's Camp marchers were "unanimously disposed to make every sacrifice for an honorable adjustment of our differences that could be required of free citizens of the United States." To further ease tension they closed their letter stating that they had no intention of invading Jackson County: "We are informed that the citizens of Jackson entertain fears that our people intend to invade their territory in a hostile manner. We assure you that their fears are groundless; such is not and never was our intentions."[40]

Smith's promise may have had just the opposite effect, since many observers knew that this army had not come so far to give in so easily. Near panic conditions gripped some Jackson Countians as they braced for war. Various representatives from Clay and Jackson Counties visited the Mormon camp to learn their next move. Joseph tried to convince them that he "had no intentions to molest or injure any people, but only to administer to the wants of our afflicted brethren; and that the evil reports which were circulated about us were false, and were circulated by our enemies to get us destroyed."[41]

Finally, on 1 July, Smith made a counterproposal that he titled "Propositions &c. of the Mormons." The prophet announced his peaceful

40. "History of Joseph Smith," *Times and Seasons* 6, no. 21 (15 January 1846): 1092.
41. "Extracts from H. C. Kimball's Journal," *Times and Seasons* 6, no. 3 (15 February 1845): 804.

intentions with a promise not to commit hostilities against any man or body of men and that his marchers would fight only to defend themselves. Then Smith made a series of proposals calling for the appointment of a dozen "disinterested men," six chosen from each side of the conflict, to reassess the value of possessions belonging to non-Mormons in Jackson County who refused to live side by side with the Saints. Once values were determined, the church would buy the property, making full payment within one year. No Saints would enter the county prior to full payment. Any damage to Mormon property would be deducted from the total sale price. If his proposal was not accepted, then Smith called for all peoples to peacefully co-exist.[42]

A huge obstacle for both sides was their lack of trust for each other. Just as the marchers discounted the Jackson County proposals, the Jackson Countians suspected Smith's propositions. Neither side was willing to compromise, making peaceful conditions impossible. Smith could only recall the violence inflicted on the Saints a year earlier, and Jackson County citizens questioned anyone who "prophesied for God." What the Missouri citizens did not know was that on 22 June, Joseph experienced an epiphany at the Fishing River demanding that the marchers end their crusade to liberate Zion. Known as the "Fishing River Revelation," this prophecy chastised the general church membership (but not the leaders) for their lack of obedience, their unwillingness to impart of their substance to the poor and afflicted, and their unwillingness to support the marchers—transgressions that forestalled at least for "a little season" the redemption of Zion. Those marchers who demanded a fight received assurance: "Behold, the destroyer I have sent forth to destroy and lay waste mine enemies; and not many years hence, they shall not be left to pollute mine heritage, and to blaspheme my name upon the lands which I have consecrated for the gathering together of my Saints."[43]

An important theme throughout the Fishing River Revelation was the realization that the Saints' army was simply not large enough to defeat the enemy that occupied Zion, and that until proper strength could be achieved, redemption of the American Holy Land and vengeance of

42. Smith's "Propositions" appeared in the *Upper Missouri Enquirer*, 1 July 1834; see Launius, *Zion's Camp*, 140–41.
43. Doctrine and Covenants 102:4a–b (LDS 105:15).

God's enemies "unto the third and fourth generation"[44] would simply have to wait. Perhaps reflecting Smith's own ambivalence on interpreting this divine message, especially considering the probability of losing a pitched battle, the prophet used language of intense violence yet ended on a peaceful note:

> Sue for peace, not only the people that have smitten you, but also to all people; and lift up an ensign of peace, and make a proclamation for peace unto the ends of the earth; and make proposals for peace, unto those who have smitten you, according to the voice of the Spirit which is in you, and all things shall work together for your good; therefore, be faithful, and, behold, and lo, I am with you even unto the end. Even so. Amen.[45]

Three circumstances make the decision to avoid battle with the Jackson Countians understandable. First, Smith surely realized that the superior forces arrayed against him outnumbered his small army and were better equipped to carry the fight to its fateful conclusion. Second, although Smith was absolutely certain of his mission of liberation, and that God favored his efforts, in the eyes of human law, his troops were the illegal invaders of the state. Although his prophetic mission was of greater importance, the lack of legal protection had to give him some pause. Finally, exhaustion and malnourishment among his ranks periodically hampered their movement and made them susceptible to illness. His faith that God's mighty arm would fight alongside his troops was tempered as he reviewed his beleaguered followers.

This last concern was soon justified. On the evening that Smith gave his Fishing River Revelation, a cholera epidemic broke out among his ranks and took a heavy toll. Joseph Smith had a mild infection, Heber C. Kimball nearly died, and Jesse Smith, Joseph's cousin, did die. From late June through August 1834, the disease struck a third of the marchers.

Cholera, brought on by contaminated water and poor sanitation, attacked the victim's digestive tract. Characterized by very high fever, chronic diarrhea, and fatal dehydration, cholera's most obvious symptom was its swiftness. Victims of the virulent disease fell from their horses, and guards

---

44. Doctrine and Covenants 102:8d (LDS 105:30).
45. Doctrine and Covenants 102:11a–d (LDS 105:38–41).

suddenly collapsed where they stood.[46] The Mormons did not introduce cholera to the region, and the disease lingered on the American frontier long after they left.[47]

In a matter of days, cholera struck area farmers and spread across the Missouri countryside. In late June 1834, Smith divided his companies to prevent his entire army from being consumed by the disease. Suspicious Missourians soon became aware of this strategy—yet another reason to oppose the invaders. Several companies of marchers left the Fishing River, arrived at the banks of Rush Creek, approximately two miles east of Liberty, Missouri, and encamped for the evening. Over the next several days, the disease took its toll as marchers fell. Eventually, thirteen marchers, including one woman, Betsy Parrish, succumbed. Local church member Algernon Sidney Gilbert died on 29 June. One burial site for some Zion's Camp victims was located "in a little bluff by the side of a small stream that emptied into Rush Creek."[48]

Ending the Zion's Camp March

ALL PROSPECTS NOW for liberating Zion ended with the failure of negotiating for the return of church properties, and the losses caused by cholera. On the last day of June, the prophet authorized Lyman Wight to order the disbanding of Zion's Camp. Each marcher received a

46. On the trails west during the 1840s, a common reference to the suddenness of death could be found in the quip, the victim of cholera "would be healthy at breakfast and dead by supper."

47. For an excellent discussion of cholera's impact on the settlement of the American frontier, see Geoffrey C. Ward, *The West* (New York: Little, Brown and Company, 1996), 4, 122, 135–36.

48. "Extracts from H. C. Kimball's Journal," *Times and Seasons* 6, no. 5 (15 March 1845): 839. In June 1958, a local farmer discovered the skeletal remains of three individuals, one being female. A decade later University of Missouri, Columbia, archaeologist F. G. Spiers issued an anatomical report confirming the possibility that the skeletons were Zion's Camp marchers. Historian Vivian W. Graybill, a member of the Reorganized Church of Jesus Christ of Latter Day Saints, linked the historic geography through early records of Zion's Camp. On 25 March 1976 the skeletons were interred in Mound Grove Cemetery in Independence. Then on 11 October 1997, at a gravesite commemoration, historians met to erect a commemorate headstone honoring the deceased Zion's Camp marchers. See Max H. Parkin, "Zion's Camp Cholera Victims Monument, Dedicatory Statement," *Missouri Mormon Frontier Foundation Newsletter* 15 (Fall 1997).

certificate verifying their honorable service, thus allowing them to return home. A few thought the order to disband cowardly, but most welcomed it. Before long, the marchers formed small parties and set out for Kirtland. Meanwhile, on 3 July Joseph called all Saints who remained in the area to gather in Liberty, Missouri, where he announced the Missouri Presidency and the creation of the High Council of Zion. David Whitmer became president and also headed the High Council. The primary task of this council, as defined by the prophet, was to address the worthiness of Clay County Saints in preparation for the occupation of Zion at the end of the "little season." Over the next several days, Joseph transacted more business with the High Council and concluded with "an appeal" that declared the marchers' peaceful intentions, apocalyptic predictions, the Second Coming, and a warning that God would prevail on the side of his chosen Saints.[49] Then, the prophet called Missouri leaders to return to Kirtland for spiritual endowment.

Joseph Smith, his brother Hyrum, Frederick Granger Williams, William McLellin, and several others began the month-long journey back to Kirtland, arriving on 1 August. During their days of travel, no doubt they reflected on their successes and failures. Certainly they learned much about their own leadership roles in a church less than five years old. By demonstrating their commitment to endure great pain and anguish, the experience identified a cadre of individuals who could be depended on to build a viable priesthood structure. Future apostles and seventies could look back on their experiences as marchers as a bond of brotherhood. The ordeal also provided a seemingly endless source of testimonies of God's blessings for the survivors. Finally, the march was a rare opportunity to bring the two churches—Kirtland and Independence—together as one. Rumblings from the Independence Saints about lack of support from brothers and sisters in Kirtland were silenced, at least for a time.

But there also seemed to be a dark side of the Zion's Camp march. On various occasions during the journey, Joseph confronted the limits of his leadership skills. This added to an incipient and recurring tradition of dissent, as others also noted the prophet's humanity. The crusade was costly

---

49. William W. Phelps, et. al., "An Appeal," as found in "History of Joseph Smith," *Times and Seasons* 6, no. 22 (1 February 1846): 1110–11, and continued in the following issue 6, no. 23 (15 February 1846): 1120–23.

in terms of lives and dollars for a budding church confronting the challenges of its own existence. Finally, in the minds of many in the church, the march dashed their hopes for a lasting pacifist presence in American society. Coming out of Zion's Camp was a long-standing militant theme that pinned the movement's success on the use of force, defensive if possible but offensive if necessary, to achieve their divine calling.

Joseph Smith Jr. discerned that a lack of spirituality among the marchers must have prevented success of the divine mission to liberate Zion. Joseph would address this need in dramatic fashion. Using the same Old Testament allegory that was so helpful in the Zion's Camp march, the prophet resorted to administrative, scriptural, and further ecclesiastical development. But his best remedy to achieve the spirituality he yearned for was temple building—a construction project initiated even before the Zion's Camp march.

CHAPTER ELEVEN

House of the Lord and the Latter Day Saint Pentecost

House of the Lord[1]

ESTABLISHING A HOUSE of the Lord should be seen as one key aspect of Joseph Smith Jr.'s broader attempt to "restore" the original, first-century church. Sending missionaries to the Lamanites to reestablish their sacred heritage; creating Zionic community in Independence, Missouri; establishing an Old Testament-oriented priesthood structure; and even revising the Bible itself were other attempts to demonstrate the link between the Middle Eastern Holy Land and the American Holy Land. In so doing, the prophet brilliantly connected to a larger social theme with Puritan roots suggesting that America was the "New Jerusalem." The Judeo-Christian tradition had anointed Hebrews as "God's chosen people" and established their temple as sacred space, the holy place where they could meet their God. And now that Joseph Smith Jr. had been instrumental in restoring the priesthood, a holy place was needed where a special endowment of "power from on high"[2] could be bestowed. The

---

1. References to the church's first capitol building in Kirtland, Ohio, almost always used the name House of the Lord in its earliest years. Modern references interchange House of the Lord, the accurate historical name, and Kirtland Temple. For the purposes of this writing, the terms will be interchanged. Also, I would like to thank Lachlan Mackay, director of historic sites for the Community of Christ, for his insightful commentary on the following two chapters.
2. Doctrine and Covenants 38:8e (LDS 38:38).

ancient Hebrews built their temple for such purposes as these and Joseph wanted nothing less.

The prophet wasted no time in pursuing his perceived divine directive to establish the "Restored Church." In late July 1831, as his followers were settling in Independence, Missouri, Joseph and Sidney Rigdon dedicated the land where God's temple would be built. Two years later, specific plans were drawn up to guide the construction process. Of course the persecution—yet another connection with Hebrew people—that followed prevented the Independence temple from being constructed. Thus, Kirtland, Ohio, an isolated community of approximately a thousand residents, became the unintended citadel for Latter Day Saintism and the alternative location for the House of the Lord. Later, this edifice would be referred to as the Kirtland Temple.

It is difficult to identify exactly how Joseph Smith Jr. conceptualized the House of the Lord. But blessed with a vivid imagination and receptive to inspired thoughts, no doubt he took great delight in the challenge. Numerous obstacles faced the prophet in getting started on the construction project. As early as 1831, the church owned no property in the Kirtland area where the edifice could be built. The members were impoverished, so financing construction meant great sacrifices had to be made. And no one within the movement had specific training even to draw up blueprints. Joseph would have to depend on his prophetic gifts and leadership skills to see this project to its successful completion.

The prophet may have taken an important first step toward conceptualizing his temple during an October 1832 missionary trip to several northeastern cities, including New York City. Accompanied by Newell Whitney, the two men walked the streets of the nation's largest metropolis. They took housing at the Pearl Street Boarding House in Lower Manhattan, just below Wall Street. During their stay, Joseph took time on 13 October to write his wife, Emma, about the marvelous buildings that surrounded him: "This day I have been walking through the most splended part of the City of New Y—the buildings are truly great and wonderful to the astonishing of evey beholder." He concluded his three-page letter with "Your affectionate husband until Death Joseph Smith Junior."[3] This may

3. Joseph Smith Jr. (New York City) to Emma Smith (Kirtland, Ohio), 13 October 1832, Community of Christ Library-Archives.

have been the prophet's first exposure to such varied architectural styles and magnificent church buildings that could be worthy of God's presence. It is entirely possible that Smith and Whitney sauntered past the Dutch Reformed Sea and Land Church built by Henry Rutgers between 1814 and 1817, with an architectural design amazingly similar to that of the eventual Kirtland Temple.[4]

The two missionaries returned to Kirtland on 7 November 1832, the day after Smith's first surviving son, Joseph's, birth. Approximately eight weeks later, on 27 December, the prophet gave his first direction on the construction project:

> Organize yourselves; prepare every needful thing, and establish a house, even a house of prayer, a house of fasting, a house of faith, a house of learning, a house of glory, a house of order, a house of God; that your incomings may be in the name of the Lord; that your outgoings may be in the name of the Lord; that all your salutations may be in the name of the Lord, with uplifted hands unto the Most High.[5]

With this inspired direction, the prophet announced the purpose of the structure and the three functions of the House of the Lord: worship, education, and, referring to the word "order," church administration.

Six months later, on 1 June 1833, Joseph delivered instruction providing even more detail:

> Verily I say unto you, It is my will that you should build an house; if you keep my commandments, you shall have power to build it; if you keep not my commandments the love of the Father shall not continue with you; therefore you shall walk in darkness. Now here is wisdom and the mind of the Lord: let the house be built, not after the manner of the world, for I give not unto you, that ye shall live after the manner of the world; therefore let it be built after the manner which I shall show unto three of you, whom ye shall appoint and ordain unto this power. And the size thereof shall be fifty and five feet in width, and let it be sixty-five feet in length, in the inner court thereof; and let the

---

4. Architectural historian Laurel B. Andrew raised this possibility. See a photograph of this Dutch Reformed church in her *The Early Temples of the Mormons: The Architecture of the Millennial Kingdom in the American West* (Albany: State University of New York Press, 1978), 44–45.
5. Doctrine and Covenants 85:36b–c (LDS 88:119–120).

lower part of the inner court be dedicated unto me for your sacrament offering, and for your preaching; and your fasting, and your praying, and the offering up your most holy desires unto me, saith your Lord. And let the higher part of the inner court, be dedicated unto me for the school of mine apostles, saith Son Ahman; or, in other words, Alphus; or, in other words, Omegus; even Jesus Christ your Lord. Amen.[6]

In a conference of high priests held on the same day that Joseph gave the above direction, he discussed specific construction plans. Conference delegates appointed Joseph Smith, Sidney Rigdon, and Frederick Granger Williams to fulfill the functions designated, including obtaining a specific plan for construction of the sacred inner court.[7] These three accepted overall responsibility to ensure that the construction would meet with the Lord's satisfaction as they understood it. With the actual dimensions now in place, construction could begin.

During the summer of 1833, as leaders made preparations, they deliberated about the fabric of the exterior. Thinking about their poverty-stricken conditions, some suggested the House of the Lord should be of the most economical construction. Lucy Mack Smith recorded the discussion and her son's response:

> Joseph requested that each of the brethren should give his views with regard to the house; and when they had all got through, he would then give his opinion concerning the matter. They all complied with his request. Some were in favour of building a frame house, but the majority were of a mind to put up another log house. Joseph reminded them that they were not building a house for man, but for God; "and shall we, brethren," said he, "build a house for our God, of logs? No, I have a better plan than that. I have a plan of the house of the Lord, given by Himself; and you will soon see by this, the difference between our calculations and His idea of things."[8]

Work soon focused on a hundred-acre tract purchased from Peter French and F. G. Williams in March 1832. The temple would be strategically perched at the top of a hill that overlooked the village of Kirtland,

6. Doctrine and Covenants 92:3a–f (LDS 95:11–17).
7. *DHC*, 1: 352.
8. Lucy Smith, *Biographical Sketches*, 202.

located just to the north of the construction site, and would be positioned east and west. Starting in early June, Hyrum Smith and Reynolds Cahoon dug trenches that outlined the temple foundation. On 23 July, a gathering of twenty-four met at the construction site and held a solemn dedication service to lay the cornerstones. From nearby quarries to the south, workers hauled sandstone blocks and rubble, and from the narrow Chagrin River, which snaked through the valley below the temple, they carted sand, gravel, and clay for the walls.

Workers had to proceed on the verbal guidance of Smith, Rigdon, and Williams, the committee of three, since there were no formal construction plans at hand.[9] The three claimed a vision on which they would rely for details. Construction proceeded slowly until fall because of scant resources, limited worker skills, the distractions from Independence, and frequent missionary trips that drew away church leaders.[10] In early October

9. Their earlier blueprint-drawing efforts exposed their lack of understanding of building design. Numerous mistakes emerged in the earlier Independence, Missouri, plan, and similar mistakes occurred in the Kirtland plan as well. For example, workers dug a foundation of insufficient width and depth to handle the enormous weight of the building. Window placements were not fully planned in advance of digging the foundation. Support piers were irregularly spaced, as were girder placements, both problems creating abnormal structural stress. These irregularities also created problems for interior construction. One example was the uneven bay spacing, which caused the vestibule wall to cut awkwardly through a window opening. Even the actual location for placing the temple was problematic due to the prevalence of loose glacial till soil and proneness to earthquake slippage. Inexperience with large-scale construction could account for Joseph's lack of concern about problems with sandy soil, since in small-scale home building this was not as problematic. But, short of divine intervention, Smith could not have known about area earthquake activity. The best analysis of the complete process of Kirtland Temple construction can be found in Elwin C. Robison, *The First Mormon Temple: Design, Construction, and Historic Context of the Kirtland Temple* (Provo, Utah: Brigham Young University Press, 1997). For an explanation of construction problems see his third chapter titled, "The First Campaign of Construction, Summer–Fall 1833," 27–44.

10. For example, for almost the entire month of October, Joseph Smith, Sidney Rigdon, and Freeman A. Nickerson were on a mission trip to Upper Canada. This was the first formal missionary venture of the church to be performed outside the United States and its territories. Because various workers were sent on missions, it meant that construction crew members rotated between departures and arrivals. For a brief explanation of Nickerson and the first international missionary venture, see Mark A. Scherer, "A Church with an International Heritage," *Saints Herald* 145, no. 12 (December 1998): 22.

1833, leaders decided to halt construction because of winter setting in, with hopes to commence again at spring thaw the following year.

As progress on the walls revealed the overall shape of the temple, a new problem emerged. The competition for building resources and the increasing numbers of believers migrating to Kirtland raised local concerns about the impact of the large Mormon presence. Tempers flared and threats of mob violence forced the decision to place guards on the walls during the night. Joseph Smith recalled an attempt to intimidate workers by firing cannon bursts on a nearby hill.[11] Heber C. Kimball, a temple worker and future church apostle, lamented in January 1834:

> The church was in a state of poverty and distress, in consequence of which it appeared almost impossible that the commandment [to build the temple] could be fulfilled, at the same time our enemies were raging and threatening destruction upon us, and we had to guard ourselves night after night, and for weeks were not permitted to take off our clothes, and were obliged to lay with our fire locks in our arms.[12]

Only the passing of the cold winter days, the melting snows, and the changing of the seasons lifted hopes for resuming construction to fulfill God's commandment.

Important Contribution of Artemus Millett

THE MAGNITUDE OF the Kirtland Temple building project required a superintendent with large-scale construction expertise. The person to accept the challenge was Artemus Millett, a newly baptized Canadian. In a consulting visit to Kirtland during the fall of 1833, Millett assessed the enormous challenges the workers faced. The master stone mason gained extensive experience in rubblework-and-stucco construction, a familiar

---

11. "The threats of the mob about Kirtland through the fall and winter had been such as to cause the brethren to be constantly on the lookout, and those who labored on the temple were engaged at night watching to protect the walls they had laid during the day, from threatened violence. On the morning of the 8th of January, about 1 o'clock, the inhabitants of Kirtland were alarmed by the firing of about thirteen rounds of cannon, by the mob, on the hill about half a mile northwest of the village." See *DHC*, 2: 2. Also see Heber C. Kimball, "Extract from the Journal of Elder Heber C. Kimball," *Times and Seasons* 6, no. 1 (15 January 1845): 771.

12. Kimball, "Extract," 771.

technique in Ontario and Quebec.[13] His suggestion to use this process to remedy so many of the problems that seemed so overwhelming brought great relief to all.

Because the approaching winter would force the closing of nearby Fairport Harbor, the primary port on Lake Erie for that region, Millett headed back to his construction business along the northern shore of Lake Ontario, in Canada. But he promised to return at spring thaw, and did so in April 1834. On his arrival in Kirtland, the buzz of preparations for the Zion's Camp march dashed his hopes to get started. He found that Joseph Smith Jr. the temple builder had become Joseph Smith Jr. the liberator.

COMMUNITY OF CHRIST LIBRARY-ARCHIVES
Kirtland Temple

Through the remainder of the spring and into the summer of 1834, the few workers who did not march with the prophet to Zion raised the walls no more than four feet above the ground.[14] Substantial progress awaited the return of the prophet and his marchers.

Completion of the House of the Lord Exterior

ON HIS RETURN from Missouri in July 1834, Joseph did not need any more incentive than he already had to complete the temple construction project. The numerous revelations prior to the march, the perceived lack of spirituality among his marchers, and his millennial expectations all refocused him to the task at hand. And the prophet did not

---

13. Rubblework is a masonry construction technique using irregular-shaped stones of differing sizes that may be roughly squared. Stucco is a plaster applied to walls that usually contains an aggregate to give the wall texture. See Robison, *The First Mormon Temple*, 197, 198.

14. Kenneth Glyn Hales, ed. and comp., *Windows: A Mormon Family* (Tucson, Ariz.: Skyline Printing, 1985), 95–96, in Robison, *The First Mormon Temple*, 46.

hesitate to pitch in with the heavy lifting when necessary. In his diary entry for 1 September 1834, he wrote: "I continued to preside over the Church, and in forwarding the building of the house of the Lord in Kirtland. I acted as foreman in the Temple stone quarry, and when other duties would permit, labored with my own hands."[15] Scaffolding rose with the walls as work continued without interruption through the winter into 1835.

Broken crockery or discarded dishes were added to the mortar. But there is no evidence that women, amid their extreme poverty, even had fine china, jewelry, or glassware to crush into the mortar, as has been suggested by long-standing tradition.[16] Without specific documentation to support such a story, it is impossible to know its origin.[17] Clearly women did make great personal sacrifice and contributed significantly to the construction of the temple, especially as workers left on mission trips. Women performed well and without hesitation the expected tasks such as cooking, spinning wool, and sewing clothes for male workers.[18] But women also drove teams

15. *DHC*, 2: 161.

16. "It has been said that the women brought their jewelry and gave it to be sold for the building of this Temple, that their best china and glass were crushed and added to the mortar that covered the outside of the building." See Inez Smith Davis, *The Story of the Church*, 227. Davis did not give any attribution to this statement.

17. Approximately fifteen years later, in *The Scarlet Letter*, author Nathaniel Hawthorne described the construction of Governor Bellingham's Mansion as exhibiting "the freshness of the passing year on its exterior, and the cheerfulness, gleaming forth from the sunny windows, of a human habitation into which death had never entered. It had indeed a very cheery aspect; the walls being overspread with a kind of stucco, in which fragments of broken glass were plentifully intermixed; so that, when the sunshine fell aslant-wise over the front of the edifice, it glittered and sparkled as if diamonds had been flung against it by the double handful. The brilliancy might have befitted Aladdin's palace, rather than the mansion of a grave old Puritan ruler. It was further decorated with strange and seemingly cabalistic figures and diagrams, suitable to the quaint taste of the age, which had been drawn in the stucco when newly laid on, and had now grown hard and durable, for the admiration of after times." See *The Scarlet Letter*, 2nd ed. (Boston and New York: Bedford/St. Martin's, 2006), 91.

    Coincidentally, Hawthorne, just a year older than Joseph Smith Jr., lived in Salem, Massachusetts, where Smith convalesced as a youth from his leg surgery between 1812 and 1813. See architectural historian Laurel Andrew's explanation of the very old building technique called "rough cast," which included mixing materials in stucco to give walls a textured look, in *The Early Temples of the Mormons*, 38.

18. "Then, every Saturday we brought out every team to draw stone to the Temple, and so we continued until that house was finished; and our wives were all the time knitting,

of oxen and hauled rocks to the temple site. Having lived in Kirtland during his youth, Aroet Hale could remember: "The Prophet required all the Church to Work on the Temple. all that was not on mishons did work all most Constant from the time it was Commenced till it was Completed Some Women & Children Labored and tended mason. One Sister I have forgot the name drove two Yoak of Cattle and haled Rock."[19] Also, Kirtlander Truman Coe observed that women of the church were asked to give up "even the necessaries of life" in order to build the temple.[20] The enormous sacrifices all the Latter Day Saints made to accomplish the herculean feat of constructing the House of the Lord during such difficult times make apocryphal stories unnecessary. Without such commitment by the women, men, and children of the movement, the House of the Lord could not have been built.

By February 1835, with the walls completed, work began on the roof. When finished, the roof, made of hand-split shakes and sawed shingles, received a paint coat of red lead pigment dissolved in linseed oil for preservation. For the stucco exterior, workers used the bluish-tinted clay and sandy pebbles from the Chagrin River combined with natural cement recently discovered from construction of the nearby Ohio Canal. Modern paint samplings revealed that workers painted the two front doors olive green. Thus, the House of the Lord took on a colorful, original appearance and glistened in the sunlight. When the exterior was enclosed, some grew concerned that the quality of materials did not equal the value of the Lord's dwelling. To remedy this concern, Joseph Young carried out

---

spinning and sewing, and, in fact, I may say doing all kinds of work; they were just as busy as any of us, and I say that those women have borne the heat and burden of those early and trying days and God will bless them for evermore. And besides all this, they have stepped forward and done the works of Sarah, and the first men of this Church have done the works of Abraham, and they will inherit the earth with them when it is redeemed and cleansed from sin. I feel to bless all such men and women, and pray my Heavenly Father to bless them in all things that will be for their good and for the honor and glory of his holy name." See Heber C. Kimball, *Journal of Discourses* 10 (6 April 1863): 165–66.

19. Aroet L. Hale, "Reminiscences," microfilm of holograph, 4, LDS Church Archives, in Robison, *The First Mormon Temple*, 47.

20. Truman Coe, "Mormonism," *The (Hudson) Ohio Observer*, 11 August 1836, 4, as found in *www.boap.org/LDS/Early-Saints/Coe.htm*. I thank Lachlan Mackay for alerting me to this resource.

Artemus Millet's plan to paint dark shadow lines on the stucco to give the appearance, at least from a distance, of cut stone masonry, a more expensive construction material during those times.[21]

An "Architectural Language" of Latter Day Saintism[22]

THE KIRTLAND TEMPLE design spoke of order and civility, a spiritual oasis in the wilds of the Western Reserve frontier, and modeled the church's "one true" theology in what believers perceived as a chaotic religious environment dominated by conflicting voices and intense competition. Of course, the architectural grammar of the House of the Lord was a foreign language to detractors in the Kirtland area, who understood only the threats posed by the Latter Day Saint presence. Skeptics had understood this presence as temporary, with Independence, Missouri, to become the capital city of the religious movement. However, construction of the religious sect's temple in Peter French's field above the village communicated a permanence that met with frustration and angst.

Before actual construction began, the prophet revealed that the design would be "not after the manner of the world."[23] However, the workers

21. Robison, *The First Mormon Temple*, 79.
22. Architectural historian Henry Glassie studied late eighteenth- and early nineteenth-century dwellings and concluded that a structural "grammar" revealed specific themes in the contemporary folk culture. Glassie noted that buildings reflected a combination of builder's skills and dweller's needs. From these influences an architectural language emerged. Glassie concluded that there was "reason in architecture," and that "old houses can be read to create statements of their designer's competence…and illustrate the mechanics of the evolution of architectural abilities." See Henry Glassie, *Folk Housing in Middle Virginia: A Structural Analysis of Historic Artifacts* (Knoxville: The University of Tennessee Press, 1975), 114. There was "reason in architecture" in the original design of the House of the Lord emerging from Glassie's two criteria—builder's skills and dweller's needs. This is an interpretive adaptation of "Material Culture, the Language of Latter Day Saintism, and the Creation of a Believable Myth," the fourth chapter in Mark Albert Scherer, "A Material Cultural Analysis of the Foundational History of Latter Day Saintism, 1827–1844" (PhD diss., University of Missouri–Kansas City, 1998), 124–61. Three valuable secondary sources provide significant informational support for this segment. They are Robison, *The First Mormon Temple*; Andrew, *The Early Temples of the Mormons*; and Roger D. Launius, *The Kirtland Temple: A Historical Narrative* (Independence, Mo.: Herald House, 1986).
23. Doctrine and Covenants 92:3b (LDS 95:15).

resorted, both outside and in, to the construction techniques with which they were most familiar. The final exterior design of the House of the Lord mixed four popular architectural styles and expressed many of the values and aspirations of the movement. The Latter Day Saints' first major building exhibited Georgian, Greek Revival, Federal, and Gothic architectural designs. Georgian architectural style was expressed in the decorative crown over front doorways, a window-door-window fenestration across the front, the quoin corner construction, and the medium-pitched roof with minimal overhang.[24] Another characteristic of Georgian style was the House of the Lord's symmetrical, box-like appearance, an element common also to the Federal style.

The triangular pediment on the front (east) façade and those found on the roofed dormers, along with dentiling[25] under the eaves and Greek fret-and-grooved fluting work on the dormers, reflected Greek Revival popularity. These features expressed appreciation for deep national roots in Greek democracy. Besides his 1832 missionary trip to New York City, Joseph Smith had other opportunities to be impressed with the Greek Revival architectural style. During his 1812 convalescence in Salem, Massachusetts, the young boy could have easily viewed the large First Baptist Church, one of the most dominant buildings in Salem. This church, completed and dedicated in January 1806, strongly resembled the Kirtland Temple in its use of Greek Revival architecture, multiple front doors, and the Federal fanlight window in the prominent triangular pediment.[26] The appreciation of Greek culture could easily be found in western and central New York. Settlers gave Greek names to their new communities such as Ithaca, Troy, and Syracuse in New York. The same appreciation is reflected in the names of Athens and Sparta, Ohio.

24. For further explanation of Georgian architectural style see Robert B. Harmon, *Georgian Architecture in America: A Brief Style Guide* (Monticello, Ill.: Vance Bibliographies, 1982).

25. Dentiling is a classical Greek architectural characteristic using uniform block and space repetitions commonly found underneath eaves or elsewhere in the triangular pediment. The term originates from the Greek word for teeth.

26. To view these architectural similarities, see *www.fbcsalemma.org/heritage.htm*. For further reading on Greek Revival architecture see Roger G. Kennedy, *Greek Revival in America* (New York: Stewart, Tabori & Chang, 1989).

Three specific features of the Kirtland Temple architecture reflected the Saints' rich heritage of the American federal republic—the cupola and belfry, oval window and fanlights, and triple-sash windows. This Federal architectural style was used widely throughout New England for government buildings, meeting houses, and domestic dwellings, and in the architecture of many buildings in the nation's capital, Washington, D.C. The Kirtland Temple cupola and its octagonal belfry, which towers on the roof more than a hundred feet from the front entrance, demonstrate the influence of Federal architect Charles Bulfinch (1763–1844).[27] From a far distance, the cupola with its belfry and weather vane was the first noticeable feature of the temple, giving the unknowing traveler the impression that the structure was a government building.

Like the cupola and belfry, the Kirtland Temple's oval window and fanlights exhibited Federal architectural influence. The prominent oval window centered in the pediment on the east façade would have reminded easterners of home. The fanlights above the two front doors and the large center window celebrated the new nation's founding.

Finally, the triple-sash windows on the north and south walls revealed construction techniques exhibiting workers' familiarity with Federal building styles. These Federal windows reflect especially the skilled craftsmanship of Brigham and Joseph Young. The window tracery pattern, perhaps the exterior's most sophisticated work, required great care and attention to detail. Workers installed the windows in November 1835, thus completing exterior construction.

What makes the Kirtland Temple's exterior architectural language so unique is the combination of its architecture styles. The exterior windows and scrollwork on the belfry and cupola demonstrated this characteristic. The colonial period of Federal construction style would not have included the arched sash. Architectural historian Laurel Andrew has observed that workers "Gothicized" the temple's Federal windows by adding pointed sashes, just as Bulfinch did with his Federal Street Church in Boston.[28] Also, temple architects placed a Roman adaptation of a Greek Ionic

---

27. Charles Bulfinch designed numerous statehouses in New England including the Massachusetts State House in Boston. An architectural adviser to Thomas Jefferson, Bulfinch designed the nation's capitol building and grounds.

28. Andrew, *The Early Temples of the Mormons*, 43.

capital on the Federal belfry.[29] The Kirtland Temple thus reflected the newer, western approaches to architectural design.[30]

Pattern Books and the Interior Design

LONG BEFORE WORKERS put the finishing touches on the exterior, other men and women diligently concentrated their efforts on the interior. Here Jacob Bump's skills and creativity as a joiner and plasterer were most noticeable. Bump did not march with Zion's Camp to Missouri, but stayed in Kirtland to draw up plans, season lumber, and direct preparations for finishing the interior.

The House of the Lord's interior expressed the creativity of American architect Asher Benjamin (1773–1845), who popularized Greek Revival designs in his published pattern books starting in 1797.[31] Bump frequently referenced them. Fluted columns and pilasters, frets, Doric and Vitruvian scrolls, and dentiled cornices adorn the lower and second floors. The prominent friezes using the guilloche pattern symbolized salvation theology and the afterlife by using the Greek letter for infinity. This design, carefully spaced so its repetition has no beginning or ending, is an appropriate physical presentation of the longevity and sacredness of the Eternal Spirit.

The most visible feature of the first and second floors is the stepped-back pulpits situated at the east and west ends of both floors. The four-tiered, elevated positioning reminded workers of the houses of worship

---

29. The Ionic capital is in the shape of a whorl and resembles the horns of a ram—a reminder that Greeks used their temples as venues for animal sacrifice to appease their gods. See Kennedy, *Greek Revival in America*, 20.

30. For a complete study of historical architecture in northeastern Ohio, see Richard M. Campen, *Architecture of the Western Reserve, 1800–1900* (Cleveland, Ohio: The Press of Case Western Reserve University, 1971).

31. Benjamin's pattern books are *The Country Builder's Assistant* (Greenfield, Mass.: Thomas Dickman, 1797); *The American Builder's Companion; or, A New System of Architecture: Particularly Adapted to the Present Style of Building in the United States of America* (Etheridge and Bliss, 1806); *The Rudiments of Architecture* (Boston: Munroe and Francis, 1814); *The Practical House Carpenter* (Boston: R. P. & C. Williams and Annin & Smith, 1830); *The Practice of Architecture* (Boston: Carter, Hendee & Co., 1833); *The Builder's Guide* (Boston: Perkins & Marvin, 1839); and *Elements of Architecture* (Boston: Benjamin B. Mussey, 1843). Primarily builders worked from the 1806 and 1830 pattern books. For pictorial examples, see Robison, *The First Mormon Temple*, 67ff.

from their New England roots. But the pulpits also symbolized the democracy of the Latter Day Saint priesthood structure, where many led worship services and engaged in theological instruction rather than acknowledging a supreme oligarchy of a few. Also associated with the temple workers' New England religious heritage are the enclosed pew boxes found on the first and second floors.

No doubt the most aesthetically pleasing feature of the lower court to the early Saints was the west window, positioned behind the pulpits. The large size served well to provide sunlight during the afternoon and early evening hours. The sophistication of the ornamented woodwork framing constantly reminded worshipers of the importance of their gathering.

Functional Purposes of the Interior Design of the House of the Lord

DIFFERENT ASPECTS OF the House of the Lord's interior design served numerous functions for the Latter Day Saint movement. The two pulpit stations reflected the bicameral nature of the church priesthood. Because priesthood structure was so new to the members, church leaders instructed them regarding each office by placing initials on the facing of the pulpits. Little documentation exists to specify what the initials actually represented; however, it is possible to surmise their meaning.[32] The west end represented the Melchisedec Order of priesthood, or higher order. Beginning at the lowest set of pulpits, they are labeled as follows: P.E.M., for the Presiding Elder Melchisedec, the presiding officer of the Elder's Quorum; M.H.P., for the Melchisedec High Priesthood, the presiding officer of the High Priest's Quorum; P.M.H., Presiding Melchisedec High Priest (representing the church Standing High Council, or even the Stake High Council); and M.P.C., for Melchisedec Presiding Council, representing possibly the First Presidency of the church or the stake presidency.

During this formative time of priesthood development, authorities made a noted separation between standing and traveling ministries. The initialing in pulpit design signified this distinction. Those who occupied

---

32. On the priesthood pulpit initials, I refer to Launius, *The Kirtland Temple*, 46–48.

Diagram illustrating the initials on the pulpits in Kirtland Temple

each of the pulpits during the dedication were standing ministers associated with the newly established stake. Quorum members in the Council of Twelve Apostles attended and participated in the dedication ceremonies but were considered "visiting dignitaries." When in Kirtland between mission trips, apostles would likely be given seats of honor on the side of the main pulpits.

At the east end of the first floor, workers constructed a nearly identical stand of pulpits under another large window positioned to emit sunlight during the morning hours. Those who occupied these pulpits led the Aaronic Order of priesthood, or the lower order. As with the west end, workers carved the initials of the different leading priesthood functions. Again from the lowest tier to the highest, they are labeled: P.D.A., Presiding Deacons Aaronic (for the Deacons Quorum Presidency); P.T.A., Presiding Teachers Aaronic (for the Teachers Quorum Presidency); P.A.P., Presiding Aaronic Priest (for the Priests Quorum Presidency); and B.P.A. to identify the Bishop Presiding over Aaronic (for the bishop who supervised Aaronic ministries and functions).

The interior design satisfactorily accommodated the functional purpose of each floor. The first floor, or lower court, was for worship services. Because both priesthoods participated in directing worship services, seating flexibility was needed. To accommodate this, free-standing benches in the pew boxes allowed worshipers to be seated facing either set of pulpits.

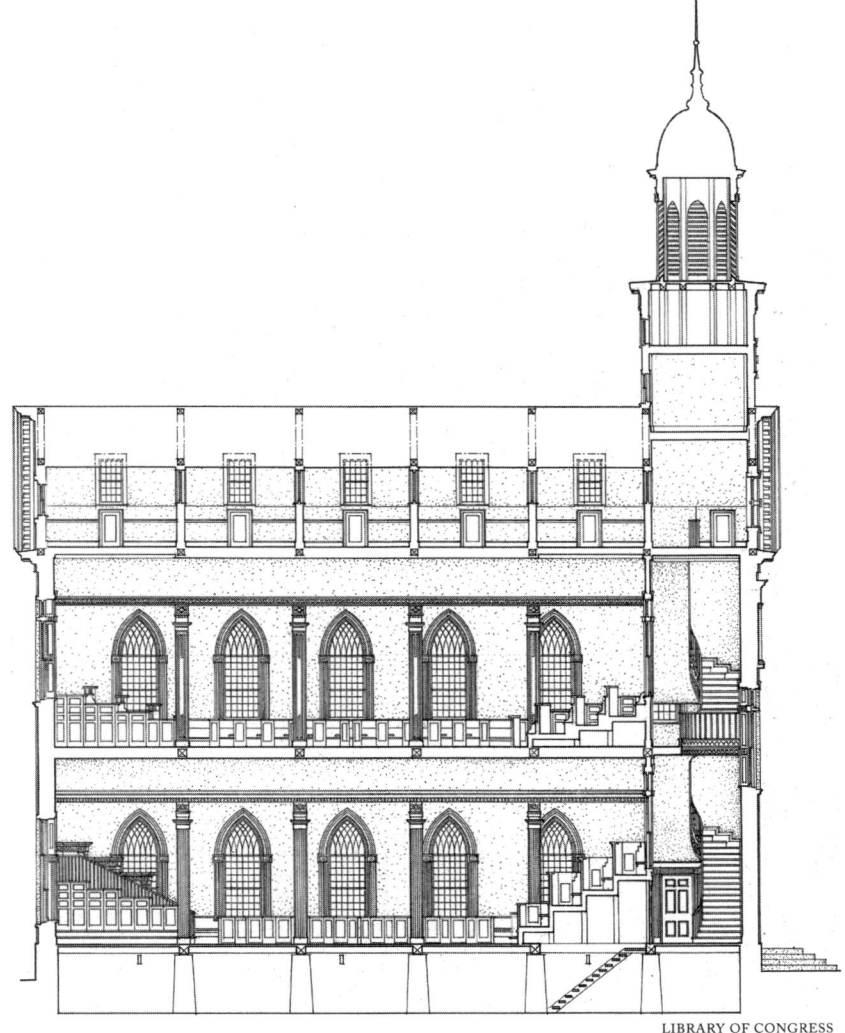

Longitudinal section, Kirtland Temple

Choir seating in the four corners of the lower court allowed for an antiphonal music experience.

The second floor, or upper court, housed the School of the Apostles, the educational function of the church. With a similar arrangement of pulpits at both ends, the second floor appeared to be modeled after the first floor. However, on close inspection, the second floor is not as ornately adorned. This may be because in August 1835 Jacob Bump became disillusioned with Joseph Smith Jr.'s leadership and left the work site in disgust, which cost the project its most skilled craftsman and his tools. The arrival a few months later of Truman Angell, a carpenter's apprentice, proved to be an acceptable replacement. Perhaps due to having less skill, Angell followed Asher Benjamin's pattern book *The Practical House Carpenter* much more closely. It is also possible that Angell considered Bump's architectural style selections outdated. Thus, the second floor exhibited less-sophisticated ornamentation.[33]

While the purposes of the lower and upper courts were revealed early in the construction process,[34] determination of the third floor's purpose was not established until the last day of 1835, shortly before its completion. When workers covered the wall and roof trusses, the result was the creation of five long, narrow rooms. To light each room, workers constructed five dormers with double-hung windows. At various times, this multipurpose area, possibly even an afterthought, provided space for the Kirtland High School. An open area running the length of the floor separated the north and south sides of the room and emptied into a spacious room at the west end. Smith chose this west end space as his administrative office. Here the prophet would spend much of his time in writing, counseling, and personal meditation.[35]

"Veiled Worship"

ONE OF THE most unique aspects of the temple interior was the presence of veils that hung from the ceiling in the lower court. As described by contemporaries, the veils of the House of the Lord were made of sewn canvas and resembled large sails.[36] Through the use of hooks and

33. Robison, *The First Mormon Temple*, 68.
34. Doctrine and Covenants 92:3e–f (LDS 95:16–17).
35. "In the afternoon I attended at the chapel to give directions concerning the upper rooms, and more especially the west room, which I intend occupying for a translating room, which will be prepared this week." See *DHC*, 2: 347.
36. Traveling through Kirtland in 1850, James F. Ryder entered the inner court and saw the veils still suspended from the ceiling. He described the canvas veils being as "heavy as sails to a ship...fastened at [the] bottom to large rollers and rigged with ropes and

rings, the veils were suspended from the ceiling. Workers raised and lowered them by crank through an ingenious rope-and-pulley system concealed in support columns spaced across the room. The inner court could be divided into quadrants and the pulpits could be concealed also. The curvature of the barrel-vaulted ceiling prevented a complete division of the room, but the veils could reach the floor as they passed through spaces between the pew boxes.

The veils performed important symbolic, spiritual, and practical functions. First mention of veils was written into the plans for the Independence, Missouri, temple, but actual implementation occurred in Kirtland. Although the veil rollers in the upper court still exist, there is no evidence that actual veils were ever installed there.

The inner court housed a special symbolic function for worshipers. In his 1 June 1833 instruction, the prophet stated: "Let the lower part of the inner court be dedicated unto me for your sacrament offering, and for your preaching; and your fasting, and your praying, and the offering up your most holy desires unto me, saith your Lord."[37] Joseph and his followers believed in the direct connection between the Hebrews of biblical times and their role in the "new dispensation" and used language to communicate that connection. Rather than calling the structure a church, Smith identified it, using the Jewish reference, as the House of the Lord, and rarely as a temple. Church members also referred to their sacred structure as "the chapel" or "stone chapel." Referring to the vestibule at times as the outer court and the large interior rooms as the inner court added to that identification. As veils played an important role in Jewish temples, having them in the House of the Lord symbolically reinforced that connection.

By facilitating different worship settings, the veils performed a vital spiritual function. The essential purpose of the House of the Lord was to provide a sacred venue for hosting the interaction between the human and the Divine, and veils facilitated the needed privacy for that encounter. The same privacy assisted ministers who performed the sacramental ordinance of foot washing and received visions.

---

pulleys at [the] top like curtains in theaters." See James F. Ryder, *Voightländer and I: In Pursuit of Shadow Catching* (Cleveland, Ohio: Imperial Press, 1902), 69, in Robison, *The First Mormon Temple*, 85.

37. Doctrine and Covenants 92:3e (LDS 95:16).

COMMUNITY OF CHRIST LIBRARY-ARCHIVES
Kirtland Temple Lower Court with veils suspended from ceiling, ca. 1920

But there was also a practical function to the veils. The veils facilitated personal meditation space as well as space for small-group meetings when the entire sanctuary was not needed. Combined with the enclosed pew boxes, the veils enabled worshipers to retain body heat in small-group services during cold spells. The veils also broke large gatherings into small ones to facilitate better participation in church services. The veils helped to fulfill the purpose of the House of the Lord.

The Dedication Service and the "Latter Day Saint Pentecost"[38]

THE MOST SIGNIFICANT church service of the entire Latter Day Saint Restoration Era occurred in the spring of 1836 during the dedication of the House of the Lord. Anticipation began to build after the

---

38. There are many accounts of the dedication service for the House of the Lord. For example, see *Latter Day Saints' Messenger and Advocate* 2, no. 6 (March 1836): 274–81, and *DHC*, 2: 410–28.

prophet announced that Sunday 27 March would be the day of dedication for the temple. When that day arrived, huge crowds gathered hours before the temple doors opened. At eight o'clock in the morning, worshipers entered through the double doors into the lower court, and the priesthood leadership took their designated seats. With the sanctuary filled to capacity, deacons opened the windows so those outside could also participate. When the front doors closed, the service began at nine o'clock with President Sidney Rigdon presiding. After scripture reading and singing, Rigdon embarked on a two-and-a-half-hour sermon using the eighth chapter of Matthew as his text. After Rigdon's discourse, each priesthood quorum stood and acknowledged the authority of Joseph Smith Jr. as "prophet and seer." When this ended, Rigdon accorded the same privilege to the entire congregation, who unanimously stood in support of the prophet[39] and sang another hymn. Then, the congregation took a short intermission.

Joseph Smith Jr. reconvened the service with the singing of the hymn "Adam-ondi-Ahman," written by newspaper editor William W. Phelps. At the conclusion of the hymn, Joseph presented each quorum of priesthood to the congregation, who sustained their ministry with their vote. Following another hymn, Smith presented his dedicatory prayer, a highlight of the day. Then the choir sang another hymn by William W. Phelps titled "The Spirit of God Like a Fire Is Burning."[40]

The dedication service then entered into a Communion ceremony of bread and wine, after which the prophet's younger brother, Don Carlos, and several others offered their testimonies of the Book of Mormon. Joseph Smith then stood and testified of his prophetic responsibilities and of receiving angelic visitations. At that point, Frederick G. Williams bore testimony that an angel had entered the sanctuary and sat down between church patriarch Joseph Smith Sr. and himself.[41]

39. This tradition continues in the Community of Christ today.
40. This is the most popular hymn of Latter Day Saintism. Because it acknowledges the powerful Pentecostal experience of the church dedication during those early years, church members traditionally stand for its singing. Because the Community of Christ today extends to nations around the world, and because this most popular hymn is the only one for which worshipers traditionally stand, Phelps's "The Spirit of God Like a Fire Is Burning" has become what might be considered the church's "international anthem."
41. *Latter Day Saints' Messenger and Advocate* 2, no. 6 (March 1836): 281.

The dedication service concluded with remarks by Hyrum Smith and Sidney Rigdon, after which Rigdon gave a closing prayer. Then the congregation shouted several hosannas and amens. Worshipers left the inner court by four o'clock in the afternoon. This ended the seven-hour dedication service, but not the spiritual manifestations.

That night, priesthood members gathered back at the temple for a meeting, and the Pentecostal experience continued. People reportedly spoke in tongues, prophesied, saw visions, heard angelic voices and singing, and witnessed strange lights on the roof of the temple. Several parishioners even observed angels hovering over the roof. Some testified of hearing a noise "like a mighty rushing wind, which filled the Temple."[42]

Because of the spiritual power of this Latter Day Saint Pentecost, and because so many people stood outside the temple, the prophet decided to hold a second dedication service the following Sunday, 3 April 1836. More than eight hundred attended the service to hear Thomas B. Marsh and David W. Patten give powerful sermons. During the afternoon Communion service, Joseph ordered the pulpit veils to be lowered to facilitate the blessing of several babies and the confirmation of new converts. This shielded the pulpit from the congregation. Joseph and Oliver Cowdery knelt in prayer and then stood. Joseph testified that as the two men rose the heavens were opened and Jesus Christ appeared to receive the temple and the sacrifices of the people. Then Moses appeared and conferred on the two men the keys of the gathering of Israel and the leading of the ten tribes from the land of the north. Elias succeeded Moses and conferred on them the gospel of Abraham. Finally, Elijah appeared, to give to the men

---

42. *DHC*, 2: 428. Also, in the last entry of Oliver Cowdery's "Sketch Book" dated Sunday, the 27th, the Second Elder wrote: "Attended on the dedication of the Lord's house. For the particulars of this great event see my account written by myself, and printed in the March No. of The Messenger and Advocate, signed C. In the evening I met with the officers of the church in the Lord's house. The Spirit was poured out—I saw the glory of God, like a great cloud, come down and rest upon the house, and fill the same like a mighty rushing wind. I also saw cloven tongues, like as of fire rest upon many, (for there were 316 present,) while they spake with other tongues and prophesied." A complete transcript of the Sketch Book is provided in Leonard J. Arrington, "Oliver Cowdery's Kirtland, Ohio, 'Sketch Book,'" *Brigham Young University Studies* 12, no. 4 (Summer 1972): 410–26.

the keys to priesthood authority and to prepare for the Second Coming.[43] Heavenly manifestations continued through the spring of 1836 as worshipers testified to various spiritual gifts.

For the westering migrant from the East who had spent the last month traveling the rough trails into the Western Reserve, passing through Kirtland Mills may have provided at least temporary release from the deep woods wilderness road. Here they could replenish provisions, feed and water stock, and share their difficulties along the trail. No doubt, seeing the Kirtland Temple on the hill would have attracted their curiosity. Unless a local resident were to explain, they would not have known immediately the building's identity or purpose. The Georgian characteristics may have signaled order amid the wilderness. The Greek Revival and Federal features may have reminded them of their democratic roots and a strong sense of patriotism. But as they reached the top of the hill they would have noticed the Gothic Revival windows signifying that this was a house of worship. The lettering on the front wall removed all doubt that this was the House of the Lord.

To summarize, the Kirtland Temple served three key purposes in the life of the early church—worship, education, and church administration. Most important, however, the House of the Lord provided sacred space for spiritual empowerment. The "Lord's House," as an early church member called it, still stands today as a physical testament to the significant sacrifices of the first generation of Latter Day Saints.[44] For future generations of believers the House of the Lord would symbolize the spiritual connection between the human and the Divine.

---

43. *DHC*, 2: 435–36. For a faithful secondary source account of the temple dedicatory events see Milton V. Backman Jr., *The Heavens Resound: A History of the Latter-day Saints in Ohio, 1830–1838* (Salt Lake City: Deseret Book Company, 1983), 294–303.

44. W., "To the Saints Abroad," *Latter Day Saints' Messenger and Advocate* 2, no. 10 (July 1836): 349. This article is signed only with the initial "W." Frederick Granger Williams was probably the author since last-name initials were frequently used to protect anonymity.

CHAPTER TWELVE

Problems in Kirtland

A Visitor with a Different Agenda: Michael H. Chandler and the Book of Abraham

STORIES ABOUT THE seer from Palmyra had spread across Ohio, New York, and Pennsylvania by the early 1830s. Newspaper accounts told of his experiences at Cumorah, and missionaries tried to direct public perception with a strong defense of the man and his mission. The young prophet's claim to command supernatural abilities to decipher ancient writings on golden plates made him quite an attraction throughout the region. Many of the curious visited the Saints in Kirtland and listened to their testimonies. Joseph Smith Jr. frequently took the time to chat, and with his handshake, they recognized something very special about him. Those who were unconvinced considered Smith a charlatan and the object of their scorn. During those times, shysters sought out the weaknesses of people and preyed on their vulnerabilities. This may have been the case when Michael Chandler, an opportunist with a questionable past,[1] trundled into Kirtland, Ohio, in the summer of 1835 with his wagon filled with Egyptian artifacts.

During the late eighteenth and early nineteenth centuries, Egyptian antiquities drew the attention of people from all over the Middle East, Europe, and America. The Egyptian government, racked with corruption,

---

1. For example, Chandler claimed that he inherited the collection from his uncle Antonio, but genealogical studies of Lebolo demonstrate no relationship. Also, Lebolo's probate records specified the disposition of his estate with no mention of a Michael H. Chandler. For further explanation see Bushman, *Rough Stone Rolling*, 286–87.

forbade some tomb raiders from benefiting from their exploitations while they secretly cooperated with others. One Italian plunderer, Antonio Lebolo, convinced the consul general of Egypt to collude with him in grave digging projects in three areas of southern Egypt near the ancient ruins of Thebes. Around 1820, with great success, the Lebolo diggers unearthed many artifacts including eleven mummies and papyri. Lebolo sold some of his antiquities to European museums and kept others.

After Lebolo's death in 1830, his family wanted to get as much money as they could for his artifacts so they decided to peddle them in the American markets. The Lebolo family hired the Trieste shipping firm of Albano Oblasser to handle the transoceanic transfer to America and to sell the treasures to the highest bidder. One to make a bid was Irishman Michael Chandler living in Philadelphia, whose great hope was to find a pharaoh's fortune hidden among his purchase. Unfortunately for Chandler, his get-rich-quick gamble busted, leaving him with four mummies and several scrolls of hieroglyphic writings.

Catering to America's fascination with such antiquities, Chandler set up a small museum in Philadelphia where, for a small price, people could view his treasures. Eventually Philadelphians grew tired of the Chandler exhibit, forcing him to take his show on the road. Perhaps a visitor to his museum told him about a seer from upstate New York, now living in the Connecticut Western Reserve, who could actually read Egyptian writings. It is possible that Chandler figured that if he could get this seer to translate the unknown language, he might be able to profit even more. It must have been worth a try since he purchased a wagon, loaded his artifacts, and headed west.

During March 1835, Chandler exhibitioned in Cleveland, Ohio, and then worked his way eastward through several small Western Reserve communities, heading toward Kirtland. According to a local newspaper, in the early spring Chandler was in Painesville, a short distance from Kirtland. A paragraph describing a mummy and one papyrus scroll appeared in the Painesville, Ohio, *Telegraph* on 27 March 1835:

> No. 1—4 feet 11 inches, female—supposed age 60; arms extended, hands side by side in front; the head indicating motherly goodness. There was found with this person a roll or book, having a little resemblance to birch bark; language unknown. Some linguists however say

they can decipher 1336, in what they term an epitaph; in black and red; many female figures.[2]

From this statement, it is evident that others attempted translation before Joseph Smith Jr. had the opportunity.

Michael Chandler and his traveling show finally arrived in Kirtland on 3 July 1835, and his entrance created quite a stir in the community. The enterprising Chandler unhitched his wagon near the unfinished House of the Lord. Lines formed quickly to view his marvels from the Middle East. After a couple of days showing the exhibit, Chandler publicly challenged the prophet to use his well-known skills to translate the papyri. This put Smith in an awkward position—if he said no to Chandler, then his followers might doubt his prophetic credentials. He had no choice but to accept. After a quick perusal, Smith told Chandler and the waiting audience that "one of the rolls contained the writings of Abraham, another the writings of Joseph of Egypt."[3]

As if to curry favor with the prophet, Chandler responded positively to Smith's discovery by issuing a written statement confirming his agreement. The document read:

> KIRTLAND, July 6, 1835.
> This is to make known to all who may be desirous, concerning the knowledge of Mr. Joseph Smith, Jun., in deciphering the ancient Egyptian hieroglyphic characters in my possession, which I have, in many eminent cities, showed to the most learned; and, from the information that I could ever learn, or meet with, I find that of Mr. Joseph Smith, Jun., to correspond in the most minute matters.
>
> MICHAEL H. CHANDLER
> Traveling with, and proprietor of, Egyptian mummies[4]

The language that Chandler used to certify Smith's interpretation must have reminded the prophet of Martin Harris's encounter in New York with Charles Anthon—perhaps a sign of further prophetic responsibility,

---

2. Painesville, Ohio, *Telegraph*, 27 March 1835, in Charles M. Larson, *...By His Own Hand Upon Papyrus: A New Look at the Joseph Smith Papyri*, rev. ed. (Grand Rapids, Mich.: Institute for Religious Research, 1992), 86.
3. *DHC*, 2: 236.
4. *DHC*, 2: 235.

or possibly Chandler played to Smith's ego by publicly acknowledging his prophetic skills.[5]

More serious issues confronted Smith because of his understanding of the nature of the papyri, however. Now that he had seen these scrolls and divined what he thought they were, he may have felt the obligation as seer to continue their translation, especially since within these scrolls were new insights into the Old Testament story. These writings complemented very well the construction of the House of the Lord. Since he and his followers were the American Old Testament people in the new and last dispensation of time, perhaps he felt it was no coincidence to be presented with this opportunity. The Seer was impressed with the need to purchase the artifacts outright.[6]

Whatever his reason, Smith hoped that Chandler's price would be reasonable. Unfortunately for the church, the Irishman's price for the complete exhibit, including mummies and papyri, was $2,400. This was a huge sum of money for a sacrificing people who were giving their all for the construction of the House of the Lord. On faith Joseph assembled a group of church member benefactors, including Joseph Coe and Simeon Andrews, to raise the money.[7] Having paid Chandler his asking price, Joseph Smith Jr. was now the proud owner of four Egyptian mummies and an arm full of papyri scrolls. Chandler left Kirtland a very rich man and, no doubt, with a smile on his face.

Joseph launched into the translation process immediately. As with his Book of Mormon translation, several of his trusted colleagues served as scribes and sat by the prophet day after day to record his thoughts. But different from his translation of the Book of Mormon, Smith did not use a seer stone to assist his divining of the hieratic symbols. John Whitmer's description is instructive of the process: "Joseph the Seer saw these Record and by the revelation of Jesus Christ could translate these records, which

---

5. Careful reading of Chandler's statement acknowledges only the extent of Smith's detailed study and not its accuracy.

6. It is also entirely possible that when Smith offered his initial interpretation he found it necessary to own the artifacts so as to control them. His credibility as a seer would remain in tact should Egyptian hieroglyphics later be deciphered.

7. Joseph Coe paid $800, as did Simeon Andrews. The remaining $800 was raised from many other believers.

COMMUNITY OF CHRIST LIBRARY-ARCHIVES

"Facsimile no. 1" from the Book of Abraham

gave an account of our forefathers, ~~even Abraham~~ Much of which was written by Joseph of Egypt who was sold by his brethren. Which when all translated will be a pleasing history and of great value to the saints."[8]

During the remaining weeks of July, Joseph focused on what he called the Abraham scrolls, translating parts of the text by the end of the month. But then he put away the project until October, when he resumed, with some interruptions, until the end of November 1835. Perhaps to record for future purposes, the Seer included in his translated works a thirty-four-page reference book of symbols and their meanings. He titled this book his

---

8. John Whitmer, *The Book of John Whitmer Kept by Commandment*, original manuscript in Community of Christ Library-Archives; reproduced in *From Historian to Dissident: The Book of John Whitmer*, ed. Bruce N. Westergren (Salt Lake City: Signature Books, 1995), 167. Strikethrough in original.

Egyptian A[l]phabet and Grammar. William W. Phelps and Warren Parrish served as scribes.

Almost seven years passed before Smith published portions of the *Book of Abraham.* He chose the 1 March 1842 issue of the church's *Times and Seasons* (Nauvoo, Illinois) for his first installment. More samples appeared serially through the remainder of the month. Historian Richard Bushman described the *Book of Abraham* writings "as an apocryphal addition to the Genesis story."[9] Within its pages are accounts of Abraham's wandering through Ur, Canaan, and Egypt. Also, according to Smith, Abraham speculated on the makeup of the cosmos, the creation story, priesthood lineage, and the nature of the Godhead.

The theological implications are considerable. The message of the *Book of Abraham* reflected the prophet's position on the most important social issue in early nineteenth-century America—slavery. Smith used the *Book of Abraham* to explain the skin color of African Americans as the "curse of Ham." The *Book of Abraham* and Smith's rewriting of Genesis in his New Translation of the Bible confirmed the cursed skin of African Americans.[10] Also establishing official policy, an August 1835 General Assembly statement announced the church's position of non-interference with slavery.[11] These interesting writings corrected the church's unjustified antislavery reputation, which stemmed from their clash with proslavery

---

9. Bushman, *Rough Stone Rolling*, 287.

10. "And he said, cursed be Canaan. A servant of servants shall he be unto his brethren. And he said, Blessed be the Lord God of Shem; and Canaan shall be his servant, *and a veil of darkness shall cover him, that he shall be known among all men.* God shall enlarge Japheth, and he shall dwell in the tents of Shem; and Canaan shall be his servant." See Joseph Smith's New Translation of the Bible ("Inspired Version"), Genesis 9:29–31. The prophet added the italicized sentence to the King James Version. Compare Genesis 9:25–27 KJV.

11. "We do not believe it right to interfere with bond servants, neither preach the gospel to, nor baptize them, contrary to the will and wish of their masters, nor meddle with, or influence them in the least to cause them to be dissatisfied with their situations in this life, thereby jeopardizing the lives of men: such interference we believe to be unlawful and unjust, and dangerous to the peace of every government allowing human beings to be held in servitude." Delegates to the church's general assembly, meeting in Kirtland, Ohio, unanimously adopted this statement of racial marginalization and canonized it. Currently it is entered as Section 112:12b–d (LDS 134:12) in the Doctrine and Covenants.

citizens in Independence, Missouri, two years earlier. Now, Latter Day Saint missionaries preaching in the antebellum American South could accurately declare Mormonism to be inoffensive to their cherished way of life based on their "peculiar institution of slavery."[12]

The *Book of Abraham* storyline demonstrates once again the vivid imagination of the prophet and his ability to intertwine theological and social issues relevant in the lives of his followers. But moving forward, Smith's interpretations of the Egyptian artifacts would raise serious questions to be answered by future generations—questions of historicity, theology, and interpretative veracity. Accepting the answers would require great faith in the prophet and would play an important role in deciding where the religious movement he led would be positioned within the Christian mainstream.

The Best of Times, the Worst of Times

THE LATTER DAY Saints reached their pinnacle of achievement in Kirtland by the summer of 1836. Their theological formation was developing well, the basic structure and keys to priesthood authority were confirmed, missionaries were having success in the field, stewardship concepts were realigned, and even new church identity was established. The dedication ceremonies of the House of the Lord and the Pentecostal outpourings lifted the spirits of believers and reinforced their millennial anticipation of Jesus Christ's Second Coming. With each powerful service in the temple, the Saints affirmed that their sacrifices were well worth it. That their prophet received new insights into the Old Testament as told from Egyptian papyri and Father Abraham affirmed his credibility in the minds of many.

Reflecting on good times, an editorialist captured the Saints' optimism in the June 1837 Kirtland newspaper the *Latter Day Saints' Messenger and Advocate*:

> Our village was all activity, all animation—the noise and bustle of teams with lumber, brick, stone, lime or merchandise, were heard from the early dawn of morning till the grey twilight of evening. The sound

---

12. Elijah Abel, a free black man, joined the church in Kirtland in 1832 and, as an exception to church practice, was called to the priesthood office of elder.

of the mechanic's hammer saluted the ear of the sluggard before the rising sun had fairly dispelled the sable shades of night, and the starting up, as if by magic, of buildings in every direction around us, were evincive to us of buoyant hope, lively anticipation, and a firm confidence that our days of pinching adversity had passed by, that the set time of the Lord to favor Zion had come, that we might almost rejoice when the world around us mourn, laugh at its calamity and mock when its fear comes.[13]

With great hopes for the future, the prophet made specific plans for the growth and prosperity that he felt was on the horizon. In 1836, Smith prepared his community redesign, titled the "Plan for Kirtland," in hopes of harnessing prosperity and organizing it for the future. His plan called for wide streets, equally divided lots, and symmetrical city blocks with right-angle corners. His Kirtland community design resembled to a certain extent his failed "Plat for the City of Zion." Perhaps the sacred social blueprint Smith sought in Independence, Missouri, could become a reality at Kirtland, Ohio.[14]

However, external and internal pressures on the movement proved the Kirtland prosperity to be temporary at best. Pressures from outside focused on political positioning on secular issues, employment practices, sales boycotts, and "wicked and vexatious lawsuits."[15] Pressures from within grew from the need to find new church resources and from disaffected church leaders and members. Smith's inability to deal effectively with all of these pressures brought to a conclusion the substantive contribution of Kirtland as the unintended capital city of Latter Day Saintism during the Restoration Era.

The intimidation brought by the ever-increasing number of Mormon converts—the same problem that caused the Saints' expulsion in Missouri—arose in Kirtland by the summer and fall of 1836. To raise revenues for the church through selling subscriptions and advertisements, the church's Literary Firm printed its first number of the *Northern Times* in February 1835. In a Whig region of Ohio, the Saints strongly supported the

---

13. *Latter Day Saints' Messenger and Advocate* 3, no. 9 (June 1837): 520.
14. Joseph Smith Jr. laid out his Plan of Kirtland in 1836. A drawing can be found in Backman, *The Heavens Resound*, 312.
15. *DHC*, 3: 11.

Jacksonian Democratic Party ticket of Martin Van Buren of New York for president and Richard M. Johnson of Kentucky for vice president in the coming 1836 national election.[16] Wagons of Mormon converts arrived every day carrying Democratic Party voters. Local Whigs already sensed a township government takeover just waiting to happen with the next election, and with each day, fears were that Geauga County government might be next unless the situation changed.[17]

Western Reserve communities, like those in New England, were obliged to take care of their poor. Food banks assisted the poor and indigent. However, local citizen overseers "warned out" any newly arrived Mormon immigrants who had no means for their own survival.[18] Secular community leaders reserved scarce resources for their own, but not for Mormon intruders.

Local businessmen applied economic pressure on church members by refusing to hire them in their mills, lumberyards, blacksmith shops, and stores, nor would mill owners process Mormon grain crops or buy their goods. Mormons suffered, especially during the winters, when food supplies were scarce. The boycott forced Mormon families to survive on goods purchased from surrounding communities, where their presence was not so intimidating. Eventually, a Mormon built his own mill so members could process their crops.

Just as pressures from without tested the faith of the Saints, pressures from within created crises as well. Economically deprived followers who left behind their successful farms in New York and Pennsylvania began to question their decision to uproot their families and follow the prophet

---

16. The 9 October 1835 issue emblazoned the Democratic Party ticket on its front page and quoted Thomas Hart Benton, stating, "Union, harmony, self-denial, concession,—everything for the cause, nothing for men,—should be the watchword, and the motto of the democratic party." *Northern Times* 1, no. 28 (9 October 1835): 1, in Community of Christ Library-Archives.

17. There was some evidence of Mormons making political inroads in Kirtland Township government. For example, Mormon Oliver Harmon Jr. was elected in 1836 to serve as overseer of the poor. Also, one of two fence viewers and one of the supervisors of the highways were Mormons. Milton V. Backman Jr. provides a statistical analysis of the ratio of Latter Day Saint and non-Latter Day Saint town officers for Kirtland Township, 1830–1839, in his *The Heavens Resound*, 339.

18. Backman, *The Heavens Resound*, 340.

Problems in Kirtland

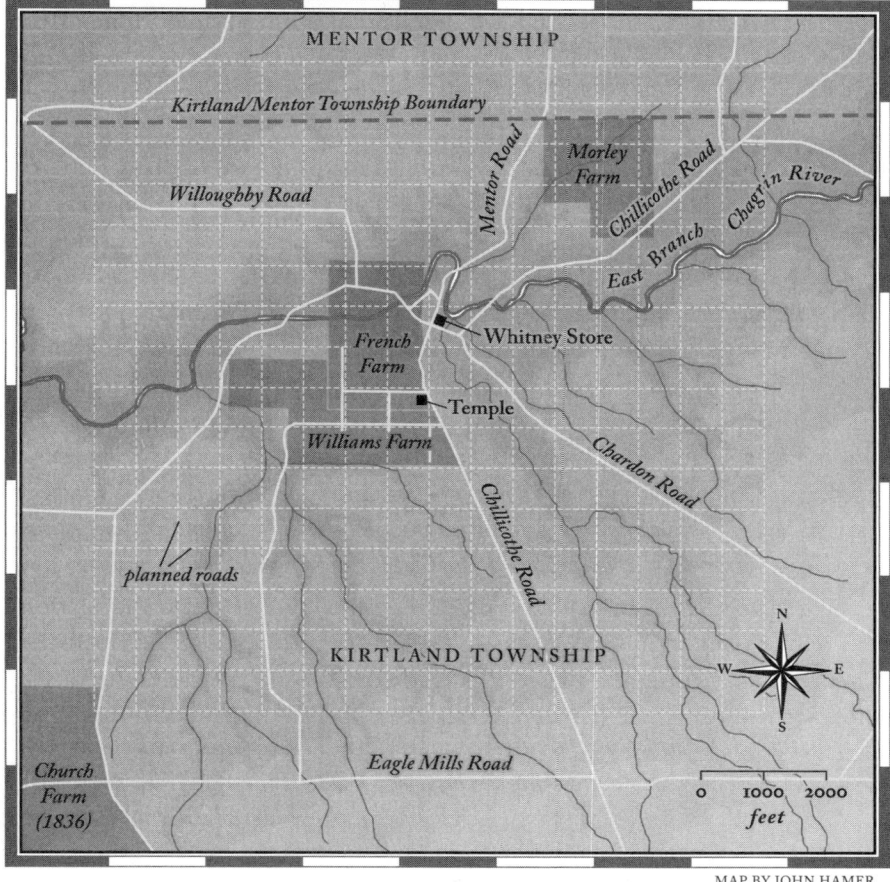

MAP BY JOHN HAMER

Joseph Smith's 1833 Kirtland Plat superimposed on the surrounding terrain

and his millennial dream to achieve their salvation. To remain financially solvent, Joseph had to find revenue sources to sustain the church and its mission. Sometime before July 1836, a church member named Burgess, who had immigrated to Kirtland, told the prophet that "a large amount of money had been secreted in the cellar of a certain house in Salem, Massachusetts, which had belonged to a widow, and he [Burgess] thought he was the only person now living, who had knowledge of it, or to the location of the house.'"[19] Without being told the actual location, the prophet took Burgess's statement seriously. Accompanied by Oliver Cowdery, Hyrum Smith, and Sidney Rigdon, the prophet left Kirtland in search of a hidden treasure of gold and silver in Salem, Massachusetts.[20]

Leaving on 25 July, the men traveled to Buffalo, and then passed through Rochester, Utica, and Albany, suggesting that they coursed along the Erie Canal, and arrived in New York City, where they spent the next week. From New York City they took another steamer to Providence, Rhode Island, and then went by rail to Boston, Massachusetts. They concluded their outbound journey by traveling the last fifteen miles to Salem.

Clearly Joseph was confused, since the treasure could be in the basement of any of a hundred houses. Evidently, the prophet was concerned about his standing with God in even pursuing such a venture with so little foreknowledge and at a time when church resources were so scarce. After Smith and his colleagues arrived in Salem, he received divine reassurance on 6 August 1836:

> I the Lord your God am not displeased with your coming this Journey, notwithstandi[n]g your follies I have much treasure in this city for you, for the benefit of Zion; and many people in the city whom I will gather out in due time for the benefit of Zion, through your instrumentality. Therefore it is expedient that you should form acquaintance with men in this city, as you shall be led, and as it shall be given you.
>
> And it shall come to pass, in due time, that I will give this city into your hands, that you shall have power over it, insomuch that they shall not discover your secret parts; and its wealth, pertaining to gold and silver, shall be yours.[21]

---

19. Ebenezer Robinson, "Items of Personal History of the Editor," *The Return* (July 1889): 105, in Van Wagoner, *Sidney Rigdon*, 181.

20. The selection of these important church leaders signaled how significant the hoped-for success of this trip was for the movement. See H. Michael Marquardt, *The Rise of Mormonism, 1816–1844* (Longwood, Fla.: Xulon Press, 2005), 431.

21. Marquardt, *The Joseph Smith Revelations*, 281. Conference delegates within the Community of Christ tradition have never canonized this statement; however, the LDS Church has. Currently it is included in the LDS Doctrine and Covenants as Section 111.

Salem, Massachusetts, held special meaning for the Seer, as his family roots ran deep there. His great-great-grandfather, Samuell Smith, and Samuell's in-law John Gould were accusers in a Salem witch trial in 1692. As he toured the area, he must have found interesting the changes in the town since his convalescence there from leg surgery as a seven-year-old while living with his Uncle Jesse. Obviously the Mormon party fully expected to receive divine knowledge of the treasure's location. But after seventeen days in Salem with no insights, they gave up and returned empty-handed to Kirtland, arriving in September.[22]

Legal Challenges and Vexatious Lawsuits

SKEPTICS BOTH INSIDE and outside the movement used the failed prophecy as an opportunity to pursue Smith in the courts. Legal challenges were not limited to the prophet's religious claims, but also focused on his commercial decision making. When necessary, the Saints responded with counter suits. The case of Joseph Smith Jr.'s pursuit of Philastus Hurlbut in 1833 is a good example. Hurlbut's membership in the church had lasted barely a month when church leaders excommunicated him on charges of sexual misconduct. Feeling victimized, Hurlbut lashed out against Joseph Smith with allegations that the so-called prophet had stolen the Book of Mormon narrative from Solomon Spaulding's writings. When Hurlbut supposedly threatened Smith's life, the prophet levied charges that led to a sensationalized trial that went into the next year.

Feeling certain of legal success against Hurlbut, and believing that God stood by his side, Smith prophesied victory in court:

> My soul delighteth in the law of the Lord, for He forgiveth my sins, and will confound mine enemies. The Lord shall destroy him who has lifted his heel against me, even that wicked man Dr. Philastus Hurlburt; He will deliver him to the fowls of heaven, and his bones shall be cast to the blasts of the wind, for he lifted his arm against the Almighty, therefore the Lord shall destroy him.[23]

---

22. D. Michael Quinn argued that the Salem trip was a continuation of Joseph Smith Jr.'s treasure-seeking habits. See Quinn, *Early Mormonism*, 262–64.

23. *DHC*, 2: 46.

When the court rendered in the prophet's favor, Joseph felt vindicated. His journal under the date of 9 April 1834 reads: "after an impartial trial, the court decided that Dr. Philastus Hurlburt be bound over, under two hundred dollar bonds, to keep the peace for six months, and pay the cost, which amounted to nearly three hundred dollars, all of which was in answer to our prayers, for which I thank my Heavenly Father."[24]

Unfortunately, not all his trial experiences were so positive. During his last two years in Kirtland, seventeen plaintiffs charged Smith with a variety of crimes, mostly associated with his indebtedness. Of these cases, four were settled out of court, nine Smith either lost or defaulted, thus requiring him to pay damages, and four were discontinued by the plaintiffs.[25] Between 1836 and 1839, Joseph Smith brought three civil suits but prevailed in only one, recovering $213.92. He lost a second case and dropped charges in a third.[26]

Joseph Smith Jr. was not the only church leader to endure legal wrangling. Parley P. Pratt and Sidney Rigdon had to defend themselves as well. The Ohio courts generally treated the Saints fairly.[27] Joseph grew tired of defending himself, however, and his frustrations emanated from those who brought the charges, and not the courts. But many of the charges were of his own making through his speculative banking solution to finance the church mission. Enormous pressures generated from forces both outside and inside the movement tested the faith of followers living in Kirtland. Since the church's most pressing problem at this time was financial, a dramatic solution had to be found.

The Kirtland Banking Venture

IT IS UNKNOWN how Joseph Smith Jr. decided on a banking venture as a source of revenue to fund the mission of the church. Almost no one

---

24. *DHC*, 2: 49.
25. Marvin S. Hill, C. Keith Rooker, and Larry T. Wimmer, *The Kirtland Economy Revisited: A Market Critique of Sectarian Economics* (Provo, Utah: Brigham Young University Press, 1977), 30–33.
26. Hill, Rooker, and Wimmer, *The Kirtland Economy Revisited*, 33fn a.
27. This is the conclusion of Edwin Brown Firmage and Richard Collin Mangrum in *Zion in the Courts: A Legal History of the Church of Jesus Christ of Latter-day Saints, 1830–1900* (Urbana: University of Illinois Press, 1988), 54.

within the movement had any experience as a banker. But the reality was that the church and its leaders became encumbered with heavy debts, and every day, the poverty-stricken Saints faced the threat of creditors calling at their doors.

Approaching 1837, Joseph must have surveyed church assets and discovered that, with rising land prices, he could sell off church-owned parcels to pay bills, but the usury charged by bankers in the Northeastern states, Cleveland, and nearby communities was an unavoidable burden. Amid what Joseph perceived as a relatively healthy regional economy, he devised a plan to create a land bank where, through the inflationary value of church properties and interest income on investments, the church could pay off debts and thus provide a stable source of income for future church mission.[28] At least that was the plan.

The economic climate for such an institution in the Western Reserve presented great opportunities for success. Ohio frontier communities were starved for credit and specie money (gold and silver coins). Although the initial offering of the Kirtland bank was in scrip (paper money), Smith must have foreseen a day in the not too distant future when his bank could support a free exchange of his paper money with hard money. Many Northeastern bankers refused to speculate on pioneers headed west for fear they would either never see their money again, or not get a good return from it.[29] Thus, local banks had natural advantages.

Also, Joseph thought he knew the approximate investment strength of the entrepreneurs within his following. In 1836, Mormons owned eight of the nine mercantile firms and eight of the thirteen manufacturing firms in Kirtland.[30] It is possible that Smith anticipated the support of these businessmen if times got tough. Being so well located between Fairport Harbor, a major Lake Erie disembarkation point, and Cleveland would

---

28. In *The Kirtland Economy Revisited*, Hill, Rooker, and Wimmer estimated that Smith held land in Kirtland worth approximately $33,000 in increased equity due to inflationary economic conditions. See page 36. The authors also calculated that in 1830 an average acre of land in Kirtland cost $7.03; by 1837 that same acre cost $33.95. See page 15.
29. Firmage and Mangrum, *Zion in the Courts*, 54.
30. This was a preindustrial era when manufacturing meant blacksmith shops; brickyards; saw, grist, and carding mills; a tannery; and a shoe shop, to name a few examples. See Hill, Rooker, and Wimmer, *The Kirtland Economy Revisited*, 13.

place a Kirtland bank in a central position to benefit from travelers westering from the East. Finally, the Kirtland area benefited from the numerous small feeder canals that connected to the north-south oriented, 309-mile Ohio Canal, completed in 1833.[31] These canals signaled to the prophet the ability to move people and products more easily across the region. Beyond the burdensome financial needs of the church, all these conditions may have given the prophet optimism to move in the direction of a church-owned land bank.

Launching the project required three important tools: an affiliated sponsoring association, a bank charter from the state of Ohio, and special plates to print the money. On 2 November 1836, Smith announced the creation of the "Kirtland Safety Society." His language suggested the need to assure investors about the security of their investments. This association would be the church's bank, yet its success also depended on the confidence of investors from the Kirtland community. Although the prophet knew his followers would participate, they had already committed their savings toward the construction of the House of the Lord and acquisition of the Egyptian artifacts. So the most significant revenues would have to come from nonmembers. Confidence was the key.

Public confidence would be bolstered by receiving authorization from the state capital through a banking charter. So the same day he created the Kirtland Safety Society, Joseph Smith dispatched Orson Hyde to Columbus, Ohio, to apply for a bank charter, and Oliver Cowdery to Philadelphia, Pennsylvania, for currency plates. Cowdery returned from Philadelphia with the plates but Hyde returned from Columbus empty-handed. Rather than facing the obvious reality and discarding the entire plan, Smith and church leaders decided to circumvent the state legislature's right to issues charters and to enforce the Ohio Banking Act of 1816. On 2 January 1837, church leaders abandoned the Kirtland Safety Society and organized the Kirtland Safety Society Anti-Banking Company. After this change, notes that came off the press bore the prefix "ANTI-" and the suffix "ING CO." next to the word BANK so that it read "ANTI- BANK ING CO." Each bill was numbered by hand, and, no doubt to lend credibility, Sidney

---

31. Billington and Ridge, *Westward Expansion*, 332–33.

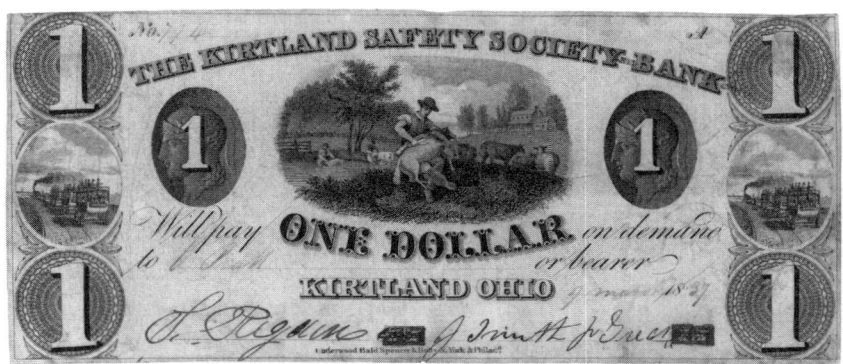

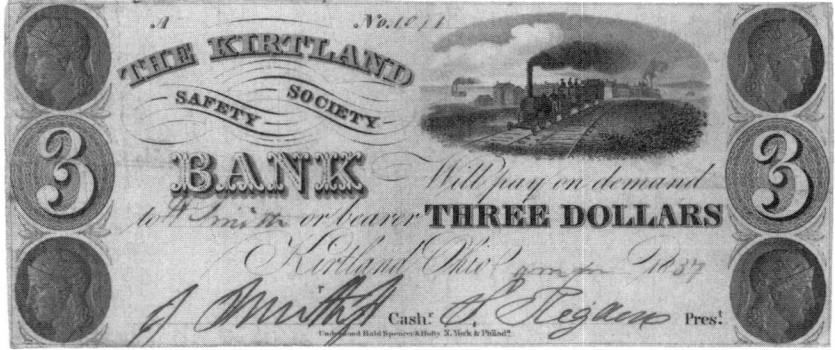

COMMUNITY OF CHRIST LIBRARY-ARCHIVES
Kirtland Safety Society notes signed by Joseph Smith and Sidney Rigdon (the word ANTI appears before BANK and the words ING CO. after BANK on the $1 bill)

Rigdon signed many of the bills as president, as did Joseph Smith Jr. as cashier.

The bank was set up in a small structure just south of the House of the Lord and the doors opened for the first day's business on 2 January 1837. The first run of bills was issued in one-, two-, and three-dollar denominations totaling approximately $10,000. Larger denominations followed, raising the value of notes issued to as much as $100,000.[32]

Within a week, observers exploited the flaws in the plan. To hasten the inevitable disaster, skeptics took out notes and then returned to the

32. Smith set the capital stock at $4 million, though the roughly 200 investors provided only $21,000 in cash. Heber C. Kimball subscribed for $50,000 in shares with his $15 cash investment. See Bushman, *Rough Stone Rolling*, 332.

bank to redeem them for specie. This initiated an unavoidable plummet in bank assets. Detractor C. G. Webb reported that, in an attempt to reverse the slide, Joseph Smith Jr. lined the shelves of the bank vault with chests marked "$1,000." Each was covered with a layer of fifty-cent silver coins. Investors who were worried about their savings could enter the vault, where Smith would open one for their viewing and heft it. As Webb reported, Smith filled the boxes with "sand, lead, old iron, stone, and combustibles." Webb described the impact of the charade: "[The chests] created general confidence in the solidity of the bank and that beautiful paper money went like hot cakes. For about a month it was the best money in the country."[33]

Webb identified correctly the approximate length of time that the bank remained viable. By the end of its third week of business, the bank floundered. On 23 January, Smith and Rigdon stopped payment, shut its doors, and drew the shades. What had been a precipitous decline in paper value now went into freefall. Within the next two weeks, the bank notes lost 88 percent of their value and investors lost all hope of any return on their investment. Joseph Smith himself was a big loser, as he had personally purchased more stock than 85 percent of the investors.

Since the signatures of Joseph Smith Jr. and Sidney Rigdon appeared on many of the bills, they could not escape blame. Now their enemies attacked with vengeance and Grandison Newell, a long-time detractor, entered the first major suit against the prophet, alleging violation of the Ohio Banking statute. At the initial hearing, held in March 1837, the judge set a trial date for October. The fall verdict held Smith and Rigdon responsible for the losses. As if to add insult to Smith's financial injury, the October judgment fined Smith and Rigdon $1,000 each. But that was only the first case against them. Lawsuits for damages by other investors stacked up

---

33. The context of this oft-cited reference should be understood and possibly challenged, as Webb was a strong critic of the prophet and his movement. From an interview with Wilhelm Wyl, in *Mormon Portraits, Joseph Smith the Prophet, His Family and His Friends* (Salt Lake City, n.p., 1886), 36; also in Oliver Olney, *The Absurdities of Mormonism Portrayed, a brief sketch* (Hancock County, Illinois: n.p., 3 March 1843), 4; also see Cyrus Smalling Letter in E. G. Lee, *The Mormons, or Knavery Exposed* (Philadelphia: n.p., 1841), 14. These primary sources are in Brodie, *No Man Knows My History*, 197. Also see Hill, Rooker, and Wimmer, *The Kirtland Economy Revisited*, 3.

during the fall of 1837, while there was little hope that either man could meet any of his debts.[34]

Problems of Apostasy

AMID ALL HIS legal and financial troubles, Smith continued uninterrupted with his prophetic task. His trip to Missouri in late September 1837 unnerved those who pursued him in the courts. Church administration problems continued as Smith, Rigdon, William Smith, and Vincent Knight arrived in the Saints' encampment at Far West, Caldwell County, Missouri, on 1 November.

As misfortunes abounded, especially the financial ones associated with the bank failure, doubts naturally focused on the prophet. The failed Salem prophecy and aborted treasure quest triggered questions in the minds of those who were already suspicious that Smith had lost his prophetic skills. By September 1837, the crisis boiled over at the church conference in Kirtland, when the members were called on to sustain church leadership. Joseph Smith Jr. and Sidney Rigdon were sustained, but delegates rejected Martin Harris, John Johnson, Joseph Coe, and Joseph C. Kingsbury because of their criticisms of the prophet. Several others, including three apostles—Luke S. Johnson, Lyman E. Johnson, and John F. Boynton—were disfellowshipped. Because David Whitmer, Oliver Cowdery, and Leonard Rich confessed their weaknesses and asked forgiveness, they regained their leadership responsibilities.[35]

The apostasy also reached deeply into the membership. Thirty priesthood members rejected the prophet and renounced their membership. Not satisfied with their actions, these former members launched a competing religious movement under the direction of the prophet's close personal friend and former secretary Warren Parrish. Reverting back to the Palmyra, New York, era, Parrish and his followers embraced the original name,

---

34. A valuable explanation of the historical, legal, and economic issues surrounding the collapse of the Kirtland community is provided in Hill, Rooker, and Wimmer, *The Kirtland Economy Revisited*.
35. *Kirtland Council Minute Book*, typescript copy, 235, in Community of Christ Library-Archives.

Church of Christ.[36] Eventually, as many as three hundred members, including about one-third of the church leadership, bolted the movement. Over time, the original three witnesses to the Book of Mormon, four apostles, and five presidents of seventy[37] left the church completely or were disciplined by surviving church leaders.

With loyalty problems not limited to Kirtland, the prophet had to set in order the Missouri church as well. At a church conference on 6–7 November 1837, members refused to sustain Frederick Granger Williams as second counselor in the First Presidency. To resolve the complaints against Williams, Smith nominated his older brother, Hyrum, who received unanimous support. Reasserting his authority, Smith disciplined David Whitmer, Oliver Cowdery, John Whitmer, and William W. Phelps, all church leaders in Missouri, for usurping too much authority. The change in the First Presidency in Missouri required another sustaining vote for Hyrum among the Kirtland Saints. These problems were indicative of the dysfunctional, bifurcated nature of the church at the time, but this issue would be resolved within the next year with the evacuation from Kirtland.

Disintegration of the Church and Kirtland Evacuation

NOTWITHSTANDING THE CONTINUED outpourings of heavenly manifestations in temple church services during the spring, and the calling of more than a hundred ministers to missions throughout North America and England, it was becoming clear that as 1837 progressed the church had approached the nadir of its existence. On their return to Kirtland on 10 December, Smith and Rigdon found the church in complete disarray and with little hope that the prophet could change things. Smith faced yet another lawsuit surrounding the bank crisis, and if found guilty, he could face being in prison for a very long time. And on 22 December, Apostle Brigham Young, feeling his life was in danger, kissed his wife and family

---

36. Thomas B. Marsh to W.[ilford] Woodruff, in *Elders' Journal* 1, no. 3 (July 1838): 36–37.
37. The seventy were special witnesses accepting missionary responsibilities. The priesthood office is based on a New Testament reference found in Luke 10. Joseph Smith Jr. selected many of the seventy from the companies who had participated in the failed Zion's Camp march a year and a half earlier.

good-bye and fled on horseback to Missouri. Violence against church leaders and members escalated, and more followed Young out of town.

As 1838 dawned, Smith and Rigdon concluded that their escape from Kirtland now was just a matter of timing. Their indefensible financial transactions associated with the anti-bank scheme, challenges from apostates, and pending trial litigation provided more than enough incentive for them to leave Kirtland. Getting the Mormons to leave the region may have been the real motive of church critics, since those who brought suit to recover losses knew that church resources were already exhausted. The numerous warrants for their arrest guaranteed that the church leaders, as fugitives from justice, could never return. During the evening of 12 January 1838, Smith and Rigdon were alerted to a posse forming to arrest them. In a rush, Joseph and Sidney made plans to rendezvous with Emma and Phebe in Norton Township, Medina County, Ohio, about sixty miles away. Then, with the posse's thundering hooves in the distance, the two men made good their escape. Thirty-six hours later, wives and families met husbands and fathers.[38] With only the basic necessities and family heirlooms in their wagons, anything left behind became the plunder of looters or was sold off to cover debts.

Those church members who remained behind were now the focus of community anger. Reprisals occurred daily as numerous homes were set ablaze. Just after midnight of 16 January, Caroline Crosby awoke from her sleep to men yelling and a bright light shining in her window.[39] Someone had torched the printing office next to the temple. Due to a favorable prevailing wind, the temple itself was only scorched. Arson was an effective method of harassment to force the Saints out of Kirtland.[40]

38. *DHC*, 3: 1–2.
39. *Autobiography of Luman Andros Shurtliff*, 30–31, in Backman, *The Heavens Resound*, 349.
40. Believer Benjamin F. Johnson identified his brother-in-law, Lyman R. Sherman, as the print shop arsonist. See Benjamin F. Johnson, "Autobiography of Benjamin F. Johnson," as found in *My Life's Review* (Independence, Mo.: Zion's Printing and Publishing, Co., 1942), 29–30. Noticing that a convenient wind would protect the temple from incineration, it is entirely possible that Sherman torched the print shop especially since the church no longer owned it at the time of its burning. Lawyers had recently attached the print shop in a lawsuit to compensate detractors. Sherman soon rose through the priesthood and joined the Quorum of Twelve Apostles in January 1839.

By February, families began their preparations to follow their prophet to Missouri. With the spring thaw, the small wagon trains headed west. Then, in early July, a major complement of nearly five hundred Saints in fifty wagons left Kirtland. The wagon train called themselves the Kirtland Camp. When the evacuation ended, a little more than one hundred Saints remained from what once had been the capital city of Latter Day Saintism and had numbered in the thousands.

Assessing the Kirtland Experience, 1831–1838

Joseph Smith Jr.'s religious movement achieved much during its seven-year presence in Kirtland. The House of the Lord exhibited the Saints' sacrificial giving. The construction project expressed their anxiousness to be identified as an Old Testament people in the New World dispensation. The prophet communicated the structure's purpose in a language of revelatory idealism focusing on worship, education, and church administration, while its workers expressed in its construction detail an architectural language demonstrating a pragmatic selection of popular architectural styles. Together this structural language of Latter Day Saintism evolved considerably from its foundation in Kirtland through the planning of a temple in Far West, Missouri, and the eventual construction of one in Nauvoo, Illinois. But for today, even more than the gleaming white edifice made of rubble stone and mortar, the Kirtland Temple symbolizes the pinnacle of spiritual achievement in the heavenly manifestations to which the Saints testified. Those Pentecostal experiences still linger in the minds of people today who hear the stories and visit the sacred structure.

During the Kirtland era, Joseph Smith continued his scriptural innovations. In revising the Bible to correct perceived errors and document his theological positions, and in his translation of the *Book of Abraham*, Smith enhanced his prophetic credentials, proving to his followers that he had not lost his powers of discernment and his ability to read unknown ancient texts. Thus, the Kirtland period was an "era of revelation." In August 1835, the General Conference delegates in Kirtland authorized the compilation of revelations given to the church into a Doctrine and Covenants, which would systematize the beliefs and laws of the church. More than sixty entries into this book were made during this period and ranged from suggestions for healthy living, laws for church governance, and a commandment to keep a regular church history, to official stances on repentance and the redemption of Zion.

But the strongest and most controversial of the church's doctrinal statements on salvation and the end times also have their roots in the Kirtland period. These theological positions may have drawn the most people to the church. The belief in three heavens afforded salvation to even the "good men of the earth," although only those baptized in the church could receive the highest glory. This provided an acceptable alternative to Calvinist views that stated God would elect only a few, and the dualist heaven-hell soteriology of more-mainline Protestant denominations. But also here in Kirtland, theological seeds were planted about the permanence of the marriage institution for both time and eternity. In the years to come, these beliefs would bloom fully and move Mormonism away from the main currents of Christian thought.

The Kirtland Mormons knew they lived in the last dispensation of time. They anxiously awaited the Second Coming and even changed their official name to reflect their dispensationalist beliefs—the Church of the Latter Day Saints. Members also knew their salvation depended on loyalty and obedience to their modern-day prophet. Those who seriously questioned the prophet's decisions were either forced out or marginalized. In either case, they established a long-standing tradition of dissent that still exists in the movement today.

In the development of the Mormon worldview, a radical shift emerged. Moving into the Connecticut Western Reserve in 1831, Mormons brought with them near-pacifist beliefs. However, events in Independence, Missouri, spurred their rejection of nonviolence. With the Zion's Camp march in the spring and summer of 1834, the prophet pursued militaristic means to redeem Zion. Although a failure, the prophet never returned the church to being one of peace and nonviolence. The world, to Joseph Smith Jr., was now one of us versus them, right versus wrong, just versus unjust, and exclusion versus inclusion. Such a simplistic view amid the complexities of frontier American society inflamed the passions of both defenders and detractors.

The Kirtland Latter Day Saints were "people of the word"—both written and spoken. In establishing at least four church newspapers,[41] they declared their beliefs on key political, social, and doctrinal issues of their times. With the Literary Firm coordinating these publications, subscription sales were to be a valuable source of income for the church. Historian Nathan O. Hatch referred to this era in American history as "the golden age of local publishing."[42] Certainly the Latter Day Saints participated in the proliferation of church periodicals that circulated throughout the American frontier. Mormon preachers also added their voices to a cacophony of vernacular preaching that dominated the American hinterland. Of all the preachers in the Kirtland period, Sidney Rigdon, with his passion for the spoken word, best exemplified this characteristic. The dramatic increase in baptisms attested to the success of Latter Day Saint missionaries in the context of intense denominational competition.[43]

Most of all, the Kirtland era, from 1831 to 1838, was pivotal because going into this time the church had yet to prove its viability. Coming out of Kirtland there would be no question that the movement had staying power. Even with all of its problems as the Saints evacuated Kirtland, their journey was in pursuit of a belief in their prophet, Joseph Smith Jr., as the one person who could direct the ushering in of the Second Coming as well as the achievement of their own salvation.

When Joseph arrived in early 1831, the viability of his movement was yet to be proved. But by the time of the exodus in 1838, the small frontier church was international with its successful missions into Canada and the British Isles, where baptisms by church missionaries dramatically increased the total membership.

Although the Saints left behind in Kirtland much of their earthly goods that could not be packed in their wagons, they took with them their hopes, dreams, and aspirations for their divine inheritance in Zion. All eyes now looked westward to the church community in Far West, Caldwell County, Missouri.

---

41. Here I refer to *The Evening and the Morning Star*, the *Latter Day Saints' Messenger and Advocate*, the *Elders' Journal*, and the *Northern Times*.
42. Hatch, *Democratization of American Christianity*, 127.
43. Hatch, *Democratization of American Christianity*, 137.

CHAPTER THIRTEEN

Finding Sanctuary and Forging Unity at Far West

Becoming One Church in Far West, Missouri: A Brief Review of the Historical Setting

ON THURSDAY 18 October 1838, Mormon soldiers, in self-righteous anger, pillaged and set fire to the northwestern Missouri communities of Gallatin, Millport, and Grindstone Fork in Daviess County. Twelve days later, as part of a massacre of Mormons at Haun's Mill in eastern Caldwell County, an anti-Mormon ruffian placed his rifle muzzle to the head of a cowering ten-year-old child and fired. What events created circumstances where seemingly rational people could justify in their own minds the commission of such atrocities? What lessons can be learned from this dark chapter in Missouri and church history? Finding answers to these questions is the focus here.

By the spring of 1834, church members who had evacuated from Jackson County had established themselves north of the Missouri River in Clay County. Their full expectation was to regain their "inheritance in Zion" by going back to where Christ's return would surely happen. In a few months, Joseph Smith Jr.'s Zion's Camp march to liberate Zion would end in failure.

The Missouri Saints' hopes of redeeming Zion faded. Mormon wagons may have passed each other in 1834 as some of the 1,200 beleaguered Jackson County Saints slowly trekked back to Kirtland while even more left Kirtland heading to Zion with great enthusiasm. As Mormons from the East migrated into Clay County, a few acquired sizable tracts of land. The increasing arrival of émigrés intimidated the citizens of Clay County, but these Missourians, at least in the near term, handled the numbers problem quite differently from those on the south side of the Missouri River in Jackson County. Although worried about the same issues as Jackson Countians, the citizens of Clay County were much more patient and willing to discuss problems. Their complaints—political intimidation, competition over land purchases, and exhaustion of local resources—must have sounded quite familiar to the Saints.

Perhaps the Mormons had learned at least some of the difficult lessons of exclusivity from their Jackson County experience, as communication and accommodation characterized their two-and-a-half years in Clay County. Between 1834 and 1836, the Saints lived in relative harmony there. However, by the end of June 1836, as Mormon numbers grew, local citizens approached the Saints with a bill of particulars that addressed their concerns about developments:

> [The Mormons'] rapid emigration, their large purchases, and offers to purchase lands, the remarks of the ignorant and imprudent portion of them, that this country is destined by heaven to be theirs are received and looked upon, by a large portion of this community, as strong and convincing proofs that they intend to make this county their permanent home, the centre and general rendezvous of their people.[1]

Adding to their list of complaints, the Clay County citizens charged that church leaders had frequent contact with Native Americans, telling them that they were "part of God's chosen people, and are destined by heaven to inherit this land." Also, citizens considered Mormons' Eastern cultural habits and their perceived opposition to slavery as barriers to their relationship. Each claim, including the antislavery charge, prompted the Saints' wholehearted rejection. But here is where the Clay Countians handled the Mormon Question differently than did their counterparts in Jackson County. Rather than resorting to violence, the Clay County citizens petitioned the Mormons to leave:

> We, therefore, in a spirit of frank and friendly kindness, do advise them to seek a home where they may obtain large and separate bodies

---

1. *DHC*, 2: 449–50.

of land, and have a community of their own. We further say to them, if they regard their own safety and welfare, if they regard the welfare of their families, their wives and children, they will ponder with deep and solemn reflection on this friendly admonition.

We want nothing, we ask nothing, we would have nothing from this people, we only ask them, for their own safety, and for ours, to take the least of the two evils. Most of them are destitute of land, have but little property, are late emigrants to this country, without relations, friends, or endearing ties to bind them to this land. At the risk of such imminent peril to them and to us, we request them to leave us, when their crops are gathered, their business settled, and they have made every suitable preparation to remove. Those who have forty acres of land, we are willing should remain until they can dispose of it without loss, if it should require years. But we urge, most strongly urge, that emigration cease, and cease immediately, as nothing else can or will allay for a moment, the deep excitement that is now unhappily agitating this community.[2]

The demands presented by Clay County officials were friendly but firm. Now the Saints had to respond.

The Mormons had two possible courses of action—one violent and the other peaceful. In a 16 August 1834 letter from Kirtland to Lyman Wight, Edward Partridge, John Corrill, Isaac Morley, and others of the High Council of Zion, Joseph Smith Jr. ordered Lyman Wight to appeal to the Missouri governor for redress of the Saints' grievances, and if he did not find satisfaction, then he was to "to endeavor to take life, or tear down houses, and if the citizens of Clay county do not befriend us, to gather up the little army, and be set over immediately into Jackson county, and trust in God, and do the best he can in maintaining the ground." Smith set the date for this "redemption of Zion" as 11 September 1836.[3]

Perhaps the Missouri Saints could not conceive of another expulsion and Zion's Camp march, even with the prophet's assurance that God was on their side; so rather than resorting to violence again, they chose the second option—peaceful accommodation. On 1 July 1836, taking only a day to decide, church leaders resoundingly rejected the charges levied earlier in

2. *DHC*, 2: 451.
3. *DHC*, 2: 145.

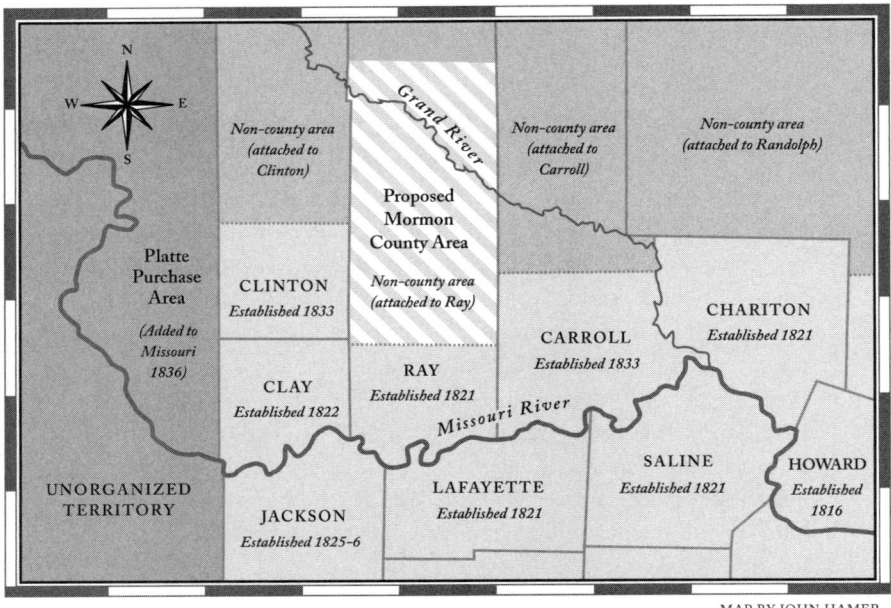

MAP BY JOHN HAMER

Northwestern Missouri in 1835, highlighting the proposed Mormon county area

the Clay County petition, but then accepted the peaceful offer by agreeing to work with county officials in finding suitable lands.

The Search for Sanctuary—the Creation of Caldwell County and Daviess County, Missouri[4]

FINDING SUITABLE LAND to call their own was not a difficult task. Even before Clay County troubles arose, a few Mormon families moved east from Clay County into an undeveloped part of northern Ray County.[5] This sizable tract of northern Missouri, chartered at statehood in Jefferson City in 1821, extended from its southern border at the banks of

4. An excellent exploration of the creation of Caldwell County is Stephen C. LeSueur, "Missouri's Failed Compromise: The Creation of Caldwell County for the Mormons," *Journal of Mormon History* 31, no. 3 (Fall 2005): 113–14.

5. Leland Homer Gentry, *A History of the Latter-day Saints in Northern Missouri from 1836 to 1839* (PhD diss., Brigham Young University, 1965, published by the Joseph Fielding Smith Institute and *Brigham Young University Studies*, 2000), 19–20.

the Missouri River northward to the Iowa Territory border. Northern Ray County was typical Missouri prairie and deemed by most as unproductive, and thus sparsely populated. These conditions seemed desirable, so respected Mormon leaders John Corrill and John Murdock viewed the land and then went to Richmond, the Ray County seat, to present a four-part petition stating the Mormon intentions: that Mormons wanted only their equal rights as property owners; that should Ray County officials desire the Saints to leave, the request would be honored assuming reasonable time to sell the land without sacrifice, and in so doing, the Saints would promise to stop further Mormon immigration into the county; that the Mormons would settle in the county only with the consent of the Ray County citizens; and last, that the Saints would honor a six-mile strip of land[6] as a buffer with Ray Countians.[7]

By early August 1836, both sides misconstrued communications. The two Mormon negotiators returned to the Saints thinking they had achieved success when they had not. However, the Ray County officials underestimated the considerable resistance from Missouri citizens, who vowed to stop Mormon encroachments. Amid all this confusion, on 8 August, William W. Phelps and John Whitmer purchased a tract of land and laid out the Mormon community of Far West, and the migration out of Clay County proceeded.

---

6. This six-mile strip of land, extending from the eastern and western boundaries separating Caldwell and Ray Counties, was called Buncombe's Strip. The Buncombe settlement near the center of the strip of land became the source for the name of the jurisdiction. LeSueur noted that the legislative origin of the strip only confused the boundary arrangements between Caldwell and Ray County settlers. The 1820 law that created Ray County awarded Buncombe's strip to Ray County, but five years later another law stated that Buncombe would be incorporated in any new county created north of Ray County. This designated Buncombe as part of Caldwell County. The Missouri legislature ended the confusion in January 1839 by attaching Buncombe to Ray County. See LeSueur, "Missouri's Failed Compromise," 124fn27. Since the 24 October 1838 Battle of Crooked River occurred within Buncombe's Strip, it is possible that Buncombe was a reward to Ray County for any losses they may have received from the Mormon War.

7. "Report of the Committee on the Part of the Mormons," *Journal History of the Church of Jesus Christ of Latter-day Saints* (30 July 1836), in LeSueur, "Missouri's Failed Compromise," 123.

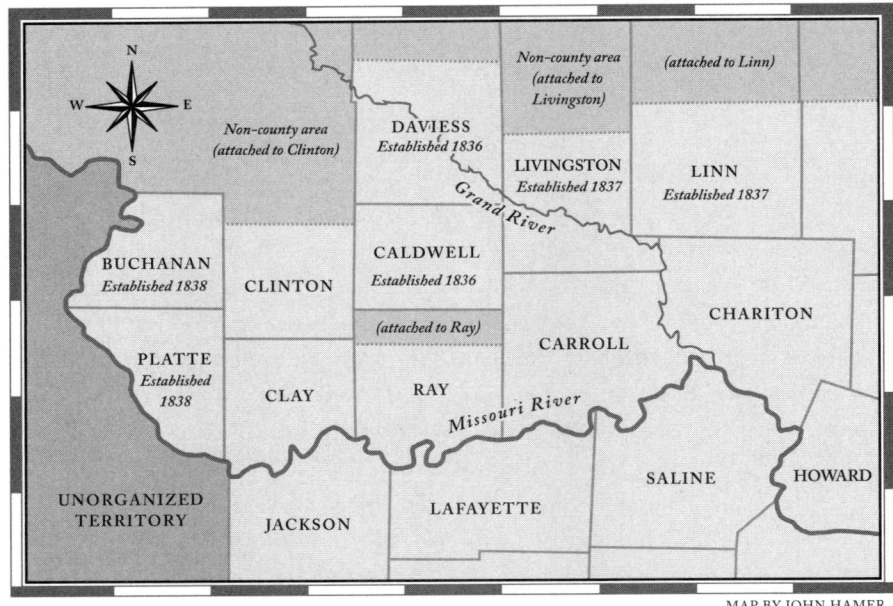

Northwestern Missouri, 1836-38

What the Latter Day Saints needed most, however, was political control, and thus legal protection, over their community. This they received when Missouri governor Lilburn W. Boggs signed legislation on 29 December 1836 that established the boundaries of Caldwell County.[8] Boggs, the consummate politician, who was obviously no great supporter of Mormon rights, needed convincing to support friendly legislation for a people he despised.[9] Four reasons motivated his signature. First was the respect

8. Alexander Doniphan's father, Joseph Doniphan, performed military service under Captain Matthew Caldwell. Alexander remembered stories told by his father about Caldwell's bravery and gallantry in battle, and thus chose to name the new county after him. Caldwell County, Kentucky, is also named after Matthew Caldwell. See *History of Caldwell and Livingston Counties, Missouri* (St. Louis: National Historical Company, 1886), 105, photocopy in Community of Christ Library-Archives.

9. Boggs was elected to the Missouri state house as senator from 1826 to 1832, then served as lieutenant governor in 1832 during the Jackson County crisis. He was a former merchant in Jackson County and personally owned property in Independence. A Missouri westerner, he knew well the political liabilities of extending his support for legislation that would provide the Mormons a Missouri sanctuary. An excellent source of information on Boggs is Joseph F. Gordon, "The Political Career of Lilburn W. Boggs,"

commanded by the legislation's sponsor, Alexander William Doniphan, Clay County representative in the Ninth Missouri General Assembly. Finding a homeland for the Mormons became Doniphan's "pet project" while he served in the state legislature.[10] Doniphan's sterling reputation along with that of other important supporters, including David Rice Atchison and William Wood, lent the credibility needed to redraw the boundaries in the unincorporated northern territories of Ray County.

Second, Doniphan's legislation received bipartisan support. Working closely with the Democrats on earlier issues,[11] Doniphan, a Whig, engendered the confidence of Democratic politicians, including the influential Democratic representative John C. Thornton. Hailing originally from Ray County, Thornton moved to Clay County where citizens elected him to represent them in the General Assembly along with Doniphan. Thornton served as speaker of the House for more than four years prior to Doniphan's legislation.[12] Together Doniphan and Thornton skillfully worked both sides of the political aisle to garner support for the redrawing of the boundaries.

COMMUNITY OF CHRIST LIBRARY-ARCHIVES
Alexander William Doniphan

A third reason Boggs signed Doniphan's Mormon homeland initiative was with hope that it would resolve the Mormon Question plaguing northwestern Missouri for half a decade. In the minds of many contemporary observers, the Mormon problem was a vexing one that seemed to

---

Missouri Historical Review 52 (January 1958): 111–22. An analysis of the politics of Doniphan's proposal is required to understand Boggs's favorable signature.

10. This term is presented in the fine biography of Doniphan by Roger Launius. See his *Alexander William Doniphan*, 37.

11. Such issues included chartering a state bank for Missouri, development of transportation infrastructure and other internal improvements, and numerous initiatives spurring economic growth within the state. See Launius, *Alexander William Doniphan*, 34ff.

12. Launius, *Alexander William Doniphan*, 37.

focus on individual rights versus the rights of the community. Because Missouri was a newly created frontier state, it faced many legal issues yet to be resolved, especially this one. By providing a sanctuary for Mormons in relatively isolated territory perceived by most to be of little worth and even less productivity, Boggs hoped Doniphan's plan would resolve this issue. Although this was unlikely, finding the land unproductive might cause the Mormons to simply go away.[13]

Doniphan's plan also addressed property rights concerns and provided economic incentives for those non-Mormon settlers already living in unincorporated, far northern reaches of Ray County and adversely affected by the legislation. Because there were no more than twenty families involved, the politicians in Jefferson City, including the governor, anticipated their protests. To accommodate their concerns, Doniphan proposed creation of a second county, just to the north of Caldwell, called Daviess County.[14] This tract of land, although similar in terrain and size, had a distinct advantage over Caldwell County—the Grand River Valley. This meandering waterway gently coursed its way northwest to southeast across Daviess County, eventually emptying into the Missouri River near DeWitt, in southeast Carroll County. Daviess County residents would find this a great asset, with its route an important link to trade and commerce.

13. That the Mormons would "simply go away" was wishful thinking for three reasons. First, Boggs knew the theological basis of the Mormon attraction for Jackson County and their desire to return to their Zion. Second, the productivity of the land was quickly being discovered by settlers. Albert Rockwood recorded this in his journal stating, "Crops are verry good, it is said there is corn enough in Caldwell Co. to last the inhabitante and the Emigration 2 years but preparations are making for 10 fold larger crops next year. This is truly a delightsome County [.] the air & warter is verry good." See Rockwood Journal, 6 October 1838, in Dean C. Jessee and David J. Whittaker, eds., "The Last Months of Mormonism in Missouri: The Albert Perry Rockwood Journal," *Brigham Young University Studies* 28, no. 1 (November 1988): 20–21. The third reason that Boggs felt that the Mormons would not simply go away comes from his understanding of the staying power and sacrifices the Mormons were enduring to stay in Caldwell County. No doubt having considered these possibilities, as consummate politician, Boggs would have hoped for this eventuality. Of course, as summer 1838 approached with open warfare breaking out in Daviess County, Boggs's hopes diminished only to be replaced by anger and vindictiveness.

14. Daviess County is named after Colonel Joseph H. Daviess who fell in 1811 at the Battle of Tippecanoe in Indiana. Daviess served under William Henry Harrison. See *History of Caldwell and Livingston Counties, Missouri*, 105.

The influx of Mormons into Caldwell County created a sellers market, yielding good prices for Caldwell acreage and thus benefiting those Missouri citizens willing to move north. Doniphan's solution placated for the most part those who protested the Mormon takeover.

Closely related to the resolution of the economics issue was the fourth motivation—the rich lands along the Missouri Platte River, to the west of Clay County. Historian Michael S. Riggs astutely noted the possibility that Mormons could move westward into this unorganized land with all its advantages.[15] The Missouri River formed the entire western border of the tract, ensuring easy accessibility, and the vast, rich bottomlands all but guaranteed abundant harvests. Also, the strategic location of a military garrison across the Missouri River (Fort Leavenworth) could provide the Mormons some physical protection and perhaps prevent further vigilante attacks. That Mormons eyed this verdant tract of land early on was signaled in a series of letters written during the fall of 1834 by William W. Phelps: "This fine tract of territory [the Missouri Platte River country] embraces land enough for two or three counties, and contrary to the observation which I wrote you last August about it, there will be further effort for annexation to this State, as soon as matters can move."[16] Riggs concluded that by giving the Mormons the worthless Caldwell prairie on Clay County's northeastern border, Doniphan protected the prize Platte country for more favorable settlement on Clay County's west.[17]

Considering these four motivations, and knowing that a Caldwell County asylum drew Mormons farther away from Jackson County, Missouri, Governor Lilburn Boggs attached his signature to the Doniphan legislation creating Caldwell and Daviess Counties, each jurisdiction being approximately twenty miles square. Missouri Mormon leaders initially understood that Doniphan's original legislation designated that the entire unorganized northern Ray County territory would be set aside for the

---

15. Michael S. Riggs, "The Economic Impact of Fort Leavenworth on Northwestern Missouri 1827–1838. Yet Another Reason for the Mormon War?" in *Restoration Studies IV*, 124–33.

16. W. W. Phelps, "Letter No. II," *Latter Day Saints' Messenger and Advocate* 1, no. 3 (December 1834): 33; Launius, *Alexander William Doniphan*, 40; Riggs, "Economic Impact of Fort Leavenworth," 128.

17. Riggs, "Economic Impact of Fort Leavenworth," 129.

Mormon sanctuary. Thus the creation of Daviess County was both a surprise and a disappointment. The Mormons had to be satisfied with a half loaf rather than the full loaf, losing half their territory but at last finding sanctuary from persecution.

Forging Unity among a Divided People

FOR SOME TIME, the prophet had struggled to maintain unity in a church that was geographically divided between northern Ohio and western Missouri. To accommodate the situation, he set up administrative officers in both locations based on what he understood as a "divine pattern." Church leaders in Ohio and Missouri naturally found it difficult to communicate and this led to misunderstandings. At times tempers flared. Periodically, the prophet called the leaders together and counseled with them in a valiant attempt to establish harmony. Such was the purpose of the 27 December 1832 admonition known as the "Olive Leaf":

> Let him offer himself in prayer upon his knees before God, in token or remembrance of the everlasting covenant; and when any shall come in after him, let the teacher arise, and, with uplifted hands to heaven, yea, even directly, salute his brother or brethren with these words: Art thou a brother or brethren, I salute you in the name of the Lord Jesus Christ, in token or remembrance of the everlasting covenant, in which covenant I receive you to fellowship, in a determination that is fixed, immovable, and unchangeable, to be your friend and brother, through the grace of God, in the bonds of love, to walk in all the commandments of God blameless, in thanksgiving, for ever and ever. Amen.[18]

In this same message, Smith instituted the ordinance of washing of feet as an act of humility. Yet, even with his best efforts, unity was still elusive because of the considerable distance that separated his people.

At the 3 May 1834 conference in Kirtland, delegates unanimously changed the legal name of the church from the Church of Christ to the Church of the Latter Day Saints. Included in the legislation were two resolves to communicate that decision throughout the church.[19] That many

---

18. Doctrine and Covenants 85:40–41 (LDS 88:131–33).
19. One resolve ordered that "this Conference recommend to the Conferences and Churches abroad, that in making out and transmitting Minutes of their proceedings,

Missouri Saints continued to refer to themselves as members by the original name suggested that unity had not prevailed.

On his arrival in Far West,[20] Smith sensed the problem of bifurcation between the Ohio and Missouri churches and announced a new name that would accomplish the unity he sought. Demonstrating once again the ability to apply his sense of the divine will to the needs of the people, the prophet took action. Within six weeks of his residence in Far West, Joseph Smith Jr. gave instruction that brought the two churches together by changing the sect name and uniting the church leadership.

> Verily thus saith the Lord unto you my servant Joseph Smith, Jr. and also my servant Sidney Rigdon and also my servant Hyrum Smith and your counselors who are, and who shall be hereafter appointed; and also unto my servant Edward Partridge and his counselors, and also unto my faithful servants who are of the High Council of my church in Zion (for thus it shall be called) and unto all the elders and people of my Church of Jesus Christ of Latter Day Saints scattered abroad in all the world; for thus shall my church be called in the last days, viz., The Church of Jesus Christ of Latter Day Saints.[21]

---

such minutes and proceedings be made out under the above title." The second resolve ordered that "these Minutes be signed by the Moderator and Clerks, and published in the *The Evening and the Morning Star*." This was to ensure the name change was legally noted in all jurisdictions throughout the church. See "Communicated," *The Evening and the Morning Star* 2, no. 20 (May 1834): 160.

20. The Smith family arrived at Far West on 13 March 1838 and the Rigdons on 4 April.

21. "An Extract of Revelation," *Elders' Journal of the Church of Jesus Christ of Latter Day Saints* 1, no. 4 (August 1838): 52. This newspaper replaced the *Latter Day Saints' Messenger and Advocate* in the fall of 1837. With 1,000 of the 1,500 subscribers to the *Messenger and Advocate* in arrears in their payment because of the financial paralysis in Kirtland, the church leaders determined that declaring the paper insolvent was the best course of action. The *Elders' Journal* prospectus was published in the last two editions of the *Messenger and Advocate*, with the transition set for the fall of 1837. Joseph Smith Jr. announced himself as editor, Sidney Rigdon as assistant editor, and Don Carlos Smith (Joseph's younger brother) as business and correspondence manager. Only two Kirtland issues of the *Elders' Journal* went to press before the church printing house was burned in November 1837. Subsequent issues were published in Far West. For a comprehensive study of the church's printing history see Wayne Ham, ed., *Publish Glad Tidings: Readings in Early Latter Day Saint Sources* (Independence, Mo.: Herald House, 1970).

In this one prophetic statement, Smith brilliantly realigned the church leadership by naming Sidney and Hyrum as his presidential counselors and Missouri president Edward Partridge and his counselors to other important leadership positions; but more important, he reestablished church identity by combining the Missouri preference for "Church of Christ" with Kirtland's "Latter Day Saints."[22]

The 26 April utterance that declared the new church name also included the command to lay out yet another city: "Let the city Far West be a holy and a consecrated land unto me, and it shall be called most holy, for the ground upon which thou standest is holy."[23] In the previous year, John Whitmer and William W. Phelps identified a suitable plat of land for Far West and located the spot for a temple. These arbitrary decisions of the Missouri leaders reflected their sense of independence from the Kirtland leadership, their millennial expectations, and their hesitancy to await instruction from some eight hundred miles away,[24] even if it was to come from the prophet. Smith's role as prophet was crucial to maintaining institutional cohesion and was never challenged seriously, at least by those who still believed in him.[25] Yet there were clear signs that he needed to

22. For a history of the church's names, see Mark A. Scherer, "'Called by a New Name': Mission, Identity, and the Reorganized Church," *Journal of Mormon History* 27, no. 2 (Fall 2001): 40–63.

23. "An Extract of Revelation," *Elders' Journal* 1, no. 4 (August 1838): 52.

24. Richard P. Howard, *The Church Through the Years*, 2 vols. (Independence, Mo: Herald House, 1991), 1: 257.

25. Of course this excludes those who dissented to start their own church, such as Warren Parrish and his remake of the Church of Christ. Historian Richard S. Van Wagoner disagrees with my assessment here. Van Wagoner argues that the numerous influential church leaders such as W. W. Phelps, Lyman Johnson, Frederick G. Williams, John Whitmer, David Whitmer, and Oliver Cowdery, all by then living in Far West, "presented a united front that seriously challenged Rigdon's and Smith's doings." See Van Wagoner, *Sidney Rigdon*, 214–15. I base my viewpoint on the fact that the entire movement rested on the shoulders of Joseph Smith Jr. His prophetic authority, truly challenged in early 1831, was resolved in instruction given in February of that year; see Doctrine and Covenants Section 43 (LDS 43). Also that church members supported the 1838 excommunications of the men listed above, including Phelps and John Whitmer, four days before Smith arrived in Far West, suggests that when offered a choice, the church members easily supported their prophet over those who contested against him. Van Wagoner's observation that while Oliver Cowdery was second elder, the church processes were more democratic, however, is a good one. From 1832 to 1838,

Finding Sanctuary and Forging Unity at Far West 291

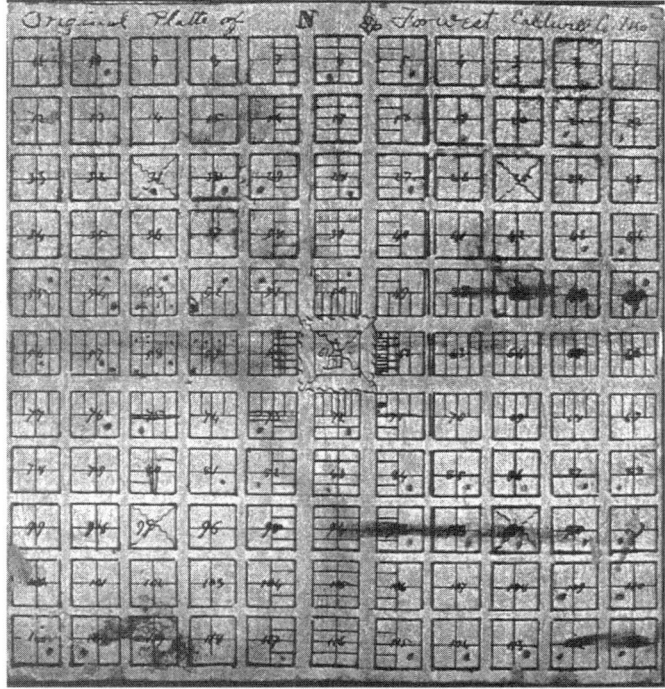

COMMUNITY OF CHRIST LIBRARY-ARCHIVES

"Sheepskin Plat" of the City of Far West, Caldwell County, Missouri, 1837, describing a city of about one square mile

assert more of his presidential prerogative. His two-prong strategy was, first, to establish the allegiance of the membership and, second, to establish a fortress presence in the minds of outsiders.

Weeding Out the Unrighteous

THE YEAR AND a half starting with the founding of Caldwell County and the Mormons' initial settlement in the closing months of 1836 and lasting through June 1838 was a rare period of peaceful coexistence between the Mormons and their neighbors. This was a time for building homes, clearing land, and organizing the community of Far

---

a noticeable transition occurred signaling a move from democratic principles to "command and compliance." See Van Wagoner, *Sidney Rigdon*, 215.

West. During these difficult times of shortages, Mormons found jobs with non-Mormon employers. Area merchants willingly sold supplies and offered credit to their new neighbors. This built trust between believer and non-believer. Missouri leader John Corrill confirmed the peaceful relations in his important history: "Friendship began to be restored between [the Mormons] and their neighbors, the old prejudices were fast dying away, and they were doing well, until the summer of 1838."[26] But now that Smith and Rigdon were settled in Far West, things would change dramatically.

Observing the difficult lessons from Kirtland, the two church leaders determined not to allow the internal dissent to emerge once again. Unity was imperative. Obedience became a test of fellowship, especially when this mandate received divine authority in June 1834: "Zion cannot be built up unless it is by the principles of the law of the celestial kingdom, otherwise I cannot receive her unto myself; and my people must needs be chastened until they learn obedience, if it must needs be, by the things which they suffer."[27] Church courts provided a venue for dealing with member complaints and transgressions, but Smith and Rigdon needed an enforcement arm that stood outside the official chain of command. To prevent a recurrence of dissident problems that were still fresh in his mind, Smith agreed to the formation of a secret security organization—the Sons of Dan, or simply the Danites, as they would later be called—that would enforce compliance with leadership directives and purge dissenters.

The source of the Danite name is as mysterious as the founding of the organization. John Corrill wrote that the clandestine organization took the name

> the Big Fan; this, I suppose, was figurative of their intentions to cleanse the chaff from the wheat. They also assumed the name of "The Daughter of Zion," and afterwards were called "Danites." Why they assumed these names I never knew, but always supposed they took it from the scriptures, which speaks of them, the first prophetically, and the last historically.[28]

---

26. Corrill, *A Brief History*, 26. Historians today see Corrill's history as a valuable window into the church story during this era because of his objective writing, a unique perspective in these difficult times.

27. Doctrine and Covenants 102:2c–d (LDS 105:5–6).

28. Corrill, *A Brief History*, 32.

But perhaps the most direct scriptural connection with the Danite name came from the Book of Daniel:

> And in the days of these kings shall the God of heaven set up a kingdom, which shall never be destroyed: and the kingdom shall not be left to other people, *but* it shall break in pieces and consume all these kingdoms, and it shall stand for ever. Forasmuch as thou sawest that the stone was cut out of the mountain without hands,...the great God hath made known to the king what shall come to pass hereafter: and the dream is certain, and the interpretation thereof sure.[29]

Missouri Mormon Reed Peck agreed with Corrill's biblical reference to the name origins but extended further the connection between the Old Testament and the Latter Day Saints by referring to the total commitment required of its members:

> As the Lord had raised up a prophet in these last days like unto Moses it shall be the duty of this band to obey him in all things, and whatever he requires you shall perform being ready to give up life and property for the advancement of the cause[.] When any thing is to be performed no member shall have the privilege of judging whether it would be right or wrong but shall engage in its accomplishment and trust God for the result.[30]

The purpose of the secret society was scriptural also: "Arise and thresh, O daughter of Zion: for I will make thine horn iron, and I will make thy hoofs brass: and thou shalt beat in pieces many people: and I will consecrate their gain unto the Lord, and their substance unto the Lord of the whole earth."[31] When it matured, the Danite organization intimidated members who criticized the prophet, forced adherence to church beliefs and practices, demanded conformity on political issues, and provided armed guards for church leaders, especially the prophet. During the summer and fall of 1838, Sampson Avard, the most prominent leader of

---

29. Daniel 2:44–45 KJV.
30. Reed Peck, *The Reed Peck Manuscript*, 1839, transcript (Salt Lake City: Modern Microfilm Co.), 10. Community of Christ Library-Archives. For the warlike purposes of the "children of Dan" see Numbers 1:38 and 2:25.
31. Micah 4:13 KJV.

the Danites, recruited a membership that grew to between three and four hundred Mormons.

Historians have long debated the prophet's involvement in this vigilante force. A careful review of documentary evidence links the prophet to the secret society from its origins to its demise. Smith attended some Danite meetings and periodically spoke to the group. That he had full knowledge of its activities is undeniable.

With his Danites in place, and their allegiance sealed by oath,[32] Smith had his own paramilitary vigilante force to root out dissidents and to enforce conformity. Because Danite tactics included probable violations of the law, Smith chose not to join the band officially, thus providing him "plausible deniability" if confronted in a court of law.[33] Through the generations, Smith's defenders have referred to his alleged statement of Danite criticism in October 1838.[34] However, as historian Stephen LeSueur has observed, Morris Phelps inserted this passage after Smith's assassination.[35]

32. The Danite oath of initiation required the candidate to raise his right hand and swear: "In the name of Jesus Christ, the son of God, I do solemnly obligate myself ever to conceal, and never to reveal, the secret purposes of this society called the Daughters of Zion. Should I ever do the same, I hold my life as my forfeiture." Sampson Avard, who headed the Danite organization, revealed this oath in a proceeding before Judge Austin A. King of the Fifth Judicial Circuit in the State of Missouri at Richmond. This criminal inquiry against Joseph Smith Jr. and others for the crime of high treason and other crimes against the State began on 12 November 1838. See "Evidence," *Document Containing the Correspondence, Orders, &C. In Relation to the Disturbances with the Mormons; And the Evidence Given Before the Hon. Austin A. King.* (Fayette, Mo.: Office of the Boon's Lick Democrat, 1841), 97. Community of Christ Library-Archives.

33. Stephen C. LeSueur raised this legal issue in his "The Danites Reconsidered: Were They Vigilantes or Just the Mormons' Version of the Elks Club?" *John Whitmer Historical Association Journal* 14 (1994): 47. I would extend LeSueur's argument, however, to suggest that since Smith and Rigdon placed Mormons Elias Higbee and John Cleminson as judge and law clerk (who was responsible for processing lawsuits) for Caldwell County, respectively, the First Presidency felt they had the necessary legal protection to refuse to answer more vexatious lawsuits. That Smith still distanced himself (at least officially) from the Danites revealed his unwillingness to take chances should lawsuits be preferred in jurisdictions outside the county. The strategy of placing Mormon supporters in positions of legal authority set a precedent for similar circumstances in Nauvoo, Illinois, a few years later.

34. See *DHC*, 3: 178–82.

35. LeSueur discovered that the official account of Smith's rejection of Danite activity was lifted almost verbatim from a Morris Phelps manuscript penned after Smith's

To exonerate Smith from Danite leadership based on Phelps's writing violates historical integrity.

Smith and Rigdon took little time to engage the Danites in addressing the problem of dissidence in the Far West community. In the spring of 1838, the apostate purge that began in the Kirtland days resumed in Far West with the excommunication of William W. Phelps and John Whitmer. Apostles, presidential counselors, Book of Mormon witnesses, Missouri presidents, seventy, and church historians all fell victim to charges of apostasy, were forced out, or simply chose to leave.[36] Most members anticipated that the Far West apostates would simply leave the church community to go their own way. When this did not happen, they forced the First Presidency to take more extreme measures. Here Sidney Rigdon took the lead, while Joseph Smith, again for his own legal protection, acted in an unofficial but supporting role.

Sidney Rigdon's "Salt Sermon" and Ultimatum[37]

THE FOUNDING OF an oath-bound secret society in June 1838 coincided with a pivotal sermon given by first counselor Sidney

---

assassination. As LeSueur observed, "The two accounts continue for several pages in parallel language, sometimes word-for-word, although the *DHC* version often cleans up the language and adds details here and there." See "Reminiscences" (Morris Phelps), MSd271, LDS Church Archives. A transcript of the Phelps manuscript is in this author's possession.

36. These expulsions included, from the church presidency—Oliver Cowdery and Frederick Granger Williams; from the Missouri church presidency—David Whitmer, John Whitmer, and William W. Phelps; from the Quorum of Twelve Apostles—John F. Boynton, Luke Johnson, Lyman Johnson, and William McLellin; from the Book of Mormon witnesses—Oliver Cowdery, David Whitmer, Martin Harris, John Whitmer, Jacob Whitmer, and Hiram Page; and church historians Oliver Cowdery, John Whitmer, and John Corrill. Added later to this growing list of leaders to become disillusioned was Thomas B. Marsh, president of the Council of Twelve, and Apostle Orson Hyde. Some individuals returned to Latter Day Saintism—for example, Frederick Granger Williams in the summer of 1838, Luke Johnson in 1846, and Oliver Cowdery in 1848.

37. The most reliable account of the church story during the Far West era is Stephen C. LeSueur, *The 1838 Mormon War in Missouri* (Columbia: University of Missouri Press, 1987). Also, to understand how church leaders asserted their authority during these historic times, see D. Michael Quinn, *The Mormon Hierarchy: Origins of Power* (Salt Lake City: Signature Books, 1994).

David (left) and John Whitmer, leaders of the church in Missouri

Rigdon in Far West. On Sunday 17 June 1838, Rigdon preached on the text of Matthew 5:13: "Ye are the salt of the earth: but if the salt have lost his savour, wherewith shall it be salted? it is thenceforth good for nothing, but to be cast out, and to be trodden under foot of men." Using more than just the biblical reference, Rigdon also invoked a revelatory warning given by Joseph in November 1831: "And upon them that hearken not to the voice of the Lord, shall be fulfilled that which was written by the prophet Moses, that they should be cut off from among the people."[38] All who gathered for the sermon understood that Rigdon's application of this scripture focused squarely on those dissidents still living in the Far West community. Without mentioning names, Rigdon accused apostates of attempting to destroy the church from within, and of numerous crimes. Reed Peck, who was in the large audience, recalled Rigdon claiming that it was "the duty of this people to trample [dissenters] into the earth and if the county cannot be freed from them any other way I will assist to trample them down, or to erect a gallows on the square of Far West and hang them up as they did the gamblers at Vicksburg and it would be an act at which the

---

38. Doctrine and Covenants 108:11e (LDS 133:63).

angels would smile with approbation."[39] Listeners knew exactly to whom Rigdon referred.

The day after Rigdon's sermon, the Danites sprang into action by issuing a letter warning dissenters that the church would not tolerate their interference; that the eighty-three signatories[40] would drive them out of the county; and that there was nothing the apostates could do to forestall their removal. The threat worked. Danite George W. Robinson, Rigdon's son-in-law, recorded the dissidents' escape by writing: "These men took warning, and soon they were seen bounding over the prairie like the scape Goat to carry of[f] their own sins."[41] Apostate families were left homeless, as their properties were seized to cover church debts.

Not all in Far West looked with favor at the apostate expulsion. John Corrill, a well-respected church member since his baptism early in 1831 and participant in nearly all major events during the Missouri period, opposed the earlier expulsions of William W. Phelps and David and John Whitmer. When he saw how church leaders handled dissidents after the "Salt Sermon," as it was to be called later, he expressed his disgust by writing in his history: "This scene I looked upon with horror, and considered it as proceeding from a mob spirit."[42] If supporter John Corrill was horrified, it is not difficult to imagine how church outsiders viewed the purge.

Sidney Rigdon's 1838 Fourth of July Oration and Ultimatum

SIDNEY RIGDON'S WELL-PUBLICIZED sermon on 17 June, along with the Danite intimidation and removal of dissidents that followed,

39. Peck, *Manuscript*, 6–7.

40. The first signatory was Sampson Avard, leader of the Danites. Other signatures included many notable church leaders including Hyrum Smith, a member of the First Presidency. The prophet's signature, however, was conspicuously missing. This was yet another opportunity for Joseph Smith Jr. to avoid prosecution should the letter be submitted as evidence in a trial.

41. George W. Robinson, "The Scriptory Book of Joseph Smith, Jr. ...," in *An American Prophet's Record: The Dairies and Journals of Joseph Smith*, ed. Scott H. Faulring (Salt Lake City: Signature Books, 1987), 187.

42. Corrill, *A Brief History*, 35. When Corrill heard the Danite plans to forcibly remove the dissenters, he secretly alerted the dissidents to make preparations.

caused Missourians to grow suspicious that church leaders were taking a new approach to their occupation of northwestern Missouri. With his Fourth of July oration, Rigdon removed all doubt. Although the Saints did not realize it, the speech was the beginning of the end of their occupation of Caldwell County, and indeed, their stay in Missouri. The church leadership pre-approved the language of this speech, and Rigdon was their effective mouthpiece. There can be no question that they intended to use this occasion to signal a shift in the direction of the church. Since this speech established a "line in the sand" framing the future relationship of the Far West Saints with their neighbors, the oration merits a careful analysis.

On the morning of 4 July 1838, Far West area residents anticipated the festivities that were planned to commemorate the nation's birth. People from across the countryside gathered as they heard Dimick Huntington's marching band tune their instruments. When Huntington gave the signal, his band launched into patriotic tunes and began their march through the square. Hundreds joined in behind the band as they paraded joyously to the temple excavation site. After the crowd arrived, they participated in the ceremonial laying of the temple cornerstones.[43] Then the church dignitaries took the stand.

The speaker for the morning was President Sidney Rigdon. In vintage fashion, Rigdon welcomed the people and quickly launched into his speech—he had an important message to send to believers and nonbelievers alike. First, Rigdon chose eloquent words, using patriotic expressions to commemorate the special day. He called for national unity during this time of celebration and rejected those who advocated for the union between church and state. Rigdon lamented the "fire of persecution"[44] the church

---

43. The church newspaper provided coverage of the festivities for the day. The committee of arrangements orchestrated each activity. The temple cornerstones were laid in order: first, the stake presidents, assisted by twelve men, set the southeast corner; second, the presidents of the elders set the southwest cornerstone assisted by twelve men; third, the church bishop, assisted by twelve men, set the northwest corner; and finally, the president of the teachers, assisted by twelve men, set the northeast corner. See "Celebration of the 4th of July," *Elder's Journal* 1, no. 4 (August 1838): 60.

44. Sidney Rigdon, *Oration Delivered by Mr. S. Rigdon on the 4th of July, 1838* (Far West, Mo.: Printed at the Journal Office, 1838), 7, photo reprint, Community of Christ Library-Archives. Also see Peter Crawley, "Two Rare Missouri Documents," *Brigham Young University Studies* 14, no. 4 (Summer 1974): 502–27.

had experienced in recent years and invoked the guarantee of rights under the Constitution (themes to which he would return). In what may have been the most direct expression of the importance of education, Rigdon discussed the need for an intelligent membership:

> Next to the worship of our God, we esteem the education of our children and of the rising generation. For what is wealth without society, or society without intelligence. And how is intelligence to be obtained?—by education. It is that which forms the youthful mind: it is that alone, which renders society agreeable, and adds interest and importance, to the worship of God. What is religion without intelligence!—an empty sound.[45]

Then slowly Rigdon redirected his oration to religious themes. By using millennial expressions, he reminded the audience to note the primacy of the times for the Second Coming, by stating

> that whether there are wars, or famines, or pestilences, or earthquakes, or distress of nations, or whatever may come according to the purposes of our God, that we may know it before hand, and be prepared for it, so that none of these things shall overtake us as a thief in the night, and while we are crying peace and safety, sudden destruction come upon us.[46]

He mentioned the need to build the Far West House of the Lord and suggested that its dual purpose of worship and education would be similar to the Lord's House in Kirtland. Quoting from Isaiah, Malachi, and even the psalmist David, Rigdon predictably compared the tribulations of the Saints with those of the peoples of the Old Testament:

> And as Moses left Egypt not fearing the wrath of the king, and refused to be called the son of Pharoah's daughter, choosing rather to suffer affliction with the people of God, than enjoy the pleasures of sin for a season, having respect to the recompense of reward. So do we, we choose to suffer affliction with the people of God, rather than enjoy the flatteries of the world for a season.

---

45. Rigdon, *Oration*, 8.
46. Rigdon, *Oration*, 10.

The Great Orator then focused on the long-suffering tribulations the Saints had waded through to get to their present circumstances:

> We have not only when smitten on one cheek turned the other, but we have done it, again and again, until we are wearied of being smitten, and tired of being trampled upon. We have proved the world with kindness; we have suffered their abuse without cause, with patience, and have endured without resentment, until this day, and still their persecutions and violence does not cease. But from this day and this hour, we will suffer it no more.

Rigdon began his closing statement in a crescendoing voice, issuing a caution:

> We warn all men in the name of Jesus Christ, to come on us no more forever, for from this hour, we will bear it no more, our rights shall no more be trampled on with impunity. The man or the set of men, who attempts it, does it at the expense of their lives. And that mob that comes on us to disturb us; it shall be between us and them a war of extermination, for we will follow them, till the last drop of their blood is spilled, or else they will have to exterminate us: for we will carry the seat of war to their own houses, and their own families, and one party or the other shall be utterly destroyed.—Remember it then all MEN.
>
> We will never be the aggressors, we will infringe on the rights of no people; but shall stand for our own until death. We claim our own rights, and are willing that all others shall enjoy theirs.

He concluded his rallying cry with:

> We therefore, take all men to record this day, that we proclaim our liberty on this day, as did our fathers. And we pledge this day to one another, our fortunes, our lives, and our sacred honors, to be delivered from the persecutions which we have had to endure, for the last nine years, or nearly that. Neither will we indulge any man, or set of men, in instituting vexatious law suits against us, to cheat us out of our just rights, if they attempt it we say wo be unto them.
>
> We this day then proclaim ourselves free, with a purpose and a determination, that never can be broken, "no never! *no never!!* **NO NEVER.**"!!![47]

---

47. Rigdon, *Oration*, 12 (emphasis in the original).

Rigdon's oratory whipped the audience into a frenzy. Members responded with ecstatic shouts of "Hosanna to God and the Lamb."[48] What the vast multitude of believers heard was a near-Pentecostal affirmation of the rightness of their cause; but what nonbelievers, sprinkled through the audience, heard was a mortal threat. What started out as a speech to celebrate the Declaration of Independence for all Americans ended up as a declaration of independence for Caldwell County Mormons.[49] The belligerent warning left no doubt of the intentions of the First Presidency as they nodded approval. The symbolism of Danite leader Sampson Avard, also sitting on the stand, signaled an endorsement of his secret band's enforcement methods. By the end of the celebration, there was no mistake about the shift from reaction to proaction. To ensure that the message was distributed far and wide, Smith ordered it to be published in pamphlet format. In August, Smith advertised the publication of Rigdon's oration in the *Elders' Journal* and encouraged all members of the church to acquire a copy.[50]

---

48. "A History, of the Persecutions, of the Church of Jesus Christ, of Latter Day Saints in Missouri," *Times and Seasons* 1, no. 6 (April 1840): 81; and Parley P. Pratt, *Autobiography*, 173–74. Ebenezer Robinson recalled that the audience shouted "Hosanna! Hosanna!! Hosanna!!! three times." See Robinson's description of events that day in "Items of Personal History of the Editor, No. 6," *The Return* 1, no. 10 (October 1889): 149. Community of Christ Library-Archives.

49. Robinson, "Items of Personal History," 148.

50. See *Elders' Journal* 1, no. 4 (August 1838): 54:

> In this paper, we give the proceedings which were had on the fourth of July, at this place, in laying the corner stones of the temple, about to be built in this city.
>
> The oration delivered on the occasion, is now published in pamphlet form: those of our friends wishing to have one, can get it, by calling on Ebenezer Robinson, by whom they were printed. We would recommend to all the saints to get one, to be had in their families, as it contains an outline of the sufferings and persecutions of the Church from its rise. As also the fixed determinations of the saints, in relation to the persecutors, who are, and have been, continually, not only threatening us with mobs, but actually have been putting their threats into execution; with which we are absolutely determined no longer to bear, come life or come death, for to be mobed any more without taking vengeance, we will not.
>
> EDITOR.

A few days after the speech, the skies darkened and a storm cloud gathered over Far West. With a sudden crash, a bolt of lightning obliterated the flag pole erected for the patriotic celebration. Several ran to see the destruction, including Joseph Smith Jr. As the prophet stepped through the splinters lying on the ground, Ebenezer Robinson heard the prophet predict that "as he walked over these splinters, so will we trample our enemies under our feet."[51] The lightning strike and Smith's prophecy symbolized the volatile environment that now existed in northwestern Missouri and what would lie ahead for the Saints in the remaining months of 1838.

Eruption of Violence against the Mormons in Carroll County

THE FOUNDATION FOR peace between the Missouri citizens and the Mormons was based on the assumption that the Mormons would settle within the confines of Caldwell County. The understanding in the minds of the governor and state legislators, who agreed to Alexander Doniphan's legislation, was that, once it was created, the Mormons would stay settled within the confines of the newly created county. This assumption created a sense of stability and peace among the Saints and their neighbors. An editorialist, probably George W. Robinson, described the setting:

> The Saints here are at perfect peace with all the surrounding inhabitants, and persecution is not so much as once named among them: every man can attend to business without fear or excitement, or being molested in any wise. There are many of the inhabitants of this town, who own lands in the vicinity, and are at this time busily engaged in cultivating them. Hundreds of acres of corn have been planted already, in our immediate neighborhood; and hundreds of acres more are now being planted. (This is the fourth day of May.)[52]

The Mormon willingness to seek permission before moving into an undesignated area, to leave if asked, and to discourage other Mormons from

---

When the Oration pamphlet appeared, the printer placed the following logo on the front cover: "Better far sleep with the dead, than be oppressed among the living."

51. Robinson, "Items of Personal History," 149.
52. *Elders' Journal* 1, no. 3 (July 1838): 34.

settling in that area sufficed to convince even many of the skeptics. All of this changed when Smith and Rigdon arrived at Far West from their Kirtland escape.

When the details of Sidney Rigdon's Salt Sermon and Fourth of July oration spread throughout the countryside, tensions mounted between the Mormons and their gentile neighbors. The spark that led to open warfare lay just over the horizon in July with Mormon families in Carroll County, and in early August with the Daviess County election.

Throughout the fourteen years of the Restoration Era, the increasing number of church members became a persistent problem. In the Kirtland, Independence, Clay County, and now Far West experiences, Gentiles were intimidated by the influx of hundreds of wagons lumbering into their area. All told, approximately ten thousand Mormons had settled in Missouri by the time of evacuation in the winter 1838–1839. But this seemingly overwhelming number was actually a localized problem, since the estimated total population of Missouri was approximately 325,000.[53] Unfortunately for the Mormons, the Missourians were not distributed equally across the state, and since most Missourians lived on the eastern side, along the Mississippi River, the sparse gentile population on the western side presented proportional challenges, thus creating an intimidating imbalance.

Even in isolated areas, the presence of just a few families moving into the area drew objections from Missouri citizens. Such was the case in DeWitt, Carroll County. The strategic location of DeWitt, on the bluff overlooking the confluence of the Grand and Missouri Rivers, presented excellent investment opportunities to land speculators. Their initial booster efforts were relatively unsuccessful since only seven of their lots were sold by 1837. Ironically, two gentile speculators,[54] motivated more by profits from land sales and less by religious prejudices, invited Mormons to move into the area. The John Murdock and George Hinkle families responded to the invitation and set the stage for confrontation. Carroll County citizens correctly anticipated that more families would follow. Here again, rumors feeding prejudices led to Mormon marginalization. Threats of reprisal

53. This demographic statistic is based on the research of Stephen LeSueur in *The 1838 Mormon War*, 35. The author based this figure on 1840 census records.

54. Eli Guthrie laid out the DeWitt settlement then sold out his interest to land speculators David Thomas and Henry Root.

surely sounded familiar to Murdock and Hinkle, but the Mormons knew they had not violated any laws by acquiring their lots; so did the Carroll County citizens. This caused some hesitation to move too quickly. After several meetings held through the spring of 1838 on what course of action to take, Missouri citizens decided that their concerns were best served by issuing warnings rather than using force.[55]

Meanwhile, undaunted by threats, Mormons poured into the area, especially with the late-June establishment of Diahman, a Mormon settlement located up the Grand River in Daviess County. By the end of September, two hundred Mormons from Canada settled in the DeWitt area, prompting a citizen response. The reprisals began as a vigilante force of one hundred fifty citizens uprooted Mormon farmers and even burned one home. When Mormons resisted with gunfire, the countryside divided into armed camps. Reinforcements from surrounding counties swelled the citizen ranks to threefold their size, while the Mormons of DeWitt barricaded themselves and awaited arrival of their reinforcements from Far West and Diahman. Full-scale siege seemed imminent as efforts to find a peaceful settlement failed.

Two important circumstances weighed heavily in the final outcome of the Carroll County conflict: the size of the citizen force, and the government inaction to find a peaceful solution. First, the near-unanimous support of the surrounding counties drew militia recruits and armaments, giving the attackers a decided advantage in the conflict. The Mormons were alerted by several non-Mormon observers of the pending disaster they and their families would suffer should fighting break out.

Second, Mormons decided to send a representative to appeal their case directly to the governor. They strategically selected Henry Root, the non-Mormon land agent, to appeal to local officials, and another non-Mormon, A. C. Caldwell, to ride to Jefferson City to plead their case

---

55. Some citizens actually opposed vigilante action. As reported in a Missouri newspaper: "We look upon it [vigilante action] as an infraction of all law and right, as a stain on the American character, and as deserving the reprehension of the press every where. If they [Mormons] have infracted the law, let its severities be inflicted to the utmost, but that one set of men should drive out another, on account of their religious, or rather bigoted, heresies, ought not to be tolerated in any land, much less in a land boasting of its freedom." See *Missouri Republican*, 18 August 1838, in LeSueur, *The 1838 Mormon War*, 57.

directly with the governor. When both emissaries returned without success, the Mormons knew the fight was their own to resolve.

Having committed resources to the conflict, some counties sent representatives to investigate the circumstances and weigh the issues causing the conflict. These agents discovered the aggressive Carroll County vigilantes and the defensive Mormons both hoping to find relief from their petitions to the government. The break in the standoff occurred when David Thomas reported to the Mormon leaders a vigilante proposal that, should the Mormons surrender, they would not be harmed and would receive a fair price for their lands. Mormon leader George Hinkle, who saw the hopelessness of their situation, accepted the terms to avoid certain massacre by the angry mob. On Thursday 11 October, the Mormons evacuated DeWitt. Exhausted from their ordeal, they headed to Daviess County, where the prophet had directed them to settle. Their arrival in this northwestern Missouri county set the stage for more confrontation with their gentile neighbors.

Daviess County Election-Day Violence and Retribution

BY THE SPRING of 1838, Joseph Smith anticipated an influx of Mormon followers from Kirtland to arrive in numbers sufficient to test the boundaries of his Caldwell County sanctuary. Because this understanding with the state legislature to remain within the county confines was unwritten and agreed to by church leaders other than himself, the prophet felt no great obligation to comply. Indeed, Joseph supported and even visited with those enduring the siege in DeWitt, Carroll County. In late June, knowing that his Kirtland followers would be arriving soon, he platted a community north of the Caldwell County line in Daviess County, in the Grand River Valley. He called the settlement "Adam-ondi-Ahman," or "the place where Adam dwelt."[56] This community reflected Joseph's penchant for identifying "sacred space," and here the prophet created a stake he called Diahman.[57]

---

56. Adam-ondi-Ahman held great spiritual significance for Joseph and his followers.

57. Traditionally, a stake is a jurisdictional designation that recognizes the presence of a highly concentrated settlement of church members.

COMMUNITY OF CHRIST LIBRARY-ARCHIVES

The Gallatin election-day brawl in August 1838

Fear of the increasing number of Mormons struck Daviess County Missourians as it had others in surrounding counties. The Mormon settlement in Daviess County was especially difficult to accept for those settlers who had sold the Caldwell County properties and moved northward, assuming the county line permanently protected them. The few Mormons who wandered into their county prior to Smith laying out Diahman seemed relatively harmless. But by August 1838, Mormon numbers had increased dramatically, making up half the population.

In the days leading up to the first county election, to be held on 6 August, rumors spread that Missourians would prevent Mormon settlers from voting. Candidates running for office knew the Mormon bloc-voting track record, usually for Democrats, and most knew they would tip the balance to determine the winner. Tensions ran high on election day as people from across the county gathered in Gallatin, the Daviess County seat. As in so many frontier elections, the whiskey flowed freely and it did not take long for tempers to flare.[58]

---

58. The Mormons ran John Lemmons as a candidate for the office of associate judge in the August election. To garner votes, Lemmons "treated to wine" potential supporters. He did not win in the election nor did he participate in the brawl on the streets of Gallatin. However, the Missouri High Council did prefer charges against him for his campaign tactics. See William Swartzell, *Mormonism Exposed....* (Pekin, Ohio: Published by the author, 1840), 31.

William Peniston, a Whig candidate for the state legislature, whose father established Millport, a nearby Daviess community, gave an inflamed speech against the Mormons. The spark was a jostle between a Missourian and a Mormon; this led to a full-scale brawl in the Gallatin street. John Butler, a large and powerful Mormon, grabbed a huge oak club, appealed to several fellow Danites in the crowd with a yell, "O yes, you Danites, here is a job for us," and waded into the fray.[59] Brief in duration, both sides were bloodied in the fight; but the thirty Mormons, considerably outnumbered, stood their ground.

The Mormons may have won the fight, but their troubles were far from over. After the confrontation in the street, the Missourians retreated but threatened to return with pistols, so the Mormons quickly headed back to Diahman. That night they stood watch, anticipating further violence. Rumors flooded into Far West the next day. John Corrill recorded that two Mormons had died and that the Daviess County citizens would not let the Mormons bury them, and that "there were gatherings on both sides."[60]

From the square at Far West Sampson Avard signaled the alarm, and one hundred fifty well-armed men assembled for the march to Diahman. Included in the marchers were Joseph and Hyrum Smith and Sidney Rigdon. They arrived at the Saints' settlement on the evening of 7 August only to find that no one had been killed and that cooler heads had prevailed. Rather than returning home, Smith determined to show their strength to area settlers as a warning about further violence.

Visiting several prominent citizens,[61] the Mormon army headed for the farm of Judge Adam Black. Smith sent riders, including Lyman Wight, Sampson Avard, and Cornelius Lott, ahead of the column. Their purpose was to get Black to sign a statement disavowing any connection with the Daviess vigilantes. The judge objected to signing anything under duress. In a heated exchange, Black answered, "I will die first." The three Mormons

59. John Lowe Butler, 1808–1860, "Autobiography," ca. 1859, typescript, Community of Christ Library-Archives.
60. Corrill, *A Brief History*, 35.
61. Mormons paid a visit also to local sheriff William Bowman and others. See William Peniston's affidavit dated 10 August 1838, and filed with Judge Austin A. King, of the State of Missouri, in Ray County, presumably Richmond, the county seat. See *DHC*, 3: 61.

reported Black's rejection to Smith and his approaching column. Smith ordered his column into battle formation. They surrounded Black's cabin. Failing a second try, Lyman Wight suggested that Black negotiate with the prophet directly. When Black agreed, Smith pressed his case with the judge, attempting to convince him that he only desired peaceful conditions throughout the countryside.[62] But one hundred fifty heavily armed men surrounding his house and family convinced Black otherwise. The judge's compromise was to write his own petition:

> I, Adam Black, a Justice of the Peace of Daviess county, do hereby Sertify to the people, *coled Mormin*, that he is bound to *suport* the Constitution of this State, and of the United State, and he is not attached to any mob, nor will not attach himself to any such people, and so long as they will not molest me, I will not molest them. This the 8th day of August, 1838.
>
> Adam Black, J.P.[63]

On exiting Black's cabin, Brigadier General Eberly, a pseudonym for Sampson Avard, physically threatened Black, stating, "If you violate the articles of agreement, *death shall be your portion!*"[64] At least for now, this ended the incident; but shortly thereafter Black, accompanied by William Peniston, still smarting from his election-day loss, and former sheriff William Bowman rode to Richmond to lodge a legal complaint against the church leaders. This began a series of lawsuits to try Smith, Lyman Wight, and others for crimes against the state.

To find remedy, Smith appealed to militia general David Atchison to bring troops to quell the violence. Almost completely surrounded with

---

62. Black's position as a Daviess County justice of the peace and officer of the court was well known to all. Smith may have recognized the legal liability of threatening a judge to sign such a petition. By sending the riders ahead, Smith would have avoided liability. However, when his emissaries reported Black's refusal, Smith must have hoped that his strength of numbers would have intimidated Black out of his silence.

63. *DHC*, 3: 59–60. This official history provides a very mellowed account of the incident. William Swartzell observed a far more inflammatory exchange between Black and the Mormons. He suggests the compromise resolution as explained here. See Swartzell, *Mormonism Exposed*, 30.

64. Swartzell, *Mormonism Exposed*, 30. LeSueur, in *The 1838 Mormon War*, identified Avard's pseudonym, 66fn30.

Daviess County enemies to the north, Carroll County enemies to the southeast, and Ray County enemies to the south, Caldwell County evolved into an armed camp. Smith successfully initiated peace overtures to Daviess residents through state senator-elect Josiah Morin and state representative John Williams, both recipients of Mormon electoral support. But this lasted only a short time. Exaggerated complaints of violence by Mormons against Missouri citizens stirred ill will on both sides.

Added to Joseph Smith's problems with his neighboring counties were further dissident challenges from within. Church members John Sapp and Nathan Marsh registered their complaints against the leaders in early September.[65] These important statements fueled the rising suspicions about Mormon depredations. These documents became useful tools against church leaders in future litigation. Also, John Corrill, who was appointed church historian on 6 April 1838, questioned the church's new stewardship policy. Sidney Rigdon said he always suspected Corrill. Smith chastised Corrill for his lack of support by saying, "If you do not act differently and show yourself approved you shall never be admitted into the Kingdom of Heaven." Smith added, "I will stand at the entrance and oppose you myself and will keep you out if I have to take a fisty cuff in doing it." Corrill returned Smith's invective with a brave rejoinder, "I may possibly get there first."[66] Having had the heated exchange, it was just a matter of time before Corrill left the fellowship. Corrill stayed with the church as long as he, his wife, and their four children could. On 17 March 1839, church leaders excommunicated the historian.

---

65. *Correspondence, Orders, &C.*, 16–17.
66. Peck, *Manuscript*, 13. Kenneth Winn interpreted Corrill's rejoinder to mean that Corrill might get to heaven first and would fight to keep Smith out. Winn provided the best treatment of John Corrill in his fine essay, "'Such Republicanism as This': John Corrill's Rejection of Prophetic Rule," in *Differing Visions: Dissenters in Mormon History*, ed. Roger D. Launius and Linda Thatcher (Urbana: University of Illinois Press, 1994), 45–75; for the verbal exchange between Smith and Corrill, see Winn's explanation, 64–65.

CHAPTER FOURTEEN

Fortress Mentality, Violence, and Expulsion from Missouri

Mormon Destruction of Gallatin, Millport, and Grindstone Fork

THE VIOLENCE IN northwestern Missouri between the citizens and the Mormons should be understood as retribution followed by retribution. Fears fed by prejudice fueled the clash of cultures. By October 1838, rampaging intruders on both sides of the dispute burned farms, killed livestock, and uprooted crops. Smith and his church leaders lost all confidence in the law to protect their civil rights.

On Monday 15 October, nearly all able-bodied men of Caldwell County armed themselves and assembled in Far West for all-out war. Smith went into the stand and addressed his followers by reminding them of the abuses they had suffered, of his petitions rejected, and the "capitulating vexations to which the church had been subject." In perhaps his most succinct statement of vigilantism, Smith appealed to his troops:

> Who is so big a fool as to cry the law! the law! when it is always administered against us and never in our favor[.] I do not intend to regard the law hereafter as we are made a set of outlaws by having no protection from it[.] We will take our affairs into our own hands and manage for ourselves...but I am determined that we will not give another foot and I care not how many come against us, 10 or 10000[.]

Fortress Mentality, Violence, and Expulsion from Missouri

God will send his Angels to our deliverance and we can conquer 10000 as easily as 10.[1]

Later in his speech, the prophet provided his troops a veiled authorization to pillage and plunder the countryside. Then Rigdon chastised pacifists, who questioned the call to arms, suggesting they should be "pitched on their horses with bayonets and placed in front of the battle."[2]

On 16 October, Smith's Far West troops marched to Diahman, where more men entered the ranks, bringing the Mormon army to nearly five hundred.[3] After a heavy snow on 17 October, the skies brightened the following day and the troops made ready. On the 18th Smith divided his army into companies and dispatched them to nearby communities. One hundred fifty men led by Apostle David W. Patten headed south from Diahman seven miles to Gallatin. They quickly took possession of the county seat and pillaged the small shops, saloons, and merchandise stores. Patten's troops left town with their plunder overflowing their wagons. As they left, they torched the town. With little or no resistance, the Mormon forces arrived back at Diahman with their loot.

Mormon troops also assaulted Millport, a small community a few miles east of Gallatin in Daviess County, and Grindstone Fork, also in Daviess County. The unit of men who marched on Grindstone Fork charaded first as citizens from Carroll County, to find out who was against them, and also to steal from the residents before they attacked.[4] As northwestern Missouri was aflame with lawlessness, local citizens expressed outrage and responded in kind. Hardly a Mormon farm was spared. Amid the violence, only property damage resulted and no lives were lost. However, vigilantes on both sides brutally turned families out into the snowy countryside to stand by as their farmhouses and possessions were reduced to ashes and livestock were slaughtered or hauled away.

1. Peck, *Manuscript*, 18–19.
2. Peck, *Manuscript*, 19. This was in reference to the objections raised by John Corrill, Reed Peck, and others.
3. Joseph Smith Jr. raised a guard unit whose specific responsibility was to procure provisions for his army in Caldwell County. He called the unit his "Fur Company" because one task was to press teams, and even some men, into service for the war. See Corrill, *A Brief History*, 37.
4. Corrill, *A Brief History*, 37.

The Fatal Mormon Mistake at Crooked River, 25 October 1838

Ray County citizens, to the south, seemed to escape the violence of the Mormon War, at least for a time. When word about the widespread destruction reached Richmond, the Ray County seat, the local militia leader, Captain Samuel Bogart, a Methodist minister, did not await orders; instead, he called out his men and marched them northward into the Buncombe Strip, the six-mile-wide line that separated Ray and Caldwell Counties. There they established a defensive line against Mormon encroachments. To ensure that Missouri militia general David Atchison knew the severity of the conditions in the area, and to justify taking the liberty of mustering his company without specific orders, Bogart wrote Atchison about his actions on 23 October 1838:

> Dear Sir:—The Mormons have burnt Gallatin and Mill Port, and have ravaged Daviess county, driven out the citizens, burnt the post office, taken all kinds of property from the citizens; have gone into Livingston county, and taken the cannon from the citizens there; they have threatened to burn Buncombe and Elk Horn [in Ray County], and have been seen near, and on the line between Ray and Caldwell. In consequence of which I have ordered out my company to prevent, if possible, any outrage on the county of Ray, and to range the line between Caldwell and Ray, and await your order and further assistance. I will camp at Field's, 12 miles north of this, to night. I learn that the people of Ray are going to take the law into their own hands, and put an end to the Mormon war.
>
> In hast, your obd't serv't,
SAMUEL BOGART.
>
> P.S. Please be explicit in your express to me as to my course.
> S.B.[5]

On the same day, 23 October 1838, Atchison returned a letter that provided Bogart the command he needed to provide his maneuver legitimacy. Atchison responded:

> HEAD QUARTERS 3d Division MISSOURI MILITIA.
> Liberty, October 23, 1838.

---

5. *Correspondence, Orders, &C.*, 48.

SIR: Your communication by express has been received. You are hereby ordered to range the line between Caldwell and Ray counties, with your company of volunteers, and prevent, if possible, any invasion of Ray county by any persons in arms whatever. You will also take care to inquire into the state of things in Daviess county, and make report thereof to me, from time to time. I will endeavor to be with you in a few days, &c.

DAVID R. ATCHISON,
Maj- Gen. 3d Div., Mo. Mi.

Captain S. Bogart.[6]

This official letter authorized Bogart's troops to repel Mormon invasion. One must wonder about both letters bearing the same 23 October date. Discovering that Bogart's letter would appear as evidence in a court hearing, it is possible that Atchison wrote out his command near the trial date and backdated it to 23 October to ensure a legal basis for Bogart's action. Although Atchison may have responded immediately with the authorization so the courier could return, it is improbable that Bogart's courier made the round trip from the Ray County encampment to Atchison in Liberty, Missouri, in one day. Because of the travel time across snowy terrain, it is doubtful that Bogart actually received Atchison's response on the 23rd.[7]

Fearing that an attack on Far West was imminent, the Mormon prophet sent out spies to Ray County to watch for "mob" movements. Considering the tense atmosphere, these observers interpreted Bogart's defensive maneuvers along the county border as a staging activity for the assault on Far West and reported back what they saw. Smith would not wait for Bogart's company to attack so he dispatched his own militia to take the fight to his enemy.

Not all were enthusiastic about Smith's move against the Missourians. These individuals were identified when Smith announced the initial

---

6. *Correspondence, Orders, &C.*, 108.
7. A heavy snowstorm in northwest Missouri a week earlier halted temporarily Smith's preparations for war on Daviess County. By the following week, either the snow was still on the ground or was melting. If the latter, the Missouri terrain would have been quite muddy. In either case, the courier's excursion would have been arduous.

call-up weeks earlier. Church historian John Corrill observed the prophet's action and lamented later:

> I now saw plainly that [the Mormons] had become desperate, and their career would soon end; for I knew that their doings would soon bring the people on them, and I dreaded the consequences. I would have been glad to have left the county with my family, but I could not get away; the decree was passed, and there was no other chance for me and the other dissenters but to pretend to take hold with the rest. I now understood that they meant to fall upon and scatter the mob wherever they could find them collected.[8]

With the mustering of Mormon troops, Corrill and the dissenters were caught in a test of faith. However, Corrill's estimation that Smith's army would "scatter the mob" reflected a significant misunderstanding with enormous implications. The engagement at Crooked River was not with a mob as in Gallatin and DeWitt, but with a regular unit of the Missouri militia. This changed everything and made even more real Corrill's concern about the "dreaded consequences" of Smith's actions.[9]

During the day of 24 October 1838, Mormon settlers fled into Far West from the south, claiming to be driven out by Bogart's troops. Shortly thereafter, Smith's spies returned from Buncombe and reported the Ray County militia assembling along the county line, suggesting they were about to invade Caldwell County. This seemed to verify the Mormon evacuees' claims. The spies also told Smith that the Missourians had captured three Mormons and planned to execute them in the morning.

8. Corrill, *A Brief History*, 37.
9. In fairness to the Mormon leadership and troops, making the distinction between a hastily organized mob and county militia units was extremely difficult. Essentially they were the same people, of course, with the difference being whether or not they marched with official sanction. Lack of uniforms and state-sponsored provisions forced the opposing sides to communicate their presence and intention. In this time of extreme emotion, and in the case of the Battle of Crooked River where the element of surprise was a key to the Mormon success, such communication was not an option. At the hearing weeks after the battle, some dissenters testified they knew that Bogart's men were official militia. Samuel Bogart and his lieutenant Asa Wild testified that they informed the Mormons they were militia. One must question the veracity of these testimonies, however. In the midst of a surprise attack, such announcement would have been of little value and probably not believed. Again, the importance of Atchison's 23 October 1838 letter could be entered as evidence of Bogart's state authorization.

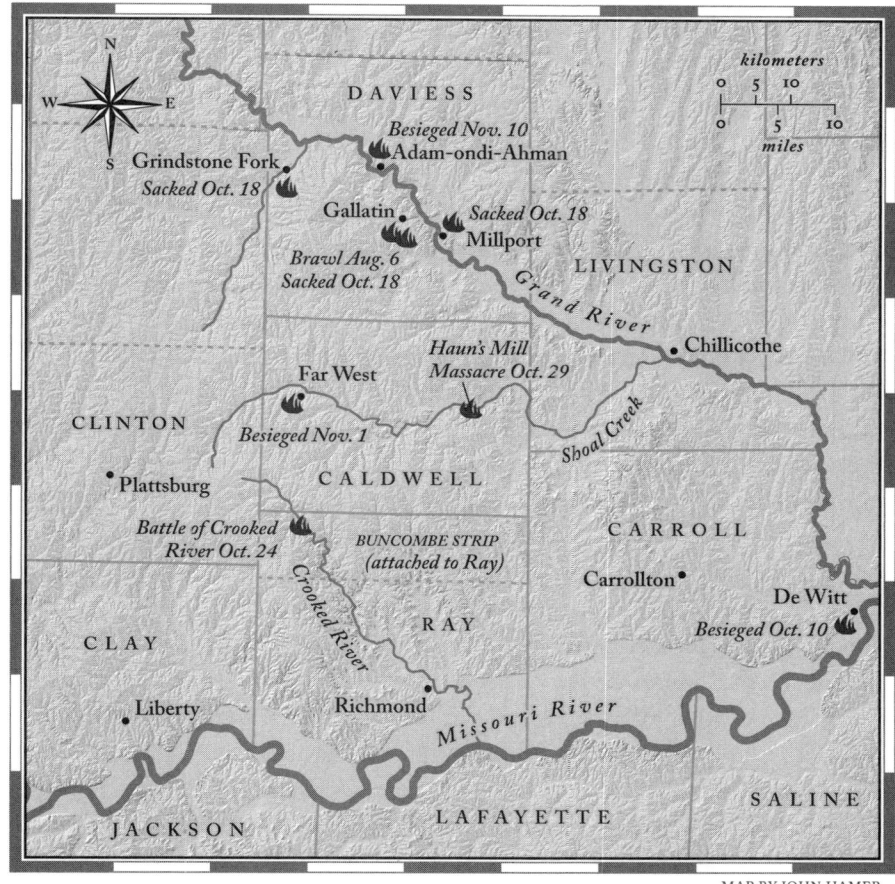

Places of conflict in the 1838 Mormon Missouri war

For the Mormon prophet, there was no time to lose. Immediately, the drum and bugle corps sounded the alarm and within minutes some fifty fully-armed Mormons gathered in the Far West square. With outrage, Smith gave the troops the marching orders: "*Go and kill every devil of them.*"[10] Then he gave the column to Apostle David Patten, beloved by his troops and given the name "Captain Fearnought" because of his

10. Letter from C. Hall and Richard Hill, *The Return* 2, no. 2 (February 1890): 216, Microfilm Collection, Community of Christ Library-Archives. They claimed that David Judy was their source.

indomitable reputation of leading his troops in the sacking of Gallatin. Patten's captain's status was consistent with his Danite rank.

Under the cloak of darkness, Patten led his troops out of Far West and headed south to the reported position of the mob intruders. He recruited twenty-five more troops along the way and crossed the county line about 3 a.m. Patten found Bogart's men asleep in their tents along Crooked River. With stealth, Patten's dismounted troops quietly approached Bogart's encampment. Just before dawn, a militia picket discovered the Mormon army. After a verbal exchange in the darkness, a single round from the picket felled Mormon Patrick O'Banion. This shot awoke the camp and the Battle of Crooked River began.[11]

With the early morning light upon them, Patten formed his battle line eighty yards across on an open field, while Bogart's men scurried from their tents to their rifle stands and into a well-protected defensive position in a slough along the riverbank. Patten suddenly realized his vulnerability when the militia's opening volley caused several of his men to fall. Patten then ordered his men to charge. The Mormons closed the distance quickly and threw themselves into the militia lines yelling "God and liberty!" Immediately the militia broke ranks and fled across the river to the other bank. Mormons opened up on the militia, who were slowed by having to wade through the water. Years later, reflecting on the scene, Mormon Hosea Stout wrote that "many a mobber was there baptised without faith or repentance under the messingers of lead sent by the brethren."[12]

Almost as quickly as it started the Battle of Crooked River ended, with the Mormon routing of the Missouri militia. When the black powder smoke cleared, saber strokes ceased, and fighting ended, three Mormons had died and seven had received wounds. During the fighting, David Patten received a ball to the abdomen that caused his death later in the day.

11. At a hearing in Richmond, Missouri, after the battle, the captain of the pickets, John Lockhart, testified as a witness for the state that he tried to get the Mormons coming through the darkness to identify themselves. Failing at that, he heard what he thought was a snap of a percussion cap. Thinking the intruders had opened fire, he raised his rifle to his shoulder and squeezed off a round into the darkness. His shot hit Patrick O'Banion. Thus, there is some question as to who actually fired the first shot of the Battle of Crooked River. For Lockhart's deposition statement see *Correspondence, Orders, &C.*, 142.

12. Reed A. Stout, ed., *Autobiography of Hosea Stout* (N.p., n.d.).

Until now, no Mormon soldier had been killed in a northwestern Missouri engagement. The Battle of Crooked River dashed the belief of some Mormons at Far West that, since God was on their side, angels would protect their righteous soldiers.[13] As Stephen LeSueur has observed, Patten became the Mormons' "first apostolic martyr."[14] Since the militia retreat was so quick and complete, amazingly only one militiaman was killed and six suffered wounds. The Mormons plundered the encampment and returned to Far West with the spoils of battle. Rumors of the skirmish, many of them false, spread quickly throughout northwestern Missouri, causing panic and suspicion.

Two Views of the 1838 Missouri Mormon War

To understand both sides of the 1838 Missouri Mormon War requires much of the reader. The historical records do not show clearly whether, before the battle, the Ray County militia actually forced Mormon settlers to flee their farms and escape into Far West, although that is what the settlers told Joseph Smith Jr. Likewise, it is just as difficult to discern the real intent of Bogart's troops. Mormon spies reported that the militia was staging for an attack, while the official communication between Bogart and Atchison suggested otherwise. Witnesses for both the prosecution and the defense at a Richmond hearing that followed the battle spoke on behalf of those whom they represented, and prejudice prevailed on both sides. Perhaps the passing of more than a century and a half affords today's reader the opportunity to view both sides more objectively.

From the Mormon view, their entire history had been one encounter after another of suffering at the hands of unorganized but effective citizen violence. Persecution seemed to follow them wherever they went. Church leaders endured vexatious lawsuits; beleaguered Saints abandoned their legally established settlements, leaving behind their personal property, which relegated them to a poverty-stricken, migratory existence. The law almost always went against them, causing great pain. To ease his followers'

---

13. Carrie Polk Johnston and W. H. S. McGlumphy, *History of Clinton and Caldwell Counties, Mo.* (Topeka, Kans.: Historical Publishing Company, 1923), 236.

14. LeSueur, *The 1838 Mormon War*, 142. Mormon soldiers Patrick O'Banion and Gideon Carter also died in the skirmish.

frustration, Smith rationalized their grief with Old Testament allegories. He assured his followers that like the children of Israel, they had stood against their gentile enemies, and God was on their side as well. But the vigilante nature of the American frontier was more than the Mormon prophet and his people could bear. At Far West, Caldwell County, Missouri, with a siege mentality, Smith took his stand.

From the perspective of the Missouri government in Jefferson City, the Mormons were constant troublemakers. The clashes with Jackson Countians and the protests of Clay Countians between 1831 and 1836 marked the Mormons as disturbers of the peace. With the 1834 Zion's Camp march, they entered Missouri to liberate their land of Zion in Jackson County without legal sanction. Only a timely hailstorm and the prophet's good sense to withdraw forestalled the disaster that would have come with a military engagement at the Fishing River with state militia troops.

Although their strange religious beliefs might have been accommodated on the spacious American frontier, the large numbers of Mormon settlers upset the important balance of power in local politics and presented undue competition for choice land acquisition. As a remedy to the Mormon Question, the state legislature provided a good-faith attempt by creating Caldwell County as a Mormon sanctuary. Because Smith arbitrarily violated the understood agreement and encouraged church leaders to find "living space" in surrounding Missouri counties, Alexander Doniphan's duly authorized sanctuary plan of 1836 did not work.

In Thomas Marsh's affidavit, given in Ray County, the dissenting apostle provided all the testimony needed to cast suspicion on Joseph Smith Jr.'s intentions:

> The plan of said Smith, the prophet, is to take this State, and he professes to his people to intend taking the United States, and ultimately the whole world.... I have heard the prophet say that he should yet tread down his enemies, and walk over their dead bodies; that if he was not let alone he would be a second Mahomet to this generation, and that he would make it one gore of blood from the Rocky Mountains to the Atlantic Ocean; that like Mahomet, whose motto, in treating

for peace, was "the Alcoran, or the Sword," so should it be eventually with us, "Joseph Smith or the Sword."[15]

Amid all this, Governor Lilburn Boggs, the consummate politician, Jackson County landowner, and merchant, received official communiqués from government representatives and militia officers that northwestern Missouri communities were in flames, local farms were plundered, and—with the Battle of Crooked River—a Mormon army, in an early dawn raid, had assaulted duly authorized elements of the Missouri militia who were positioned in a defensive posture. Being no great respecter of Mormon rights, when Boggs received numerous letters from Missouri citizens petitioning for a redress of their grievances, he answered with his "final solution" to the Mormon Question: force Mormons to leave the state or face annihilation. Boggs issued his infamous extermination order on 27 October 1838 in a letter to General John B. Clark at the headquarters of the Missouri State Militia in Jefferson City. In this letter, Boggs stated that "the Mormons must be treated as enemies, and must be exterminated or driven from the State if necessary, for the public peace—their outrages are beyond all description."[16]

COMMUNITY OF CHRIST LIBRARY-ARCHIVES
Governor Lilburn Boggs of Missouri

Actually, the Mormon leadership had used extermination language months before Boggs. When Sidney Rigdon took the stand in front of the Saints in Far West on 4 July 1838, he admonished his listeners that "it shall be between us and them *a war of extermination,* for we will follow them, till the last drop of their blood is spilled, or else they will have *to exterminate* us: for we will carry the seat of war to their own houses, and their own families, and one party or the other shall be utterly destroyed.

---

15. *Correspondence, Orders, &C.,* 58. Thomas B. March (also Marsh) swore this statement before Henry Jacobs, justice of the peace for Ray County on 24 October 1838.

16. *Correspondence, Orders, &C.,* 61.

Remember it then all MEN."[17] The official order to remove or annihilate the Mormons eliminated all of Smith's options and set into motion the last days of Latter Day Saintism in Missouri for more than an entire generation.[18]

The Massacre at Haun's Mill

THE CITIZENS IN the northwestern Missouri communities learned of the successful Mormon attack and organized their defenses while the two Mormon strongholds, Far West and Diahman, prepared as well. Prejudice against each other developed quickly. Even their best neighborly efforts could not break through each other's fears, especially after Gallatin, Millport, Grindstone Fork, and Crooked River. Only in isolated circumstances did Mormons and Missouri citizens live together in relative harmony. For example, non-Mormons living on farms near Shoal Creek in far eastern Caldwell County knew mill owner Jacob Haun[19] as a hard worker and fair man who provided reliable milling services. Area residents overlooked Haun's religious beliefs and accepted his friendship; however, their feelings would soon change.

During the summer and fall of 1838, residents of Livingston and Daviess Counties, to the east and north of Caldwell County, harassed the steady stream of Mormon immigrants traveling across their territory by scaring wagon teams, rerouting wagons, and detaining men for brief periods of time, dumping provisions and confiscating weapons and supplies.

17. Rigdon, *Oration*, 12 (italics added for emphasis).
18. Slowly and quietly Reorganized Latter Day Saints began to return to Jackson County, Missouri, during and after the American Civil War in the 1860s. By that time, many of the original Missouri citizens who held such contempt for the Mormons had either passed on or forgotten their harsh feelings. The Reorganized Latter Day Saints, embracing more moderate theological positions, were less of a threat to nonbelievers. For a discussion of this moderation, see Alma R. Blair, "The Reorganized Church of Jesus Christ of Latter Day Saints: Moderate Mormons," in *The Restoration Movement: Essays in Mormon History*, ed. F. Mark McKiernan, Alma R. Blair, and Paul M. Edwards (Independence, Mo.: Herald House, 1979), 207–30.
19. Jacob Haun moved from Green Bay, Wisconsin, to northern Missouri before Caldwell County was created. This made him one of the first Mormons to move to this region of the state. Having some milling experience, he contracted with Jacob Meyers Jr. to build a grist and saw mill at a convenient bend in Shoal Creek.

By the end of October, Livingston and Daviess County "regulators" drilled frequently and prepared at a moment's notice for a possible Mormon attack. When the Mormons set fire to several local communities and engaged in what most understood was a preemptive strike at Crooked River, the Missouri regulators decided they could not await another predawn raid. Their focus was a Mormon hamlet on Shoal Creek in eastern Caldwell County known as Haun's Mill.

In the mid-1830s, Jacob Haun operated his grist mill on Shoal Creek, just four miles west of the Livingston County line. Haun's mill was one of several located along the strategic stream.[20] Jacob Myers built his mill just upstream from Haun. Thus, Haun's location was called by some as simply "the mills."[21] Shoal Creek's current was strong enough to power saw and grist mills, and its water was deep and reliable enough to irrigate farm fields. Being so close to the county line made his settlement the first friendly community Mormon travelers would encounter on arriving in Caldwell County. Haun's hamlet, actually not more than a dozen cabins housing a few families, and James Houston's blacksmith shop were situated about sixteen miles east of Far West. More important, Haun provided grain provisions and milling operations for Mormon immigrants, whose stores were mostly emptied by the time of their arrival. Typically, there were more families living in wagons and tents at Haun's Mill than in its buildings.

On 25 October, the day of the Battle of Crooked River, the approximately seventy-five Mormons who occupied Haun's Mill received unwelcome visitors. Nehemiah Comstock, of Livingston County, and his twenty riders entered the settlement and demanded the surrender of all weapons and ammunition. Hesitant to do so, but fearing the possibility of violence, most Saints complied with Comstock's demand. Three days after

---

20. Across from Haun's mill, Jacob Myers and his son, Jacob Jr., partnered to build and run their own grist and saw mill operation. Robert White also built a mill on the creek nearby, and Joshua Whitney built a mill on the creek a few miles downstream, in Livingston County. For a faithful account of the Haun's Mill massacre, see Alexander L. Baugh, "A Call to Arms: The 1838 Mormon Defense of Northern Missouri" (PhD diss., Brigham Young University, 1996), 253–98.

21. *Correspondence, Orders, &C.*, 82.

Comstock's visit, citizen and Mormon representatives negotiated an agreement that would allow both sides to live in peace.[22]

Not all Missourians supported the peace agreement conditions, nor were the Mormons willing to let down their defenses simply on a promise. Under the leadership of David Evans, Mormon pickets and night watchmen took positions on the settlement's perimeter and arranged a fortress position at Houston's blacksmith shop in the center of the hamlet. Should an attack from the north occur—the most likely scenario—then the women and children would escape across the creek and into the woods, and the thirty-five to forty men would defend the hamlet from the protection of the blacksmith shop.

Through the day on Monday 29 October, local citizen volunteers and Livingston, Carroll, Ray, and Daviess County regulators gathered about eight miles northeast of Haun's Mill. By noon the next day, some 200 men led by William and Thomas Jennings headed to Haun's Mill, arriving between three and four in the afternoon. Using a heavily timbered area a few hundred yards north of the hamlet for cover, the troops dismounted and divided into three companies. Quietly they surrounded the settlement on the north, east, and west sides, leaving only the south as an escape route, just as the Mormon defensive plan anticipated. The attackers blackened their faces and donned red bandanas as they snuck into position for the assault. Then the pickets discovered them. Facing overwhelming numbers, Evans immediately raised a white flag to surrender and yelled for quarters. On seeing the signal, the attackers opened fire. Their opening volley ripped through the hamlet, splintering tree branches, breaking windows, and sending women and children scurrying for safety. Thirty-two men and four boys hustled into the blacksmith shop and returned fire.

In a matter of minutes, the Mormons realized the vulnerability of their defensive position. The log walls of the blacksmith shop were neither chinked nor daubed. Although this condition was excellent for ventilation of the forge, it afforded less protection than anticipated against musket balls. Thirty-six people jammed into the eighteen-foot-square structure meant that balls passing through the walls could hardly miss hitting a

---

22. Baugh argued that the disarming and peace negotiations were part of a well-orchestrated plan to weaken Mormon defenses in preparation for an attack. Citizens wanted to reduce resistance as much as possible for the assault; see "Call to Arms," 262.

defender. Because the Mormons were concentrated in a fixed position, the Missourians could focus a withering fire into the structure from three directions. When Evans saw his men fall, he made a second surrender plea; but dodging bullets, he fled for the woods.

Soon the men and boys inside the blacksmith shop exhausted their ammunition. Nineteen men bolted out the south door for the woods but only six made it to safety, as thirteen suffered wounds (from which three died). When the defenders could no longer return fire, the blacksmith shop became a slaughterhouse. As weapons silenced and the smoke cleared, the regulators rushed through the south door and saw bodies heaped on the floor. The attackers finished off several wounded and discovered three boys unharmed. Nine-year-old Charlie Merrick broke away from his captors and made it outside, where he was gunned down. The two sons of Warren Smith—Sardius, age ten, and Alma, age seven—cowered beneath the bellows. One ruffian shot Alma in the hip, leaving Sardius to plead for his life. Then an attacker from Carroll County, referred to as Mr. Glaze, put his musket muzzle behind Sardius's ear and squeezed the trigger, killing the boy instantly.[23]

The atrocities continued outside the blacksmith shop as ruffians walked through the hamlet, abusing the wounded. They plundered the wagons, tents, and log cabins for anything worth carrying off. Then they left the carnage behind, completing their plan of destruction. From the first shot fired to the last, the assault lasted about an hour. Eyewitness Joseph Young, Brigham's older brother, estimated that the attackers fired some sixteen hundred rounds at the Mormon defenders.[24]

23. "Joseph Young's Narrative of the Massacre at Haun's Mill," *DHC*, 3: 185. Also in Johnston and McGlumphy, *History of Clinton and Caldwell Counties*, 241–43. The author of *History of Caldwell and Livingston Counties, Missouri* disagreed with Joseph Young's identification of Mr. Glaze of Carroll County as the man who killed young Sardius Smith. This author emphatically claimed that William Reynolds, from Livingston County, shot the boy.

24. Young had the good fortune to be in his cabin on the south side of the creek, away from the attackers, when the assault began. Although fired upon, he and his family made good their escape. Young claimed to have heard that each of the intruders fired an average of seven shots, thus totaling "upwards of sixteen hundred shots" at the Mormon defenders. Young provided his explanation of the massacre in an affidavit sworn before C. M. Woods, circuit court clerk of Adams County, Illinois, on 4 June 1839. See "Joseph Young's Narrative of the Massacre at Haun's Mill," *DHC*, 3: 183–86.

The massacre at Haun's Mill

After the invaders left, the moans of the wounded defenders broke the eerie silence. Slowly, those who had escaped into the woods returned to tend to the survivors. As the sun set on the hamlet, the gruesome task of bandaging wounds began, while through the night some of the wounded died. The next morning, concerns spread among the survivors that the marauders might return to continue the slaughter. This prompted a decision about burying the dead. Winter came early in 1838, freezing solid the northwestern Missouri prairie. Digging graves for each of the dead jeopardized more lives with the delay, so several men gathered fourteen bodies and slid them into an unfinished well. Ten-year-old Sardius Smith was the last corpse interred; then workers filled in the mass grave as best they could. The Mormons gathered what they could carry and quickly left for Far West. Nehemiah Comstock and another contingent of ruffians returned hours later to find the hamlet abandoned and the dead buried, so they left.[25]

The final death toll from the massacre reflected a lopsided fight. All told, the Mormons suffered seventeen killed and fourteen wounded. Only

---

25. "A History of the Persecution, of the Church of Jesus Christ, of Latter Day Saints in Missouri," *Times and Seasons* 1, no. 10 (August 1840): 149–50.

four Mormons who fought escaped injury. Inside the blacksmith shop, William Champlin drew dead bodies over himself and faked death. Jacob Foutz received a thigh wound and also pretended to be dead. Only three Missourians received wounds—John Hart, an arm wound; John Renfrow, a lost thumb; and Allen England, a severe thigh wound.[26] Almost all the fifty women and children made it to the woods unharmed.[27]

The Surrender of Far West, Missouri

ON WEDNESDAY 31 October, the Haun's Mill evacuees slowly drifted into Far West only to find their capital city under siege. Until the Battle of Crooked River, the prophet had succeeded in avoiding bloodshed when confronted by his enemies. Even with his bellicose speeches, easy as they were to make, he truly regretted the loss of life and preferred to avoid hostilities if at all possible. His actions at the Fishing River in June 1834, and now at Far West, demonstrated the prophet's willingness to set aside his great faith built on his assurance that God was on his side and that angels would protect them. He allowed his frustrations to cloud his judgment by sending his army to the Crooked River, and now he and his movement would suffer great persecution. Because his troops had confronted regular militia and not a ragtag mob a week earlier at the Crooked River, his enemies would come at him with a vengeance.

During the previous evening of Tuesday 30 October, Mormon lookouts spotted a huge militia column approaching Far West from the south. The troops were heavily armed with siege weaponry and were empowered by the Missouri governor's extermination order. Panic spread through the Mormon city as Smith ordered a barricade to be erected on the outskirts of town. As the evening sun set, the militia bivouacked on the banks of Goose Creek, about a mile south and in plain view.

Lyman Wight arrived with one hundred fifty volunteers from Diahman the next day, bolstering spirits in the town. Still, the militia army, numbering about twenty-five hundred, almost tripled the Far West defenders. By now, messengers had informed Joseph of the Haun's Mill massacre.

---

26. *History of Caldwell and Livingston Counties, Missouri*, 150.
27. Mary Steadwell was the only woman wounded in the fighting. She received a gunshot wound to her hand. See *DHC*, 3: 324. Also see Baugh, "Call to Arms," 271–72.

Although he still did not know how many of his followers had died in the attack, the news clearly had a temporizing effect. He no doubt projected the enormous potential loss of life that stood before him. As he surveyed his own breastworks, now extending for nearly three-quarters of a mile, and then the overwhelming numbers of militia arrayed in their encampment at Goose Creek, he determined that his defenses could never hold and decided that a negotiated peaceful settlement was his only recourse.

Five negotiators under the leadership of Mormon colonel George Hinkle, commander of the Caldwell County militia, left Far West for the encampment.[28] On their arrival, militia adjutants denied a meeting because the commandant was too busy with his preparations for the assault, but the men were told to return at two o'clock in the afternoon. The negotiating team instead saw General Alexander Doniphan, who informed them that General David Atchison had been relieved and that General Samuel D. Lucas now commanded the armies. With no progress, the team returned to Smith at Far West and shared the bad news that Lucas, the hated perpetrator of violence in Jackson County, directed the opposing armies. Sensing doom, Smith told his representatives to "beg like a dog for peace," so at the appointed time, the team met with Lucas and received his terms.[29]

Far West, Missouri, was almost totally isolated from outside communications. The church newspaper, the *Elder's Journal*, reflected this isolation. Editors issued the *Journal*'s last number in August 1838 with internal articles transacting church business, scriptural exegesis, conference notes, and a description of the Fourth of July festivities. Certainly the church leadership had other pressing priorities and frequently communicated directly with the people, thus reducing the importance of the newspaper. The only current outside news reported in the paper came from Diahman, but again this provided only church information. So for the first time, the Mormons learned about the governor's extermination order from

---

28. The five members of the negotiating team were George Hinkle, Reed Peck, John Corrill, William W. Phelps, and Arthur Morrison. Stephen LeSueur noted that Smith selected three opponents of the war—Peck, Corrill, and Phelps—as negotiators. Morrison was a judge with an excellent legal background, but the spokesperson was to be Hinkle. See LeSueur, *The 1838 Mormon War*, 161.

29. Corrill, *A Brief History*, 41; and Peck, *Manuscript*, 24.

Fortress Mentality, Violence, and Expulsion from Missouri 327

The Mormon surrender at Far West

General Lucas during the negotiations, and they were shocked at the development.

Of his four specific demands,[30] Lucas insisted that Joseph Smith, Sidney Rigdon, Lyman Wight, Parley P. Pratt, and George W. Robinson surrender as hostages and that those who participated in the Battle of Crooked River would face trial. Should the hostages not be handed over, then Far West would be reduced to ashes. Lucas gave them an hour to submit to his ultimatum. The team members quickly returned to Far West. They had seen firsthand the impressive militia preparations and forcefully argued for surrender. Smith called for better terms but the negotiators said there simply was not time. In his 1839 history, John Corrill recorded Joseph's concern about the safety and welfare of his people, when the prophet

---

30. Lucas issued four specific demands of the Mormons: (1) To give up the leaders of the Church of Jesus Christ of Latter Day Saints to be tried and punished; (2) to make an appropriation of the property of all who had taken up arms, for the payment of their debts, and indemnify for the damage done by them; (3) that the rest of the membership of the church should leave the state under the protection of the militia, but should be permitted to remain under protection until further orders were received from the commander-in-chief; and (4) to give up their arms of every description, which would be receipted for. See *Correspondence, Orders, &C.*, 73.

stated "he would rather go to prison for twenty years or even die rather than to allow his people to be exterminated."[31]

When Smith consented to the demands, Corrill and Peck jumped on their horses and rode full speed toward the militia camp only to find that Lucas had not waited for their response. Anticipating that Smith would never surrender, he had marched his men forward to within six hundred yards of the Far West breastworks. Corrill and Peck found Lucas positioning his cannon to bombard the town when they told him of Smith's surrender.

Hinkle then brought Smith and the church leaders to Lucas who, to everyone's surprise, promptly declared them not hostages but his prisoners. Having fulfilled his responsibility of delivering up the men, Hinkle left the meeting bewildered and headed back to the town. As he swung around on his saddle and looked back, the militia troops had surrounded the church leaders and were jeering at them. That night the prisoners lay on the cold, wet ground with angry guards watching over them.

Meanwhile, back in Far West, the defenders prepared for a battle, as they fully anticipated their leaders would return. Many remembered Sidney Rigdon's belligerent Fourth of July oration and the command that Mormons should fight to the death anyone who came upon them. When the leadership did not return, a misunderstanding of the negotiations led to charges that Hinkle had betrayed the prophet by giving him over to the enemy.[32] Hinkle, as chief negotiator, followed his orders just as he understood them. He got the impression that as church president, Smith might be able to arrive at more favorable terms. Even Lucas suggested the church leadership would be hostages to be released after the final negotiations rather than becoming his prisoners. Lucas, not Hinkle, was responsible for violating their agreement. Later Hinkle, Corrill, Phelps, and Peck were branded as traitors. But they denied the accusations that they had given over the church leadership to the militia as prisoners. Eventually, the four

---

31. Corrill, *A Brief History*, 41.

32. After Hinkle agreed to the four surrender terms, he asked Lucas for another day for the terms to be implemented. Hinkle offered the Mormon leadership as hostages to be held overnight in the militia camp as an assurance that the conditions of surrender would be met. This bartering of the church leadership seemed consistent with Smith's admonition to find any agreement possible.

men joined a lengthy list of church leaders to be forced out of the fellowship.[33]

Certainly the church leaders felt betrayed, especially when Lucas confronted Smith with the decision to surrender the city or stand by and watch it destroyed. At eight o'clock in the morning on 1 November, Smith sent a message to Hinkle ordering the surrender of the city. The Saints were stunned as ninety minutes later the militia marched within two hundred yards to collect the Mormons' weapons. With great frustration, approximately six hundred Mormon soldiers came out from behind the barricade, threw down their weapons, then slowly returned to the town square, escorted by guards who goaded them to resist.[34] None did.

The one last issue remaining was the status of Diahman, the other Mormon stronghold. News of Far West's surrender spread quickly into Daviess County. With the church leadership in militia custody, resistance seemed futile and could not be justified, so community leaders capitulated without a fight. The 1838 Missouri Mormon War ended with complete Mormon humiliation.

Incarceration, Harassment, and the Exodus

THE FIRST DAY of November 1838 was an extremely difficult one for the prophet and his people. Once again, Latter Day Saint efforts to build an insular Zionic community as they understood it had been thwarted in violent confrontation. As at every other stop along the church's journey, the Saints were marginalized, persecuted, and uprooted. Now they faced yet another uncertain future.

---

33. The debate as to Hinkle's role in this episode remains unresolved among historians. For an indictment of Hinkle, see James B. Allen and Glen M. Leonard, *The Story of the Latter-day Saints* (Salt Lake City: Deseret Book Company, 1976), 128. For an interpretation that absolves Hinkle, see Trudy Herendon, "George March Hinkle: Elder of the Mormon Church Hero or Traitor?" *Missouri Mormon Frontier* [*Newsletter*] 33 (January–April 2004): 1–18. This article of the Missouri Mormon Frontier Foundation, Jackson County, Missouri, is comprehensive in its explanation of Hinkle's history and is in part a reprint from the *Henckel Genealogical Bulletin: A Research Compendium* 34, no. 2 (Fall 2003): 1345–64.

34. This number is established in *History of Caldwell and Livingston Counties, Missouri*, 138.

By evening, the Mormon prisoners found themselves standing at a judgment bar. But this time the bar was a drumhead military court martial.[35] Seven Mormon leaders—Joseph Smith Jr., Sidney Rigdon, Hyrum Smith, Lyman Wight, Amasa Lyman, Parley P. Pratt, and George W. Robinson—stood trial for treason against the state in front of General Lucas and his chief officers.[36] Protests of this action came from the Saints and the militia. Most notably, Generals Alexander Doniphan and Hiram Parks strenuously challenged the legitimacy of the trial, but to no avail.

When the officers of the court martial handed down the guilty verdict, Lucas ordered Doniphan to take the prisoners into the public square at Far West and shoot them at nine o'clock in the morning. Doniphan's selection to carry out the sentence was strategic due to his reputation in Jefferson City. By facilitating the execution, he would have legitimized Lucas's decision to try the civilians. Doniphan realized this as well and would not conspire with Lucas. Instead, he rendered his judgment of the illegal process in a letter to Lucas: "It is cold-blooded murder. I will not obey your order. My brigade shall march for Liberty [Missouri] to-morrow, at 8 o'clock; and if you execute those men, I will hold you responsible before an earthly tribunal, so help me God!" The next morning, instead of witnessing the state-sponsored atrocity, Doniphan ordered up his Clay County troops, who were fully supportive of him, passed in review of the prisoners and General Lucas, and then marched out of Far West.[37]

35. Hill, *Joseph Smith*, 242; Bushman, *Rough Stone Rolling*, 370.
36. Lyman Wight, a Mormon defendant, was a colonel in the Daviess County militia and could have received a legitimate court martial. Why this circumstance was not pursued is a mystery. George Hinkle was a militia colonel also but was not brought before Lucas as a defendant. This convinced many Mormons of Hinkle's complicity in surrendering the prophet.
37. *History of Caldwell and Livingston Counties, Missouri*, 137; LeSueur, *The 1838 Mormon War*, 183. Doniphan biographer Roger D. Launius determined that Doniphan's motivations were based on the general's "fairness and sense of justice." Launius did acknowledge the benefits to Doniphan's law practice in defending the Mormons by suggesting that his image as a young lawyer was enhanced by taking up their cause. Researching Missouri State Archives records, Launius discovered that Doniphan did receive $67.35 from the state for his eleven days of active duty but did not mention any payments of legal fees. See Launius, *Alexander William Doniphan*, 66 and 66fn55.
   Historian Ronald E. Romig surmised that Doniphan's motives were not quite so altruistic. In conversation with the author, Romig observed that Smith and the

Alexander Doniphan's flagrant insubordination in early November 1838 saved the prophet's life and no doubt the entire movement. On the following morning, rather than executing the prisoners, the militia ordered the Saints to sign over their property deeds to pay for the damages inflicted during the Battle of Crooked River and the expenses for the troop deployment. Then, in front of the huge gathering, Joseph and the other prisoners climbed into wagons, bid the Saints farewell, and under heavy guard left Far West for Jackson County, to be held in preparation this time for civil court proceedings.

The Saints in Far West were left to fend for themselves at the mercy of irate Missouri militiamen. Totally defenseless Far West residents saw their homes ravaged, men whipped, livestock shot for food and sport, and crops destroyed. Some women received abusive treatment at the hands of the militia guard, including reports of rape. The weeks ahead would be some of the most difficult times in the Mormon Restoration Era.

General Lucas allowed his prisoners to return to their homes to get provisions for their sixty-mile journey to Independence, and their pending legal ordeal. Heavily guarded, each man collected his things and said good-bye to his family. Joseph Jr. gave Emma a passionate hug as their son Joseph, now just days before his sixth birthday, grabbed his father's leg and said, "Father, is the mob going to kill you?" A disgusted guard intervened

---

church leadership had racked up a hefty legal bill over the previous two years, and that Doniphan acted in his own financial self-interest in wanting to keep Smith alive. On behalf of the church, Bishop Edward Partridge deeded to Alexander Doniphan and his law partner Amos Rees 111 acres of prime Jackson County land valued at $5,000. The deed's date, 28 November 1838, is coincident to Doniphan's agreement to once again represent the Saints while they were jailed in Richmond, and eventually Liberty, Missouri. Whether the deed transfer was payment in arrears or in advance for legal services is impossible to tell. See Accretion Papers, Community of Christ Library-Archives.

LDS historian Brigham H. Roberts noted that Smith paid out $50,000 for his legal fees while in Missouri. But Smith regarded his expenditure as a worthless investment, stating that he "received very little in return; for sometimes they were afraid to act on account of the mob, and sometimes they were so drunk as to incapacitate them for business. But there were a few honorable exceptions." See Roberts's, *The Missouri Persecutions* (Salt Lake City: George Q. Cannon & Sons Co., 1900), 272. Accurately establishing "intent" remains the most difficult arena of inquiry within the historical discipline.

by striking the boy with the side of his sword and scolded him saying, "You little brat, go back; you will see your father no more."[38]

Under the security of three hundred troops commanded by Brigadier General Moses Wilson, the wagon procession arrived in Independence in a couple of days. Much to their surprise, the prisoners were well received by the Independence citizens. From there Joseph wrote Emma in Far West on 4 November, "We have been protected by the Jackson County boys, in the most genteel manner, and arrived here in midst of a splended parade…instead of going to [jail] we have a good house provided for us and the kindst treatment."[39]

The church leaders had spent just four days in Independence when militia general John B. Clark replaced Lucas. Clark's first order was to move the prisoners to Richmond, Ray County, for a court of inquiry before Judge Austin A. King of the Fifth Circuit Court, who had the proper jurisdiction. The hearing lasted from 12–28 November. Joining the original prisoners were some fifty others charged with participating in the Battle of Crooked River. During the hearings, witnesses for both sides jousted with accusations. Judge King facilitated a one-sided presentation of the evidence. When Joseph Smith took the stand, he lashed out at the unfairness of the proceedings, quoted scripture, and blasted those who spoke against him, saving his most vitriolic charges for his own dissenters, who lined up against him. On 24 November, Judge King released twenty-three of the prisoners for lack of evidence.[40] A day later, King released or admitted to bail all the other prisoners except Lyman Wight, Caleb Baldwin, Hyrum

---

38. There are slightly varying descriptions of this scene particularly as to how the guard actually responded. Suffice it to say, the rough treatment had a powerful impact on the young lad as he saw his father shoved away by the guards. See Baugh, "Call to Arms," 152; Newell and Avery, *Mormon Enigma*, 75; and Mark H. Forscutt, "Commemorative Discourse on the Death of Mrs. Emma Bidamon," *Saints' Herald* 26, no. 14 (15 July 1879): 213.

39. Joseph Smith Jr. to Emma Smith at Far West, 4 November 1838, photocopy, Joseph Smith Papers, Community of Christ Library-Archives. Also see Joseph Smith III and Heman C. Smith, *The History of the Reorganized Church of Jesus Christ of Latter Day Saints*, 8 vols. (Independence, Mo.: Herald House, 1967), 2: 295–96.

40. The released prisoners included Thomas Marsh, Orson Hyde, John Whitmer, George Hinkle, John Corrill, Reed Peck, and Sampson Avard. When asked, Avard laid blame for Danite activities squarely with the prophet.

Smith, Alexander McRae, Sidney Rigdon, and Joseph Smith Jr.[41] Still, the jail facilities were overcrowded, so the Mormon leaders were transferred to the jail in Liberty, Clay County, Missouri, twenty-five miles west of Richmond.

On 30 November, Joseph and the others climbed down into the fourteen-foot-square Liberty Jail dungeon and began what became a four-month stay. Joseph faced charges of treason (for calling out the Caldwell County militia to establish a Mormon kingdom against the State of Missouri) and murder (of the militiaman during the Battle of Crooked River). That the prisoners would be incarcerated in Liberty made it convenient for Alexander Doniphan and Amos Rees who agreed once again to represent as counsel their Mormon friends.

During Smith's months of incarceration, the one diversion granted by his jailers was the opportunity to write letters. Most of his letters went to Emma and his family. Representative is the letter he wrote from Richmond to Emma in Far West, dated 12 November 1838:

> Tell the children that I am alive and trust I shall come and see them before long. Comfort their hearts all you can, and try to be comforted yourself.... For Christ's sake, tell little Joseph he must be a good boy; Father loves him with a perfect love; he is the Eldest [and] must not hurt those that [are] Smaller than him but comfort them. Tell little Frederick, Father loves him with all his heart; he is a lovely boy. Julia is a lovely little girl; I love her also, She is a promising child; tell her, Father wants her to remember him and be a good girl.... Little Alexander is on my mind continualy. Oh my affectionate Emma, I want you to remember that I am a true and faithful friend to you; and the children, forever. My heart is entwined around yours forever and ever; Oh, may God bless you all.[42]

When Emma Smith learned of the prison transfer, she took the first of three trips from Far West to see her husband and to shuttle various family members of those incarcerated with him. She arrived with Young Joseph and Phebe Rigdon, and they spent the night in the dungeon with

---

41. *DHC*, 3: 210–12.
42. Joseph Smith Jr. to Emma Hale Smith, 12 November 1838, photocopy, Joseph Smith Papers, Community of Christ Library-Archives; also see Newell and Avery, *Mormon Enigma*, 76.

their loved ones. She returned approximately three weeks later, arriving on 20 December with the wife of Caleb Baldwin, and stayed two days. On her third and last visit, in late January 1839, Emma brought Mary Fielding Smith, still weak from the premature birth of a son, to see her husband, Hyrum. Again joining his mother in the wagon was Young Joseph. During this January visit, Lyman Wight recorded the prophet blessing presumably his son as his successor.[43] This was perhaps the most difficult of the three trips, but the travelers endured the forty-mile journey in the bitterly cold winter weather.

By late January 1839, the membership had been organized under the Committee for Removal to leave the state.[44] Facing a difficult 200-mile winter journey, the Saints organized into three groups. Those who felt the imperative to get out of the state as quickly as possible headed northward just over the state line to Iowa Territory, journeyed eastward to the Mississippi River, and then crossed over into Illinois. A second party trekked eastward through Livingston County, and then across the state. The third directed their wagon teams southeast for a short distance, passed through Carroll County, followed the Missouri River briefly, then traveled northeastward and crossed over the Mississippi River into Quincy, Illinois. By March, the evacuation of the members out of Missouri was essentially complete.

Meanwhile, the wretched conditions in Liberty Jail affected the mental and physical condition of its occupants. Most of the prisoners endured the dampness and cold, but Alexander McRae and Sidney Rigdon had to deal with special challenges. McRae stood at six feet six inches and could not stand upright in the dungeon, which had only a six-foot ceiling,[45]

43. Wight did not provide the actual name of the boy who received the blessing. Based on the circumstances, most have assumed that Young Joseph was the recipient. See Lyman Wight to editor, *Northern Islander*, July 1855, Lyman Wight Letterbook, Community of Christ Library-Archives.

44. Far West Committee on Removal, minutes 1839, January–April, MS 2564, LDS Family and Church History Department Archives, Salt Lake City, Utah.

45. Liberty Jail, built in 1833, cost six hundred dollars and faced east. Special attention was paid to the possibility of prisoners tunneling to obtain their freedom, so workers built four-foot-thick outside walls, then provided a one-foot interior space filled with loose rock. The interior walls were made of rough-hewn oak logs. The prison had two rooms—an upper room for jailers and the lower dungeon with an earthen floor. Only

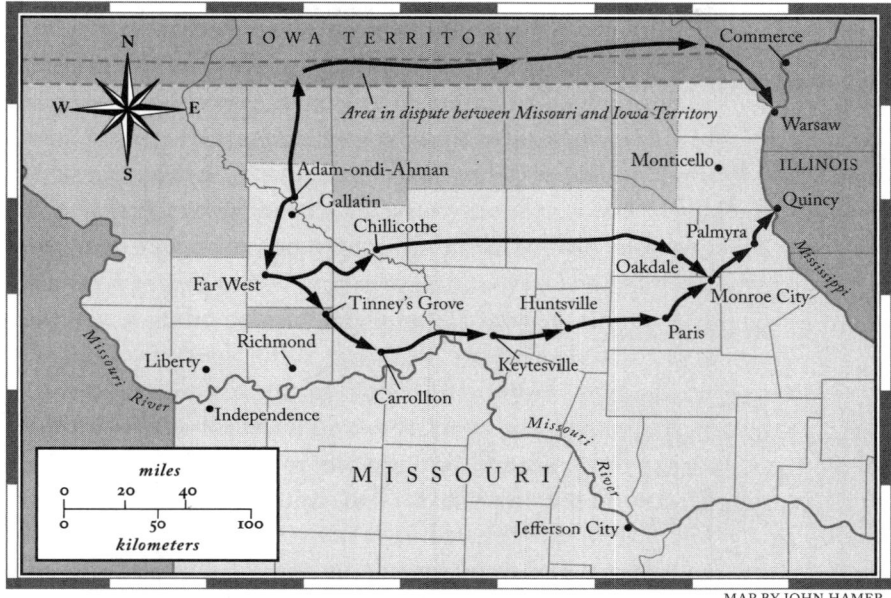

The Mormon exodus from Missouri, 1838–39

and Rigdon's mental health had often been an issue after being thrown by a horse when he was seven years old and dragged a considerable distance before being rescued. His brutal beating at the Johnson farm in Hiram, Ohio, in March 1832 exacerbated his condition, causing periods of melancholia.[46] Now, languishing for more than four months in the dank Liberty Jail reduced Rigdon's tolerance to survive the harsh conditions.

Jailers noted Rigdon's fragile condition, prompting an early court appearance for the prisoners. On 25 January 1839, the prisoners walked into the courtroom of Joel Turnham, a Clay County judge. Alexander Doniphan represented all but Rigdon, who represented himself. The room filled quickly with Mormon haters as litter bearers carted Rigdon into the courtroom. Rigdon accepted the opportunity to make a statement before

---

two narrow windows with heavy iron bar grates provided light and ventilation. The best description of the physical construction of the jail and the significance of Mormon occupation is provided in Leonard J. Arrington, "Church Leaders in Liberty Jail," *Brigham Young University Studies* 13, no. 1 (Autumn 1972): 20–26.

46. For an analysis of Rigdon's mental condition, see Van Wagoner, *Sidney Rigdon*, 117–18.

the court. Too weak to stand, from his cot the great Mormon orator recalled the years of persecution, beatings, robbings, hunger, and destitution suffered by the Latter Day Saints. The persuasiveness of his speech overwhelmed his prosecutors, won over even the most angry of listeners, and secured his release. Years later, Doniphan, an orator in his own right, recalled, "Such a burst of eloquence it was never my fortune to listen to, at its close there was not a dry eye in the room, all were moved to tears." One spectator who had arrived to lynch the Mormon leader grabbed his hat, walked through the audience, and collected one hundred dollars to cover Rigdon's exodus from Missouri.[47]

Fearing for his life, Rigdon returned to jail for his own protection. Then, in the dark of night on 5 February, Rigdon left the jail on foot to meet his son-in-law, George Robinson, waiting with horses. He rendezvoused with his wife, Phebe, three miles out of town, and in a carriage probably driven by his son-in-law, they headed east, making their way across the state. They rode fast through the countryside, avoiding public roads, sleeping during the day, and traveling at night. When they arrived at night at the western bank of the Mississippi River, Rigdon did not want to await the sunrise, so he paid two canoeists to paddle them across to sanctuary in Quincy, Illinois.[48]

Meanwhile, Smith and the remaining prisoners faced more litigation, this time in Gallatin, Daviess County. On 8 April, they stood before a grand jury that returned indictments for arson, riot, burglary, treason, and receiving stolen goods. This time, in Thomas C. Burch's court, Amos Rees and Peter H. Burnett, from Doniphan's law firm, represented the prisoners in their long-awaited opportunity to finally defend themselves in an actual trial. The prophet feared he could not receive a fair trial in any northern Missouri county. Burch agreed and changed the venue to Columbia, Boone County. Shortly after the decision, Daviess County sheriff William Morgan and four deputies escorted the prisoners to a wagon and headed east and then south toward Columbia.

On 16 April, the second day of their trek to Columbia, the guards and prisoners camped for the night. The guards began drinking heavily,

---

47. *Saints' Herald* 31, no. 31 (2 August 1884): 490.
48. Van Wagoner, *Sidney Rigdon*, 255.

leaving open the opportunity for the prisoners to escape. No one knows whether they actually escaped or were simply released. But Joseph Smith III, in his memoirs, recalled a visit from two men at Nauvoo, Illinois, who demanded eight hundred dollars and the replacement of a horse as payment for the escape, suggesting the prisoners had bribed the guards.[49] On the sixth day of their journey, Joseph and the other escapees arrived at the Mississippi River, crossed it, and entered Quincy.

One last item of church business in Missouri had its origins in a prophetic statement made on 8 July 1838. When he asked the Lord's will concerning certain of the twelve apostles, Smith prophesied, "Next spring let [the missionaries] depart to go over the great waters, and there promulgate my gospel, the fullness thereof, and bear record of my name. Let them take leave of my Saints in the city of Far West, on the 26th day of April next, on the building spot of my house, saith the Lord."[50] Obeying the directive, six apostles and approximately twenty other church members left their Illinois sanctuary and secretly retraced their journey across hostile Missouri territory. They timed their travel so they would arrive on the prophesied date, gathering after midnight at the temple site. After a quick meeting, they scurried back to Quincy, satisfied that they had fulfilled God's will and were now qualified to make their journey overseas. They then departed for a mission to England. In the weeks that followed, virtually all the loyal Saints had left Missouri, bringing to an end nearly a decade of trying to establish their Zion in that land.

Reflections on the Far West Experience

THE PROBLEMS SURROUNDING the Mormons moving west did not originate in Missouri, but emerged from the deep-seated frustrations that came from their unfulfilled millennial expectations initiated at the church's beginnings in upstate New York. Their inability or unwillingness to find acceptable ways of expressing their values clashed

---

49. Mary Audentia Smith Anderson, "The Memoirs of President Joseph Smith," *Saints' Herald* 81, no. 46 (13 November 1934): 1454.

50. *DHC*, 3: 46–47. Although this instruction is not canonized in the Community of Christ tradition, the LDS Church chose to place it in their Doctrine and Covenants as Section 118, where it remains today.

with the culture of other migrants to the American West. In every setting, the Mormons, as a minority, confronted the challenges of majority rule in a democratic society. At the time of their organization in upstate New York, Smith's followers willingly participated by living within social norms. For example, on 6 April 1830 they met the New York state criterion to organize, and at their second conference, in June, officially accepted the church leadership and a statement of official beliefs—the "Articles and Covenants of the church of Christ." However, their move toward isolation and their rejection of compromise led to their persecution. The Mormon belief in insular communitarianism, their theological arrogance, and their increasingly large numbers proved to be a volatile combination, resulting in an extermination order.

Just as important, the intolerance held by non-Mormons on the American frontier contributed significantly to the inflamed relations with their Mormon neighbors. Not exclusively against the Mormons, this intolerance spread against other minorities, including Native Americans, African Americans, Irish, and Hispanics. Because non-Mormons relied on frontier vigilantism to resolve their problems, anyone was threatened who jeopardized their perceived independent rights as citizens.

Missourians were prone to assign guilt by association. When Mormon missionaries shared their Book of Mormon with Native Americans, citizens assumed that Mormons were forging alliances against them—an assumption that prevailed during the Far West period. All it took for trigger-happy Westerners to view Mormons as abolition advocates was a poorly worded title in an Independence newspaper editorial. Because many of the Saints originated in antislavery New England and probably retained their accents, "Free People of Color" was all it took to ignite violence, which extended through the years of Mormon occupation in Missouri, ending in their expulsion. In neither case were the Mormons attempting to be strong advocates for other minorities.

Fortunately for the non-Mormons, the courts were on their side, as were most politicians. Exaggerated claims and even blatant lies were sufficient to garner support of elected officials. State and local government offices assisted them in the marginalization process, especially when rumors of the prophet's alleged attempt to overthrow the state government spread across the countryside. Always there was just enough truth to persuade skeptics that the Mormons threatened Missourians' lifestyle. When the pressure became too great, violence broke out with murderous consequences. All told, as the Far West experience demonstrated, the Mormon Question in Missouri defied simplistic answers.

In retrospect, the main participants on both sides of the Mormon expulsion went on to lead interesting lives. Alexander Doniphan achieved hero status in the Mexican-American War. In 1849, David Rice Atchison, senator from Missouri, was serving as president pro tem of the United States Senate when Zachary Taylor won the election of 1848. Taylor, a religious man, refused to be sworn in on Sunday 4 March 1849, and because Vice-President-Elect Millard Fillmore also was not sworn in, this meant that Atchison, former Doniphan law partner and respected by the Saints at Far West, served as president of the United States for one day. Peter H. Burnett, who had defended the prisoners in Thomas Burch's courtroom at Gallatin in April 1839, migrated west to California to become its first governor after statehood.

COMMUNITY OF CHRIST LIBRARY-ARCHIVES
Brigham Young in his late forties

The political career of Lilburn Boggs declined after Mormon expulsion. Most Missouri politicians condemned his extermination order of late October 1838 as a violation of republican values, yet they chose not to rescind it. Indeed, the extermination order was not officially rescinded until 25 June 1976, by then-governor Christopher S. Bond. After the Mexican-American War, Boggs moved to California and served as the alcalde (chief administrator) of California's northern district prior to statehood.

Many church leaders removed from the rolls during the Far West period returned to the fellowship with their statements of contrition. These included Orson Hyde, William W. Phelps, and Thomas B. Marsh. Other dissenters chose not to return, including David and John Whitmer, and the heady church historian John Corrill.[51] The Danite organization officially ended after Far West; however, many continued unofficially to perform Danite functions through the next decade.

Finally, the Far West period was pivotal for the evolution of the Latter Day Saint church, and especially for its prophet. When the state militia removed the leadership from the Far West square, many felt their time with the prophet had come to an end. It did not take long for discussions to emerge about the future of the church and who would lead now that the entire First Presidency of Joseph Smith Jr., Sidney Rigdon, and Hyrum Smith faced execution. That the Saints looked to Brigham Young, charter member of the Council of Twelve Apostles, to keep the movement together and lead them out of Missouri, had significant future implications.

The months of imprisonment had a lasting impact on the prophet. Eminent Mormon historian Leonard J. Arrington considered the months of Smith's incarceration as "a time of testing."[52] Joseph's letters during this time demonstrated unusual eloquence, deep reflection, and profound insight. He wrote of his frustrations by calling down the forces of heaven on his enemies for inflicting such suffering on his followers, yet encouraged all to find redemption in their suffering. But he also tempered his language against other religions, calling the Saints to have respect for other faith communities. He even acknowledged the mistakes made by church leaders, including his own.[53]

Clearly, the prophet used this time to formulate the long-term future of his church and to establish an immediate course of action. He decided to engage in the political system by writing a petition for redress of grievances and with a personal visit to Washington, D.C., within six months

---

51. LeSueur noted that Corrill was elected to the Missouri state legislature. A highlight of his political career was his failed attempt to pass legislation to prevent religious swindling crimes by prohibiting anyone from "prophesying or speaking in the name of the Lord." During the debate on his bill he told the other legislators that the bill was necessary "to prevent the recurrence of the evils heretofore experienced with the Mormons." See *Missouri Republican*, 25 January 1839, as cited in LeSueur, *The 1838 Mormon War*, 260. The bill failed to pass by a vote of 44 to 41.

52. Arrington, "Church Leaders," 26.

53. An excellent analysis of Joseph Smith Jr.'s letters during this period can be found in Bushman, *Rough Stone Rolling*, 380–85. Also see Arrington, "Church Leaders," 24–25.

of his escape. His electioneering in Illinois, and even his candidacy in the approaching presidential election of 1844, followed later.

John Corrill's assessment summed up his own view of the Mormon experience, and also why he left the movement:

> When I retrace our track, and view the doings of the church for six years past, I can see nothing that convinces me that God has been our leader; calculation after calculation has failed, and plan after plan has been overthrown, and our prophet seemed not to know the event until too late. If he said go up and prosper, still we did not prosper; but have labored and toiled, and waded through trials, difficulties, and temptations, of various kinds, in hope of deliverance. But no deliverance came.[54]

From Liberty Jail, the prophet himself may have realized this also. But he was determined more than ever to chart a new course if he could escape the manacles of his captors just one more time. The reunion with his family and friends in Quincy, Illinois, during the spring of 1839 offered the prophet a new beginning. But the next five years would reveal his willingness to accept only some of the lessons of his history.

Conclusion to the Middle Period of the Restoration

THE MIDDLE YEARS of the Restoration, from 1830 through 1839, peaked in 1836 in Kirtland, Ohio, as the Latter Day Saints dedicated a House of the Lord for their sacrament offerings, preaching, fasting, prayers, and offering up their most holy desires to their God.[55] The Pentecostal outpourings at the dedication service had a lasting impact and surfaced in their testimonies and writings for generations to come. Still, they were a divided people with a divided identity.

Joseph Smith Jr. resolved the issue of church identity. Two churches—in Ohio and Missouri—proved unworkable. The prophet united the two wings into one at Far West in 1838. From that point, until his death, he was the embodiment of the Church of Jesus Christ of Latter Day Saints.

But church members confronted firsthand the violent nature of American frontier society. This confrontation resulted in the persistent

54. Corrill, *A Brief History*, 48.
55. Language taken from Doctrine and Covenants 92:3e (LDS 95:16).

presence of persecution, which followed them wherever they went. They responded by breaking loose from their upstate New York pacifist moorings. Mostly out of frustration, but always feeling that God was on their side, they accepted violent solutions to achieve their aspirations of being a specially chosen people in the New World to usher in the Second Coming of Christ.

The membership demonstrated the depth of their loyalty to their president even when he confronted the limits of his prophetic leadership. Under the most difficult of circumstances, the vast majority continued with him on the journey even though it meant loss of life, property, and their material prosperity. Smith recognized their sacrifices and brought more than sixty revelatory messages that provided divine assurance and eased their burdens.

Now the journey would take them to western Illinois to create yet another sacred community, but with new safeguards. Nauvoo, the newest Mormon enclave, would become a Mormon city-state affording protection not found in previous settings. With this new community, the Restoration Era would enter its final period.

The Late Period of the Restoration

❧

1839 to 1844

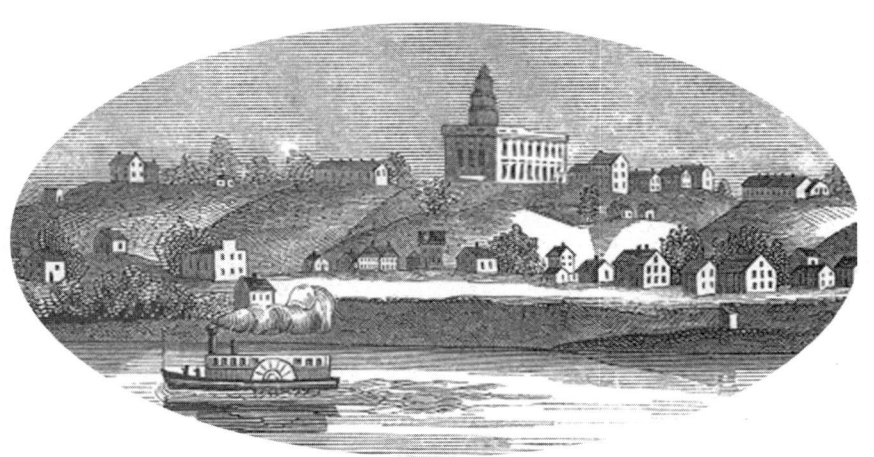

NAUVOO

CHAPTER FIFTEEN

Nauvoo, Illinois: Creating a New Community on the Mississippi

Awaiting Prophetic Direction

WHILE THE CHURCH leadership languished in Liberty Jail, the Saints worried about the church's future and certainly their own. Five thousand followers committed their all to the prophet's ushering in of the Second Coming. Believers delivered their own salvation into the hands of the prophet. When the Saints crossed the Mississippi River into Illinois in late 1838, some wondered if this was all for naught.

Quincy, Illinois, residents had heard the stories of the Saints' persecution. With sympathy they opened their homes to many of the haggard exiles, while other Saints settled in encampments on the outskirts of town. Now, the Missouri expatriates waited and wondered while they endured the cold winter elements. The Saints would use this time to heal from their persecution and to plan their future.

Considerable debate arose on whether to scatter or remain together—important voices counseled that the Saints should scatter, while others counseled to retain the gathering. President Sidney Rigdon, Bishop Edward Partridge, and High Priest William Marks spoke on behalf of many in the movement who were already making plans for departure at spring thaw. However, when senior apostle Brigham Young arrived, he called for a reorganization of the church—any plans for dispersion would be temporary only.[1]

When Joseph Smith arrived at the western bank of the Mississippi River and stared across at Quincy, Illinois, on the other side, he may have wondered about his potential reception. Dressed in a blue coat with a high collar, a black hat with its wide brim pulled down, and an unshaven face, Smith inconspicuously climbed onto the ferry and rode over to the Illinois side. Earlier rumors of Joseph's escape had reached the Saints, so Emma asked family friend Dimick Huntington to stand watch at the boat dock for her husband's arrival. When the deck hands lowered the ferry boardwalk to the Illinois riverbank, Joseph disembarked. From a distance Huntington recognized the prophet and ran up to him. Joseph quickly hushed him and asked about his wife and children. After arranging for a second horse, the two men quietly rode through the back alleys of Quincy to the outskirts of town and then the three miles to the home of Judge John and Sarah Cleveland, who were providing Emma and the family shelter in their home. Emma heard the riders and peered out the window. With her amazing gift of discernment, she immediately recognized her husband, burst from the house, and met him in the front yard with a loving embrace.[2]

Joseph Smith Jr.'s escape from certain execution rejuvenated his commitment to lead his people. Over the next month, the prophet directed his attention to finding suitable land to build yet another—his fourth—City of God. Time was of the essence now that spring had arrived. Although their membership included mechanics, carpenters, blacksmiths, and wainwrights, generally the Mormons were an agricultural people. They looked to the land not only for their sacred space but also for their sustenance. Planting season had arrived, and land acquisition and preparation were imperative.

1. Apostle John Taylor supposedly heard a remark made by Sidney Rigdon: "Brethren, every one of you take your own way, for the work seems as though it had come to an end." See John Taylor, "Unity of the Saints," *Journal of Discourses* 11 (1867): 25. Rigdon's statement may have reflected his understanding of the prophet's feelings at low ebb as they sat hopelessly in Liberty Jail facing execution. Also, Taylor's remembrances should be understood in the context of a twenty-five year separation from the event and the animosities the Quorum of Twelve Apostles held toward Rigdon during the power struggle after Smith's assassination.

2. This episode is told well in Newell and Avery, *Mormon Enigma*, 81–82.

Nauvoo, Illinois: Creating a New Community on the Mississippi   347

MAP BY JOHN HAMER

The vicinity of Nauvoo, Illinois

Suitable land lay some fifty miles north of Quincy on a peninsula that had been the site of an abandoned community called Commerce. Curiously, Joseph changed the name to Nauvoo, a Hebrew reference to a "beautiful situation or place." Only in Smith's imagination could this land be called beautiful since it was a stagnant-water swampland with a few abandoned structures.[3] The church purchased even more land on the Iowa

3. Joseph Smith Jr. described how deserted Commerce was when he arrived: "When I made the purchase…there were one stone house, three frame houses, and two block houses, which constituted the whole city of Commerce. Between Commerce and Mr. Davison Hibbard's, there was one stone house and three log houses, including the one

Territory side in Lee County.[4] Together, this land, on both sides of the river some twelve miles north of Keokuk and eight miles south of Fort Madison, provided the venue for the last chapter of the Restoration Era.

Similar to Kirtland, Ohio, the geography on the Illinois side included towering bluffs that could be seen easily for miles and flats next to the river.[5] This land offered Smith yet another opportunity to be "city builder." He platted his community in June 1839 according to the lines of the initial land survey, excluding the property lines of Commerce itself. This was different from his designs for Independence, Missouri. Eventually the Nauvoo City Council rectified this exception by eliminating those old boundaries altogether. The Nauvoo plat was the picture of order, suitable only for a holy city—one hundred fifty squares of four acres, with each square divided into four one-acre lots. Wide streets running at ninety-degree angles east and

---

that I live in, and these were all the houses in the vicinity and the place was literally a wilderness." See *History of the RLDS Church*, 2: 367; *DHC*, 3: 375.

4. This historic tract of land was designated in 1824 by the United States Congress as the "Half Breed Tract." Because the 119,000 acres between the Des Moines and the Mississippi Rivers south of Fort Madison was prime land, it attracted land speculators, traders, trappers, and soldiers from nearby forts. These men took women as wives and concubines from the area's original occupants, the Sac and Fox tribes. Unceremoniously, the offspring that populated the area were called "half breeds." The definition of half breed was anyone who was "part Indian and didn't wear a blanket." The original treaty disallowed occupants to sell or convey the land; but when in 1834 the land was opened for transfer, speculators swarmed the area for what they could get. One competing land agent was Isaac Galland, who made a questionable claim on a sizable tract of land. Holding a checkered reputation, Galland found the Saints a vulnerable clientele and offered to sell his interest in some of his Lee County, Iowa Territory, and Commerce, Illinois, property. Galland's terms of no money down and long years to pay were favorable to the impoverished Saints. On 4–6 May 1839, Smith called a General Conference, the first since his Missouri escape, and the delegates voted unanimously to make the purchase of land. However, through his manipulations, unbeknown to the Mormons, Galland transferred land to them with questionable title. See Robert Bruce Flanders, *Nauvoo: Kingdom on the Mississippi* (Urbana: University of Illinois Press, 1965), 30ff. This did not become a major problem until Mormon occupation ended, leaving a web of title challenges for Joseph Smith Jr.'s widow, Emma Hale Smith, to untangle.

5. Of course there is no comparing the huge Mississippi River with its nationwide transportation system to the Chagrin River, wide and deep enough only to service several mills and to hold baptismal services. My observation focuses more on Smith's tendency to settle near a reliable water supply and where there was a prominent point to locate the House of the Lord.

west, north and south, divided the acreage. Smith's original plat provided for a river canal to wend its way through the city.

Almost immediately Smith sent out the word for the Saints to gather. The First Presidency carefully monitored settlement patterns, using land sales to church members where possible to retire the purchase debt. With the rising tide of immigrants arriving in the area, the church leadership benefited from inflationary conditions to cover the losses from the poor, who could not pay. Members were supposed to receive permission from the church leadership to settle in Nauvoo—a lesson learned from Independence, Missouri. However, many indigent families ignored the directive and arrived in Nauvoo without any means to settle. The losses from these unauthorized settlements lasted only a year, when at the October 1840 conference the First Presidency announced that those who moved to Nauvoo without recommendation from the branches where they resided should be "disfellowshipped."[6]

Building the Nauvoo Community

THE GROWING PAINS of Nauvoo were similar to those of other nineteenth-century communities of its size.[7] Although the millennial motivation to populate Nauvoo was unique to this western Illinois community, the problems associated with the gathering were quite similar. As believers obediently arrived, the sound of hammers and saws rang out through the newly created streets. A review of two Nauvoo newspapers—the church's official organ, the *Times and Seasons*, and the *Nauvoo Neighbor*—revealed the diversity of occupations in the community. One could find

6. *DHC*, 4: 205. Receiving a recommendation from a local church official before one could "gather" established a precedent that found expression during the Reorganization Era. Joseph Smith Jr.'s grandson Frederick Madison Smith, second prophet of the Reorganized Church of Jesus Christ of Latter Day Saints, set similar conditions for members wishing to gather to Jackson County in the 1920s during the early years of his thirty-one-year tenure as church president. When moving, RLDS members needed to obtain a letter of removal, certifying they were members in good standing. The letter was to be presented to the pastor of the new branch to which they moved.

7. This is the observation of Kenneth W. Godfrey in his informative essay, "The Nauvoo Neighborhood: A Little Philadelphia or Unique City Set upon a Hill?" in *Kingdom on the Mississippi Revisited: Nauvoo in Mormon History*, ed. Roger D. Launius and John E. Hallwas (Urbana: University of Illinois Press, 1996), 72–93.

the services of carpenters, hatters, blacksmiths, portraitists, clock smiths, trappers, coal miners, fishermen, teachers, publishers, lawyers, broadsword instructors, and mapmakers. Domestic needs were also addressed in the advertisements, including remedies for ailments and even the eradication of bedbugs, a persistent problem throughout the era:

> *Bedbugs.*—Do not fail to treat these odiferous marauders to mercury whenever they make their appearance. To prepare it for application, put a small quantity—say a tea spoon full—into a tumbler and break in the white of two eggs. Then make an egg beater by splitting into the end of a stick crosswise and inserting two flat pieces of wood or goose quill. Put the wheel end of this into the tumbler and taking the upper end into the palms of the hands, roll it as in beating eggs, till the mercury is fully incorporated. Apply it in small quantities with a feather. It will remain for years and the bedbugs will sooner take another pew than endure it an instant. Pour the melted quick silver and eggs, for mercy's sake, till all the bugs in the country have the *cramp*.[8]

Of great concern to Nauvoo residents was their ability to sustain their personal economy. Since the church leadership was the primary broker of land, settlers were financially obligated to the church for their homes and farms. But church members never lost their penchant for communalism, even in the Nauvoo settlement. Because the challenges of surviving a frontier lifestyle could be overwhelming, by working together, as in so many other burgeoning cities in America, the Nauvoo community grew quickly.

Economic associations soon emerged.[9] Citizens set prices, established quality standards, and empowered a police force for their safety. Formally established economic associations watched over the sale of grain crops; potato, wood, and pork prices; and housing construction.

Supervision of quality control by Nauvoo citizens had been superseded by church leaders, since the Quorum of Twelve Apostles approved the regulators' decisions. This symbolized the overarching presence of the church in all aspects of Nauvoo life. With the arrival of spring 1841, the

---

8. "Bedbugs," *Nauvoo Neighbor* 3, no. 9 (2 July 1845): 2. Microfilm Collection, Community of Christ Library-Archives.

9. Godfrey, "The Nauvoo Neighborhood," 75.

editor of the *Times and Seasons* expressed optimism about the building process in the community:

> Every where we see men of industry, with countenances beaming with cheerful content, hurrying to their several occupations and scenes of labor. The sound of the ax, the hammer, and the saw, greet your ear in every direction. Notwithstanding the discouraging circumstances under which the saints were thrown, shipwrecked as it were, upon this shore, they have indeed wrought wonders. Habitations are reared for miles in every direction, and others are springing up, and ere we are aware of their existence, and are filled with happy occupants.[10]

Even with the heavy demand for labor, Nauvoo had its impoverished population but in numbers no more or less significant than other cities of the era.[11]

As colorful as it was, there was also a dark side to the community. Since Nauvoo was a "river town" it faced special challenges, including criminal activity. Hancock County sheriff Minor R. Deming frequently placed notices in the *Neighbor* calling for the apprehension of fugitives from the law.[12] Church leaders took aggressive steps to root out criminals in their community by identifying, publicizing, and then prosecuting perpetrators.[13] An undesirable element emerged from within the ranks of both nonmember and Mormon Nauvooans. Articles in the church newspaper warned readers to be wary of suspicious activities around them. In a piece titled "Look Out for Thieves!!" the editor wrote:

> This place has been infested of late with a gang of *thieves*, insomuch that property of almost all kinds, has been unsafe unless secured with bolts and bars; cattle and hogs have been made a free booty. The community are awake to ferret them out, and have already made some inroads among them; the measures that are taking, have created a

---

10. "Miscellaneous," *Times and Seasons* 2, no. 11 (1 April 1841): 368.
11. Godfrey, "The Nauvoo Neighborhood," 74.
12. M. R. Deming, "MURDER! $200 Reward!" *Nauvoo Neighbor* 3, no. 9 (2 July 1845): 3.
13. Bill Shepard, "Stealing at Mormon Nauvoo," *John Whitmer Historical Association Journal* 23 (2003): 91–110. In this excellent analysis, Shepard discussed the reaction of Joseph Smith Jr. and Hyrum Smith to these individuals, to events that influenced the evolution of their policy of dealing with the "undesirable element," and the contrasting approaches of Brigham Young during the post-assassination period in Nauvoo.

general *alarm* among the midnight *pilagers*, and they are making *tracks* as fast as possible. As it is very possible that some may escape JUSTICE, and palm themselves upon an unsuspecting community, we give this notice as a timely warning, that all may be on the look out. We sincerely hope that all those who escape justice here, will soon be overtaken in their wickedness—ALTON [Illinois] is a suitable place for all such characters.[14]

By mid-December 1840, the gravity of criminal activity had accelerated, requiring church leaders to name names. Four "notorious thieves" escaped from the Hancock County sheriff's custody, and citizens were cautioned "to be on their guard" for them. The four escapees were James R. Bingham, Alanson Brown, David Holman, and Artemus Johnson. These men, being held over for trial, jumped their five-hundred-dollar bond.[15]

Over time, when persecution against Mormons in Nauvoo increased, the church leadership differentiated their treatment of church members who stole from Gentiles versus Mormons who stole from each other. A precedent of the church hierarchy accepting goods stolen from Gentiles dates back to the Far West period. Such windfall donations were considered as tithing, or perhaps, out of a sense of guilt, free-will offerings. Although authorities generally used the ill-gotten loot to assist the poor, this became an obvious source of conflict with each occurrence.[16]

As in most frontier towns in the early nineteenth century, life was not easy, and at times, quite hazardous. In the early days of Mormon habitation, the geography prevented easy settlement. An extensive limestone strata, heavy clay deposits, and high bluffs trapped water from the numerous springs in the area and created swampy conditions. Most knew of the

---

14. "LOOK OUT FOR THIEVES!!" *Times and Seasons* 2, no. 1 (1 November 1840): 204.
15. "BEWARE OF THIEVES!!" *Times and Seasons* 2, no. 4 (15 December 1840): 256.
16. For more on this subject see Michael S. Riggs, "From the Daughters of Zion to 'The Banditti of the Prairies': Danite Influence on the Nauvoo Period," *Restoration Studies VII*, ed. Joni Wilson and Ruth Ann Wood (Independence, Mo.: Herald House, 1998), 95–106. Riggs observed Mormon Justus Morse's reference to a Danite robbing of a gentile store in McDonough County, Illinois, as having "sucked the milk of the gentiles" (96). Also see LeSueur, *The 1838 Mormon War*, 117–20. LeSueur documented goods taken from the gentile communities of Millport, Gallatin, and Grindstone Fork in northwest Missouri.

hazards associated with such conditions but did not know specifically what caused some people to escape sickness and others to become afflicted.

Summer was frequently referred to as "the sickly season," no doubt because of the infectious mosquitoes that brought the "ague," or malaria.[17] During the first summer of 1839, residents found themselves in the throes of a malarial epidemic. Joseph Smith's journal records the dimensions of affliction of his people's suffering. The fever forced the cancellation of meetings and required ministers to tend to the stricken. Many claimed great healings, while others succumbed. In his 28 July entry, the prophet admonished church members to "set their houses in order, to make clean the inside of the platter, and to meet on the next Sabbath to partake of the Sacrament... [so that] we might be enabled to prevail with God against the destroyer, and that the sick might be healed."[18] The prophetic counsel acknowledged cleanliness and spiritual preparation as key to survival.

The sickly season of 1840 was worse, however, with even more deaths throughout the city. Anticipating yet a third difficult summer, Smith warned travelers in his "Proclamation to the Saints Scattered Abroad" in January 1841 with a reminder of the disease that plagued the Saints at Nauvoo. The fever peaked that summer and then subsided. Once workers drained the swampy areas through trenching a system of ditches, the sickly season shortened, but not without taking its toll. At times, so many people died that individual funerals were impractical. Sidney Rigdon suffered with the ague for nearly a year,[19] and the Smith family was not immune from the

---

17. The term "sickly season" frequented articles in the *Times and Seasons*: "as the sickly season is past, and we have made large additions to our establishment," 2, no. 1 (1 November 1840): 203; "It was then thought by many that its days would not be long in the land, and that at any rate it would not survive the sickly season," 4, no. 11 (15 April 1843): 161; "This together with the sickness of some of our hands during the late sickly season, has caused us to be behind the day of publication," 4, no. 20 (1 September 1843): 312; "as it was in the sickly season, many feeble persons, thrown out into the scorching rays of the sun," 6, no. 16 (1 November 1845): 1017.

18. *DHC*, 4: 4–5.

19. Joseph Smith Jr. to John C. Bennett, 8 August 1840, *DHC* 4: 178; Van Wagoner, *Sidney Rigdon*, 267.

fever, as it took the life of the prophet's father and patriarch of the church, Joseph Smith Sr., and the prophet's younger brother, Don Carlos Smith.[20]

Expectations and Realities of the Nauvoo Economy

THE STRUCTURE OF the Nauvoo economy demonstrated that Joseph Smith Jr. had learned at least some lessons from his Kirtland experience. Outside creditors considered church assets as deriving from the labor of his followers, from the land where they settled, and from his word as prophet-president. Smith expected the Saints to labor heroically in building the Nauvoo economy, and overall, the people responded favorably. Most held more than one occupation while working their church-assigned one-acre plot. This small amount of land did not prevent those with resources from expanding their holdings by purchasing property outside the boundary of the community. Joseph Smith, as trustee-in-trust for church holdings and chief Nauvoo real estate broker, sold the lands, hoping that profit from an assumed inflationary spiral would finance the initial acquisition of land hosting the Nauvoo community. Church members' prosperity meant the needs of the poor could be met and larger contributions could fill church coffers. At least that was the plan.

The prophet, however, underestimated the success of his British missionaries. The "push factors" of worker abuse and high unemployment in a depressed economy in Great Britain accentuated by the "pull factor" of a theology of spiritual salvation of all believers in the afterlife deposited thousands of European immigrants on the bank of the Mississippi River at Nauvoo. Two missionary ventures into the British Isles proved very successful. Heber C. Kimball and Orson Hyde proselytized between 1837 and 1838. Seven other apostles followed a year later, ministering in Preston, Manchester, Liverpool, the Isle of Man, and in Ireland.[21] In the first three years of the British Mission, starting in 1837, Mormon elders baptized 1,417 souls. By 1841, Mormon baptisms produced 8,425 members. During the

20. *History of the RLDS Church*, 2: 538; also see "Death of General Don Carlos Smith," *Times and Seasons* 2, no. 20 (16 August 1844): 503–504.

21. From Kirtland, Ohio, Smith sent two apostles, Heber C. Kimball and Orson Hyde, to Great Britain. These two men headed a delegation of elders from Canada. The seven who followed were Brigham Young, Orson Pratt, Parley P. Pratt, Willard Richards, George Albert Smith, John Taylor, and Wilford Woodruff.

Nauvoo, Illinois: Creating a New Community on the Mississippi 355

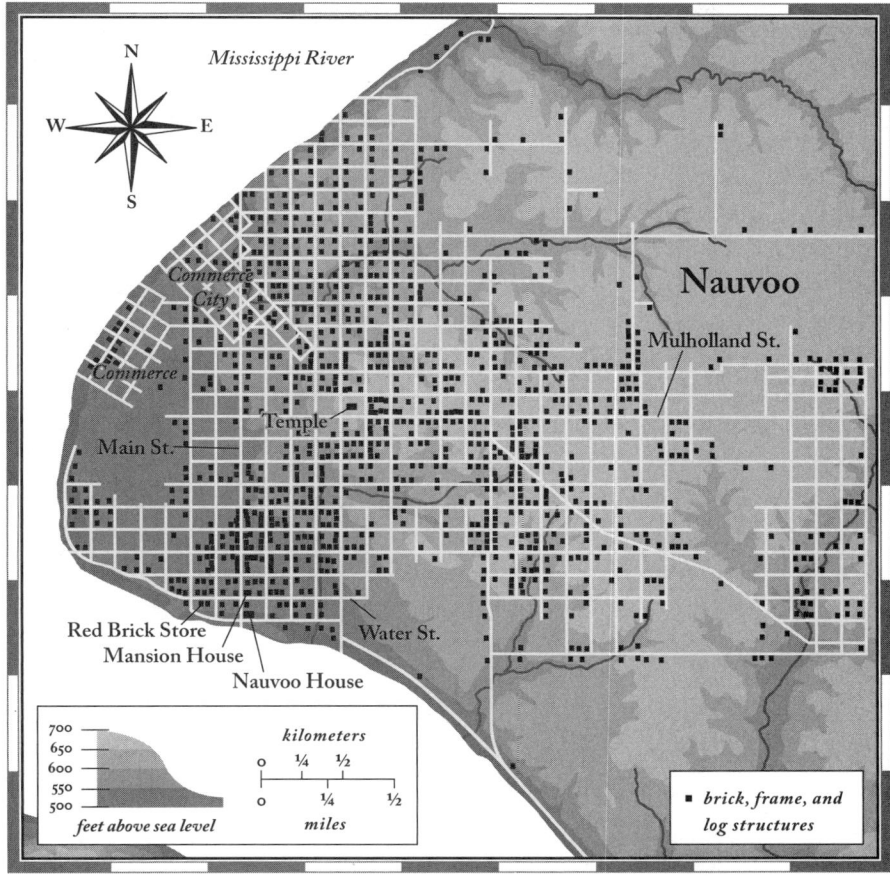

COMMUNITY OF CHRIST LIBRARY-ARCHIVES

Nauvoo at its greatest extent, 1846

five years of the Mormon presence in Nauvoo, nearly five thousand British Saints gathered there, the vast majority of whom were impoverished at the time of their arrival.[22] With great expectations, these converts fully anticipated that the church would care for them.

22. See the analysis of British immigration in Flanders, *Nauvoo*, 58ff. Although this work is dated, his conclusions have not been substantially challenged. Indeed, Flanders's book remains the gold standard for any study of the Nauvoo period from 1839–1846. The estimate of five thousand British immigrants is consistent with the more recent analysis of Fred E. Woods in *Gathering to Nauvoo* (American Fork, Utah: Covenant Communications, 2002), 153–54. Woods's analysis builds on earlier immigration

The first group—of 240 immigrants—gathered to Nauvoo in 1840. More than eleven hundred arrived the following year. Smith and the church leaders felt obligated to find space within the Nauvoo community for this large number of people—a task that placed enormous strain on the community and church economy. With a struggle, Smith met the first payment of $3,000 to Horace Hotchkiss, who held the note on 400 acres of church properties around Commerce. But as the immigrant numbers increased with the passing of time, Smith's plan to build the economy faltered and Hotchkiss grew impatient for his second payment, due in the summer of 1841.

Smith exhausted almost all of the church's resources to meet the first payment, and now had only one viable resource left to make the second—the property assets of the Saints yet to gather to Nauvoo. In a creative financing scheme, the prophet sent a team of church representatives to the East to encourage members to gather to Nauvoo, but before doing so, to sign over their property titles to the church in exchange for land of similar value in the Nauvoo area. On arrival, the prophet would then deed over the eastern land titles to Hotchkiss to satisfy the Mormon debt.

These resources were considerable, as were the number of Saints still living in the East. As late as 1843, there were fourteen branches of the church in the Boston vicinity alone, representing more than eight hundred church members.[23] Since the opportunities for title-trading were significant, Joseph sent his brothers Hyrum and William with Isaac Galland. The selection of Galland to represent the church was strategic, since he was a new convert, had experience with title ownership, and was close to Hotchkiss. Unfortunately, Galland was of suspicious character. At first, the financing scheme seemed to work, but then a disagreement arose between Smith and Hotchkiss over payment details. Resolving the issue took great pains by the prophet, the support of a church conference, and an apostolic

---

studies in Andrew Jenson, "Church Emigration," *The Contributor* 12, no. 12 (October 1891): 441–50. The last recorded immigrant company to set sail for Nauvoo left Liverpool, England, on 16 January 1846 with forty-five converts under the leadership of Hiram Clark. Because of missing records, the actual number of British immigrants to Nauvoo is based on estimates.

23. As of a church conference held at Boylston Hall, in Boston, 793 church members, 33 elders, and 43 other officers attended these fourteen congregations. See *DHC*, 5: 268.

epistle to the eastern Saints about the urgency of gathering so the church debt could be met.[24]

Another important issue related to the Nauvoo economy centered on banking practices. The usual banking and lending institutions found in other contemporary communities of similar size were absent from Nauvoo. A shortage of money and a difficult Kirtland history explain why. As stated earlier, most immigrants exhausted their personal income during their travel, but many had the negotiable titles of the properties they had left behind and were happy to exchange them for property in their new community. Still, little money could be exchanged for goods and services. Thus, a substantial barter economy emerged out of necessity. The absence of specie reduced somewhat the need for banking and lending institutions. It is clear, however, that for the city to continue its development, at some point these financial institutions would be necessary. Until then, merchants kept records of transactions with customers and ran their businesses on what little monies could be tendered.

Perhaps more than anything, the lessons of the Kirtland bank crisis had burned into the prophet's memory. Although he may have been tempted once again to start a bank, the thought of attempting to build confidence among his own people, who also remembered the anti-bank scheme, stirred little interest. The Latter Day Saints possessed few resources and neither did the gentile community. Printing money once again garnered little support among the church leaders, who had taken heavy losses in Kirtland. The Nauvoo economy would have to grow on its own without the customary banking and lending institutions.

To promote economic development, Smith encouraged the creation of joint-stock associations. Two examples demonstrate the usefulness of these associations—the Nauvoo Coach and Carriage Manufacturing Association and the Agricultural and Mechanical Association. With the developing economy, consumers were concerned about equity for the products that were bartered. Common questions arose about the fairness of trading one product for another. To regulate these trades, the economic associations took responsibility for ensuring the quality of construction and product worthiness. The Nauvoo Coach and Carriage

---

24. Brigham H. Roberts, *Comprehensive History of the Church of Jesus Christ of Latter Day Saints*, 6 vols. (Provo, Utah: Brigham Young University Press, 1965), 2: 8–10.

Manufacturing Association set standards of quality during the construction process to ensure the products qualified for barter, and church leaders monitored regulators' decisions.

As the local economy matured, the Nauvoo Agricultural and Mechanical Association exemplified Joseph's economic hopes. The association was established to raise money through the sale of shares "for the promotion of agriculture and husbandry in all its branches, and for the manufacture of flour, lumber, and such other useful articles as are necessary for the ordinary purposes of life."[25] At fifty dollars a share, the capitalization was set at $100,000, with the possibility of tripling the total value. This association was Smith's answer to the need for more industry in the city. Most important, the Agricultural and Manufacturing Association had the endorsement of the State of Illinois, through the city charter. After Kirtland, lawful authorization was always an issue.[26] Unfortunately, the realities of sparse money reserves for investment plagued the Agricultural and Manufacturing Association as it did the other associations. It is a tribute to the perseverance of the Saints that the Nauvoo economy grew so well even with these enormous obstacles.

Arrival of John Cook Bennett and the Paramount Importance of the Nauvoo City Charter

MISSING FROM EACH community experiment along the Latter Day Saint journey, at least until now, was the legal and physical protection required to build the kingdom of God. Because the Nauvoo City Charter provided this protection, its importance cannot be overstated. But Joseph, inexperienced in the ways of accomplishing these protections, needed help. In a seemingly fortuitous turn of events he became acquainted with Dr. John Cook Bennett. This remarkable individual seemed to personify the solution to Joseph's needs.

---

25. *DHC*, 4: 303.
26. "An Act to Incorporate the City of Nauvoo," as found in *History of the RLDS Church*, 2: 468–75; *DHC*, 4: 239–45. The legislative authority of the Nauvoo City Council is explained in "Of the Legislative Powers of the City Council," *History of the RLDS Church*, 2: 476–79; *DHC*, 4: 245–48.

Bennett, a man of considerable accomplishment, had all the qualities to which the prophet aspired. He held the military rank of brigadier general of the Invincible Dragoons, a cavalry unit in the Illinois militia. He was also the state's quartermaster general, and thus a man of notable influence in the state capital. With professional medical training, Bennett was also well educated.[27]

After an extensive letter-writing campaign with the Mormon prophet, Bennett arrived in Nauvoo in the late summer of 1840, with the intent of being baptized. Thus, it is not surprising that Smith befriended Bennett.[28] Historians have debated for generations why Bennett took such great interest in Joseph Smith Jr. and the Mormon Church. It seemed that the two men sensed in each other mutual opportunities to accomplish their own ends.

COMMUNITY OF CHRIST LIBRARY-ARCHIVES

John Cook Bennett dressed as major general of the Nauvoo Legion

From her first meeting with Bennett, Emma Smith sensed something suspicious about him. Perhaps it was his brutal treatment when he

---

27. After leaving the Nauvoo area in the spring of 1845, Bennett lectured at the Botanico-Medical College in Ohio. He had published extensively on the healthful qualities of the tomato in 1837–1838. See Andrew F. Smith, *The Saintly Scoundrel: The Life and Times of Dr. John Cook Bennett* (Urbana and Chicago: University of Illinois Press, 1997), 144.

28. Historian Andrew Smith listed five reasons why the two men struck up such a close friendship. Bennett, a former preacher, knew the Bible very well and was an excellent public speaker. Smith, always fascinated with military issues, took great interest in Bennett's control of the distribution of arms and equipment around the state—an opportunity that might be useful in the future. Bennett's arrival in Nauvoo just before Joseph Sr. died weakened the prophet's sensibilities, making him more susceptible to Bennett's machinations. In the late summer of 1840, with most of the Council of Twelve on missions, there was a leadership vacuum in Nauvoo. Bennett offered counsel on difficult matters, normally provided by others close to the prophet. Finally, Bennett persuaded Smith of his loyalty to the movement, and in the months that followed, proved his friendship as complete and unconditional. For excellent biographical coverage of Bennett's life see Andrew Smith's *The Saintly Scoundrel*. For the explanation of Bennett's relationship with the prophet, mentioned above, see 56–58.

pulled her son Joseph's tooth with a "turn key," causing profuse bleeding, which prompted Emma to question Bennett's medical credentials and personal motives. After that difficult encounter, Emma, a woman of uncommon knowledge of medicinal healing methods, refused Bennett's prescribed treatments. When Bennett arrived in Nauvoo, he stayed with the Smith family for thirty-nine weeks. But after the tooth-pulling incident, Bennett decided to move to other living quarters in Nauvoo and away from Emma's watchful gaze. From then on, Bennett's visits were occasional and usually at mealtime.[29]

Just a month after Bennett arrived in Nauvoo, a church conference asked Smith, Bennett, and Robert B. Thompson, Smith's personal secretary, to "draft a bill for the incorporation of the town of Nauvoo, and other purposes." The same conference legislation designated Bennett to push the incorporation measure through the state legislature.[30] The language of the proposed charter emerged from discussions between Smith and Bennett.[31] After the conference, Bennett headed for Springfield with the recommended language for a city charter that included provisions from other Illinois cities of similar size.[32]

Bennett used his considerable power of persuasion to lobby both Democratic and Whig lawmakers to support the charter language. This was an election year and Nauvoo's dramatic population growth had caught the eye of both parties. Certainly Bennett reminded the politicians of this

29. Newell and Avery, *Mormon Enigma*, 91–92.
30. *History of the RLDS Church*, 2: 467; *DHC*, 4: 205.
31. There is a long-standing debate as to who should get the credit for the language that gave such all-encompassing freedoms to the Nauvoo community. Smith claimed credit; however, his inexperience calls into question its authenticity. Bennett also laid claim to the success but could not have left for Springfield without the prophet's blessings. Thus, both should share in the success of the liberal charter.
32. Actually there were only five other cities in Illinois with populations comparable to Nauvoo even at this early date: Chicago received its charter declaring it a city in March 1837. Alton, a few miles upriver from St. Louis, Missouri, was Chicago's closest rival in size in 1840. Alton residents received city status with their charter in July 1837. Galena achieved city status and their charter in 1839, followed by Springfield, the state capital, in 1840. Quincy, the largest Illinois community on the Mississippi River, reached city status a few months after Springfield. An informative analysis of the charters of the six Illinois cities can be found in James L. Kimball Jr., "The Nauvoo Charter: A Reinterpretation," in Launius and Hallwas, *Kingdom on the Mississippi Revisited*, 30–47.

fact. Neither party wanted to be seen as opposing such a potentially large voting bloc. When it came time to consider the charter legislation, floor leaders quickly pushed the bill to a vote, and it passed with little change.[33]

To gain passage, Bennett had skillfully garnered support from politicians normally opposed to such initiatives. For example, the Democratic secretary of state, Stephen A. Douglas, who generally opposed such incorporations, assisted the bill through the process. But at least one Whig politician—the state representative from Springfield—had plenty of reason to oppose incorporation as well. During the 1840 presidential election, which had occurred just weeks earlier, church leaders counseled members to vote in favor of Whig nominee and eventual winner William Henry Harrison.[34] Fearing their political control as too obvious, church leaders encouraged the membership to strike the Whig candidate at the end of the list of presidential electors, and instead vote for the Democratic elector, James Ralston.[35] This would give the appearance that the Mormons were not catering to any political party. The eliminated Whig elector was a little-known member of the Illinois House of Representatives named Abraham Lincoln. In this 1840 presidential election it was clear that the Mormons were more anti-Van Buren (D, New York) than they were pro-Harrison (W, Ohio).[36] Still, Representative Lincoln voted in favor of the Nauvoo charter and even congratulated Bennett on his successful lobbying effort.[37] As will be seen, Bennett's promise of political payback would bode ill in the Mormons' future.

---

33. The legislative process may be followed in Flanders, *Nauvoo*, 9.
34. Historian Andrew Smith speculates that Whigs were favored over Democrats due to the difficult treatment the Democrats, especially sitting president Martin Van Buren, gave the Mormons during the Missouri crisis. See Andrew Smith, *The Saintly Scoundrel*, 58.
35. An inspection of the actual ballots found that approximately two hundred votes had Lincoln's name scratched out and replaced with James Ralston's name. See Flanders, *Nauvoo*, 223.
36. This is the conclusion of Robert Flanders in *Nauvoo*, 223.
37. Andrew Smith, *The Saintly Scoundrel*, 58–61.

Nauvoo City Charter: The Mormon "Magna Charta"

The Nauvoo city charter was the single most important political document of the late Restoration Era. From its provisions, Joseph Smith Jr. gained almost every protection he needed to build his city successfully. In their "Proclamation to the Saints Scattered Abroad," published in the *Times and Seasons*, the First Presidency appropriately identified the newly acquired city charter as the church's "magna charta."[38] The charter's long list of enabling provisions shaped the Nauvoo community from 1841 through 1844. Since this document was so pivotal to future events in western Illinois, three specific aspects merit close inspection: the city government; a systematized framework for community education that included the University of the City of Nauvoo, the Nauvoo Seminary, and the common schools; and the Nauvoo Legion.

The Nauvoo City Government. The city charter provided for a strong city council with the ability to appoint and remove officials at their pleasure. Initially, the council included four aldermen and nine councilors, plus the mayor. As a council, these men could pass any ordinance not "repugnant" to either the United States or Illinois constitutions. Although this provision seemed all-empowering, any overextension of this authority would rescind the entire charter, along with all its provisions and powers.

The city judicial system resided in a municipal court. As in similar city charters in Illinois, the mayor presided over the court as its chief justice, and the four aldermen served as associate justices. The governor of the state commissioned the justices, and the mayor held "exclusive jurisdiction of all cases arising under the ordinances of the corporation." Any citizen could appeal any individual decision made by the mayor or aldermen to the municipal court; however, since these officers sat together as that court, their collective wisdom could supersede their individual decisions. Appeals from the municipal court could be sent to the Hancock County circuit court, provided that the originating municipal trial included a jury of twelve peers.

---

38. "Proclamation to the Saints Scattered Abroad," *Times and Seasons* 2, no. 1 (15 January 1841): 274. At this time the First Presidency included Joseph Smith Jr., Sidney Rigdon, and Hyrum Smith. This proclamation can also be found in *History of the RLDS Church*, 2: 501–505; *DHC*, 4: 267–73.

Perhaps the most important provision of the municipal courts was the authorization to issue writs of *habeas corpus* in all cases arising from city ordinances. A writ of *habeas corpus* is an order to have a prisoner brought before a judge at a specific time and place as a legal protection to determine if a detainee has been afforded due process. Such protective authorization was not uncommon for a mayor in Illinois communities. These early years of the new American nation were highlighted by legal experimentation as just one of many efforts to build the fledgling democracy. As overly broad as these judicial powers appear today, they seemed reasonable to Illinoisans when compared with those of other municipalities of that era. Through this power, church leaders could use city court authority to find relief from the harassing arrest warrants from other legal jurisdictions, thus ending the plethora of vexatious lawsuits so prevalent in past years.[39]

In Nauvoo, the enormous authority invested in the office of the mayor created a nearly unparalleled opportunity for a legal union between church and state. The prophet would not miss this chance to move the community in exactly that direction. In an age of Jeffersonian democracy, such a move would threaten nonbelievers across the region. The first step in this direction was the election of John Cook Bennett as Nauvoo's first mayor in early 1841.[40]

THE UNIVERSITY OF THE CITY OF NAUVOO, THE COMMON SCHOOLS, AND THE NAUVOO SEMINARY. A second key provision of the Nauvoo City Charter included the creation of a comprehensive community educational system that included a city university. Rather than

---

39. The power of issuing writs of *habeas corpus* in the Nauvoo charter followed the Alton, Illinois, precedent established just a year earlier on 1 June 1839. This power had the effect of the municipal court superseding the county court. Prior to the influx of Mormons settling in Nauvoo, Alton, another Mississippi river town, was the next largest municipality to rival Chicago in size. See Kimball, "The Nauvoo Charter," 40–43. For a specific definition, see http:www.u-s-history.com/pages/h1451.html#H. Historian James Kimball accurately identified the early nineteenth century as a "testing ground" to determine the proper relationships between judicial bodies at every level in American government. See his "The Nauvoo Charter," 42–43.

40. In his inaugural address, Bennett publicly announced his five priorities in his mayoral agenda: to prohibit all bars, tippling houses, and dram shops; to create a University of the City of Nauvoo; to organize the Nauvoo Legion; to construct a wing dam on the Mississippi River; and to drain the lowlands along the Mississippi. See "Inaugural Address," *Times and Seasons* 2, no. 8 (15 February 1841): 317–18.

being unique to Nauvoo, the inclusion of a university reflected what historian Don Harrison Doyle described as a "booster ethos" among western communities to attract migrants to settle within their boundaries. In the earliest days of the American republic, the framers of the Constitution set aside Section 16 of every federal township to be dedicated by state and territorial legislatures "for the use of schools." In 1848, the next generation of national leaders added a second square mile, Section 36, for the same purpose. All saw education as a key to national prosperity. Establishing a city university, just one of many important attractions to lure westering peoples, was a necessity in the "open race" that drove the development of the nation's interior.[41]

Three imposing problems confronted the successful development of the Nauvoo city university: providing adequate institutional monies for buildings; recruiting qualified faculty; and keeping tuition affordable to attract a student body. Because most frontier towns could not meet those challenges, as historical geographer Donald W. Meinig observed, the West was soon littered with "ghost colleges."[42] In developing his University of the City of Nauvoo, Joseph Smith attempted to succeed where so many other communities had failed.

Among the Mormons, the need for higher education was quite evident. In addition to his mayoral responsibilities, John C. Bennett accepted the position of university chancellor. On 3 February 1841, in his mayoral inaugural address, Bennett criticized prevailing education methods when

---

41. Don Harrison Doyle, *The Social Order of a Frontier Community, 1825–70* (Urbana: University of Illinois Press, 1978), 63. See Doyle's fourth chapter for a fuller explanation of the "booster ethos." The evolution of Jacksonville, Illinois, located approximately seventy-five miles southeast of Nauvoo, demonstrates how educational institutions contemporary to the founding of the University of the City of Nauvoo were so important to attracting settlers. The success or failure of such institutions could determine the community's fate. Citizens of Jacksonville lost out to Springfield in the competition to receive the new state capital from its earlier location in Vandalia. So Jacksonville community leaders refocused their efforts in developing other public institutions including Illinois College, established just ten years before the Saints arrived at Commerce. Along with an asylum for the insane, promoted personally by Dorothea Dix, and an institution for the deaf and mute, Illinois College sustained Jacksonville's future as Illinois's "city of institutions" (79).

42. Meinig, *The Shaping of America*, 2: 252–53.

he identified a gap between what was learned and what was really understood. He lamented to his audience:

> Every boarding school Miss is a Plato in petticoats, without an ounce of that genuine knowledge…to escape perils with which she must necessarily be encompassed. young people are taught to use a variety of hard terms, which they understand but imperfectly;—to repeat lessons which they are unable to apply;—to astonish their grand-mothers with a display of their parrot-like acquisitions;—but their mental energies are clogged and torpified with a variety of learned lumber, most of which is discarded from the brain long before its possessor knows how to use it. This is the quackery of education.[43]

Having a high-quality faculty would prevent such "perils." Eleven months later, in a *Times and Seasons* article, Chancellor Bennett announced his faculty. Teaching mathematics and English literature was Orson Pratt, whose command of knowledge in these subjects, as described by the editor, was "equaled by few, and surpassed by none this side of the great waters." Orson Spencer was to teach languages. Spencer, a college graduate, was rather unique among his contemporary Mormons. He had graduated from Union College in New York, received seminary training in divinity, and was considered "a ripe scholar, and well fitted for the department to which he has been elected by the Regents." Finally, Sidney Rigdon accepted the appointment to instruct in rhetoric and *belles lettres*, subjects in which he was "deeply learned."[44] Other proposed classes included arithmetic; algebra; geometry; conic sections; plane trigonometry; mensuration; surveying; navigation; analytical, plane, and spherical trigonometry; differential and integral calculus; philosophy; and chemistry.[45] Students were expected to pay a five-dollar tuition fee per quarter, payable semi-quarterly and in advance.[46]

---

43. John C. Bennett, "Inaugural Address," *Times and Seasons* 2, no. 8 (15 February 1841): 317.

44. "University of the City of Nauvoo," *Times and Seasons* 3, no. 4 (15 December 1841): 630–31.

45. *Belles lettres* is an artistic style of writing known for its beauty and poetic tone rather than for didactic or informational content. Mensuration is a branch of applied geometry that involves finding the measurement of lines, surfaces of solids, and angles.

46. *Times and Seasons* 2, no. 20 (10 August 1841): 517.

In a "Proclamation to the Saints Scattered Abroad," in the 15 January 1841 issue of *Times and Seasons*, the First Presidency of Joseph Smith, Sidney Rigdon, and Hyrum Smith addressed the importance of, and purpose for, the University of the City of Nauvoo:

> The "University of the City of Nauvoo," will enable us to teach our children wisdom—to instruct them in all knowledge, and learning, in the Arts, Sciences and Learned Professions. We hope to make this institution one of the great lights of the world, and by and through it, to diffuse that kind of knowledge which will be of practical utility, and for the public good, and also for private and individual happiness. The Regents of the University will take the general supervision of all matters appertaining to education from common schools up to the highest branches of the most liberal collegiate course. They will establish a regular system of education, and hand over the pupil from teacher to professor, until the regular gradation is consummated, and the education finished.[47]

The university board of regents interlocked with the city council and placed tight control over the curriculum and put instruction into the hands of a few powerful men.

There is no evidence that the University of the City of Nauvoo program moved significantly beyond its planning into anything other than conferring a few ceremonial degrees. In the competition for the time and resources of Nauvoo citizens, the university fared poorly. Far more successful were the "common schools" that developed in the community. The structure of the common school system in Nauvoo followed the four political divisions of the city, called wards. Three school wardens supervised the educational program in their ward. Teachers in each ward had to procure a certificate of competency from the University of the City of Nauvoo chancellor and registrar.[48] Textbook adoption also required recommendation from the chancellor and regents. Careful examination of curriculum offerings and textbook selections reveals that common-school subject matter and instruction differed little from that of secular communities.

---

47. "Proclamation to the Saints Scattered Abroad," 274–75.
48. "Common Schools," *Times and Seasons* 3, no. 4 (15 December 1841): 632.

The Nauvoo Seminary was an educational institution similar to today's high school and provided a connection between the elementary-oriented common school system and the city university. The historical name is somewhat misleading in modern-day language. No religious course instruction occurred at the seminary; rather, the curriculum was based on that found in New England high schools. Primary course work focused on practical studies of English grammar, writing, geography, arithmetic, algebra, bookkeeping, and history. Most seminary classes convened in a building one block northeast of the temple, while others met in the homes of instructors.[49]

From the church's earliest days, the leadership realized the value of an educated membership that could grasp innovative doctrinal concepts and religious practices. Wherever the church journeyed, they established schools, and the community in western Illinois was no exception. Yet the primary purpose of education was preparation for responsible membership in the church. This demonstrated an awareness that publicly supported education was a factor in the community's success and contributed significantly to Nauvoo becoming the second largest city in Illinois by 1844.

THE NAUVOO LEGION. When Illinois achieved statehood in December 1818, Article 5 of its new constitution provided for the organization of a state militia. This was not an unusual provision for American citizens residing on the western frontier. All free able-bodied males, with "negroes, mulattoes and Indians excepted," between ages eighteen and forty-five years of age, were to be "armed, equipped, and trained as the General Assembly may provide by law."[50] Many Illinois communities formed their own militia units in conjunction with this statute. Although commissioned by the state government "to provide for the common defense" of its citizens in times of conflict, during times of peace the militias were mere

---

49. See the seventh chapter titled, "Common Schools," in Calvin V. French, "Organization and Administration of the Latter Day Saint School System of Free Education, Common School through University at Nauvoo, Illinois, 1840–1845" (master's thesis, Temple University, 1965), 53–63, in Community of Christ Library-Archives.

50. This language taken from the Illinois Revised Statutes, 1845, was based on an earlier Illinois Militia Code of 1833. An excellent article on the Nauvoo Legion, and one primary source for this explanation, is Hamilton Gardner, "The Nauvoo Legion, 1840–1845: A Unique Military Organization," in Launius and Hallwas, *Kingdom on the Mississippi Revisited*, 48–61.

COMMUNITY OF CHRIST LIBRARY-ARCHIVES

Lieutenant General Joseph Smith Jr. reviewing Nauvoo Legion troops, 1844

tools to instill patriotism. With the usual pomp and circumstance, the local militia paraded on national holidays and appeared at official community functions.

The Illinois Constitution set guidelines on militia organization but empowered city charters to provide specifics based on community resources and frontier defense needs. For Nauvoo, the Twelfth Illinois General Assembly authorized the formation with various requirements on such matters as court martial proceedings, how the legion might be used, and who might call the troops to arms (both mayor and the governor).[51] The Nauvoo Legion was born of Nauvoo City Council legislation passed on 8 February 1841. Section 4 of the enabling ordinance designated the ranks of

---

51. In a very technical sense the Nauvoo Legion was not a regular unit of the Illinois state militia, but Section 25 of the city charter required the performance of the same duties. The fine distinction is explained in Gardner's article, "The Nauvoo Legion," 51–54.

its general officers. The chief commanding officer was accorded the rank of lieutenant general. Only one other military general in American history up to that time had achieved such a high rank—George Washington.[52] The Illinois constitution reserved the lesser major general rank to command local and state militias, but with Joseph Smith Jr. an exception was made.[53]

Smith was not without experience in training and commanding troops in the field. The Zion's Camp march in 1834, and his troop incursions at Far West before his arrest in 1838, groomed the prophet in military leadership and decision making. However, these earlier opportunities were far different from commanding the Nauvoo Legion, since the prophet's authority was state sponsored and not personally assumed.

The Nauvoo Legion was more than simply social and ceremonial, like most of the other militia units, and Smith turned it into his own private army. He confirmed his intentions on 8 January 1841 by stating: "The Nauvoo Legion…will enable us to perform our military duty by ourselves, and thus afford us the power and privilege of avoiding one of the most fruitful sources of strife, oppression, and collision with the world." He tempered his personal use of his army by promising "to show our attachment to the state and nation, as a people, whenever the public service requires our aid, thus proving ourselves obedient to the paramount laws of the land."[54] This was a notable change of attitude when compared with his frustration with the law during the Far West persecution crisis in October 1838, when he

---

52. Gardner's research identified two other lieutenant generals before the end of the Civil War. Winfield Scott received the rank of brevet lieutenant general for his meritorious service in the Mexican-American War, although certain limitations were placed on his actual functions. On 28 February 1864, in a special act of Congress, Ulysses S. Grant received the rank of lieutenant general. See "The Nauvoo Legion," 53.

53. Gardner suggests that the rationale for this exception remains unexplained. However, it is possible that since local militias were mostly ceremonial and any abuse of commanding officers would render their official positions null and void, the appointment was allowed. Also, Bennett's lobbying persuasions based on Mormon voting power could still be felt in Springfield. Allowing a lieutenant general in Nauvoo could curry favor with the Mormon vote. Some lawmakers may have anticipated that Bennett himself might have commanded the militia. With his considerable experience, and already earning high rank within the state militia, having a lieutenant general in Nauvoo could be allowed.

54. "Proclamation to the Saints Scattered Abroad," also found in *History of the RLDS Church*, 2: 503; *DHC*, 4: 269.

complained to an audience: "Who is so big a fool as to cry the law! the law! when it is always administered against us and never in our favor. I do not intend to regard the law hereafter as we are made a set of outlaws by having no protection from it. We will take our affairs into our own hands and manage for ourselves."[55] Times and circumstances definitely were changed, demonstrating Joseph's flexibility to now work within the law rather than attempt to circumvent it.

Recruitment of troops into the legion produced sizable numbers in a relatively short time. In September 1841, nearly fifteen hundred men joined the ranks, and by May of the following year, the numbers reached two thousand. By 1844, under Smith's leadership, the legion numbers swelled to nearly five thousand, making it the largest armed force in Illinois and the single largest local militia in the United States.[56] At this time in American history, only 8,500 soldiers served in the entire United States Army.[57] Such military power appealed greatly to Smith, as evidenced in the flamboyant uniforms he wore. Festooned in a lieutenant general's collar bars, golden epaulettes, belt buckle, and vest buttons, a high-collared shirt, a finely decorated sword with a scrimshaw handle and brass scabbard on his hip, a gold braided cummerbund, in shiny black knee-high boots, and a medallioned, ostrich-plumed hat, Smith delighted in his role as commanding officer.[58]

Commanders of local militias extended to their peers from surrounding communities their compliments and the courtesy of reviewing each other's troops. This provided ample opportunity to showcase each other's training and accomplishments. These were mostly ceremonial affairs that included parades and picnic-basket meals. But when Smith mustered his legion for review, it is possible to imagine training exercises where

55. Peck, *Manuscript*, 18–19.
56. Robert V. Remini, *Joseph Smith* (New York: Penguin Putnam, Inc., 2002), 149; Quinn, *Origins of Power*, 632–33. Historians disagree on the actual numbers of the Nauvoo Legion but concur on the identification of Smith's legion as the largest state-sanctioned militia force in America.
57. See Quinn's observation on this statistic in his *Origins of Power*, 106. To retrieve the total size of the United States Army during the Nauvoo period, Quinn referred to Thomas H. S. Hamersly, *Regular Army Register of the United States, 1779–1879* (Washington: By the author, 1880), 212–13.
58. Portraitist Sutcliffe Maudsley captured this in 1842 in the only painting of Smith while he was alive. An image of Joseph Smith in uniform appears on page 442.

his troops used live ammunition. With deafening cannon volleys, coordinated musket fire, and roaring charges across open fields, Smith's purpose seemed to be to intimidate observers and raise suspicions about how the prophet would utilize his troops. Historian Robert B. Flanders observed that Smith's Nauvoo Legion was his "symbol of quasi-sovereignty."[59]

Beyond the theological focus of Nauvoo, the three secular components—the city charter with its *habeas corpus* provision, the University of the City of Nauvoo, and the Nauvoo Legion—ornamented community life in Nauvoo. The constant influx of immigrants seeking a new life, and assurances of an afterlife, guaranteed the vitality and longevity of the city while led by the prophet. Being situated on the great river also guaranteed the inherent problems of crime, but a city police force, constable, legion, justice of the peace, and even an informal Danite presence, served well to maintain law and order.

Seeking Redress in the Nation's Capital: The Evolution of Mormon Political Involvement

DURING HIS INCARCERATION in Missouri and eventual escape in the spring of 1839, Joseph Smith Jr. had ample opportunity to ponder the tragic events of northern Missouri and to consider how to redress the losses wreaked upon his followers and himself personally. Typically, Mormon petitions to local and state government officials had fallen on deaf ears. Except for those few apostates who had left the church, cohesion among the general membership remained essentially firm. Ironically, the reversals in Missouri and Kirtland engendered a feeling of oneness and a sense of identity.[60]

Still, the prophet hoped to hold accountable the individuals who had sponsored the events that drove the Saints out of their Zion. He believed that satisfaction could only be achieved in Washington, D.C. Between April and October 1839, the Saints put their grievances and property loss damages in writing. A high council meeting decision in Nauvoo in late

---

59. Flanders, *Nauvoo*, 109.

60. Today, that same sense of persecution pervades many of the Restoration churches and provides the same sense of cohesion felt during this historic period of the church story.

October 1839 empowered Joseph to go to the nation's capital to achieve redress.[61] On 29 October, Joseph, Sidney Rigdon, Elias Higbee, and Orrin Porter Rockwell loaded their necessary provisions in the back of a two-horse carriage and trundled off, with their hopes that the rightness of their grievances would sway the president of the United States and Congress to impeach the Missouri government for neglecting their obligation to guarantee American citizens their First Amendment rights.[62]

During their journey to the East, Sidney's delicate health became a problem. Stopping at Springfield, Illinois, the team picked up physician Robert D. Foster, whose task was to administer to Rigdon during the difficult journey. Eventually Rigdon's condition worsened and the articulate church spokesman had to be left behind along with his physician and Orrin Porter Rockwell. This allowed Smith and Higbee to travel more quickly to the nation's capital, anticipating the others would arrive later. Unfortunately, all letters of recommendation were written specifically for Rigdon. To remedy this problem, Rigdon wrote a letter recommending Smith and Higbee, who now were to complete Rigdon's mission to lay before national politicians the Mormon petition for redress.

Arriving in Washington on Thursday 28 November, Smith and Higbee found a room at the Gadsby Hotel, ironically located on the corner of Missouri and Third Streets. The next day, the men went to the White House and knocked on the front door. When it was opened, they introduced themselves and asked to see President Martin Van Buren. Immediately they were ushered to the living quarters on an upper floor, where they presented their letters of introduction to Van Buren.[63]

President Van Buren read one of the many letters Smith gave him, then looked up with a half-frown and said, "What can I do? I can do nothing for you! If I do anything, I shall come into contact with the whole state of Missouri." This did not end the conversation, however. Smith and

---

61. *History of the RLDS Church*, 2: 376ff; *DHC*, 4: 16.
62. Church leaders placed blame primarily on Missouri governor Lilburn Boggs and his extermination order. Because Illinois residents at Quincy favorably received the Saints, they were exonerated from any grievances. In fact, a prominent group of Illinois-based politicians wrote letters of introduction including Illinois U.S. senator Richard M. Young and Governor Thomas Carlin. See Van Wagoner, *Sidney Rigdon*, 265–66.
63. *History of the RLDS Church*, 2: 402–403; *DHC*, 4: 24.

Higbee pressed their arguments to persuade Van Buren to reconsider the sufferings of the Saints. Van Buren inquired about the Saints' religious beliefs and heard the two church leaders' testimonies.[64] The two men left their meeting unimpressed with the president's lack of response.

From the White House, Smith and Higbee rode up Pennsylvania Avenue to the halls of Congress. They consulted first with the Illinois delegation in the House of Representatives on how best to push through their redress legislation. But during his visit, Joseph viewed with skepticism the ability and character of the nation's representatives. After several days of lobbying on behalf of the Saints, Smith left Higbee in Washington while he headed for Philadelphia to meet with church members there. He gave numerous sermons and lifted spirits.

Meanwhile, Higbee gave a ninety-minute speech before a joint committee of senators and representatives in a Senate committee room. He rehearsed the plight of the Saints and their expulsion from Missouri. Missouri senator Lewis Linn (1795–1843) and Missouri representative John Jameson (1802–1857) listened as Higbee laid out his argument calling for redress.[65] In another hearing the following day, Linn and Jameson engaged Higbee on the particulars of his story, especially on who was responsible for the abuses. After several more days of hearings, the chairman, New Jersey senator Garret Dorset Wall (1783–1850), reported the committee decision against the Saints. Wall stated that they could find redress only in the courts and legislature of Missouri. In Higbee's final letter to Smith he expressed his frustration: "I feel now that we have made our last appeal to all earthly tribunals; that we should now put our whole trust in the God of Abraham, Isaac, and Jacob. We have a right now which we could heretofore so fully claim—that is, of asking God for redress and redemption, as they have been refused us by man."[66]

---

64. "The Prophet's Letter to Hyrum Smith—Reporting State of Affairs at Washington," 5 December 1839, *DHC*, 4: 39–42.

65. While Smith traveled through the eastern states, Higbee sent him a letter that provided an update on his progress in seeking redress. Dated 20 February 1840, Higbee felt somewhat intimidated at first to indict Missourians with these two men sitting on the committee. But Higbee launched into his plea undaunted.

66. Elias Higbee to Joseph Smith Jr., 26 February 1840, from Washington [D.C.], *History of the RLDS Church*, 2: 403–4; *DHC*, 4: 88.

In a last-ditch effort, Joseph Smith also took his case to South Carolina senator John C. Calhoun but received no support. Smith described his interview with the influential Southern politician "whose conduct towards me very ill became his station."[67] Shortly thereafter, Smith and Higbee took the long journey home to Nauvoo, arriving safely on Wednesday 4 March 1840. They could only report that "popular clamor and personal aggrandizement were ruling principles of those in authority." Smith cursed the political career of Martin Van Buren, stating, "May he never be elected again to any office of trust or power, by which he may abuse the innocent and let the guilty go free."[68]

Mormon Political Influence in Western Illinois

WITH THE FRUSTRATION of his Washington trip fresh on his mind, Smith officially charted an initial course of political impartiality in state politics. He had seen enough of posturing and disingenuousness from the nation's leaders, so he declared his neutrality and told his followers to vote as they wished on the issues of the day. But his nonalignment was short-lived when it dawned on him that, with the ever-increasing number of Mormons in Hancock County, he could strongly influence, if not control outright, the results of elections and referenda in western Illinois.

Political influence in Hancock County emanated from Smith's control of the municipal-government political machinery in Nauvoo. Here again was the value of the city charter, which vested strong power in the mayor, aldermen, and the nine councilors.[69] Although this authority was municipally oriented, its influence extended throughout western Illinois.

The all-important *habeas corpus* clause saved Joseph Smith from extradition to Missouri in June 1843 on a four-year-old arrest warrant for treason against the state. Missouri governor Thomas Reynolds (1796–1844)

67. *History of the RLDS Church*, 2: 402; *DHC*, 4: 80.

68. *DHC*, 4: 89. Van Buren ran for reelection in 1840 but lost to the Whig candidate, William Henry Harrison of Indiana. Always engaged in the American political scene after his presidency, Van Buren accepted the nomination for the presidency from the Free Soil Party in 1848, but lost to another Whig candidate, Zachary Taylor.

69. Robert S. Wicks and Fred R. Foister, *Junius and Joseph: Presidential Politics and the Assassination of the First Mormon Prophet* (Logan: Utah State University, 2005), 22.

sent his warrant to Springfield, Illinois, to the attention of Illinois governor Thomas Ford. Fulfilling his legal obligation, Ford issued the warrant for Smith's arrest but alerted Springfield judge James Adams, a personal friend and newly converted Mormon. Adams sent an express rider to Nauvoo to signal the alarm, only to discover that Joseph had taken his family to visit Emma's sister near Dixon, Illinois, some two hundred miles northeast. The arresting officers, Hancock County constable Harmon T. Wilson and Jackson County, Missouri, sheriff Joseph Reynolds, arrested Smith on 22 June and escorted him, under heavy guard, to a tavern near Dixon's Ferry on the Rock River.

When word spread of Joseph's arrest, partisan lawyers flocked to Smith's defense to curry Mormon support at the polls in the coming August election. Campaigning for the Sixth Congressional District seat in the United States House of Representatives, and quite conveniently just six miles away at the time of the arrest, was Whig lawyer Cyrus Walker, who gained access to the prisoner and swapped Mormon support for his legal assistance.[70] The arresting officers accepted the writ of *habeas corpus*, allowing the warrant to be legally reviewed by a justice of the peace. Of course, Smith chose the municipal justice in Nauvoo for his review. Together, Wilson, Reynolds, Walker, and the Smith family traveled to Joseph's city.

At the outskirts, the entourage met a column of forty riders from Nauvoo, who escorted them parade-like into town. That afternoon the prophet addressed a huge crowd and explained his ordeal. Presumably his *habeas corpus* strategy had worked. Then he introduced Cyrus Walker to the Saints and openly called for their support of his candidacy, as promised.[71] With the huge Mormon voting bloc seemingly in hand, Walker left Nauvoo confident of his electoral victory. With the passing of time, however, that support eroded.

70. Historians Wicks and Foister, in *Junius and Joseph*, suggested that Smith's arrest was a conspiracy and that Walker's campaign took him to the Dixon, Illinois, area was no coincidence. The authors assessed the charge of conspiracy, promoted by Walker's Democratic Party opposition, as "convincing even if chiefly circumstantial" (41–42).

71. Before turning the crowd over to Walker, Smith turned to him and, in an ironic twist, whispered in a voice loud enough for people to hear, "These are the greatest dupes, as a body of people, that ever lived, or else I am not so big a rogue as I am reported to be." See Wicks and Foister, *Junius and Joseph*, 40.

As the late summer election approached, rumors spread through western Illinois that the prophet's older brother, Hyrum, had an interest in running for the national Congress as a Democratic candidate. Supposedly, Hyrum offered the Mormon vote to Walker's opponent, Democrat Joseph P. Hoge, in a *quid pro quo* for support in his own election in 1843. But this had the potential to split the Mormon vote and weaken their political influence. A local newspaper edited by Mormon leader John Taylor, the *Nauvoo Neighbor*, offered letters addressing both candidates but supported Hoge rather than the prophet's recommended candidate, Cyrus Walker. The *Neighbor* also announced that Hyrum Smith would speak on the election on the coming Saturday.[72]

Before a very large crowd gathered on 7 August, just two days before the election, Hyrum gave a stump speech, admonishing the Saints on "how to vote, and whom to support if they considered their own interest and good of the place." Hyrum called for a vote for Hoge. In the audience, William Law, second counselor in the First Presidency, sensed the mood of the crowd swaying against the advice of the prophet, so he took the stand and reminded listeners that Hyrum's advice was not based on revelation. Thus, the word of the prophet should prevail—vote for Walker.

Law felt good as he stepped down but then saw Hyrum return to the stand. This time Hyrum told the audience that he knew for certain how the Saints were to vote for "he had sought to know, and knew from knowledge that would not be doubted, from evidences that never fail, that Mr. Hoge was the man, and it was for the interest of this place and people to support him." Hyrum then held up a makeshift placard with writing that prophesied, "Thus saith the Lord, those that vote [for Hoge] shall be blessed; those who do not shall be accursed." Much to William Law's dismay, the church patriarch claimed divine light to support the Democrat, and the audience cheered.[73]

William Law had done all he could to support Joseph Smith's earlier statements. Now only the prophet could clarify the proper course of action.

72. *Nauvoo Neighbor* 1, no. 14 (2 August 1843): 2. Microfilm Collection, Community of Christ Library-Archives.

73. This account is ably presented in Wicks and Foister, *Junius and Joseph*, 45–46. They cited the *Macomb (Illinois) Weekly Journal*, 22 January 1877, and the *New York Weekly Tribune*, 26 August 1843, as their sources of information.

The next day, Joseph took the stand to resolve the issue. He complimented Cyrus Walker as "a high-minded man," and acknowledged the Whig candidate as the person to get his vote. But then he told the audience that Walker "withdrew all claim to your vote and influence if it will be detrimental to your interest as a people."

The prophet's statement released the Saints to throw their support for Hoge, especially when he informed them of a conversation he had had with Hyrum earlier in the day: "Brother Hyrum tells me this morning that he has had a testimony to the effect that it would be better for the people to vote for Hoge; and I never knew Hyrum to say he ever had a revelation and it failed." Then, still standing in front of the crowd, Joseph chastised his second counselor, stating, "I never authorized Brother Law to tell my private feelings, and I utterly forbid these political demagogues from using my name henceforth and for ever."[74] William Law, innocent in his attempt to support the prophet, felt publicly humiliated.

When the vote returns came in, Hoge won handily by prevailing especially in Nauvoo, Hancock County, Illinois. Two observations are important from this August 1843 election. First, it demonstrated the enormous power of the Mormon voting bloc and their potential role in determining future elections in Illinois. Second, the Saints proved their unreliability by tossing their support back and forth at the mere whim of church leaders. In the world of nineteenth-century frontier American politics, dependability was crucial to achieving political "return favors." That the Saints would switch so readily generated considerable suspicion from both the Democrats and the Whigs, thus negating much of the Mormon political advantage.

For Joseph Smith Jr., his late 1839 trip to Washington and the congressional election of 1843 taught difficult lessons about engaging in politics. That fall, he made one last attempt to find support in the nation's capital. Knowing that 1844 was a presidential election year, Smith sent a letter to those politicians he anticipated would seek the nation's highest office—Democrats John C. Calhoun of South Carolina, Lewis Cass of Michigan, Richard M. Johnson of Kentucky, and Martin Van Buren of

---

74. *DHC*, 5: 526. This embarrassment signaled an emerging rift between Smith and Law that would culminate with the second counselor leaving the church within a year to launch his own church and to publish his own newspaper, the *Nauvoo Expositor*.

New York, and Whig Henry Clay of Kentucky. In his letter, Smith once again outlined Mormon suffering and requested to know their response to his claims should they win the presidency. Only Calhoun and Clay responded.[75] Both used vague language, arguing the limited powers of the federal government to preempt the decisions made at the state level. In fairness to the politicians, the proper relationship between the states and the federal government loomed over most issues they confronted during their tenure in office. Only with a civil war would the issue be resolved.

Prestigious Visitors from the East

BEFORE ILLINOIS'S POLITICAL conventions, the Smiths received two important visitors from Massachusetts—Charles Francis Adams (1807–1886), son of former United States president John Quincy Adams, and Josiah P. Quincy Jr. (1802–1882), the former president's nephew. The men arrived at the dock in Nauvoo because they had heard about the Mormon prophet and wanted to meet him. Josiah Quincy, son of a Harvard president and soon to be elected mayor of Boston, kept close watch on the American scene for influential people. For sixty-four years, his extensive journaling focused on such notable figures as John Adams, the Marquis de Lafayette, Daniel Webster, John Randolph, and Andrew Jackson. Forty years later, Quincy's journaling appeared in book format in his *Figures of the Past: From the Leaves of Old Journals*, published in Boston in 1884. The last chapter of Quincy's book is a detailed account of his 15 May 1844 visit with Adams to the Nauvoo Mansion House and a day-long conversation with Prophet Joseph Smith Jr.[76]

This amazing interview revealed much about the prophet's theological and political viewpoints. At times in his recollection, Quincy was skeptical of Smith's claims, using such descriptors as "wild talk," "fanatic, impostor, and charlatan," and "blasphemous," but also Quincy used complimentary language such as "a fine-looking man," "self-reliant," and stated that the prophet spoke "with a quiet superiority that was

---

75. *History of the RLDS Church*, 2: 708–713.
76. Quincy's account is titled "Joseph Smith at Nauvoo." See Josiah Quincy, *Figures of the Past: From the Leaves of Old Journals*, 6th ed. (Boston: Roberts Brothers, 1884), 376–400, Vault Collection, Community of Christ Library-Archives.

Mansion House in Nauvoo with the hotel wing attached at right

overwhelming."[77] The author even compared Smith's demeanor to Andrew Jackson's, observing that "the prophet's hold upon you seemed to come from the balance and harmony of temperament which reposes upon a large physical basis."[78]

Quincy's description of Joseph Smith at their first meeting is very informative. As they were introduced in the doorway of the Mansion House, Quincy saw "a hearty, athletic fellow, with blue eyes standing prominently out upon his light complexion, a long nose, and a retreating forehead. He wore striped pantaloons, a linen jacket, which had not lately seen the washtub, and a beard of some three days' growth." Quincy could hardly believe that "this was the founder of the religion which had been preached in every quarter of the earth."[79]

After discussions on a variety of topics and a personal tour of the temple construction site, the party returned to the Mansion House, where Joseph showed the two visitors his mother's Egyptian antiquities

---

77. Quincy, *Figures of the Past*, 393.
78. Quincy, *Figures of the Past*, 387.
79. Quincy, *Figures of the Past*, 380.

collection.[80] Absolutely certain of his interpretation of the mummies and papyri, Smith turned everyone's attention to one mummy and said: "I want you to look at that little runt of a fellow over there. He was a great man in his day. Why, that was Pharaoh Necho, King of Egypt!" Smith also identified on the parchment the handwriting of Abraham, Moses, and Aaron. Quincy asked about the drawing of a serpent walking on a pair of legs, questioning "the propriety of providing the reptile in question with this unusual means of locomotion." Smith answered the inquiry again without any hesitation or doubt: "Why, that's as plain as a pikestaff. Before the Fall snakes always went about on legs, just like chickens. They were deprived of them, in punishment for their agency in the ruin of man."[81] The two well-educated visitors must have been astonished at the prophet's explanation.

After having penned Smith's amazing explanations of the Egyptian exhibitry, Josiah Quincy cautioned his readers that "any hasty interpretation of him is inadequate." At the end of their visit, the Bostonians heard Smith's strategy for running for the presidential chair: "Finally, he told us what he would do, were he President of the United States, and went on to mention that he might one day so hold the balance between parties as to render his election to that office by no means unlikely." It seemed clear that Adams and Quincy understood the seriousness of Smith's prophetic and political aspirations.

Perhaps Josiah Quincy's most profound comments about the Mormon prophet both introduced and concluded his chapter. Quincy began with a prediction about Smith:

> It is by no means improbable that some future text-book, for the use of generations yet unborn, will contain a question something like this: What historical American of the nineteenth century has exerted the most powerful influence upon the destinies of his countrymen? And it is by no means impossible that the answer to that interrogatory

---

80. Smith referred to the collection as his mother's because he claimed that she paid $6,000 of her own money for it (though not exactly accurate). Also he told the men that she received the revenues from tours and asked them to pay her for the tour. Quincy described the prophet's statement: "'Gentlemen,' said this *bourgeois* Mohammed, as he closed the cabinets, *'those who see these curiosities generally pay my mother a quarter of a dollar.'*" See *Figures of the Past,* 387.

81. Quincy, *Figures of the Past,* 386–87.

may be thus written: *Joseph Smith, the Mormon prophet.* And the reply, absurd as it doubtless seems to most men living, may be an obvious commonplace to their descendants.[82]

Then, Quincy ended his chapter by reiterating Smith's importance to his and future generations:

> Born in the lowest ranks of poverty, without booklearning and with the homeliest of all human names, he had made himself at the age of thirty-nine a power upon earth. Of the multitudinous family of Smith, from Adam down (Adam of the "Wealth of Nations," I mean), none had so won human hearts and shaped human lives as this Joseph. His influence, whether for good or for evil, is potent to-day, and the end is not yet.
>
> I have endeavored to give the details of my visit to the Mormon prophet with absolute accuracy. If the reader does not know just what to make of Joseph Smith, I cannot help him out of the difficulty. I myself stand helpless before the puzzle.[83]

Josiah Quincy and his travel partner, Charles Francis Adams, admitted that their stop in Nauvoo to meet the Mormon prophet was coincidental; thus, to draw the conclusion on the importance of Smith's contribution reveals how impressed the two men were with the prophet. Now, with the passing of more than two hundred years since Joseph Smith Jr.'s birth, the curious insights of Quincy's writings and the accuracy of his assessment of the prophet's perplexing nature seem truly prophetic.

The Smith chapter in Quincy's book is one of the most important documents to emerge concerning the closing months of the prophet's life. Its great significance is in the disinterested nature of the author, his willingness to rank Smith alongside such influential people, and the prophetic nature of his introduction and conclusion. Unfortunately, our generation is not any closer to understanding the true nature of Joseph Smith Jr.'s complex personality and motivation, even with all the valiant attempts of his modern biographers. The Mormon prophet remains the puzzle today that Quincy said he was.

82. Quincy, *Figures of the Past*, 376.
83. Quincy, *Figures of the Past*, 400.

CHAPTER SIXTEEN

The Evolution of Joseph Smith's Theology

❡

Nature of the Godhead

DETERMINING THE MAINSTREAM of Protestant Christianity on the American frontier in the Second Great Awakening is difficult at best—the river of thought on the subject is both deep and wide. Establishing theological consensus on the nature of the godhead within the Christian community was quite impossible between, and even within, the denominations of Joseph Smith's day. Members of the Methodist, Catholic, Presbyterian, and Baptist movements, though officially maintaining a trinitarian stance, actually held varying views. The discourse generally focused on whether the one God appeared in the form loosely stated as the three-in-one (trinitarian), whether the Holy Spirit was a divine entity (but not deity) separate from the Father and Son (binitarian), or whether God was God and thus did not need the Son to express divine purpose (unitarian).[1]

1. Tertullian (c.155–c.220 CE) was one of the earliest Christian writers to use precise, careful language in explaining the trinitarian concept of three distinct persons in one individual deity. Binitarianism was coined in 1890 to describe the views of those early Christian theologians who believed in two personages in the godhead, while the Holy Spirit maintained a separate and mystical existence reflecting the mind of God. The unitarian view—that there is but one member of the godhead—was coined in 1600 to identify a strong antitrinitarian movement that began in Europe and was eventually transplanted in America. For a development of these differing views of the godhead in the context of Mormonism, see two valuable essays: Van Hale, "Defining the Contemporary Mormon Concept of God," 7–15, and Dan Vogel, "The Earliest, Mormon

Sorting through the prophet's theological beliefs has confounded researchers through the generations. Arriving at a consensus has been nearly impossible. However, it remains clear that Joseph Smith's theology evolved over time. By the time he located in Nauvoo, and with the development of the temple rituals, his theology had reached its culmination.

Many early-nineteenth-century theologians used the term "modalism" in reference to the nature of the deity. This term, though similar to trinitarian views today, emphasized the difference in roles of the deity and dwelt less on the issue of personhood. At various points during the Latter Day Saint journey, either practically or officially, the church started with a modalistic view of the godhead. Then, by the mid-1830s, church leaders shifted to a binitarian emphasis on God the Father and Jesus Christ, God's Son. With the move to Nauvoo and the strong influences of the temple, the church became "tritheistic," that is, believing in three separate gods.[2]

Perhaps the first view of Joseph Smith's understanding of the nature of the godhead is found during his experience in the Palmyra grove. As explained earlier, only after twenty years of theological maturation did the prophet conclude that God the Father and Jesus Christ were separate physical beings. To summarize, in the first three explanations of the Grove Experience, starting in 1831–1832 and continuing through 1835, Joseph Smith told his story with only one member of the godhead appearing to him.[3] Then in 1840, he changed his story to include two separate deities, and stayed with this until his death.[4] The inconsistency in his story

---

Concept of God," 17–33, in *Line upon Line: Essays on Mormon Doctrine*, ed. Gary James Bergera (Salt Lake City: Signature Books, 1989).

2. Although there are some differences in terminology and definitions, many historians have observed this shift in theology. Representative of this general agreement is Vern G. Swenson, "The Development of a Holy Ghost in Mormon Theology," in Bergera, *Line upon Line*, 28–29.

3. The earliest recorded account of the First Vision was Joseph Smith's written statement in his Kirtland Letter Book, written sometime in 1831 or 1832; the second was an 1834 letter forwarded to William W. Phelps for publication in the Kirtland, Ohio, *Latter Day Saints' Messenger and Advocate* 1 no. 3 (December 1834): 42–43, written by Oliver Cowdery and approved by the prophet; and the third was in Joseph Smith's private journal under the date 9 November 1835.

4. This 1840 account was in response to a request for information from Mormon missionary Orson Pratt who was in Edinburgh, Scotland. Two later accounts of the First Vision were placed in the Nauvoo, Illinois, *Times and Seasons*. See Smith's letter to John

becomes quite understandable if placed in the context of Joseph's theological maturing process. It is also very evident throughout his writings and public statements.

The Book of Mormon expresses inconsistent language on the nature of the godhead. In some verses, the Father, Son, and Holy Spirit are three expressions of the one God. Zeezrom, for example, asked Amulek two important questions on the nature of the godhead: "Is there more than one God?" Amulek answered, "No." Then, Zeezrom followed with "Is the Son of God the very eternal Father?" and Amulek answered, "Yea, he is the very eternal Father of heaven and of earth...and he shall come into the world to redeem his people."[5] Also, the title page of the Book of Mormon was written to prove that "JESUS is the CHRIST, the ETERNAL GOD."[6] Yet the Third Book of Nephi suggests a distinct binitarian separation:

> Behold I have given unto you my gospel, and this is the gospel which I have given unto you, that I came into the world to do the will of my Father, because my Father sent me; And my Father sent me that I might be lifted up upon the cross; and after that I had been lifted up upon the cross, I might draw all men unto me: That as I have been lifted up by men, even so should men be lifted up by the Father, to stand before me, to be judged of their works, whether they be good or whether they be evil.[7]

This inconsistency signals some uncertainty about Smith's own views on this complex theological issue.

Further insight into Smith's early views of the godhead came during the opening months of church organization in June 1830 and took on a revelatory tone. Originally the statement was labeled "The Articles and Covenants of the Church of Christ." Church members

---

Wentworth, which was printed in the 15 March 1842 issue of the Nauvoo newspaper, and also in Joseph Smith's history recorded in the *Times and Seasons* periodically between March and April of the same year. See *Times and Seasons* 3 no. 6 (15 March 1842): 706–10ff. For the best analysis of the differing accounts of the First Vision, see Howard, "Joseph Smith's First Vision" in *Restoration Studies I*, 95–127.

5. Alma 8:81–82, 93–96 (LDS 11:28–29, 38–39).

6. Dan Vogel made this observation in "The Earliest Mormon Concept of God," in Bergera, *Line upon Line*, 23.

7. III Nephi 12:25–27 (LDS 17:13–14).

determined that it should be entered into the Doctrine and Covenants as Section 17:

> Wherefore the almighty God gave his only begotten Son, as it is written in those scriptures which have been given of him: he suffered temptations but gave no heed unto them; he was crucified, died, and rose again the third day; and ascended into heaven to sit down on the right hand of the Father, to reign with almighty power according to the will of the Father, that as many as would believe and be baptized, in his holy name, and endure in faith to the end, should be saved: not only those who believed after he came in the meridian of time in the flesh, but all those from the beginning, even as many as were before he came, who believed in the words of the holy prophets, who spake as they were inspired by the gift of the Holy Ghost, who truly testified of him in all things, should have eternal life, as well as those who should come after, who should believe in the gifts and callings of God by the Holy Ghost, which beareth record of the Father, and of the Son, which Father, Son, and Holy Ghost are one God, infinite and eternal, without end.[8]

Although some elements of trinitarianism are present in the opening and closing sentences, this scripture focuses on the roles of each member of the godhead rather than their physical separation, and thus expresses modalistic qualities. The "Articles and Covenants" were foundational to church organization and received a unanimous vote of support by members attending the church conference held in Fayette Township, New York, on 9 June 1830. Since church members included this view of the godhead in the Doctrine and Covenants, it took on canonized status.

Shortly after the move to Kirtland, Ohio, and with Smith's extended access to Sidney Rigdon and his scholarly biblical understanding, a significant transition on the nature of the godhead became noticeable as church leaders moved to a new position—binitarianism. The church elders attended a series of classes in the unfinished House of the Lord through the winter of 1834–1835. Joseph Smith and Sidney Rigdon prepared a series of seven lectures on theology and faith. A forceful nonrevelatory statement in the fifth Lecture of Faith informed the audience as follows: "There are two personages who constitute the great matchless, governing and supreme

---

8. Doctrine and Covenants 17:5a–h (LDS 20:21–28).

power over all things—by whom all things were created and made, that are created and made, whether visible or invisible: whether in heaven, on earth, or in the earth, under the earth, or throughout the immensity of space—They are the Father and the Son." Later in the lecture, the Holy Spirit was identified as "the mind of God."[9]

In April 1835, another binitarian statement appeared in the Kirtland, Ohio, *Latter Day Saints' Messenger and Advocate*. "I was not a professor at the time, nor a believer in sectarian religion, but a believer in God, and the Son of God, as two distinct characters, and a believer in sacred scripture." Here church newspaper editor William W. Phelps addressed an inquiry to the newspaper and provided a lengthy response based on his earlier pre-membership experiences.[10]

On 16 February 1832, in Hiram, Ohio, at the farm of convert John Johnson, the prophet and Sidney Rigdon were revising the Gospel of John in the King James Version of the Bible. In the presence of a dozen loyal onlookers, the two men experienced a vision. Referred to as the Vision of the Three Glories, this became Section 76 in the Doctrine and Covenants. Rigdon provided revealing language for the revelation: "wherefore, as it is written, they [the order of Melchisedec] are gods, even the sons of God; wherefore all things are theirs, whether life or death, or things present, or things to come, all are theirs, and they are Christ's, and Christ is God's; and they shall overcome all things."[11] Although much can be read into Rigdon's word choices, the beginnings and possible credibility of a doctrine of plural gods, even in the Old Testament context, gained currency during the Kirtland era.[12]

9. The seven Lectures of Faith were included in the 1835 Doctrine and Covenants as the "doctrine" component, with the remainder directed to the "covenants" of the church. Actual authorship of the series has been debated. For a historical background of the evolution of church canon, see H. Michael Marquardt, *The Joseph Smith Revelations: Text and Commentary* (Salt Lake City: Signature Books, 1999). Marquardt's discussion of the pivotal August 1835 church conference in Kirtland, Ohio, where the Lectures of Faith were canonized, can be found on pages 12–16.

10. *Latter Day Saints' Messenger and Advocate* 1, no. 8 (April 1835): 115.

11. Doctrine and Covenants 76:5h (LDS 76:58–60).

12. In borrowing polytheistic language, Joseph Smith could look, once again, to his understanding of the Garden of Eden story in Genesis. The biblical author associated the power of understanding the difference between good and evil with the power of

Although the *Book of Abraham* did not receive canonized status in the Church of Jesus Christ of Latter-day Saints, headquartered in Salt Lake City, Utah, until years after Joseph Smith Jr.'s death, the writing clearly demonstrated Smith's thinking on the plural and physical nature of God. In the opening years of the Reorganized Church of Jesus Christ of Latter Day Saints, which formed in the decades following the assassination of Joseph Smith Jr., church leaders did not canonize the *Book of Abraham*; however, they did embrace some of the *Book of Abraham*'s theology. This included belief in the book's view of a plural godhead.[13]

Ambiguity from former years concerning the nature of the godhead turned to clarity with two important sermons Joseph Smith gave in the months just before his assassination. The first, and most important, was a funeral oration given in a church conference in April 1844, and the second approximately six weeks later, in a popular grove meeting place near the temple construction site.

The Humanity of a Plural Godhead: The King Follett Discourse and the Prophet's Last Sermon

ON 7 APRIL 1844, Joseph Smith gave what may have been his most theologically significant sermon as prophet of the church. His close friend King Follett[14] died during the construction of a well in Nauvoo,

---

being gods: "For God doth know, that in the day ye eat thereof, then your eyes shall be opened, and *ye shall be as gods*, knowing good and evil" (italics added for emphasis), Genesis 3:10 IV; cf. 3:5 KJV.

13. See "Council of Twelve Minutes," Book A (2 May 1865): 13, Community of Christ Library-Archives. The Reorganized Church of Jesus Christ of Latter Day Saints, now called Community of Christ, does not recognize the *Book of Abraham* as scripture. Also, the belief in the plurality of gods was eliminated by the RLDS Church by the 1870s.

14. Follett was a native of Vermont and moved to Cuyahoga County, Ohio. He was baptized in the spring of 1831, at age 41. Follett experienced persecution at Far West by serving a jail sentence in Richmond, Missouri, on charges of robbery. He escaped his imprisonment in July 1839 but was recaptured. He was the last Mormon prisoner to be set free from a Missouri jail, and on his release in October 1839, he joined his family in Nauvoo. See *DHC*, 3: 360, 401–402. Follett was at the bottom of a well, rocking the walls. The men above were lowering a bucket of rocks down to him when the rope broke. The accident was fatal.

and Smith used this occasion to pronounce publicly his most-far-reaching theological statement. In his sermon, the prophet addressed a variety of topics dealing with his understanding of the cosmos, salvation, the nature of the godhead, and the afterlife. Most important, the "King Follett Discourse," as far as it is correctly recorded, is the clearest representation of the prophet's view of the character of God as an exalted human. Preaching from the stand before thousands, the prophet stated:

> God himself was once as we are now, and is an exalted man, and sits enthroned in yonder heavens! That is the great secret. If the veil were rent today, and the great god who holds this world in its orbit, and who upholds all worlds and all things by his power, was to make himself visible, I say, if you were to see him today, you would see him like a man in form like yourselves in all the person, image, and very form as a man; for Adam was created in the very fashion, image and likeness of god, and received instruction from, and walked, talked and conversed with him, as one man talks and communes with another.[15]

By assigning human attributes to God, especially in a funeral sermon, Smith intended his thoughts as pastoral ministry to mourners. But the huge congregation received so much more. Joseph had positively stated that members, "by going from one small degree to another, from a small capacity to a great one; from grace to grace, from exaltation to exaltation, until you attain to the resurrection of the dead, and are able to…sit in glory, as do those who sit enthroned in everlasting power" could become gods, although lesser ones. This language revealed Smith's evolved theology of the godhead.[16]

Smith admonished his followers to join him in the learning process of divinity: "Here then is eternal life, to know the only wise and true God. You have got to learn how to be Gods yourselves; and to be kings and priests to God, the same as all Gods have done." This Gnostic-like view of the afterlife put within reach of the believer their own divinity.[17] The

15. The King Follett Discourse is found in "Conference Minutes," *Times and Seasons* 5, no. 15 (15 August 1844): 612–17. Willard Richards, Wilford Woodruff, Thomas Bullock, and William Clayton participated in recording this pivotal sermon.

16. An earlier (February 1832) reference to the human nature of the deity can be found in Doctrine and Covenants 76:5g–h (LDS 76:57–60).

17. *Times and Seasons* 5, no.15 (15 August 1844): 614.

oration bolstered the faith of followers and no doubt astonished nonbelievers in the crowd.

Through the years, many viewed the King Follett sermon with skepticism for several reasons. As early as August 1897, writing for the Board of Publication of the Reorganized Church of Jesus Christ of Latter Day Saints, church historian Heman C. Smith summarized his objections to the Follett Sermon in the church's official history, the *History of the Reorganized Church of Jesus Christ of Latter Day Saints.* The church historian did not want to repeat what he considered heretical beliefs, so he simply referred the reader to the August 1844 *Times and Seasons* synopsis and justified his rejection of the Nauvoo heresies with four reasons. First, he acknowledged that the Seer's sermon was very lengthy, while the *Times and Seasons* summary was only five pages. He concluded that such a brief review could not present accurately the prophet's complete teachings on the subject. Second, the Follett sermon was not printed until after the prophet's death and thus could not receive his review for accuracy or his endorsement. Third, Heman Smith claimed that the Follett sermon's style varied widely from other speeches and writings of the prophet, thus casting even more doubt on its authenticity. And last, the church historian questioned the memory of those who recorded the prophet's sermon, claiming that there was "no evidence that a *verbatim* report was made when delivered."[18] Heman Smith's critique in the Reorganized Church's history was an official effort to place theological distance between the church then headquartered in Lamoni, Iowa, and the church headquartered in Salt Lake City, Utah.

Joseph Smith Jr. gave another sermon that revealed his view of the godhead, on 16 June 1844, just eleven days before his death. In the grove east of the temple in Nauvoo, Smith removed any doubts about the pluralistic nature of the godhead:

> I wish to declare I have always and in all congregations when I have preached on the subject of the Deity, it has been the plurality of Gods. It has been preached by the Elders for fifteen years.
>
> I have always declared God to be a distinct personage, Jesus Christ a separate and distinct personage from God the Father, and that the Holy Ghost was a distinct personage and a Spirit: and these three constitute three distinct personages and three Gods. If this is

---

18. *History of the RLDS Church,* 2: 735–36.

in accordance with the New Testament, lo and behold! we have three Gods anyhow, and they are plural: and who can contradict it?[19]

Feeling the need to justify his view, Smith then gave his congregation a lesson in the Hebrew language. The prophet explained that the Hebrew translation of the Bible's opening sentence verified the existence of more than one god. Smith reasoned:

> An unlearned boy must give you a little Hebrew. *Berosheit baurau Eloheim ait aushamayeen vehau auraits*, rendered by King James' translators, "In the beginning God created the heaven and the earth." I want to analyze the word *Berosheit*. *Rosh*, the head; *Sheit*, a grammatical termination, The *Baith* was not originally put there when the inspired man wrote it, but it has been since added by an old Jew. *Baurau* signifies to bring forth; *Eloheim* is from the word *Eloi*, God, in the singular number; and by adding the word *heim*, it renders it Gods. It read first, "In the beginning the head of the Gods brought forth the Gods," or, as others have translated it, "The head of the Gods called the Gods together."[20]

The prophet told his audience that he had received this instruction from God and from the witness of the Holy Ghost.[21] As he progressed with his sermon, Smith rejected trinitarianism without reservation: "Many men say there is one God; the Father, the Son and the Holy Ghost are only one God! I say that is a strange God anyhow—three in one, and one in three! It is a curious organization."[22]

Smith cited the *Book of Abraham* as his textual information source, and then gave further rationale by providing insight into the makeup of the divine family:

---

19. *DHC*, 6: 474.
20. *DHC*, 6: 475. This lesson in Hebrew is similar to one the prophet gave during the King Follett Discourse in April 1844. See *Times and Seasons* 5, no. 15 (15 August 1844): 614. Community of Christ Seminary scholar Wayne Ham concluded that Joseph's translation and explanation represent as much his own speculation as they do any knowledge of the Hebrew language he may have had.
21. *DHC*, 6: 475.
22. *DHC*, 6: 476.

If Abraham reasoned thus—If Jesus Christ was the Son of God, and John discovered that God the Father of Jesus Christ had a Father, you may suppose that He had a Father also. Where was there ever a son without a father? And where was there ever a father without first being a son? Whenever did a tree or anything spring into existence without a progenitor? And everything comes in this way. Paul says that which is earthly is in the likeness of that which is heavenly, Hence if Jesus had a Father, can we not believe that *He* had a Father also? I despise the idea of being scared to death at such a doctrine, for the Bible is full of it.[23]

Thomas Bullock recorded this historic sermon until rain brought the service to an abrupt end.

The belief in the humanity of God predates even church organization and shows the influence of the prophet's family upbringing. In late 1829, Lucy Mack Smith received a visit from "three delegates" of the Presbyterian congregation in Palmyra, New York, who wanted an explanation for the Smiths' absence from their public worship, and further information about the Book of Mormon. During their conversation, the visitors raised the issue of God's character. Responding to their questions, the prophet's mother told the visitors, "The different denominations are very much opposed to us. The Universalists are alarmed lest their religion should suffer loss, the Presbyterians tremble for their salaries, the Methodists also come, and they rage, for they worship *a God without body or parts*, and they know that our faith comes in contact with this principle."[24]

By the end of spring 1844, the Latter Day Saint theology clearly embraced the concept of plural gods. The prospects for Latter Day Saints to achieve divinity in the afterlife separated the movement from competing faith communities but attracted thousands of seekers on the American frontier, holding great concern for their salvation. These beliefs also edged Latter Day Saintism further out of the Christian mainstream.

---

23. *DHC*, 6: 476.
24. Lavina Anderson, *Lucy's Book*, 467.

Importance of the Nauvoo Temple

THE NAUVOO TEMPLE offered a primary venue where members could, through their gospel of works, prepare and possibly achieve their salvation. "Exaltation" became their contemporary term for salvation. A preliminary form of "endowment" had been introduced at the dedication of the Kirtland House of the Lord. Heber C. Kimball recalled that Joseph Smith Jr. had convened a 23 June 1834 meeting in Clay County, Missouri, to identify the first elders to receive their "endowment."[25] Then, on 15 February 1835, the prophet challenged the newly created Quorum of Twelve Apostles: "Tarry at Kirtland until you are endowed with power from on high." The prophet continued his counsel:

> You need a fountain of wisdom, knowledge and intelligence such as you never had. Relative to the endowment, I make a remark or two, that there may be no mistake. The world cannot receive the things of God. He can endow you without worldly pomp or great parade. He can give you that wisdom, that intelligence, and that power, which characterized the ancient saints; and now characterizes the inhabitants of the upper world.[26]

The Kirtland understanding of endowment was dramatically different from the Nauvoo understanding, however. As beliefs evolved during the transition from Ohio to Illinois, the endowment theology evolved also, from a promise that missionaries would be empowered with special gifts "from on high" so they could accomplish a great and marvelous work, to "secret knowledge" that prepared the soul for celestial life. Smith's ritualization of this secret knowledge became the central focus of the temple in Nauvoo. Smith based the Nauvoo temple rites on Gnostic understandings revealed only to the prophet, who then extended his authority to supervise the implementation of that secret knowledge to the Council of Twelve.

---

25. *DHC*, 2: 112–13; "Heber C. Kimball's Journal," *Times and Seasons* 6, no. 3 (15 February 1845): 804–805. These elders were Edward Partridge, William W. Phelps, Isaac Morley, John Corrill, John Whitmer, David Whitmer, Algernon Sidney Gilbert, Peter Whitmer Jr., Simeon Carter, Newel Knight, Parley P. Pratt, Christian Whitmer, Solomon Hancock, Thomas B. Marsh, and Lyman Wight. Gilbert died shortly after the ceremony.

26. *DHC*, 2: 197.

Joseph Smith positioned his church in the nationwide dispute on the nature of the marriage covenant between those who viewed it as strictly a civil ceremony, like the Puritans and Anglicans, and those who viewed the covenant as a sacrament, like the Methodists and Baptists. Smith embraced the sacramental view of marriage and saw his prophetic prerogative as transcending human law in order to fulfill God's law. He considered all civil marriages as valid for "time" only but not for "eternity." Yet during the Kirtland days, Smith had not yet conceived the Nauvoo meaning of being sealed for eternity or how to accomplish it. This is reflected in his personal letters to Emma Hale Smith. Historian Richard S. Van Wagoner has observed that as late as 1840 the prophet occasionally ended his letters to Emma with "your husband till death" above his signature.[27] For a marriage to be sealed for eternity, those who performed the ceremony required priesthood authority, to which the prophet held the keys, and the proper venue for the ritual was within the sacred walls of a dedicated temple. That there are no known sealings in the Kirtland Temple signaled that the sealing ritual was a later elaboration.

COMMUNITY OF CHRIST LIBRARY-ARCHIVES

Nauvoo Temple (as it appeared ca. 1846)

---

27. The prophet may have borrowed the idea of making a distinction between marriage for time and eternity from contemporary perfectionist preacher Robert Matthews, also known as "Matthias the Prophet." Matthews linked the stewardship of community property with wives of his followers. Smith and Matthias met in Kirtland in the mid-1830s and parted ways shortly after their meeting. Matthias's influence may have lingered, however. See Van Wagoner, *Sidney Rigdon*, 7–9; also see Brodie, *No Man Knows My History*, 407–409.

Works versus Grace and Baptism for the Dead: Pope Leo X, Martin Luther, and Joseph Smith Jr.

OF ALL THE temple rituals that developed during the Nauvoo era, baptism for the dead is of particular importance, since the sacrament was the only temple ritual performed that survived the transition from the Restoration Era to the Reorganization Era. For the Nauvoo Saints, this sacrament was the first to be performed in their temple and has a fascinating origin.

As stated earlier, at every stop along the Latter Day Saint journey, the prophet was intent on meeting the spiritual needs of his people. Joseph Smith's theology always seemed to be a work in progress. He would contemplate the great theological issues of the day and respond to his followers with a revelation of what he perceived reflected the mind and will of God.

Personal salvation seemed always to be before the prophet for his consideration. No doubt he pondered the great issue of works versus grace. The Great Theological Debate of the sixteenth century, couched in terms of personal salvation, turned on the question simplistically posed: "Can humans 'on this side of the veil' specifically determine events that happen on the 'other side of the veil'?" Briefly stated, Pope Leo X (1475–1521) of the Roman Catholic Church said yes, and Martin Luther (1483–1546), an Augustinian monk and German university professor, said no. This complex theological issue pitted Leo's view of salvation as justified by works against Luther's view that salvation could be justified only by faith.

By the time of Nauvoo, the prophet carefully pondered the question, especially during the late summer of 1840 as his father, Joseph Sr., lay on his deathbed. With his family gathered around him, the church patriarch called for Joseph Jr. and shared his concern about his oldest son, Alvin, who had died seventeen years earlier. Since this was long before church organization, Alvin's baptism into Latter Day Saintism was impossible. According to church beliefs, Alvin would be considered one of the unbaptized "honorable men of the earth" identified in Section 76 of the Doctrine and Covenants. But by the conditions of this revelation, Alvin could attain only the terrestrial world, a lesser glory, whereas the rest of the Smith family, already baptized, would be in celestial, or the highest, glory.[28] Tragically, the family would remain separated for eternity.

Evidently, the prophet's epiphany on 21 January 1836, in Kirtland, Ohio, where Joseph Smith claimed to see the celestial kingdom, did not satisfy the dying patriarch:

> The heavens were opened upon us, and I beheld the celestial kingdom of God, and the glory thereof, whether in the body or out I cannot tell—I saw the transcendant beauty of the gate through which the heirs of that Kingdom will enter, which was like unto circling flames of fire, also the blasing throne of God, whereon was seated the Father and the Son.—I saw the beautiful streets of that Kingdom, which had the appearance of being paved with gold—I saw father Adam, and Abraham and Michael[29] and my father and mother, my brother Alvin, that has long since slept, and marvled how it was that he had obtained an inheritance in that Kingdom, seeing that he had departed this life, before the Lord had set his hand to gather Israel the second time and had not been baptized for the remission of sins.[30]

It may be that in that special moment Joseph Sr. recalled the harsh condemnation that Reverend Benjamin B. Stockton had given during Alvin's funeral sermon in November 1823 about the unwillingness of the deceased to be baptized. No doubt this still weighed heavily on all the family.

In cases like this, Joseph Jr. frequently referred to biblical scripture. It is possible that he recalled the apostle Paul's statement to the Corinthian Christians, which raised the issue of their salvation through baptism:

> For he hath put all things under his feet. But when he saith all things are put under him, it is a manifest that he is excepted, which did put all things under him. And when all things shall be subdued unto him,

28. Doctrine and Covenants 76:5–7 (LDS 76:30–113).

29. Michael was another name for Adam. Oliver Cowdery recorded that "I have been informed from a proper source that the Angel Michael is no less than our father Adam." See Oliver Cowdery to John Whitmer, 1 January 1834, Oliver Cowdery Letterbook, 15, Henry E. Huntington Library, San Marino, California, in Marquardt, *The Joseph Smith Revelations*, 278. That Smith would use both names may suggest this theological understanding was not fully evolved by that time.

30. The prophet had this vision at Kirtland, Ohio, on 21 January 1836; recorded in his 1835–1836 "Journal," original in LDS Archives. For a contextual explanation see Marquardt, *The Joseph Smith Revelations*, 278–79.

then shall the Son also himself be subject unto him that put all things under him, that God may be all in all. Else what shall they do which are baptized for the dead, if the dead rise not at all? Why are they then baptized for the dead? And why stand we in jeopardy every hour?[31]

Smith used this interrogative scripture to introduce to the church the possibility that by proxy a deceased person could be baptized vicariously by a living friend or relative. This tenet became known as baptism for the dead.

Once again the prophet met a considerable need of not only his family, but also his followers. The sacred journey of his people had taken a heavy toll as unbaptized friends and relatives were either left behind or buried in graves along the trail. The salvation of the unbaptized meant that they could not enjoy citizenship in celestial glory, but through proxy baptism the Saints could make that opportunity available.

Yet at the same time, another problem weighed on the prophet. Temple construction progressed far too slowly. The daily struggle of living and their commitment to other building projects limited how much time church members could give to temple construction. Ingeniously, Smith resolved the two problems—proxy baptisms and temple construction—with one solution. First, with Joseph Jr.'s initiation of baptism for the dead, he satisfied his father's concern and that of others. Now, at least by proxy, Alvin had the opportunity to attain celestial glory. Second, because vicarious baptisms were performed in the Mississippi River, the prophet declared that the ritual was too sacred to be done in public view and ordered that further baptisms were to be done only inside the temple. This gave the needed incentive for workers to redouble their commitment to work on the temple.

Just as he anticipated, believing that the souls of deceased unbaptized family and friends awaited their proxy baptism, workers spent long days laboring diligently so that at least the basement and the font could be covered and dedicated. On 8 November 1841, the Saints met in a solemn

---

31. I Corinthians 15:27–29 KJV. This is the only reference to baptism for the dead in the entire Bible.

ceremony to consecrate the facility, and three weeks later dozens were baptized for deceased friends and family.[32]

Although the temple font was the primary venue for the ritual baptism, other elders continued baptizing for the dead in the Mississippi River as late as 1843. In a 2 May 1843 letter to her friends and family, gentile Nauvoo resident Charlotte Haven recalled her observance of a proxy baptismal ceremony during a stroll along the Mississippi River outside Nauvoo:

> We followed the bank toward town, and…spied quite a crowd of people, and soon perceived there was a baptism. Two elders stood knee-deep in the icy cold water, and immersed one after another as fast as they could come down the bank. We soon observed some of them went in and were plunged several times. We were told that they were baptizing for the dead who had not had an opportunity of adopting the doctrines of the Latter Day Saints. So these poor mortals in ice-cold water were releasing their ancestors and relatives from purgatory! We drew a little nearer and heard several names repeated by the elders as the victims were douched, and you can imagine our surprise when the name George Washington was called. So after these fifty years he is out of purgatory and on his way to the "celestial" heaven! It was enough, and we continued our walk homeward.[33]

At this point in his life, it was clear that Joseph Smith Jr. took Pope Leo's argument and adopted a theology of works. Although he at times acknowledged the grace of God as very important, in the Mormon prophet's opinion, what happened in time could definitely impact what would happen in eternity.[34]

32. The prophet designed a great basin measuring sixteen feet long, twelve feet wide, and four feet deep. It rested seven feet above the floor on the backs of twelve meticulously carved, life-size wooden oxen (representing the twelve tribes of Israel). Eventually stone oxen replaced the wooden originals. A thirty-foot well dug in the basement near the font provided water for the font. See Flanders, *Nauvoo*, 198–99.

33. Charlotte Haven to Family Members, 2 May 1843, in William Mulder and A. Russell Mortensen, eds., *Among the Mormons: Historic Accounts by Contemporary Observers* (Lincoln: University of Nebraska Press, 1973), 122–23.

34. Historian Dan Vogel speculated that the roots of a theology of works could be found as early as the period of revival in Palmyra, New York. That Smith did not have an emotional moment of commitment where he fell to the ground being slain in the spirit, as called for in many of the local revivals, signaled the prophet's move toward a theology of works. See Vogel, *Making of a Prophet*, 153–54.

Celestial and Plural Marriage

NO THEOLOGICAL PRACTICE moved Mormonism farther away from the Judeo-Christian mainstream than the institution of plural marriage. The presence of Joseph Smith's speculative perceptions of the Divine's intent about alternative marital relationships can be traced throughout the church story. Questions of the doctrine's origin and Joseph Smith's specific involvement have been sources of disagreement within the movement and are among the most frequently studied aspects of the church's history.

THE SPECTRUM OF OPINION. After Joseph Smith III affiliated with the movement to reorganize the church in April 1860, the controversial issue of polygamy became a foundation stone in the wall of separation between the Latter Day Saint church headquartered in the Salt Lake Valley and the Latter Day Saint church headquartered in the Midwest. Through the generations, a range of viewpoints has developed about the prophet's involvement. Historical argumentation on Smith's alleged participation can be best understood when viewed on a "spectrum of opinion." At one end of the spectrum are those who exonerate the prophet entirely of any involvement. They blame the aberrant marital institution on either John Cook Bennett's "spiritual wife system"[35] or Brigham Young's "gross materialistic leadership."[36] One step removed from this position on the spectrum are historians who have avoided placement of blame by admitting only that Smith must have known about the existence of the practice and defer to other analyses.[37] At the polar opposite end of the spectrum are those who identify Joseph Smith as the author, originator, and first practitioner of the marital practice.[38] Not far from this pole is the "contextual approach," which holds that polygamy was the unintended consequence of the inception of Joseph Smith's Nauvoo temple cultus beginning in 1840 with baptism for the dead. Further, this suggests that polygamy evolved

---

35. *History of the RLDS Church*, 2: 732.
36. Davis, *Story of the Church*, 489.
37. Edwards, *Our Legacy of Faith*, 108–109.
38. Richard S. Van Wagoner, *Mormon Polygamy: A History* (Salt Lake City: Signature Books, 1986); Todd Compton, *In Sacred Loneliness: The Plural Wives of Joseph Smith* (Salt Lake City: Signature Books, 1998).

from an intricate system of family-oriented rituals and culminated in plural marriage.[39] Additionally, some have concluded that Joseph was involved, but later came to believe the doctrine was a mistake and wanted to rid the church of it. Contemporary documentary evidence has significantly impacted all of these positions. Today, all those who carefully study the issue in its historical context will find themselves somewhere on this spectrum.

Any historically sound exploration of Smith's involvement must answer several crucial questions: What do we mean in using the term "polygamy"? When was polygamy first practiced within the movement and who was involved? How could the practice be rationalized in the early nineteenth century? And, in a religious movement tightly controlled by the words and deeds of an authoritarian prophet, could church members have practiced polygamy without his knowledge or permission? These complex questions have been the focus of entire books. This explanation can only address the surface issues.

Since Western culture today is strongly committed to monogamous marriage, it becomes easy to impose a guilty verdict and harsh sentence on early Mormon practitioners of polygamy. In this discussion it will be important to avoid the hazard of judgmentalism, especially considering the conflicted nature of the evidence that both refutes and supports Joseph Smith's involvement in the issue. Rendering judgment on Smith's alleged involvement depends on what evidence one is willing to accept. If an unquestionably authenticated "smoking gun document" written in Joseph's hand, where he freely admits to being the author of polygamy, is the only evidence one will accept, then one can rightfully claim that Joseph Smith Jr. is innocent of all charges, because, as of this writing, no such document exists. However, if one accepts a veritable mountain of circumstantial evidence and the personal accounts, letters, diaries, newspaper accounts, and sworn testimonies of those who admit direct involvement, then one could identify Joseph Smith Jr. as the first polygamist of Mormonism.

PUBLIC DENIAL OF OFFICIAL POLYGAMOUS BELIEFS AND PRACTICE. Joseph Smith Jr. and other leaders took numerous occasions to publicly reject allegations that they either endorsed or practiced polygamy. Two good examples of this appeared in the official church

---

39. Richard P. Howard, "The Changing RLDS Response to Mormon Polygamy: A Preliminary Analysis," *Restoration Studies III*, 157, 158.

newspaper. Minutes from a 15 April 1842 General Conference reported both Hyrum Smith's and Joseph Smith's rejection of rumors about the practice of plurality. Hyrum "spoke in contradiction of a report in circulation about Elder [Heber C.] Kimball, B[righam]. Young, himself, and others of the Twelve, alleging that a sister had been shut in a room for several days, and that they had endeavored to induce her to believe in having two wives." Following his older brother, Joseph Jr. "spoke upon the subject of the stories respecting Elder Kimball and others, showing the folly and inconsistency of spending any time in conversing about such stories or hearkening to them."[40]

Church leaders also announced in the 1 February 1844 issue of the *Times and Seasons* administrative action against elders who were taking such liberties:

> As we have lately been credibly informed, that an Elder of the Church of Jesus Christ, of Latter-day Saints, by the name of Hiram Brown, has been preaching Polygamy, and other false and corrupt doctrines, in the county of Lapeer, state of Michigan. This is to notify him and the Church in general, that he has been cut off from the church, for his iniquity; and he is further notified to appear at the Special Conference, on the 6th of April next, to make answer to these charges.[41]

Both Joseph Jr. and his brother Hyrum, two presidents of the church, attested to the notice. Such public statements offered plausible deniability against charges, especially since the exposed practice of polygamy would have violated bigamy laws. How to address this difficult issue placed the prophet in a quandary.

THE ORIGINS OF POLYGAMY: INDISCRETION OR SACRED RITE?[42] The practice of polygamy within Mormonism can possibly be traced back to the prophet's early involvement with women other than his wife, Emma. According to testimony given years later, it was alleged that Joseph Smith Jr. was involved in three extramarital relationships between

---

40. "Conference Minutes," *Times and Seasons* 3, no. 12 (15 April 1842): 763. These were the minutes for the 6 April 1842 General Conference.
41. "Notice," *Times and Seasons* 5, no. 3 (1 February 1844): 423.
42. What the prophet may have seen as the divinely directed restoration of an Old Testament practice likely would have been seen by others as marital infidelity.

1830 and 1835. By 1830, rumors of a liaison between Joseph Smith and one Eliza (also Elizabeth) Winters spread throughout northern Pennsylvania, where Joseph and Emma were living. Adding to the rumors were reported statements made between the prophet and Martin Harris claiming that "adultery was no crime." Area resident Levi Lewis heard Harris state that "he did not blame Smith for attempting to seduce E. W. (Eliza Winters)."[43] Some historians speculate that these rumors may have prompted Joseph and Emma's unexpected move back to upstate New York in the late summer of 1830.[44]

A second alleged affair was with Nancy Marinda Johnson of Hiram, Ohio. Some have connected this liaison with Joseph's brutal beating, tarring, and feathering, which occurred 24 March 1832. That the mobbers were accompanied by a Dr. Dennison, whose job was to castrate the young prophet during the assault, offered some credibility to that connection; and that the doctor lost his nerve and refused to perform the operation dramatically changed church history.[45]

Joseph Smith Jr.'s alleged third indiscretion was with one Fanny Ward Alger. Fanny's parents, Samuel and Clarissa Hancock Alger, moved to the Kirtland area sometime between 1826 and 1828. Fanny, the fourth of eleven children, was born on 20 September 1816. In early 1835, Emma needed a maidservant to help with household chores and with raising the family, so she offered the position to Fanny, then nineteen years old, who gladly accepted. Benjamin Johnson, infatuated with the attractive and eligible young woman, described Fanny as "A varry nice & Comly young woman about my own age. towards whoom not only mySelf but every one

---

43. These statements were made almost five decades later. See Hiel Lewis, "That Mormon History: Reply to Elder Cadwell," *Amboy Journal* 24 (6 August 1879): 1, as cited in Vogel, *Early Mormon Documents*, 4: 296–97, 314.

44. Newell and Avery, *Mormon Enigma*, 64; Van Wagoner, *Mormon Polygamy*, 4.

45. In 1884, Clark Braden made this accusation in his debate with E. L. Kelley in *Public Discussion of the Issues between The Reorganized Church of Jesus Christ of Latter Day Saints and The Church of Christ (Disciples)* (St. Louis: Christian Publishing Company, [1884]), 202. Also see Brodie, *No Man Knows My History*, 119. In April 1842, Nancy Marinda did enter into the "new and everlasting covenant" (polygamy). Historian Todd Compton suggested that fear of Smith gaining control over their farms was the primary motivation of the Hiram, Ohio, mobbers. See his *In Sacred Loneliness*, 230–31.

Seemed *partial* for the ameability of her character and it was whispered eaven then that Joseph *Loved her*."[46]

Emma greatly appreciated Fanny and treated her like a daughter. Thus, it was quite surprising when Emma abruptly kicked Fanny out of her house. The family of Ann Eliza Webb took in Fanny until her parents from Mayfield, Ohio, could arrive and take custody of their daughter.

Quietly the Alger family left Kirtland in September 1836 and headed west. At Dublin, Indiana, Fanny met and married Solomon Custer, who, at nineteen years, was her same age.[47] The couple raised nine children and probably stayed in east-central Indiana, and no longer affiliated with Latter Day Saintism. The rest of Fanny's family remained with the church, moved to western Illinois by 1842, and then migrated west in 1846.[48]

In July 1872, William McLellin, one of the original members of the Council of Twelve, wrote a lengthy letter to Joseph Smith III about his father, the Seer. Included in this fascinating holograph are the details of Emma's discovery of her husband together with Fanny.[49] In the letter

46. Dean R. Zimmerman, *I Knew the Prophets, An Analysis of the Letter of Benjamin F. Johnson to George F. Gibbs, Reporting Doctrinal Views of Joseph Smith and Brigham Young* (Bountiful, Utah: Horizon, 1976), 38, in Newell and Avery, *Mormon Enigma*, 66. See Don Bradley, "Mormon Polygamy before Nauvoo? The Relationship of Joseph Smith and Fanny Alger" in *The Persistence of Polygamy: Joseph Smith and the Origins of Mormon Polygamy*, ed. Newell G. Bringhurst and Craig L. Foster (Independence, Mo.: John Whitmer Books, 2010), 14–58.

47. Two years later when Joseph fled from Kirtland to Far West, he passed through Dublin, Indiana, and unsuccessfully tried to find work cutting cordwood and sawing logs. Whether Joseph and Emma ran into Fanny is unknown. That those fleeing the law from Kirtland should pass through east-central Indiana is quite understandable since by the late 1830s the routes were a well-developed part of the National Road system. Richmond, Indiana, settled as early as 1800, just a few miles northeast of Dublin, was a primary hub point of the main trunk of the National Road. The church did have a presence in Dublin by the time the Smith family traveled through in early 1838. A local church member sold his tavern and gave the Smith family $300, which financed the next two months of their journey to Far West. For an excellent map of National Road development, see Meinig, *The Shaping of America*, 2: 226. Newell and Avery provided an explanation of the monetary gift in *Mormon Enigma*, 69.

48. Compton, *In Sacred Loneliness*, 30–40.

49. William McLellin learned about Latter Day Saintism probably from Samuel Harrison Smith and Reynolds Cahoon, and received baptism in 1831. He was an assistant teacher in the School of the Elders, and in 1835, he entered the Council of Twelve Apostles as a charter member. In 1838, McLellin was excommunicated because he had lost

McLellin stated: "Again I told [your mother, Emma Hale Smith] I heard that one night she missed Joseph and Fanny Alger. She went to the barn and saw him and Fanny in the barn together alone. She looked through the crack and saw the transaction!!! She told me this story was verily true."[50] Not surprisingly, this indiscretion strained the Smith marriage. McLellin wrote Joseph III that his father had promised to desist but Emma was not convinced of his contrition. Joseph then "called in Dr. [Frederick Granger] Williams, O. Cowdery, and S. Rigdon to reconcile Emma. But she told them just as the circumstance took place. He found he was caught. He confessed humbly, and begged forgiveness. Emma and all forgave him."[51] Eventually McLellin identified the actions of Joseph and Fanny in the haymow as Smith's first "sealing," but his reference was probably more pejorative than evidential. In either case, the encounter between the prophet and the maidservant had a lasting impact.

It did not take long for rumors to spread throughout the Ohio countryside about the prophet's indiscretions and the possibility that polygamy had been initiated. Obviously this was a public relations problem for the church through the spring of 1835.[52] As summer approached, the pressure for an official response intensified. To quell the rumors, and hopefully put the issue behind them, Smith agreed to go on a missionary tour through

---

confidence in the Presidency. On leaving the church, he studied medicine. He eventually moved to Independence, Missouri, where he died in April 1883.

50. W. E. McLellin to Joseph Smith III, July 1872, Independence, Jackson County, Missouri, P13f213, Community of Christ Library-Archives. In the letter, written more than forty years later, the old apostle misspelled his own name, confused Joseph III's birth date, and the time of the incident.

51. McLellin repeated his story of the Smith-Alger affair to a reporter, who placed the account in the 6 October 1875 *Salt Lake Tribune*. See Van Wagoner, *Mormon Polygamy*, 6.

52. The prophet had performed at least nineteen public marriages by 1837. This was especially controversial, since technically Smith was not legally recognized to perform these weddings. None were more controversial than the Goldwaithe-Knight marriage in 1835. Lydia Goldwaithe had married Calvin Bailey in the fall of 1828. Two years later the couple had a healthy baby girl named Roseanna. Then, Calvin took to the bottle and abused his wife and child. On 12 February 1832, another child, Edwin Bailey, was born but lived just one day. The difficult birth almost took Lydia's life as well. Out of

Michigan with Frederick Granger Williams, and leave the matter for Oliver Cowdery and William W. Phelps to resolve.

While the Michigan missionaries were away, Cowdery and Phelps called for a General Conference in Kirtland in mid-August. In this official convening of the church—one of the most important of the entire Kirtland period—Cowdery and Phelps attempted to remove all doubts about where the church stood on marriage. The two men acknowledged the rumors as the purpose for the statement, then specifically stated the official church position on marriage for both members and nonmembers to understand: "Inasmuch as this Church of Christ has been reproached with the crime of fornication, and polygamy: we declare that we believe that one man should have one wife; and one woman but one husband, except in case of death, when either is at liberty to marry again."[53] Although not a revelation from their prophet, conferees unanimously approved the document's insertion in the Doctrine and Covenants, thus canonizing the position. That the declaration had the desired effect among the Gentiles remained

---

money to pay for his drinking habit, Calvin deserted his family, forcing friends to rescue Lydia and Roseanna.

In the spring of 1835, after Lydia Bailey's conversion to Mormonism, she moved to Kirtland and eventually settled into Hyrum Smith's boardinghouse. Also living there was widower Newel Knight. After a courtship, Newel asked for Lydia's hand in marriage and for the prophet to perform the vows. The couple immediately confronted two obstacles—Lydia was still married to Calvin, and Joseph Smith Jr. did not have a license to marry them. The decision to go ahead with the vows has been the focus of a protracted debate in church history, especially considering that just four months earlier a church conference had unanimously passed a resolution establishing only monogamous marriage covenants. Arguing that the Knight-Bailey marriage was legal since none of the prophet's marriages were ever challenged is William G. Hartley in "Newel and Lydia Bailey Knight's Kirtland Love Story and Historic Wedding," *Brigham Young University Studies* 39, no. 4 (2000): 6–22. Also claiming Smith's legitimacy is M. Scott Bradshaw, "Joseph Smith's Performance of Marriages in Ohio," *Brigham Young University Studies* 39, no. 4 (2000): 23–69. Other historians challenged the legality of Smith's marriages. For example, see Quinn, *Origins of Power*, 88. Also see Brooke, *The Refiner's Fire*, 212. Both Quinn and Brooke referred to the marriage as "bigamous." Historian Richard Van Wagoner described the decision to marry the couple without a license as "a bold display of civil disobedience." See *Mormon Polygamy*, 7.

53. Doctrine and Covenants 111:4b (not in LDS editions).

doubtful, but it did inform the members as to official church beliefs on the sacrament of marriage—at least for then.[54]

Three years later the Saints packed their wagons with their physical possessions and trundled off to Far West, Caldwell County, Missouri, to follow their prophet. They also took with them the organization of the First Presidency, Quorums of the Twelve Apostles and Seventy, a bicameral priesthood, their beliefs in the *Book of Abraham*, a strong emphasis on education, and the sacred memories of their Pentecostal experience at the dedication of the House of the Lord.

For those most closely associated with the prophet, the Smith-Alger affair simmered along their 800-mile journey to northwestern Missouri. Two factions emerged on the embarrassing issue, pitting Smith and Rigdon[55] on one side and the Whitmers, Cowdery, and Phelps on the other. Eventually, the latter men were tried in a church court for their membership and among the charges against Cowdery was language that caused the Kirtland indiscretions to resurface. George Washington Harris, a member of the Far West High Council, testified in Cowdery's trial that he had overheard a conversation between Cowdery, Smith, and Thomas B. Marsh where Cowdery "seemed to insinuate that Joseph Smith Jr. was guilty of adultery, but when the question was put [to Joseph]... he answered No." This conversation allegedly occurred on 6 November 1837.[56] Approximately three months later, Cowdery bristled in a letter to his brother, Warren, on 21 January 1838, referencing the Smith-Alger ordeal: "A dirty, nasty, filthy affair of his and Fanny Alger's was talked over in which I strictly declared that I had never deviated from the truth on the matters, and as I supposed was admitted by himself."[57]

54. Newell and Avery stated that the statement on marriage "did little to stem rumor and gossip, but it reassured church members." See *Mormon Enigma*, 67. Also, because the language of Phelps and Cowdery remained essentially unchanged, the prophet must have approved of this language.

55. Eventually, Smith and Rigdon would have their own falling out over the polygamy issue in Nauvoo when Smith allegedly propositioned Rigdon's unmarried daughter Nancy to become his polygamous wife on 9 April 1842.

56. *Far West Record*, 167.

57. Oliver Cowdery to Warren Cowdery, 21 January 1838, "Letters of Oliver Cowdery," 80–83. This quote taken from *New Mormon Studies CD-ROM: A Comprehensive Resource Library*, "Diaries, Journals, and Letters." The original letter is in the Huntington

The accusations required a response, so the prophet convened a church court. On Wednesday 11 April 1838, in a High Council meeting at Far West, Elder Seymour Brunson preferred nine charges against Oliver Cowdery, the second charge stating: "For seeking to destroy the character of President Joseph Smith, Jun., falsely insinuating that he was guilty of adultery."[58] The second charge and five others were sustained, which brought Cowdery's excommunication.[59]

With the guilty verdict of the trial made public, Oliver Cowdery, the second elder, a witness to the Book of Mormon plates and the primary scribe, who had experienced ordination with the prophet to the Aaronic and Melchisedec priesthoods, and missionary to the Lamanites, joined many other church founders as outcasts of the movement. The other defendants were also convicted and their membership removed. Indeed, by fall 1838, the end of the Far West era, ten of the original twelve apostles and nearly all eleven witnesses to the Book of Mormon were no longer with the church.

Those on the spectrum of opinion who accept Joseph Smith Jr.'s involvement in polygamy note the heavy toll this issue took on Emma Hale Smith, the prophet's wife. On 12 July 1843, the prophet allegedly pronounced a secret revelatory statement authorizing polygamy that admonished Emma to be faithful and true to her husband, and threatened her salvation: "And I command mine handmaid, Emma Smith, to abide and cleave unto my servant Joseph, and to none else. But if she will not abide

---

Library, San Marino, California. Oliver Cowdery's letters are reproduced in Stanley R. Gunn, *Oliver Cowdery: Second Elder and Scribe* (Salt Lake City: Bookcraft, 1962).

58. *DHC*, 3: 16. Because polygamy was not mentioned in any of the nine charges, Brunson implicitly made a distinction between polygamy and adultery. The legal technicality protected the marriage sacrament from public exposure and criminality.

59. The next day, on 12 April 1838, Cowdery wrote an eloquent letter of defense that addressed the charge preferred against him. His language reflected his understanding of his constitutional rights, and to some of the charges admitted guilt based on those rights. He avoided acrimonious countercharges and concluded with an acknowledgment of the High Council's sincerity. He closed his letter thusly: "With consideration of the highest respect, I am Your obedient servant. O Cowdery." See *Far West Record*, 165–66.

this commandment she shall be destroyed, saith the Lord; for I am the Lord thy God, and will destroy her if she abide not in my law."[60]

Anticipating Emma's intense opposition to polygamy, the question arose: Who would tell her? Joseph did not want to be the one to break the news, and volunteers from his intimate circle of advisers were not quickly forthcoming. Joseph's earlier attempts to broach the sensitive subject with Emma had met with dismal failure. Hyrum, being the good brother-in-law, volunteered to go with Joseph to tell her, after Joseph wrote out the ten-page statement. Joseph's personal secretary, William Clayton, wrote of Emma's response: "After it [the revelation] was wrote Presidents Joseph and Hyrum presented it and read it to E[mma] who said she did not believe a word of it and appeared very rebellious."[61]

In private conversations of Nauvoo residents throughout the spring of 1843, the subject of "plurality" arose frequently. Members of the secretly designated Anointed Quorum received their special temple endowment, but Emma could not, due to her rejection of the polygamous celestial marriage system. This weighed heavily on her. By May 1843, she could no longer withstand the pressure. Biographers Linda King Newell and Valeen Tippets Avery construct a solid case that on 23 May, Emma stood by as High Priest James Adams from Springfield, Illinois, married Joseph to Emily and Eliza Partridge, daughters of Edward Partridge, in the Mansion House. Then, in the next week, on a cold and rainy day of 28 May, Emma was sealed to Joseph for time and eternity. Her "rebellious" opposition was an outpouring of frustration from the months of pressure from her husband to accept the "new and everlasting covenant." Plural marriage was the only doctrine that she ever opposed.[62]

ACKNOWLEDGMENT AND REJECTION. As will be seen, the polygamy issue took its toll on the movement. Attacks came from both outside and inside the movement once the practice became exposed. Just days before his arrest in June 1844, the prophet met with Nauvoo Stake president William Marks to discuss how best to address the polygamy

60. The Church of Jesus Christ of Latter-day Saints accepts this statement as revelatory. See Doctrine and Covenants 132:54 (LDS).

61. George D. Smith, ed., *An Intimate Chronicle: The Journals of William Clayton*, six journals (Salt Lake City: Signature Books, 1991), 2: 110.

62. Newell and Avery, *Mormon Enigma*, 142–43.

that had spread throughout the priesthood leadership. Marks was a very close friend of the Smith family and commanded enormous respect among the membership. Marks left the following record of his conversation with Joseph Smith:

> Joseph, however, became convinced before his death that he had done wrong; for about three weeks before his death, I met him one morning in the street, and he said to me, Brother Marks, I have something to communicate to you, we retired to a by-place, and set down together, when he said: "We are a ruined people." I asked, how so? He said: "This doctrine of polygamy, or Spiritual-wife system, that has been taught and practiced among us, will prove our destruction and overthrow. I have been deceived." He said, "in reference to its practice; it is wrong; it is a curse to mankind, and we shall have to leave the United States soon, unless it can be put down, and its practice stopped in the church. Now" said he, "Brother Marks, you have not received this doctrine, and how glad I am. I want you to go into the high council, and I will have charges preferred against all who practice this doctrine, and I want you to try them by the laws of the church, and cut them off, if they will not repent, and cease the practice of this doctrine;" and said he, "I will go into the stand, and preach against it, with all my might, and in this way we may rid the church of this damnable heresy."[63]

COMMUNITY OF CHRIST LIBRARY-ARCHIVES
William Marks

Events outran Smith's opportunity to preach against it, and Marks was forced out of Nauvoo (with his membership intact, however) in the struggle for power after the prophet's assassination. But this statement acknowledged in veiled language Smith's involvement in the doctrine and also his rejection of it once he saw the long-term damage it was wreaking

---

63. William Marks, "Epistle," *Zion's Harbinger and Baneemy's Organ* 7, no. 3 (July 1853): 53, Microfilm Collection, Community of Christ Library-Archives.

on the movement. Because of this aberrant marital practice the Latter Day Saint tradition would have to carry these events of the Restoration Era as their burden of history.

Ancient Linguistic Translation: *The Pure Adamic Language, the* Book of Abraham, *the Greek Psalter, and the Kinderhook Plates*

THE PURE ADAMIC LANGUAGE. Joseph Smith Jr.'s translation of the Book of Mormon, the *Book of Abraham*, the Greek Psalter, and the Kinderhook Plates demonstrated his fertile imagination and inspired genius. These writings also revealed much about the powerful, contemporary nineteenth-century cultural influence, the prophet's theological development, and the pressure he felt to fulfill his perceived responsibilities as intermediary between God and the church membership. Throughout Joseph Smith's life, he expressed an enthusiasm for learning original languages in search of their purest meaning: "My soul delights in reading the word of the Lord in the original, and I am determined to pursue the study of the languages, until I shall become master of them. At any rate, so long as I do live, I am determined to make this my object; and with the blessing of God, I shall succeed to my satisfaction."[64] But these writings also exposed the prophet's humanity.

As prophet, Joseph felt the obligation to understand completely the mind and will of God. He believed that there was a pure and direct language spoken between Adam and God before Adam's fall. This language left nothing to be misinterpreted since it was free from human error. For a modern-day prophet of God, learning such a language would perfect his leadership and facilitate exactly the ushering in of the Second Coming. His strong desire to have this divine knowledge dated back to his younger years and was inseparably connected to his mystical speculations. He saw the use of seer stones to receive revelations, which were later canonized

---

64. *DHC*, 2: 396.

in the Doctrine and Covenants, as taking him to the brink of divine understanding.[65]

Joseph Smith identified with the Adam of the Genesis story. The Seer believed that Adam was a deified being before his Fall in the Garden of Eden. That Adam could communicate on a par with God evidenced his divinity. The pure and undefiled Adamic language was lost at the Fall, however. Joseph yearned to recover it, because knowing that language would allow him to communicate directly with God.[66] Through divine inspiration Joseph felt he had learned some terms but not the complete language. His identification of Adam-ondi-Ahman as well as the various names given to specific individuals and locations in the Doctrine and Covenants Sections 77 and 81 may have been early attempts to use Adamic expressions of this divine language.[67]

65. Many of the early inclusions in the 1835 Doctrine and Covenants were dictated through the use of his seer stone. These include Sections 2, 6, 7, 10, 12, 13, 14, and 15 (LDS 3, 6, 7, 11, 14, 15, 16, and 17). See Marquardt and Walters, *Inventing Mormonism*, 188, 195fn51; and Richard P. Howard, "Latter Day Saint Scriptures and the Doctrine of Propositional Revelation," in Vogel, *The Word of God*, 9.

66. Historian John L. Brooke demonstrated the importance of knowing this Adamic language as "another critical link with the intellectual world of seventeenth-century hermeticism." See his *The Refiner's Fire*, 196–97. Hermeticism was an exploration of the enchanted practices of witchcraft, conjuring, counterfeiting, and alchemy. Applied to the religious context, the philosophy believed in the definite possibility of direct interaction between God and human beings. Hermeticism emerged as a social movement in 1463 in Renaissance Italy on the discovery of a collection of lost ancient texts in Macedonia three years earlier. Because these writings were attributed to Hermes Trimegistus, a pagan divine being, they were called the *Corpus Hermeticum*. This body of writing became an Egyptian Genesis. Hermetic understanding was quite empowering and neatly complemented Smith's theological speculations. Not unique to the Latter Day Saints, various aspects of hermeticism could be found in many other contemporary religions. These included, for example, the Anabaptists, Quakers, Seekers, and Spirituals. As one historian observed: "Hermeticism raised humans from the status of a pious and awestruck observer of God's wonders and encouraged them to operate with His universe by using the powers of the cosmos to their own advantage. Using their intellect, humans could perform marvelous feats—it was no longer humans *under* God, but God *and* humans." See Peter J. French, *John Dee: The World of an Elizabethan Magus* (London: Routledge and K. Paul, 1972), 76, 85, in Brooke, *The Refiner's Fire*, 11.

67. In Section 77 (LDS 78), perhaps to hide their identity, the Seer gave pseudonyms to the various individuals to whom the revelation was directed. For example, Newell K. Whitney was Ahashdah; Joseph Smith was Gazelam, or Enoch; and Sidney Rigdon was Pelagoram. The prophet repeated this practice a month later in Section 81 (LDS

Accurately, historians have referred to Joseph Smith as a "modern-day Moses," who led his people on a diaspora to find sacred land where Zion could be achieved. But he also saw himself as a "modern-day Adam" because he thought the Adamic language held the keys that could unlock the mysteries that separated humanity from divinity. Such empowerment was needed to accomplish his prophetic task, and he felt the obligation to pursue every avenue available to him in order to succeed.

THE *BOOK OF ABRAHAM*. Smith's responsibilities as a "prophet, seer, and revelator" and his high expectations for his office were confirmed in Book of Mormon scripture: "Now Ammon said unto him, I can assuredly tell thee, O king, of a man that can translate the records: for he has wherewith that he can look, and translate all records that are of ancient date: and it is a gift from God."[68] Events at Kirtland, Ohio, during the summer of 1835, provided an excellent opportunity for him to combine his interest in ancient linguistics and his prophetic skills.

The *Book of Abraham* also revealed insights into the prophet's understanding of the cosmos, and even creation itself. In the fourth chapter of Abraham, Smith promoted polytheism in his creation story. Not one God but a committee of gods worked in collaboration on the plan of Creation:

> And then the Lord said: Let us go down. And they went down at the beginning, and they, that is the Gods, organized and formed the heavens and the earth. And the earth, after it was formed, was empty and desolate, because they had not formed anything but the earth; and darkness reigned upon the face of the deep, and the spirit of the Gods was brooding upon the face of the waters.
>
> And they (the Gods) said: Let there be light; and there was light. And they (the Gods) comprehended the light, for it was bright; and they divided the light, or caused it to be divided, from the darkness. And the Gods called the light Day, and the darkness they called Night. And it came to pass that from the evening until morning they called night; and from the morning until the evening they called day;

---

82), referring to Oliver Cowdery as Horah or Olihah, and Martin Harris as Shalemanasseh or Mehemson. The geographic identity of Kirtland, Ohio, became the Land of Shinehah (81; LDS 80). In Sections 100 and 102 (LDS 91 and 93) Joseph Smith becomes Baurak Ale. These code names are generally not used in recent LDS editions.

68. Mosiah 5:72 (LDS 8:13).

and this was the first or the beginning of that which they called day and night.

And the Gods also said: Let there be an expanse in the midst of the waters, and it shall divide the waters from the waters. And the Gods ordered the expanse, so that it divided the waters which were under the expanse from the waters which were above the expanse; and it was so, even as they ordered. And the Gods called the expanse, Heaven. And it came to pass that it was from evening until morning that they called night; and it came to pass that it was from morning until evening that they called day; and this was the second time that they called night and day.[69]

When compared with the translation of the Book of Mormon, the translation process of the *Book of Abraham* was different in at least three ways. First, where the Book of Mormon translation took just thirteen months (and mostly within nine), work on the *Book of Abraham* extended over a nine-year period. Second, Smith used a seer stone and hat in translating portions of the Book of Mormon, yet there is no evidence that Smith used artifactual assistance in translating the Egyptian papyri. Third, with the exception of the sealed portions, Joseph Smith completed his work on the Book of Mormon, but whether Joseph actually finished the *Book of Abraham* remains quite uncertain. Scrutiny of the Egyptian artifacts after the prophet's death would raise very serious questions about the accuracy of his interpretation.

After the assassination of Joseph Smith Jr., his mother, Lucy Mack Smith, assumed curatorial responsibilities for the artifacts. Evidently, William Smith, the prophet's youngest brother, sold them in the mid-1840s with the intent of repurchasing them, but never did. An extant certificate of sale dated 26 May 1856 proved that the artifacts were conveyed to a Mr. A. Combs.[70] The collection was then divided, with most going to a Chicago museum and the remainder to an interest in St. Louis. Then, in 1871, the Great Chicago Fire supposedly incinerated the entire Chicago collection, including the papyri, but the collection had been removed from the museum before the fire and was saved from the inferno.

69. Abraham 4:1–8. See *The Pearl of Great Price* (Salt Lake City: The Church of Jesus Christ of Latter-day Saints).

70. Photocopy of the original, Community of Christ Library-Archives.

Almost three generations later, Edward Heusser, an associate of the Combs family, conveyed the papyri to the Metropolitan Museum of Art in New York City in 1947. The papyri remained in storage for the next twenty years until they were discovered in 1967. The discovery set the stage for translation of the Egyptian hieroglyphics using modern, sophisticated understanding. The results revealed the papyri to have no connection to Joseph Smith's interpretation. Rather, the prophet's speculative writings emerged from his creative imagination in the last years of his life.[71]

THE GREEK PSALTER. In mid-April 1842, the Smith family proudly exhibited their Egyptian artifacts to inquirers. At the same time that the prophet was publishing his *Book of Abraham* translations, one Henry Caswell arrived in Nauvoo. Caswell was an academic scholar of religion and eventual author of numerous books during the 1840s, including two on contemporary Mormonism. Caswell heard about the prophet's amazing gift for translating ancient texts so he decided to test the prophet by presenting an ancient Greek manuscript of the psalms to the prophet for his inspection. The prophet determined that the writings were the same as the reformed Egyptian on the Book of Mormon plates. Caswell described his encounter:

> [Smith] boldly pronounced [the psalter] to be a "*Dictionary of Egyptian hieroglyphics.*" Pointing to the capital letters at the commencement of each verse, he said, "Them figures is Egyptian hieroglyphics, and them which follows is the interpretation of hieroglyphics, written in the *reformed Egyptian* language. Them characters is like the letters that was engraved on the golden plates."

Caswell then suspected that Smith knew he had been entrapped because the prophet bolted out of the Mansion House, jumped into his carriage, and swiftly rode away without providing opportunity for Caswell to question him.[72]

THE KINDERHOOK PLATES. The prophet's translation skills were tested again a year later when a group of men brought to Nauvoo six

---

71. An excellent and more in-depth analysis of the *Book of Abraham* is found in Howard, *Restoration Scriptures*, 193–210.

72. Henry Caswell, *The Prophet of the Nineteenth Century; or, the Rise, Progress, and Present State of the Mormons, or Latter Day Saints....* (London: J. G. F. & J. Rivington, 1843), 223–24, Vault Collection, Community of Christ Library-Archives.

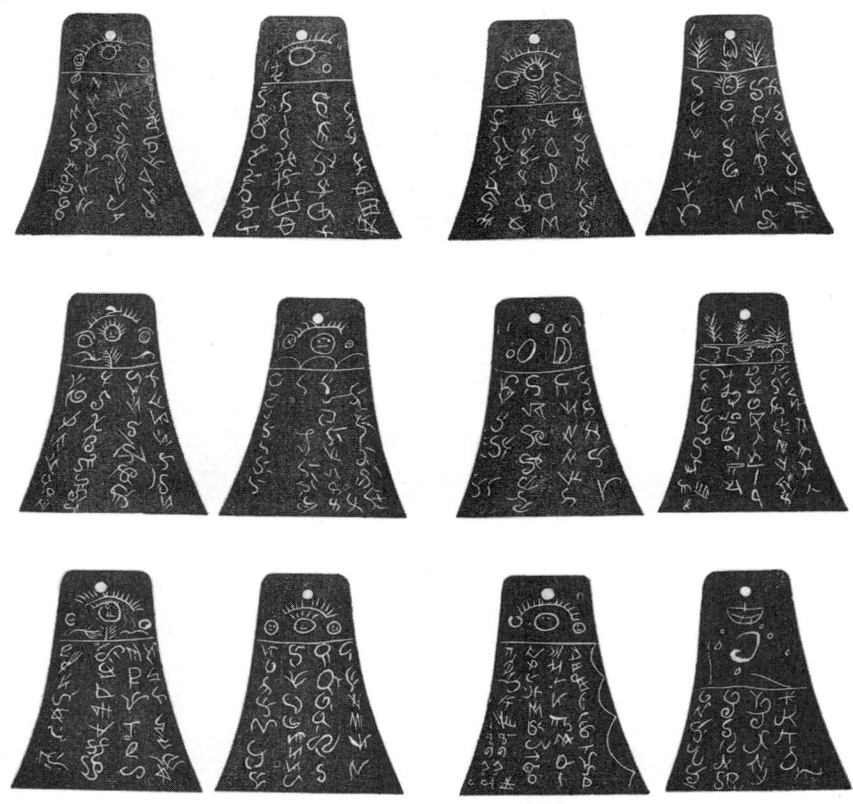

Facsimile of the Kinderhook Plates

brass "plates" that they claimed to have recovered from a mound near Kinderhook, Pike County, Illinois. In an elaborate ruse to trick the prophet, the men explained how they had discovered the plates next to a skeleton, and claimed the plates were genuine. The men entrusted the plates to the prophet to translate them. On inspecting the plates, the prophet agreed. William Clayton, the prophet's scribe, witnessed the discussion and recorded it in his journal under the date of Monday 1 May 1843: "I have seen 6 brass plates which were found in Adams County.... President Joseph has translated a portion and says they contain the history of the person with whom they were found and he was a descendant of Ham through the loins of Pharaoh king of Egypt, and that he received his kingdom from the ruler of heaven and earth."[73] Clayton inaccurately identified Kinderhook as being in Adams County; however, the editors of the *Times and Seasons* corrected the mistake in their extended coverage in the 1 May 1843 issue.[74] The *Times and Seasons* gave more background detail by reprinting an article from the *Quincy Whig*.[75]

Not until eleven years after the prophet's death was the conspiracy exposed. In 1855, testimony revealed that one of the conspirators, Bridge Whitton, a Kinderhook blacksmith, had fabricated the plates and co-conspirator Robert Wiley etched the lettering using a nitric acid and beeswax process.[76] Another conspirator, Wilbur Fugate, confessed his role as well in June 1879. The plates, in the shape of a bell and measuring between five and six inches long, disappeared for decades. Then, in 1920, similar to the *Book of Abraham* papyri, one plate was discovered, actually mislabeled, in the collection of the Chicago Historical Society. An independent chemical analysis performed in 1980 verified the Kinderhook Plate as shaped from brass alloy, and the scribing, probably through the nitric acid and beeswax process, as consistent with nineteenth-century technology.[77]

Besides through the Book of Mormon, Smith showed his creative genius and the extent of his skill to translate ancient languages by providing scriptural resources for his people through pure Adamic language, the *Book of Abraham*, the Greek Psalter, and the Kinderhook Plates. However, in so doing, Joseph Smith edged Latter Day Saintism even further toward the banks and clearly out of the Judeo-Christian mainstream with his claims. This was not of great concern for the Mormon prophet, however, who anticipated with fervor the Second Coming, as well as his role in it.

The theological innovations that Joseph Smith Jr. introduced over a fourteen-year period ending in Nauvoo, Illinois, in June 1844 collided with secular events and added to a momentum that became unstoppable down

---

73. William Clayton, *An Intimate Chronicle: The Journals of William Clayton*, ed. George D. Smith (Salt Lake City: Signature Books, 1991), 100.
74. "Ancient Records," *Times and Seasons* 4, no 12 (1 May 1843): 185–86.
75. "Singular Discovery—Material for another Mormon Book," *Times and Seasons* 4, no. 12 (1 May 1843): 186–87.
76. W. P. Harris to W. C. Flagg, 25 April 1855, in "A Hoax.: Reminiscences of an Old Kinderhook Mystery," *Journal of the Illinois State Historical Society* 5 (July 1912): 271–73.
77. Palmer, *An Insider's View*, 30–34.

a slippery slope. Smith's identification of a systematic doctrine of celestial marriage, initiated toward the end of the slippery slope, contributed to his demise. However, other theological precepts such as the importance of prophetic leadership, an open scriptural canon, the Americanization of the Judeo-Christian tradition, and creative stewardship principles have had a lasting impact.

CHAPTER SEVENTEEN

Secrecy as a Condition for Church Survival

The Need for Secrecy

FOR SUCH A public figure as Joseph Smith Jr., it seems ironic that secrecy was a dominant feature of his life.[1] So many aspects of his life required nondisclosure. His First Vision encounter, his marriage elopement, his retrieving and the translation process of the Book of Mormon plates, and his numerous revelations and epiphanies are just a few examples. In the Book of Mormon, writing with disfavor, Smith told of secret organizations such as the Gadianton robbers, yet he also created a secret organization, the Danites, at Far West in 1838. This was Smith's first experiment in structuring a covert organization. Danite activity ebbed during the transition from Far West to Nauvoo. However, in December 1843, the prophet indirectly revitalized the Danites by appointing many of its members to serve on a Nauvoo police force.[2]

If resorting to secrecy was useful to the prophet in the early and middle periods of the Latter Day Saint Restoration Era, it became an imperative in the late period, from 1839 to 1844. As Nauvoo, Illinois,

---

1. The prophet's psychobiographer William D. Morain observed that the need for secrecy emerged from "the dissociated corner of [Smith's] mind." See Morain, *The Sword of Laban*, 203.

2. For a list of Danite members of the Nauvoo police force, see Quinn, *Origins of Power*, 116–17; appendix 2, "Mormon Security Forces, 1833–47," 469–78; and appendix 3, "Danites in 1838: A Partial List," 479–90. Smith publicly announced his police force at a city council meeting on Friday afternoon 29 December 1843.

417

developed, various aspects of its community life and church theology required the strictest secrecy.

For example, in a May 1842 assembly of the Female Relief Society, Smith addressed the issue of secrecy:

> Put a double watch over the tongue…[You] should be chasten and reprove and keep it all in silence, not even mention them again.… One request to the Prest. [Emma Hale Smith] and society, that you search yourselves—the tongue is an unruly member—hold your tongues about things of no moment. A little tale will set the world on fire…lest in exposing these heinous sins, we draw the indignation of a gentile world upon us (and to their imagination just, too). It is necessary to hold an influence in the world and thus spare ourselves an extermination.[3]

This counsel cautioned the women about the hazards of rumor and its consequences on the movement. Temple rituals and the practice of celestial marriage and polygamy also required the strict silence of its participants. But there were other crucial and concealed components of Nauvoo life that included the initiation of Freemasonry, as well as Joseph's plans for the building up of the kingdom of God and his establishment of an Anointed Quorum. Common to all of these innovations was a sworn oath of secrecy.

The Craft of Freemasonry, which played an integral role in community life and the development of the Nauvoo church theology, reinforced Smith's culture of concealment. Many early leaders had embraced the Craft before their affiliation with the church, including Hyrum Smith (Mount Moriah Lodge No. 112, Palmyra, New York), Heber C. Kimball (Victor Lodge No. 303, Victor, New York), Newell K. Whitney (Meridian Orb Lodge No. 10, Painesville, Ohio), and George Miller (Widow's Son Lodge No. 60, Albemarle, Virginia).[4] Ironically, that the Book of Mormon considered secret societies as dangerous and abominable reflected the volatile, anti-Masonic atmosphere that existed during the translation

---

3. Newell and Avery, *Mormon Enigma*, 115.
4. Michael W. Homer, "'Similarity of Priesthood in Masonry': The Relationship between Freemasonry and Mormonism," *Dialogue: A Journal of Mormon Thought* 27, no. 3 (Fall 1994): 16.

process.⁵ In September 1826, the abduction and murder of William Morgan, caused by his exposé of Freemasonry, led to a nationwide scare. Morgan was temporarily jailed in Canandaigua, New York, not far from Palmyra. Also, it is entirely possible that in the fall of 1830, when Joseph Sr. served his sentence in the debtors prison in Canandaigua, his cell mate was Eli Bruce, who had been charged with Morgan's murder.⁶ Speculations about Morgan's

COMMUNITY OF CHRIST LIBRARY-ARCHIVES
Sunstone from the Nauvoo Temple

---

5. "Masonry gives rogues and evil-minded characters an opportunity of visiting upon their devoted victim, all the ills attending combined power, when exerted to accomplish destruction. It works unseen, at all silent hours, and secret times and places; and, like death when summoning his diseases, pounces upon its devoted subject, and lays him prostrate in the dust. Like the great enemy of man, it has shown its cloven foot, and put the public upon its guard against its secret machinations." See William Morgan, *Illustrations of Masonry by one of the Fraternity who has devoted thirty years to the subject...* (N.p.: William Morgan, 1827), viii. This quote is taken from an edition published approximately a year after Morgan's abduction. The original edition was published by David C. Miller of Batavia, New York. For an online version of *Illustrations* see http://www.utlm.org/onlinebooks/captmorgansfreemasonrycontents.htm.
   A comparable Book of Mormon scripture is from Alma 17:63–65 (LDS 37:30–32): "For behold, they murdered all the prophets of the Lord who came among them to declare unto them concerning their iniquities; and the blood of those whom they murdered, did cry unto the Lord their God, for vengeance upon those who were their murderers; And thus the judgments of God did come upon these workers of darkness and secret combinations; yea, and cursed be the land for ever and ever unto those workers of darkness and secret combinations, even unto destruction, except they repent before they are fully ripe. And now my son, remember the words which I have spoken unto you: trust not those secret plans unto this people, but teach them an everlasting hatred against sin and iniquity." See Vogel, *Making of a Prophet*, 243.

6. Eli Bruce entered into his diary under the date 5 November 1830: "Not so much pain in my head as yesterday. Had a long talk with the father of *the Smith*, (Joseph Smith,) who, according to the old man's account, is the particular favorite of Heaven! To him Heaven has vouchsafed to reveal its mysteries; he is the herald of the latter-day glory. The old man avers that he is commissioned by God to baptize and preach this new

anti-Masonic writing dominated conversation across upstate New York and dramatically impacted Joseph Jr. and his family.[7] But more important for the prophet, Freemasonry provided a direct link to Old Testament times—a link he could not ignore.

During his tenure as Nauvoo mayor, John C. Bennett was the prime mover of establishing Freemasonry in Nauvoo.[8] But in Joseph Smith Jr., Bennett found a more than willing supporter. After receiving the required "dispensation" from Abraham Jonas, grand master of the Illinois Masonic Lodge, preparations were made for initiating the Nauvoo Lodge on 15 March 1842. That evening, the prophet received the first-degree rites and the next night he rose to the sublime degree, thus expediting within a day or so an elaborate process that took others many years to achieve.[9]

COMMUNITY OF CHRIST LIBRARY-ARCHIVES
Moonstone from the Nauvoo Temple

With Craft encouragement, Smith could identify with yet another Old Testament figure, King Solomon. Both men were titular leaders of their people, designated "sacred space" through the construction of temples, sought divine wisdom in their decision making, and initiated temple rituals to bring their followers closer to their God. The timing of the installation of the Nauvoo Lodge with the development of temple rituals is significant. The prophet appreciated the long-standing Masonic tradition

doctrine. He says that our Bible is much abridged and deficient; that soon the Divine will is to be made known to all, as written in the *new Bible*, or *Book of Mormon*." See Vogel, *Early Mormon Documents*, 3: 4.

7. Not long after the death of her husband, Lucinda Morgan joined the Mormon movement. Many in the scholarly church history community identify Lucinda as a plural wife of the prophet. See Todd Compton's useful explanation in his *In Sacred Loneliness*, 43–54.

8. Andrew Smith, *Saintly Scoundrel*, 75–77; Flanders, *Nauvoo*, 247.

9. There is a rather conspicuous omission of Nauvoo Freemasonry from the eight-volume history of the RLDS Church. However, it is mentioned in the *DHC*, 4: 550–52.

of strict secrecy and found it useful in the development of his own temple rituals. These rituals included secret symbols, words, signs, and penalties. Less than two months after his Masonic installation, on Sunday 1 May 1842, Joseph preached in the grove on the "keys of the kingdom." He explained:

> The keys are certain signs and words by which false spirits and personages may be detected from true, which cannot be revealed to the Elders till the Temple is completed. The rich can only get them in the Temple, the poor may get them on the mountain top as did Moses. The rich cannot be saved with charity, giving to feed the poor when and how God requires, as well as building. There are signs in heaven, earth and hell; the Elders must know them all, to be endowed with power, to finish their work and prevent imposition. The devil knows many signs, but does not know the sign of the Son of Man, or Jesus. No one can truly say he knows God until he has handled something, and this can only be in the holiest of holies.[10]

The sacred "something" referred to in his statement was too secret to identify even in his own historical record.

The earliest meetings of the Nauvoo Lodge were held in various secluded venues, including a room over Henry Miller's house[11] and the upper room of the Red Brick Store. But Joseph recognized immediately these venues were inadequate for the potentially significant divine insights that could emanate from the Craft. Within a year, in June 1843, the cornerstones of the Nauvoo Lodge's own temple

COMMUNITY OF CHRIST LIBRARY-ARCHIVES
Masonic apron owned by Joseph Smith Jr.

---

10. Flanders, *Nauvoo*, 248; *DHC*, 4: 608.
11. Hansen, *Quest for Empire*, 60–61.

were laid, and the Masonic temple was dedicated on 5 April of the next year. At its dedication, Smith proudly proclaimed the new structure as "the most substantial and best finished of all Masonic Temples in the Western States."[12] Such quick construction evidenced Freemasonry's importance to Nauvoo community life.

Not all early Latter Day Saints embraced Freemasonry, however. Martin Harris was an active anti-Mason and a member of the Palmyra anti-Masonic vigilance committee in 1827. William W. Phelps edited two anti-Masonic newspapers during his early years in New York. Also, George Washington Harris, a close associate of William Morgan in Batavia, New York, eventually married his widow, Lucinda Morgan, in a public ceremony. Neither Phelps nor George Washington Harris petitioned for initiation during their stay in Nauvoo.

COMMUNITY OF CHRIST LIBRARY-ARCHIVES

Joseph Smith's Red Brick Store in Nauvoo

But these men were the exception, as Smith's enthusiasm for Freemasonry was infectious. By the end of the summer of 1843, more than two hundred fifty candidates received initiation into the Nauvoo Lodge, which elevated in degrees approximately the same number.[13] During the period of Mormon occupation of western Illinois and eastern Iowa, no less than six Mormon lodges received their dispensations. Initiations soared to seven hundred members at a time when only one hundred Masons occupied non-Mormon lodges across the state of Illinois. This threatened greatly

12. *DHC*, 6: 287.

13. Homer, "Similarity of Priesthood," 29–30.

the gentile leadership structure of the Grand Lodge in Springfield, which, in October 1843, revoked the Nauvoo Lodge's dispensation to function.

Undaunted by the revocation, Smith continued initiating lodge brothers without informing the Illinois Grand Lodge. The practice of strict secrecy enabled the continued observance of the Craft, at least for a period of time. Within months, Smith saw the need to eliminate what he perceived as corruptions in the Craft rituals, and eventually withdrew his participation. Of course, most of the Mormon membership followed Smith out of the Craft. Masonic ritualism definitely influenced, and eventually gave way to, temple ritualism.

The Masonic standard of secrecy applied to the women of Nauvoo as well. In the newly organized Female Relief Society, the prophet and church leaders sent a written message that counseled Society members to be watchful for men attempting to seduce women under the authority of the church leadership.

> We have been informed that some unprincipled men...have been guilty of such crimes—We do not mention their names, not knowing but what there may be some among you who are not sufficiently skill'd in Masonry as to keep a secret.... Let this epistle be had as a private matter in your Society, and then we shall learn whether you are good masons. We are your humble servants in the Bonds of the New & Everlasting Covenant. Joseph Smith, Hyrum Smith, Heber C. Kimball, Willard Richards, Vinson Knight, and Brigham Young.

Ironically, Joseph used "New & Everlasting Covenant" in his 12 July 1843 statement on polygamy, and the term became a preferred expression for the Mormon marital institution. Also, evidence would soon reveal that some of those who signed the written message to the Relief Society actually took plural wives and thus were among those about whom the women were cautioned.

The Oath of Secrecy and the Council of Fifty

VITAL TO JOSEPH Smith Jr.'s secret underground was the authority he vested in a "special council" of decision makers established "to organize the political kingdom of God in preparation for the second coming of Christ." Participants used numerous references to the council including "Special Council," the "Kingdom of God," the "Council of the Kingdom," the "Living Constitution,"[14] and the "Council of the Gods." Smith even referred to the council in public as "YTFIF." The oath of secrecy that each councilmember swore was based on the personal trust the prophet had with each person. Also, conspicuously missing from the council membership list were his two counselors in the First Presidency, Sidney Rigdon and William Law. The timing of these omissions suggests the presence of conflict within the First Presidency.[15]

Joseph wrote in his diary under the date of the preliminary meeting of 10 March 1844 that of the Council of Fifty membership "he required perfect secrecy." Each member was sworn under the penalty of death to withhold all information from the public about the council's actions. Password initiations to the Council of Fifty were similar to those in the temple endowment ceremony.[16]

The purpose of the Council of Fifty included the creation of a political kingdom with laws that superseded the federal government and even the United States Constitution, all in preparation for the Second Coming. Those specially chosen for the council proved their ability to maintain other oaths of silence. Many were Danites and Masons, and many embraced polygamy or gave family members into polygamous marriages. Some had received the secretive second anointing. These multi-layered oath relationships were important to build the trust to participate in "building the kingdom of God." Interestingly, no member of the Quorum of Seventy or even the prophet's younger brother, Samuel, who had received his second anointing, received membership in the Council of Fifty. The prophet's trust

14. The term comes from the failure of a council committee to successfully rewrite the Constitution of the United States to conform to the political kingdom of God. On 18 April 1844, Orson Pratt confessed the committee's failure, at which time Joseph Smith Jr. prophesied to the entire council a resolution to the issue by claiming, "Ye are my constitution." Forty years later Pratt remembered the statement to mean that rather than having a written constitution, the focus of their failed efforts, the council itself was a "living constitution." For further explanation see Quinn, *Origins of Power*, 131.

15. In the spring of 1842, the prophet greatly offended the Rigdon family with his alleged polygamous proposal to Sidney's daughter Nancy. William Law's opposition to the church's real estate policies, political involvement, and the "new and everlasting covenant" no doubt caused distrust as well. On 16 April 1844, Law was excommunicated.

16. Quinn, *Origins of Power*, 129.

extended to some nonmembers. He based his decision to invite Gentiles into the secret fellowship on his perception that ultimately the political kingdom of God would extend to those not baptized, and thus they needed representation also.

Clearly the millennial expectation dominated the agenda of the Council of Fifty while they addressed secular issues of the day. These issues included sending international ambassadors to England, France, Russia, the Republic of Texas, and Mexico-owned California. But Smith was concerned about domestic tranquility as well. Reports identified safety problems for United States citizens migrating into the borderlands of Texas and Oregon. He was also concerned about the relationship between American citizens and Native Americans, and those subjected to the abuse of "robber... and the desperado." To address national and international problems, on 26 March 1844 Smith petitioned Congress to empower him to raise one hundred thousand armed volunteers to protect the rights and liberties of American citizens against foreign invasions and domestic feuds. Four days later, Smith sent his petition to President John Tyler.[17] Using his experience in leading men into battle and his Nauvoo militia rank as lieutenant general, Smith felt equal to the task. Such notoriety could elevate him to a national personality, and his expeditionary force could prove useful in his plans to redeem Jackson County in the future.

But even with these credentials, his march to the most public office in the land required much secret planning. The more his grand designs developed and the more people he entrusted with them, the more vulnerable he became. Exposure of various aspects of church ritual and his political aspirations would have dire consequences for his personal safety and jeopardized unity within his movement.

---

17. *DHC*, 6: 275–77, 281–82.

CHAPTER EIGHTEEN

Joseph Smith Jr., Presidential Candidate in the Election of 1844

Substantive Steps to Build the Kingdom of God

THE MOST AMBITIOUS responsibility of the Council of Fifty was to promote the election of Joseph Smith Jr. for the presidency of the United States. The prophet grew frustrated with ambitious state politicians, who promised much and delivered little, and national politicians, who acknowledged the legitimacy of his pleas yet lacked the courage to act. As he moved into the new year, Smith carefully considered his options. Having such low regard for politicians, on 29 January 1844, he approached his trusted Council of Twelve with these realities and they responded with a proposal that he run for the presidency of the United States.

Joseph Smith's frustrations boiled over from his thwarted attempts to find redress from the persecution of his movement in the past and his inability to build the kingdom in preparation for the millennial future. But Smith had learned a valuable lesson from his difficult and frustrating history. During the Kirtland years, the Zion's Camp march to forcibly liberate Zion in Independence, Missouri, and the extra-legal banking venture to finance the movement ended in failure. At Far West, aggression against the northern Missouri communities of Millport, Grindstone Fork, and Gallatin, and the Mormon attack on a state militia unit at Crooked River, forced the Saints to flee for their lives to Illinois. Now, in Nauvoo, the prophet's appeals to Illinois governor Thomas Ford prompted excuses that state-level assistance would cause civil war, and national politicians entangled

Smith's petitions for federal government support with the ongoing debate over states' rights.

Meaningful change could only happen by working within government rather than from outside it. This time the Mormon revolution would plot to overturn the federal government from within. However, this became a balancing act requiring considerable secrecy because Smith's prime directive was to usher in the kingdom of God in preparation for the Second Coming. From the very beginning, this was Smith's mandate from heaven, but secular governments stood in his way. His municipal government in Nauvoo established a veritable kingdom on the Mississippi River that was a microcosm of what he intended for the entire nation and ultimately the world.

In a church conference held in Nauvoo on 8 April 1844, the prophet took an important step to define the kingdom of God. He extended the borders of Zion from its original designation of Independence, Jackson County, Missouri, to include the entire nation. He told his audience:

> You know there had been great discussion in relation to Zion—where it is, and where the gathering of the dispensation is, and which I am now going to tell you. The prophets have spoken and written upon it; but I will make a proclamation that will cover a broader ground. *The whole of America is Zion itself from north to south, and is described by the Prophets, who declare that it is the Zion where the mountain of the Lord should be, and that it should be in the center of the land.* When Elders shall take up and examine the old prophesies in the Bible, they will see it.[1]

This proclamation caused the church leadership to broaden their understanding of their responsibilities. Smith realized that his current leadership structure was inadequate to meet the new challenge, so he approached his newly formed Council of Fifty with the question. Their decision was to nominate Joseph Smith Jr. for the presidency of the United States, and then from that powerful seat, the prophet could direct the creation of the kingdom of God from sea to shining sea.

His presidential nomination came as no surprise to Joseph since an article in the 1 October 1843 *Times and Seasons*, which he no doubt

---

1. *DHC*, 6: 318–19.

approved, had posed the question "Who Shall Be Our Next President?" Although not naming the prophet specifically, the reader could hardly avoid the obvious suggested answer.[2] Earlier yet, in July 1842, Smith had signaled a shift in the reading of the Book of Daniel passages that identified the "stone…cut out of the mountain without hands"[3] from being only spiritual to being political in interpretation. Smith divined that "the kingdom and dominion, and the greatness of the kingdom under the whole heaven, shall be given to the people of the saints of the Most High, whose kingdom is an everlasting kingdom, and all dominions shall serve and obey him"[4] and that this would be manifest under his leadership in the political context. The prophet anticipated a premillennial government supervised by the Mormon leadership, free from corrupt secular political discourse, and focused on theocratic ethics. Smith's kingdom of God would superimpose revelatory law upon human law, thus creating a theocracy whose dominion would extend over all the earth.[5]

The kingdom of God could be instituted only with Joseph Smith Jr. in the presidential chair. To accomplish this feat amid the coming presidential election season, events would have to move quickly. On 11 April 1844, acting under their authority, the Council of Fifty secretly coronated, ordained, and anointed Joseph Smith as "King, Priest, and Ruler over Israel on Earth."[6] Great care had to be taken to ensure the candidate's true motive remain hidden.

Other issues relating to the prophet's presidential election were selecting a running mate, creating a campaign platform, and organizing a

2. *Times and Seasons* 4, no. 22 (1 October 1843): 343–44.
3. Daniel 2:45 KJV.
4. Daniel 7:27 KJV.
5. For an explanation of the strong millennial connection see Hansen, *Quest for Empire*, 13–14.
6. William Clayton, a personal secretary to Joseph Smith Jr. and the Council of Fifty, recorded in his journal the instruction the prophet gave the Council: "Verily thus saith the Lord, and this is the name by which you shall be called, the Kingdom of God and his Laws, with the Keys and power thereof, and judgment in the hands of his servants, Ahman Christ." See George D. Smith, ed., *An Intimate Chronicle: The Journals of William Clayton* (Salt Lake City: Signature Books, 1991), 153. Clayton also mentioned the Council vote to support Joseph: "President Joseph was voted our P[rophet] P[riest] and K[ing] with loud Hosannas" (129).

campaign strategy. The selection of a vice-presidential candidate revealed much about Smith's motivation for his use of national politics to accomplish his sacred mandate. The prophet weighed carefully who would be the best person to be at his side during the campaign of 1844, but then gave the task of actual selection to his Anointed Quorum. This specially designated body of believers were recipients of their temple endowment, a sacred temple rite that offered individuals salvation should they remain faithful to God's commandments as defined by the prophet during their remaining days on this side of the veil. Composed of approximately sixty people, mostly couples, the Anointed Quorum grew from the participants in Smith's sacred prayer circles, which emerged in early May 1842. Many were members also of the Council of Fifty, although some of those were excluded.[7] That the Anointed Quorum assumed the task of choosing Smith's running mate, rather than the Council of Fifty, whose responsibility it was to organize the political campaign for the kingdom of God, signaled that Smith's intent was the ultimate union of church and state. With the election of the Mormon prophet and king, the United States' presidential chair would become a theocratic throne.

The Anointed Quorum selected the newly converted James Arlington Bennet[8] from New York as their choice to complete the Mormon ticket. Brigham Young baptized Bennet, a New York City newspaper publisher and hotelier on Long Island, in 1843. In selecting Bennet, the quorum may have been lured by New York's thirty-six Electoral College votes, the single largest of any of the twenty-seven states in the Union. Winning New York and adding Illinois's seven electoral votes to their total, Smith would be almost a third of the way to the 138 electoral votes needed for victory. Selecting an Easterner would balance the western candidacy of Joseph Smith; and that Bennet was a businessman with some means of

---

7. For example, the second counselor in the First Presidency, William Law, was dropped from the Anointed Quorum on 7 January 1844, and Lyman Wight was added on 14 May 1844. The best chronology of the make-up and actions of the Anointed Quorum can be found in Quinn, *Origins of Power*, 491ff. For a succinct explanation of the temple endowment and second anointing in the context of Smith's presidential ambitions, see Wicks and Foister, *Junius and Joseph*, 90–91.

8. The candidate's last name has been variously spelled "Bennett." For example, see Van Wagoner, *Sidney Rigdon*, 332.

financial support meant he could contribute significantly to a barren campaign treasure chest. Bennet was an excellent choice as a running mate.⁹

Smith approved the vice-presidential nomination and commissioned Willard Richards to inform Bennet of their decision. Richards did so on 4 March 1844. Not long after Richards sent his letter, rumor spread through Nauvoo that Bennet was not native-born and thus was ineligible for a presidential ticket.¹⁰ The rumor was false but was believed, so the Quorum met again to consider an alternative. This time, their choice was Solomon Copeland of Paris, Henry County, Tennessee. Although little is known about Copeland, that he was not a member of the church raised concern in the Anointed Quorum. However, Copeland's military background was a popular credential for national candidates. These considerations were resolved when Copeland rejected the offer.

In an interesting move, perhaps to gain a broader perspective from the two previously failed nominations by the Anointed Quorum, Smith assigned the vice-presidential selection to the Council of Fifty. During a 6 May council session, the members proffered the name of Sidney Rigdon, who enthusiastically accepted. Council of Fifty member Jedediah Grant recalled Rigdon's response:

> After listening to the instructions and viewing the order of the council, and the manifestations of the power of God through Elder [Joseph] Smith, [Rigdon] leaped for joy, and walked around the room as sprightly as a boy in his gayest frolics. Exclaiming, "Joseph, Joseph! Thou servant of the most High God, I will never leave nor forsake thee, for mine eyes now see what Kings and Prophets desired to see and hear."...Brother Joseph you have tried to shake me off for several

---

9. On 22 April 1842, John C. Bennett, chancellor of the University of the City of Nauvoo, conferred an honorary degree on Bennet. *DHC*, 4: 600–601.

10. *DHC*, 6: 244. The rumor was that Bennet was born in Ireland, thus violating the United States Constitutional requirement for the occupant of the presidential chair. See Article II, Section 1: "No person except a natural born Citizen, or a Citizen of the United States, at the time of the Adoption of this Constitution, shall be eligible to the Office of President; neither shall any Person be eligible to that Office who shall not have attained to the Age of thirty-five Years, and been fourteen Years a Resident with the United States." Bennet declined the nomination anyway.

years, but you cannot do it, I will hold on to the skirts of your garment, I am now determined never to let you go."

With his nomination, Rigdon saw an opportunity to heal his relationship with the prophet, which had been strained through the previous two years. Now Joseph had his running mate, completing the third-party ticket of Joseph Smith Jr. of Illinois and Sidney Rigdon of Pennsylvania. Although both men lived in Nauvoo, their campaign literature aptly identified Smith and Rigdon as hailing from different states.[12]

Positioning on the Issues: Smith's Campaign Platform

IN EARLY FEBRUARY 1844, Smith and his political advisers worked diligently to construct a campaign platform on which he could run. On 9 February, he publicly stated his position on nearly all the important political issues of the day. In a tract, actually penned mostly by William W. Phelps, the prophet's closest political adviser,[13] titled *General Smith's Views of the Powers and Policy of the Government of the United States*, Smith proved to be a serious candidate even though he faced overwhelming electoral challenges.[14] He introduced his *Views* by quoting the Declaration

11. Jedediah Grant, *A Collection of Facts Relative to the Course Taken by Elder Sidney Rigdon in the States of Ohio, Missouri, Illinois, and Pennsylvania* (Philadelphia: Brown, Bicking & Gilbert, 1844), 16. Another observer of Rigdon's spectacle, Orson Hyde, added that Rigdon "began to speak, then to shout, then to dance, and threw his feet so high that he lost balance, and came well nigh falling over backwards upon the stove." Also see Orson Hyde, *Speech of Elder Orson Hyde, Delivered Before the High Priest's Quorum, in Nauvoo, April 27th, 1845, Upon the Course and Conduct of Mr. Sidney Rigdon, and Upon the Merits of His Claims to the Presidency of the Church of Jesus Christ of Latter-day Saints* (Liverpool: James and Woodburn, 1845), 8–9. Both the Grant and Hyde quotes are from Van Wagoner, *Sidney Rigdon*, 332.

12. That the candidates hailed from different states informed the public that the ticket met the qualification outlined in the Twelfth Amendment to the Constitution: "The Electors shall meet in their respective states, and vote by ballot for President and Vice-President, one of whom, at least, shall not be an inhabitant of the same state with themselves."

13. W. W. Phelps knew much more about national and international politics than Smith. See Bruce A. Van Orden, "William W. Phelps's Service in Nauvoo as Joseph Smith's Political Clerk," *Brigham Young University Studies* 32, nos. 2 and 3 (Winter/Spring 1991): 88, 90.

14. *History of the RLDS Church*, 2: 713–26.

Title illustration from Joseph Smith's 1844 presidential platform

of Independence and the Constitution of the United States. He referred to Benjamin Franklin and to previous presidents, from George Washington to John Quincy Adams, with great appreciation. Not surprisingly, Smith indicted Van Buren as a "miserable sycophant" for his duplicity on slavery and other issues.

Then Smith moved into his rationale for running by demanding redress for persecuted citizens (a less-than-veiled reference to his own plight). He called for public affirmation that the president of the United States in fact retained power to use the military to suppress rebellion and mobs. Having spent so much time in jail cells, Smith had witnessed prisoner abuse, so he advocated turning penitentiaries into seminaries of learning. Next, Smith established his position on a number of key issues that confronted the nation starting with the vexing social issue of slavery. His language showed his agreement with the prevailing view of slaves as personal "property" of their owners. Yet he called for the elimination of slavery by 1850, with Congress to subsidize slave owners with "a reasonable price" from government revenues received from federal land sales. Smith demanded efficiency in national and state governments as a way to reduce taxes and spending and sided with Whigs with his support for a national bank.

Joseph Smith did not limit his platform to domestic policy issues but addressed foreign policy as well. He insisted on international rights on the high seas. On the issue of territorial expansion, he stated that if, by their petition, Texas applied for admission, the United States should extend "the right hand of fellowship," and the same should be offered to Mexico and Canada. As relations between Great Britain and the United States cooled over the boundary dispute regarding Oregon Territory, Smith simply stated, "Oregon belongs to this government honorably,"[15] suggesting his alignment with northern Democrats.

On 9 February 1844, Smith's *Views* hit the streets and became one of the most widely spread literary pieces ever distributed by the church. By the end of the month, John Taylor had printed some 1,500 copies. Still not enough, *Views* was republished in Nauvoo; Pittsburgh and Philadelphia; Pontiac, Michigan; Kirtland; and New York City. More information about Smith's plans emerged from newspaper interviews. For example, in mid-April 1844, the prophet declared:

> As the "*world is governed too much*," and there is not a nation or dynasty, now occupying the earth, which acknowledges Almighty God as their lawgiver, and as "crowns won by blood, by blood must be maintained," I go emphatically, virtuously, and humanely for a THEO-DEMOCRACY, where God and the people hold the power to conduct the affairs of men in righteousness and where liberty, free trade, and sailor's rights, and the protection of life and property shall be maintained inviolate for the benefit of ALL.[16]

Smith's observation revealed his willingness to breech Thomas Jefferson's "wall of separation" between government and religion.

Church leaders quickly launched the presidential campaign by commissioning more than three hundred missionaries to the states and even to

---

15. *General Smith's Views of the Powers and Policy of the Government of the United States* (Nauvoo, Illinois: printed by John Taylor, 1844), Pamphlet Collection, Community of Christ Library-Archives.
16. "History of Joseph Smith," *Latter Day Saints' Millennial Star* 23 (22 June 1861): 391, Microfilm Collection, Community of Christ Library-Archives.

Wisconsin Territory to proclaim the candidacy of their prophet. Council of Twelve president Brigham Young ordered that

> [All] able Elders...will preach the truth in righteousness, and present before the people "General Smith's Views of the Powers and Policy of the General Government," and seek diligently to get up electors who will go for him for the Presidency. All the Elders will be faithful in preaching the Gospel in its simplicity and beauty, in all meekness, humility, long-suffering and prayerfulness; and the Twelve will devote the season to traveling, and will attend as many conferences as possible."[17]

Within a month Joseph Smith Jr.'s campaign for the presidency of the United States was well organized and in full swing.

To make official his candidacy, and hopefully to gain valuable publicity, Smith needed to be nominated at state and national party conventions. The state convention convened on 17 May 1844, in the upper room of Smith's Red Brick Store. Delegates threw their support joyously to the prophet.

At the national level, Whig party favorite Henry Clay received his nomination by acclamation on 1 May 1844 in Baltimore, Maryland, and the Democrats met to nominate their candidate, James Knox Polk of Tennessee, at the end of the month in the same city. Thus, it made sense that Smith would follow suit and plan for a national nominating convention in Baltimore, as well. The Mormons scheduled their convention for mid-July. However, due to Smith's assassination in June, the convention assembled but chose neither to nominate nor to endorse any other candidate for the presidency.[18]

To the surprise of many local observers, Joseph Smith Jr. did win an informal election shortly after he launched his presidential campaign. On the Mississippi River packet-steamer *Osprey*, navigating regularly between Nauvoo and St. Louis, passengers conducted a straw poll among the presidential aspirants. Both men and women voted, with election results that

---

17. For a list of the political missionaries and their assigned states and territories, see *DHC*, 6: 335–40. Young's commissioning statement is found at the end of that list.
18. *Davenport (Iowa) Gazette* 3, no. 52 (August 15, 1844): 2, transcript, John J. Hajicek, *Newsclippings from Iowa and Illinois 1841–1849* (Burlington, Wis.: John J. Hajicek, 1992), 79.

heavily favored Smith. In the Wednesday 8 May 1844 issue of the *Nauvoo Neighbor*, the editor reported:

> General Joseph Smith, 26 gentlemen, 3 ladies
> Henry Clay (Whig), 6 gentlemen, 2 ladies
> Martin Van Buren (Democrat), 2 gentlemen, 0 ladies.[19]

Even skeptics who knew that Smith had virtually no chance of moving from the Mansion House to the White House conceded that should the election be close, Smith's electoral votes could possibly determine the outcome or at least throw the election into the House of Representatives. Neither the Democrats nor the Whigs wanted this to happen. Smith's independent political party was without a formally announced name—a detail no doubt on the national convention agenda. However, with a formal, fully functioning national campaign apparatus in place that included seasoned campaign advisers and candidate handlers on staff, a comprehensive campaign platform established, more than three hundred "political missionaries" scattered throughout the country spreading the political gospel, and the Council of Fifty to guide the process, Smith was certain to become at least a minor national figure on the American political scene.

Overwhelming Problems at Home

THE MORMON PROPHET faced significant problems at home, both among his church leaders and with outside forces in western Illinois. The collision of these two important influences in Smith's life ultimately led to his arrest, along with his older brother, Hyrum. Joseph Smith Jr.'s final chapter would focus on his attempts to resolve dissent originating at the highest levels of church administration.

Some within the movement who had observed Smith dabble in Freemasonry, initiate secretive temple rituals that included his speculations on polygamous celestial marriage, establish an underground ecclesiastical government tasked with his election to the presidency of the

---

19. "For President, Gen. Joseph Smith, Nauvoo, Illinois," *Nauvoo Neighbor* 2 no. 2 (8 May 1844): 2. It is interesting to note that those who conducted the straw poll offered the franchise to women, a privilege not constitutionally extended until 1920. An analysis of the straw poll suggests the possibility that an overwhelming number of passengers were Mormons.

United States, call for the destruction of the United States government to be replaced with a theocratic kingdom of God, and all the while heard his public denials, believed the prophet was taking the church away from its fundamental mission. The last straw for these concerned church members may have been the decision of the Council of Fifty to covertly coronate, ordain, and anoint the prophet as "King, Priest and Ruler over Israel on Earth" on 11 April 1844.

The person with the highest authority to rein in the prophet and most willing to do so was William Law, appointed second counselor in the First Presidency in early April 1841. A man of significant personal resources and possessor of great respect among the church community, William Law could effectively question the direction the prophet was taking the church. Unfortunately for Law, the Council of Fifty excommunicated him in an extra-legal church trial on 18 April, which eliminated his access to the secretive, internal decision making.[20] Rather than follow the example of the previously excommunicated second counselor, Oliver Cowdery, who had left the church community at Far West in 1838, at least for the present, Law stayed in Nauvoo and initiated a two-pronged strategy to deal with the crisis that he felt faced the church. His first effort was to form his own "Reformed Mormon Church" just three days after his excommunication. Law's followers wanted to restore the church back to its spiritual roots and repudiate the secretive exercises that had steered the church away from the Christian mainstream.

Smith took the Reformed Church seriously when he learned that on 12 May some three hundred people attended to hear a series of sermons that blasted his alleged spiritual-wife doctrine and his attempts to combine church and state. The timing of these sermons coincided with the prophet's same-day public proclamation that he would be "one of the instruments of setting up the kingdom of Daniel by the word of the Lord" and his intention to "lay a foundation that will revolutionize the whole

---

20. In an irregular move, the Council of Fifty made the decision for Law's excommunication rather than an ecclesiastical church court. Added to the proceedings were the names of Wilson Law and Robert D. Foster. None of the accused was a member of the Council of Fifty. For a discussion of the irregularities see Quinn, *Origins of Power*, 125–27.

world."[21] Such claims bolstered charges that Smith had simply gone too far and had moved the church in the wrong direction.

More significantly, William Law believed that the best way to deal with what he perceived as abuse was to expose the secrecy of Joseph Smith's theological extremism. On 7 May, a delivery wagon rolled into Nauvoo carting a printing press for the Law brothers. Three days later, the Laws published their prospectus for a new Nauvoo newspaper, the *Nauvoo Expositor*. It took a month to prepare the first and only issue of the *Expositor*, which hit the streets of Nauvoo on 7 June 1844. Fifteen resolutions highlighted in the *Expositor* signaled their discontent and suggested where the prophet had led the people astray. Two examples are:

> Resolved 4th, That the hostile *spirit* and *conduct* manifested by Joseph Smith, and many of his associates towards Missouri, and others inimical to his purposes, are decidedly at variance with the true spirit of Christianity, and should not be encouraged by any people, much less by those professing to be the ministers of the gospel of peace.
>
> Resolved 14th, That we hereby notify all those holding licences to preach the gospel, who know they are guilty of teaching the doctrine of other Gods above the God of this creation; the plurality of wives; the unconditional sealing up against all crimes, save that of sheding innocent blood; the spoiling of the gentiles, and all other doctrines, (so called) which are contrary to the laws of God, or to the laws of our country, to cease preaching, and to come and make satisfaction, and have their licences renewed.[22]

Many of the charges listed by the Laws were associated with rites performed by priesthood leaders in the privacy of the Nauvoo Temple. The *Expositor* was not the first effort to reveal to the public the secretive temple rituals. Two years earlier, John C. Bennett had published exposés in the *Sangamo Journal* (Springfield, Illinois) and in his book titled *History of the Saints*. But those within the movement knew that Bennett was prone to exaggeration and misrepresentation.[23] Bennett had little legitimacy among believers, so it was easy for him to be dismissed. Joseph Smith's response to

21. Quinn, *Origins of Power*, 644.
22. *Nauvoo Expositor* 1, no. 1 (7 June 1844): [2].
23. Homer, "Similarity of Priesthood," 47.

Prospectus of the Nauvoo Expositor

Bennett's claims against the church, which Smith published in the church-sponsored *Times and Seasons*, marginalized his accuser.[24]

With William Law, however, the circumstances were different. The second counselor tapped a source of discontent that had grown over time with blatant duplicity, unexplained rumors, and public statements that seemed to verify dissenter suspicions. Where Bennett left Nauvoo with

24. "To the Church of Jesus Christ of Latter Day Saints, and to All the Honorable Part of Community," *Times and Seasons* 3, no. 17 (1 July 1842): 839–42.

few major allies, Law received strong support from some very influential church members, including his brother, Wilson Law, major general in the Nauvoo Legion; Robert D. Foster, surgeon-general; Austin Cowles, brevet brigadier general of the Nauvoo Legion, justice of the peace, and Nauvoo High Council member; Seventy James Blakeslee; and Chauncey Higbee and Charles Ivins, both prominent businessmen.[25]

Smith could not easily discredit these church leaders or defend against the challenges they posed. Now serving as mayor, the prophet presented his case against the dissidents to the Nauvoo City Council and declared that the *Expositor* "is a nuisance, and stinks in the nose of every honest man."[26] On Monday evening 10 June 1844, the Nauvoo Legion stood by while Nauvoo law officers carried out Mayor Smith's order to destroy the *Expositor* press.[27] This action initiated a series of events that outran Smith's ability to control and eventually resulted in his demise.

---

25. Flanders, *Nauvoo*, 308.

26. "Nauvoo City Council Minutes," 8–10 June 1844, as presented in John E. Hallwas and Roger D. Launius, *Cultures in Conflict: A Documentary History of the Mormon War in Illinois* (Logan: Utah State University Press, 1995), 153.

27. See *DHC*, 6: 448:

> *To the Marshal of said City, greeting.* You are here commanded to destroy the printing press from whence issues the *Nauvoo Expositor*, and pi the type of said printing establishment in the street, and burn all the *Expositors* and libelous handbills found in said establishment; and if resistance be offered to your execution of this order by the owners or others, demolish the house; and if anyone threatens you or the Mayor or the officers of the city, arrest those who threaten you, and fail not to execute this order without delay, and make due return hereon.
>
> By Order of the City Council,
> Joseph Smith, Mayor
>
> Marshal's Return—"The within-named press and type is destroyed and pied according to order, on this 10th day of June, 1844, at about 8 o'clock p. m."

CHAPTER NINETEEN

Escape, Apprehension, and Assassination

Promises Made, Promises Broken

NEWS OF THE *Expositor* destruction traveled fast to nearby Carthage and Warsaw. Within a matter of days, crowds formed in both western Illinois communities to hear agitated speeches challenging the rationale for the destruction of the *Expositor*. Inflamed newspaper articles by Thomas C. Sharp, editor of the *Warsaw Signal*, invoked the same extermination language that the Mormons had heard seven years earlier. On 12 June, Sharp wrote:

> We hold ourselves at all times in readiness to cooperate with our fellow citizens in this state, Missouri, and Iowa, to exterminate—UTTERLY EXTERMINATE, the wicked and abominable Mormon leaders, the authors of our troubles.... War and extermination is inevitable! Citizens ARISE, ONE and ALL!!!—Can you stand by, and suffer such INFERNAL DEVILS! To rob men of their property and rights, without avenging them. We have no time for comment, every man will make his own. LET IT BE MADE WITH POWDER AND BALL!!![1]

People felt threatened by events in Nauvoo. The article exposed the outsider frustration, which had boiled over to vigilantism.

Suspicions that Smith and the Mormon leadership were "above the law" were confirmed when the prophet and seventeen others were arrested

---

1. "The Nauvoo Expositor," *Warsaw Signal*, 12 June 1844, 2, Microfilm Collection, Community of Christ Library-Archives.

on the morning of 17 June. The defendants appeared before the non-Mormon but very friendly judge, Daniel H. Wells. After hearing both sides of the indictment that Smith ordered the destruction of the press, Wells dismissed the charges and released the prisoners.[2] Like the foiled extradition attempt a year earlier, it appeared as though Smith would escape prosecution again.

With tension in the air, on the 18th Smith called out the Nauvoo Legion and the police force, totaling some five thousand men, all for the protection of the city. This official command became very problematic later, as Smith's enemies interpreted it as a treasonous, offensive measure rather than defensive in nature. With the Legion assembled before him, Smith climbed onto a platform across Water Street from the Mansion House and gave his last address to his people. For ninety minutes the prophet, dressed in full military uniform, alerted them to possible attack by surrounding enemies, and vowed his willingness to fight to the death to defend their community: "Will you stand by me to the death, and sustain at the peril of your lives, the law of our country, and the liberties and privileges which our fathers have transmitted unto us, sealed with their sacred blood?" The audience shouted a tumultuous "Aye!" Then, dramatically the lieutenant general drew his sword and thrust it toward the sky. With unswerving determination he yelled, "I have unsheathed my sword with a firm and unalterable determination that this people shall have their legal rights, and be protected from mob violence, or," he assured them, "my blood shall be spilt upon the ground like water, and my body consigned to a silent tomb!"[3] The pageantry and resoluteness of the prophet's oratory left an indelible impression, allayed fears, and assured Nauvoo citizens that he would protect them, or die in the attempt.

During the next week, Joseph Smith and Governor Thomas Ford exchanged letters, forcing the prophet to justify his actions. Unconvinced, the governor informed Smith of his pending arrest. But Ford did guarantee *"the safety of all such persons as may thus be brought to this place from Nauvoo*

---

2. *History of the RLDS Church*, 2: 738; Court documents were placed in the *DHC*, 6: 488–91.

3. *DHC*, 6: 499.

Lieutenant General Joseph Smith Jr. speaking to the Nauvoo Legion and citizens from the stand across from the Mansion House on the corner of Water and Main Streets in Nauvoo

either for trial or as witness for the accused."[4] This was a promise far beyond the governor's ability to keep.

With his arrest a foregone conclusion, everyone around Smith agreed that incarceration would mean his death. So Smith privately contemplated his best course of action—to escape while there was still time. Joseph secretly planned evacuation of his own family and his brother Hyrum's

---

4. *History of the RLDS Church*, 2: 742; *DHC*, 6: 537.

family, and then the rest of the church members would follow.⁵ But for now, the prophet decided to escape arrest. As the sun set on the evening of 22 June, Joseph, Hyrum, Willard Richards, and Orrin Porter Rockwell climbed into a leaky skiff, pushed away from the Nauvoo shoreline, and rowed across the Mississippi River to the Iowa side. The two-mile journey became hazardous as Rockwell rowed against the rain-swollen current. The passengers had to bail water with their boots to avoid the boat being swamped; yet they made it to the other side successfully but soaked.

Word of the prophet's escape hit the Nauvoo streets with shock. Just days earlier, Smith had given his stirring speech assuring his absolute loyalty, and now he had deserted his followers during their time of greatest need. To make matters worse, rumors circulated throughout that mobs were forming against the community.

On 23 June, the thunder of hooves from the twenty members of a Carthage posse could be heard in the distance. They arrived in Nauvoo with a warrant from the governor to arrest the prophet. Only Porter Rockwell, who had just returned, knew where the escapees were, and, of course, he remained silent. After the posse left town, church leaders Reynolds Cahoon and Hiram Kimball went to the Mansion House and demanded that Emma write her husband to persuade him to return. She did so and sent the letter with her trusted nephew, Lorenzo Wasson. Rockwell agreed to escort the three men to the prophet's hiding place.

The men found the fugitives in the early afternoon packing provisions to continue their flight, and the conversation was not cordial. As Joseph read Emma's letter, Cahoon could hold back his frustration no longer. He blurted out, "You always said if the church would stick to you, you would stick to the church, now trouble comes and you are the first to run!" Kimball complained as well. Together, Cahoon, Kimball, and even his close nephew, Wasson, called the prophet's actions cowardly and stated that the mobs would destroy all their possessions and leave everyone

5. Joseph told Emma to prepare for a trip by steamboat to Portsmouth, Ohio, where he would contact them and continue east. Whether Joseph actually intended for these plans to be carried out remains a mystery. He made no further entries in his personal journal after 22 June 1844. Others wrote that the prophet intended to lead the church into the western territories. Events at Carthage Jail left to other leaders the future of the church. See Newell and Avery, *Mormon Enigma*, 185–86.

homeless. They reminded him that the governor did, after all, guarantee his safety should he surrender.

The accusation of cowardice struck Smith like a thunderbolt and stopped him in his tracks. After pausing for somber reflection, the prophet then looked at the men and said, "If my life is of no value to my friends it is of none to myself." Joseph then turned to Porter Rockwell and asked, "What should I do?" Rockwell answered, "You are the oldest and ought to know best; as you make your bed, I will lie with you." Then Joseph looked at Hyrum, who advised, "Let us go back and give ourselves up, and see this thing out." Joseph stared away and then said, "If you go back I will go with you, but we shall be butchered." Hyrum assured his younger brother, "No, no; let us go back and put our trust in God, and we shall not be harmed. The Lord is in it. If we live or have to die, we will be reconciled to our fate."[6] Late that afternoon, the men arrived back in Nauvoo to await their arrest.

COMMUNITY OF CHRIST LIBRARY-ARCHIVES
Joseph Smith III (age about 10)

Joseph spent the evening with his family and arose early the next day, 24 June 1844. He called for his family and closest friends to gather in the north room of the Mansion House. He sat his eldest son, Joseph, in a chair and gave him a father's blessing. His language was specific, clear, and understood by those in the room. The prophet conferred a blessing, not of specific appointment to church leadership since the boy was just eleven years old, but of succession by "right of lineage," as Joseph III would explain many years later. Actually, this was not the first such blessing. A year earlier in the Red Brick Store, the prophet had

6. *DHC*, 6: 549–50.

anointed his son Joseph's head with oil, and offered a blessing using very similar language.[7]

After the blessing, Joseph kissed each family member and then said to them, "I go as a lamb to the slaughter, but if my death will atone for any faults I have committed during my lifetime I am willing to die."[8] It was time for Joseph to surrender himself to authorities in Carthage, the seat of government in Hancock County. His escort to Carthage waited outside. Mournfully he rode away but returned later that afternoon to everyone's surprise, but he was not a free man. Joseph had called out the militia on 18 June when he was being pursued by a posse that held a warrant for his arrest. Governor Ford requested that he officially disarm the Nauvoo Legion, which was technically still mustered. After issuing the order to disarm the Legion, Joseph and Emma gave each other their farewells at six o'clock in the late afternoon—the last time they would see each other alive. Years later, in an 1856 interview, Edmund C. Briggs, a leader in the efforts to reorganize the church, asked Emma about this emotional parting:

> I [Briggs] then said to her: "Did Joseph have any knowledge or premonition of his death before it took place?" She replied: "Yes, he was expecting it for some time before he was murdered. About the time he wrote those letters that are in the Book of Covenants he was promised if he would go and hide from the church until it was cleansed he should live until he had accomplished his work in the redemption of Zion, and he once left home intending not to return until the church, was sifted and thoroughly cleansed; but, his persecutors were stirring up trouble at the time, and his absence provoked some of the brethren to say he had run away, and they called him a coward, and Joseph heard of it, and he then returned, and said, 'I will die before I will be called a coward.' He was going to find a place and then send for the

---

7. These blessings should not be misidentified as prayers of prophetic succession. Certainly Joseph III did not consider them as such. In a letter composed in 1896, Joseph Smith III could not remember that his father used the word "ordain" in any of the blessings, but simply said "Whether this may be considered an ordination or not, it was a setting apart by blessing, and I have so considered it." See Joseph Smith III to J. M. Stubbart, Octavia, Nebraska, 19 May 1896, Joseph Smith III Letterbook, 6: 458–59, Vault Collection, Community of Christ Library-Archives.

8. Mary B. (Smith) to Ina (Smith) Coolbrith, 27 March 1908, Vault Collection, Community of Christ Library-Archives.

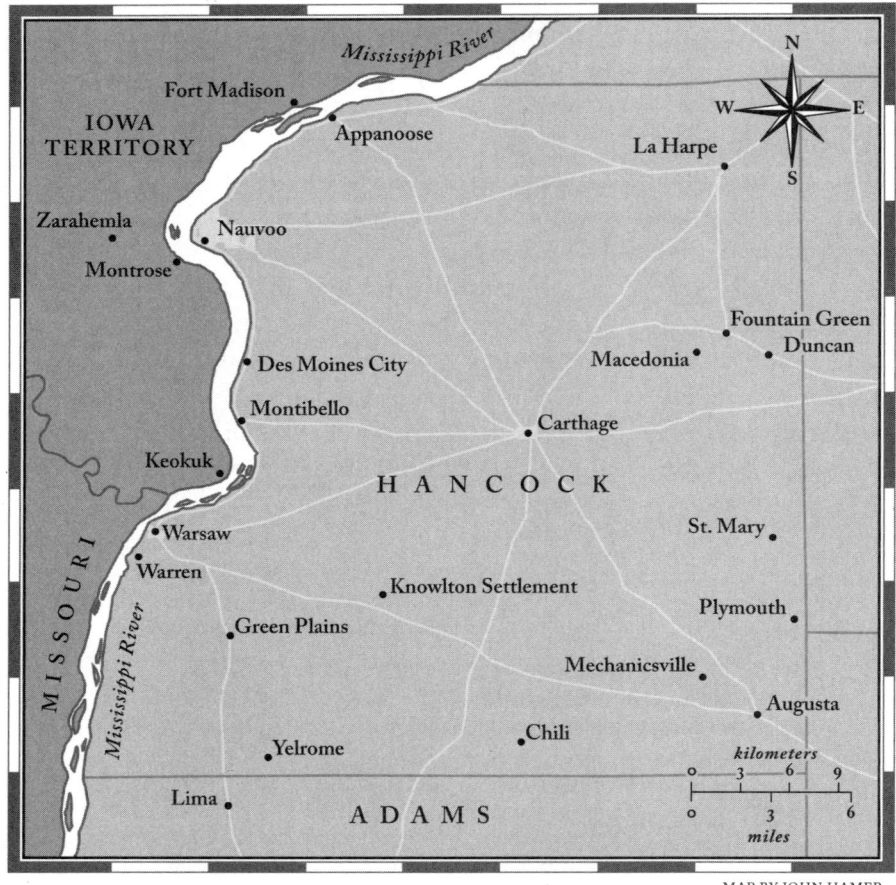

Hancock County, Illinois, in 1844

family, but when he came back I felt the worst I ever did in my life, and from that time I looked for him to be killed, and had felt so bad about it, that when he was murdered I was not taken by surprise, and did not feel so bad as I had for months before."

While she talked to us the tears flowed from her large, bright eyes like rain, and I could see in every act affection for Joseph.[9]

---

9. Edmund C. Briggs, "A Visit to Nauvoo in 1856," *Journal of History* 9, no. 4 (October 1916): 453–54.

Carthage Trials and Tribulations

By 1845, Hancock County was the most populous county in the state of Illinois with its 22,559 residents. At least half were followers of Joseph Smith Jr. Except when the Fifth Judicial Circuit sat for trial, Carthage was a rather typical western Illinois community with a few hundred permanent residents. But the Hancock County seat was a well-known venue for jurisprudence in western Illinois history. Many famous lawyers tried cases there, including Orville H. Browning, Archibald Williams, Stephen A. Douglas, and Abraham Lincoln. Also, historic decisions for the state of Illinois would be rendered in Carthage besides the Mormon prophet's in June 1844.[10]

Joseph, Hyrum, and their escort finally arrived in Carthage just before midnight on 24 June. The brothers turned themselves in the next morning amid a hostile atmosphere. The first charge against the Mormon prophet was for inciting riot, but the trial was deferred. As he and the others rose before the judge and started to walk out of the courtroom, authorities confronted the defendants, and Joseph and Hyrum were charged this time with treason.[11] The treason charge, weak at best, sufficed to bind over the men for trial and prevent their return to the safety of their Mormon citadel, Nauvoo.

Smith had faced treason charges before—the first being at Far West in November 1838. He had evaded those charges then, and now the prophet hoped that he could do it again. Unfortunately, this time would be different. Enforcement officers escorted them to Carthage Jail at the outskirts of town, as it turned out, more for protection than incarceration. Spectators called for their immediate execution, and it is likely that if members of the

---

10. Dallin H. Oaks and Marvin S. Hill, *Carthage Conspiracy: The Trial of the Accused Assassins of Joseph Smith* (Urbana: University of Illinois Press, 1975), 2–3. For example, almost a year later, in May 1845, a twenty-one-year-old Irishman named William Fraim, a deckhand on a Mississippi River steamer, was found guilty of killing a man in a drunken brawl. In this trial, spectators witnessed the only man ever to receive a hanging sentence in Hancock County. Fraim's unsuccessful defense was argued by a Springfield, Illinois, lawyer named Abraham Lincoln. Fraim was hanged three weeks after Lincoln's failed appeal of the sentence.

11. *History of the RLDS Church*, 2: 741.

guard appointed by the governor to protect the prisoners had had their way, they would have been happy to accommodate.

The prophet, safe in the jail for now, was in an impossible situation. He spent the next two days receiving visitors, reflecting about his life's struggles, and writing letters to various people, including his wife, Emma. He could no longer control events, and his charismatic personality, friendly handshake, and divine insights could no longer help him escape his predicament. He knew it and seemed resigned to his fate.

Assassination of the Prophet in Carthage, Illinois[12]

AS WITH SO many aspects of the church story, our understanding of crucial events has evolved over time. Such is the case with the events in Carthage Jail in late June 1844. The traditional understanding of the Carthage assassination has been based on Apostle Willard Richards's story. His credential of being in the jail when the attack happened and being just one of two survivors has naturally outweighed other interpretations. Richards published his account in the 1 August 1844 *Times and Seasons*.[13] However, from the details he provided it is possible to question the accuracy of some of his claims. Thus, it is important to consider other accounts as well in order to gain a fuller understanding.

During the few days of their incarceration, visitors streamed in and out of their jail cell, including Illinois governor Thomas Ford and Colonel Thomas Geddes of the Illinois state militia. But most were Mormon supporters and close friends. Some stayed through the night. On one evening, eight men slept on the cold jail cell floor. During the day, these men served as letter couriers and lookouts. Among these visitors were Joseph's bodyguard, Stephen Markham; Welsh convert and ship captain Dan Jones;

---

12. This account is a synthesis of several scholarly accounts of the tragic events at Carthage, Illinois. I am particularly appreciative and strongly influenced by Robert Wicks and Fred Foister in their *Junius and Joseph*. Another excellent interpretation is in Oaks and Hill's *Carthage Conspiracy*. Documentary support is provided in Hallwas and Launius's *Cultures in Conflict*. The traditionally accepted account of the assassination by Willard Richards is found in his "Two Minutes in Jail," *Times and Seasons* 5, no. 14 (1 August 1844): 598–99.

13. Richards, "Two Minutes in Jail," 598–99.

Apostles Willard Richards and John Taylor; and Mormon loyalists John S. Fullmer and Cyrus H. Wheelock.

Thursday 27 June 1844 was like so many hot and humid days in western Illinois. The month had been usually rainy and the normally dusty roads were a quagmire. After lunch, the brief shower, which ended by four o'clock, was not unexpected. The men raised the windows in the second-floor sitting room in hopes that a breeze would cool the room. Joseph and Hyrum were completing their third day in jail.

Rumors of assassination ran rampant through the countryside and in Carthage. Fearing the worst, Fullmer smuggled into the jail cell his single-barreled boot pistol, and Wheelock brought his six-barreled Allen's Patent Pepperbox. With some hesitation, the Smith brothers accepted the armaments.[14] At least now, the prisoners could defend themselves should an attack come.

Illinois governor Thomas Ford ordered elements of the Carthage Grays, a local militia unit, to ensure the prisoners' safety. Ford's selection of the Grays was suspect at best since several within the units had publicly threatened the lives of the Smith brothers just two days earlier. The governor's decision was possible evidence of his indirect participation in a conspiracy to end the lives of the Smith brothers.[15]

As the afternoon progressed, there was a somber mood among the men in the jail. With the other visitors on errands, only Willard Richards and John Taylor remained with the prisoners. The prophet had foretold his death on numerous occasions over the last fourteen years, but somehow had always escaped. Neither the visitors over the previous two days nor his cell mates could raise his depressed spirits. Hyrum read three accounts of prison escape episodes and the Three Nephites story from the Book of Mormon but not even that could bring a smile. His hopes for yet another miracle faded and time passed slowly. Joseph asked John Taylor, who had a

14. With the presentation of the weapons, Hyrum expressed to his younger brother his reservation. Joseph received the Pepperbox and gave it to Hyrum saying, "You may have to use this." Hyrum resisted, "I hate to use such things or to see them used." Joseph replied, "So do I, but we may have to, to defend ourselves." Seeing no other option, Hyrum took Wheelock's pistol. See *DHC*, 6: 607–608.

15. Two valuable studies to promote a conspiratorial theme are Oaks and Hill's *Carthage Conspiracy* and Wicks and Foister's *Junius and Joseph*.

beautiful tenor voice, to sing a popular song based on Matthew 25, "A Poor Wayfaring Man of Grief."

After supper, about five o'clock, a commotion broke the silence as a lookout spied a mob coming from Carthage toward the jail. The mob had painted their faces with gunpowder, mud, and water in a meager attempt to hide their identity. When they arrived at the jail, the prisoners heard angry voices yell for their surrender (evidently the assailants knew that the prisoners were not locked up in their dungeon cells). Following a brief scuffle with the guards,[16] several mobbers discharged their weapons up the second floor stairway. Then, after reloading, they charged up the stairs to the landing and attempted to burst their way into the room, only to find the prisoners blocking the door. One intruder fired through the door, striking Hyrum in the face just to the left side of his nose. His legs stiffened where he stood and he fell backward, striking the floor, and exclaimed: "I am a dead man."

Seeing his brother fall, Joseph cried out, "O dear! Brother Hyrum!" In a fit of rage, the prophet brandished the six-shot pistol provided the previous evening by Cyrus Wheelock and charged the door, which was still unopened. Pressed hard against the wall next to the door, Joseph opened it just enough to thrust his pistol around the casing. He snapped his revolver six times but only three barrels discharged, with his bullets striking three of the mobbers.[17] With his weapon emptied, he retreated across the room.

The intruders thrust their weapons through the doorway and opened up on the prisoners. Standing next to the window, Taylor was struck in the leg by a ball fired from the mob below; another shot, aimed at his chest, hit his pocket watch instead, at five o'clock, sixteen minutes, twenty-six

16. As part of the conspiracy, it is entirely possible that the small detachment of Carthage Grays who stood guard in the stairway had loaded their weapons with blanks. Eyewitness young William Hamilton reported that during the scuffle, the guards opened up on the mobbers at a distance of only twenty feet, yet no one was hit. Nor did the intruders take revenge on the guards for firing, but only pushed them out of the way.

17. William Vorhees (spelled also Vorhis and Voras) was wounded in the left shoulder, Charles Gallagher was grazed on the side of the face, and John Willis (spelled also Wills and Mills) received a bullet in the right wrist. As he was being carried from the jail, Willis proudly yelled to bystanders, "I shot Hyrum! And Joe shot me!" See William M. Daniels, Grand Jury Testimony, October 1844, Community of Christ Library-Archives.

seconds causing him to fall to the floor. Taylor rolled under the bed nearby and lay motionless. A third ball, fired from the doorway, struck Taylor's left hip and blew away a large piece of flesh.

As all this was happening, Richards claimed that he stood behind the door and took broad swipes with his cane at the half-dozen barrels protruding through the doorway but evidently without effect. The room quickly filled with gun smoke as the firing continued. A ball from the doorway grazed Hyrum's leg and yet another ripped through his chest and entered his head, below the jaw.

COMMUNITY OF CHRIST LIBRARY-ARCHIVES
The assassination of Joseph Smith

Amid the confusion and smoke, and perhaps as the men in the doorway reloaded their weapons, Joseph ran to the window and looked on the mob below. With an explosion, a single volley from the doorway hit Joseph in his right thigh but only caused a minor wound. Joseph had just enough time to climb through the window and perch on the sill; then he raised his arms and yelled the opening words of the Masonic distress call: "O Lord, My God."[18] Either he lost his balance and fell or he jumped to the pavement some fifteen feet below, at the feet of the angry mob. The prophet, landing hard on his side, was stunned.

Still, Joseph had only received one ball and it was certainly not fatal. Slowly the prophet moved one leg and then the other when a mobber grabbed him and propped him up against the well curb near where he had

---

18. The remainder of the Masonic plea was, "Is there any love for the widow's son?"

fallen. Surprisingly, during those next brief moments, no one stepped forward to shoot Joseph. Perhaps they could not find it in themselves to shoot a former Masonic brother. But pushing their way through the crowd were men from the stairway. Four assassins from Warsaw took their positions in front of the fallen prisoner, shouldered their rifles, and on command, fired at almost point blank.[19] The Mormon prophet slumped over dead.[20]

When he heard the huge explosion of the four-man firing squad, Richards, still in the upper room, ran to the window. He may have heard someone in the crowd yell the alarm that the Nauvoo Legion was coming through the woods. Rumors swirled through the day that a detachment was on the way to liberate the prisoners. Although it was only one person's imagination, his alarm was enough to quickly disperse the mob. Richards then rushed for the door when he heard Taylor's faint plea to take him too. The huge Mormon apostle easily pulled Taylor from beneath the bed, dragged him into the dungeon cell, and covered him with straw. Then, Richards awaited the return of the assassins to finish him off. However, the gunmen fled from the scene with the others. Except for a slight wound to his earlobe, Richards remained unscathed.[21]

19. The men who charged up the jail stairway and assaulted the prisoners were carefully selected from elements of the Warsaw militia. Jacob C. Davis, captain of the Warsaw Rifle Company, William N. Grover, captain of the Warsaw Cadets, and Major Mark Aldrich, commander of the Warsaw Independent Battalion, chose twenty men based on their courage and fighting skills. These twenty men were "to go and kill Joseph and Hiram Smith in the jail at Carthage." See Daniels, Grand Jury Testimony, October 1844.

20. Whether or not Joseph was alive when he hit the pavement has been debated. In his published account, Willard Richards claimed that the prophet was dead as he fell out the window; however, eyewitnesses below testified that Smith was still alive, thus necessitating the firing squad. That Joseph received five bullet wounds, four of them from the mob at point blank range, suggests that the prophet was still alive. Also, when Smith fell from the window Richards was still behind the door in the gun-smoke-filled room, making it nearly impossible for him to determine the status of the victim. Richards could not have seen Smith hit the pavement and admittedly did not go to the window until after the firing squad had discharged their weapons. See the argumentation on this point in Wicks and Foister, *Junius and Joseph*, 178.

21. Some historians who have closely studied the Richards account have discovered inaccuracies. For example, by his own admission, the prophet received only one ball in the upper room—the wound to his right leg. This would not have proved fatal, although Richards claimed that Joseph was dead when his body hit the ground, from his fall.

Multiple Causes for the Prophet's Assassination

NO ONE REASON can adequately explain why there was such hatred of Joseph Smith Jr. in western Illinois. Rather, a combination of forces stirred the anger against the Saints in general, and their leader specifically. Theological beliefs certainly played a role, but the church's potential domination of statewide Masonic organizations as well as county, state, and national politics was even more offensive. The greatest anger however grew from the prophet's exploitation of judicial privileges granted by his municipal charter. In the minds of area citizens, Joseph Smith Jr. had placed himself above the law during a time when people considered anti-republican behavior as a threat to their democratic institutions.

Religious beliefs entered into the milieu but only as a pretext for the destruction of the *Expositor*. Although the introduction of secretive salvific rites, including aberrant marital practices, offended some members of the church and were a key to understanding Smith's aspirations for a millennial future, those who gathered outside Carthage Jail on that fateful day in late June considered the prophet's religious thinking as relatively inconsequential. Opponents of Latter Day Saintism were willing to grant basic First Amendment protection even to the Mormons; besides, there were better reasons to assassinate the leaders.

Area newspapers seriously objected to Smith's religion, but more to lampoon the beliefs than use them as a direct reason for assassination. For example, in a February 1844 issue of the *Warsaw Message*, a rabid anti-Mormon sheet, was a poem titled "Buckey's Lamentation for Want of

---

Richards, still hiding behind the door, could not have known that. Second, Richards claimed that more than one ball came through the door before it opened. Today's tour guides at Carthage Jail are adamant that the existing door is the original. But there is only one bullet hole in the door, thus calling into question Richards's claim. Third, that Richards was completely hidden behind the door is also suspect. Willard Richards was a very large man, weighing more than three hundred pounds. The doorjamb is only about four inches from the north wall. There is no way that such a large man could remain hidden behind the door without being detected. The door could not have swung open very far with him standing behind it. Evidently, amid the confusion, the intruders ignored Richards altogether, especially since they were after the two Smith brothers. It is possible, therefore, to give Richards the benefit of the doubt on this point. See the argumentation on the various interpretations of what happened in Carthage Jail in Wicks and Foister, *Junius and Joseph*, 178–80fn76.

More Wives."[22] Using bird imagery, the poet exposed the identities of the two daughters of Bishop Edward Partridge (Emily Dow and Eliza M. Partridge), Eliza R. Snow, and Lydia Knight, the wife of Vinson Knight. These women were among the alleged plural wives of the prophet:

> He sets his snares around for all—
> And very seldom fails
> To catch some thoughtless PARTRIDGES
> SNOW-birds or KNIGHT-ingales![23]

A second satirical twenty-two verse sonnet appeared in the *Warsaw Signal* in April 1844. The fictitious poet, Buckey, confronted the Mormon prophet in the form of a rhyme. The twelfth and thirteenth verses portrayed Smith's amorous pursuit of Sidney Rigdon's daughter Nancy. Allegations suggested that the first counselor's daughter had rebuffed the prophet's overtures to become one of his plural wives. When his attempt was made public, Smith escaped criticism by claiming he was only challenging the limits of her virtue, and with her denial she passed the test. "Buckey's" poem described Smith's seduction:

> 12
> Although you tried, by priestly power
> To make this gentle creature cower
> And eat her words, that you might tower
> In priestly pride;
> But strong in truth, she in that hour
> Told you you lied.
>
> 13
> And when you found it would not do,
> Then like a coward [patroon], you
> Acknowledg'd what she had said was true
> Unto her sire;

---

22. It is possible that the *Warsaw Message* typesetter misspelled Buckey's name. Other references refer to this fictitious character as "Buckeye." For accuracy purposes, the name will be identified as spelled. Also between February and April 1844 owners changed the name of their newspaper from the *Warsaw Message* to the *Warsaw Signal*. Microfilm Collection, Community of Christ Library-Archives.

23. "Buckeye's Lamentation for Want of More Wives," *Warsaw Message*, 7 February 1844, 2.

> But then you'd nothing more in view
> Than just to try her—[24]

During the days following the murders, certainly church leaders viewed their religious faith as the primary reason for the Carthage assault. Joseph and Hyrum were viewed as martyrs for the faith. The earliest promotion of this view came in an *Extra* edition of the *Nauvoo Neighbor* on 30 June 1844; then on the following day, editors republished the article in the church's official organ, the *Times and Seasons*:

> They fell as Martyrs amid this tornado of lead, each receiving four bullets! John Taylor was wounded by four bullets in his limbs but not seriously. Thus perishes the hope of law; thus vanishes the plighted faith of the state; thus the blood of innocence stains the constituted authorities of the United States, and thus have two among the most noble martyrs since the slaughter of Abel, sealed the truth of their divine mission, *by being shot by a Mob for their religion!*[25]

Understandably, by couching the reasons for assassination in religious overtones, the surviving church leaders could sanctify the murders and bestow lasting martyrdom on the deceased brothers.

For their gentile neighbors, however, the strange Mormon religion played a far lesser role in the assassination. Area Masons had much to fear from the dramatic growth of the Craft in Nauvoo. The possibility of Joseph Smith Jr. gaining control of Freemasonry in Illinois by virtue of swamping Craft elections with overwhelming Mormon numbers was very real. This was Smith's intent since it would increase his power to implement his political aspirations in the coming year. Thus, even with his personal rejection of the Craft, Freemasonry could still be used as a stepping stone toward achieving political control of the state.

---

24. "The Buckey's First Epistle to Jo," *Warsaw Signal*, 25 April 1844, 1.
25. The *Neighbor Extra* hit the streets of Nauvoo at 3 o'clock on Sunday afternoon 30 June 1844. The lead article was titled "Awful Assassination! The Pledged faith of the State of Illinois stained with innocent blood by a Mob!" in *Nauvoo Neighbor,—Extra:* (30 June 1844): 1. The next day, the *Times and Seasons* ran essentially the same article as "Awful assassination of JOSEPH AND HYRUM SMITH!—The pledged faith of the State of Illinois stained with innocent blood by a Mob!" See *Times and Seasons* 5, no. 12 (1 July 1844): 560.

The dramatic increase of Mormon immigrants, who would become voters, proved a considerable asset as Smith pursued his political goals. Controlling the entire municipal government was no problem, but gaining influence at the county and state levels posed special challenges that required a careful strategy—a strategy immediately recognized by politicians across the state and from both the Democratic and Whig political parties.

At the national level, the announcement of Smith for the presidency of the United States only confirmed what many Illinoisans suspected. Few believed that Smith could win; however, in a close presidential campaign, Smith could influence the outcome in return for concessions on his numerous demands. By the spring of 1844, the presidential election was shaping up to be very close.

But perhaps the greatest cause for the assassination was the anger that grew from Joseph Smith Jr.'s anti-republican efforts to combine church and state. The Nauvoo municipal charter provided seemingly unlimited protection for the prophet. The *habeas corpus* shelter was Smith's best legal weapon in his arsenal of special privileges. Most evident was his escape from extradition during his confrontation with Missouri officers in Dixon, Illinois, in 1843. Many felt the parade procession of Smith and his family riding into Nauvoo made a mockery of the law, and no Illinois politician had the courage to oppose him. The Mormon vote was just too powerful.[26]

---

26. When election officials tallied the Hancock County, Illinois, votes in the presidential election the following November, the Democratic Party nominee, James Knox Polk of Tennessee, won by a margin of almost 2 to 1. See Wicks and Foister, *Junius and Joseph*, 226. In an ironic twist, religious foment did enter the presidential campaign of 1844 with the introduction of "Manifest Destiny" as an issue. With definite religious overtones to this issue, pious Calvinists saw national expansion as God's will. During the very heated campaign season, Democrats attacked Henry Clay's morality, claiming he violated every tenet of the Ten Commandments. See the widely circulated leaflet titled: "Henry Clay's Moral Fitness for the Presidency, Tested by the Decalogue." This claim stemmed from Clay's alleged revelry, brothel visits, drinking, and gambling. Another handbill cautioned:

> Christian Voters!
> Read, Pause and Reflect!
> Mr. Clay's
> Moral Character

For all these reasons, pressure increased to eliminate the Mormon obstacle in one of two ways: burn Nauvoo, the Mormon citadel, to the ground and leave "its men, women, and children...to the disposal of the soldiers," or assassinate its titular leader, Joseph Smith Jr.[27] The assassination on 27 June partly resolved the issue.

Conclusion to the Late Period of the Restoration

THE ENTIRE ASSASSINATION ordeal took only a matter of minutes, but with it, the Mormon journey entered a new phase. No longer could followers rely on revelatory utterings from their prophet Joseph Smith Jr. to address their spiritual needs. His death created a significant power vacuum, originally intended to be filled only by Jesus Christ at the Second Coming.

Future generations would disagree on a final assessment of the Restoration Era. Some would view Nauvoo Latter Day Saintism as the pinnacle of achievement of the "fullness of the gospel," while others would view the developments as escalating theological extremism ending in the "dark and cloudy days." Along with the high achievement of being a truly unique, American expression of key elements of the Old and New Testaments, the posterity of Latter Day Saintism would also have to carry some formative events of the Restoration Era, including polygamy, as their burden of history.

The Latter Day Saint movement during the Restoration Era exhibited symptoms of an American cultural schizophrenia that defies simple explanation. The host nation of Smith's Restoration movement, just more than two generations old, was torn between those wanting to retain their small-farm, rural way of life, while others worked toward an American life of urban industrialism. The national government based its sovereignty on the inalienable rights to life, liberty, and the pursuit of happiness for

---

See "1844: Polk and Manifest Destiny," in Paul Boller, *Presidential Campaigns* (New York: Oxford University Press, 1985), 78–83.

27. George T. M. Davis, *An Authentic Account of the Massacre of Joseph Smith, the Mormon Prophet, and Hyrum Smith, His Brother, Together with a Brief History of the Rise and Progress of Mormonism, and All the Circumstances Which Led to Their Death* (St. Louis, Mo.: Chambers and Knapp, 1844), 80–81, in Wicks and Foister, *Junius and Joseph*, 165.

its people, yet excluded significant segments of its population, including slaves, Native Americans, and women.

Reflecting similar conflict, Joseph Smith Jr.'s religion was birthed with a "peace gene"[28] as the movement functioned in Kirtland, Ohio, only to launch a military invasion aimed at retaking Jackson County, Missouri, and eventually, to draft its young men into the nation's largest state militia, in Nauvoo. The one God Joseph Smith Jr. encountered alone in the Sacred Grove at Palmyra, New York, at least as initially recorded between 1831 and 1832, became many gods ten years later in Nauvoo, Illinois. The public expression of monogamy established in the Book of Mormon text in 1830, and by unanimous church conference action in Kirtland in 1835, evolved secretly into polygamy at Nauvoo in 1843. Condemnation of secretive organizations as stated in their American scripture gave way to active involvement in one of the most secret societies—Freemasonry. The opposition to abolition at Kirtland and the public rejection of freeing slaves at Far West, Missouri, ended in an 1844 presidential campaign platform that advocated the end of slavery by no later than 1850. Latter Day Saintism emerged in April 1830 under the shelter of the freedom of religion protections of the "establishment clause" of the First Amendment, yet this same movement sponsored a presidential candidate in the election of 1844 who advocated the complete destruction of that wall of separation between church and state. Finally, the prophet of Mormonism, whose family roots ran deep into the nation's fight for national independence from King George III of England, was himself ordained king by secret coronation in early 1844.

Throughout his fourteen-year tenure as leader of the Mormon Restoration Era, the charismatic Joseph Smith Jr. pressed the limits of his prophetic leadership. Evidences of this tendency could be seen in his translation of the Book of Mormon, in his varying accounts of his epiphany in the Palmyra Grove, in the Zion's Camp march, in seeking to elude crushing debt with the Kirtland Bank venture, and in his military strategy during the Mormon War in Missouri.

28. Historian Richard P. Howard identified evidences of a "peace gene" in three important aspects of the early movement: statements found in the Doctrine and Covenants, the church's hymnody, and in official actions and statements by church leaders and conferences. See his "The Quest for Traces of a Peace Gene in Restoration History," *John Whitmer Historical Association Journal* 23 (2003): 45–58.

At Nauvoo, Illinois, Smith's desire to determine not only the future of his followers but also the future of neighboring Gentiles went beyond his ability to control events. Like so many great leaders both before and after him, Smith fell victim to the consequences of his own decision making.

During the brief visit of Josiah Quincy and Charles Francis Adams to Nauvoo in May 1844, the prophet escorted the men by buggy to his proudest architectural achievement—the Nauvoo Temple. Although it was still a construction site, Smith no doubt shared the importance of the ministries that emanated from that sacred space. After the visit, as the men rode down the hill back to the Mansion House, the skies opened up and a heavy rain turned the dusty roads into a quagmire. As the team pulled the wagon through the mud, Quincy remarked on the prophet's autocratic control over his community since "the prophet being absolute in Nauvoo, no man could be arrested or held without his permission." Curiously, Smith ignored the comment. So a short time later, Quincy again raised the issue. In his diary the Bostonian recorded his observation and Smith's eventual response:

> It seems to me, General, I said, as he was driving us to the river, about sunset, that you have too much power to be safely trusted to one man. "In your hands or that of any other person," was the reply, "so much power would, no doubt, be dangerous. I am the only man in the world whom it would be safe to trust with it. Remember I am a prophet!"[29]

Quincy wrote in his comment that this demonstrated Smith's sense of humor, but the admission revealed much about how the prophet viewed himself, and it foretold of much larger problems that loomed ahead, not only for the prophet but also for the religious movement he led.

Frequently during his earlier life Smith had confronted the consequences of his decision making. Whether considered as divine intervention or just good fortune, each time, he fortuitously seemed to escape certain doom. History is replete with famous people who, under similar circumstances, assumed invulnerability.[30] Smith's followers viewed him as their

---

29. Quincy, *Figures of the Past*, 397.
30. Numerous Roman emperors, Napoleon Bonaparte, United States presidents, Confederate general Robert E. Lee, and even infamous dictators like Benito Mussolini and

modern-day Moses,[31] who acted as intermediary between them and God. His words were the words of God and to be taken only with the greatest of loyalty —adherents' salvation hinged on their obedience to his inspired counsel. Bolstered by the powers of the Nauvoo municipal charter, Smith retained unparalleled legal protections, and with the city militia, his personal bodyguards, and the city police force, Smith had his own army to enforce his decisions. On occasion he was wise and judicious with this power, but as he moved through the spring of 1844, he committed politicide by destroying the *Nauvoo Expositor*. This misstep accelerated his slide down a slippery slope and ended with his demise in Carthage, Illinois. Whether he was blinded by ambition or based his judgments on honorable intentions depends on how one interprets his words and deeds. In either case, Joseph Smith Jr., a man of meager upbringing, became an American prophet, and as historian Jan Shipps has argued, established "a new religious tradition" that is now claimed by millions of people around the world.[32]

But the Restoration Era is far more than a biography of Joseph Smith Jr. It is the story of thousands of people who individually made

---

Adolf Hitler are examples of historical figures who assumed the same sense of invulnerability, only to discover the tragic realities of their assumption. Within a ministerial context, Henry Ward Beecher, the great spiritual leader of the late 1860s and 1870s, and his extramarital "nest hiding" affair with Elizabeth Tilton, proved that the secret desire to integrate sexual and spiritual fulfillment continued on into the Victorian Era. Televangelists Jim Bakker and Jimmy Swaggart are modern popular ministers who confronted their seeming invulnerability. An excellent account of the Beecher fall from grace is Altina L. Waller, *Reverend Beecher and Mrs. Tilton: Sex and Class in Victorian America* (Amherst: University of Massachusetts Press, 1982). I would like to thank James Doty for alerting me to this interesting source.

31. On numerous occasions, the prophet identified with Moses. As early as June 1830, Smith's encounters with God were portrayed through the experiences of Moses in Doctrine and Covenants Section 22 (LDS Moses 1). This was first printed in the Nauvoo *Times and Seasons* 4, no. 5 (16 January 1843): 71–73. Smith repeated his comparison to Moses the following September. See Doctrine and Covenants 27:2a (LDS 28:2): "But, behold, verily, verily I say unto thee, No one shall be appointed to receive commandments and revelations in this church excepting my servant Joseph Smith, Jr., for he receiveth them even as Moses."

32. Eminent historian Jan Shipps, who is unaffiliated with Latter Day Saintism, has spanned the great historical divide between true believers and modern skeptics of the Latter Day Saint movement. Her widely recognized, landmark interpretation is found in *Mormonism: The Story of a New Religious Tradition*.

life-changing decisions to follow his prophetic dictates and who joined in the Latter Day Saint diaspora—pulling up stakes, moving, and settling, again and again—over a brief, fourteen-year period. Their journey took them from Colesville, Fayette, and Palmyra, New York, to Kirtland, Thompson, and Hiram, in the Connecticut Western Reserve of Ohio. Some went to the far western reaches of the nation—to Independence, Liberty, and DeWitt, Missouri—to settle. Then they were called to gather together at the Mormon sanctuary at Far West, Caldwell County, Missouri, but were forcibly removed to western Illinois. For many, this location ended the Restoration Era journey when they moved into settlements in and around Nauvoo, in Hancock County. Many hoped that where they settled each time would be their final destination to await the Second Coming, only to have their expectations unfulfilled by circumstances seemingly beyond their control.

Not long after the Carthage assassination a chorus of different voices arose to fill the leadership vacuum. Each man argued his case as to why he was the "one mighty and strong" to lead the people. How followers responded to this confusion and other daunting challenges that lay just over their horizon and beyond determined the future of Latter Day Saintism.

EPILOGUE

Legacy of the Restoration Era as Foundation for the Continuing Journey

WITHIN A DECADE of the Carthage assassination a small group of devotees, born out of the many issues raised in the *Nauvoo Expositor* protest, assessed the events of the Nauvoo period and searched for remedies to the theological excesses of those difficult days. In the early 1850s they called for a "New Organization" of the original church and placed great confidence in their belief that the true successor would come from the "seed of Joseph." Because of their concerns about the Seer's authoritarian leadership style, they required a successor who would include other leaders and even the membership in determining the prophetic direction of the church. In Joseph Smith III, these followers found their prophetic successor, and under his leadership the "New Organization" of the church became the Reorganized Church of Jesus Christ of Latter Day Saints, and eventually Community of Christ.

Era of Reorganization

JOSEPH III AND his mother, Emma Hale Smith, arrived in Amboy, Lee County, Illinois, during the evening of 5 April 1860, and attended a prayer service. The next day, the small gathering of Saints, numbering not more than three hundred, extended the hand of fellowship, and in so doing, launched what would become the Reorganized Church of Jesus Christ of

Latter Day Saints. Joseph III's opening years of administration revealed his patience in redirecting the movement toward moderation.[1] Emma Hale Smith, the "First Lady of Latter Day Saintism," contributed significantly to her son's leadership. Ever the supporter of her husband, and now her oldest son, Emma's faith, courage, compassion, and perseverance impacted her entire generation and had a lasting influence up to today. Her strength of character significantly bolstered the fledgling Reorganization, adding to the legitimacy of her son as prophet. Emma's contribution factored heavily amid an unsettled, competitive environment where numerous church leaders claimed succession to the church presidency.

Dissent characterized Latter Day Saintism almost from the start. Because Joseph Smith Jr. did not establish clearly the line of succession, his church fractured and members dispersed among numerous claimants. Brigham Young, president of the Quorum of Twelve Apostles, led a majority of the Saints to the Wasatch Range and the Salt Lake Valley. With their great hopes for isolation, they prospered, but not without their own trials and tribulations.

Many dissenting movements died out within a matter of years, and others, after the first generation. With the Reorganized Church of Jesus Christ of Latter Saints under the prophetic leadership of Joseph III, the story was quite different. Over his fifty-four year tenure, Young Joseph, as his friends called him, dealt skillfully with controversial issues by choosing a leadership style and decision-making process considerably different from his father's. Using a gradualist theological approach, Joseph III steered his Reorganized Church toward the Christian mainstream, rather than away from it.

Joseph Smith III bequeathed to future leaders a legacy of firm but moderate leadership. His successor, Frederick Madison Smith, sought a new social contract with the church membership. Joseph III's oldest son, known by his friends as Fred M., brought a different leadership style to the prophetic task. This change brought crisis to the church, but it also established "supreme directional control" in the hands of the president of the church.

---

1. The theme of moderation was introduced by historian Alma R. Blair in "Moderate Mormons," 201–24.

Frederick M. Smith provided the church a Zionic vision more like his grandfather's than his father's. Fred M. embraced a social gospel approach to human needs. He both initiated and further developed community projects, such as a major health care facility, rest home, and cemetery in Independence, Missouri, in the 1920s. He moved the institutional headquarters to Independence and challenged members to build a huge Auditorium to facilitate his growing church's administrative processes. But the difficult circumstances of the Great Depression and a world war dashed his personal hopes for success before his death in 1946.

Era of Worldwide Community

ISRAEL ALEXANDER SMITH took the reigns from his older brother in a time of transition. Emerging from the years of economic depression and war, Israel's prophetic ministry took a more pastoral approach. He called members to unity and healing in hopes of providing stability as the Reorganized Church grew in strength and membership. Israel benefited greatly from those who encircled him in the church leadership. These included the pastoral ministry of his cousin Elbert Aoriul Smith, the son of David Hyrum Smith, and the conservative stewardship guidance of G. Leslie DeLapp. Late in Israel's administration, a shift in church direction became noticeable—the movement of the church into the world.

The closing years of Israel Smith's presidential administration, and those of his successor, half-brother William Wallace Smith, continued to move the church to worldwide community. Cultural forces rapidly moved the institution from sect to denomination, from "remnant church" to "church in international mission."[2] The globalization of church resources took ministers into new international settings and forced leaders to find answers to questions for which they were not prepared, especially among the non-Western peoples of Africa and Asia. A series of Joint Council seminars through the mid-1960s and early '70s convened to address this deficit of understanding. Controversial discussions, based on the disclosure of a series of position papers and a newly developed church school curricu-

2. Historian Richard P. Howard made this observation as he studied the carefully worded language of the "Statement on Objectives, No. 5," that grew out of the Joint Council Seminars of 1967. For Howard's complete explanation, see his *The Church Through the Years*, 2: 366–69.

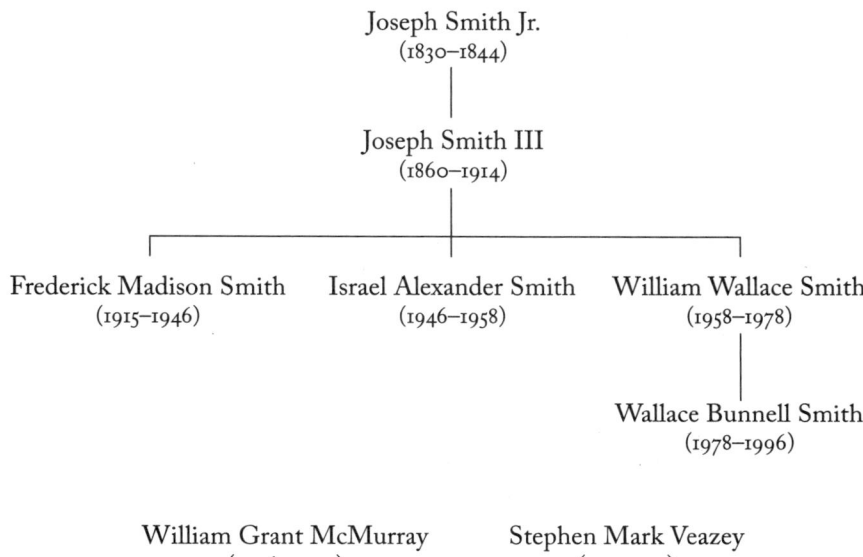

Presidents of the church (with the years of their tenure)

lum, reflected new directions in church thought. In 1976, W. Wallace announced his retirement and selected his son, Wallace B. Smith, as prophet-president designate. The possibility of the prophet's retirement symbolized new directions as the church moved into the 1980s, while Wallace B. Smith challenged the church to have a "faith to grow."

The paradigm shift involving new approaches in theology, scripture, and history, however, placed considerable strain within the church fellowship. Brewing for decades, the clash between worldviews reflecting cultural monism versus cultural pluralism came to a head in 1984 when church president Wallace B. Smith felt directed to extend ecclesiastical authority to women.[3] For the next five years the membership pressed the limits of common consent at all jurisdictional levels of church organization.

As the church moved into the 1990s, a focus on educating the membership followed a long-standing tradition in the church story. From its very beginning, church leaders saw the need to educate as a remedy to cope with new understandings, membership and priesthood responsibilities,

3. Doctrine and Covenants 156:9.

and the rapidly changing world around them. As specific needs arose, numerous affiliated organizations outside the church's administrative structure emerged and contributed significantly in the closing decades of the twentieth century.[4] With the dedication of the Temple in Independence to peace, reconciliation, and healing of the spirit, still new initiatives focused on international mission. An emphasis on a theology of peace and justice found considerable support in many circles.

In September 1995, Wallace B. Smith presented a pastoral letter to the church in which, following the precedent set by his father, he announced his retirement plans and proposed W. Grant McMurray as his successor as president. Although succession from father to son was broken with Israel A. Smith in 1946, now the role of church president extended beyond the Smith family. McMurray challenged church members to focus their ministry on social needs within their community and to become "a prophetic people." Through his presidential appointments, women entered the leading quorums of the church.

Church identity became a primary issue as McMurray called for institutional transformation by the year 2000. In 2001 the corporate name changed to Community of Christ to more accurately reflect church mission. During McMurray's tenure the church embraced a new stewardship philosophy and redesigned administrative jurisdictions to better accommodate congregational life. Community of Christ entered yet another chapter when, in November 2004, McMurray announced his resignation from the church presidency. He chose not to designate a successor and a World Conference convened in early June 2005 to confirm the selection of Stephen M. Veazey to lead the church. In his inaugural address to the church, President Veazey challenged the membership to "share the peace of Jesus Christ."[5]

---

4. Perhaps the best example is Outreach International, established in 1979 to help men and women in poor communities overcome the effects of poverty and create new futures for themselves and their communities. See their Web site at *www.outreach-international.org*.

5. Stephen M. Veazey, "Share the Peace of Jesus Christ," *Herald* 152, no. 7 (July 2005): 11–21.

A Unique People with a Common Story

THERE IS NO question that the Latter Day Saints of the Restoration Era were distinctive in their beliefs and how they encountered the enormous challenges of their culture. They sought an Old Testament identity in what they perceived as a New Testament setting within the new American nation.[6] As unique as their story may be, still the Latter Day Saint narrative is about a people who bravely faced their trials and tribulations knowing that their personal salvation was at stake. Yet their human response to what they perceived as their call to fulfill God's purposes parallels so many other peoples in earlier eras of biblical and Christian history.

For many today the story of Latter Day Saintism is an important source of pride (in a very positive way). An inadequate human response at times to a professed understanding of divine call does not detract from their commitment to a collective cause much greater than they are individually. The Latter Day Saints of the first generation were a scriptural people who found some solace in the heavy burdens they carried. Modern-day believers find the same solace.

The Restoration Era established a legacy for future followers to build their own churches. For more than a century, members of the Reorganized Church of Jesus Christ of Latter Day Saints built on Restoration Era foundation stones that included prophetic leadership from the "seed of Joseph Smith Jr.," an open canon of scripture and the Book of Mormon, a lay priesthood, and the need for continued education and training. Joseph Smith III perpetuated the Restoration Era legacy but with moderation. Young Joseph's interpretation of Zionic living, to be achieved inclusively in the communities where his followers lived rather than in an exclusive, isolated sacred space, is one of many examples of how the Seer's oldest

---

6. The most direct evidence comes from Joseph Smith Jr.'s written response to an inquiry about church identity and beliefs after his arrival at Far West, Missouri, in 1838: "The fundamental principles of our religion is the testimony of the apostles and prophets concerning Jesus Christ, 'that he died, was buried, and rose again the third day, and ascended up into heaven'; and all other things are only appendages to these, which pertain to our religion. But in connection with these, we believe in the gift of the Holy Ghost, the power of faith, the enjoyment of the spiritual gifts according to the will of God, the restoration of the House of Israel, and the final triumph of truth." See *Elders' Journal* 1, no. 3 (July 1838): 44.

son tempered his father's religious excesses. Indeed, in this regard the son learned the lessons of his father's history.[7]

Building on the groundwork of both the Restoration and Reorganization Eras, Community of Christ thus far has drawn from the presence of a "peace gene," has demonstrated a strong appreciation for ecumenism,[8] has expanded the role of women in priesthood ministry to include leadership responsibilities at the highest levels of church administration, and has extended, even further, the church's ministry into new national settings. Today's Community of Christ, in its mission "to proclaim Jesus Christ and promote communities of joy, hope, love, and peace," seems to be more than just an extension of a historical tradition established during earlier eras, but may well be a reinterpretation of it as it meets the challenges of the twenty-first century. Thus, the journey continues.

---

7. In his 1909 prophetic statement, Joseph Smith III challenged followers that the Zionic enterprise meant "living and acting honestly and honorably before God and in the sight of all men, using the things of this world in the manner designed of God, that the places where they occupy may shine as Zion, the redeemed of the Lord" (Doctrine and Covenants 128:8c).

8. A city ordinance passed in Nauvoo, Illinois, acknowledged the legality of other denominations within the city limits. *An Ordinance in relation to Religious Societies.* Sec. 1.: "Be it ordained by the City Council of the City of Nauvoo, That the Catholics, Presbyterians, Methodists, Baptists, Latter Day Saints, Quakers, Episcopalians, Universalists, Unitarians, Mahommedans, and all other religious sects and denominations, whatever, shall have free toleration, and equal privileges in this city, and should any person be guilty of ridiculing, abusing, or otherwise depreciating another, in consequence of his religion, or of disturbing, or interrupting any religious meeting, within the limits of this city, he shall on conviction thereof before the Mayor, or Municipal Court, be considered a disturber of the public peace, and fined in any sum not to exceed five hundred dollars, or imprisonment not exceeding six months, or both, at the discretion of said Mayor, or Court." See "To the Elders and Churches Abroad," *Times and Seasons* 4, no. 23 (15 October 1843): 363–64.

In 2011, the National Council of Churches of Christ in the USA voted to receive Community of Christ into full membership. See "National Council Approves Church for Membership," *Herald* 158, no. 2 (February 2011): 20–21.

Resources

BIBLIOGRAPHIC ESSAY

"Travelers on the New Mormon History Trail": Community of Christ Contributions to the New Mormon History Movement[1]

THE WRITINGS IN Latter Day Saint history by those affiliated with the Community of Christ (formerly known as the Reorganized Church of Jesus Christ of Latter Day Saints) from the early 1960s to the present reflect the general characteristics of the New Mormon History movement. This movement emerged in response to the desire of many historians to break away from the old debating paradigm of either attacking or defending the legitimacy of Mormonism. Going beyond the tired argument of which church, LDS or RLDS, was the true successor to the early church of Joseph Smith Jr., participants in the movement chose topics that focused on the lives of grassroots members, both male and female, leaders and followers. Movement historians also applied modern critical research methods in their attempts to understand Latter Day Saintism. No longer would their studies be constructed as battering rams or immoveable defenses of decisions made by historical figures. Paul M. Edwards explains

---

1. This bibliographic essay is taken, with minor modifications, from my contribution to Newell G. Bringhurst and Lavina Fielding Anderson, eds., *Excavating Mormon Pasts: The Historiography of the Last Half Century* (Salt Lake City: Greg Kofford Books, 2004), 253–72; used by permission. The term "New Mormon History" was coined by historian Moses Rischin in "New Mormon History," *The American West* 6 (March 1969): 49.

this approach in "The New Mormon History," *Saints Herald* 133, no. 11 (November 1986): 12–14, 20.

In this essay, I describe how the Community of Christ history community, including both baptized members and those closely associated with the church, pursued with professionalism previously unavailable historical materials, using a wide variety of techniques and research methods. These scholars manifested a penchant for grassroots topics while they emphasized a holistic approach in their quest for authentic accounts of the Latter Day Saint movement. Because of the vast quantity of scholarship from this community of history scholars, another characteristic of the New Mormon History movement, this essay highlights only certain foundational books, periodicals, journal articles, and academic capstone projects within the historical field of research on the Restoration movement. Finally, I discuss briefly the important contributions of the John Whitmer Historical Association to the corpus of literature focusing on the church story.

Community of Christ Historians Blazing the New Mormon History Trail

ROBERT BRUCE FLANDERS blazed the trail into the New Mormon History movement for those in the Community of Christ in his *Nauvoo: Kingdom on the Mississippi* (Urbana: University of Illinois Press, 1965). Based on his University of Wisconsin doctoral dissertation, Flanders offered a critical account of Joseph Smith's attempts to build a Mormon economic and political city-state on the Illinois banks of the Mississippi River (v–vi). The book's longevity may well be the best testament to its enormous contribution. Though written more than four decades ago, *Nauvoo* is still the single most important political, social, and economic work on the topic.

Many historians associated with the Community of Christ followed Flanders's lead by looking critically at topics ranging from the historical context of early nineteenth-century American society to significant events in the landscape of Latter Day Saintism in the opening decade of the twenty-first century. Perhaps the most important Community of Christ official to travel the New Mormon History trail was Richard P. Howard, church historian from 1965 to 1994. His role in modernizing the church's historical processes cannot be overstated. Assisted by able staff in the church's library-archives and by W. Grant McMurray, then assistant history commissioner and later church president, Howard introduced professional standards of collection, preservation, and the cataloging of church historical materials that became the grist for the mills of serious historians. Under Howard's direction, this fertile institutional repository opened new vistas to scholars, thus generating a vast array of historical interpretations about the origins and development of the religious movement.

Early in Howard's thirty-year career, he focused on the evolution of church scriptures. The result of his exploration was *Restoration Scriptures: A Study of Their Textual Development* (Independence, Mo.: Herald House 1969; rev. ed., 1995). This important work consists of three parts: the Book of Mormon, Joseph Smith's "New Translation" of the Bible, and the Doctrine and Covenants. Howard provided the reader with almost a hundred pages of appendices (220–314) that included photographic facsimiles of manuscripts pivotal to the development of Latter Day Saint scripture.

Of unique interest to Community of Christ readers is Richard Howard's careful analysis of the *Book of Abraham*, written by Joseph Smith Jr. between 1835 and 1842 (rev. ed., chapter 12). Since the early Reorganized Church did not canonize the *Book of Abraham*, most Community of Christ members know very little of the writing. Thus, Howard's careful study assisted the reader (at least those associated with the church headquartered in Independence) to understand the book as a product of the first Mormon prophet's "theological reflection, aided by his intuitive powers of mental imagery." Howard summarized his analysis by stating: "Whatever the early Saints felt about the Book of Abraham, it seems not to have been either an inspired or scholarly translation. Joseph Smith referred to himself as a revelator and translator. He often used those terms interchangeably. His work as translator, however, did not equip him as a linguist of Egyptian language symbols" (204).

A significant early contribution to the New Mormon History movement is Wayne Ham's *Publish Glad Tidings: Readings in Early Latter Day Saint Sources* (Independence, Mo.: Herald House, 1970). This intellectual history was based on the accurate assumption that valuable insights can be gleaned from a close inspection of the original literature of the times. Ham crafted brief historical explanations of *The Evening and the Morning Star*

(1832–1834), the *Latter Day Saints' Messenger and Advocate* (1834–1837), the *Elders' Journal* (1837–1838), and the *Times and Seasons* (1839–1844). Then, by highlighting selected portions of these early writings, Ham identified the pressing issues, emotional responses, and decisions by church leaders that drove the religious movement in the early years.

Edward A. Warner, in "Mormon Theodemocracy: Theocratic and Democratic Elements in Early Latter-Day Saint Ideology, 1827–1844" (PhD diss., Iowa University, 1973), dispelled the popular notion that Mormonism was completely theocratic in its views of church-state relations. To construct his persuasive argument, Warner drew on extensive research to discuss a necessary tension between theocratic characteristics of the Mormon Church institution (centralized in the prophetic office and hierarchized in a graded system of priesthood offices) and the democratic characteristics (decentralized prerogatives among the Mormon membership). Critical of historical orthodoxy, Warner concluded that these characteristics were neither oppositional nor mutually exclusive, for early Mormons saw them conjoined into one theodemocratic system (10, 44–45).

Graceland College, Lamoni, Iowa

THE NEW MORMON History movement gained strong support among the faculty at Graceland College (now Graceland University), the church-sponsored institution of higher education located in Lamoni, Iowa.[2] Leading support came from Paul M. Edwards, professor of history and philosophy, who wrote *The Hilltop Where: An Informal History of Graceland College* (Lamoni, Iowa: Venture Foundation, 1972). This book is more than a nostalgic look at the first seventy-five years of the Graceland story since Edwards outlined the difficult decision-making involved in setting directions for the denominational college, its physical construction and educational offerings, and the achievements of its faculty members and students. In his concluding chapter, Edwards gave a

2. In November 1999, the Graceland College Board of Trustees and World Church leaders agreed to change Graceland's institutional name to Graceland University. The decision grew from the addition of numerous academic programs that ranged far beyond traditional liberal arts college offerings. The new name became effective on 1 June 2000. For a brief explanation of the decision, see "From Graceland College to Graceland University," *Saints Herald* 147, no. 4 (April 2000): 158.

philosophical commentary, challenging the reader to look critically at society and appreciate the important role that higher education played in shaping it (140–43).

Among Community of Christ members, few have had a greater teaching influence than Graceland history professor Alma R. Blair. "The Reorganized Church of Jesus Christ of Latter Day Saints: Moderate Mormons," in *The Restoration Movement: Essays in Mormon History*, ed. F. Mark McKiernan, Alma R. Blair, and Paul M. Edwards (Lawrence, Kans.: Coronado Press, 1972; rev. ed., Independence, Mo.: Herald House, 1992), may be his most significant writing in terms of defining foundational issues of identity. Blair was the first modern professional historian to observe that those who joined the Reorganization did so for reasons ranging far beyond lineal succession (203). Although the Community of Christ is rooted in the fourteen years of common history it shares with the Salt Lake church, it attracted those who stood against Brigham Young and the doctrine of polygamy, the belief in a plurality of gods, theological speculations about preexistence and exaltation, and the practice of baptism for the dead. Blair concluded that the Reorganized Church earned its reputation as moderate Mormons (219).

Larry E. Hunt, also of Graceland's history faculty, forged from his doctoral dissertation a two-volume biography, *F. M. Smith: Saint as Reformer* (Independence, Mo.: Herald House, 1982). By placing the second prophet of the Reorganized Church in the historical context of the Mugwump political movement during America's Gilded Age at the turn of the twentieth century, Hunt brilliantly demonstrated that Smith's institutional reforms were in alignment with the larger social reform movement and concluded that the RLDS prophet, though more comfortable among his church followers and in the pulpit, would also have fit well in secular political circles advocating similar social reforms (1:17).

Perhaps the most provocative professor of history at Graceland University has been William D. Russell. Representative of Russell's insightful questioning is "The Historicity of the Book of Mormon and the Use of the Sermon on the Mount in III Nephi" in *Restoration Studies II: A Collection of Essays About the History, Beliefs, and Practices of the Reorganized Church of Jesus Christ of Latter Day Saints,* ed. Maurice L. Draper (Independence, Mo.: Herald House, 1982). Joining others in a thoughtful critique of the

Book of Mormon's historical veracity, Russell interrogated the organizational format, language, cultural characteristics, and authors' biases evident in the III Nephi account. Russell concluded that "the Book of Mormon should not be regarded as a historical account of ancient people who inhabited the Americas" (197).

Following the Trail Blazers

MOTIVATED BY THE belief that much can be learned from the literary works of the man who led the Reorganized Church through two world wars and the nation's greatest economic depression, Norman D. Ruoff compiled *The Writings of President Frederick M. Smith*, 3 vols. (Independence, Mo.: Herald House, 1978–81). Drawing articles from the movement's primary publication, the *Saints' Herald*, radio and pulpit sermons, and civic group talks to reveal the priorities of Smith's presidential leadership, Ruoff's three volumes identified the three major themes of F. M. Smith's presidency: Zion, stewardship, and education. This important research tool, absent of specific interpretive insights, required readers to draw their own conclusions about F. M. Smith's intellectual and spiritual leadership.

F. Mark McKiernan was a leader in the Community of Christ history community from the 1960s until his untimely passing in 1997. His most significant contribution, *The Voice of One Crying in the Wilderness: Sidney Rigdon, Religious Reformer, 1793–1876* (Lawrence, Kans.: Coronado Press, 1971; 2nd ed., Independence, Mo.: Herald House, 1986), reflected New Mormon History themes. Reprinted eight times by two publishers, *Rigdon* became the definitive early work on the great Mormon orator until Richard Van Wagoner's *Sidney Rigdon: A Portrait of Religious Excess* (Salt Lake City: Signature Books, 1994) emerged more than two decades later. McKiernan found in Rigdon's life many of the great religious themes of the era, introducing him as "a man with a vision, a quest, and a mission" (11) and "a refraction of the religious tendencies held by millions of early nineteenth-century Americans who were greatly concerned about the fate of their eternal souls and joined one religious denomination after another" (12). McKiernan concludes that Rigdon's obituary should have quoted

Mark 1:3—that Rigdon was truly "The voice of one crying in the wilderness, Prepare ye the way of the Lord" (145).

McKiernan made a second important contribution by editing, with Roger D. Launius, *An Early Latter Day Saint History: The Book of John Whitmer Kept by Commandment* (Independence, Mo.: Herald House, 1980). The editors introduced Whitmer as an individual who "stood at the very thresholds of great power and authority within the restored church but never attained the authority nor the recognition that [he] probably deserved" (9). Less than a year after the church's organization, Joseph Smith Jr., through instruction dated 8 March 1831, called Whitmer to "write and keep a regular history" (Doctrine and Covenants 47:1a; LDS 47:1), thus replacing Oliver Cowdery, who was on a mission to the West. The RLDS Church acquired the John Whitmer manuscript history from the Whitmer family in 1903. Five years later, church historian Heman C. Smith published parts of the history in the RLDS *Journal of History* but the full version was not available except in manuscript until McKiernan and Launius completed their edition. A wealth of explanatory footnotes contextualized this nineteenth-century document.

F. Mark McKiernan joined Graceland faculty members Alma R. Blair and Paul M. Edwards in editing a significant collection of thirteen essays on Latter Day Saint history in *The Restoration Movement: Essays in Mormon History*. Leading historians, both inside and outside Reorganized Latter Day Saintism, contributed essays on crucial topics. In addition to the high quality of the content and skillful interpretation, *The Restoration Movement* demonstrated the collegiality of New Mormon History scholars by spanning the theological divide between the two churches. After its original publication in 1973 by Coronado Press in Lawrence, Kansas, Herald House in Independence, Missouri, acquired the copyright and has added two printings to the five earlier ones.

The Prolific Era of Historical Writings in the 1980s

DURING THE DECADE of the 1980s, historians provided many significant analyses of crucial issues related to the church story. Any essay on RLDS contributions to Mormon historiography must include the works of historian Roger D. Launius, who first became interested in church history as a baccalaureate student at Graceland College. His experiences as a summer intern at the Community of Christ historic properties in Nauvoo, Independence, and Kirtland solidified his career as a professional historian and a prolific researcher of Restoration history topics. In *Zion's Camp: Expedition to Missouri, 1834* (Independence, Mo.: Herald House, 1984), Launius transformed his master's thesis from Louisiana State University into a book-length narrative documenting that the march was an attempt by church leaders to regain lost land in Jackson County, boost the morale of the victimized Saints, and provide them with money and supplies. In addition to these purposes, Launius also noted how Zion's Camp assisted the Mormon prophet in creating an ecclesiastical structure and finding appropriate candidates to fill the positions. Because the participants assumed positions in the developing church hierarchy, Launius observed that "Zion's Camp—either intentionally or by accident—served as a crucible out of which the prophet forged a more powerful and efficient church organization. [Smith's] contact with the most committed and talented men of the church during the expedition greatly aided in the development of church administration" (8). Launius did not intend to levy judgments by fixing blame for failure of the march (and failure, it was, in terms of restoring the Saints to their Jackson County lands) but gave a fair accounting of the doomed efforts of liberation.

Following the narrative format in *Zion's Camp*, Launius produced a historical account of the first Mormon temple in *The Kirtland Temple: A Historical Narrative* (1986). After discussing the conceptualization of a temple, Launius identified the temple as a dream of the membership through that dream's beginning, realization, and shattering. The author also discussed "The Kirtland Temple Suit" (chap. 5), calling the legal action brought by the RLDS Church "the most spectacular event bearing on the history of the Kirtland Temple, save its dedication" (100). Six informative appendices provide a list of those who received a special blessing for assisting in the temple construction, elements of the dedication service on 27 March 1836, accounts by those who reported visitations of Jesus Christ in the weeks following the dedication, the church's petition in the Kirtland Temple suit, and the court's opinion (171–98). Unfortunately, this volume is not illustrated, a deficiency Launius remedied with informative historic photographs in the thirty-one-page *Illustrated History of the Kirtland*

Temple (Independence, Mo: Herald House, 1986), which included explanatory essays.

Roger Launius's most significant early contribution to the New Mormon History was his research on Joseph Smith III, founder of the Reorganized Church. This project began as his doctoral dissertation at Louisiana State University, and expanded to a book-length work. *Joseph Smith III: Pragmatic Prophet* (Urbana: University of Illinois Press, 1988) became the first modern biography of Joseph, the Seer's eldest son. Launius characterized Joseph Smith III as a consensus builder whose priorities were "unity and commonality, steadfastness of purpose, and rightness of action" (x). Because Joseph Smith III was a second-generation Latter Day Saint, the author observed that the young Smith "was not as overcome by the awe of the spiritual vision as those who had gone before; he was able to take aspects of the grandiose dreams of his father, separate the logical from the impractical, and build on them" (xi). Launius concluded that Joseph III's "career represents an important case study in the union of principle and pragmatism in American religious history" (369). For this important work, Launius received the 1989 Evans Biography Award from the Center for Regional Studies at Utah State University.

A prolific researcher and writer, Launius was also the first to produce a book-length social history exploring the experiences of black Americans in the Reorganized Church. Echoing Ralph Ellison's influential 1953 novel *The Invisible Man,* Launius titled his work *Invisible Saints: A History of Black Americans in the Reorganized Church* (Independence, Mo.: Herald House, 1988) because, as Ellison had described society's overall neglect of the needs of blacks, the RLDS Church has "left its small black membership out of the mainstream of the movement" (9). Launius admitted the difficulty of performing this work—a white man trying to adequately, even accurately, portray the black person's experience within the church. Hearteningly, he concluded that the Community of Christ stood in the national mainstream because of its response to the social needs of black Americans and, therefore, reflected American egalitarianism (12). Other writings by Launius will be discussed below.

Administrative Biography Series

IN THE MID-1980S, historian Paul M. Edwards observed that an intense focus on the first fourteen years of the Restoration movement limited the horizons of a historical understanding of the Reorganized Church. To broaden the view, he pursued a project with the cooperation of Herald Publishing House to promote investigations into the growth of the Reorganized Church as an institution. Thus, the Administrative Biography Series was designed to advance the historical understanding of the work of the Reorganized Church presidents, with Edwards agreeing to be the series editor. As of this writing, four works have been completed.

Edwards launched the series with *The Chief: An Administrative Biography of Fred M. Smith* (Independence, Mo.: Herald House, 1988), very much an insider's history as the nicknames in the title indicate. Frederick Madison Smith, oldest son of Joseph Smith III, presided over the church for nearly a third of the twentieth century. Edwards portrayed him as a figure of controversy and paradox, presiding over an institution in transition. F. Henry Edwards, the author's father, served in the Quorum of Twelve Apostles for more than twenty-three years and in the First Presidency for twenty years, and was married to Fred M.'s daughter, Alice. Paul Edwards's writings reflect his affection for his grandfather; indeed, many stories are first-person accounts. In addition to serving at times as a participant-observer, he astutely analyzes and interprets Fred M.'s sometimes controversial efforts to make his religious institution into a modern church (272).

Roger D. Launius contributed the second volume to the Administrative Biography Series. With a tighter focus, the author retraced his steps from his earlier works on the subject and produced *Father Figure: Joseph Smith III and the Creation of the Reorganized Church* (Independence, Mo.: Herald House, 1990). Here, Launius argued that "by background, temperament, training, and, in some instances, clairvoyance, [Joseph Smith III] charted a cautious, practical, and basically moderate course for a people" (12). He analyzed the success of young Smith's leadership style in forging a new religious institution and in shepherding the Reorganized Church for fifty-four years.

Norma Derry Hiles produced the third work in the Administrative Biography Series. With Fred M.'s successor, Israel Alexander Smith, as her subject in *Gentle Monarch: The Presidency of Israel A. Smith* (Independence, Mo.: Herald House, 1991), Hiles offered a warm biography of the least-researched and least well-known president of the Reorganized Church. Unfortunately, only three of the eight chapters explored the uncharted terrain of Israel Smith's presidential administration lasting from 1946 to 1958. An epilogue of five memory tributes concluded *Gentle Monarch*, with a statement from Israel's half-brother and presidential successor, W. Wallace Smith, who "looked to [his] big brother with respect and admiration" (197). Although Hiles charted a narrow path, serious historical analysis of the crucial years of Israel A. Smith and his contribution to Reorganized Latter Day Saintism still remains to be done.

Maurice L. Draper contributed the fourth book to the series with *The Founding Prophet: An Administrative Biography of Joseph Smith, Jr.* (Independence, Mo: Herald House, 1991). In it, he mapped out the origins and development of Latter Day Saintism by examining the Seer's role in major aspects of life in the early church. Draper's credentials as a former member of the Quorum of Twelve Apostles and counselor in the First Presidency added to his writing the interesting dimension of someone who had wrestled with similar administrative issues. His twelfth chapter, highlighting the missionary fervor of the early Saints, was particularly effective. Draper wrote with a seasoned understanding of the historical and theological issues inherent with his subject and exemplified principles of the New Mormon History by articulating his personal biases at various points so that the reader could evaluate their impact. For example, when introducing the theological issue of pre-mortal existence, a significant Nauvoo doctrine that went west with Brigham Young but did not thrive in the Reorganization, Draper stated: "I personally find such ideas to be theologically unsound and irrational" (188). Written in an engaging style, *The Founding Prophet* is an excellent addition to the Administrative Biography Series.

General Surveys

RESPONDING TO THE influences of the New Mormon History movement, general agreement arose on the need to replace Inez Smith Davis's well-loved but quite outdated *The Story of the Church* (1934). Historians Paul M. Edwards and Richard P. Howard responded to the need for a general survey of church history that could reinterpret the Reorganized Church story using modern historical methods. In the popular *Our Legacy of Faith: A Brief History of the Reorganized Church of Jesus Christ of Latter Day Saints* (Independence, Mo.: Herald House, 1991), Edwards surveyed the church story from its historical setting in post-revolutionary America to the 1980s. The author also included a valuable appendix of important events in church history and a list of World Church leaders.

As a capstone to his career as church historian, Richard Howard produced his *The Church Through the Years*, 2 vols. (Independence, Mo.: Herald House, 1992, 1993). Howard's first volume began with an insightful explanation of the contribution that the discipline of history makes in the reader's life. Eloquently, Howard explained his purpose: "The capacity to be thankful for our heritage rests in the power of memory. A central purpose of these pages is to help the church remember the lives, struggles, hopes, and joys of those who make up our history. Let us be glad for the faith and the good works of those who sacrificed, toiled, and rejoiced in one another to create and keep alive this household of faith" (1:20).

Howard began volume 2 with the search of first-generation "Josephites" for Restoration members lost in the decade and a half after the prophet's death, and concluded with an exploration of issues surrounding the construction of the Temple in Independence. An appendix included the five sections of the Doctrine and Covenants that appeared in a separate historical appendix in the 1970 edition and were later removed by action of the church's 1990 World Conference. Also, Howard added W. Wallace Smith's letter of instruction related to his resignation as prophet-president of the Reorganized Church. Finally, Howard's selected readings section is thorough and comprehensive. Perhaps the greatest weakness of Howard's two-volume work is found in its limited index. Nevertheless, *The Church Through the Years* remains the best general work that focuses on the Reorganized Church story.

The Reorganized Church and the Theme of Dissent

CLARE D. VLAHOS, in "The Challenge to Centralized Power: Zenas H. Gurley, Jr., and The Prophetic Office" (*Courage: A Journal of History, Thought, and Action* 1, no. 3 [March 1971]: 141–58), laid the groundwork for discussing the recurring theme of dissension. Vlahos used Gurley's challenge to Joseph III's authority in the early 1880s to demonstrate the controversial nature of prophetic power in leading the church.

Tensions surrounding the exercise of prophetic authority became the focus of attention for Reorganized Church members a decade later. The 1980s were the most turbulent period in the history of the Community of Christ, not even excepting Fred M.'s controversial drive for "supreme directional control." That the Reorganized Church history community should reflect this theme of dissent in their scholarship is not surprising. Mormonism suffered shattering schisms after the death of the prophet Joseph Smith in June 1844. During these difficult times, many individuals in various leadership positions testified of being divinely ordained or prophetically appointed to lead the Restoration movement. These movements emphasized different aspects of the institutional structure and theology that evolved from Palmyra, New York. Historian Steven L. Shields skillfully charted the histories and theologies of these various churches in *Divergent Paths of the Restoration*, 4th rev. ed. (Los Angeles: Restoration Research, 1990).

Other historians also recognized the 1980s as a decade of disruption. Roger D. Launius and W. B. "Pat" Spillman co-edited *Let Contention Cease: The Dynamics of Dissent in the Reorganized Church of Jesus Christ of Latter Day Saints* (Independence, Mo.: Graceland/Park Press, 1991). The nine essays in this book analyzed various aspects of religious dissent, particularly in the context of the Reorganized Church. To inform the reader of the long-standing tradition of dissent within the movement that officially reorganized in Amboy, Illinois, on 6 April 1860, Spillman observed, "The Reorganized Church of Jesus Christ of Latter Day Saints began as an organization of dissenters—those who disagreed with others who claimed to inherit the prophetic mantle after the assassination of Joseph Smith, Jr. Since its earliest days, members of the church have cherished their independence of thought and freedom of expression" (10). Launius and Spillman successfully represented the broad spectrum of opinions on the controversial issue of dissent.

Roger D. Launius expanded his 1991 project on RLDS dissent to the larger history of the Mormon movement in *Differing Visions: Dissenters in Mormon History* (Urbana: University of Illinois Press, 1994) with co-editor Linda Thatcher. The editors solicited essays from scholars within RLDS, LDS, and unaffiliated history communities, who mined numerous research repositories for little-known information about the leaders of separatist movements. In his foreword to *Differing Visions*, Leonard J. Arrington introduced the reader to common themes such as the various interpretations of Joseph Smith's life and death, the range of motivations for separation (usually not self-serving), and the phenomenon that those who had once associated with the Restoration movement, even as dissenters, could seldom fully reject it (x–xi). *Differing Visions* is a crucial work in understanding the historical context of dissent as a key characteristic of Latter Day Saintism.

Conflict between Mormonism and the "old settler" culture surrounding Nauvoo in the early 1840s became the focus of *Cultures in Conflict: A Documentary History of the Mormon War in Illinois* (1995), edited by John E. Hallwas and Roger D. Launius (Logan: Utah State University Press, 1995). The editors used nearly a hundred historical documents to reveal dimensions of the clash between these two divergent cultures in western Hancock County, Illinois. Arranged in chronological order, the documents were divided into six periods within the era: the coming of the Mormons, the origins of the conflict, the trouble in Nauvoo, the murders in Carthage, the trial of the accused assassins and vigilante violence against outlying settlements, and the exodus in February 1846 and the battle of Nauvoo in September 1846. Hallwas and Launius explored regional archives and personal papers of contemporary individuals, some of which had never been published before, to present a well-balanced contemporary understanding of the mid-nineteenth-century Mormons who lived within their separatist community. A valuable historical and interpretive headnote prefaces each document. In their introduction, Hallwas and Launius criticized leading Mormon scholars for their orthodox approach to the Mormon dilemma at Nauvoo, stating that the standard religious persecution theme only partially explained the murders of Joseph and Hyrum Smith. Rather, "conflict between these groups arose because of their strikingly different cultural values. The experience of people in Hancock County during the 1840s demonstrates the inevitable conflict between theocratic and democratic government, the danger of demonizing other people, and the self-deceptions fostered by the myths of innocence and political righteousness" (8).

The same two historians joined forces to collect previously published essays in *Kingdom on the Mississippi Revisited: Nauvoo in Mormon History* (Urbana: University of Illinois Press, 1996). Launius and Hallwas selected fourteen essays representing the best scholarship on the Mormons of the Mississippi River town. Because the Reorganized Church holds the "elect lady" in such high esteem, many in the RLDS history community may see "The Lion and the Lady: Brigham Young and Emma Smith" by Valeen Tippetts Avery and Linda King Newell (198–213) as the best essay in the collection (originally printed in the *Utah Historical Quarterly* 48 [Winter 1980]: 81–97). Avery and Newell recounted the struggle, courage, and persistence that Emma Hale Smith Bidamon exhibited in the difficult years after the murder of her husband. An exhaustive bibliographic essay on secondary sources at the end of the book (251–67) provided an added value to the work.

Makers of Church Thought Series

THE MAKERS OF CHURCH THOUGHT SERIES is a collection of extended essays about five men who brought leadership skills to the Reorganization in very important ways. Series editor Paul M. Edwards again launched this series and modeled the collection of works with *F. Henry Edwards: Articulator for the Church* (Independence, Mo.: Herald House, 1995). Edwards, this time writing about his father, searched for the proper descriptor. He looked past "theologian," "doctrinaire," "historian," and "apologist," and chose "articulator," because F. Henry Edwards gave "words to the strongly held but hazily understood beliefs of his generation of church members" (10). Paul Edwards included a thirty-five-page list of books and articles written by his father, to symbolize the powerful influence F. Henry had on the evolution of church thought. The author concluded: "[F. Henry Edwards's] writings and addresses cover the intellectual history of the movement for half a century. The impact of his contribution is observable today both in the doctrine of the movement and in the lives of those people for whom he was a significant aid in the formation of their own beliefs" (125).

Alan D. Tyree wrote *Evan Fry: Proclaimer of Good News* (Independence, Mo.: Herald House, 1995), the second volume in the Makers of

Church Thought Series. Evan Fry was a prominent radio minister for the RLDS Church from 1938 until just before his death in 1958. A contemporary of F. Henry Edwards, Fry offered the church his gift of "presenting complex ideas in simple language and through illustrations that endeared him to his audience" (7). Tyree argued that Fry, though blazing no new theological paths for the Reorganized Church, became "the church's best-known proclaimer of the gospel" (9).

Henry K. Inouye's *Roy A. Cheville: Explorer of Spiritual Frontiers* (Independence, Mo.: Herald House, 1996), the third volume in the Makers of Church Thought Series, offered more than just a monographic biography of a Reorganized Church leader. Inouye placed Cheville in the context of twentieth-century Latter Day Saint history. Far more theoretical than the other series authors, Inouye demonstrated his training in religious philosophy in his analysis of Cheville's theology. At times, the focus on Cheville got lost in the author's discussions of process theology, existentialism, rationalism, and personal relations with the Cosmic Personality (81).

The fourth volume of the Makers of Church Thought Series, *Arthur A. Oakman: An Artist with Words* (Independence, Mo.: Herald House, 1997) by Maurice L. Draper, added significantly to an understanding of the architects of modern church beliefs. Consistent with other series authors' approaches to their subjects, Draper argued that the greatest contribution that this long-serving apostle made to the Reorganization was in his ability to communicate with the membership. Draper wrote: "Oakman's verbal artistry was best demonstrated in his oral expressions, as in preaching, lecturing, and prophetic utterances. Voice inflections, posture and gestures, and facial expressions accompanying his choice of words added to the motivational power of delivery. His persuasive public address style stimulated his hearers to share his faith commitments long after the specific content of his message might have been forgotten" (17).

Instead of using a chronological format in his exploration of Oakman's ministry, Draper presented Oakman's views on a variety of theological subjects, including the nature of the deity, incarnation, revelation, and foundations of the faith, just to name a few. Although claiming this approach as Oakman's preference (21), the author sacrificed the valuable historical contextualization of his subject.

Wayne Ham's study, *Geoffrey F. Spencer: Advocate for an Enlightened Faith* (Independence, Mo.: Herald House, 1998), focused on the significant contribution of one of the Reorganized Church's leading thinkers. Ham acknowledged Spencer's preference to avoid being considered a trained theologian. Instead Spencer "endeavored to discern the significant elements in the contemporary experience of the church and to state these in each situation with sufficient reasonableness and clarity that they could provide the basis for a consensus among church leaders" (10). This work is the fifth, and most recent, book in the Makers of Church Thought Series.

General Interest Works

THE SIGNIFICANT CONTRIBUTION by Community of Christ to the New Mormon History movement can be seen throughout the historical landscape. The scholarship of L. Madelon Brunson, Barbara Hands Bernauer, Isleta L. Pement Wehner, Paul M. Edwards, and Roger D. Launius is representative of this contribution. These intellectuals have produced a number of leading studies.

Madelon Brunson's excellent study of the role of women in the early years of Mormonism and the Reorganization in *Bonds of Sisterhood: A History of the RLDS Women's Organization, 1842–1893* (Independence, Mo.: Herald House, 1985) was very timely. Brunson, then RLDS Church archivist, published her work at the time of the first ordination of women into the RLDS priesthood. In *Bonds of Sisterhood*, she identified the female experience in the Reorganization as a paradox—women were integrated into the organization and essential aspects of the church, yet they were excluded from decision making (9). Brunson argued that as women determined their own participation in the church, some responded with the fear that their actions threatened the church structure. In her research, Brunson found that "the sisters did not intend damage to the institution or infringement of the priesthood system. Some of the women, however, believed exclusion of half the membership from substantial activities paralyzed the church as the body of Christ" (12–13). In *Bonds of Sisterhood*, Brunson provided the best historical treatment on women's participation in early Mormonism and the Reorganized Church.

Barbara Hands Bernauer, assistant archivist in the Community of Christ Library-Archives, investigated the mystery and discovery of the actual burial location of Joseph the Seer and his brother Hyrum. Appropriately titled, "Still 'Side by Side': The Final Burial of Joseph and Hyrum Smith," *John Whitmer Historical Association Journal* 11 (1991): 17–33, Bernauer received acclaim for this superior research and writing when her article won the John Whitmer Historical Association's Best Article award in 1992. Two years later, she published her extensive essay in booklet format, and it remains the definitive work on this topic. An added personal dimension guided her research since Bernauer is the granddaughter of W. O. Hands, who supervised the 1928 archaeological dig in Nauvoo.

Any discussion of Community of Christ historians traveling the New Mormon History trail must include a statement on the church's official publisher, Herald Publishing House. Isleta L. Pement and Paul M. Edwards coauthored *A Herald to the Saints: History of Herald Publishing House* (Independence, Mo.: Herald House, 1992), in which they argued that beginning with the day when Joseph Smith Jr. and Oliver Cowdery first walked the Book of Mormon manuscript into the printing establishment of Egbert B. Grandin in Palmyra, New York, every generation of Latter Day Saintism has realized the communicative value of the written word. From their extensive research, Pement and Edwards concluded that, although publishing technology has gone through dramatic changes, the original purpose of Herald Publishing House—to serve as a natural viaduct to the people—has changed very little (10–11). The authors showed how Herald Publishing House has played an indispensable role for the history community of the Community of Christ, since the vast majority of the New Mormon History scholarship emerged from its presses.

Roger D. Launius, in *Alexander William Doniphan: Portrait of a Missouri Moderate* (Columbia: University of Missouri Press, 1997), offered a fresh look at one of the most important figures in Missouri's pre-Civil War history. Doniphan was a "household name" after the 1846 war with Mexico, which paved the way for annexing the territory that eventually became New Mexico and Arizona. Launius argued that Doniphan charted a path of moderation in the face of the social extremism that surrounded him (xii–xiii). Those who have studied the history of Latter Day Saintism know well that Doniphan's moderation saved Joseph Smith from execution at Far West in 1838; yet Launius showed how this important event was but one demonstration of a lifelong pursuit of accommodation without compromise of personal principles. Launius's best example of this characteristic was Doniphan's effort to mediate compromise between unionists and slave owners at the state and national levels. Launius described Doniphan's dejection as the Civil War broke out during the spring and summer of 1861:

> [Doniphan] had worked...to preserve peace and to secure the rights of all sides in the sectional conflict. This effort had come to very little. Missouri did not secede, and he believed that was the right decision, but it brought no serenity to his soul. With a foot in both camps, passionately in favor of the Union and believing in its highest ideals while maintaining his proslavery leanings, Doniphan wrestled with his conscience over the crisis and his response to it. All he could do was to declare neutrality, work for justice as he understood it, and long for peace (254).

From this scholarly treatise, Launius reminded the reader of the importance of seeing the history of Latter Day Saintism in the larger context of American history.

Scholarly Historical Journals and Articles

IT IS IMPOSSIBLE to review adequately more than thirty years of journalistic scholarship by historians associated with the RLDS–Community of Christ tradition. The panorama of topics is simply too vast. This section provides a small, but representative, sample of pivotal journal articles on historical topics. The criteria for this selection centered on interpretations that either initiated or accompanied shifts in the understanding of historic events. Not surprisingly, these articles generated initial controversy but gained general acceptance over time. This is not to suggest a complete agreement among the membership of the church on these interpretations, but it does acknowledge each author's significant contribution to his or her specific field of inquiry.

COURAGE: A JOURNAL OF HISTORY, THOUGHT, AND ACTION. Coinciding with the New Mormon History movement, three important journals served as venues for innovative interpretations. The first, *Courage:*

A Journal of History, Thought, and Action, published its pilot issue in April 1970 as a means of expression for independent thought. *Courage* had no official connection with either the then-RLDS Church or Graceland College, even though it was published in Lamoni, Iowa. *Courage* was edited, however, by individuals associated with the RLDS Church who were convinced that a free discussion of issues was necessary for the well-being of the church and its members. The editorial committee of *Courage* announced their intentions in "Critical Function of Courage," *Courage: A Journal of History, Thought, and Action*, pilot issue (April 1970): 49–52. Financial deficits ended the venture in 1973 after just nine issues were published. Still, *Courage* was the crucible from which future intellectual journals associated with the Reorganized Church would be forged.

Courage hosted several leading articles in church history during its three-year lifespan. For example, Richard P. Howard in "The 'Book of Abraham' in the Light of History and Egyptology," *Courage*, pilot issue (April 1970): 33–47, suggested that the interesting work "represents simply the product of Joseph Smith, Jr.'s imagination, wrought out in the midst of what to him must have been a very crucial and demanding and complex set of circumstances" (45). Howard concluded by encouraging scholars to recognize the integrity of the *Book of Abraham* as a historical fact, while at the same time purging its associations of historicity.

A second crucial article, Richard Howard's "Latter Day Saint Scriptures and the Doctrine of Propositional Revelation," *Courage* 1, no. 4 (June 1971): 209–25, appeared at a time when professional standards of analysis were being applied to church history and theology. Howard, as both church historian and leading scriptorian, highlighted the inherent problems of scriptural inerrancy and provided a primary voice in a church-wide discussion on the issue.

Wayne Ham's "Problems in Interpreting the Book of Mormon as History," *Courage* 1, no. 2 (September 1970): 15–22, prepared in its original form in the 1960s as a "Position Paper" for the Curriculum Consultation Committee, challenged readers to openly espouse a nonhistorical view of the Book of Mormon. In presenting nine specific criticisms in such areas as the story of the book's coming forth, narrative, propensity to reflect in detail the religious concerns of the American frontier, the developed Christological perspectives, ethical implications as binding on all, use of biblical passages, specific use of Isaiah, anachronisms, and changes in later editions, Ham demonstrated the difficulties of considering the Book of Mormon as literal history. In his conclusion, Ham called for liberating the Book of Mormon from traditional problems associated with the obligation of accepting it unquestioningly as a pure and undefiled history. Instead, Ham regarded the Book of Mormon as "a product of the American frontier" to be honored as "an interesting artifact of the Restoration movement in the nineteenth century" so that it could be enjoyed as a "fascinating piece of literature for the very first time" (21).

W. B. "Pat" Spillman, in "On Conceptualization of Zion," *Courage* 3, no. 1 (Fall 1972): 37–43, contributed to new understanding about the meaning of "Zion" in both its theological and historical contexts. Spillman identified three distinct conceptions of Zion within Reorganized Latter Day Saintism: a city, a condition in the hearts and minds of the people, and a process of becoming. He did not argue any specific viewpoint but called for constant reinterpretation in the context of Zion's meaning to each generation.

RESTORATION STUDIES. Since 1980, historians associated with the Community of Christ have used *Restoration Studies: A Collection of Essays About the History, Beliefs, and Practices of the Reorganized Church of Jesus Christ of Latter Day Saints* to publish their research and findings. This valuable resource has served for more than twenty-five years as a forum to express, as well as challenge, orthodoxy over the range of matters listed in the journal's subtitle. Various scholars have served on the editorial board that supervised production of the nine volumes, to date, of *Restoration Studies*. From the first volume produced in association with the 1980 sesquicentennial celebration of the movement, articles were selected on the basis of their contribution to "pursue truth 'wherever it may lead'" (Maurice L. Draper, "Preface," *Restoration Studies I: A Collection of Essays About the History, Beliefs, and Practices of the Reorganized Church of Jesus Christ of Latter Day Saints* [Independence, Mo.: Herald House, 1980]: 9).

Several significant *Restoration Studies* articles have had lasting impact on the journey taken by the church history community. Richard P. Howard, "Joseph Smith's First Vision: An Analysis of Six Contemporary Accounts," *Restoration Studies I* (1980): 95–117, set the tone in the Community of Christ for reinterpreting events in the early Restoration years.

Howard's account added significantly to the work on the same topic by other notable historians such as Fawn M. Brodie and Dean C. Jessee. After weighing six different portrayals of Joseph Smith Jr.'s experience in the grove by using a rubric of fourteen criteria, Howard noted the specific differences in each account. Then, he cautioned against oversimplification and directly denied the validity of using his research as ammunition for either attack or defense. Instead, he concluded that the varying explanations point out the complexities associated with "interpreting events that are beyond history" (116–17).

One *Restoration Studies* article, written for the sesquicentennial edition, made history itself in addition to providing an authoritative account of presidential succession in the Reorganized Church. D. Michael Quinn, in "The Mormon Succession Crisis of 1844," *Brigham Young University Studies: A Multidisciplinary Latter-day Saint Journal* 16, no. 2 (Winter 1976): 187–233, had earlier identified eight succession concepts that Joseph the Seer had at least partially implemented during his lifetime. In *Restoration Studies*, W. Grant McMurray, in "'True Son of a True Father': Joseph Smith III and the Succession Question" (*Restoration Studies I* [1980]: 131–145), summarized relevant points from Quinn's article. Then, McMurray described the pivotal revelatory experiences of Jason W. Briggs and Zenas H. Gurley Sr. in southern Wisconsin during the fall of 1851 that led to the creation of the "New Organization," a small gathering of Saints yearning for a president who would be a lineal descendant of Joseph the Seer. The most obvious candidate was Joseph III, his oldest son. After a description of "Young Joseph's" hesitation to assume the prophetic mantle, McMurray, who was Richard Howard's assistant history commissioner, described key events that led to Joseph III's ordination, the issues Smith saw as central to succession, and the role of lineage in RLDS succession. The title comes from Joseph III's August 1861 "First General Epistle of the President" (*True Latter Day Saints' Herald* 2, no. 6 [August 1861]: 121–124). The twenty-eight-year-old prophet referred to himself as "a true son of a true father" as he launched his fifty-four-year tenure as the first prophet-president of the Reorganized Church. Sixteen years after this article's publication, McMurray made history in his own right by beginning his tenure as the sixth prophet-president of the Reorganization, the first non-Smith to hold that office.

John Whitmer Historical Association Journal. Since its beginning in 1972, the John Whitmer Historical Association (JWHA) has provided Community of Christ historians, and those affiliated with other religious movements, a forum to share the fruits of their research in an annual conference. JWHA's independent status from any religious institution has allowed for free scholarly exploration of historical issues. Numerous papers from these conferences have been published in its annual *Journal,* which first appeared in 1981. Over the years, many controversial issues have appeared in its pages, still a lively tradition. Again, space limitations allow the mention of only a few benchmark essays that have strongly impacted historical thought among those affiliated with the Reorganization.

Richard P. Howard's "The Changing RLDS Response to Mormon Polygamy: A Preliminary Analysis," *John Whitmer Historical Association Journal* 3 (1983): 14–29, was a history-making article since it courageously moved away from the traditional RLDS position that Joseph Smith Jr. was not the author of Nauvoo polygamy. Howard, as church historian, revealed the diversity of responses to polygamy in the early Reorganization, then explained the factors influencing the development of polygamy in Nauvoo. After a brief discussion of responses from both the gentile and Mormon communities, Howard provided a nine-point summary. He referred to strong evidence that the entrance of polygamy into the Mormon community at Nauvoo was "accidental" because the situation of deceased spouses had not been foreseen in the development of temple "sealing" rituals in either Kirtland or Far West. Howard concluded: "Once Joseph Smith, Jr., came to see the harm being done to the church, he sought the help of [William] Marks to use all their combined power to put down polygamy in the church. However, by that time things had gone too far" (25). Even though Howard concluded that extant evidence only indirectly connected Joseph the Seer to the actual initiation of Nauvoo polygamy, such a conclusion caused much controversy among some RLDS members, especially when, three years later, his article was reprinted under the same title in *Restoration Studies III* (Independence, Mo.: Herald House, 1986): 145–62.

Don H. Compier's "The Faith of Emma Smith," *JWHA Journal* 6 (1986): 64–72, was first part of the JWHA spring lecture series in 1986; but because of the ordination of women, accepted by RLDS World Conference action in 1984, and with the first ordinations occurring the next year, his work became even more important. Compier highlighted Emma Smith's strong influence in the evolution of Mormonism, particularly during the difficult Nauvoo years and the emergence of the Reorganization. The first half of the article focused on the powerful presence of Methodism in Emma's early life and how Emma expressed that religious influence in the development of the Word of Wisdom, charitable and quasi-political activities through the Female Relief Society of Nauvoo, and especially in the Elect Lady's demand for marital loyalty. According to Compier, Emma expressed her commitment to Latter Day Saintism after the martyrdom by affirming the validity of the Book of Mormon, her love for Joseph Jr., and her strenuous efforts to see his "New Translation of the Bible" published (66–67).

Also, Community of Christ president W. Grant McMurray chose the *JWHA Journal* to respond to criticism by historian Roger D. Launius ("The Reorganized Church, the Decade of Decision, and the Abilene Paradox," *Dialogue: A Journal of Mormon Thought* 31 [Spring 1998]: 47–65); philosopher Paul M. Edwards ("Christ-centered Boredom: History and Historians," *JWHA Journal* 18 [1998]: 21–37); and sociologist Danny L. Jorgensen ("Beyond Modernity: The Future of the RLDS Church," *JWHA Journal* 18 [1998]: 5–20). These scholars critiqued the direction of the contemporary RLDS Church. In "History and Mission in Tension: A View from Both Sides," *JWHA Journal* 20 (2000): 34–47, McMurray charted the interaction between his years of service as assistant church historian, World Church secretary, and then member of the First Presidency with his training in historical methodology and noted a distinctive tension. McMurray exposed the inherent problems of incorporating history and mission into scholarly writings and acknowledged a point "where the work of the historian ends and the work of the theologian begins." In addressing his critics, McMurray counseled historians to be "acutely aware of motivations and predilections" to confuse history and theology, particularly in the examination of the relationship between faith, history, and mission.

The closing session of the 30th annual meeting of the John Whitmer Historical Association at Nauvoo, Illinois, in late September 2002, was titled, "The Singing Saints: A Festival of Hymns and Hymnody." Conference attendees participated in a hymnfest led by Richard Clothier, Junia Braby, and Brett Jagger. Participants representing a variety of Latter Day

Saint traditions gave background readings to specially selected historical hymns. Where possible, the organizers used original music scores. In a historic first, the program was preserved on a CD and inserted into the back cover of the special conference edition.

A highlight of JWHA conferences is the Sterling M. McMurrin Lecture Series delivered in commemoration of an amazing scholar and educator. Paul M. Edwards, in "Christ-centered Boredom: History and Historians," launched this plenary session presentation in the 1997 annual meeting. Since then many important scholars have used this opportunity to make significant observations about the progress of historical writings within the church history community. Historians such as Richard P. Howard, Mario S. DePillis, Stephen C. LeSueur, and D. Michael Quinn have used the McMurrin Lecture as a forum to challenge thinking and blaze trails into new fields of study. Most memorable was the sixth annual lecture, presented in 2002 by Robert Bruce Flanders in "Nauvoo on My Mind" (*JWHA Journal* 23 [2003]: 13–20). Given in Nauvoo, Illinois, on the thirtieth anniversary of the history association, Flanders reflected on his own career since tenure as the first president of the association, in 1972. He encouraged listeners to see the history of Nauvoo as more than just a controversial episode in the church story; rather, Nauvoo was a genetic marker of church identity to be continually explored for new understandings.

John Whitmer Historical Association Books

THE JOHN WHITMER Historical Association has provided an important forum for historical research projects. Three works published by this association are particularly significant, two by LDS historians. First, Marjorie Newton's *Hero or Traitor?: A Biographical Study of Charles Wesley Wandell* (Independence, Mo.: Independence Press, 1992) focused on the missionary most responsible for founding both the LDS and RLDS churches in Australia. Second, Gregory A. Prince's *Having Authority: The Origins and Development of Priesthood During the Ministry of Joseph Smith* (Independence, Mo.: Independence Press, 1993) is the best treatment on the Mormon bicameral priesthood in its historical setting. A third monograph, by Matthew Bolton, titled *Apostle of the Poor: The Life and Work of Missionary and Humanitarian Charles D. Neff,* was published in 2005 by John Whitmer Books. This fine work was the first title in the historical association's imprint. Bolton's biography chronicled the late RLDS apostle's early life, conversion to the church, rise to church leadership, and pivotal role in the church's worldwide expansion in the 1960s and 1970s. The author demonstrated how Neff's experience as a naval officer in World War II and his missionary work among the poor in the developing world fostered a deep social conscience, leading him to found several humanitarian organizations, such as the Community of Christ–sponsored Outreach International, and to challenge the causes of human suffering throughout the world.

Academic Capstone Projects

SEVERAL CAPSTONE ACADEMIC works make worthy contributions to Community of Christ historical scholarship. Four of these are representative. In 2003 Kimberly L. Loving completed his master of arts in religion degree through Graceland University, Lamoni, Iowa, with his thesis, "Ownership of the Kirtland Temple: Legends, Lies, and Misunderstandings." This scholarly study delved into the context in which the Reorganized Church of Jesus Christ of Latter Day Saints legally acquired title to the House of the Lord in Kirtland, Ohio. Loving combined his legal skills with historical methods to provide a unique view of the litigation. This study demonstrated that the actual judicial findings dispel a long-established mythology that emerged after the litigation by claiming that the legitimacy of ownership rests solely on principles of property abandonment, and for no other reason. Thus, this historical analysis of the Kirtland Temple litigation of 1879 and 1880 substantiated neither the traditional claim of the legitimacy of Joseph Smith III's presidential succession, nor the assertion that the Reorganized Church of Jesus Christ of Latter Day Saints wrestled ownership from the Church of Jesus Christ of Latter-day Saints.

In 1995, Richard A. Waugh completed his doctor of philosophy degree in geography at the University of Wisconsin–Madison. His dissertation, "Sacred Space and the Persistence of Identity: The Evolution and Meaning of an American Religious Utopia," examined the development of sacred space within the RLDS Church. In this fascinating study, Waugh assessed such concepts as Zion and the construction and placement of temples using postmodern criteria. A third academic capstone project is the 1998 University of Missouri–Kansas City doctoral dissertation by Mark A. Scherer, titled "A Material Cultural Analysis of the Foundational History of Latter Day Saintism, 1827–1844." Scherer's work is a qualitative, interdisciplinary exploration of early nineteenth-century material culture and educational practices. Scherer found that early church members practiced a "language of Latter Day Saintism" in their choice of architectural styles as well as in their educational institutions and practices. The author argued that Joseph Smith Jr. launched his movement by observing an important principle of material culture studies when the budding prophet included the testimonies of witnesses who "saw and touched" the Book of Mormon plates: "seeing is believing, but feeling is truth." Three fields of inquiry in the study of material culture—structuralism, symbolism, and functionalism—provided a framework for this analysis.

Representative of the important research and writing from students in the Community of Christ Seminary is the integrative master's thesis titled "A Journey toward the Ordination of Women in the Community of Christ: A Historical Literature Review" by Becky L. Savage (Graceland University, 2005). Savage's examination covered historical literature published over a one-hundred-fifty-year period. She argued that the heralded message that "all are called" did not mean that "all are eligible" and that women persevered through adversity with tenacious and visionary leadership. Savage concluded that cyclical experiences of women's organizations, and sociological and theological influences and revelatory experiences could be best understood in the context of church publications.

Conclusion

BIBLIOGRAPHIC ESSAYS, LIKE the stream of time, seem to be without beginning and without end. A flood of scholarship occurred before and after the scope of this writing. It is a daunting task to attempt historiographical coverage of more than thirty years of scholarship in such a brief essay. Just as sculptors reveal as much about themselves as about their subject, this essay portrays some of the stronger influences on my personal exploration of the Latter Day Saint story from the perspective of historians associated with the Community of Christ. I caution readers against concluding that because a certain article or book is not mentioned, the work is neither influential nor meritorious. Rather, this essay reveals the need for further comprehensive and unbiased studies of historical literature on Latter Day Saintism, especially those that provide a more in-depth focus on the history of the Reorganized Church, now called the Community of Christ. In important ways, and through resources such as these, this church history community has made a significant contribution by blazing trails across the New Mormon History field of inquiry.

SELECTED BIBLIOGRAPHY

Books and Articles

Allen, James B., and Glen M. Leonard. *The Story of the Latter-day Saints.* Salt Lake City: Deseret Book Company, 1976.

Ambrose, Stephen E. *Undaunted Courage: Meriwether Lewis, Thomas Jefferson, and the Opening of the American West.* New York: Ambrose-Tubbs, 1996.

"An Act to provide for the Incorporation of Religious Societies." In *Laws of the State of New-York, Revised and Passed at the Thirty-Sixth Session of the Legislature,* passed April 5, 1813. Albany, N.Y.: H. C. Southwick & Co., 1813.

Anderson, Lavina Fielding, ed. *Lucy's Book: A Critical Edition of Lucy Mack Smith's Family Memoir.* Salt Lake City: Signature Books, 2001.

Anderson, Mary Audentia Smith. *Ancestry and Posterity of Joseph Smith and Emma Hale, With Little Sketches of Their Immigrant Ancestors All of Whom Came to America between the Years 1620 and 1685, and Settled in the States of Massachusetts and Connecticut.* Independence, Mo.: Herald Publishing House, 1929.

Anderson, Mary Audentia Smith, ed. "The Memoirs of President Joseph Smith (1832-1914)." Serially presented. *Saints' Herald* 81–84 (6 November 1934–31 July 1937).

Anderson, Richard Lloyd. *Joseph Smith's New England Heritage: Influences of Grandfathers Solomon Mack and Asael Smith.* Salt Lake City: Deseret Book Company, 1971.

Anderson, Robert D. *Inside the Mind of Joseph Smith: Psychobiography and the Book of Mormon.* Salt Lake City: Signature Books, 1999.

Andrew, Laurel B. *The Early Temples of the Mormons: The Architecture of the Millennial Kingdom in the American West.* Albany: State University of New York Press, 1978.

Arrington, Leonard J. *Brigham Young: American Moses.* New York: Alfred A. Knopf, 1985.

Arrington, Leonard J. *Charles C[.] Rich: Mormon General and Western Frontiersman.* Provo, Utah: Brigham Young University Press, 1974.

Arrington, Leonard J. "Church Leaders in Liberty Jail." *Brigham Young University Studies* 13, no. 1 (Autumn 1972): 20–26.

Arrington, Leonard J. "Oliver Cowdery's Kirtland, Ohio, 'Sketch Book.'" *Brigham Young University Studies* 12, no. 4 (Summer 1972): 410–26.

Austin, Emily. *Mormonism; or, Life Among the Mormons*. Madison, Wis.: Cantwell, 1882.

"Awful Assassination of JOSEPH AND HYRUM SMITH!—The Pledged Faith of the State of Illinois stained with innocent blood by a Mob!" *Times and Seasons* 5, no. 12 (1 July 1844): 560.

Backman, Milton V. Jr. *The Heavens Resound: A History of the Latter-day Saints in Ohio, 1830–1838*. Salt Lake City: Deseret Book Company, 1983.

Baugh, Alexander L. "A Call to Arms: The 1838 Mormon Defense of Northern Missouri." PhD. diss., Brigham Young University, 1996.

Benjamin, Asher. *Elements of Architecture*. Boston: Benjamin B. Mussey, 1843.

Benjamin, Asher. *The Builder's Guide*. Boston: Perkins & Marvin, 1839.

Benjamin, Asher. *The Country Builder's Assistant*. Greenfield, Mass.: Thomas Dickman, 1797.

Benjamin, Asher. *The Practical House Carpenter*. Boston: R. P. & C. Williams and Annin & Smith, 1830.

Benjamin, Asher. *The Practice of Architecture*. Boston: Carter, Hendee & Co., 1833.

Benjamin, Asher *The Rudiments of Architecture*. Boston: Munroe and Francis, 1814.

Benjamin, Asher (with Daniel Raynerd). *American Builder's Companion; or, A New System of Architecture: Particularly Adapted to the Present Style of Building in the United States of America*. Boston: Etheridge and Bliss, 1806.

Bestor, Arthur. *Backwoods Utopias, The Sectarian and Owenite Phases of Communitarian Socialism in America: 1663–1829*. Philadelphia: University of Pennsylvania Press, 1967.

Billington, Ray Allen, and Martin Ridge. *Westward Expansion: A History of the American Frontier*. 5th ed. New York: Macmillan Publishing Co., 1982.

Blair, Alma R. "The Reorganized Church of Jesus Christ of Latter Day Saints: Moderate Mormons." In *The Restoration Movement: Essays in Mormon History*. Edited by F. Mark McKiernan, Alma R. Blair, and Paul M. Edwards. Independence. Mo.: Herald Publishing House, 1979, 201–24.

Blanchard, Paula. *Margaret Fuller: From Transcendentalism to Revolution*. New York: Delacorte Press/Seymour Lawrence, 1978.

Boller, Paul. *Presidential Campaigns*. New York: Oxford University Press, 1985.

Book of Commandments for the Government of the Church of Christ. Zion [Independence, Mo.]: W. W. Phelps & Co., 1833.

Book of Doctrine and Covenants. Independence, Mo.: Herald Publishing House, 1990.

Bradshaw, M. Scott. "Joseph Smith's Performance of Marriages in Ohio." *Brigham Young University Studies* 39 (2000): 23–69.

Briggs, E. C. Letter to Joseph Smith III. *Saints' Herald* 31, no. 25 (21 June 1884): 396–97.

Briggs, Edmund C. "A Visit to Nauvoo in 1856." *Journal of History* 9, no. 4 (October 1916): 453–54.

Brodie, Fawn M. *No Man Knows My History: The Life of Joseph Smith, The Mormon Prophet*. 2nd ed. rev. New York: Alfred A. Knopf, 1995.

Brooke, John L. *The Refiner's Fire: The Making of Mormon Cosmology, 1644–1844*. Cambridge: Cambridge University Press, 1994.

Brown, Dee. *Bury My Heart at Wounded Knee: An Indian History of the American West*. New York: Harcourt/Holt, Rinehart & Winston, 2007.

Bruce, Dickson D. Jr. *And They All Sang Hallelujah: Plain-Folk Camp-Meeting Religion, 1800–1845*. Knoxville: University of Tennessee Press, 1974.

Bushman, Richard L. *Joseph Smith and the Beginnings of Mormonism*. Urbana: University of Illinois Press, 1984.

Bushman, Richard L. *Joseph Smith: Rough Stone Rolling, A Cultural Biography of Mormonism's Founder*. New York: Alfred A. Knopf, 2005.

Butler, John Lowe. "Autobiography." Typescript. Community of Christ Archives, Independence, Missouri.

Butler, Jon. "Magic, Astrology, and the Early American Religious Heritage, 1600–1760." *American Historical Review* 84 (April 1979): 317–346.

Caldwell, Matthew. *History of Caldwell and Livingston Counties, Missouri*. St. Louis: National Historical Company, 1886.

Campen, Richard M. *Architecture of the Western Reserve, 1800–1900*. Cleveland: The Press of Case Western Reserve University, 1971.

Cannon, Donald Q., and Lyndon W. Cook, eds. *Far West Record: Minutes of The Church of Jesus Christ of Latter-day Saints, 1830–1844*. Salt Lake City: Deseret Book Company, 1983.

Caswell, Henry. *The Prophet of the Nineteenth Century; or, the Rise, Progress, and Present State of the Mormons, or Latter Day Saints....* London: J.G.F. & J. Rivington, 1843.

Collette, D. Brent. "In Search of Zion: A Description of Early Mormon Millennial Utopianism as Revealed through the Life of Edward Partridge." Master's thesis, Brigham Young University, 1977.

Compton, Todd. *In Sacred Loneliness: The Plural Wives of Joseph Smith.* Salt Lake City: Signature Books, 1998.

Corrill, John. *A Brief History of the Church of Christ of Latter Day Saints (Commonly Called Mormons) Including an Account of Their Doctrine and Discipline, with the Reasons of the Author for Leaving the Church.* St. Louis: Printed for the Author, 1839.

"Council of Twelve Minutes," Book A, 2 May 1865. Vault Collection. Community of Christ Library-Archives, Independence, Missouri.

Cross, Whitney R. *The Burned-over District: The Social and Intellectual History of Enthusiastic Religion in Western New York, 1800–1850.* Ithaca, N.Y.: Cornell University Press, 1982.

Davis, Inez Smith. *The Story of the Church: A History of the Church of Jesus Christ of Latter Day Saints, and of Its Legal Successor, the Reorganized Church of Jesus Christ of Latter Day Saints.* 6th ed. Independence, Mo.: Herald Publishing House, 1959.

Dibble, Philo. *History of the Life of Philo Dibble, Sr.* N.p., n d. Community of Christ Library-Archives, Independence, Missouri.

Document Containing the Correspondence, Orders, &C. In Relation to the Disturbances with the Mormons; And the Evidence Given Before the Hon. Austin A. King. Fayette, Mo.: Office of the Boon's Lick Democrat, 1841.

Doyle, Don Harrison. *The Social Order of a Frontier Community, 1825–70.* Urbana: University of Illinois Press, 1978.

Edwards, Jonathan. *An Account of the Life of the Reverend Mr. David Brainerd....* Edited by Norman Pettit. New Haven, Conn.: Yale University Press, 1985.

Edwards, Paul M. *Our Legacy of Faith: A Brief History of the Reorganized Church of Jesus Christ of Latter Day Saints.* Independence, Mo.: Herald Publishing House, 1991.

Ellis, Joseph J. *American Sphinx: The Character of Thomas Jefferson.* New York: Vintage Books, 1998.

Epperson, Steven. "The Grand Fundamental Principle: Joseph Smith and the Virtue of Friendship." *Journal of Mormon History* 23 (Fall 1997): 77–105.

Fairfield, Roy P., ed. *The Federalist Papers: A Collection of Essays Written in Support of the Constitution of the United States.* 2nd ed. Baltimore: Johns Hopkins University Press, 1986.

Firmage, Edwin Brown, and Richard Collin Mangrum. *Zion in the Courts: A Legal History of the Church of Jesus Christ of Latter-day Saints, 1830–1900.* Urbana: University of Illinois Press, 1988.

First Baptist Church, Salem, Massachusetts. "Our Heritage." www.fbcsalemma.org/heritage.htm.

Flake, Chad J., ed. *A Mormon Bibliography, 1830–1930: Books, Pamphlets, Periodicals, and Broadsides Relating to the First Century of Mormonism.* Salt Lake City: University of Utah Press, 1978.

Flanders, Robert Bruce. *Nauvoo: Kingdom on the Mississippi.* Urbana: University of Illinois Press, 1965.

Ford, Thomas. *History of the State of Illinois, from Its Commencement as a State in 1818 to 1847.* Chicago: S. C. Griggs and Co., 1854.

Forscutt, Mark H. "Commemorative Discourse on the Death of Mrs. Emma Bidamon." *Saints' Herald* 26, no. 14 (15 July 1879): 209–17.

Foster, Lawrence. *Religion and Sexuality: Three American Communal Experiments of the Nineteenth Century.* New York: Oxford University Press, 1981.

Franklin, John Hope. *From Slavery to Freedom: A History of African Americans.* 8th ed. New York: Alfred A. Knopf, 2000.

French, Calvin V. "Organization and Administration of the Latter Day Saint School System of Free Education, Common School through University at Nauvoo, Illinois, 1840–1845." Master's thesis. Temple University, 1965.

Gardner, Hamilton. "The Nauvoo Legion, 1840–1845: A Unique Military Organization." In *Kingdom on the Mississippi Revisited: Nauvoo in Mormon History.* Edited by Roger D. Launius and John E. Hallwas. Urbana: University of Illinois Press, 1996, 48–61.

Gentry, Leland Homer. "A History of the Latter-day Saints in Northern Missouri from 1836 to 1839." PhD. diss. Brigham Young University, 1965.

Glassie, Henry. *Folk Housing in Middle Virginia: A Structural Analysis of Historic Artifacts.* Knoxville: The University of Tennessee Press, 1975.

Godfrey, Kenneth W. "The Nauvoo Neighborhood: A Little Philadelphia or Unique City Set upon a Hill?" In *Kingdom on the Mississippi Revisited: Nauvoo in Mormon History.* Edited by Roger D. Launius and John E. Hallwas. Urbana: University of Illinois Press, 1996, 72–93.

Godwin, Parke. *A Popular View of the Doctrine of Charles Fourier.* Philadelphia: University of Pennsylvania Press, Inc., 1972.

Golemba, Henry L. *George Ripley.* Boston: G. K. Hall & Co., 1977.

Goodrich, Samuel. *Reflections of a Lifetime.* 2 vols. New York: n.p., 1856.

Green Mountain Boys. Letter to Thomas C. Sharp, 15 February 1844, 3, Thomas C. Sharp and Allied Anti-Mormon Papers, Beinecke Rare Book and Manuscript Library, Yale University, New Haven, Connecticut.

Gunn, Stanley R. *Oliver Cowdery: Second Elder and Scribe.* Salt Lake City: Bookcraft, 1962.

Hale, Van. "Defining the Contemporary Mormon Concept of God." In *Line upon Line: Essays on Mormon Doctrine.* Edited by Gary James Bergera. Salt Lake City: Signature Books, 1989, 7–15.

Hallwas, John E., and Roger D. Launius. *Cultures in Conflict: A Documentary History of the Mormon War in Illinois.* Logan: Utah State University Press, 1995.

Ham, Wayne, ed. *Publish Glad Tidings: Readings in Early Latter Day Saint Sources.* Independence, Mo.: Herald Publishing House, 1970.

Hamer, John. *Northeast of Eden: A Historical Atlas of Missouri's Mormon Country.* Ann Arbor, Mich.: Published by the author, 2004.

Handbook of Chemistry and Physics. Cleveland: The Chemical Rubber Publishing Company, 1962.

Hansen, Klaus J. *Mormonism and the American Experience.* Chicago: University of Chicago Press, 1981.

Hansen, Klaus J. *Quest for Empire: The Political Kingdom of God and the Council of Fifty in Mormon History.* East Lansing: Michigan State University Press, 1967.

Harmon, Robert B. *Georgian Architecture in America: A Brief Style Guide.* Monticello, Ill.: Vance Bibliographies, 1982.

Harris, W. P. Letter to W. C. Flagg. 25 April 1855. In "A Hoax: Reminiscences of an Old Kinderhook Mystery." *Journal of the Illinois State Historical Society* 5 (July 1912): 271–73.

Hartley, William G. "Newel and Lydia Bailey Knight's Kirtland Love Story and Historic Wedding." *Brigham Young University Studies* 39, no 4 (2000): 6–22.

Harvey, Van A. *The Historian and the Believer: The Morality of Historical Knowledge and Christian Belief.* Urbana: University of Illinois Press, 1996.

Hatch, Nathan O. *The Democratization of American Christianity.* New Haven, Conn.: Yale University Press, 1989.

[Herendon, Trudy]. "George March Hinkle: Elder of the Mormon Church Hero or Traitor?" *Missouri Mormon Frontier [Newsletter]* 33 (January–April 2004): 1–18.

Hill, Donna. *Joseph Smith: The First Mormon*. Garden City, N.Y.: Doubleday & Company, 1977.

Hill, Marvin S., C. Keith Rooker, and Larry T. Wimmer. *The Kirtland Economy Revisited: A Market Critique of Sectarian Economics*. Provo, Utah: Brigham Young University Press, 1977.

Homer, Michael W. "'Similarity of Priesthood in Masonry': The Relationship between Freemasonry and Mormonism." *Dialogue: A Journal of Mormon Thought* 27, no. 3 (Fall 1994): 1–113.

Howard, Richard P. "An Analysis of Six Contemporary Accounts Touching Joseph Smith's First Vision." In *Restoration Studies I: A Collection of Essays About the History, Beliefs, and Practices of the Reorganized Church of Jesus Christ of Latter Day Saints*. Edited by Maurice L. Draper and Clare D. Vlahos. Independence, Mo.: Herald Publishing House, 1980, 95–117.

Howard, Richard P. "Beating Solomon Spaulding's Poor, Dead Horse One More Time." *Saints Herald* 124, no. 9 (September 1977): 37.

Howard, Richard P. *Restoration Scriptures: A Study of Their Textual Development*. Rev. and enl. Independence, Mo.: Herald Publishing House, 1995

Howard, Richard P. "The Changing RLDS Response to Mormon Polygamy: A Preliminary Analysis." In *Restoration Studies III: A Collection of Essays About the History, Beliefs, and Practices of the Reorganized Church of Jesus Christ of Latter Day Saints*. Edited by Maurice L. Draper and Debra Combs. Independence, Mo.: Herald Publishing House, 1986, 145–162.

Howard, Richard P. *The Church Through the Years*. 2 vols. Independence, Mo.: Herald Publishing House, 1991, 1993.

Howard, Richard P. "The 'History of Joseph Smith' in Its Historical Setting." Serially presented. *Saints' Herald* 119 nos. 7–10 (July–October, 1972).

Howard, Richard P. "The Quest for Traces of a Peace Gene in Restoration History." *John Whitmer Historical Association Journal* 23 (2003): 45–58.

Howe, E. D. *Mormonism Unvailed: or, a Faithful Account....* Painesville, Ohio: Published by the Author, 1834.

Jackson, Richard H. "The Mormon Village: Genesis and Antecedents of the City of Zion Plan." *Brigham Young University Studies* 17, no. 2 (Winter 1977): 223–40.

Jessee, Dean. "Joseph Knight Recollection of Early Mormon History," *Brigham Young University Studies* 17, no. 1 (Autumn 1976): 29–39.

Jessee, Dean C., ed. *The Papers of Joseph Smith*. 3 vols. Salt Lake City: Deseret Book Co., 1989.

Jessee, Dean C., and David J. Whittaker, eds. "The Last Months of Mormonism in Missouri: The Albert Perry Rockwood Journal." *Brigham Young University Studies* 28, no. 1 (Winter 1988): 5–41.

Johnson, Benjamin F. *The Autobiography of Benjamin Johnson: My Life's Review*. Independence, Mo.: Zion's Printing and Publishing Co., 1947.

Johnston, Carrie Polk, and W. H. S. McGlumphy. *History of Clinton and Caldwell Counties, Mo*. Topeka, Kans.: Historical Publishing Company, 1923.

Kennedy, Roger G. *Greek Revival in America*. New York: Stewart, Tabori & Chang, 1989.

Kimball, Heber C. "Advancement of the Saints...." *Journal of Discourses* 10 (1865): 233–38.

Kimball, Heber C. "Building the Temple...." *Journal of Discourses* 10 (1865): 163–69.

Kimball, James L. Jr. "The Nauvoo Charter: A Reinterpretation." In *Kingdom on the Mississippi Revisited: Nauvoo in Mormon History*. Edited by Roger D. Launius and John E. Hallwas. Urbana: University of Illinois Press, 1996, 39–47.

Kious, W. Jacquelyne, and Robert I. Tilling. *This Dynamic Earth: The Story of Plate Tectonics*. Washington, D.C: US Geological Survey, 2003.

Kirtland Council Minute Book, Typescript Copy. Community of Christ Library-Archives, Independence, Missouri.

Kling, David W. "New Divinity Schools of the Prophets, 1750–1825: A Case Study in Ministerial Education." *History of Education Quarterly* 37, no. 2 (Summer 1997): 187.

Knight, Newell. *Scraps of Biography*. Salt Lake City: Juvenile Instructors Office, 1883.

Lancaster, James E. "The Method of Translation of the Book of Mormon." *John Whitmer Historical Association Journal* 3 (1983): 51–61.

Larson, A. Karl, and Katherine Miles Larson, eds. *Diary of Charles Lowell Walker*. Vol. 2. Logan: Utah State University Press, 1980.

Larson, Charles M. ...*By His Own Hand Upon Papyrus: A New Look at the Joseph Smith Papyri*. Rev. ed. Grand Rapids, Mich: Institute for Religious Research, 1992.

Launius, Roger D. *Alexander William Doniphan: Portrait of a Missouri Moderate*. Columbia: University of Missouri Press, 1997.

Launius, Roger D. *The Kirtland Temple: A Historical Narrative*. Independence, Mo.: Herald Publishing House, 1986.

Launius, Roger D. *Zion's Camp: Expedition to Missouri, 1834*. Independence, Mo.: Herald Publishing House, 1984.

Laws of the State of New York, Revised and Passed at Thirty-Sixth Session of the Legislature. 2 Vols. Albany, N.Y.: H. C. Southwick and Co., 1813.

Lee, E. G. *The Mormons, or Knavery Exposed*. Philadelphia: n.p., 1841.

LeSueur, Stephen C. "Missouri's Failed Compromise: The Creation of Caldwell County for the Mormons." *Journal of Mormon History* 31, no. 3 (Fall 2005): 113–144.

LeSueur, Stephen C. *The 1838 Mormon War in Missouri*. Columbia: University of Missouri Press, 1987.

LeSueur, Stephen C. "The Danites Reconsidered: Were They Vigilantes or Just the Mormons' Version of the Elks Club?" *John Whitmer Historical Association Journal* 14 (1994): 35–51.

Lewis, Jan Ellen, and Peter S. Onuf, eds. *Sally Hemings & Thomas Jefferson: History, Memory, and Civic Culture*. Charlottesville: University Press of Virginia, 1999.

Limerick, Patricia Nelson. *The Legacy of Conquest: The Unbroken Past of the American West*. New York: W. W. Norton & Company, 1988.

Mack, Solomon. *A Narraitve of the Life of Solomon Mack....* Windsor, [Vt.]: By the author, 1811.

Marini, Stephen A. *Radical Sects of Revolutionary New England*. Cambridge, Mass.: Harvard University Press, 1982.

Marquardt, H. Michael. *The Joseph Smith Revelations: Text & Commentary*. Salt Lake City: Signature Books, 1999.

Marquardt, H. Michael. *The Rise of Mormonism, 1816–1844*. Longwood, Fla.: Xulon Press, 2005.

Marquardt, H. Michael, and Wesley P. Walters. *Inventing Mormonism: Tradition and the Historical Record*. Salt Lake City: Smith Research Associates, 1994.

Marsden, George M. *Jonathan Edwards: A Life*. New Haven, Conn.: Yale University Press, 2003.

McLellin, W. E. Letter to Joseph Smith III, Independence, Missouri, July 1872. Community of Christ Library-Archives, Independence, Missouri.

McLoughlin, William G. *New England Dissent, 1630-1833: The Baptists and the Separation of Church and State*. 2 Vols. Cambridge, Mass.: Harvard University Press, 1971.

Meinig, D. W. *The Shaping of America: A Geographical Perspective on 500 years of History*. 3 Vols. Vol. 2: *Continental America, 1800-1867*. New Haven, Conn.: Yale University Press, 1993.

Meyerhoff, Hans, ed. *The Philosophy of History in Our Time*. Garden City, N.Y.: Doubleday Anchor Books, 1959.

Morain, William D. *The Sword of Laban: Joseph Smith Jr. and the Dissociated Mind*. Washington, D.C.: American Psychiatric Press, 1998.

Morgan, Captain William. *Illustrations of Masonry by one of the Fraternity who has devoted thirty years to the subject* .... N.p.: William Morgan, 1827. http://www.utlm.org/onlinebooks/captmorgansfreemasonrycontents.htm.

Mulder, William, and A. Russell Mortensen, eds. *Among the Mormons: Historic Accounts by Contemporary Observers*. Lincoln: University of Nebraska Press, 1973.

Murdock, S. Reed. *John Murdock: His Life and his Legacy*.... Layton, Utah: Summerwood Publishers, 2000.

Newell, Linda King, and Valeen Tippetts Avery. *Mormon Enigma: Emma Hale Smith*. Urbana: University of Illinois Press, 1994.

Oaks, Dallin H., and Marvin S. Hill. *Carthage Conspiracy: The Trial of the Accused Assassins of Joseph Smith*. Urbana: University of Illinois Press, 1975.

"Old Soldier's Testimony, The." *Saints' Herald* 31, no. 4 (4 October 1884): 643–45.

Olney, Oliver. *The Absurdities of Mormonism Portrayed, a brief sketch*. Hancock County, Ill.: N.p., 1843.

Palmer, Grant H. *An Insider's View of Mormon Origins*. Salt Lake City: Signature Books, 2002.

Parkin, Max H. "Zion's Camp Cholera Victims Monument Dedication." *Missouri Mormon Frontier Foundation Newsletter* 15 (Fall 1997): 2–6.

Peck, Reed. *The Reed Peck Manuscript*. Salt Lake City: Modern Microfilm Co., 1965.

Persuitte, David. *Joseph Smith and the Origins of the Book of Mormon*. Jefferson, N.C.: McFarland & Company, Inc., 1985.

Pratt, Orson. *The Prophetic Almanac for 1846*. New York: New York Messenger, 1846.

Pratt, Orson. "Remarkable Visions," 1848. Pamphlet series. Liverpool: R. James, 1851.

Pratt, Parley P. Jr., ed. *Autobiography of Parley Parker Pratt*. Salt Lake City: Deseret Book Company, 1976.

Pratt, Parley Parker. *History of Late Persecutions of the Church of Latter Day Saints.* N.p., 1840. Community of Christ Library-Archives, Independence, Missouri.

Priest, Josiah, *The Wonders of Nature and Providence Displayed....* Albany, N.Y.: By the Author, 1826.

Prince, Gregory A. *Having Authority: The Origins and Development of Priesthood during the Ministry of Joseph Smith.* John Whitmer Historical Association Monograph Series. Independence, Mo.: Independence Press, 1993.

Quincy, Josiah. *Figures of the Past: From the Leaves of Old Journals.* 6th ed. Boston: Roberts Brothers, 1884.

Quinn, D. Michael. *Early Mormonism and the Magic World View.* Rev. ed. Salt Lake City: Signature Books, 1998.

Quinn, D. Michael. "Jesse Gause: Joseph Smith's Little-Known Counselor." *Brigham Young University Studies* 23 (Fall 1983): 487–93.

Quinn, D. Michael. "Joseph Smith's Experience of a Methodist 'Camp Meeting' in 1820." *Dialogue: A Journal of Mormon Thought.* Paperless: E-Paper #3, expanded Version. www.dialoguejournal.com/excerpts/e3.pdf

Quinn, D. Michael. "Joseph Smith III's 1844 Blessing and the Mormons of Utah," *John Whitmer Historical Association Journal* 1 (1981): 12–27.

Quinn, D. Michael. *The Mormon Hierarchy: Origins of Power.* Salt Lake City: Signature Books, 1994.

Radke, Andrea G. "We Also Marched: The Women and Children of Zion's Camp, 1834." *Brigham Young University Studies* 39, no 1 (2000): 147–65.

Remini, Robert V. *Joseph Smith.* New York: Penguin Putnam, Inc., 2002.

Rigdon, Sidney. *Oration Delivered by Mr. S. Rigdon on The 4th of July, 1838.* Far West, Mo.: Printed by the [*Elder's*] Journal Office, 1838.

Riggs, Michael S. "From the Daughters of Zion to 'The Banditti of the Prairies': Danite Influence on the Nauvoo Period." In *Restoration Studies VII: A Collection of Essays About the History, Beliefs, and Practices of the Reorganized Church of Jesus Christ of Latter Day Saints.* Edited by Joni Wilson and Ruth Ann Wood. Independence, Mo.: Herald Publishing House, 1998, 95–106.

Riggs, Michael S. "The Economic Impact of Fort Leavenworth on Northwestern Missouri, 1827–1838. Yet Another Reason for the Mormon War?" In *Restoration Studies IV: A Collection of Essays About the History, Beliefs, and Practices of the Reorganized Church of Jesus Christ of Latter Day Saints.* Edited by Marjorie B. Troeh and Eileen M. Terrill. Independence, Mo.: Herald Publishing House, 1988, 124–33.

Roberts, Brigham H. *The Missouri Persecutions.* Salt Lake City: George Q. Cannon & Sons Co., 1900.

Roberts, Brigham H. *Studies of the Book of Mormon.* Edited by Brigham D. Madsen. 2nd ed. Salt Lake City: Signature Books, 1992.

Robinson, Ebenezer. "Items of Personal History of the Editor, No. 6." *The Return* 1 (October 1889): 149.

Robison, Elwin C. *The First Mormon Temple: Design, Construction, and Historic Context of the Kirtland Temple.* Provo, Utah: Brigham Young University Press, 1997.

Romig, Ronald E. "Law of Consecration: Antecedents and Practice at Kirtland, Ohio." In *Restoration Studies VI: A Collection of Essays About the History, Beliefs, and Practices of the Reorganized Church of Jesus Christ of Latter Day Saints.* Edited by Wayne Ham and Joni Wilson. Independence, Mo.: Herald Publishing House, 1995, 191–205.

Saunders, Benjamin. Interviewed by William H. Kelley, September 1884. In "Miscellany," Community of Christ Library-Archives, Independence, Missouri.

Scherer, Mark A. "A Church with an International Heritage." *Saints Herald* 145, no. 12 (December 1998): 506.

Scherer, Mark Albert. "A Material Cultural Analysis of the Foundational History of Latter Day Saintism, 1827–1844." PhD. diss. University of Missouri at Kansas City, 1998.

Scherer, Mark A. "'Called by a New Name': Mission, Identity, and the Reorganized Church." *Journal of Mormon History* 27, no. 2 (Fall 2001): 40–63.

Schirmer, Sherry Lamb, and Richard D. McKinzie. *At the River's Bend: An Illustrated History of Kansas City, Independence, and Jackson County.* Woodland Hills, Calif.: Windsor Publications, Inc., 1982.

Shepard, Bill. "Stealing at Mormon Nauvoo." *John Whitmer Historical Association Journal* 23 (2003): 91–110.

Shipps, Jan. *Mormonism: The Story of a New Religious Tradition.* Urbana: University of Illinois Press, 1985.

Smith, Andrew F. *The Saintly Scoundrel: the Life and Times of Dr. John Cook Bennett.* Urbana: University of Illinois Press, 1997.

Smith, George D., ed. *An Intimate Chronicle: The Journals of William Clayton.* 6 Journals. Salt Lake City: Signature Books, 1991.

Smith, Joseph Jr., trans. Book of Mormon. Authorized Edition. Independence, Mo.: Board of Publication of the Reorganized Church of Jesus Christ of Latter Day Saints, 1908.

Smith, Joseph Jr. "The King Follett Discourse." *Times and Seasons* 5, no. 15 (15 August 1844): 612–17.

Smith, Joseph Jr. (New York City). Letter to Emma Smith (Kirtland, Ohio), 13 October 1832. Community of Christ Library-Archives, Independence, Missouri.

Smith, Joseph Jr. Letter to Emma Hale Smith. 12 November 1838. Joseph Smith Papers. Community of Christ Library-Archives, Independence, Missouri.

Smith III, Joseph. "Last Testimony of Sister Emma," *Saints' Herald* 26, no. 19 (1 October 1879): 289–90.

Smith III, Joseph. Letter to J. M. Stubbart. Octavia, Nebraska, 19 May 1896. Joseph Smith III Letterbook, 6: 458–59. Community of Christ Library-Archives, Independence, Missouri

Smith, Lucy. *Biographical Sketches of Joseph Smith the Prophet and his Progenitors for Many Generations*. Liverpool, England: S. W. Richards, 1853. Reprint. Independence, Mo.: Herald Publishing House, 1969.

(Smith) Mary B. Letter to Ina (Smith) Coolbrith, 27 March 1908. Community of Christ Library-Archives, Independence, Missouri.

Smith, William. *William Smith on Mormonism....* Lamoni, Iowa: Herald Steam Book and Job Office, 1883.

"Statement of J. W. Peterson Concerning William Smith." 1 May 1921. Miscellaneous Letters and Papers. Community of Christ Library-Archives, Independence, Missouri.

St. John Stott, Graham. "Just War, Holy War, and Joseph Smith Jr." In *Restoration Studies IV: A Collection of Essays About the History, Beliefs, and Practices of the Reorganized Church of Jesus Christ of Latter Day Saints*. Edited by Marjorie B. Troeh and Eileen M. Terril. Independence, Mo.: Herald Publishing House, 1988, 134–141.

Swartzell, William. *Mormonism Exposed....* Pekin, Ohio: Published by the author, 1840.

Swenson, Vern G. "The Development of a Holy Ghost in Mormon Theology." In *Line upon Line: Essays on Mormon Doctrine*. Edited by Gary James Bergera. Salt Lake City: Signature Books, 1989, 89–101.

Taylor, John. "Unity of the Saints." *Journal of Discourses* 11 (1867): 20–27.

Thomas, Mark D. *Digging in Cumorah: Reclaiming Book of Mormon Narratives*. Salt Lake City: Signature Books, 2000.

Thorton, Russell. "Cherokee Population Losses During the Trail of Tears: A New Perspective and a New Estimate." *Ethnohistory* 31, no. 4 (1985): 289–300.

Tyler, Alice Felt. *Freedom's Ferment: Phases of American Social History from the Colonial Period to the Outbreak of the Civil War.* New York: Harper & Row, 1962.

Van Wagoner, Richard S. *Mormon Polygamy: A History.* Salt Lake City: Signature Books, 1986.

Van Wagoner, Richard S. *Sidney Rigdon: A Portrait of Religious Excess*, Salt Lake City: Signature Books, 1994.

Vogel, Dan. *Indian Origins and the Book of Mormon: Religious Solutions from Columbus to Joseph Smith.* Salt Lake City: Signature Books, 1986.

Vogel, Dan. *Joseph Smith: The Making of a Prophet.* Salt Lake City: Signature Books, 2004.

Vogel, Dan. "The Earliest Mormon Concept of God." In *Line upon Line: Essays on Mormon Doctrine.* Edited by Gary James Bergera. Salt Lake City: Signature Books, 1989, 17–33.

Vogel, Dan. "The Locations of Joseph Smith's Early Treasure Quests." *Dialogue: A Journal of Mormon Thought* 27, no. 3 (Fall 1994): 197–231.

Waller, Altina L. *Reverend Beecher and Mrs. Tilton: Sex and Class in Victorian America.* Amherst: University of Massachusetts Press, 1982.

Ward, Geoffrey C. *The West.* New York: Little, Brown and Company, 1996.

Werner, M. R. *Brigham Young.* New York: Harcourt, Brace and Company, Inc., 1925.

Whitmer, David. *An Address to All Believers in Christ by a Witness to the Divine Authenticity of the Book of Mormon.* Richmond, Missouri: David Whitmer, 1887.

Whitmer, John. *The Book of John Whitmer Kept by Commandment.* Community of Christ Library-Archives, Independence, Missouri.

Wicks, Robert S., and Fred R. Foister. *Junius and Joseph: Presidential Politics and the Assassination of the First Mormon Prophet.* Logan: Utah State University, 2005.

Wight, Lyman. Letter to Editor, *Northern Islander*, July 1855. Lyman Wight Letterbook. Community of Christ Library-Archives, Independence, Missouri.

Winchester, Simon. *Krakatoa: The Day the World Exploded, August 27, 1883.* New York: HarperCollins Publishers, 2003.

Winn, Kenneth H. *Exiles in a Land of Liberty: Mormons in America, 1830–1846.* Chapel Hill: The University of North Carolina Press, 1989.

Winn, Kenneth H. "'Such Republicanism as This': John Corrill's Rejection of Prophetic Rule." In *Differing Visions: Dissenters in Mormon History*. Edited by Roger D. Launius and Linda Thatcher. Urbana: University of Illinois Press, 1994.

Wirthlin, LeRoy S. "Nathan Smith (1762–1828) Surgical Consultant to Joseph Smith." *Brigham Young University Studies* 17, no. 3 (Spring 1977): 319–37.

Woods, Fred E. *Gathering to Nauvoo*. American Fork, Utah: Covenant Communications, 2002.

Wright, David P. "Isaiah in the Book of Mormon: Or Joseph Smith in Isaiah." In *American Apocrypha: Essays on the Book of Mormon*. Edited by Dan Vogel and Brent Lee Metcalfe. Salt Lake City: Signature Books, 2002, 157–234.

Wyl, Wilhelm. *Mormon Portraits, Joseph Smith the Prophet, His Family and His Friends*. Salt Lake City: N.p., 1886.

Newspapers and Periodicals

Amboy (Illinois) Journal, August 6, 1879.

Daily Missouri Republican (St. Louis), 9 August 1833.

Elders' Journal of the Church of the Latter Day Saints (Kirtland, Ohio), October 1837–November 1837.

Elders' Journal of the Church of Jesus Christ of Latter Day Saints (Far West, Missouri), July 1838–August 1838.

Evening and the Morning Star, The (Independence, Missouri), June 1832–July 1833.

Evening and the Morning Star, The (Independence, Missouri)–Extra, 16 July 1833.

Evening and the Morning Star, The (Kirtland, Ohio), December 1833–September 1834.

Latter Day Saints' Messenger and Advocate (Kirtland, Ohio), October 1834–September 1837.

Latter-Day Saints' Millennial Star, The, 19 November 1864.

Nauvoo (Illinois) Expositor, 7 June 1844.

Nauvoo (Illinois) Neighbor—Extra, 30 June 1844.

Nauvoo (Illinois) Neighbor, 2 August 1843–2 July 1845.

Northern Times (Kirtland, Ohio), October 9, 1835.

(Hudson) Ohio Observer, 11 August 1836.

Times and Seasons (Commerce, Illinois), November 1839–April 1840.
Times and Seasons (Nauvoo, Illinois), May 1840–15 February 1846.
Warsaw (Illinois) Message, 7 February 1844.
Warsaw (Illinois) Signal, 25 April 1844–12 June 1844.
Zion's Harbinger and Baneemy's Organ (St. Louis, Mo.), July 1853.

Documentary Collections

Roberts, Brigham H., ed. *Comprehensive History of the L.D.S. Church of Jesus Christ of Latter Day Saints*, 6 vols. Provo, Utah: Brigham Young University Press, 1965.

Roberts, Brigham H., ed. *History of the Church of Jesus Christ of Latter Day Saints. Period I. History of Joseph Smith, the Prophet; by Himself.* 6 vols. Salt Lake City: Deseret Book Company, 1896–1912.

Smith, Joseph III, and Heman C. Smith. *The History of the Reorganized Church of Jesus Christ of Latter Day Saints.* 4 vols. Lamoni, Iowa: Herald Publishing House, 1896–1903.

Vogel, Dan, comp. and ed. *Early Mormon Documents.* 5 vols. Salt Lake City: Signature Books, 1996–2003.

INDEX

A

Aaronic Priesthood, 248
Adair, James, 97
Adam-ondi-Ahman, 305
    hymn written by William W. Phelps, 253
    means the place where Adam dwelt, 305
Adams, James (Judge)
    sends express rider from Springfield, Illinois, to alert the prophet about a pending arrest warrant in June 1843, 375
Adams, Charles Francis, 378, 381, 459
Adams, John Quincy, 16, 378, 432
Albany, New York, 41, 73, 84, 97, 134, 135, 160, 236, 266, 487, 493, 494
Alger, Fanny Ward, 401
    family quietly leaves Kirtland, Ohio, 402
    marries Solomon Custer, 402
Allen, Charles
    Independence, Missouri, mob tars and feathers, 199
American Archimagus, 98
American frontier, xxi, 13, 21, 23, 116, 147, 148, 202, 204, 231, 318, 338, 391
    and the proliferation of church periodicals, 278
    and vernacular preaching, 278
    violence on, 181
American Holy Land, 229
    Joseph Smith Jr. links America with Middle Eastern Holy Land, 234
American scripture, 88, 95, 115, 116, 167, 170, 177, 204, 458
Americanized Christianity, 13
Americanized the Judeo-Christian tradition, 96
An Address to All Believers, 118, 130, 497
Anderick, S. F., 49
Anderson, Mary Audentia Smith, 29, 337, 487
Andrews, Simeon, 259
Angell, Truman, 250
Anointed Quorum, 407, 418
Anthon, Charles, 85, 258
Article of Agreement, 45
Articles and Covenants of the Church of Christ, The, 128, 338
Articles of Confederation, 15
articling, 45
assassination, xix, 434, 448, 453, 455, 456, 457
Atchison, David Rice, 308
    receives letter from Samuel Bogart informing of the general lawlessness in northwestern Missouri, 312
    redraws unincorporated territories of Ray County, Missouri, to define Caldwell County, 285
    responds to Bogart's letter, 313
    Richmond, Missouri, law firm retained by Latter Day Saints in Independence, Missouri, 200
    successful Washington D.C. politician, 339
Austin, Emily, 185, 487
Avard, Sampson, 294, 297, 301, 307, 332
    leader of Danites, 293
    uses Eberly as pseudonym, 308

B

Baldwin, Caleb, 332, 334
Baltimore, Maryland, 434

baptism for the dead, 394, 396
Barden, Jerusha (Hyrum Smith's first wife), 129
Battle of Crooked River, 283, 314, 316, 319, 321, 325, 327, 331, 332, 333
    dashed beliefs in angelic protection against enemies, 317
Beaver, 31
Benjamin, Asher, 246, 250, 488
Bennett, John C., 358, 359
    as Chancellor of the University of the City of Nauvoo, 364
    brigadier general in the Illinois militia, 359
    power of persuasion in Illinois legislature to gain city charter, 360
    quartermaster general of the Illinois state militia, 359
Benton, Thomas Hart, 264
Black, Adam (Judge), 307
    authors petition under duress, 308
Bogart, Samuel
    Methodist minister and Missouri milita captain, 312
Boggs, Lilburn W., 287, 319, 339, 372
    as alcalde of California's northern district prior to statehood, 339
    as Missouri governor signs legislation creating Caldwell County, 284
    as Missouri lieutenant governor during Zion's Camp March, 224
    consummate politician, four reasons to sign legislation to create Caldwell County, 284
    offers to mediate violence during persecution in Independence, Missouri, 201
Bond, Christopher S. (Missouri Governor) rescinds Extermination Order in June 1976, 339
Book of Abraham, 256, 261, 262, 276, 387, 390, 405, 409, 411, 412, 413, 415
    theological speculations, 261
Book of Commandments, 124, 126, 155, 170
    first attempt to collect and print revelatory statements, 187
    press destroyed in Independence, Missouri, 199
Book of Mormon, xxi, 22, 28, 39, 53, 64, 74, 75, 81, 88, 89, 91, 92, 93, 95, 96, 97, 98, 99, 100, 101, 105, 109, 111, 114, 115, 116, 118, 120, 128, 137, 138, 146, 148, 168, 169, 174, 177, 205, 209, 210, 253, 259, 267, 295, 338, 384, 391, 406, 409, 411, 412, 413, 415, 417, 418, 419, 449, 458, 467, 487, 492, 494, 496, 497
    and all things in common, 204
    as American scripture, 146, 167, 170
    as chief proselytizing tool, 145, 169
    as expression of Joseph Smith Jr.'s religious genius, 138
    composition and dimension issues, 110
    disposition and publication issues, 117
    first opportunity to present with Native American Cattaraugus tribe, 170
    Hurlbut's attack of, 209
    poor reception in Jackson County, Missouri, 215
    proselytizing change of approach from original purpose, 178
    recent scholarship issues, 113
    shared with Cattaraugus tribe, 170, 177
    shared with Delaware tribe, 174
    shared with Shawnee tribe, 174
    shared with Wyandotte tribe, 172
    story basics, 92
    three interpretative schools of thought on origins and authorship, 113
    Three Witnesses eventually leave the church, 274
    witness issues, 104
boosterism, on the American frontier, 23, 303, 364
Booth, Ezra, 158
    as Methodist preacher in Western Reserve, 154
    defection from church, 210
Boston, Massachusetts, 18, 20, 26, 29, 36, 41, 143, 160, 245, 266, 356, 378, 490, 494
Boston Tea Party, 29
Boudinot, Elias, 97
Bowman, William (Daviess County sheriff), 308

Brainerd, David, 55, 56, 489
Brewster, James Colin, 71
Bridgman, Peter G. (nephew of Josiah Stowell), 74
Briggs, Edmund C., 108, 445, 488
British Mission successes, 1837-1841, 354
Brodie, Fawn M., 34, 83, 115, 206, 210, 272, 393, 401, 488
Brook Farm, 26
Bruce, Dickson D. Jr., 52, 488
    four-step process of conversion in early nineteenth century, 52
Bruce, Eli, 419
Buffalo, New York, 170, 171, 182, 266
Bulfinch, Charles, 245
Bump, Jacob
    as joiner and plaster on the House of the Lord, 246
Buncombe Strip, 312, 314
    separating Ray and Caldwell Counties, 312
Burch, Thomas C. (Judge)
    allows venue change from Gallatin to Columbia, Missouri, 336
Burnett, Peter H.
    Doniphan's law partner represents Mormon prisoners in Gallatin courtroom, 336
    first governor of the State of California, 339
Butler, John L.
    in the Daviess County Election fight, 307
Butler, Jon, 74, 489

C

Cahoon, Reynolds, 211, 238, 402, 443
Cake and Beer Shop, 44
Cairo, Illinois, 172
Calhoun, John C. (South Carolina Senator), 374, 377
Campbell, Alexander (efforts led to emergence of the Disciples of Christ), 115, 116, 144, 145, 208
Carlin, Thomas (Illinois Governor), 372

Carroll County, Missouri, 303
Cass, Lewis, 377
Caswell, Henry, 413, 489
Catholics, 24, 468
Center Place of Zion (Jackson County, Missouri)
    as geographic center for redemption of the world, 166
Chandler, Michael H., 256, 257
    arrives in Kirtland, Ohio, 258
    as opportunist, 256
    exhibitions in Cleveland, Ohio, 257
    exploits Joseph Smith Jr.'s ego, 259
Charles I, King of England, 29
Chase, Willard, 73, 80
Chenango County, New York, 72, 81
Chevalier, Michael, 143
China markets, 34
Christian mainstream, xxii, 262, 277, 382, 398, 415, 436, 463
Christian primitivism, 96, 166
church as remnant to church in mission, xiv
Church of Christ, 19, 124, 126, 130, 134, 135, 147, 161, 188, 195, 198, 202, 274, 288, 290, 384, 404, 489
Church of the Latter Day Saints, 162, 174
    name change to bring harmony, 288
church organization, formal, 121
    baptismal service, 129
    importance of the first Tuesday of April, 131
    issues of legal incorporation, 131
    more spiritual than legal, 136
    no documentary evidence of any marriages performed or property acquired, 134
    traditional story, 124
Cincinnati, Ohio, 172
Clark, John B.
    Missouri militia general replaces Samuel D. Lucas, 332
Clark, William, 16, 176
    Superintendent of Indian Affairs, 176
clash of cultures, 178, 205

Clay, Henry, 378
Clayton, William, 388, 407, 414, 415
Cleaveland, Moses, 142
Cleveland, Ohio, 112, 246, 257, 491
Cobb, Polly Harris, 86
Coe, Joseph, 183, 259, 273
Cole, Abner, 73
Colesville, New York, 77, 126, 127, 130, 134, 182, 183, 185, 186, 187, 461
   prophet bolsters spirits in settlement in Zion, 186, 187
Commerce, Illinois, 347, 348, 364
communitarian, 14, 26
communitarian principles and Acts 2, 204
Community of Christ, xiv, xix, 4, 46, 49, 90, 113, 119, 127, 146, 190, 196, 235, 253, 260, 266, 273, 284, 293, 294, 301, 307, 308, 312, 316, 319, 330, 332, 333, 334, 337, 350, 351, 376, 378, 387, 401, 403, 413, 433, 440, 445, 450, 455, 462, 466, 468, 489, 492, 496, 497
Comstock, Nehemiah, 321
Connecticut Land Company, 142
Connecticut Western Reserve, 141, 144, 145, 148, 150, 154, 243, 257, 461
Constitution of 1789, 15, 299
Corps of Discovery (Louisiana Purchase Exploratory Party), 16
Corrill, John (early church historian), 161, 198, 199, 200, 216, 281, 283, 292, 295, 297, 307, 309, 311, 314, 326, 327, 332, 340, 341, 392, 489, 497
   excommunicated at Far West, Missouri, in March 1839, 310
   expresses disgust at the Salt Sermon purge, 297
   heated exchange with the prophet, 309
   informs Lucas of the prophet's surrender at Far West, 328
Council of Fifty
   different references to, 424
   international ambassadors sent from, 425
   promotion of Smith for president of the United States, 1844, 426
   purpose of, 424
   US domestic issues and the, 425

Cowdery, Lyman, 48, 101
Cowdery, Oliver, 3, 48, 60, 66, 88, 89, 91, 99, 100, 101, 102, 104, 105, 106, 111, 117, 119, 124, 126, 127, 128, 129, 130, 132, 155, 160, 162, 170, 174, 176, 178, 199, 254, 264, 266, 270, 272, 273, 274, 290, 295, 383, 395, 404, 405, 406, 436, 487, 490, 494
   as Lamanite Mission leader, 170
   ordained assistant president of the High Priesthood on 5 December 1834, 162
   to Philadelphia for currency printing plates, 270
Crawford, Charles, 97
cultural influences, 13, 97, 105, 114
Cummins, Richard (Shawnee Indian agent), 176
Cumorah, 64, 76, 77, 78, 111, 113, 117, 222, 256, 496

D

Danites, 294, 295, 297, 417, 424, 493
   allegiance sealed by oath, 294
   Daughter of Zion, 292
   in the Daviess County election fight, 307
   quick reaction force to intimidate dissenters, 297
   Sons of Dan, 292
Dartmouth College, 48, 101, 137
Dartmouth Medical College, 37
Daviess County, Missouri, 279, 282, 286, 288, 303, 304, 305, 306, 308, 309, 311, 313, 320, 322, 329, 330, 336
Davis, Inez Smith, 131, 241, 398, 489
   promotes traditional understanding of formal church organization, 131
Declaration of Independence, 19, 301, 432
Delaware tribe, 99, 174, 175, 177
Deming, Minor R. (Hancock County, Illinois, sheriff), 351
DeWitt, Carroll County, Missouri, 303
dispensationalism, 277
Dix, Dorothea, 25, 364
Dixon, Illinois, 375

Index

DNA-testing, 5
Doctrine and Covenants, 124, 148, 157, 215, 261, 266, 337, 386, 394, 395, 404, 458
   canonizes traditional understanding of formal church organization, 131
   systematized the beliefs and laws of the church, 276
doctrine of salvation, 57
Doniphan, Alexander W., 285, 286, 287, 302, 318, 326, 333
   as Clay County state representative to the Ninth Missouri General Assembly, 285
   assists the creation of Caldwell County, 285
   hero status in the Mexican American War, 339
   protests legitimacy of Far West court-martial trial, 330
   recalls Rigdon's courtroom defense in January, 1839, 336
   represents Liberty Jail prisoners, 335
   Richmond, Missouri, law firm retained by Latter Day Saints in Independence, Missouri, 200
Douglas, Stephen A.
   Illinois secretary of state, 361
Dow, Lorenzo, 20, 57
Dow, Neal, 25
Dunklin, Daniel (Missouri Governor), 199, 200, 219, 224
   determination to withhold militia support for Zion's Camp marchers, 224
Durfee, Lemuel, 45, 46, 49, 115, 132, 133
Dutch Reform Sea and Land Church built by Henry Rutgers, 236
dysfunctional family (Smith family), 114

E

E Pluribus Unum, 18
Easty, Mary, 29
ecclesiastical structure (of the new church), 160
Edwards, Jonathan, 56, 489, 493

Egyptian Alphabet and Grammar, 261
Eight Witnesses (to the Book of Mormon), 108
Eighteen Hundred and Froze to Death (1816), 40
Electoral College, 16, 429
Emerson, Ralph Waldo, 17
England, 13, 14, 15, 17, 23, 27, 28, 29, 30, 31, 33, 38, 41, 42, 56, 71, 74, 137, 143, 166, 245, 247, 274, 325, 355, 425, 458, 487, 493, 496
Era of Good Feeling, 16
Era of Restoration, xix, xxi
Eras of active reform, 6
Eras of pastoral consolidation, 6
Erie Canal, 42, 182, 266
Evans, David, 322, 323
Evening and the Morning Star, The, 124, 126, 134, 161, 166, 187, 194, 196, 227, 278, 288, 497
   press further west than any other in the United States in 1832, 188

F

Far West, Missouri, xxii, 65, 88, 185, 191, 193, 273, 276, 278, 279, 289, 290, 292, 295, 296, 297, 298, 302, 303, 307, 311, 313, 315, 317, 318, 319, 320, 321, 324, 325, 326, 327, 328, 329, 330, 331, 332, 333, 338, 339, 340, 352, 369, 387, 402, 405, 406, 417, 426, 436, 447, 458, 461, 494
   and all-out war, 310
   area Mormon settlers arrive for protection in late October 1838, 314
   Haun's Mill survivors drift into, 325
   House of the Lord, 299
   House of the Lord as launching point for mission to Europe, 337
   initially layed out by Phelps and John Whitmer, 283
   Mormon Question defies simplistic answers, 339
   Patten's troops head for Ray County under cloak of darkness, 316
   problems of apostasy, 291
   reflections and lessons, 337

Fayette, New York, 39, 102, 105, 106, 108, 110, 123, 124, 126, 127, 128, 129, 130, 131, 134, 146, 147, 168, 170, 177, 385, 461
Fayette, New York, Branch, organization on 11 April 1830 confused with initial organization, 128
Federal architectural style, 244, 245
Federal Land Act of 1820, 23
Federalist Papers, 94, 490
Female Relief Society, 423
First Vision, xxi, 51, 52, 53, 60, 61, 65, 66, 67, 136, 137, 383, 417
  evolutionary development approach, 66
  questioning the traditional account, 59
  traditional account, 61
Fishing River revelation
  chastises Zion's Camp marchers, 229
  sue for peace, 229
Flournoy, Jones Hoy, 186
Ford, Thomas (Governor of Illinois), 110, 375, 426, 441, 449, 490
Fort Madison, Iowa Territory, 348
Foster, Robert D., 440, 443
  as physician, joins trip to Washington D.C. with Joseph Smith Jr. October 1839, to tend to an ailing Sidney Rigdon, 372
Fourier, Charles, 25, 490
Fourth of July Oration of Sidney Rigdon, 297
France, 16, 24, 425
Free People of Color, 195, 196
French and Indian War, 31, 137
French, Peter, 237
Fuller, Sarah Margaret, 17

G

Galland, Isaac, 356
Gallatin, Daviess County, Missouri, 279, 306, 307, 310, 311, 312, 314, 316, 320, 336, 339, 352, 426
Garden of Eden, 205, 206, 207, 386
Gates, Lydia, 31
Gates, Theophilus Ransom, 165
Gause, Jesse, 161, 187, 212, 213, 494

apostatizes, begins a lasting tradition of dissent, 213
fell short as original counselor in First Presidency, 211
Georgian architectural style, 244, 491
ghost colleges, 21, 364
Gilbert, Algernon Sidney, 183, 392
  dies during Zion's Camp March, 231
  Independence, Missouri, mob destroys general store, 199
Gilbert, John H., 109, 119
ginseng, 33
globalization, xiv, 464
glossolalia (speaking in tongues, visions and healings), 145
Gnosticism, 388, 392
golden plates, 75, 101, 256, 413
Goodrich, Samuel, 20, 490
Gothic architectural style, 244
Gould, John, 29, 267
Grandin, Egbert B., 105, 109, 118, 119
Great American Desert, 205
Greek Psalter, 409, 415
Greek Revival architectural style, 244, 246, 492
Green Mountain Boys (Vermont), 71, 490
Grindstone Fork, Daviess County, Missouri, 279, 310, 311, 320, 352, 426
guardian spirits, 109

H

Hale, Alva, 81
Hale, Aroet, 242
Hale, Elizabeth, 83
Hale, Isaac, 83, 84, 113, 115
Hancock, Levi, 223
  as Zion's Camp marcher, 223
Hanover, New Hampshire, 48, 101, 210
Harmony, Pennsylvania, 25, 48, 53, 77, 81, 83, 84, 85, 86, 87, 91, 100, 101, 106, 111, 126, 134
Harris, Martin, 81, 84, 88, 99, 104, 105, 106, 108, 109, 111, 113, 118, 120, 127, 162, 183, 258, 273, 295, 401, 422
  chooses not to petition for masonic initiation in Nauvoo, 422

loses 116 pages of the Book of Mormon, 86
Harrison, William Henry, 361
Haun, Jacob, 320, 321
Haun's Mill, 320, 321, 322, 323, 325
　hamlet on Shoal Creek in Caldwell County, 321
　in eastern Caldwell County, Missouri, 279
Haven, Charlotte
　witnesses a proxy baptism in the Mississippi River, 396
Hawthorne, Nathaniel, 17, 241
Hemings, Sally, 5, 493
hermetic influences, 137
Hibbard, Billy, 57
Higbee, Elias, 294
　travels to Washington D.C. with Joseph Smith Jr. October 1839, 372
High Council of Zion, 232
Hinkle, George, 303, 326, 330, 332
　and the defense of Carroll County Saints, 305
　escorts the prophet to General Lucas, 328
　negotiates the surrender of Far West, 326
Hispanics, 338
Hoge, Joseph P. (Democratic politician)
　receives Mormon votes, wins handily in congressional election 1843, 377
　seeks Mormon political support, 376
Hotchkiss, Horace
　holds note on properties around Commerce, Illinois, 356
House of the Lord (Far West, Missouri), 299
House of the Lord (Kirtland, Ohio), 217, 234, 235, 242, 243, 246, 247, 251, 252, 258, 259, 262, 270, 271, 276, 348, 385, 392, 405
　and the architectural language of Latter Day Saintism, 243
　and veiled worship, 250
　architecture as mixture of four styles, 244
　as Latter Day Saint pentecost, 254
　as physical testament to church member sacrifices, 255
　as venue for Kirtland High School, 250
　completion of exterior, 240
　Elijah appears in vision, 3, 254
　four factors delaying construction, 238
　function of the inner court, 251
　functional purposes of the interior design, 247
　Jesus Christ appears in vision, 3, 254
　Moses appears in vision, 3, 254
　need for economical construction, 237
　pulpit lettering, 247
　service of dedication, spring 1836, 252
　significant role of women in construction, 241
　symbol of spiritual connection between the human and the divine, 255
　three functions, 236
　use of Jewish reference, 251
Houston, James
　blacksmith at Haun's Mill, 321
Howard, Luther, 42
Howe, Eber D.
　editor of the Painesville, Ohio *Telegraph*, 209
Hubble, Laura
　prophetess challenger, 210
Hudson River, 31
Hungary, 24
Huntington, Dimick, 298
　meets the prophet at the boat dock in Quincy, Illinois, 346
Huntley, Hannah, 30
Hurlbut, Doctor Philastus, 209, 267, 268
Hyde, Orson, 146, 163, 216, 220, 224, 295, 332, 339, 354, 431
　emissary to Governor Dunklin during Zion's Camp March, 224
　goes to Columbus, Ohio, for a bank charter, 270

I

Independence, Missouri, xxii, 24, 33, 46, 49, 90, 110, 113, 119, 124, 134, 146, 151, 152, 155,

161, 163, 170, 174, 180, 183, 184, 188, 190, 193, 196, 201, 205, 211, 214, 215, 217, 218, 219, 234, 235, 238, 243, 251, 260, 262, 263, 273, 282, 284, 289, 293, 294, 301, 307, 308, 312, 313, 316, 319, 321, 327, 330, 331, 332, 333, 334, 338, 348, 349, 350, 351, 376, 378, 387, 389, 402, 413, 426, 433, 440, 445, 450, 452, 455, 464, 488, 489, 491, 492, 494, 495, 496, 497
and the plan for cleanliness, 191
and the Secret Constitution, 197
as Center Place of Zion, 190
as sacred geography, 186
description of terrain and first white settlers, 183
extended boundaries of the New Jerusalem, 191
land dedicated for the Temple in Zion, 235
Mormons spurred rejection of non-violence, 277
Plat of the City of Zion, 190
prominence on western border of the United States, 179
Indian Removal Act, 1830, 172
inheritance, eternal, 30, 150, 179, 180, 181, 182, 183, 185, 189, 201, 205, 206, 220, 225, 278, 279, 395
Ireland, Shadrach, 13, 14, 15
Italy, 24

J

Jackson, Andrew, 16, 19, 21, 24, 184, 197, 378, 379
Jackway, Hiram, 49
Jameson, John (Missouri Representative), 373
Jefferson, Thomas, 5, 16, 18, 19, 23, 176, 197, 245, 433, 487, 489, 493
Jennings, Samuel, 45
Jennings, Thomas, 322
Jennings, William, 322
Jenson, Andrew, 105, 355
Johnson, Benjamin F., 402, 492
Johnson, Elsa
  healed by Joseph Smith Jr., 154
Johnson, John, 154
Johnson, Luke S.
  disfellowshipped apostle, 273
Johnson, Lyman E.
  disfellowshipped apostle, 273
Johnson, Richard M. (senator, Kentucky, vice president), 264, 377
Jonas, Abraham
  grand master of the Illinois Masonic Lodge, 420
Judeo-Christian tradition, 115, 138, 205, 234

K

Kelley, William H., 46, 49, 495
Keokuk, Iowa Territory, 348
Kidd, William (Captain), 71
Kimball, Heber C., 163, 206, 226, 239, 241, 271, 354, 392, 418, 492
  nearly dies during Zion's Camp March, 230
Kinderhook Plates, 409, 415
King Follett Discourse, 388, 389
King, Austin A. (Judge)
  hearing of those charged with prosecuting Battle of Crooked River, 332
Kirtland anti-bank venture
  and the importance of public confidence, 270
Kirtland Camp, 276
Kirtland High Council
  established on 17 February 1834, 162
Kirtland, Ohio, xxii, 24, 53, 66, 71, 124, 145, 151, 160, 170, 171, 177, 182, 193, 218, 234, 235, 252, 254, 256, 261, 263, 276, 287, 292, 348, 354, 383, 385, 386, 395, 411, 458, 487, 495
  and Acts 2, 203
  and emigration patterns, 143
  and Joseph Smith Jr. stirring passion in the Western Reserve, 154
  and problems of apostasy, 273
  as citadel for Latter Day Saintism, 235
  becomes seat of the Church of Christ, 160

cannon barrage near the House of the Lord, 217
church proves viability, 278
disintegration and evacuation of the church, 274
Kirtland Safety Society, 270, 273
Kirtland Temple (see House of the Lord [Kirtland, Ohio])
Kirtland, Turhand, 142
Knight, Joseph, 77, 78, 91, 111, 126, 127, 186, 210, 492
Knight, Newell, 130, 182, 183, 186, 392, 492
Knight, Polly (possible first deceased church member), 210

L

labeling strategy, 74
Lafayette, Marquis de, 378
Lake Ticonderoga, 31
Lamanite Missionaries, 145, 172, 173, 176, 178
 become Gentile Missionaries, 178
 travel three hundred miles on foot from St. Charles to Independence, Missouri, in deep snow, 173
Lane, George, 60
Lansing, R. R., 118
Last Testimony of Emma Smith Bidamon, 91, 111, 113, 496
Latter Day Saintism, 13, 19, 20, 26, 145, 146, 207, 235, 243, 253, 263, 295, 394, 399, 402, 415, 453, 457, 458, 460, 463
 and the curse of Cain, 204
 and the important role of sacred geography, 180, 184, 186, 193, 305
 and theology of exclusion, 202
 debate over the demise of the movement after Far West, 345
 dispensational beliefs, 277
 early believers were people of the village, 184
 evacuation of the Saints from Kirtland, Ohio, 276
 lack of appeal to African Americans, 197

 last days in Missouri for an entire generation, 320
 militarist means to redeem Zion, 277
 multiple heavens versus mainline Christian dualism, 277
 reaches pinnacle of achievement during Kirtland period by summer 1836, 262
 structural language of, 276
Latter Day Saints' Messenger and Advocate, 66, 262
law of consecration, 14, 150, 160, 181, 213, 214, 215
 as communal directive, 151
Law, William, 376, 424, 429, 436, 437, 438
 berated by the prophet for vocalizing support for Smith's candidate, Cyrus Walker, 377
 voices support for the Whig Cyrus Walker in congressional election in August 1843, 376
Lebanon, New Hampshire, 36
Lebolo, Antonio (Italian archeologist), 257
Lemmons, John, 306
Lewis, Joshua, 186
Lewis, Meriwether, 16, 176, 487
Lincoln, Abraham
 supports granting Nauvoo city charter, 361
 Whig elector in 1840 presidential election, 361
Linn, Lewis (Missouri Senator), 373
Litchfield, Connecticut, 57
Literary Firm (of Kirtland), 263, 278
Livingston County, Missouri, 320, 321, 329
Louisiana Territory, 16
Lucas, Samuel D., 330, 331
 demands four conditions for the surrender of Far West, 327
 Missouri milita general commanding assault on Far West, 326
 orders execution of Mormon prisoners at Far West, 330
Luther, Martin
 Augustinian monk and the theology of grace, 394

Lyme, Connecticut, 30

M

Macedon, New York, 44, 78
Mack, Jason, 31, 34
Mack, John, 30
Mack, Lydia (Lucy's mother), 42
Mack, Sarah Bagley, 30
Mack, Solomon, 30, 31, 64, 487, 493
Mack, Stephen, 14, 16, 31, 32, 34, 132, 205, 282, 294, 295, 447, 466, 487, 493
Madison, James, 16, 94
malaria, 353
Manchester, New York, 48, 51, 53, 77, 80, 81, 83, 84, 86, 101, 108, 110, 118, 124, 126, 127, 128, 129, 130, 132, 133, 134, 136
Mann, Horace, 25
Mansion House, 378, 379, 407, 413, 441, 443, 444, 459
Manuscript Found
   historical novel authored by Solomon Spaulding, 209, 267
Marks, William, 345
Marsh, Thomas B., 163, 254, 274, 295, 318, 332, 339, 392, 405
Massachusetts Bay colony, 28
McBride, Reuben
   Zion's Camp March song, 219
McKune, Joshua, 83
McLellin, William, 228, 232, 295, 402
   as negotiator for Zion's Camp marchers, 227
McMurray, W. Grant, 466
McRae, Alexander, 333
   in Liberty Jail, 334
Melchisedec Priesthood, 161, 163, 247, 386, 406
Melville, Herman, 17
Merrick, Charlie
   nine year old child killed at Haun's Mill, 323
metallic plates, 48, 53, 74, 75, 76, 77, 78, 79, 80, 83, 84, 85, 87, 88, 89, 90, 91, 92, 98, 104, 105, 106, 108, 109, 110, 111, 112, 113, 115, 117, 406, 413, 414, 415, 417

meteor shower
   after Saints exodus from Independence, Missouri, 201
militia, 304, 314, 318, 319, 327, 328, 330, 332, 368, 369, 370, 425, 426, 445, 449, 452, 458, 460
Millennial Harbinger, 115
Millett, Artemus, 239
   key role in construction of the House of the Lord, 239
Millport, Daviess County, Missouri, 279
Mitchell, Samuel L., 85
Monroe, James, 16
Moor's Charity School, 48
Moredock, Esquire, 40
Morgan, Lucinda, 420, 422
Morgan, William
   author of freemasonry exposé in 1826, 419, 422
Morgan, William (Daviess County, Missouri, sheriff), 336
Morley, Isaac, 144, 171, 198, 281, 392
   as stock New England family settling in Western Reserve near Kirtland Mills, 144
   provides room for the Smith's in spring 1831, 152
Mormon War in Missouri
   assault at Haun's Mill, 322
   burning to the ground of Grindstone Fork in Daviess County, Missouri, 311
   court-martial of seven Mormon leaders at Far West, 330
   Daviess County election day fight, 306
   ends without a shot fired, 329
   engagement at Crooked River, 314
   eruption of violence, 302
   Far West ravaged after surrender, 331
   Hinkle, Corrill, Phelps, and Peck branded as traitors, 328
   Missouri citizen casualties at Haun's Mill, 325
   Missouri militia casualties at Battle of Crooked River, 317

Mormon casualties at Battle of
    Crooked River, 316
Mormon casualties at Haun's Mill, 324
Mormon marginalization, 303
Mormon troops charade as Carroll
    County citizens to gain information
    and steal from Grindstone Fork
    residents, 311
Mormons set fire to northwestern
    communities, 310
prejudice and fear as a primary cause
    for war, 320
rumors feed prejudice, 303
Salt Sermon sparks confrontation, 303
the prophet tells troops to live off the
    land, a euphemism to plunder the
    countryside, 311
Mormonism Unvailed, 210
Moroni, 75, 77, 93
Murdock, John, 153, 171, 283, 303
Murdock, Julia Clapp (wife of John
    Murdock), 153
Myers, Jacob, 321

N

Naples, Illinois, 222
Native Americans, 22, 24, 56, 92, 96, 97, 98,
    99, 114, 138, 172, 174, 175, 176, 205, 215, 280,
    338, 458
    taking the gospel to, 170
    Trail of Tears, 24
Nauvoo, Illinois, xxii, 21, 24, 53, 111, 126, 162,
    182, 191, 193, 261, 276, 294, 337, 348, 349,
    350, 351, 352, 353, 354, 355, 356, 357, 358, 359,
    360, 361, 362, 363, 364, 366, 367, 368, 369,
    370, 371, 374, 375, 376, 377, 378, 381, 383,
    387, 388, 389, 392, 393, 394, 397, 405, 407,
    413, 417, 418, 420, 421, 422, 425, 426, 427,
    430, 431, 433, 436, 437, 438, 439, 440, 441,
    442, 443, 444, 445, 446, 447, 452, 455, 456,
    457, 458, 459, 460, 461, 462, 468, 488, 490,
    494, 495
    banking practices, 357
    building community, 349
    concern for residents to sustain their
        personal economy, 350
    created by Nauvoo City Charter, 367
    criminal activity, 352
    economic associations, 350
    general impoverishment of
        membership, 357
    Hebrew reference to beautiful situation
        or place, 347
    push and pull immigration factors, 354
    quality control by the Council of
        Twelve, 350
    shortage of money, 357
    sickly season, 353
Nauvoo Agricultural and Mechanical
    Association
    exemplifies the prophet's economic
        hopes, 358
Nauvoo City Charter, 360, 492
    allows Smith to control municipal
        government political machine, 374
    forms city government structure, 362
    issues writs of *habeas corpus*, 363
    Mormon "magna charta," 362
    shapes Nauvoo community, 362
Nauvoo Common School System, 367
Nauvoo Expositor, 377, 437, 439, 440, 453,
    460, 462
Nauvoo Legion
    basic qualifications, 367
    popularity of forming community
        militias, 367
    size, 370
    Smith delights in his role as
        commanding officer, 370
    Smith turns into his own private army,
        369
Nauvoo Mayor, 363
Nauvoo Municipal Court, 362
Nauvoo Neighbor, 349, 351, 376, 455, 497
Neely, Albert (Justice), 73
New England, 28, 41, 144, 247
New England Puritanism, 17, 137
New Harmony, Indiana, 25

New Mormon History, 468, 469, 470, 471, 472, 473, 474, 475, 476, 479, 480, 481, 487
New Portage Ohio,
   staging camp for Zion's Camp Marchers, 221
Newell, Grandison
   sues Smith for money fraud in Kirtland, 272
Northern Times, 263
Norwich, Vermont, 40, 41
Noyes, John Humphrey, 25

O

O'Banion, Patrick, 316, 317
   first to fall at Battle of Crooked River, 316
Ohio Banking Act of 1816, 270, 272
Ohio Canal, 242, 270
olive leaf revelation, 214, 288
Omandagus, 222
Oneida, New York, 25
osteomyelitis, 37
Owen, Robert, 25

P

pacifist, 233, 277
Page, Hiram, 105, 210, 295
Painesville, Ohio, 109, 146, 148, 210, 257, 258, 418
Palmyra, New York, 28, 42, 44, 45, 46, 48, 49, 52, 53, 59, 60, 64, 70, 73, 81, 82, 84, 86, 100, 109, 114, 115, 118, 119, 120, 124, 131, 132, 137, 146, 256, 273, 383, 391, 397, 418, 422, 458, 461
Parks, Hiram, 330
Parrish, Betsy
   dies during Zion's Camp March, 231
Parrish, Warren, 261, 290
   prophet's close friend and former secretary disaffected, 273
Partridge, Edward, 147, 148, 171, 180, 183, 186, 198, 214, 215, 225, 281, 289, 290, 330, 345, 392, 407, 454, 489
   as Painesville, Ohio, hatter, 146
   baptism in Seneca River, upstate New York, 11 December 1830, 146
   contention with Sidney Rigdon, 213
   Independence, Missouri, mob tars and feathers, 199
   institutes Law of Consecration and Stewardship, 160
Patten, David W., 163, 254
   as Captain Fearnought, 315
   leads Mormon army into Gallatin and pillages local businesses, 311
   Mormonism's first apostolic martyr, 317
   shot at Battle of Crooked River, 316
peaceful coexistence with neighbors
   1834-1836, 280
   1836-1838, 291
Peck, Reed, 293, 297, 309, 311, 326, 332, 370, 494
   observes the agitated mood of listeners of Rigdon's Salt Sermon, 296
   on origins of Danite name, 293
Peniston, William, 307, 308
Perfectionists, 25
Perkins, Cyrus, 38
persecution, xxii, 64, 65, 127, 195, 288, 298, 302, 325, 336, 345, 352, 371, 387, 426
   and Free People of Color, 195
   arson as tool, 275
phalanxes, 25
Phelps, Morris, 294
Phelps, William W., 156, 179, 187, 188, 194, 195, 197, 198, 214, 215, 216, 232, 261, 274, 287, 290, 295, 297, 326, 339, 386, 392, 404, 422, 431
   as counselor in the Presidency of the Missouri church, 162
   chooses not to petition for masonic initiation in Nauvoo, 422
   composes "Adam-ondi-Ahman" hymn, 253
   composes "The Spirit of God Like a Fire Is Burning" hymn, 253
   lays out the community of Far West, Missouri, 283

Philadelphia, Pennsylvania, 24, 25, 97, 120, 270, 272, 349, 373, 431, 433, 488, 490, 493
  venue for Michael Chandler's Egyptology museum, 257
Poe, Edgar Allen, 17
Poland, 24
polygamy, xiv, 99, 213, 398, 399, 400, 403, 404, 405, 406, 407, 416, 418, 424, 458
  New and Everlasting Covenant, 423
Pope Leo X
  and the theology of works, 394
Poultney, Vermont, 48, 98, 100
Poverty Year (1816), 40
Pratt, Orson, 33, 59, 126, 163, 189, 190, 354, 383, 424, 494
  instructs mathematics and English Literature in the University of the City of Nauvoo, 365
Pratt, Parley, 170, 171, 177, 195, 224, 268
  as Lamanite missionary, 145
  emissary to Governor Dunklin during Zion's Camp March, 224
  escapes bull dog attack during Lamanite Mission, 171
  incarceration and escape during Lamanite journey, 171
  mission from Independence to Kirtland, 217
  returns to St. Louis to get travel papers, 177
Presbyterianism, 115
president of the United States, 16, 22, 339, 432
Priest, Josiah, 97, 494
priesthood, 3, 20, 53, 88, 90, 150, 161, 162, 166, 187, 201, 203, 210, 212, 213, 232, 234, 247, 248, 253, 254, 255, 261, 262, 273, 274, 393, 405, 406, 465, 467
  prophet concretizes revelations with publication of Doctrine and Covenants, 163
Printer's Manuscript (of the Book of Mormon), 119
problem of numbers (persistent and looming), 338
  among Illinois freemasons, 455
  at Diahman, 306
  in Clay County, Missouri, 280
  in Daviess County, Missouri, 306
  in DeWitt, Carroll County, Missouri, 303
  in Far West, Missouri, 303, 305
  in Hancock County, Illinois, 374
  in Independence, Missouri, 188
  in Kirtland, Ohio, 263
  in Nauvoo, Illinois, 356
  on the American frontier, 318
Protestants, 24
Providence, Rhode Island, 266
Puritan, 15, 17, 29, 166, 234, 241
  puritan ethic, 28
  puritan tradition, 17
Putney, Vermont, 25

Q

Quincy, Illinois, 336, 341, 346
  residents hear stories of persecution from Saints, 345
Quincy, Josiah P., Jr.
  Biographer of important American figures, 378
  physical description of the prophet, 379
  profound comments about the prophet
  predicts Smith's powerful future influence on American society, 380
Quorum of Twelve Apostles, xiv, 295, 346, 392, 463
  maintains quality control in Nauvoo, 350
  original quorum chosen in 1835, 162

R

Randolph, Vermont, 33, 36, 44, 378
Rathbun, Robert
  Independence, Missouri, mob destroys blacksmith shop, 199
Ray County, Missouri, 225, 226, 282, 283, 285, 286, 287, 307, 309, 312, 313, 314, 317, 318, 319, 332
Rees, Amos, 330, 336
  law partner of Doniphan and Atchison, 333

reformed hieroglyphics, 85, 99
religious pluralism, 14, 204
Restoration Era, 7, 26, 28, 263, 303, 331, 348, 362, 394, 400, 457, 458, 460, 467
Reynolds, Joseph (Jackson County, Missouri, sheriff)
    arrests the prophet and attempts extradition, 375
Reynolds, Thomas (Missouri Governor), 374
Rich, Caleb, 56, 57
Rich, Charles, C., 212
Rich, Leonard
    disfellowshipped but confessed and returned to leadership responsibililities, 273
Richards, Willard
    and traditional story of Carthage assassination events, 448
    escapes to Iowa Territory with prophet to avoid arrest, 443
Rigdon, Phebe
    rendevouzes with husband Sidney to leave Missouri in early February 1839, 336
    visits husband in Liberty Jail, 333
Rigdon, Sidney, 116, 145, 147, 148, 156, 161, 171, 183, 203, 208, 209, 211, 212, 235, 237, 238, 253, 266, 268, 272, 273, 289, 295, 297, 298, 307, 309, 319, 327, 328, 330, 333, 334, 340, 345, 346, 362, 366, 385, 386, 424, 430, 431, 454, 496
    and early theological themes, 144
    as Campbellite preacher, 144
    closes House of the Lord dedicatory service with prayer, 254
    conversion to Latter Day Saintism, 146
    declares keys of the kingdom lost to the movement in July 1832, 211
    declining health in Liberty Jail, 335
    dedicates sacred land in Zion, 186
    exemplifies passion for the spoken word on the American frontier, 278
    flees with Smith from Kirtland, Ohio, 275
    gives Fourth of July Oration, 1838, 297
    gives Salt Sermon, June 1838, 296
    instructs rhetoric and *belles lettres* in the University of the City of Nauvoo, 365
    president of Kirtland anti-bank, 271
    primary theological themes of communalism and millennialism, 144
    Salt Sermon sparks animosities, 303
    suffers from malaria (ague) in Nauvoo, 353
    suffers from melancholia, 335
    travels to Washington D.C. with Joseph Smith Jr. October 1839, 372
Roberts, B. H., 96, 100, 330, 357, 378, 494, 495
Robinson, Ebenezer, 301, 302
Robinson, George W., 297, 327, 330, 336
    Far West editorialist compliments peaceful setting of Saints living amongst Missouri citizens prior to the prophet's arrival, 302
    observes dissidents escaping Far West due to Salt Sermon, 297
Rockwell, Caroline, 129
Rochester, New York, 118, 146, 266
Rockwell, Electa, 129
Rockwell, Orrin Porter, 129, 372
    escapes to Iowa Territory with prophet to avoid arrest, 443
    travels to Washington D.C. with Joseph Smith Jr. October 1839, 372
Rockwell, Sarah, 129
Root, Henry, 303, 304
Royalton, Vermont, 42
Ruland, John
    subagent for William Clark, Superintendent of Indian Affairs, 177
Rush Creek (near Liberty, Clay County, Missouri)
    burial location of Zion's Camp Marchers, 231
Rutgers, Henry, 236
Ryder, James F., 250

S

Sacagawea, 16
St. Louis, Missouri, 172, 457
Saints' Advocate, 91, 111
Salem, Massachusetts, 15, 39, 41, 241, 244, 266, 267, 273
    and witchcraft trial in 1692, 267
    treasure hunting mission in July 1836, 265
Salt River
    staging area for Zion's Camp Marchers, 222
Salt Sermon of Sidney Rigdon, 296
Sandusky, Ohio, 170, 172
Saunders, Benjamin, 46, 127, 132, 495
Scandinavia, 24
Scotland, 25, 383
Second Coming, 3, 14, 145, 150, 165, 179, 183, 186, 193, 201, 232, 255, 262, 277, 278, 299, 345, 415, 424, 427, 457, 461
    beliefs of Saints in Zion, 189
second sight, 109, 113
seer stone, 71, 76, 86, 87, 88, 89, 90, 91, 111, 115, 209, 210, 222, 239, 241, 259, 262, 272, 276, 293, 347, 397, 398, 412, 428, 455
Seneca Falls, New York, 102
Shakers, 14, 25, 212
Sharon, Vermont, 28, 32, 36, 46, 71
Sharp, Thomas C., 71, 490
    editor of the Warsaw, Illinois, newspaper, 440
Shattuck, Lemuel, 25
Shays, Daniel, 18
Shays's Rebellion, 58
Sherman, Eleazer, 57
slavery, 15, 18, 195, 196, 197, 261, 280, 432, 458
slippery treasures, 109
Smith, Alexander Hale, 91, 333
Smith, Alma
    seven year old child killed at Haun's Mill, 323
Smith, Alvin, 33, 42, 44, 45, 48, 73, 86, 87, 152, 153, 394, 395, 396
Smith, Alvin (first child of Emma and Joseph), 83

Smith, Asael, 29, 30, 46, 487
Smith, Catherine, 33
Smith, Don Carlos, 33, 42, 129, 289
    at House of the Lord dedication service, 253
    dies in Nauvoo from the ague, 354
Smith, Elias (no relation), 57
Smith, Emma Hale, 29, 48, 53, 74, 77, 78, 81, 83, 84, 86, 87, 91, 99, 100, 111, 112, 113, 115, 152, 153, 154, 155, 158, 160, 235, 275, 331, 332, 333, 346, 348, 360, 393, 401, 402, 403, 406, 407, 418, 443, 445, 448, 462, 463, 487, 490, 493, 495, 496
    adopts the Murdock twins, 154
    birth of Joseph III without Joseph Jr. present, 160
    chosen to select hymns, 187
    loses Baby Joseph Murdock on 29 March 1832, 160
    receives letter from Joseph dated 4 November 1838 about incarceration in Independence, Missouri, 332
    second of three trips to visit her husband in Liberty Jail, 334
    Smith family issues in Kirtland, 152
    stays with John and Sarah Cleveland in Quincy, Illinois, 346
    suspicious of John C. Bennett, 359
    takes first of three trips to Liberty Jail, 333
    third of three visits to see her husband at Liberty Jail, 334
    uncommon knowledge of medicinal healing methods, 360
    with Joseph visits sister near Dixon, Illinois, in June 1843, 375
Smith, Ephraim, 33
Smith, Ethan (Congregationalist Pastor), 98, 99, 100, 101
Smith, Frederick M., 463, 464
Smith, Heman C., 389
Smith, Hyrum, 33, 44, 46, 48, 49, 84, 100, 101, 105, 124, 126, 128, 129, 137, 162, 182, 210, 216, 222, 232, 238, 254, 266, 274, 289, 290, 297, 330, 333, 334, 340, 351, 356, 362, 366, 373, 376, 377, 403, 407, 418, 442, 443,

444, 447, 449, 450, 451, 455, 457
and the defense of Diahman, 307
as Palmyra, New York, school trustee, 101
claims revelatory authority to support Democrat Hoge against Whig Walker in August 1843, 376
rides to Hiram, Ohio, to alert Joseph Jr. about Rigdon's declaration that the keys of the kingdom are lost, 212
throws Mormon votes to the Democrat Joseph Hoge in congressional election in August 1843, 376
Zion's Camp recruiting tour into Michigan, 220
Smith, Israel A., 466
Smith, Jesse (prophet's cousin)
dies during Zion's Camp March, 230
Smith, Jesse (prophet's uncle), 39, 267
Smith, Joseph III, 91, 108, 111, 162, 332, 334, 337, 398, 402, 403, 444, 445, 462, 463, 467, 468, 488, 493, 494, 496
Bennett pulls tooth, 360
birth 6 November 1832, 160
pleading for his father's release in Far West square, 331
sees father in Liberty Jail, 333
Smith, Joseph Jr., xxi, xxii, 6, 13, 16, 22, 26, 27, 28, 36, 38, 39, 51, 53, 59, 60, 66, 67, 72, 74, 75, 85, 88, 94, 96, 97, 98, 99, 102, 108, 110, 113, 114, 115, 116, 117, 121, 123, 126, 127, 128, 132, 134, 136, 137, 138, 147, 160, 161, 165, 170, 206, 209, 210, 211, 218, 233, 234, 235, 238, 240, 241, 250, 251, 253, 256, 258, 259, 263, 266, 267, 268, 271, 272, 273, 274, 276, 278, 279, 281, 289, 290, 294, 297, 302, 311, 317, 318, 330, 332, 333, 340, 346, 347, 348, 349, 351, 353, 354, 362, 369, 371, 373, 377, 378, 381, 387, 394, 395, 399, 403, 409, 415, 417, 420, 423, 424, 427, 428, 431, 435, 447, 453, 455, 456, 457, 458, 460, 463, 467, 493, 495, 496
1832 most difficult year of his life to that point, 213
achievements during Kirtland era, 276
and Manuscript History (1839), 126
and the Election of 1844, 426
and the Gnostic view of the afterlife, 388
and the Kirtland anti-bank venture, 268
and the Second Coming, 165
arrest near Dixon, Illinois, and extradition attempt in June 1843, 375
arrested as disorderly person and imposter, 74
arrives in Quincy, Illinois, after his Missouri incarceration, 346
as chief real estate broker in Nauvoo, 354
as modern-day Adam, 409, 410, 411
as modern-day Moses, 170
as prophet and seer, 253
as religious genius, 96, 116, 138, 180, 409, 415, 458
as Seer from Palmyra, 256
as Trustee-in-Trust for church holdings in Nauvoo, 354
assigns human attributes to God, 388
authors Caractors, 84
bases Nauvoo temple rituals on Gnostic understandings, 392
begins translation of Egyptian papyri, 259
calls for Saints to gather in Nauvoo, Illinois, 349
changes church name through revelation to bring unity, 289
chastises pacifists who oppose his call to arms at Far West, Missouri, 311
conceptualizes House of the Lord architecture, 235
confused during treasure hunt mission to Salem, Massachusetts, in summer 1836, 266
connects believers with Hebrews of biblical times, 165, 166, 167, 169, 170, 179, 259
considered either prophet or charlatan, 208
curses Martin Van Buren's political career, 374

describes Egyptian antiquities
  collection in Mansion House, 379
discerns lack of spirituality among
  Zion's Camp marchers as cause for
  failure, 233
discusses Saints' plight with President
  Martin Van Buren, 372
dualist view of his world around him,
  277
early childhood, 36
enflames passions in American society,
  277
family ancestry, 28
flees with Rigdon from Kirtland, Ohio,
  275
gives last sermon revealing distinct
  personages in the Godhead, 389
ignores gentlemen's agreement with
  Missouri state legislature to keep
  Mormon settlements within
  Caldwell County, 305
impressed by John C. Bennett's
  credentials, 359
incarceration in the Liberty, Missouri,
  jail, 333
Kirtland anti-bank cashier, 271
lashes out against Austin King's unfair
  trial proceedings, 332
learned lessons in Nauvoo from the
  Kirtland economic experience, 354
learns difficult lessons about national
  politics in 1839 trip to nation's
  capital, 377
leg surgery during youth, 36
legal challenges and vexatious lawsuits,
  267
lieutenant general rank in the Nauvoo
  Legion, 369
lines Kirtland bank shelves with chests
  to create illusion of solvency, 272
moves to control Hancock County,
  Illinois, politics, 374
offers dedicatory prayer in the House of
  the Lord, 253
offers King Follett Discourse, 387

orders Hinkle to surrender Far West,
  329
parentage and difficult times, 33
places Latter Day Saint stamp on the
  apostle Paul's stewardship concepts,
  203
positions church on the nationwide
  dispute on the nature of the
  marriage covenant, 393
predictable pattern of conversion, 51
purchases Egyptian artifacts, 259
receives faulty intelligence from spies
  about militia on southern border of
  Caldwell County, 314
seeks redress in Washington, D.C., 371
sets redemption of Zion for 11
  September 1836, 281
struggles to maintain unity between
  Ohio and Missouri churches, 288
tours lower Manhattan, New York, in
  October 1832, 160
versus Philastus Hurlbut lawsuit, 267
wagon ride to Harmony, Pennsylvania,
  in December 1827, 81
Smith, Joseph Sr., 28, 30, 33, 34, 39, 41, 44,
  45, 46, 50, 64, 71, 76, 77, 78, 105, 114, 124,
  127, 162, 253, 359, 394, 395
common laborer with low wages, 46
dies in Nauvoo from the ague, 354
travels to Palmyra for first time, 42
Smith, Lucy (youngest daughter of Joseph
  and Lucy Mack Smith), 33
Smith, Lucy Mack, 28, 30, 46, 64, 77, 78,
  80, 89, 101, 106, 110, 114, 118, 119, 211, 212,
  237, 391
Smith, Mary Fielding
  visits Hyrum in the Liberty Jail, 334
Smith, Nathan, 37, 38, 497
Smith, Robert, 28
Smith, Samuel (great grandfather), 29
Smith, Samuel Harrison, 33, 48, 49, 105, 402
Smith, Samuell (great, great, grandfather),
  29
Smith, Sardius
  ten year old child killed at Haun's Mill,
  323

Smith, Sophronia, 33, 36, 49
Smith, Wallace Bunnell, 465
Smith, William, 33, 90, 91, 113, 127, 128, 163, 273, 496
    describes translation process of metallic plates in 1891, 90
Smith, William Wallace, 464, 468
South Bainbridge, New York, 73, 77, 100
Spencer, Orson
    instructs Languages in the University of the City of Nauvoo, 365
    unique in membership as a college graduate, 365
spiritual wifery, 14
Stafford, Cornelius R., 127
Stevenson, Edward, 105, 108
Stockton, Benjamin B. (Reverend)
    preaches Alvin Smith's funeral, 395
Stout, Hosea
    describes Mormon success in routing Bogart's troops at Crooked River, 316
Stowell, Josiah, 72, 77, 78

T

Tambora Volcano, 40
Taylor, John, 346, 354, 376, 433, 449, 452, 455, 496
temperance movement, 25
Thompson, Robert B.
    prophet's personal secretary in Nauvoo, 360
Thoreau, Henry David, 17
Thornton, John C., 285
    Speaker of the House in Missouri legislature, 285
Three Witnesses (Book of Mormon), 105, 118
Tiffany, Joel, 111, 113
Times and Seasons, 53, 88, 111, 117, 123, 126, 218, 219, 226, 228, 231, 232, 239, 261, 301, 324, 349, 351, 352, 353, 362, 363, 365, 366, 383, 388, 389, 390, 392, 415, 427, 428, 438, 448, 455, 460, 468

title-trading
    property swap for land in the Nauvoo, Illinois area, 356
Topsfield, Massachusetts, 29, 30
transcendentalism, 17
translation process, 53, 74, 84, 87, 88, 89, 91, 92, 99, 102, 106, 117, 259, 412, 419
treasure seeking, 53, 70, 71, 74, 77, 87, 114
treatment for the insane, 25
trinitarianism, 96, 382, 383, 390
Tucker, Pomeroy, 44, 132
Tunbridge, Vermont, 30, 32, 33, 36
Turley, Theodore, 110
Turnham, Joel (Clay County, Missouri, Judge), 227
    hears case against Rigdon on 25 January 1839, 335
typhus, 36, 37, 39, 48

U

Unitarianism, 17
United States Constitution, 136
Universalism, 50, 56, 57, 137, 391
University of the City of Nauvoo, 20, 21, 362, 363, 364, 365, 366, 371, 430
    as ghost college, 364
    created by Nauvoo City Charter, 363
    curriculum, 365
    faculty, 365
Urim and Thummim, 76, 78, 80, 88, 89, 90, 91, 98, 108, 111
Utica, New York, 43, 84, 266
utopian, 17, 25, 26

V

Van Buren, Martin, 264, 377
Veazey, Stephen M., 466
View of the Hebrews, 98, 99, 100
Vision of the Three Glories, 156, 210

W

Walker, Cyrus (Whig politician and lawyer)
    swaps legal assistance for political

support in the U.S. Congressional election, August 1843, 375
wall of separation between church and state, 22
Wall, Garret Dorset (New Jersey Senator), 373
Walters, Luman, 73
warning out, 41
Warsaw Signal, 440, 454, 455, 498
Washington, George, 18, 31, 197, 369, 397, 405, 422
Wayne Sentinel, 100
Wayne's Landing
  Missouri River portage used by Saints during exodus from Independence, Missouri, 201
Webb, C. G.
  and Kirtland bank fraud, 272
Webster, Daniel, 378
Weed, Thurlow, 118
Wentworth Letter, 126
Wentworth, John, 111, 126, 383
Westbury, Massachusetts, 26
Whiskey Rebellion, 18
White River Valley, 71
Whitmer, Christian, 105, 392
Whitmer, David, 91, 104, 105, 106, 108, 118, 130, 131, 133, 162, 232, 273, 274, 290, 295, 392, 497
  as president of the Missouri church, 162
Whitmer, Elizabeth Ann, 105
Whitmer, Jacob, 105, 295
Whitmer, John, 88, 92, 105, 109, 110, 124, 162, 198, 259, 260, 274, 290, 294, 295, 297, 332, 339, 351, 392, 395, 458, 492, 493, 494, 495, 497
  as counselor in the Presidency of the Missouri church, 162
  lays out the community of Far West, Missouri, 283
Whitmer, John C., 105
Whitmer, Mary Musselman, 105
Whitmer, Peter Jr., 105, 129, 392
Whitmer, Peter Sr., 187
Whitney, Newell K., 148, 160, 187
  and missionary trip to New York City with Joseph Smith Jr. in October 1832, 235
Wight, Lyman, 145, 161, 171, 217, 222, 231, 281, 307, 308, 327, 330, 332, 334, 392, 429, 497
  appeals to Missouri governor for redress of grievances, 281
  arrives with one hundred fifty volunteers for the defense of Far West, 325
  claims witness to the prophet offering a succession blessing, 334
  recruiting tour into Michigan, 220
Wilds, Sarah, 29
Willers, Dietrich, Jr., 102
Williams, Frederick Granger, 161, 171, 213, 216, 232, 237, 274, 295, 404
  administers funds for the Zion's Camp March, 221
  ordained as counselor in the First Presidency, 161
Wilson, Harmon T. (Hancock County constable), 375
Wilson, Moses
  escorts Mormon prisoners from Far West to Independence, Missouri, 332
Windham, New Hampshire, 29
Winters, Eliza (Elizabeth), 401
witchcraft, practice of, 29
Woburn, Massachusetts, 57
Word of Wisdom, 162
Wright, David P., 93, 114, 497
Wyandotte tribe, 177
year without a summer (1816), 40

Y

Young, Brigham, 163, 212, 214, 220, 221, 238, 245, 268, 273, 282, 321, 334, 340, 351, 354, 357, 398, 402, 429, 434, 463, 487, 488, 489, 490, 491, 494, 495, 497, 498
  flees from Kirtland, Ohio, 274
  successfully argues for the reorganization of the church after Far West, 345
  tells soldier to order rattlesnake out of

camp during Zion's Camp March, 221
Young, Joseph (Brigham's older brother)
  eyewitness to Haun's Mill massacre, 323
  paints lines on House of the Lord exterior, 243

Z

Zelph (Lamanite warrior chieftain), 222
Zion's Camp March
  and seventies recruitment, 163
  becomes an invading army, 225
  ending the march, 231
  epiphanies, 221
  peace flag, 223
  problems in timing low recruitment, and finances, 220
  sagging morale, 222
  Saints outnumbered, 226
  spread of cholera, 221, 230, 231
  torrid pace, 221

ABOUT THE AUTHOR

Mark Albert Scherer became the Community of Christ World Church historian in 1995 after more than twenty years in public education. He has been an associate professor of history and continues as an adjunct faculty member of Community of Christ Seminary at Graceland University. Born and raised in Independence, Missouri, he attended Graceland College (Lamoni, Iowa) from 1968 to 1972 and graduated with a bachelor's degree in history. In 1977, he received a master's degree in American history from the University of Missouri–Kansas City. There, he completed a doctor of philosophy degree in interdisciplinary studies (history and education) in 1998. Scherer's doctoral dissertation is titled "A Material Cultural Analysis of the Foundational History of Latter Day Saintism, 1827–1844." His writings have appeared in a number of scholarly journals. In 2003–2004, Scherer served as president of the John Whitmer Historical Association.

Scherer's family heritage is steeped in the Community of Christ tradition. His father, Albert A. Scherer, was a missionary assigned to the Netherlands after the Second World War. Scherer holds the priesthood office of high priest. He enjoys reading, exploring, and making sense of the past. He is a bona fide political junkie, plays golf, and enjoys being with his family (although not necessarily in that order). In 1976, Scherer married Rita L. Hawley of Independence, Missouri. They have two sons, Brett and Bryan.